Issues in Adolescent Psychology

Edited by **Dorothy Rogers**

State University of New York at Oswego

Issues in Adolescent Psychology

second edition

Appleton-Century-Crofts

Educational Division

New York *Meredith Corporation*

Contributors

Ronald L. Akers

Gordon W. Allport

Shirley S. Angrist
Carnegie-Mellon University

Albert Bandura
Stanford University

Marc D. Baranowski
University of Wisconsin

Robert C. Bealer
Pennsylvania State University

Vern L. Bengtson
University of Southern California

Henry B. Biller
University of Rhode Island

Daniel G. Brown
*United States Public Health Service,
Atlanta, Georgia*

William V. Burlingame
University of North Carolina

Gary A. Davis
University of Wisconsin

John Demos
Brandeis University

Virginia Demos

S. N. Eisenstadt
Hebrew University

Glen H. Elder, Jr.
University of North Carolina

David Elkind
University of Rochester

James L. Fenner

Richard Flacks
University of Chicago

Edgar Z. Friedenberg
State University of New York at Buffalo

Stephen R. Graubard
Brown University

Eugene L. Gaier
State University of New York at Buffalo

Douglas H. Heath
Haverford College

Jerome Kagan
Harvard University

Kenneth Keniston
Yale University

Stanley Krippner
Wagner College

Jack Levin
Northeastern University

Eleanore B. Luckey
University of Connecticut, Storrs

David B. Lynn
University of California, Davis

Clyde O. McDaniel, Jr.
*Urban Laboratory in Education, Atlanta,
Georgia*

Don Merten

Howard A. Moss
*National Institute of Mental Health,
Bethesda, Maryland*

FRANK MUSGROVE
                    University of Manchester

ROLF E. MUUSS
                            Goucher College

GILBERT D. NASS
                    University of Connecticut

SAMUEL H. OSIPOW
                        Ohio State University

HERBERT A. OTTO

SARAH T. OTTO

DOROTHY ROGERS
        State University of New York at Oswego

HANS SEBALD
                    Arizona State University

LAWRENCE SCHIAMBERG
                    University of South Dakota

GARY SCHWARTZ
        *Institute of Juvenile Research, Chicago,
                        Illinois*

G. H. SEWARD
                University of Southern California

ARLENE SKOLNICK
            University of California, Berkeley

JAMES L. SPATES
            Hobart and William Smith Colleges

EDWARD A. SUCHMAN
                    University of Pittsburgh

HERSCHEL D. THORNBURG
                        University of Arizona

POVL W. TOUSSIENG
    *Youth Counseling and Child Development
        Center, Oklahoma City, Oklahoma*

IRVING B. WEINER
                    University of Rochester

MELFORD S. WEISS
                    Sacramento State College

STEPHAN D. WEISS
                University of Massachusetts

FERN K. WILLITS
                Pennsylvania State University

R. C. WILLIAMSON
                            Lehigh University

PATTY WIRTH
            High School Student, Middle West

To My Students

Preface

This volume provides supplementary reading material for a college course in adolescent psychology. It has been prepared to accompany and complement the editor's text, *The Psychology of Adolescence, Second Edition,* but the issues presented here are so universal and so broad in scope as to be of interest to anyone concerned with adolescents.

This second edition presents twenty-one issues, or topics involving issues, arranged under six general headings. An introduction to each issue analyzes its significance, examines its present status, and summarizes the applicable research, presenting a sampling of opinions from authorities holding many different views. To enable students to explore topics in greater depth, reference lists and suggested additional readings accompany each section. A glossary at the end of the book defines unfamiliar terms used in the reading selections.

This edition represents a thorough revision of the successful first edition. Three new topics have been added, concerning adolescents' relationships to the family, to drugs, and to modern technological society. Of the forty-four selections, four-fifths are new in the second edition; and the annotated lists of readings at the end of each topic have been completely updated. The great majority of both the reading selections and the suggested additional readings were written within the last five years and thus present the most current thinking on issues. While some represent a particular side of an issue, many provide a broad background for the discussion of some issue-charged area.

For the teacher, the issues approach to adolescent psychology permits interesting variations in course organization and instruction. Several students may investigate each topic, and then, as a panel, discuss it before the class; or students may select specific issues as subjects for term papers. Often they may supplement library research with original studies of their own. For instance, on the subject of adolescent image, a student might interview persons of different age groups concerning their views of the adolescent. Sometimes two or more instructors within the department may discuss a topic informally before combined classes of their students. The investigation of issues seems to excite student interest more readily than does a conventional survey of subject matter.

Various criteria have governed the choice of issues to be included in this volume. Some have been selected for their relevance to students' own special concerns.

Students are particularly interested in such topics as dating, sex role, and youth culture, but they should also become acquainted with those which have attracted special attention from researchers, for example, the relative importance of stress during adolescence. Certain issues, such as the meaning of adolescence and the adolescent image, have been considered noteworthy for a long time; other topics, among them drugs and alienation, have attracted attention more recently. Some of the topics (the adolescent and creativity, the storm-and-stress hypothesis) represent specific issues; others (biological sex role, social-sex role) are not issues as such but encompass areas which involve unresolved questions.

Other criteria guided the specific choice of readings. When authorities hold distinctly different points of view with regard to a topic, selections were chosen to represent these varied positions. In complex topics, where problems are relatively undifferentiated and involved, selections have been used which help to sort out the jigsaw puzzle of ideas. Some selections have been included because they were especially well-written, lucid, or provocative. In general, the authors are authorities in the areas with which they deal, and collectively they provide a wide range of philosophies and points of view. Most are psychologists; in a few cases they are authorities in related disciplines; and one was herself an adolescent. This should make clear that walls do not exist between disciplines and that different areas of knowledge and different age levels may effectively contribute to each other.

Books of readings in general have certain merits. Within a small space, they offer a range of subject matter written by experts in the field. A book of readings about issues possesses additional merits, for it presents several valid, though differing, points of view relating to the same topics. While textbooks may provide excellent summaries of research, space limitations preclude their presenting source materials, except for brief quotations. This book is intended to supply the materials needed to supplement the texts.

I wish to express to the staff of the Penfield Library at Oswego my appreciation for their invaluable assistance — especially to Jane Wright, Claire Merlehan, Grace Manwaring, and Jane Morrison. I am also grateful to Ann Hoefer and Cherie Blanchard for their competent clerical assistance.

D. R.

Contents

part one

General Issues Concerning Adolescence

1

The Nature and Meaning of Adolescence

Books and articles — both popular and professional — which deal with adolescence disagree widely on the precise meaning of the term. Adolescence is variously treated as a specific span of years, a stage in development, a subculture, a state of mind, or a combination of these concepts. For example, every teenager is considered "an adolescent." Yet we may say that an adult's behavior seems "adolescent," meaning that he is behaving in a silly, irresponsible way. Or we may label a child as "preadolescent," but the exact moment when the child arrives at adolescence proper is uncertain. The result has been confusion as to what adolescence signifies. We may ask: Is it possible, or even desirable, to attempt a more precise definition? Do we need different viewpoints toward adolescence? Whenever we use the term should we specify, within the context, the particular frame of reference being employed?

Let us take a closer look at various definitions of adolescence. The term itself is derived from the Latin *adolescere,* meaning to grow to maturity. In this sense of growth, adolescence is a process rather than a period, a process of evolving from child to adult. More precisely, adolescence is often defined as a stage in physical development (Rogers, 1972, p.?).

The term *pubescence,* or preadolescence, generally refers to the period of about two years preceding puberty and to the physical changes which take place during that time. This period is marked by a spurt in physical growth, by changes in body proportions, and by the maturation of primary and secondary sex characteristics. The climax of pubescence, called *puberty,* is distinguished by certain indications of sexual maturity: in girls by the *menarche,* or first menstruation, in boys by several signs, probably the most valid being the presence of live spermatozoa, or male reproductive cells, in the urine. Early adolescence, in the biological sense, dates from the onset of the pubescent growth spurt until about a year after puberty, when the new biological functions have been pretty well established. Late adolescence is even less definite in duration, lasting until physical growth is relatively complete and early adulthood begins.

Adolescence may also be defined chronologically — Hurlock (1956, pp. 27-28), for one, has designated preadolescence as the age period from 10 through 12;

early adolescence as the age period from 13 through 16; and late adolescence as from ages 17 through 21. It is true that, on the one hand, such chronological definitions can prove distorting, in that neither psychological nor biological maturity proceeds at the same rate in all individuals; nor do all aspects of biological or psychological maturity develop at the same rate in the same individual. A boy who has experienced puberty because of glandular malfunction may remain a child in every other sense. On the other hand, specific ages, as points of reference, can prove useful for certain purposes, particularly legal ones. For example, the age of 18 is quite significant in the legislation of many countries (Rosenmayr, 1968). What criterion, other than the chronological one, could logically be used to determine when an individual may be licensed to drive, may obtain a marriage license, or may vote? In addition, the age-stage from 13 to 18 years is important in terms of external manifestations of biological maturation; while during the age-stage from 18 to 24, almost no outward physical changes are visible.

The study of adolescence may also be approached in a theoretical frame of reference. The phenomenologist emphasizes the adolescent's perception of himself and his environment. The field theorist is concerned with how elements within the adolescent's experience fit together into meaningful patterns. The psychoanalytic approach, which is built on Freudian theory, provides a prototype for children's development. Whether this prototype may be considered valid or not has been widely disputed, but no psychologist questions the impact of psychoanalytic theory on the psychology of adolescence. The psychoanalyst portrays early life stages as highly significant in the individual's development, and each stage as important for all that follows. The prototype of the child at each stage involves certain libidinal and aggressive energies, as well as frustrations, defenses, and anxieties.

Still another approach to adolescence is developmental — that is, adolescence is treated in relation to other stages of development, and in terms of the psychological dynamics involved. Eisenberg (1965) considers in particular the special role that adolescence plays in total development, in helping the individual to establish an identity.

Another approach to adolescence is sociological. Social adolescence is largely a creation of the Western world. In this context, the adolescent is one who has outgrown the social status of the child but has not yet been accorded the mature privileges of the adult. In the sociological sense, the status of the adolescent varies with certain conditions. The lower-class boy who leaves school at 18 to help support the family may be judged a man, while the girl of 20 who has no job and lives at home is looked upon, and treated, as an adolescent.

Related to the sociological frame of reference is the cross-cultural one. In this approach, adolescence is viewed in terms of the duties and privileges assigned to, or denied to, youth in various cultures through the world and at different times in history. Certain constants, which have characterized adolescent development regardless of culture, may identified. Once the general cross-cultural concepts have been established, it is easier to detect variations in the over-all pattern within specific cultures.

Cross-cultural studies of primitive societies have highlighted the contrast between the ritualistic methods these primitive peoples follow in socializing their young and the almost total lack of such practices among modern Western societies. According to Bauman (1967), both historical and primitive societies meticulously prescribed new duties for young people as they moved from one age-stage to another, and stylized *rites de passage* were developed to mark the transition of individuals from childhood to adulthood. However, in modern societies we find only a few vestiges of such rituals, as in high school and college graduation exercises. In contrast to the primitive societies' clear pattern or roles and duties, in modern industrial societies the passing from childhood to adolescence is like a "transition to nowhere." An individual proceeds into an ill-defined no-man's-land. He is not accorded, after puberty, the duties and privileges of an adult but remains in a somewhat dependent status. In other words, observes Bauman, young people today remain "children," in the sociocultural sense of that term, to a greater age. Moreover, there is "a tendency for the role of the child to absorb completely the whole ground available for training for adult life, implying the complete abolition of 'the apprenticeship of youth' [p. 329]."

Closely allied to the cross-cultural consideration of adolescence is the historical approach. However, rather than comparing widely different cultures at the same period of history, this approach considers those cultures from "the long view," as their attitudes toward youth changed over the course of the centuries. Since present-day customs, attitudes, and behaviors characteristic of adolescents have their roots in the past, this approach is essential to an understanding of present-day youth. However, as Muuss (1971) points out, one difficulty in tracing very early or prescientific ideas of adolescent development is that prior to the twentieth century, adolescence was not treated as a distinct stage of human development. In fact, the word "adolescence" first appeared in the fifteenth century, suggesting that historically, observations about adolescents were not made in reference to a specific age-stage but simply occurred within the general context of the terms "child" and "adult" in human development.

In the first selection in this chapter, Demos and Demos review early writings and research concerning adolescence and help to place this age period in historical perspective. An analysis of writings from the period 1800 to 1875 reveals almost no usage of the word "adolescence" during this time and only limited concern with this stage of human development. The "discovery" of adolescence after 1900 was related to various changes in American life, particularly to changes in family relationships within a new urban and industrial order.

The second reading, by Muuss, fuses the historical and physical appoaches to adolescence and focuses on a phenomenon widely neglected by developmental psychologists — the appearance of puberty at an earlier age now than was the case some decades ago. The author indicates some of the medical, educational, and social implications of this accelerated development, both for society and for the adolescent himself.

It is unlikely that psychologists will ultimately agree on the best way to define adolescence. Perhaps, as scientific data proliferate, concepts of adolescence, within the various frames of reference, will become more easily identifiable. Meantime, we shall have to muddle along, adapting to imprecise and constantly shifting concepts of the term.

REFERENCES

BAUMAN, Z.   Some problems in contemporary education. *International Social Science Journal*, 1967, *19*(3), 325–337.

EISENBERG, L.   A developmental approach to adolescence. *Children*, July–August 1965, *12*(4), 131–135.

HURLOCK, E.   *Child development.* (3rd ed.) New York: McGraw-Hill, 1956, 27–28.

MUUSS, R. E. (ED.)   *Adolescent behavior and society: A book of readings.* New York: Random House, 1971. Pp. 3–22.

ROGERS, D.   *The psychology of adolescence.* (2nd ed.) New York: Appleton-Century-Crofts, 1972.

ROSENMAYR, L.   Towards an overview of youth's sociology. *International Social Science Journal*, 1968, *20*(2), 286–315.

Adolescence in Historical Perspective

JOHN DEMOS   VIRGINIA DEMOS

The authors review early research concerning adolescence. Before 1900, little attention was paid to this stage of human development. The relatively recent "discovery" of adolescence is related to changes in the American way of life and particularly to changes in family relationships within a new urban and industrial order.

The idea of adolescence is today one of our most widely held and deeply imbedded assumptions about the process of human development. Indeed most of us treat it not as an idea but as a *fact*. Its impact is clear in countless areas of everyday life—in newspapers, magazines, and books; in various forms of popular entertainment; in styles of dress and of language. Its causes and meaning have been repeatedly analyzed in the work of psychologists and sociologists. Its effects are endlessly discussed by teachers, social workers, officers of the law, and parents everywhere.

Yet all of this has a relatively short history. The concept of adolescence, as generally understood and applied, did not exist before the last two decades of the nineteenth century. One could almost call it an invention of that period; though it did incorporate, in quite a central way, certain older attitudes and modes of thinking. It will be our purpose in this paper to describe the roots and the growth of the concept, to the point in the early twentieth century when it had become well established in the public consciousness. We shall limit our attention to developments in the United States, since adolescence was on the whole an American discovery.

We shall begin with a sketch of some common ideas about childhood and "youth" during the period 1800–1875, as revealed in two kinds of sources: (1) a rapidly developing literature of child-rearing advice, and (2) a large body of books and pamphlets directed to the young people of the country and bearing especially on their "moral problems." Then we shall summarize the activities of the "child-study movement" (beginning in about 1890) and in particular the work of the psychologist G. Stanley Hall, for there the concept of adolescence can be examined at its source. And finally we shall propose a hypothesis for drawing together these various types of material and above all for explaining the relationship between the *idea* of adolescence and the social phenomena to which it was a response. It is here that questions of family life will come most fully into view, since adolescence was, we believe, profoundly related to certain fundamental changes affecting the internal structure of many American homes. But this matter of the connection between "ideas" and "facts," between major cultural assumptions like adolescence and the social realities in which they develop, presents extremely tricky problems. It lurks as an uncom-

From J. Demos & V. Demos, Adolescence in historical perspective. Reprinted from the *Journal of Marriage and the Family,* November 1969, *31*(4), 632–638. By permission.

fortable presence behind most serious study that bears in one way or another on the history of the family. The difficulty lies in the nature of the evidence available to historians, which comprises for the most part a variety of written materials. It is much easier, therefore, to construct a history of ideas *about* the family than of the family as such.

The present paper cannot pretend to resolve such problems; indeed it may serve chiefly to illustrate them. But it is at least our intention to keep sight of the important distinctions. And if the bulk of our efforts are directed toward the realm of "ideas," it is only because this seems the logical way to begin.

The literature of child-rearing advice is one of the most revealing, and least exploited,[1] sources for the history of the American family. Its beginnings can be located in the early part of the nineteenth century; and it has been growing steadily, and changing in character, ever since. Before about 1825 relatively few books on child-rearing could be found in this country, and those that were available came chiefly from England.[2] In general, they were mild in tone and full of simple moral homilies strung endlessly together. They do not, in short, seem to have been directed to any very pressing needs or problems in the lives of their readers.

After 1825 the situation, for this country at least, changed rapidly. Child-rearing books by American authors began to appear, some of which went through numerous editions and sold many thousands of copies.[3] This development was owing to several different factors. In the first place it was related to a deepening interest in the fact of childhood itself as a distinct period of life and one which was little comparable to the years of maturity. Secondly, it expressed the broad impulse of nationalism that engulfed the country at this time. English books on child-rearing could no longer be regarded as suitable to American conditions. Finally, the new and authentically "native" literature on this subject reflected deep anxieties about the quality of American family life.[4]

Most of the concern which was evident in these books related to problems of authority. In one form or another they all imparted the same message: the authority of parents must be established early in a child's life and firmly maintained throughout the years of growth. Even the smallest infant reveals a "willfulness" that "springs from a depraved nature and is intensely selfish."[5] This must be suppressed by strict training in obedience, or it will rapidly develop beyond the possibility of control with dire implications for the later (adult) personality.

These injunctions seemed all the more necessary because—so many people thought—parental authority was steadily on the wane. In describing the average home, the writers of the child-rearing books repeatedly used words like "disorder," "disobedience," "licentiousness," and above all "indulgence" (i.e., of the children). Statements such as the following were typical:

> It must be confessed that an irreverent, unruly spirit has come to be a prevalent, an outrageous evil among the young people of our land. . . . Some of the good old people make facetious complaint on this. . . . "There is as much

[1]We know of only three attempts to confront this material directly: Bernard Wishy, *The Child and the Republic,* Philadelphia: University of Pennsylvania Press, 1968; Robert Sunley, "Early Nineteenth-Century American Literature on Child-Rearing," in *Childhood in Contemporary Cultures,* ed. by Margaret Mead and Martha Wolfenstein, Chicago: University of Chicago Press, 1955, pp. 150–167; and Elaine V. Damis, *The History of Child-Rearing Advice in America from 1800–1940,* unpublished honor's thesis, Radcliffe College, 1960.

[2]See, for instance, Juliana Seymour, *On the Management and Education of Children,* London, 1754; and Miss Appleton, *Early Education,* London, 1821.

[3]Parallel to this increase in books on child-rearing, there developed at this time a new kind of magazine directed specifically to "mothers." *Mother's Magazine* and the *Mother's Assistant* were prominent examples. Both seem to have achieved a wide circulation within a very few years. The magazines, in turn, were closely related to the movement for "maternal associations." These societies, operating at the local level and devoting their energies largely to the discussion of child-rearing problems, became quite a vogue in the 1820s and 1830s. All of this demonstrates further the heightened interest in motherhood—and thus childhood—that characterized the period.

[4]These anxieties were a matter of great complexity and wide ramifications. Indeed they must be understood as relating not only to conditions internal to the family but also to the wider social climate of the time. For some useful discussion of all this, see Bernard Wishy, *The Child and the Republic.*

[5]H. W. Bulkeley, *A Word to Parents,* Philadelphia: Presbyterian Board of Publication, 1858, p. 12.

family government now as there used to be in our young days," they say, "only it has changed hands."[6]

This seeming change in the traditional family pattern had other dimensions as well. Thus many authors noted the growth of a kind of "child-centered" attitude and condemned it out of hand. More and more parents, for example, appeared to feel compelled to show off their children before any and all guests. Similarly, there was in many households far too much concern with efforts to amuse and entertain the young.[7] Children who were often made the center of attention in this manner would inevitably become conceited and selfish. Another alarming development was the increasing tendency of children to seek social satisfactions outside of the family, among groups of their own peers. Mrs. Lydia Child, whose *Mother's Book* went through many editions, returned again and again to the theme that "youth and age are too much separated."[8] She and many of her contemporaries decried the "new custom" of holding parties exclusively for young people[9] and urged that parents should always be the closest friends and confidants of their children.

Lest it be imagined that Americans of the nineteenth century had no special concern whatsoever for the period which we now call adolescence (and which in their day was simply termed "youth"),[10] we must turn to another category of books that were written specifically *for* the "youth" of the time and about their particular problems. The general nature of these writings is implicit in their titles: *A Voice to Youth; How to be a Man; Papers for Thoughtful Girls; The Young Lady's Companion; On the Threshold; Lectures to Young Men.*

From all of these works there emerges quite clearly a sense of "youth" as a critical transition period in the life of nearly everyone. It is a time, first of all, when people are extremely impressionable, extremely open to a wide range of outside influences. It is—to quote Joel Hawes's *Lecture to Young Men* (1832)—

> pre-eminently . . . the forming, fixing period. . . . It is during this season, more than any other, that the character assumes its permanent shape and color. [11]

Words such as "pliant," "plastic," and "formative" appear again and again in the discussions of youth.

Because of this characteristic openness, young people are vulnerable to many kinds of "danger." To begin with, boys and girls entering their teens experience a sudden and sharp upsurge of the "passions." They become highly emotional; their mood fluctuates unpredictably from exuberance to melancholy. Henry Ward Beecher, whose *Lectures to Young Men* were among the best known examples of the genre, declared:

> A young man knows little of life; less of himself. He feels in his bosom the various impulses, wild desires, restless cravings he can hardly tell for what, a sombre melancholy when all is gay, a violent exhilaration when others are sober. [12]

In keeping with their Victorian conventions, these writers never directly mentioned the phys-

---

[6]Warren Burton, *Helps to Education,* Boston: Crosby and Nichols, 1863, pp. 38–39. Similar observations can be found in the writings of foreign visitors to this country. See Arthur W. Calhoun, *A Social History of the American Family,* New York: Barnes and Noble, 1945, pp. 17–19, for some extensive discussion of this travel literature. See also Max Berger, *The British Traveller in America,* New York: Columbia University Press, 1943.

[7]On this matter see, for example, Lydia M. Child, *The Mother's Book,* Boston: Carter, Hendee and Babcock, 1835, p. 94; and Burton, *op. cit.,* pp. 74–75, 92.

[8]Child, *op. cit.,* p. 95.

[9]See *ibid.,* p. 138; also *Mother's Magazine,* 1, pp. 42–45.

[10]The word "adolescence" was known in the nineteenth century, but we have found only a very few cases of its use in the literature on child-rearing and "youth."

[11]Joel Hawes, *Lectures to Young Men,* Hartford, Connecticut: Cooke & Co., 1832, p. 35. See also Child, *op. cit.,* p. 125.

[12]Henry Ward Beecher, *Lectures to Young Men,* Boston: J. P. Jewett & Co., 1844, p. 21. Beecher actually delivered these lectures to an audience of young people in Boston before publishing them. Such was also the pattern for many of the other works of this kind. For a similar comment on the turmoil characteristic of youth, see Henrietta Keddie, *Papers for Thoughtful Girls,* Boston: Crosby and Nichols, 1860, p. 1.

iological changes that occur at puberty, in particular the strong new charge of sexual energy and tension. Occasionally one finds an allusion to "internal revolutions" and "occult causes, probably of a physical kind"[13]; but for the most part people were content to define youth in the above terms, that is, as a vast outpouring of the emotions.

As if to complement these disruptive changes within the personality, the world at large was full of "seductive temptations," of inducements to all manner of wicked and ruinous behavior. As Beecher said,

These wild gushes of feeling, peculiar to youth, the sagacious tempter has felt, has studied, has practiced upon, until he can sit before that most capacious organ, the human mind, knowing every step and all the combinations.[14]

Here, then, was the wider, social dimension of the problems which confront the young person. The world lies in wait for him, and "ardent, volatile, inexperienced, and thirsting for happiness," he is

exceedingly liable to be seduced into the wrong paths—into those fascinating but fatal ways, which lead to degradation and wretchedness.[15]

There are, at this stage of life, dangers both within and without.

Most of the material considered so far has been drawn from the period 1825–1850. As the years passed and the century neared its end, the picture of youth that we have been describing was embellished somewhat in certain important respects. Thus, for example, the sexual factor began to receive some attention.[16] And some writers were struck by a kind of aimlessness and indecision that seemed increasingly common among American young people. Theodore T. Munger,

whose book *On the Threshold* was published in 1881, declared that

Young men of the present years . . . are not facing life with that resolute and definite purpose that is essential both to manhood and to external success. . . . [They] hear no voice summoning them to the appointed field, but drift into this or that, as happens.[17]

Moreover, towards the end of the century, many writers identified the "dangers" and "temptations" which threatened youth directly with urban life. Something of this had been implicit from the beginning, but now it came clearly into the open.[18] The city loomed as the prime source of corrupting influences for the young. Its chaotic social and economic life, its varied population, its frenzied commercial spirit, and its dazzling entertainments were all sharply antagonistic to proper growth towards adulthood.

At roughly the same time, meanwhile, the formal concept of adolescence was receiving its first public expression. The immediate context of this development was a new movement for systematic "child study," inspired and guided by G. Stanley Hall. Hall was, of course, one of the major figures in the early history of American psychology. After a lengthy period of study in Germany, he became in 1881 a professor at Johns Hopkins, and six years later he accepted the presidency of Clark University. There he remained for the rest of his life, presiding over a wide range of research and teaching activities.

The aim of the child-study movement was to enlist large numbers of ordinary citizens in a broad effort to deepen both public and scientific understanding of human development. The mothers who belonged to the various local organizations were encouraged to keep detailed records of the behavior of their children and to participate in regular discussions about such rec-

[13]Isaac Taylor, *Home Education,* New York: D. Appleton & Co., 1838, p. 131.

[14]Beecher, *op. cit.,* p. 21.

[15]John M. Austin, *A Voice to Youth,* New York: J. Bolles, 1838, p. 1.

[16]See, for example, Elizabeth Blackwell, *Counsel to Parents on the Moral Education of Their Children,* New York: Brentano's Literary Emporium, 1879.

[17]Theodore T. Munger, *On the Threshold,* Boston: Houghton Mifflin & Co., 1881, p. 5. See also William A. Mowry, *Talks with My Boys,* Boston: New England Publishing Company, 1885, pp. 30 ff.; and Philip S. Moxon, *The Aim of Life,* Boston: Roberts Brothers, 1894, pp. 11-29.

[18]See, for example, George H. Hepworth, *Rocks and Shoals,* Boston: American Unitarian Association, 1870; and Mowry, *op. cit.*

ords. They were also exposed to, and themselves reflected back, the major themes in Stanley Hall's own work—not least, his theory of adolescence.

The essentials of Hall's view of adolescence appeared in one of his earliest papers on psychology: "The Moral and Religious Training of Children," published in 1882 in the *Princeton Review*. The great point of departure, then as later, was the idea of "storm and stress," of severe crisis characterized by

lack of emotional steadiness, violent impulses, unreasonable conduct, lack of enthusiasm and sympathy. . . . The previous selfhood is broken up . . . and a new individual is in process of being born. All is solvent, plastic, peculiarly susceptible to external influences.[19]

The suggestions contained in this article were subsequently elaborated in much greater detail by some of Hall's students at Clark. Efforts were made to link the adolescent "crisis" with a wide range of personal and social phenomena—with religious conversion, for example,[20] and with the rising rate of juvenile delinquency.[21] Hall himself provided the capstone to this whole sequence of activity, with the publication in 1904 of his encyclopedic work, *Adolescence: Its Psychology, and Its Relations to Physiology, Anthropology, Sociology, Sex, Crime, Religion, and Education.* It is impossible to summarize here the many ideas and vast assortment of data embraced therein, but certain underlying themes can at least be singled out. From the very start Hall's thinking had been profoundly influenced by Darwinism, and the psychology he proposed was explicitly bound to an evolutionary, or "genetic" model. He urged a kind of "archaeology of the mind," in which all the various stages in the development of human consciousness would be rediscovered

and understood in their proper order.[22] A key link here was the theory known as "recapitulation," which affirmed that every individual "lives through" each of the major steps in the evolution of the race as a whole. Adolescence assumed a special importance in this scheme, for it represented (and "recapitulated") the most recent of man's great developmental leaps. The adolescent, Hall believed, reveals truly enormous possibilities of growth and "is carried for a time beyond the point of the present stage of civilization."[23] This is not, however, an easy situation, for it encompasses a variety of contradictions and "antithetic impulses." Among the impulses which Hall paired in this context were hyperactivity and lassitude, happiness and depression, egotism and self-abasement, selfishness and altruism, gregariousness and shyness, sensitivity and cruelty, radicalism and conservatism. Caught in the midst of so much change and conflict, the adolescent was bound to experience "storm and stress" more or less continuously.

Hall's work on adolescence quickly exerted a considerable influence in many different directions. Its impact was clear in general texts on psychology,[24] studies of education,[25] the new literature on child-rearing,[26] and a variety of books on child labor, religious training, vocational guidance, and the like.[27] Even critical comments showed the extent to which the idea

[19]G. Stanley Hall, "The Moral and Religious Training of Children," in *Princeton Review* (January, 1882), pp. 26–48. This essay was later republished in a slightly revised form in *Pedagogical Seminary*, 1, pp. 196–210.

[20]See E. D. Starbuck, *The Psychology of Religion,* New York: Ginn & Co., 1899; and an essay by the same author, "A Study of Conversion," in *American Journal of Pyschology*, 8, pp. 268–308.

[21]See Edgar J. Swift, "Some Criminal Tendencies of Boyhood: A Study in Adolescence," in *Pedagogical Seminary*, 7.

[22]See G. Stanley Hall, *Adolescence*, New York: D. Appleton & Co., 1904, Vol. 2, pp. 61, 69.

[23]See the "epitome" of Hall's theories by G. E. Partridge, *The Genetic Philosophy of Education*, Boston: Sturgis & Walton Co., 1912, p. 31.

[24]For example, James R. Angell, *Psychology*, New York: H. Holt & Co., 1904. See especially p. 358.

[25]See George H. Betts, *The Mind and Its Education*, New York: D. Appleton & Co., 1906; P. M. Magnusson, *Psychology as Applied to Education*, New York: Silver, Burdett and Company, 1913; and Arthur Holmes, *Principles of Character-Making,* Philadelphia: J. B. Lippincott Company, 1913.

[26]See William McKeever, *Training the Boy,* New York: Macmillan Company, 1913; and *Training the Girl*, New York: Macmillan Company, 1914; also W. B. Forbush and Catherine M. Burrell, *The Mother's Book,* New York: The University Society, Inc., 1919.

[27]See George B. Mangold, *Child Problems,* New York: The Macmillan Company, 1910; George A. Coe, *Education in Religion and Morals,* New York: F. H. Revell Company, 1904; and Meyer Bloomfield, *The Vocational Guidance of Youth,* Boston: Houghton Mifflin Company, 1911.

of adolescence had captured the public imagination: there were those who complained that "we are today under the tyranny of the special cult of adolescence."[28]

Hall's reputation was, however, relatively short-lived. From the very beginning his theories of adolescence aroused at least some criticism. Men like E. L. Thorndike (himself an important figure in the history of American psychology), Charles H. Judd, and Irving King charged him with many forms of exaggeration and overstatement.[29] And after 1925 his work went rapidly into eclipse. Many scholars came to feel that it was unreasonable to view growth in terms of set "stages" of any kind whatsoever. Margaret Mead, in her famous study of Samoan children, tried to show that adolescent "storm and stress" are a function of certain *cultural* determinants.[30] By contrast, Hall was seen as the representative of an outmoded, wholly physiological orientation.[31] Moreover, his fervent, almost missionary approach to his subject, his florid writing, his long-range goal of race improvement—all this came to seem irrelevant, or even offensive, to later generations of psychologists.

Thus G. Stanley Hall has been largely forgotten, if not rejected outright. Yet, we suggest, he has left his mark all the same. Hall's critics denied the validity of considering personal growth in terms of "stages"; but we still regard adolescence in just such a context. His critics accused him of having greatly exaggerated "storm and stress" phenomena, and yet today more than ever we view adolescence in exactly those terms. In fact, the "special cult of adolescence" seems to have lost no strength at all. And it was Hall, more than anyone else, who fixed it in our imagination.

It would be easy to overstate the element of innovation in Hall's thinking. If we compare the kind of adolescence that he was describing with some of the ideas that were current just before his time,[32] we find a considerable degree of continuity. His achievement lay in reshaping certain aspects of popular belief about youth, combining them with some of the most exciting new ideas in science (i.e., evolution), gathering data on a large scale, and presenting the whole in a persuasive and meaningful fashion.

Yet certain questions about the rise of the concept of adolescence remain. What larger developments in American society did it reflect? To what popular attitudes, or needs, or anxieties, did it minister? We offer, in conclusion, the following very tentative suggestions—some of which we have simply lifted from contemporary thinking about adolescence in the fields of psychology and sociology.[33]

We propose, as a starting point, the long-term transformation of the United States from an agricultural into an urban and industrial society; for this change—which has, of course, been basic to so much of our history during the last 150 years—has exerted a profound influence on the structure of American families. Consider that most farm families are characterized by a high degree of internal unity. Children and adults share the same tasks, the same entertainments, the same friends, the same expectations. Their is a continuum between the generations. The child appears not so much as a child per se but as himself a potential farmer; he is, then, a miniature

[28]Frank O. Beck, *Marching Manward*, New York: Eaton & Mains, 1913, p. 38.

[29]See E. L. Thorndike, *Notes on Child-Study*, in *Columbia University Contributions to Philosophy, Psychology, and Education*, 8:3–4, p. 143; also Thorndike's article, "Magnitude and Rate of Alleged Changes at Adolescence," in *Educational Review*, 54, pp. 140–147. See too Charles H. Judd, *The Psychology of High School Subjects*, Boston: Ginn & Company, 1915; and Irving King, *The Psychology of Child Development*, Chicago: University of Chicago Press, 1903, pp. 222 ff.

[30]Margaret Mead, *Coming of Age in Samoa*, New York: W. Morrow and Company, 1928.

[31]On this point Hall was somewhat misrepresented. It is true that he regarded the critical changes of adolescence as proceeding from within; but he also spent much effort in analyzing various factors in our *environment*—which, he felt, greatly accentuated adolescent distress. See Hall, *Adolescence, op. cit.*, Vol. 1, pp. xv, 321 ff., 348 ff., 376 ff.; and Vol. 2, pp. 59–60.

[32]*Ibid.*, pp. 5–8.

[33]We have tried to draw together ideas from several different sources, chief among them: Kenneth Keniston, "Social Change and Youth in America," *Daedalus* (Winter, 1962), pp. 145–171; Erik H. Erikson, "Youth: Fidelity and Diversity," *Daedalus* (Winter, 1962), pp. 5–27; Ruth Benedict, "Continuities and Discontinuities in Cultural Conditioning," in *Psychiatry*, 1, pp. 161–167; Kingsley Davis, "The Sociology of Parent–Youth Conflict," *American Sociological Review*, 5, pp. 523–535.

model of his father. Such, we would argue, was the prevalent situation in nearly *all* the families of this country before the nineteenth century.

But when Americans began to move to the city, all this changed. City children, for example, do not often have a significant economic function within the family as a whole. (Or alternatively—as in the case of poor children employed as factory hands—their work is likely to be quite different from that of their parents.) Moreover, they are thrust into close proximity with other families and have the opportunity to form numerous contacts among their own peers. Thus there develops in the urban setting an important "discontinuity of age-groups."[34] Children and adults are much more obviously separated from each other than is ever the case in a rural environment.

This second configuration was starting to show itself in some American families during the early part of the nineteenth century, and perhaps it helps to explain the material presented in our opening section. Now—i.e., with the new, typically urban family structure—childhood as such is "discovered"; it is no longer feasible to regard children simply as miniature adults. Now, too, "child-centered" families become possible. The behavior of the young is increasingly seen as bizarre and also as appropriate to their particular time of life. A new tolerance for such behavior develops, and parental authority appears to weaken.[35] Finally, there is an obvious place for a literature on child-rearing.

Most cultures with sharp discontinuities of this kind possess a system of "age-grading," which defines the various steps in the transition from childhood to adulthood.[36] In many cases there are elaborate initiation rites to dramatize this change. But our society lacks such rites; ceremonies like confirmation and graduation exercises are losing whatever significance in this regard they once had. It is in such situations, as Kenneth Keniston has suggested, that a "youth culture" is likely to develop. "Youth culture" may be defined, somewhat carelessly, as institutionalized adolescence. It refers, of course, to the special way of life characteristic of large groups of young people of approximately the same age. It is more than a simple substitute for formal age-grading and initiation rites. It is not, Keniston writes,

so obviously transitional . . . [but is] . . . more like a waiting period . . . a temporary stopover in which one can muster strength for the next harrowing stage of the trip.

Its pattern is "not always or explicitly anti-adult, but it is belligerently *non*-adult."[37] In many respects adulthood looks rather forbidding when compared with the life of a child, and youth culture reflects some reluctance to bridge this gap.

It is pertinent to recall at this point the deep concern of many nineteenth-century Americans about the growth of peer-group contacts. We suggest that these people were witnessing the rudimentary beginnings of a youth culture. Of course, there were none of the artifacts so prominent in our own modern-day youth culture (e.g., "rock 'n roll," "teen magazines," special kinds of dress, and so forth). But the very fact of "wanting to be with and for [their own] kind"[38] was significant. By about 1900 the situation had become more clear. The many and varied writings on "gangs," on juvenile delinquency, and on vocational guidance all show some feeling for the special characteristics of a youth culture.

Keniston argues that a second kind of discontinuity—that between specific generations—is also important in the formation of youth culture. By this he means a clear separation between the parents and the children within an individual family. In such cases the situation of the parents offers no viable goal at which their children may aim. Intra-family conflict is likely to become chronic, and the adolescent is on his own in the

---

[34]The phrase is Kenneth Keniston's. See his article cited above.

[35]This may have been *only* a matter of appearance. The reality may have been quite different; indeed parental authority seems, if anything, stronger in the nineteenth century than in the eighteenth. But the fact that children were now more visible and more often approached in their own terms was interpreted by many observers as a symptom of decadence and loosened family bonds.

[36]Ruth Benedict, "Continuities and Discontinuities in Cultural Conditioning," *Psychiatry*, 1, p. 165.

[37]Keniston, *op. cit.*, p. 161.

[38]William B. Forbush, *The Boy Problem,* Chicago: The Pilgrim Press, 1901, p. 20.

formation of an identity. This pattern is characteristic of societies with a high rate of social change and a plurality of alternatives in regard to careers, moral codes, and life styles. The young person shrinks from such a bewildering array of choices and becomes part of the youth culture, where a clear-cut, if temporary, identity comes ready-made.

All of this seems to describe nineteenth-century America fairly well, especially the new life of the cities. Social and economic change was everywhere apparent; ambitions were high; there was an astonishing diversity of people, ideologies, occupations. The disparity between generations was assumed; it became, indeed, a part of the national mythology. Immigrant families presented an especially dramatic case in point; likewise those families in which the children of uneducated parents had the chance to go to school. Thus, once again, there was the youth culture.

The growth of the concept of adolescence was the final step in this long and somewhat devious process. It was the response to an observable *fact* —the fact of a youth culture, of many young people seemingly in distress (or at least behaving in ways that distressed their elders). Americans needed some means of understanding the problems of, and the problems created by, these young people. We have tried to show them groping toward such an understanding through much of the nineteenth century. And we have located, chiefly in the work of G. Stanley Hall, a kind of culmination of these efforts: the first comprehensive theory of adolescence in modern history.

Adolescent Development and the Secular Trend

ROLF E. MUUSS

The author describes changes that have taken place in adolescent growth patterns during the past few centuries, and conjectures future directions and broader implications of this trend.

Today's children grow faster, experience the adolescent growth spurt earlier, reach puberty earlier, and attain their adult height earlier. These patterns of accelerated growth are described as the "secular trend." Evidence indicates that the total process of growth is speeding up so that children and adolescents are taller than their coevals were sixty or seventy years ago. In addition, and less pronounced, the final adult height is increasing slowly, even though adult stature is reached at an earlier age. While there is some disagreement in respect to the specific amount of change which has taken place over any given historical period of time, there is no disagreement about the basic trend. Allowing for considerable individual variation and assuming the continuation of the present trend, it has been estimated that in the United States the normal healthy son will be as much as one inch taller and ten pounds heavier than his father. The normal healthy girl will be a half to one inch taller, two pounds heavier and will experience menarche about ten months earlier than her mother. Boys are more strongly affected by the secular trend than girls, as boys in general react more strongly to various influences, "ranging from malnutrition in Central Europe to the effects of radiation in Hiroshima" (Tanner, 1968). The acceleration of physical growth appears to have its correlates in other areas of development as well. Attitudes, interests, dating patterns and heterosexual activities, educational changes, certain health problems, and even the legal recognition of the end of adolescence (e.g. voting age) are changing in the same direction, pointing to the close interrelatedness of physical, social, attitudinal, and educational development.

Data that support the secular trend in respect to change in body size, body weight and age of sexual maturation are not confined to the United States but come from different geographic regions and a large variety of national and ethnic groups: Chinese, Japanese, New Zealander, Italian, and Polish as well as American Negroes and whites.

In a comprehensive review and analysis of all available data for American boys over an eighty-year period, Meredith (1963) generalized that the stature of North American boys had increased. He found that fifteen year old white boys were 13.1 cm or 5¼ inches taller in 1955 than in 1870 which means an increase of 8.5% in relative stature. Negro youths, age fifteen, gained 9.5 cm or 5.8% in the period from 1890 to 1930. During the same period, Negro youths, age of seven were a year and a half more advanced approximately 6.9. kg or 15.2 lbs. The average weight increase in white boys age fifteen, between 1870 and 1955, was 15 kg or 33 lbs., a change of 30% in body weight (Figure 1).

In a Swedish study, school children above the age of seven were a year and a half more advanced in their overall physical development, and

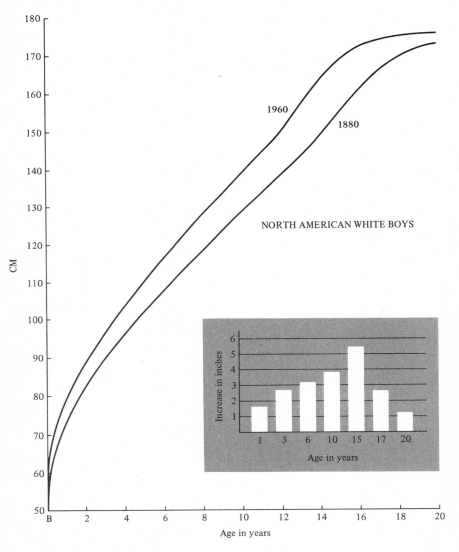

Figure 1. Schematic curves of mean stature for 1880 and 1960. Inset shows differences between the curves at selected ages. From Meredith, H. V. Change in the stature and body weight of North American boys during the last 80 years.

In *Advances in Child Development and Behavior*, L. P. Lipsett & C. C. Spiker (Eds.), N.Y.: Academic Press, Vol. 1, 1963, p. 90. Used by permission of the author and the publisher.

8–17 cm taller in 1938 than school children in 1883. The adolescent growth spurt occurred a year earlier and the velocity of the height growth was greater for the 1938–39 group (Broman, Dahlberg, & Lichtenstein, 1942). In Puerto Rico, eight to ten year old children, attending private schools were found to be 4 cm taller than their coevals thirty years earlier (Knott & Meredith, 1963). Boys from socioeconomically favored families attending Marlborough College in England were measured at an average age of sixteen and a half in 1873 and averaged 65.5 inches tall. Eighty years later, boys of the same age in the same school, probably from families of similar socioeconomic status, were 69.1 inches tall, a gain of 4.1 inches or about ½ inch per decade. The relatively small gain for the last two groups might be explained on the basis that these children came from relatively wealthy families who seem to benefit less from the secular trend than children from the lower socioeconomic classes (Tanner, 1962). Toronto school children of the age thirteen to fourteen were found to be three inches taller in 1939 than thirteen to fourteen year olds were in 1892. Comparative studies in Hamburg, Germany report that twelve year olds in the 1960s are as large as fifteen year olds were in 1875. Similar evidence since the middle of the nineteenth century could be multiplied extensively. According to less scientific sources, the average height of the first colonists who landed in Jamestown is supposed to have been less than five feet. The average height of American sailors in the war of 1812 is estimated as five feet two inches, which explains why the decks of the USS Constitution did not need to be more than five feet six inches high (J. McV. Hunt, 1969).

The secular trend means that children not only grow faster at an earlier age but even as adults they are taller than their fore-fathers; however, the difference for the final adult height is not as great as during the period of the adolescent growth spurt when the effects of the secular trend are most noticeable. Carter (1966) maintains that the total gain in height over the last century in Britain is no more than 1–½ inches; Meredith (1963) finds a change in adult height of 1.3. inches or 3.4 cm for an eighty-five year period; Tanner (1968), in contrast, reported an increase in adult height of 2½ to 3½ inches during the last century. In addition, the final adult height is attained at an earlier age. Boys in 1880 did not reach their full final adult height until they were twenty-three, twenty-four, or even twenty-five years old, while today the average male reaches his adult height at the age of eighteen. Girls, at the turn of the century, reached their adult height at eighteen or nineteen while the average today has dropped to sixteen.

Most research data deal with height and weight measures. However, the same phenomenon can be observed in other body dimensions. The knights' armor in medieval European castles serve as powerful illustrations of the secular trend since the armor seem to be made to fit average ten to twelve year old American boys of today. The seats of the famous La Scala opera house in Milan, Italy, which was constructed in 1776–1778, were 13 inches wide. Thirty years ago most states outlawed seats that were less than 18 inches wide. In 1975 comfortable seats will need to be 24 inches wide. The feet of the American male at the present time grow ⅓ of an inch every generation which means an upward change of one shoe size per generation. Today the shoes worn by the average male are 9 to 10B, while his grandfather in all probability wore a size 7 shoe.

The secular trend not only includes physical size and weight, but also maturation of the reproductive system. Thus acceleration in development is also reflected in the declining age of onset of puberty. Most available research data use as their criteria the average age of a girl's menarche. Corresponding acceleration of sexual maturation for boys has also been reported in the literature. A summary of the available evidence which has been collected from various sources, different national samples and different historical periods, has been presented by Tanner (1962) and is reproduced here (Figure 2). Even though there is some variation from one national sample to another, the overall pattern that emerges is an impressive illustration of the secular trend in sexual maturation. Menarche in the Norwegian data, which goes back to 1840, occurs on an average at the age of seventeen. Since then it has tended to occur approximately four months earlier per decade. By 1960 the reported average age of menarche was thirteen and the trend continues so that today it already occurs in the twelfth year of life and may approach the age of twelve by the turn of the century.

The effects of the secular trend are most pronounced during pubescence as the comparison of Meredith's growth curves (Figure 1) clearly shows and consequently height and weight comparisons during this developmental period yield more impressive differences than at an earlier or a later age. It is also during the pubescent period that the emotional impact and social awareness of generational differences in growth patterns are most pronounced. Parents may well remember the age when they attended their first dance, had their first date, received or gave their first kiss, and the mother, the age when she experienced menarche. And the frequently heard parental comparison, "When I was your age . . ." may actually be accurate if one considered the chronological age alone, but is less appropriate if one considers the changes which are produced by the secular trend. Furthermore, the effects of the secular trend may be compounded by social pressure toward earlier dating and romantic involvement with the opposite sex.

Several interesting questions need to be raised concerning the secular trend, although answers to these questions need to be considered as hypotheses at best and some may be no more than interesting conjectures until more solid evidence becomes available.

1. *When did the secular trend begin?* Apparently the change in man's growth patterns is a relatively recent phenomenon. Specific evidence to answer this question is hard to find since most available research studies compare data collected in the mid-twentieth century with data that were collected in the mid-nineteenth century. One study, to be cited in more detail later, indicates that there was relatively little height gain between 1740–1830 but that following 1830 the secular trend began and gained momentum after 1875 (Kiil, 1939). In agreement with this, Lenz (1959) quotes a Danish study which reported no change in height before 1845, but an acceleration of growth following that date. It has been proposed by Backman (1948), based on an extensive review of the literature, that the age of menarche was fourteen to fifteen years in ancient times and in the Middle Ages. The average age of menarche

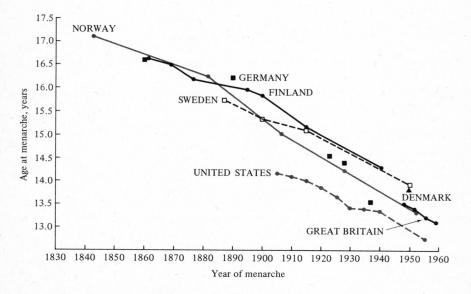

Figure 2. Secular trend in age at menarche 1830–1960.
From Tanner, J. M. *Growth at Adolescence.* Oxford: Blackwell Scientific Publications, 1962, p. 153. Used by permission of the publisher.

began to rise about 1500 and continued to increase until the end of the 18th century. At around 1800 the average age of menarche in Northern Europe was seventeen and a half to eighteen years. In the beginning of the nineteenth century with the impact of the industrial revolution the trend reversed itself and the age of menarche began to decline, an observation that is well supported by Tanner's (1962) data (Figure 2). In general, presently available evidence seems to place the acceleration of the adolescent growth spurt and the secular trend toward the end of the 18th or the beginning of the 19th century.

2. *How long is the secular trend to continue?* If one were to assume that the present rate of change of one inch gain per generation continues and then projects this trend to the year 4000, man would have doubled his standing height and have reached an average of eleven to twelve feet. And if the age of menarche would continue to decline by four months per decade, by 2240 the average four year old would experience menarche. Krogman, a well known physical anthropologist, believes that there is a boundary to the ultimate size of man, just as other species seem to have size boundaries. He predicts that the secular trend will slow down when man reaches an average height of six feet. Jensen (1969) who approaches the issue from a genetic point of view, argues that the increase of heterozygosity — that is, the state of possessing genetically dissimilar genes in regard to a given characteristic — will wear off. Reduction in heterozygosity will slowly result in a leveling off effect of the secular trend. While some sources maintain that the secular trend continues unabated (Tanner, 1962), others maintain that the trend is already beginning to slow down, at least in the United States (Jensen, 1969).

3. *What is responsible for the change in the timing of man's growth patterns?* Two very different theories have been advanced to explain man's accelerated growth in physical development: (1) diet and environmental conditions, and (2) hybrid vigor. At the present time it appears to be impossible to say that one of these factors is entirely or even predominantly responsible while the other is not.

The most obvious factors that may contribute to the secular trend are nutritional considerations: better balanced diets, more emphasis on vitamins, proteins and minerals rather than an increase in calories. However, the effects of the secular trend are more pronounced in the lower socioeconomic classes than in the middle and upper classes, which are more likely to practice dietary knowledge. It is known that middle and upper class children are taller, heavier, and menstruate earlier than children from the lower socioeconomic strata of society. Evidence to this effect can be found in the Broman, Dahlberg, and Lichtenstein (1942) study; their data distinguish between elementary and secondary school pupils at least for the ages ten through fourteen. Since Sweden at the time of the study had a dual track educational system, it can be assumed that many more children from the higher socioeconomic strata of society attended secondary schools. On all measurements reported, the secondary school pupils scored higher, an observation that is more pronounced in 1883 than in 1938. However, "the secular trend has over-ridden the social class differences, and though these still exist, the average boy of today is taller at all ages than the upper class boy of 1878" (Tanner, 1962, p. 147). In support of the nutritional hypothesis, it has been found that the secular trend is interrupted and even reversed during periods of famine and economic crises (Tanner, 1968). There are also other factors which are related to better health care, especially prenatal care, immunization against disease and reduction in serious childhood disease. Furthermore, it appears "that the mechanism which causes the secular shift must be operating within the first few years of life" (Donovan, 1965, p. 35) if not in the prenatal period of development. The change in family size from six children in the mid-nineteenth century to two or three children in the mid-twentieth century has also contributed to the secular trend. Children from small families have been found to be consistently larger and menstruate earlier than children from large families. However, this fact by itself does not constitute a sufficient explanation. It could account for some change but not for the phenomenon per se (Tanner, 1962). Since electricity has become widely available, children tend to spend more hours awake and under illumination — and if one can draw analogies from animal studies — this influences the rate of growth and accelerates sexual maturity. Other factors that may contribute to the secular trend include more leisure time, better child care, laws against child labor, improvement in housing and climate control, changes in temperature and humidity, as well as improvement in the standard of living in general.

As part of the hybrid vigor hypothesis it has been suggested that the invention of the bicycle in 1871, and the invention of the steam engine may have contributed to the secular trend. These technological inventions provided increasing freedom to travel and to select one's mate outside the narrow confines of the village. This change in the pattern of mate selection caused a progressive "breaking down of genetic isolates, that is, of the tendency for marriages to be contracted between members of the same village community" (Tanner, 1961, p. 150). Thus the change in the timing of the growth pattern and the change in the adult height receive a genetic explanation.

It has been estimated that ten to twenty percent of the variance in height is due to genetic dominance, so that the mean of the offspring of two parents will not be halfway between the parents but slightly closer to the taller parent. Outbreeding increases heterozygotes in the population with a consequent increase in height. This heterosis due to outbreeding also enhances growth rate and early maturation as amply demonstrated in numerous experiments in animal breeding (Jensen, 1969, p. 229).

One set of Norwegian data (Kiil, 1939), collected over a 200 year span, fit into the chronology of this hypothesis. Between 1740 and 1830 there was little evidence for gain in height. Betwen 1830 and 1875, with the availability of the bicycle, the height gain was found to be .3 cm per decade. After 1875 with the availability of better means of transportation the height gain increased further to .6 cm per decade. Additional support for this hypothesis can be found in the data presented by Hulse (1957). He observed in Swiss mountain villages that if both parents came from the same village their children, as adults, were 2 cm shorter than if the parents came from different villages.

The available evidence does not identify one specific factor which is responsible for the secular trend. The phenomenon is complex and in all probability the interaction of several of the factors discussed may contribute to it. A more definitive answer to the question of causation awaits further research.

4. *What are the social, attitudinal, and educational correlates of the secular trend?* While the following discussion does not imply a simple cause–effect relationship, the secular trend in physical growth has its correlates in many other areas of development in that certain interest patterns and attitudinal changes as well as social sexual interests and social sophistication seem to occur at an earlier age today than even a generation ago. The effect of this change is most pronounced during the adolescent period and most noticeable in respect to the time when adult privileges are granted by parents or demanded by youths. Some of the contemporary adolescent problems and conflicts, especially the present concern with the "generation gap," may be better understood if one were to consider the earlier biological maturation of youth as contrasted with their chronological age which usually serves as the frame of reference for parents and teachers. On a more general level, even the structure of the curriculum, the amount and kind of knowledge acquired, and the changes in mental ability follow the direction of the secular trend in physical development.

Mary Cover Jones (1960) gives evidence for this trend, even though, in contrast to the studies on physical growth patterns, historically speaking, her article covers a much shorter period of time. Ninth graders in 1953 had attitudes and interests which were much like those held by eleventh graders twenty-five years earlier. The data from the more recent sample indicate that adolescents have become more serious, are more tolerant, show greater social sophistication and sexual interests than their coevals in 1935. Harris (1959) compared the interest patterns and concerns of junior and senior high school students in 1935 with those of subjects in 1957. For both sexes the more recent data reveal an increased interest in love, marriage, home, and family, as well as a greater social awareness as indicated by an increased preference for the item "getting along with other people."

Broderick and Fowler (1961) reported that the frequently observed sex cleavage found in fourth grade sociometric tests and interpreted as a lack of interest — if not outright hostility and antagonism — toward the opposite sex is disappearing. They found that the sex cleavage is being replaced by greater and earlier cross sex friendships, interest in the opposite sex, dating, romantic attachment, and kissing. Ninety percent of this sample of fifth graders already had sweethearts, sixty-five percent had been kissed by the opposite sex, and forty percent had already dated. Kuhlen and Houlihan (1965), contrasting data on adolescent heterosexual interest obtained in 1942 with data obtained by the same procedure in 1963, provide further evidence that heterosexual interests have become significantly more pronounced in the more recent sample.

On a more practical level, considerable concern is expressed by many parents regarding their daughters' desire to use lipstick, nail polish, training bras, nylon stockings, perfume, and other paraphernalia of sex appeal, and their indications of sex interest at an earlier age. The changing patterns for boys is [sic] expressed in earlier smoking, drinking, use of drugs, having dates, and desiring physical intimacies on their dates. This concern with earlier sex appeal, heterosexual interest, and sexual intimacy of today's adolescents has found expression in a number of articles which recently have appeared in the slick cover journals. Havighurst writes in 1963, "within the past generation, the ages at which boys and girls begin dating, going to boy–girl parties, learning to dance, and other precursors of courtship and marriage have all decreased, so that junior high school is now a theater of rather active social life of a sort which formerly was thought more appropriate for the senior high school" (p. 160). Since then the pattern for junior high school has already been more widely accepted and the concern today is with the heterosexual interest in elementary school.

Curriculum changes in the public schools have also followed the patterns of the secular trend in physical development in that certain subjects are being taught at an earlier age. Some of these changes are related to other factors, such as improved technology, new methods of teaching, and changing educational and psychological theory, as

well as political and business reasons, nevertheless, the direction of change is the same as that of the secular trend. Content areas such as calculus, consumer education, or "personality and dating" are no longer the prerogative of the college curriculum but are taught increasingly more in high schools, just as elementary school children learn different number systems, such as the binary system, and receive instruction about drugs as well as sex education.

The head width and the face width (Knott & Meredith, 1963), the size of the face (Hunter & Garn, 1969), and the circumference of the head have increased, which may well have resulted in an increase in the size of the brain. One might speculate whether this physical change could have contributed to the acceleration of children's ability to learn, to think, and to reason. There is evidence that average mental test scores have increased from generation to generation in different cultures; e.g., World War II draftees scored approximately one standard deviation higher than World War I draftees (Tuddenham, 1948), and draftees in the 1960s scored ½ standard deviation higher than World War II draftees (Humphreys, 1969). To what extent changes in the patterns of physical development and changes in mental test creasing school attendance, better education, and the mass media of communication and even increased exposure to and experience with testing would most likely contribute to increased intelligence test scores.

It is known that the period of adolescence is also expanding upward in that modern industrialized and computerized society requires increasingly more education, thus prolonging the period of dependency and immaturity which the status of being a minor and being a student implies. "Without the challenge of independent responsibility . . . the duration of training tends to limit emotional maturity which is a vital component in the equipment of anyone who hopes to achieve wisdom" (Kubie, 1958). In addition, the increase of affluence in society permits the postponement of the assumption of responsibility in its young and makes possible the longer period of schooling.

On the other hand, the overall effects of the secular trend and its social-emotional correlates constitute a prolongation of the adolescent period downward since pubescence and adolescence begin considerably earlier today than at the turn of the century.

5. *What are the broader implications of the secular trend?* The social, medical, educational, and psychiatric consequences of the secular trend and particularly of a continuation of the speeding up of man's physical and sexual development are hard to assess at this time. Although the phenomenon has already evoked some concern and a great deal of speculation it has stimulated only a limited amount of research. The interrelatedness of developmental acceleration with other social trends does not allow the singling out of the secular trend as the sole cause of any one contemporary social, medical, or psychiatric issue, and no claim is made here to that effect. Nevertheless, the direction of such changes are [sic] consistent with the secular trend in that there is an acceleration of the time schedule of social and educational phenomena and at least of some medical problems. Furthermore, knowledge of the secular trend may contribute to a better understanding of such social issues as the demand for the lowering of the voting age, the demand for student participation in the decision-making processes of universities, colleges, and even high schools. The trend is also reflected in the dropping of the average age for marriages, which is preceded by a decline in the age of dating and courtship (Broderick, 1961), and a slow increase of physical intimacies and sexual intercourse at an earlier age. The resulting social-medical problems of increased venereal disease and illegitimate birth at an earlier age have been widely publicized. There is evidence that a new face shape and face size have emerged, which means "that present-day orthodontists may well be working toward cosmetic ideals thirty to fifty years old" (Hunter & Garn, 1969). Furthermore, the proportion of youngsters under sixteen arrested for narcotic offenses, as well as the general phenomena of drug use and drug addiction, have increased drastically since 1950 in the adolescent age range and even in pre-adolescence.

Some biologists and geneticists have suggested that in order to solve the problems of overpopulation, lack of nutrition, and pollution of air and water we should not only continue to be concerned with changing the environment, but in addition, we should consider changing man himself. Future man would be considerably reduced in size in order to change the ratio between the excessive size of man in relationship to the existing environment and resources. This would constitute a drastic reversal of the secular trend.

Curriculum changes of the school reflect educational acceleration. In addition, the present reorganization of the public school system itself reflects the trend toward earlier maturation. In some school systems the sixth grade has been taken out of the elementary school structure and in combination with the seventh grade and the eighth, has resulted in a new educational concept —the middle school. Other school systems are contemplating similar moves. Schools recognize that pubescent growth changes have been accelerated to the extent that the junior high school needs to be relocated age-wise and re-named.

Some authors with psychiatric or clinical orientations write about the discrepancy between an acceleration in physical, social, and educational development in today's youth with a simultaneous deceleration in emotional and ethical maturity. This developmental discrepancy is interpreted as one of the reasons for increased conflict and crises in adolescence. The available research evidence for such a discrepancy is sparse, and where the assessment of deceleration in emotional and ethical maturity has been attempted (Englemann, 1962), the interpretations and generalizations seem to go beyond the data presented. Heath (1968) concludes on the basis of extensive personality test data which were obtained from entering Haverford freshmen since World War II: "Compared to the students of even just a decade ago, the contemporary student has become an increasingly intellectualized and inhibited person whose energies are directed more toward himself and his own interest than toward others with whom he has become progressively less emotionally involved" (p. 63). The similarity between Heath's (1962) findings, even though obtained from different national groups, different age levels, and by way of different methodology, is noteworthy. Heath continues further in his analysis of historical changes. "In comparison to the student of the forties and fifties, the students of the sixties have become increasingly more over-controlled, inhibited, and tend to be more defensive and intellectually efficient" (p. 63). Quotes from the professional literature concerning the "psychological retardation of today's youth" (Seidman, 1963) and "accelerated physical development and retarded emotional development" (Otterstadt, 1960) could be multiplied. If such a discrepancy between physical, intellectual, social-sexual development on the one hand and emotional, ethical, and moral development on the other hand does exist during adolescence, it would be a significant conceptual contribution to the understanding of adolescent conflict, crises, and difficulties. However, while acceleration of physical, social, and educational development is well-supported by available evidence, the simultaneous deceleration in emotional, ethical, moral, or psychological development must be considered at this time as an interesting hypothesis which, even though it has some support, is in need of further empirical verification.

REFERENCES

BACKMAN, G. Die beschleunigte Entwicklung der Jugend. Verfruhte Menarche, verspätete Menopause, verlängerte Lebensdauer. *Acta Anatomica,* 1948, *4,* 421–480.

BRODERICK, C. B., & FOWLER, S. E. New Patterns of Relationships Between the Sexes Among Preadolescents. *Marriage and Family Living,* 1961, *23,* 27–30.

BROMAN, B., DAHLBERG, G., & LICHTENSTEIN, A. Height and Weight During Growth. *Acta Paediatrica,* 1942, *30,* 1–66.

CARTER, C. O. *Human Heredity.* Baltimore: Penguin Books, 1962.

DONOVAN, B. T., & VAN DER WERFF TEN BOSCH, J. J. *Physiology of Puberty.* Baltimore: The Williams and Wilkins Co., 1965.

ENGELMANN, W. Reifungsentwicklung und Reifungsveränderungen im gefühlsbetonten Wertungsbereich unserer Jugend. *Psychologische Rundschau,* 1962, *13,* 131–140.

HARRIS, D. B. Sex Differences in the Life Problems and Interests of Adolescents, 1935 and 1957. *Child Development,* 1959, *39,* 453–459.

HAVIGHURST, R. J. Do Junior High School Youth Grow Up Too Fast? *The Bulletin of the National Association of Secondary School Principals,* 1963, *47,* 151–162.

HEATH, D. H. *Growing Up in College.* San Francisco: Jossey-Bass, 1968.

HULSE, F. S. Exogamie et Héterosis. *Archives Suisse D'Anthropologie Générale,* 1957, *22,* 103–125.

HUMPHREYS, L. New Perspectives on Intelligence. Lecture delivered at the Maryland Psychological Association Annual Meeting, April 25, 1969.

HUNT, J. MC V. Has Compensatory Education Failed? Has it Been Attempted? In *Environment, Heredity, and Intelligence.* Reprint Series No. 2 compiled from *Harvard Educational Review,* 1969, 130–152.

HUNTER, W. S., & GARN, S. M. Evidence for a Secular Trend in Face Size. *The Angle Orthodontist,* 1969, *39,* 320–323.

JENSON, A. R. Reducing the Heredity–Environment Uncertainty. In *Environment, Heredity, and Intelligence.* Reprint Series No. 2 compiled from *Harvard Educational Review,* 1969, 209–243.

JONES, M. C. A Comparison of the Attitudes and Interests of Ninth-Grade Students over Two Decades. *Journal of Educational Research,* 1960, *51,* 175–186.

KIIL, V. Stature and Growth of Norwegian Men during the Past 200 years. *Skr. Norske Vidensk. Akad.,* 1939, No. 6.

KNOTT, V. B. Stature, Leg Girth, and Body Weight of Puerto Rican Private School Children Measured in 1962. *Growth,* 1963, *27,* 157–174.

KNOTT, V. B., & MEREDITH, H. V. Body Size of United States Schoolboys at Ages from 11 Years to 15 Years. *Human Biology,* 1963, *35,* 507–513.

KUBIE, L. S. *Neurotic Distortions of the Creative Process.* Lawrence: University of Kansas Press, 1958.

KUHLEN, R. G., & HOULIHAN, N. B. Adolescent Heterosexual Interest in 1942 and 1963. *Child Development,* 1965, *36,* 1049–1052.

LENZ, W. Ursachen des gesteigerten Wachstums der heutigen Jugend. *Wissen. Veröff. deut. Gesellsch. Ernäh.,* 1959, *4,* 1–33.

MEREDITH, H. V. Change in the Stature and Body Weight of North American Boys during the last

80 Years. In *Advances in Child Development and Behavior*. L. P. Lipsitt & C. C. Spiker (Eds.), N.Y.: Academic Press, Vol. 1, 1963, 69–114.

OTTERSTADT, H. Akzeleration und Stoffplan. *Psychologische Rundschau*, 1960, *11*, 45–51.

SEIDMANN, P. *Moderne Jugend*. Zurich & Stuttgart: Rascher Verlag, 1963.

TANNER, J. M. Earlier Maturation in Man. *Scientific American*, 1968, *218*, 21–27.

TANNER, J. M. *Growth at Adolescence*. Oxford: Blackwell Scientific Publications, 1962.

TUDDENHAM, R. D. Soldier Intelligence in World Wars I and II. *American Psychologist*, 1948, *3*, 54–56.

Chapter 1: Suggested Additional Readings

COMMITTEE ON ADOLESCENCE, GROUP FOR THE ADVANCEMENT OF PSYCHIATRY. *Normal Adolescence*. New York: Charles Scribner's Sons, 1968. This short book discusses adolescence from the psychiatric point of view, in terms of biological, cultural, and psychological determinants.

DWYER, J., & MAYER, J. Psychological effects of variations in physical appearance during adolescence. *Adolescence*, 1968–69, *3*, 353–380. This article concerns psychological effects of deviations in physical appearance during adolescence, including early and late maturing, sex appropriateness of physique, overweight, and cultural ideals of attractiveness.

KIELL, N. *The universal experience of adolescence*. New York: International University Press, 1964. The author's main thesis is that the internal turmoil and external disorder of adolescence are universal and are only moderately affected by cultural determinants. Using a psychoanalytic frame of reference, he cites research relating to various cultures to test his point of view, and concludes that, in the more literate, achieving societies, adolescent turmoil is common.

KNEPLER, A. Adolescence: An anthropological approach. In G. D. Winter and E. M. Nuss (Eds.), *Identity and Awareness*. Oakland, N. J.: Scott, Foresman, 1969, Pp. 201–216. This comparative evaluation of adolescence in American and primitive societies highlights the cultural factors involved in defining adolescence.

MUUSS, R. E. Theories of adolescent development—their philosophical and historical roots. *Adolescence*, 1966, *1*(1), 22–44. The writer traces theories and philosophies of human development from ancient times to the early twentieth century, discussing in particular the contributions of the early Greeks, the medieval Christians, Comenius, Locke, Rousseau, and Charles Darwin.

MUUSS, R. E. *Theories of adolescence* (2nd ed.) New York: Random House, 1968. The author considers various theories proposed to explain the nature of adolescence.

PESKIN, H. Pubertal onset and ego functioning. *Journal of Abnormal Psychology*, 1967, *72*, 1–15. A model of pubertal growth based on psychoanalytic ego psychology was applied to the study of early and late maturation in boys. Patterns of mobility and expressiveness proved to relate to patterns of physical maturation. The length of an individual's latency period appeared to influence the post-pubertal impulse-controlling mechanism of his personality.

ROSENMAYR, L. Towards an overview of youth's sociology. *International Social Science Journal*, 1968, *20*(2), 286–315. The author cites relevant research concerning a broad range of topics about adolescence, including the notion of youth, sociocultural variations of adolescence, adolescent peer and dating behaviors, types of adolescent socialization, and others. The approach is cross-cultural, involving data concerning the youth of many lands.

2

The Adolescent Image

The adolescent image—or society's view of the adolescent—has tended to run the gamut from rather brutal caricature to somewhat saccharine adulation. The indictments of youth have a venerable history. Over two thousand years ago, Socrates described youth as disrespectful of their elders, and as tyrants—not servants—of their households. "They are also mannerless," said Socrates, "and fail to rise when their elders enter the room. They chatter before company, gobble up dainties at the table, cross their legs, and tyrannize over their teachers."

Such indictments have continued down the ages. Robert Nixon (1964), a psychiatrist, views the majority of youth as maladjusted—and under the blanket term "maladjusted" he includes the conformists, the abnormals, and the rebels. Normal youth, who comprise a minority, he describes as being introspective but not schizophrenic, self-concerned, self-critical, and self-appraising; the existence of these psychologically normal youth, he believes, makes it possible to identify the unhealthy majority.

Hurlock's (1966) view of the majority of adolescents is no more positive than Nixon's. She describes modern youth as a new species, with several dominant traits. They are conformists, following the herd whether for good or bad. They are preoccupied with status symbols and anxious to be identified with the leading crowd; since they are also anti-intellectual, their eagerness for higher education merely reflects a desire to secure better jobs and to meet "the right people." They are irresponsible and addicted to the philosophy, "Let John do it." Lacking respect for the older generation, for rules, and for laws, today's teenagers, Hurlock concludes, are turning into second-rate students and citizens.

Others perceive youth's weaknesses, but view them somewhat more benignly. On the basis of a nationwide study of adolescents, Leidy and Starry (1967) conclude that this then is the American adolescent—a bewildering amalgam of conflicting moods and motives, habits and dreams. At times he seems all energy and innocent optimism; then again he is cynical and wise beyond his years. His values seem sometimes distorted, his attitudes a bit bizarre. He pays too much attention to his friends and what he sees on television, and not enough attention to his parents and what he hears in school. He is aware of his many conflicts and problems (knows that adults, finally, are responsible for many of them) and realizes that he may never resolve them at all [p. 12].

At the other extreme are those writers whose opinion of teenagers wallows in sentiment. According to Davidson (1957), the teenager is a scapegoat, whose "basic crime is merely that he is over 12 and under 20." In Davidson's opinion, current teenagers are "stronger, smarter, more self-sufficient, and more constructive than any other generation in history." Others are more analytical than judgmental in describing adolescents. Throughout Friedenberg's *The Vanishing Adolescent,* we find passages which collectively represent his concept of youth. In one such passage, he calls adolescents "cliquish and clannish, but not usually smug or parochial." Adolescents are generally "sound and stable" in judgment, and their mistakes are the result of factors beyond their experience. Boys he characterizes as vain, with a very personal vanity. More concerned with their personal appearance than are girls, boys bask in physical acclaim like "alligators on a log," while girls find satisfaction in attractiveness because it produces interesting relationships.

Paulston (1968), like Friedenberg, takes a tolerant view of youth's eccentricities. She describes adolescents as "mildly and temporarily insane, to the extent that diverted psychic energy obstructs their being the 'whole' individuals they really are [p. 374]."

Other writers warn against unwarranted over-generalizations about youth, and in fact, the tendency is growing among psychologists to refuse to portray the adolescent in terms of a single image. Even in a society devoted to publicity, notes Denney (1962), youth have a great capacity for concealment, and this penchant for masquerade, coupled with the wide emotional range of youth and the rapid pace of change during the youthful years, makes it difficult to fit youth into meaningful categories. Similarly, Sorenson (1962) speaks of society's "confused image of youth." Society cannot even make up its mind how to designate the adolescent. Is he a "youth," a "teenager," or just a "young person?" In any event, he is generally seen as an individual in transition. In no other stage of the life cycle, Sorenson quotes Erikson as saying, are the promise of finding oneself and the threat of losing oneself so closely allied.

Thornburg (1971), too, points out the growing tendency to distinguish among different categories of adolescence. Most generalizations just do not apply to all sorts of youth. For his part, Thornburg differentiates three groups of youth in particular: high school, non-college, and college youth.

The matter of teen image is important for various reasons. For one, an individual's self-image is importantly affected by the way others view him. In turn, the way he views himself—as worthwhile or stupid, as responsible or trustworthy, as stable or flighty—will affect how he deals with his environment. If he views himself as competent and successful, he will persist longer against difficulty than if he sees himself as mediocre in attainment (Douvan & Adelson, 1958). A healthy self-concept is also important for an individual's mental health. Adolescents who have stable, realistic self-concepts make better adjustments to life. (Spivack, 1956). Moreover, adults' views of teenagers in turn affect adolescents' relations to the adult world. Adults who look on teenagers as responsible are more likely to elicit their cooperation. Youth can hardly relate to, and profitably be guided by, adults who regard them with antagonism.

Hess and Goldblatt (1957) reported that adolescents, as a group, believed themselves subject to condemnation, criticism, and general devaluation by adults. Adolescents claimed that the older generation perceived them as sloppy, irresponsible, unreliable, and inclined toward destructive and antisocial behavior. These same adolescents credited themselves with an acceptable degree of achievement, though acknowledging they were in a subordinate status to adults. They were also generous in their views of adults, and tended to idealize adulthood. What is the effect of these conflicting images? Perhaps a moderate overestimation of adults may help motivate the adolescent to seek maturity. However, adolescents who simultaneously over-idealize adults and yet believe themselves disparaged by adults may encounter difficulties in ego development.

It becomes obvious that while society has many images of the adolescent, the adolescent also has several images of himself. The image varies with time, the place, the circumstance, and above all, with the viewer. Seen through the eyes of a small child, the adolescent appears very big and very wise; to the older person, the teenager seems still "wet behind the ears." This kaleidoscopic image of youth is reflected in the diversity of views presented in the two reading selections that follow. In the first, Friedenberg portrays youth as thwarted by an environment which inhibits them and fails to permit them to be all they are capable of becoming, and he criticizes society's image of the teenager as being unwholesome and unfair. The second article, by Otto and Otto, counterbalances Friedenberg's negative portrayal with a new image that emphasizes youth's strengths and gives them something worthwhile to live up to. At the present time, perhaps the only valid image is a confused image, reflecting youth's uncertain position in the world today.

REFERENCES

DAVIDSON, B.   18,000,000 teenagers can't be wrong. *Collier's*, January 4, 1957, p. 13.

DENNEY, R.   American youth today: A bigger cast, a wider screen. *Daedalus*, 1962, *91*, 124–145.

DOUVAN, E., & ADELSON, J.   The psychodynamics of social mobility in adolescent boys. *Journal of Abnormal Psychology*, 1958, *56*, 31–44.

FRIEDENBERG, E. Z.   *The vanishing adolescent.* Boston: Beacon Press, 1959.

HESS, R. D. & GOLDBLATT, I.   The status of adolescents in American society: A problem in social identity. *Child Development*, 1957, *28*, 459–468.

HURLOCK, E. B.   American adolescents of today—A new species. *Adolescence*, Spring 1966, *1*(1), 7–21.

LEIDY, T. R., & STARRY, A. R.   The American adolescent—A bewildering amalgam. *The National Education Association Journal*, October 1967, *56*, 8–12.

NIXON, R. E.   Psychological normality in the years of youth. *Teachers College Record*, 1964, *66*(1), 71–79.

PAULSTON, C. B.   On creativity and teaching. *Teachers College Record*, January 1968, *69*(4), 369–377.

SORENSON, R.   Youth's need for challenge and place in society. *Children*, July–August, 1962, *9*(4), 131–138.

SPIVACK, S. S.   A study of a method of self-acceptance and self-rejection. *Journal of Genetic Psychology*, 1956, *88*, 183-202.

THORNBURG, H. D.   Peers: Three distinct groups. *Adolescence*, 1971, *6*(21), 59–76.

The Image of the Adolescent Minority

EDGAR Z. FRIEDENBERG

In America, says Friedenberg, adolescent boys are perceived as a "hot-blooded minority," and "cut down." Girls, by contrast, are simply wasted, and the wastage continues all their lives. Each sex suffers from the special type of discrimination accorded it. The boy's quality of experience is "starved and repressed," while the girl simply fails to develop at all.

In our society there are two kinds of minority status. One of these I will call the "hot-blooded" minorities, whose archetypical image is that of the Negro or Latin. *In the United States, "Teen-agers" are treated as a "hot-blooded" minority.* Then, there are the "long-suffering minorities," whose archetype is the Jew, but which also, I should say, includes women. Try, for a second, to picture a Jewish "teen-ager," and you may sense a tendency for the image to grate. "Teen-agers" err on the hot side; they talk jive, drive hot-rods and become juvenile delinquents. Young Jews talk volubly, play the violin, and go to medical school, though never on Saturday.

The minority group is a special American institution, created by the interaction between a history and an ideology which are not to be duplicated elsewhere. Minority status has little to do with size or proportion. In a democracy, a dominant social group is called a majority and part of its dominance consists in the power to arrange appropriate manifestations of public support; while a subordinate group is, by the logic of political morality, a minority. The minority stereotype, though affected by the actual char-acteristics of the minority group, develops to fit the purposes and expresses the anxieties of the dominant social group. It serves as a slimy coating over the sharp realities of cultural difference, protecting the social organism until the irritant can be absorbed.

Now, when one is dealing with a group that actually is genetically or culturally different from the dominant social group, this is perhaps to be expected. It is neither desirable nor inevitable, for xenophobia is neither desirable nor inevitable; but it is not surprising.

What is surprising is that the sons and daughters of the *dominant* adult group should be treated as a minority group merely because of their age. Their papers are in order and they speak the language adequately. In any society, to be sure, the young occupy a subordinate or probationary status while under tutelage for adult life. But a minority group is not merely subordinate; it is not under tutelage. It is in the process of being denatured; of becoming, under social stress, something more acceptable to the dominant society, but essentially different from what its own growth and experience would lead to. Most

From Edgar Z. Friedenberg, "The Image of the Adolescent Minority." *Dissent,* Spring 1963. Reprinted by permission of *Dissent* and the author.

beasts recognize their own kind. Primitive peoples may initiate their youth; we insist that ours be naturalized, though it is what is most natural about them that disturbs adults most.

The court of naturalization is the public school. A high school diploma is a certificate of legitimacy, not of competence. A youth needs one today in order to hold a job that will permit even minimal participation in the dominant society. Yet our laws governing school attendance do not deal with education. They are not *licensing* laws, requiring attendance until a certain defined minimum competence, presumed essential for adult life, has been demonstrated. They are not *contractual;* they offer no remedy for failure of the school to provide services of a minimum quality. A juvenile may not legally withdraw from school even if he can establish that it is substandard or that he is being ill-treated there. If he does, as many do, for just these reasons, he becomes *prima facie* an offender; for, in cold fact, the compulsory attendance law guarantees him nothing, not even the services of qualified teachers. It merely defines, in terms of age alone, a particular group as subject to legal restrictions not applicable to other persons.

Second-Class Citizen

Legally, the adolescent comes pretty close to having no basic rights at all. The state generally retains the final right even to strip him of his minority status. He has no right to *demand* the particular protection of *either* due process or the juvenile administrative procedure—the state decides. We have had several cases in the past few years of boys eighteen and under being sentenced to death by the full apparatus of formal criminal law, who would not have been permitted to claim its protection had they been accused of theft or disorderly conduct. Each of these executions has so far been forestalled by various legal procedures,[1] but none in such a way as to establish the right of a juvenile to be tried as a juvenile; though he long ago lost his claim to be treated as an adult.

In the most formal sense, then, the adolescent

[1]Two were finally hanged this past June, five years later.

is one of our second-class citizens. But the informal aspects of minority status are also imputed to him. The "teen-ager," like the Latin or Negro, is seen as joyous, playful, lazy, and irresponsible, with brutality lurking just below the surface and ready to break out into violence.[2] All these groups are seen as childish and excitable, imprudent and improvident, sexually aggressive, and dangerous, but possessed of superb and sustained power to satisfy sexual demands. *West Side Story* is not much like *Romeo and Juliet;* but it is a great deal like *Porgy and Bess.*

The fantasy underlying this stereotype, then, is erotic; and its subject is male. The "hot-blooded" minorities are always represented by a masculine stereotype; nobody asks "Would you want your son to marry a Negro?" In each case, also, little counter-stereotypes, repulsively pallid in contrast to the alluring violence and conflict of the central scene, are held out enticingly by the dominant culture; the conscientious "teen-ager" sold by Pat Boone to soothe adults while the kids themselves buy *Mad* and *Catcher;* the boy whose Italian immigrant mother sees to it that he wears a clean shirt to school every day on his way to the Governor's mansion; *Uncle Tom.* In the rectilinear planning of Jonesville these are set aside conspicuously as Public Squares, but at dusk they are little frequented.

One need hardly labor the point that what the dominant society seeks to control by imposing "hot-blooded" minority status is not the actual aggressiveness and sexuality of the Negro, the Latin, or the JD, but its own wish for what the

[2]A very bad—indeed, vicious—but remarkably ambivalent reenactment of the entire fantasy on which the minority status of the teen-ager is based can be seen in the recent movie *13 West St.* Here, the legal impotence of the "teen-ager" is taken absolutely for granted, and sadistic hostility of adults against him, though deplored, is condoned and accepted as natural. Occasional efforts are made to counterbalance the, in my judgment, pornographic picture of a brutal teen-age gang by presenting "good" teen-agers unjustly suspected, and decent police trying to resist sadistic pressure from the gang's victim, who drives one of its members to suicide. But despite this, the picture ends with a scene of the gang's victim—a virile-type rocket scientist—beating the leader of the gang with his cane and attempting to drown the boy in a swimming pool—which the police dismiss as excusable under the circumstances. A Honolulu paper, at least, described this scene of attempted murder as "an old-fashioned caning that had the audience cheering in its seats."

British working classes used to call "a nice game of slap-and-tickle," on the unimpeachable assumption that a little of what you fancy does you good. This, the well-lighted Public Squares cannot afford; the community is proud of them, but they are such stuff as only the driest dreams are made of. These are not the dreams that are wanted. In my experience, it is just not possible to discuss adolescence with a group of American adults without being forced into the topic of juvenile delinquency. Partly this is an expression of legitimate concern, but partly it is because only the JD has any emotional vividness for them.

I would ascribe the success of *West Side Story* to the functional equivalence in the minds of adults between adolescence, delinquency, and aggressive sexuality. Many who saw the show must have wondered, as I did, why there were no Negroes in it—one of the best things about Juvenile Delinquency is that, at least, it is integrated. Hollywood, doubtless, was as usual reluctant to show a member of an enfranchised minority group in an unfavorable light. But there was also a rather sound artistic reason. Putting a real Negro boy in *West Side Story* would have been like scoring the second movement of the *Pastorale* for an eagle rather than flute. The provocative, surly, sexy dancing kids who come to a bad end are not meant realistically. Efforts to use real streets-adolescents in *West Side Story* had to be abandoned; they didn't know how to act. What was depicted here was neither Negro nor white nor really delinquent, but a comfortably vulgar middle-class dream of a "hot-blooded" minority. In dreams a single symbolic boy can represent them all; let the symbol turn real and the dreamer wakes up screaming.

Adolescents are treated as a "hot-blooded" minority, then, because they seem so good at slap-and-tickle. But a number of interesting implications flow from this. Slap-and-tickle implies sexual vigor and attractiveness, warmth and aggression, salted with enough conventional perversity to lend spice to a long dull existence. Such perversity is a kind of exuberant overflow from the mainstream of sexuality, not a diversion of it. It is joyous excess and bounty; extravagant foreplay in the well-known marriage-bed; the generosity of impulse that leads the champion lover of the high school to prance around the shower room snapping a towel on the buttocks of his team-mates three hours before a hot date, just to remind them that life can be beautiful.

Experience Repressed

When a society sees impulsiveness and sexual exuberance as minority characteristics which unsuit the individual for membership until he is successfully naturalized, it is in pretty bad shape. Adolescents, loved, respected, taught to accept, enjoy, and discipline their feelings, grow up. "Teen-agers" don't; they pass. Then, in middle-age, they have the same trouble with their former self that many ethnics do. They hate and fear the kinds of spontaneity that remind them of what they have abandoned, and they hate themselves for having joined forces with and having come to resemble their oppressors.[3] This is the vicious spiral by which "hot-blooded" minority status maintains itself. I am convinced that it is also the source of the specific hostility—and sometimes sentimentality—that adolescents arouse in adults. The processes involved have been dealt with in detail by Daniel Boorstin, Leslie Fiedler, Paul Goodman, and especially Ernest Schachtel.[4] Their effect is to starve out, through silence and misrepresentation, the capacity to have genuine and strongly felt experience, and to replace it by the conventional symbols that serve as the common currency of daily life.

Experience repressed in adolescence does not, of course, result in amnesia, as does the repression of childhood experience; it leaves no temporal gaps in the memory. This makes it more dangerous, because the adult is then quite un-

[3] Cf. Abraham Kardiner and Lionel Ovesey's classic, *The Mark of Oppression* (New York: Norton, 1951), for a fascinating study of these dynamics among American Negroes.

[4] Daniel Boorstin, *The Image.* New York: Atheneum, 1962; Leslie Fiedler, "The Fear of the Impulsive Life." *WFMT Perspective,* October, 1961, pp. 4–9; Paul Goodman, *Growing Up Absurd.* New York: Random House, 1960, p. 38; Ernest Schachtel, "On Memory and Childhood Amnesia." Widely anthologized, cf. the author's *Metamorphosis.* New York: Basic Books, 1959, pp. 279–322. A more systematic and profound treatment, I have since learned, is to be found in Norman Brown, *Life Against Death.* Middletown, Wesleyan University Press, 1959.

aware that his memory is incomplete, that the most significant components of feeling have been lost or driven out. We at least know that we no longer know what we felt as children. But an adolescent boy who asks his father how he felt on the first night he spent in barracks or with a woman will be told what the father now thinks he felt because he ought to have; and this is very dangerous nonsense indeed.

Whether in childhood or in adolescence, the same quality of experience is starved out or repressed. It is still the spontaneous, vivid and immediate that is most feared, and feared the more because so much desired. But there is a difference in focus and emphasis because in adolescence spontaneity can lead to much more serious consequences.

This, perhaps, is the crux of the matter, since it begins to explain why our kind of society should be so easily plunged into conflict by "hot-blooded" minorities in general and adolescent boys in particular. We are consequence-oriented and future-oriented. Among us, to prefer present delights is a sign of either low or high status, and both are feared. Schachtel makes it clear how we go about building this kind of character in the child—by making it difficult for him to notice his delights when he has them, and obliterating the language in which he might recall them joyfully later. This prepares the ground against the subsequent assault of adolescence. But it is a strong assault, and if adolescence wins, the future hangs in the balance.

The Adolescent Girl

In this assault, adolescent boys play a very different role from adolescent girls and are dealt with unconsciously by totally different dynamics. Adolescent girls are not seen as members of a "hot-blooded" minority, and to this fact may be traced some interesting paradoxes in our perception of the total phenomenon of adolescence.

Many critics of the current literature on adolescence—Bruno Bettelheim[5] perhaps most cogently—have pointed out that most contemporary writing about adolescents ignores the adolescent

[5]In "Adolescence and the Conflict of Generations," *Daedalus*, Winter, 1962, p. 68.

girl almost completely. Bettelheim specifically mentions Goodman and myself; the best novels about adolescents of the past decade or so have been, I think there would be fair agreement, Salinger's *The Catcher in the Rye*, John Knowles' *A Separate Peace,* and Colin MacInnes' less well known but superb *Absolute Beginners*. All these have adolescent boys as heroes. Yet, as Bettelheim points out, the adolescent girl is as important as the adolescent boy, and her actual plight in society is just as severe; her opportunities are even more limited and her growth into a mature woman as effectively discouraged. Why has she not aroused more interest?

There are demonstrable reasons for the prominence of the adolescent boy in our culture. Conventionally, it is he who threatens the virtue of our daughters and the integrity of our automobiles. There are so many more ways to get hung up on a boy. "Teen-agers," too, may be all right; but would you want your daughter to marry one? When she doesn't know anything about him except how she feels—and what does that matter when they are both too young to know what they are doing; when he may never have the makings of an executive, or she of an executive's wife?

For this last consideration, paradoxically, also makes the *boy*, rather than the girl, the focus of anxiety. He alone bears the terrible burden of parental aspirations; it is his capacity for spontaneous commitment that endangers the opportunity of adults to live vicariously the life they never manage to live personally.

Holden, Finny, and the unnamed narrator of *Absolute Beginners*, are adolescent boys who do not pass; who retain their minority status, their spontaneous feelings, their power to act out and act up. They go prancing to their destinies. But what destiny can we imagine for them? We leave Holden in a mental hospital, being adjusted to reality; and Finny dead of the horror of learning that his best friend, Gene, had unconsciously contrived the accident that broke up his beautifully articulated body. The Absolute Beginner, a happier boy in a less tense society, fares better; he has had more real contact with other human beings, including a very satisfactory father, and by his time there is such a thing as a "teen-ager," little as it is, for him to be. On this basis, the Beginner can identify himself; the marvelous book ends as he rushes out onto the tarmac at London Airport, bursting through the customs barrier, to stand at the foot of the gangway and greet a planeload of astonished immigrants by crying, "Here I am! Meet your first teen-ager."

Political Disinterest

There are still enough Finnys and Holdens running around free to give me much joy and some hope, and they are flexible enough to come to their own terms with reality. But the system is against them, and they know it well. Why then, do they not try to change it? Why are none of these novels of adolescence political novels? Why have their heroes no political interests at all? In this respect, fiction is true to American life; American adolescents are notably free from political interests. I must maintain this despite the recent advances of SANE kids and Freedom Riders; for, though I love and honor them for their courage and devotion, the causes they fight for are not what I call political. No controversy over basic policy is involved, because nobody advocates atomic disaster or racial persecution. The kids' opponents are merely in favor of the kind of American society that these evils flourish in, and the youngsters do not challenge the system itself, though they are appalled by its consequences.

Yet could they, as adolescents, be political? I don't think so; and I don't know that I would be pleased if they were. American politics is a cold-blooded business indeed. Personal clarity and commitment are not wanted in it and not furthered by it. I do not think this is necessarily true of all politics; but it becomes true when the basic economic and social assumptions are as irrational as ours.

Political effectiveness in our time requires just the kind of caginess, pseudo-realism, and stereotyping of thought and feeling; the same submergence of spontaneity to the exigencies of collective action, that mark the ruin of adolescence. Adolescents are, inherently, anti-mass; they take things personally. Sexuality, itself, has this power to resolve relationships into the immediate and interpersonal. As a symbol the cocky adolescent boy stands, a little like Luther, an obstacle to

compromise and accommodation. Such symbols stick in the mind, though the reality can usually be handled. With occasional spectacular failures we do manage to assimilate the "teen-age" minority; the kids learn not to get fresh; they get smart, they dry up. We are left then, like the Macbeths, with the memory of an earlier fidelity. But Lady Macbeth was less resourceful than ourselves; she knew next to nothing about industrial solvents. Where she had only perfume we have oil.

The Girl as Woman

This is how we use the boy, but what about the girl? I have already asserted that, since she is not perceived as a member of the "hot-blooded" minority she cannot take his place in the unconscious, which is apt to turn very nasty if it is fobbed off with the wrong sex. Is she then simply not much involved by our psychodynamics, or is she actively repressed? Is she omitted from our fanatics or excluded from them?

It may seem very strange that I should find her so inconspicuous. Her image gets so much publicity. Drum-majorettes and cheerleaders are ubiquitous; *Playboy* provides businessmen with a new *playmate* each month. Nymphets are a public institution.

Exactly, and they serve a useful public function. American males are certainly anxious to project a heterosexual public image, and even more anxious to believe in it themselves. None of us, surely, wishes to feel obligated to hang himself out of respect for the United States Senate; it is, as Yum-Yum remarked to Nanki-Poo, such a stuffy death. I am not questioning our sincerity; the essence of my point is that in what we call maturity we feel what we are supposed to feel, and nothing else. But I am questioning the depth and significance of our interest in the cover or pin-up girl. Her patrons are concerned to experience their own masculinity; they are not much interested in her: I reject the celebration of "babes" in song and story as evidence that we have adolescent girls much on our minds; if we did we wouldn't think of them as "babes." I think, indeed, that in contrast to the boy, of whom we are hyperaware, we repress our awareness of the girl. She is not just omitted, she is excluded.

The adolescent heroine in current fiction is not interpreted in the same way as the adolescent hero, even when the parallel is quite close. Her adolescence is treated as less crucial; she is off-handedly accepted as a woman already. This is true even when the author struggles against it. *Lolita,* for example, is every bit as much a tragic heroine of adolescence as Holden is a hero—she isn't as nice a girl as he is a boy, but they are both victims of the same kind of corruption in adult society and the same absence of any real opportunity to grow up to be themselves. Lolita's failure is the classic failure of identity in adolescence; and Humbert knows this and accepts responsibility for it; this is the crime he expiates. But this is not the way Lolita—the character, not the book—is generally received. Unlike Holden, she has no cult and is not vouchsafed any dignity. It is thought to be comical that, at fourteen, she is already a whore.

A parallel example is to be found in Rumer Godden's *The Greengage Summer.* Here the story is explicitly about Joss's growing up. The author's emphasis is on the way her angry betrayal of her lover marks the end of her childhood; her feelings are now too strong and confused, and too serious in their consequences, to be handled with childish irresponsibility; she can no longer claim the exemptions of childhood. But what the movie presented, it seemed to me, was almost entirely an account of her rise to sexual power; Joss had become a Babe at last.

One reason that we do not take adolescent growth seriously in girls is that we do not much care what happens to people unless it has economic consequences: what would Holden ever be, since he never even graduates from high school; who would hire him? He has a problem; Lolita could always be a waitress or something; what more could she expect? Since we define adulthood almost exclusively in economic terms, we obviously cannot concern ourselves as much about the growth of those members of society who are subject from birth to restricted economic opportunity. But so, of course, are the members of the "hot-blooded" minorities; though we find their hot-bloodedness so exciting that we remain aware of them anyway.

But girls, like Jews, are not supposed to fight back; we expect them, instead, to insinuate themselves coyly into the roles available. In our society, there are such lovely things for them to be. They can take care of other people and clean up after them. Women can become wives and mothers; Jews can become kindly old Rabbis and philosophers and even psychoanalysts and lovable comic essayists. They can become powers behind the power; a fine old law firm runs on the brains of its anonymous young Jews just as a husband's best asset is his loyal and unobtrusive wife. A Jewish girl can become a Jewish Mother, and this is a role which even Plato would have called essential.

Effects of Discrimination

Clearly, this kind of discrimination is quite different from that experienced by the "hot-blooded" minorities and must be based on a very different image in the minds of those who practice it and must have a different impact upon them. Particularly, in the case of the adolescent, the effect on the adult of practicing these two kinds of discrimination will be different. The adolescent boy must be altered to fit middle-class adult roles, and when he has been he becomes a much less vital creature. But the girl is merely squandered, and this wastage will continue all her life. Since adolescence is, for boy and girl alike, the time of life in which the self must be established, the girl suffers as much from being wasted as the boy does from being cut down; there has recently been, for example, a number of tragic suicides reported among adolescent girls, though suicide generally is far less common among females. But from the point of view of the dominant society nothing special is done to the female in adolescence—the same squeeze continues throughout life, even though this is when it hurts most.

The guilts we retain for our treatments of "hot-blooded" and "long-suffering" minorities therefore affect us in contrasting ways. For the boy we suffer angry, paranoid remorse, as if he were Billy the Kid, or Budd. We had to do our duty, but how can we ever forget him? But we do not attack the girl; we only neglect her and leave her to wither gradually through an unfulfilled life; and the best defense against this sort of guilt is selective inattention. We just don't see her; instead, we see a caricature, not brutalized as in the case of the boy, to justify our own brutality, but sentimentalized, roseate, to reassure us that we have done her no harm, and that she is well contented. Look: she even has her own telephone, with what is left of the boy dangling from the other end of the line.

A Lonely Ride

This is the fantasy; the reality is very different, but it is bad enough to be a "Teen-ager." The adolescent is now the only totally disfranchised minority group in the country. In America, no minority has ever gotten any respect or consistently decent treatment until it began to acquire political power. The vote comes before anything else. This is obviously true of the Negro at the present time; his recent advances have all been made under—sometimes reluctant—Federal auspices because, nationally, Negroes vote, and Northern Negroes are able to cast a ballot on which their buffeted Southern rural fellows may be pulled to firmer political ground. This is what makes it impossible to stop Freedom Rides; just as the comparative militance of the Catholic Church in proceeding toward integration in Louisiana may have less to do with Louisiana than Nigeria, which is in grave danger of falling into the hands of Black Muslims. People generally sympathetic with adolescents sometimes say, "Well, it really isn't fair; if they're old enough to be drafted, they're old enough to vote," which is about as naive as it is possible to get.

Can the status of the "teen-ager" be improved? Only, presumably, through increased political effectiveness. Yet, it is precisely here that a crucial dilemma arises. For the aspirations of the adolescent minority are completely different from those of other minorities. All the others are struggling to obtain what the adolescent is struggling to avoid. They seek and welcome the conventional American middle-class status that has been partially or totally barred to them. But this is what the adolescent is left with if he gives in and goes along.

In the recent and very moving CORE film, *Freedom Ride,* one of the heroic group who suffered beatings and imprisonment for their efforts to end segregation says, as nearly as I can recall, "If the road to freedom leads through the jails of the South, then that's the road I'll take." It may be the road to freedom; but it is the road to suburbia too. You can't tell which the people are headed for until they are nearly there; but all our past ethnic groups have settled for suburbia, and the people who live there bear witness that freedom is somewhere else.

I am not sure there *is* a road to freedom in America. Not enough people want to go there; the last I can recall was H. D. Thoreau, and he went on foot, through the woods, alone. This still may be the only way to get there. For those with plenty of guts, compassion, and dedication to social justice, who nevertheless dislike walking alone through the woods, or feel it to be a Quixotic extravagance, a freedom ride is a noble enterprise. Compared to them, the individual boy or girl on a solitary journey must seem an anachronism. Such a youngster has very little place in our way of life. And of all the criticisms that might be directed against that way of life, this is the harshest.

A New Perspective of the Adolescent

HERBERT A. OTTO   SARAH T. OTTO

Society, say Otto and Otto, has shaped a traumatized image of the teenager who proceeds to live up to the label. A new perspective of the adolescent is offered "as a means of regenerating the image of the teenager and as an opening wedge toward breaching the cultural conspiracy." In the new image, the adolescent is portrayed as clarifying and developing his identity, and making substantial progress in self-actualization. He is perceived as "a growth catalyst" who represents "the wave of the future."

In a society which is "image-conscious" the image of the adolescent has become succeedingly less favorable over the years. The words "adolescent" and "teenager" are increasingly associated with "juvenile delinquent" and "trouble-maker." The public media of communication have contributed materially to the shaping of a traumatized or deformed image of the teenager. To cite but one example which could be duplicated on a national scale many times: a recent dance in Salt Lake City attended by over 3,000 adolescents resulted in fights, which police estimated involved about sixty persons. Approximately two per cent of those attending were therefore involved in what the newspapers subsequently headlined as a "Full-Scale Teenage Riot." The (sometimes) unwitting but consistent shaping of a distorted image of the teen-ager by the media of communications raises a number of questions: (a) Does the distorted image of the teenager fostered by the public media affect the self-system and self-image of our young people? (b) Does the adult perception of the adolescent erect a barrier between him and

the adult world? and (c) Does this barrier impede the development of both the adolescents' and adults' potential? A new perspective of the adolescent is long overdue.

As a part of the Human Potentialities Research Project at the University of Utah, a number of studies (Healy, 1965; Souba, 1965) have been conducted to determine the nature of the adolescent's strengths and personality resources. One outcome of these studies was the gradual emergence of a new perspective of the adolescent.

The role of the adolescent in contemporary culture has been both misunderstood and distorted. *We can speak of a cultural conspiracy in the sense that major "culture carriers," the adults, appear to enter into a tacit agreement to stereotype and label the adolescent. The adolescent keeps his part of the agreement by conforming to the label.* A vicious cycle is thus set in motion. Our lack of understanding of what the adolescent *can* contribute denies him his true function in relation to society and social institutions. We

From Herbert A. Otto and Sarah T. Otto, A New Perspective of the Adolescent. Reprinted from *Psychology In The Schools*, 1967, 4(1), 76-81, by permission of the authors and publisher.

have closed our eyes to the fact that the adolescent has a vital function in relation to our institutions. Equally important, by not understanding the essential nature of the adolescent's role, *the adult denies himself a substantial measure of growth which is possible through his relationship to the adolescent.*

The image of the teenager combined with the culture conspiracy operate to suppress the development of human potential both in the adolescent as well as the adult. The following New Perspective of the adolescent is suggested as a means of regenerating the image of the teenager and as an opening wedge toward breaching the cultural conspiracy.

THE ADOLESCENT IS FULLY ENGAGED IN THE PROCESS OF CLARIFYING AND DEVELOPING HIS IDENTITY—HE ISSUES THE CHALLENGE THAT FORMATION IS A LIFE-LONG UNDERTAKING

There is a growing awareness in professional and lay circles that identity formation is an integral part of adult existence and does not cease until death. This process is often referred to as "the search for identity." It would be more correct to call it *"the ongoing development of identity."* This ongoing development of identity involves the searching out of latent and unrealized aspects and fragments of the self, thus bringing greater wholeness to the total self structure.

Closely related to this process is the concept of the open-self system. The open-self system is characterized by an attitude toward self and life which has the qualities of open-endedness and flexibility. Flexibility and being accessible to new ideas, new experiences, new viewpoints is an index to the individual's psychological health.

The measure of health is flexibility, the freedom to learn through experience, the freedom to change with changing internal and external circumstances, to be influenced by reasonable argument, admonitions, exhortation and the appeal to emotions; the freedom to respond appropriately to the stimulus of reward and punishment, and especially the freedom to cease when sated. The essence of normality is flexibility in all of these vital ways. The essence of illness is the freezing of behavior into unalterable and insatiable patterns (Kubie, 1958, pp. 20–21).

The self of the teenager particularly has the elements of an open-ended system. Many aspects of his functioning have not as yet become frozen and are highly labile. Much of what appears to be erratic functioning is actually *purposive and developmental,* a manifestation of the open-self system in an accelerated state of growth. If we accept the view that identity formation (the ongoing unfoldment of our uniquely individual abilities and powers) is a life-long process, *then the adolescent becomes the highly visible symbol of a challenge.* He challenges us to enter more fully into the searching out of that which is latent and unfulfilled; he challenges us to enter more fully into this process which brings wholeness to the structure of the self and which is a means of developing our identity.

As a part of developing his identity, the adolescent is engaged in an ongoing search for truth, for the meaning of life and death.[1] The adolescent is involved in searching out the meaning of existence. In contradistinction, for many adults the search for the meaning of existence is frozen into systems and certainties, *whereas it is the quality of search which lends vitality and joy to life.* The adolescent's quality of search can, for the adult, become a source of stimulation and inspiration.

THE ADOLESCENT IS AT A POINT OF MAJOR IMPETUS IN SELF-ACTUALIZATION AND UNFOLDMENT—HE SYMBOLIZES THE HUMAN POTENTIAL ACTIVELY COMMITTED TO SELF-REALIZATION

Many well-known behavioral scientists (Gordon Allport, 1955; Carl Rogers, 1961; Abraham Maslow, 1962; Margaret Mead, 1966; and Gardner Murphy, 1958, to name only a few) subscribe to the hypothesis that the average healthy

[1]In 1954 suicide was the fifth-ranking cause of death in the age brackets fifteen to nineteen. By 1962 it was the third most common killer of youth.

human being is functioning at a fraction of his potential. This recognition is not restricted to this country. There is a clear awareness by Russian scientists of the importance of the human potential. In an official publication of the U.S.S.R. dated November, 1964 reporting the work by Vasili Davydov of the Moscow Institute of Psychology, we find the following under the heading of "Inexhaustible Brain Potential":

The latest findings in anthropology, psychology, logic and physiology show that the potential of the human mind is very great indeed. "As soon as modern science gave us some understanding of the structure and work of the human brain, we were struck by its enormous reserve capacity," writes Yefremov. (Ivan Yefremov, eminent Soviet scholar and writer) "Man, under average conditions of work and life, uses only a small part of his thinking equipment . . .

"If we were able to force our brain to work at only half of its capacity, we could, without any difficulty whatever, learn 40 languages, memorize the Large Soviet Encyclopedia from cover to cover, and complete the required courses of dozens of colleges."

The statement is hardly an exaggeration. It is the generally accepted theoretical view of man's mental potentialities.

How can we tap this gigantic potential? It is a big and very complex problem with many ramifications. (*U.S.S.R.,* 1964, pp. 42–43.)

The recognition that healthy humanity is operating at 10 to 15 percent of its potential represents the major challenge of this age. Yet very few people consciously select the development of their potential as a life goal and then systematically and planfully proceed to actualize this potential.

The adolescent is, for the most part, clearly aware that a great deal is potential within him and that the realization of this potential will determine the course of his future. He is at the same time instrumentally engaged in self-actualization and in becoming what he can be. He represents to everyone the human potential energetically engaged in self-realization, self-actualization and unfoldment.

THE ADOLESCENT IS A GROWTH CATALYST

The teenager extends an invitation to adults to participate in growth. If this invitation is accepted and the adult is able to open himself, the teenager by the quality of his being and the nature of his interaction can trigger growth in adults. Since the essence of his being is growth and *becoming,* the adolescent offers both a challenge and opportunity to grow with and through him.

If we grant that the matrix of interpersonal relationships is the major medium of personality growth and if we acknowledge that the multiple and complex relationships between family members are for both parents and children a means of development and fulfillment, then it becomes clear that what the adolescent brings to the family is of a high order of quality. He offers parents an opportunity to break established and restricted habit patterns, habitual modes of perception and habitual modes of relating. By the keen and discerning nature of his observations and the honesty of his confrontations ("Mother, you are often afraid of life," "Father, you are too much of a stick-in-the-mud.") he brings into existence a moment which can be grasped for insight and self-understanding—an opportunity to root out cherished yet destructive stereotypes one has about oneself.

The teenager in the home through the quality of his relationships presents to his parents the chance to regain the spontaneity, freshness and vitality so often buried beneath the cares and routines of adult existence. This, for the parents, usually comes at a time of life when it is most needed.

Unless the adult acquires the perspective or recognition that the adolescent functions as a catalyst, minimal change in the adult can be expected. *Outlook inevitably determines outcomes.* The very same principle also holds for the professional. His perceptions and emotional meanings (how he sees the adolescent and what he means to him) determine whether in the course of the professional relationship with the adolescent the professional will open himself to growth.

The adolescent by the nature of his qualities, his fundamental honesty, idealism and by virtue of his capacity to ask searching questions of life and experience creates multiple occasions for the examination, reassessment and regeneration of adult and familial values. Finally, the ideational flow or wealth of ideas of the adolescent (if allowed to proceed unimpeded) can lead to creative exchange and better communication between all family members. If understood and allowed to function in his natural role, the adolescent becomes a growth catalyst par excellence for parents and for the family as a whole.

THE ADOLESCENT REPRESENTS A FORCE FOR SOCIAL AND INSTITUTIONAL REGENERATION

It has long been recognized that the teenager is a very astute critic of our social and institutional structures and is able to ask penetrating questions and raise fundamental issues. Unfortunately, this ability has largely been dismissed as a manifestation of "rebellion" and "revolt against authority." This is the equivalent of throwing out the baby with the bath water.

The adolescent brings to the social scene an idealism, integrity and commitment to values which penetrate to the very heart of dysfunctional institutions and social structures. He contributes a fresh viewpoint and often shows a keen ability for organizational analysis. If an institution shows lack of soundness in its functioning, the teenager will not accept this as the status quo but will ask "Why?" and call for change and reform. Perhaps more than the adult, the teenager recognizes the extent to which personality is indebted for its functioning to the social structures and inputs which form its environment. *The rebellion of the adolescent against institutions may stem from an awareness that social disorganization is related to personal disorganization and that a healthy self demands a healthy society.*

The adolescent represents a vital resource which has never been adequately tapped for institutional regeneration and renewal. There appears to be a partial awareness that the adolescent *can* make a contribution toward our institutional structures. In recent times a growing number of mayors of municipalities (and even governors and legislative bodies of states) have voluntarily relinquished their offices for a day to teenagers. Many of these officials have found it profitable to listen to the comments and suggestions of teenagers following their "term" in office. In the process of institutional evaluation and renewal, the adolescent represents a much neglected resource: he can make a significant contribution as co-investigator and partner, in efforts directed toward the study, improvement and the regeneration of our institutions.

THE ADOLESCENT'S HEALTHY BODY SENSE AND CAPACITY FOR SENSORY AWARENESS IS AN INDICATOR OF INDIVIDUAL POTENTIAL

The adolescent is noted for a *healthy narcissism,* a healthy pride in his growing, developing body. He is also noted for his ability to enjoy fully the sights, sounds and smells of the wonderful world which surrounds him. This heightened sensory awareness, *joie de vivre,* and life-affirmative outlook need not be restricted to the period of adolescence. There is every indication that adults whose physical systems suffer from lack of proper exercise (with a consequent dulling of sensory capacities) can regain healthy body tonicity and body sense and experience an increase in sensory function by entering into a regime of physical conditioning and sensory awareness training. For the adult, the regaining of a healthy body sense usually brings with it not only an increased enjoyment of life and living, but also increased energy, drive and interest—qualities for which the teenager is noted.

It has been a finding from the Human Potentialities Research Project (Otto, 1964) that the development of a healthy body sense via a physical conditioning regime appears to have a markedly positive effect on the self-image and self-concept as well as the self-confidence of adults. The adolescent through his healthy body sense and quality of sensory functioning, issues an invitation to the adult to regain a soundness of physical well-being, pride in the body and increased enjoyment of living which is the potential of every man and woman.

THE ADOLESCENT REPRESENTS THE WAVE OF THE FUTURE

In many ways the adolescent is a cultural innovator. For example, the widespread acceptance by the adult world of the "new sound" and the plethora of new dances (the frug, the watusi) had their origin in an extended period of teenage enthusiasm and support of these forms of expression and communication. Certain styles of apparel and popular sports (surfing, for example) have first found favor with the teenager and then been adopted by the adult world. The innovative contribution of the adolescent to the cultural mainstream is much more pervasive than suspected—and largely ignored.

Ignoring the contribution of the adolescent is but another subtle manifestation of the conformity pressures which are exerted on youth with special care. Among the institutions our educational system plays a dominant role in delimiting the development of the individual's unique capacities. This fact is repeatedly rediscovered by investigators, most recently by Friedenberg's research (1963) which makes clear that "through pressures both direct and indirect the schools encourage or demand that the student relinquish his autonomy, sacrifice his personal desires and often reject his particular excellence on behalf of institutional and social considerations which themselves are often trivial." One step in the right direction is the recognition by some professionals that *adolescenthood* just as *adulthood* is a distinct entity rather than a period of transition. "As long as adolescence is conceptualized as an in-between stage, the adolescent has no status in his own right" (Maier, 1965). And we might add, we attach minimal worth and dignity to an in-between stage.

The adolescent symbolizes and is the wave of the future. The nature of his being and *the quality of his developing self* foreshadow the man of tomorrow. He is the citizen and leader of the years to come and should be the pride and hope of the generation which is moving into his shadows. The tragedy of this generation is that through its distorted view of the teenager it is both shaping him and inviting the anger and contempt which will be an inevitable harvest.

True understanding of the close *interrelationship between all members of the family called man must lead to the development of a new perspective of the teenager* which more accurately reflects his real function and contribution. The adolescent is the living symbol of man's unfolding possibilities—of the human potential actively engaged in the process of self-realization.

REFERENCES

ALLPORT, G. W. *Becoming: basic considerations for a psychology of personality.* New Haven: Yale University Press, 1955.

FRIEDENBERG, E. Z. *Coming of age in America.* New York: Random House, 1963.

HEALY, S. L. Adolescent strengths: strength concepts of adolescents. Unpublished master's thesis, Graduate School of Social Work, University of Utah, 1965.

KUBIE, L. S. *Neurotic distortion of the creative process.* Lawrence, Kansas: University of Kansas Press, Porter Lectures, Series 22, 1958.

MAIER, H. W. Adolescenthood. *Social Casework,* 1965, *46,* 3–6.

MASLOW, A. H. *Toward a psychology of being.* New York: Van Nostrand, 1962.

MEAD, M. Culture and personality development: human capacities. In H. A. Otto (Ed.), *Explorations in human potentialities.* Springfield, Ill.: Charles C. Thomas, 1966.

MURPHY, G. *Human potentialities.* New York: Basic Books, 1958.

OTTO, H. A. The personal and family strength research projects—some implications for the therapist. *Mental Hygiene,* 1964, *48,* 447–450.

ROGERS, C. R. *On becoming a person.* Boston: Houghton Mifflin, 1961.

SOUBA, C. E. Revision of inventory of personal resources, form "A." Unpublished master's thesis, Graduate School of Social Work, University of Utah, 1965.

U.S.S.R., Soviet life today. Pedagogical quests, 1964 (Nov.), 42–45.

Chapter 2: Suggested Additional Readings

GLADSTON, R. Adolescense and the function of self-consciousness. Mental Hygiene, 1967, *51*(2), 164–168. The writer expands on the theme that the adolescent's most compelling task is the establishment of a sense of self-confidence, to replace reliance upon parents. The key to understanding the many deviations in adolescents lies in self-consciousness.

HURLOCK, E. B. American adolescents of today—a new species. *Adolescence,* Spring 1966, *1*(1), 7–21. Hurlock portrays American adolescents of today as a new species, different from adolescents of other times and other places in the world. She sees them as knowledgeable and sophisticated, but also as bored, unhappy, lazy, and neurotic; and she analyzes some of the factors responsible for this situation.

LEIDY, T. R., & STARRY, A. R. The American adolescent—a bewildering amalgam. *National Education Association Journal,* October 1967, *56,* 8–12. Findings from a nation-wide survey reveal how American adolescents look at the world around them. Among the topics covered in the survey were school, dating and assuming responsibility.

NEWSWEEK. The teenager. In Winter, G. D., & Nuss, E. M. (Eds.), *The young adult: Identity and awareness.* Glenview, Ill.: Scott, Foresman, 1969. Pp. 42–74. This article reports a study of a cross-section of young people, ages 15 to 17, across the United States. The teenagers were questioned about the persons they admire; their attitudes toward the world they live in; their recreations and activities; their health; and their opinions about the characteristics of their culture.

PRESTON, C. E. Self-perceptions among adolescents. *Psychology in the Schools,* 1967, *4*(3), 254–256. This investigation of the hypothesis that there would be demonstrable differences in how adolescents perceived themselves or their situations, depending on their current situations, was confirmed for girls and to a lesser extent for boys. An important part of the adolescent image is the way the adolescent perceives himself.

ROSENBERG, M. *Society and the adolescent self-image.* Princeton, N.J.: Princeton University Press, 1965. Rosenberg made an extensive study of adolescent self-esteem and related it to achievement and interpersonal skills. Adolescents with high and low self-esteem described themselves somewhat differently.

SEBALD, H. *Adolescence: A sociological analysis.* New York: Appleton-Century-Crofts, 1968, Chapter 1. The author discusses the various age-grades during adolescence, which range from the individual who has just experienced puberty to the one on the threshold of adulthood.

part two

Issues Relating to the Adolescent's Personality Development

3

Persistence of Personality Traits: The Significance of Adolescent Experience

The special significance of adolescent experience for successful development of adult personality has generally been accorded little attention by psychologists. Until recently, we have been disposed to think of personality as having become stabilized by late childhood almost beyond the possibility of fundamental change. However, some data indicate that adolescent behavior patterns are still fluid, thus simultaneously presenting a challenge and opportunity to secondary school teachers and other persons in a position to influence the development of youth (Hess, 1963).

The extent to which adolescent personality can be influenced for the better—and precisely which personality traits are most amenable to change—has not been finally established. Some studies have indicated considerable stability in certain traits and less persistence in others. In one study (Frantz, 1971) of changes that had occurred since high school among a group of young people aged 21–23, the greatest changes were in the social area, with the majority having become more gregarious and friendly. They changed least in traditional beliefs, domestic habits, and degree of conformity. Few differences were found between those individuals who attended college and those who did not, which supports the conjecture that college may not significantly modify personality. In another study of "typical" students," grades 9 through 13, Thompson (1968) found that the way a student responds to a personality inventory in grade nine is related to the way he will respond four years later. However, the data also suggest that an individual is somewhat better adjusted as a college freshman than he was as a high school freshman, and that males perhaps experience more family strain as college freshmen than they did four years earlier. With regard to social and family attitudes, males also experience greater changes through the period of grades 9 through 13 than do females,

The modifiability of traits also relates to sex. Using TAT stories as the basis for testing, Nawas (1971) studied male and female subjects first as adolescents and again as young adults eight years later. In both ego sufficiency and complexity, males manifested a significant increase during this period, while females demonstrated a highly significant decrease. Nawas concluded that the assumption of continuity in human development is too simplistic, even misleading, because human behaviors change more than is commonly believed. This same study offered evidence that American males and females are differentially affected by developmental changes in their roles. In other words, the American culture is dominated by values that favor the male, and despite legislation aimed at equality of the sexes, the cultural lag between male and female still exists.

However, many other studies reveal considerable persistence of basic personality traits. According to their research, most individuals stubbornly insist on remaining themselves. They live out their lives apparently circumscribed by the boundaries of a genetically sealed destiny. These studies covered periods of varying length and included individuals at various stages of life. For men, traits which have proved stable from early childhood to maturity include "ease of anger arousal" and "sexual behavior"; for women "passive withdrawal from stressful situations" and "dependency on the family" were stable traits (Honzik, 1965, p. 81).

In another study (Witkin, Goodenough, & Karp, 1967), stability of cognitive style, especially as revealed in field behaviors, was studied for one group of individuals ages 8 to 13 years, and in another group ages 10 to 24 years. A progressive increase in field dependence was evident up to age 17, with no further change from then until age 24. In a field-dependent mode of perceiving, perception is dominated by the overall organization of the field. There is relative inability to perceive parts of a field as discrete. Thus, field-dependent persons have limited ability to differentiate experiences in the world about them.

For some traits, adolescence seems to be critical; that is, characteristics which stabilize during this period persist into adulthood and even beyond. Moreover, certain traits apparent in adolescence prove more predictive of later personality than do childhood manifestations of these traits. In a study of Fels Institute (Kagan & Moss, 1962), the correlation of birth-to-age-three ratings on "aggressive retaliation" was only .19, but at the age period 10–to–14, the correlation rose to .47. Behaviors relating to sex and dependency, in particular, stabilized in early adolescence and remained highly persistent through early adulthood. Behaviors which deviated from social norms were correspondingly less stable. Thus, aggressive behaviors in women and dependent behaviors in men, both frowned upon in our society, indicated less stability from adolescence to maturity than did socially accepted aggressive behaviors in men and dependent behaviors in women. Adolescent behaviors that were not subject to strong social pressures were often apparent ten or fifteen years later. For example, intellectual striving and mastery behaviors, which are accepted for both sexes, proved highly persistent from high school years through early adulthood.

Similarly, a study of the same students (Carlson, 1965), first in the sixth grade and later as high school seniors, revealed that girls became more socially oriented, and boys more personally oriented, with the years. Growth in self-esteem, which is less dependent than other traits on changing concepts of sex role, proved to be the same for both sexes.

An interesting finding in the Fels study was the so-called "sleeper effect." A trait, apparently dormant for a while, would reappear. For instance, the degree of passivity and fear of bodily harm, as demonstrated during the age period birth-to-three-years, proved more predictive of love-object dependency in adult men than did later assessments of these traits.

One especially comprehensive and well-known study (Oden, 1968), begun more than forty years ago, concerns individuals originally testing in the top one percent of the population. Extensive data have been kept on this group, involving all sorts of behaviors. A comparison of the interests, abilities, and personality characteristics in childhood and youth revealed few significant changes. All the evidence has indicated that the superior child becomes the superior adult. However, men have lived up to their vocational potential far more than women, reflecting their different role in society.

All these various findings raise significant questions with regard to adolescents. In the Oden study, was the persistence of traits from childhood to adulthood due to genetic factors or to constant factors in environment? If the cause was environmental, might not undesirable, yet stubbornly persistent, traits be altered, given proper environmental engineering? If certain apparently less desirable traits do resist change, how best may the individuals involved be helped to adapt to them? Might not schools reward a broad range of achievement, so that fewer adolescents would find themselves disadvantaged? For example, if it be conceded that relatively passive boys are unlikely to transform into aggressive adults, why not somehow make participation in less active pursuits as rewarding as participation in football or boxing? Again, might it not be well to reserve judgment, if boys and girls indicate a lapse in certain approved traits, such as dependability? Might it not be a case of "sleeper effect"? Perhaps certain internal readjustments are taking place, and more stable characteristics will reappear. Of course, such reappearance should not be taken for granted, and the lapse would warrant attention if the return of the desirable traits were unusually delayed.

Moreover, to the extent that traits first apparent in adolescence persist into adulthood, should we not determine how such long-lasting traits are formed? That is, what sort of experiences seem to have an unusually "stamping-in" effect? If intellectual attitudes established during the teens tend to persist, then it becomes imperative to learn how to establish favorable attitudes.

Meantime, it should be kept in mind that individuals differ in the modifiability of their traits. Some persons appear to act out scripts handed them in childhood. Like plants drawn to the light, they appear irresistibly drawn to their fate. Other individuals follow a more uneven life style, and they manage to free themselves from the role destiny seemed to have decreed.

We must remember, also, that certain traits prove more persistent in some children than in others. How may teachers and parents learn to distinguish between children whose traits can and should, or cannot or should not, be changed? Sometimes a socially deviant trait, such as a considerable degree of introversion, may be optimum for the individual concerned. Perhaps the child is a researcher-in-the-making, who will be compelled to spend long hours alone. Or perhaps a somewhat dependent boy may make his best long-term adjustment through continuing to play a passive role. Any effort to make him assertive might simply leave him anxious and discontented with himself.

The first of the following selections, by Kagan and Moss, summarizes research from the Fels study, quoted above. It treats the persistence of certain behaviors from birth through adolescence. The second selection, by Skolnick, reveals considerable stability shown by males and females in certain characteristics over a period of twenty years, in accord with the differences in pressures on the two sexes and the differential role accorded them in society. Males tended to remain stable in aggression and power, females in achievement and, to some degree, in affiliation.

REFERENCES

CARLSON, R.   Stability and change in the adolescent's self-image. *Child Development,* 1965, *36,* 659–666.

FRANTZ, T. T.   Student and nonstudent change. *College Student Personnel,* 1971, *12*(1), 49–53.

HESS, R. D.   High school antecedents of young adult achievement. In R. Grinder (Ed.) *Studies in adolescence.* New York: Macmillan, 1963. Pp. 401-414.

HONZIK, M. P.   Prediction of behavior from birth to maturity. *Merrill-Palmer Quarterly,* 1965, *12,* 81.

KAGAN, J., & MOSS, H. A.   *Birth to maturity.* New York: Wiley, 1962.

NAWAS, M. M.   Change in efficiency of ego fuctioning and complexity from adolescence to young adulthood. *Development Psychology,* 1971, *4*(3), 412–415.

ODEN, M. H.   The fulfillment of promise: 40-year follow-up of the Terman gifted group. *Genetic Psychology Monographs,* 1968, *77,* 3–93.

THOMPSON, O. E.   Student values in transition. *California Journal of Educational Research,* 1968, *19,* 77–86.

WITKIN, H. A., GOODENOUGH, D. R. & KARP, S. A.   Stability of cognitive style from childhood to young adulthood. *Journal of Personality and Social Psychology,* 1967, *7*(3), 291–300.

The Stability of Passive and Dependent Behavior From Childhood Through Adulthood

JEROME KAGAN **HOWARD A. MOSS**

This article reports the results of a study of a group of "normal" adults from the Fels longitudinal research population for whom data were available from birth through adolescence. Specifically, the findings relate to stability of passive and dependent behaviors. Such behaviors proved quite stable for women, but minimally stable for men, reflecting differential pressures on the sexes.

A basic assumption of developmental theory is that adult behaviors are often established in early childhood. Although retrospective reports obtained from the verbal protocols of adults support this assumption, it has been difficult to produce a more objective demonstration of the long term stability of childhood behavior patterns. This unhappy state of affairs is a consequence of the expense and difficulty associated with collecting long term longitudinal information on a large sample of children. Only extensive, longitudinal research programs, as exemplified by the Berkeley Growth Study or the Fels Research Institute, can furnish the answers to this developmental problem.

This paper presents one set of results which have emerged from a recent study of a group of "normal" adults from the Fels longitudinal research population for whom extensive information was available from birth through adolescence. The findings deal specifically with the long term stability of passive and dependent behavior in the face of situations which are frustrating and/or demand problem solving activity. This particular behavioral variable was chosen for initial analysis because theoretical essays on personality development emphasize that the early dependence of the child on the parent is of the utmost importance in shaping his future personality. That is, the development of a variety of adult motives and behaviors are based on the quality and intensity of the dependent relationship with the mother and mother-substitute figures. Further, psychological symptoms are theoretically attributed to inconsistency in the gratification of the child's dependent overtures and/or to denial or inhibition of dependent motives or behavior.

In addition to the longitudinal material, each subject was recently assessed during early adulthood by means of both interview and test procedures. The adult assessment was focused on the behavior variables of dependency, aggression, achievement, and sexuality and on the degree of conflict and type of defensive responses associated with behavioral strivings in these areas. It was anticipated that there might be important sex differences with respect to occurrence of these behaviors, and the assessment procedures were designed to detect these potential sex differences.

Method

THE SAMPLE

The subjects (*Ss*) in this analysis were 27 male and 27 female Caucasian adults born between 1930 and 1939 who had recently been through a comprehensive assessment program which included an average of five hours of tape recorded interview and a variety of test procedures. The *Ss* were between 20 and 29 years of age at the time of the assessment. In addition, these *Ss* had fairly complete longitudinal records from 3 to 10 years of age. The *Ss* were predominantly middle class but came from a variety of vocational backgrounds including agricultural, skilled labor, tradesmen, and professional groups. The religious affiliations of the group included 43 Protestants, 10 Catholics and 1 Jewish subject. The mean Wechsler-Bellevue IQ of the group was 120 with an IQ range of 97 to 142.

INTERVIEW VARIABLES: ADULT ASSESSMENT

Each *S* was interviewed by the senior author for approximately five hours over two to three sessions. *The interviewer had absolutely no knowledge of any of the longitudinal information on the Ss.* Since these *Ss* had been studied by psychologists for over 20 years, rapport was usually excellent, and defensive and evasive answers were infrequent. Following the interviews, each *S* was rated (7-point scale) on 59 variables. Six of these adult interview variables dealt specifically with passive and dependent behavior; abridged definitions of these variables follow:

Degree to which dependent gratifications were sought in choice of vocation. This variable assessed the degree to which security was an important aspect of job choice, the degree to which the subject looked to his employer for gratification of his dependent needs, reluctance to shift jobs because of temporary loss of security. For nonworking women, emphasis was placed on her attitudes about the importance of security in her husband's job.

Degree of dependent behavior toward a love object. This variable assessed the degree to which the subject sought advice and emotional support from a love object (sweetheart, husband, wife), degree to which the subject looked for stability and wisdom in a love object, degree to which responsibility for decision making was given to love object.

Degree of dependent behavior with parents. This variable assessed the degree to which the subject looked for advice, support, emotional encouragement, and nurturance from one or both parents.

Degree of dependent behavior toward nonparental figures. This variable assessed the degree to which the subject sought advice, emotional support, and nurturance from nonparental figures who were not love objects, e.g., friends, relatives, and teachers.

Tendency to display behavioral withdrawal in the face of anticipated failure. This variable assessed the frequency and consistency with which *S* tended to withdraw from tasks and situations which he thought were difficult to master and in which failure was anticipated.

Degree of conflict over dependent behavior. This variable assessed the degree to which the subject avoided placing himself in dependent positions, his derogation of dependent behavior in self and others, and his emphasis on the value and importance of independent behavior.

A random sample of 32 taped interviews were independently studied and rated. The interrater reliabilities for the six dependency variables ranged from .63 to .82 with an average coefficient of .74.

PROCEDURE FOR EVALUATION OF CHILDHOOD BEHAVIOR

The junior author, who had no knowledge of the adult psychological status of the *Ss,* evaluated narrative reports based on direct observation of the child in a variety of situations. Summaries of interviews with the child and the mother were also available. The observation reports were based on (a) semiannual visits to the home in which a staff member observed the child interact with mother and siblings for a two to four hour period, (b) semiannual or annual observations of the child in the Fels experimental nursery school and day camp settings, (c) interviews with the child, and (d) observations of the child in the classroom. After studying this material, the psychologist rated each child for a comprehensive set of variables (7-point scale). The rater studied the material for each *S* for ages 3 to 6 and made his ratings. Following a period of interpolated work, he then studied all the material for each *S* for ages 6 to 10 and again made the ratings. A period of approximately six months intervened between the evaluation of the material for any one child for ages 3 to 6 and 6 to 10. The rater felt that retroactive inhibition was sufficiently intense to mask any halo effect of the preschool ratings upon the later ratings made for 6 to 10 years of age. That is, the amount of material studied and the large number of variables rated militated against the recall of specific ratings over such a long period of time. In addition, the high degree of interrater reliability for these ratings supports the above statement. Independent ratings of the four childhood dependency variables by a second psychologist produced satisfactory interrater reliabilities. The product-moment correlations for each variable were all in the .80's with an average reliability of .86. The four childhood variables which involved passive and dependent behavior were defined as follows:

Tendency to behave in a passive manner when faced with environmental obstacles or stress (rated for ages 3 to 6 and 6 to 10). This variable assessed the degree to which the child was behaviorally passive in the face of external frustrations and failed to make any active mastery attempts to obtain desired goal objects following frustration. The rating of a passive behavioral reaction emphasized withdrawal from the frustration but included whining, crying, and soliciting help.

Tendency to seek support, nurturance, and assistance from female adults when under stress: general dependence (rated for age 3 to 6). This variable assessed the *S's* behavioral tendency to obtain assistance, nurturance, or affection from mother and other female adults when confronted with a threat to his well-being, a problem, or loss of a desired goal object. Dependent behavior included seeking out adults when faced with a problem or personal injury, reluctance to start a task without help or encouragement, seeking assistance of others, seeking affection from and close contact with female adults.

Tendency to seek affection and emotional support from female adults (rated for ages 6 to 10). This variable assessed the degree to which the child sought affection or emotional encouragement from mother or mother substitute figures. Evidence included kissing, holding hands, clinging, seeking encouragement or proximity to female adults.

Tendency to seek instrumental assistance from female adults (rated for ages 6 to 10). This variable assessed the degree to which the child sought instrumental help with specific problems from mother, teachers, or other female authority figures. Instrumental dependent acts included seeking help with tasks, seeking help when physically threatened.

As mentioned above the average interrater reliability for these four variables was + .86.

The distributions for both the childhood and interview variables were normal. Product-moment correlations were computed between each of the childhood variables and the six interview based dependency variables obtained in adulthood with separate analyses for males and females.

TACHISTOSCOPIC PERCEPTION

After the interviews and interview ratings were completed, each adult *S* was seen for a variety of test procedures, one of which was a tachistoscopic perception task. A series of 14 scenes were drawn to suggest action in the areas of dependency, aggression, sexuality, and physical danger. Three motivationally neutral, control pictures were also included.[1] For nine of the 14 pictures, separate pairs of illustrations were made for males and females so that the sex of the central figure was the same as the sex of the subject. The pictures were black and white line drawings with minimal background details. A brief description of the three dependency pictures follows:

1. A young adult in the foreground (male for male *Ss* and female for female *Ss*) is on his knees clutching to the waist of a figure of the same age but of opposite sex who is standing and looking forward. The figure on the floor is looking up at the face of the standing figure.

2. A young adult in the foreground (male for male *Ss* and female for female *Ss*) has his arms extended in an imploring gesture toward an adult of the same sex who is standing in the background with his back to the figure in the foreground.

3. A young adult (male for male *Ss* and female for female *Ss*) is seated on a chair with head buried in the abdomen of an adult of the opposite sex who is standing and comforting the seated figure.

The 14 pictures were presented seven times at seven different exposure speeds and in six different orders. The seven speeds ranged from .01 to 1.0 seconds. The pictures were shown initially at the fastest exposure (.01 second), and each succeeding series was presented at a slower exposure speed. All exposures were above the threshold and all *Ss* reported seeing something at each exposure. The *S* sat in a light-proof room, 22 in. from a flash-opal milk glass screen. The image was projected from the back of the screen, and the field was constantly illuminated by a 35 mm. projector (30 ft-candles at the screen). The subject was told to state for each picture (a) the sex of each figure, (b) the approximate ages of each figure, and (c) what each figure on the picture was doing. The *S* was given three practice pictures to adapt him to the task and its require-

[1]Photostats of the 14 stimuli are available upon request.

ments, and the entire protocol was electrically recorded and transcribed verbatim.

The protocols were scored for recognition threshold for each picture. Recognition threshold was defined as the first series at which the picture was described accurately and all succeeding trials were accurately described. The distribution of recognition thresholds differed among the 14 pictures and was markedly skewed either to the low or high end of the scale. Thus, the distribution of recognition thresholds for each picture was divided at the median into early and late recognition groups for statistical operations.

Results

STABILITY OF DEPENDENT BEHAVIOR

Table 1 presents the product-moment correlations between the childhood and adult ratings of passive and dependent behavior.

The major result is that passive and dependent behaviors were fairly stable for females but not for males. For girls the ratings of passivity during ages 6 to 10 correlated significantly with the adult ratings of a dependent orientation in vocational choice, dependency on love object, dependency on parents, and withdrawal to failure. Childhood passivity was inversely correlated with adult conflict over dependent behavior. That is, females who were passive as children were apt to accept the dependent behavior in adulthood and show minimal anxiety over their dependent motives. Only dependent behavior toward nonparental figures failed to show a significant, positive correlation with the childhood ratings of passivity. Similarly, the childhood ratings of both instrumental and emotional dependency on female adults, for girls aged 6–10, predicted adult ratings of dependency on love object, dependency on parents, and withdrawal to anticipated failure situations.

For the men there were only two significant correlations between the childhood dependency ratings and those based on the adult interview. Boys who were high on instrumental dependency for ages 6 to 10 were high on dependent behavior towards nonparental figures in adulthood. Second, emotional dependence during ages 6 to

Table 1. Correlations Between Passive-Dependent Behavior in Childhood and Adulthood

Childhood Variables	Adult Dependency Variables											
	Dependency in Vocation		Dependency on Love Object		Dependency on Parents		Dependency on Others		Withdrawal to Failure		Dependency Conflict	
	M	F	M	F	M	F	M	F	M	F	M	F
Passivity (ages 3 to 6)	−.07	.24	.10	.23	−.28	.25	.04	.19	.06	.26	.03	.01
Passivity (ages 6 to 10)	.11	.73**	.25	.36*	−.20	.54**	.04	.06	.21	.52**	−.26	−.63**
General Dependence (ages 3 to 6)	−.06	.21	.13	.20	−.07	.07	.11	−.06	.12	.00	.05	.26
Emotional Dependence (ages 6 to 10)	.21	.08	.18	.37*	.02	.51**	−.02	.06	.35*	.37*	−.12	−.31
Instrumental Dependence (ages 6 to 10)	.19	.39*	.06	.58**	.14	.32	.37*	.01	.09	.39*	−.04	−.17

* *p* < .05, one tail.
**p < .01, one tail.

10 was positively correlated with adult withdrawal to failure.

Of the 18 correlations between each of the three childhood variables for ages 6 to 10 and the six adult variables, 60 per cent were significant in the expected direction for females, while only 9 per cent were significant for the men.

Tables 2 and 3 present the intercorrelations among the childhood and adult interview variables respectively.

The correlations among the passive and dependency variables between ages 3 to 6 and 6 to 10 were generally more consistent for girls than for boys. That is, for girls the correlations among passivity and general dependence for ages 3 to 6 and the three variables for ages 6 to 10 were all consistently high. For boys the stability of the passivity rating for ages 3 to 6 and 6 to 10 was quite high. However, the relationships between passivity for 3 to 6 and the two dependency behaviors

Table 2. Intercorrelations Among Childhood Dependency Variables

	Passivity (6 to 10)		Gen. Dep. (3 to 6)		Emot. Dep. (6 to 10)		Instr. Dep. (6 to 10)	
	M	F	M	F	M	F	M	F
Passivity (3 to 6)	.82**	.76**	.74**	.83**	.26	.80**	.38	.79**
Passivity (6 to 10)	—	—	.40*	.63**	.43*	.65**	.53**	.61**
General Dependence (3 to 6)	—	—	—	—	.37	.61**	.38*	.63**
Emotional Dependence (6 to 10)	—	—	—	—	—	—	.60**	.79**
Instrumental Dependence (6 to 10)	—	—	—	—	—	—	—	—

* *p* < .05, two tails.
**p < .01, two tails.

Table 3. Intercorrelations Among Adult Dependency Values

	Dependence Love Object		Dependence Parents		Dependence Others		Withdrawal		Dependence Conflict	
	M	F	M	F	M	F	M	F	M	F
Dep. Vocation	.61**	.42*	.53**	.49**	.12	−.10	.41*	.50**	−.61**	−.56**
Dep. Love Object	—	—	.24	.54**	.48**	.16	.49**	.54**	−.66**	−.50**
Dep. Parents	—	—	—	—	.39*	.03	.44**	.57**	−.59**	−.71**
Dep. Others	—	—	—	—	—	—	.38*	−.15	−.46**	.15
Withdrawal	—	—	—	—	—	—	—	—	−.57**	−.70**
Dep. Conflict	—	—	—	—	—	—	—	—	—	—

* $p < .05$, two tails.
**$p < .01$, two tails.

for 6 to 10 were not as high as they were for girls. This finding suggests that overt seeking of affection and/or instrumental aid in school-age boys begins to be dissociated from a passive withdrawal reaction to problem situations.

The intercorrelations among the adult dependency variables were generally positive for both sexes. Dependency on parents and dependency on love objects were each associated with withdrawal to failure and negatively related to conflict over dependency. It is interesting to note that women who are dependent on their parents tended to be dependent on their love object but not on friends or authority figures. Men, on the other hand, who were dependent on their parents tended to be dependent on friends and authority figures rather than on a love object. Dependency on parents and friends usually involves instrumental aid with problems, while dependency on a love object more often included the soliciting of emotional support and affection. It will be recalled that one of the two significant correlations for males between childhood and adult dependency involved instrumental dependency for ages 6 to 10 with adult dependency on nonparental authority figures. Emotional dependency for boys age 6 to 10 showed no correlations with the adult dependency variables. Thus, male dependent behavior is apt to emphasize the seeking of instrumental assistance with problems, while females are likely to seek affection and emotional support in addition to instrumental aid.

It is important to note that passive and dependent behavior for ages 6 to 10 showed a better relation to adult dependent behavior than the ratings for 3 to 6 years of age. This finding indicates that important age changes occur between ages 3 and 10 and that behavior displayed during the first few years of school is a better index of adult functioning than the earlier preschool behavior patterns.

TACHISTOSCOPIC PERCEPTION OF DEPENDENT PICTURES

There were significant sex differences in recognition threshold for the three dependency pictures with the females recognizing all three pictures earlier than the males. The scene that depicted a person imploring a same sexed adult . . . yielded the most significant sex difference ($p < .001$, two tails). The picture of the adult on his knees clutching on to an opposite sexed adult . . . and that of the seated adult holding on to an opposite sexed adult . . . yielded sex differences significant at the .005 and .08 levels, respectively, for two tails. The aggressive pictures, on the other hand, produced opposite results, for the females recognized two of the four aggression pictures significantly later than the men ($p < .01$, two tails). There were no significant sex differences for the sex, physical danger, or three neutral scenes.

There was not a highly consistent relationship between recognition threshold for the dependent scenes and the interview ratings of dependency conflict. Only recognition of the scene that illustrated a man on his knees in front of a woman . . . showed a relation to dependency conflict, and this held only for males. The males who were above the median in recognition threshold for this scene (late recognition) were rated as more conflicted over dependent behavior than males who recognized this picture early ($p = .07$, two tails). For the females, recognition threshold for the dependency pictures showed no significant relation to ratings of dependency conflict.

Discussion

The results support a basic hypothesis of developmental theory which states that the acquisition of certain adult response patterns begins in early childhood. The differential stability of passive-dependent behavior for men and women is probably the result of several factors. However, one set of processes which may contribute to this phenomenon is derived from the commonly accepted hypothesis that passive and dependent behavior is less punished in females than in males. Further, females are often encouraged to be passive while men are expected to be independent and autonomous in the face of frustration. Parental and peer group punishment for passive and dependent behavior should result in some inhibition of this behavior in males. Thus, we would not expect this class of behavior to be as stable for men as for women. Studies of both overt behavior and fantasy (2, 3, 4, 6, 7) all indicate that dependent responses are more frequent for girls than for boys. Further, the sex stereotypes presented by communication media fit this description. The analysis of children's books by Child, Potter, and Levine (1) indicated that girls are portrayed as passive while boys are presented as independent and heroic. Finally, a study of the likes and dislikes of 10-year-old children (5) confirms the belief that girls accept passive behavior as more appropriate for their sex role than do boys.

The present tachistoscopic threshold data support the notion that men are more conflicted over dependent behavior than women. It will be recalled that the women recognized all three scenes depicting dependent behavior much earlier than the men. This finding suggests that the tendency to perceive dependent behavior in adults is much weaker in men than it is in women. One possible cause of this "weaker perceptual hypothesis" is that dependent action is less acceptable to men, i.e., that men are more conflicted over dependent behavior. This conclusion finds support in the correlation, for men, between late recognition of dependency . . . and the interview rating of dependency conflict.

Detailed analysis of the 54 cases indicates that there was a greater proportion of men, than women, who shifted from high dependency during childhood to independent behavior as adults. The women tended to be either dependent or independent for both childhood and adulthood. For example, in comparing emotional dependence for ages 6 to 10 with adult dependency on parents, not one female showed a major shift from high dependency in childhood to low dependency in adulthood. For the men, however, 20 per cent were rated very dependent during the ages 6 to 10 and very independent in adulthood.

The authors do not suggest that passive and dependent behavior in girls is rigidly fixed at school age and that change is a rare or unusual phenomenon. It must be kept in mind that the social milieu of these particular subjects remained rather constant throughout their lives. Their familial and extrafamilial environments were not disrupted to any marked degree. The parents and peers of these Ss retained their same values, their reference groups remained constant, and, in most cases, their geographical travel was limited. Thus, the degree of behavioral stability obtained for these females might not hold for populations that are more mobile or transient, for different ethnic or class samples, or for people subjected to major traumata during adolescence and early adulthood.

Implicit in these results is a strategy for certain research problems in developmental psychology. It would appear that a select group of theoretically relevant behaviors become clearly established as preferential response tendencies as early as 6 to 10 years of age. This means that one can study the child longitudinally without having to wait 15 or 20 years before asking important questions of the data. Since the current philosophy of financial support for research allows an investigator to chart a 5 to 10 year program, it is now feasible for one investigator to see the products of a longitudinally oriented project in a reasonable length of time.

Although case history material can never prove an hypothesis, it often facilitates scientific communication by placing some flesh on the skeleton of a correlation matrix. The following case material is presented to give the reader a clearer picture of the material upon which our childhood evaluations were based and to illustrate dramatically the degree of constancy of behavioral passivity for two specific individuals.

CASE A. Miss A is a 21-year-old, unmarried woman, who was in her senior year in an Eastern college. She was one of the most independent women in our sample and one who showed a strong reaction against dependent behavior in a wide variety of situations. As an adult she was described as a woman with a very strong need for recognition by others combined with a striving for achievement related goals. She had a strong desire to nurture others and often sought out situations in which she could give advice, support, and encouragement to peers. Miss A stated during the interview that she liked to keep her personal problems to herself. She did not like to discuss her personal problems because she felt that this behavior made her appear "helpless and weak." Statements like this indicate very strong conflict and anxiety over being in a passive-dependent position with other people. She was trying to sever any semblance of a dependent relation with her mother and derogated the latter because the mother seemed to be dependent upon her for companionship. Miss A sometimes felt lonely but said that she fights these feelings and tries to be able to live with them, for she does not like to admit that she needs friends or companionship. Her relationship with men seems to be consistent with the above pattern, for she tends to withdraw from heterosexual relationships that become too intense. Miss A said that she does not like men that make demands upon her, and she avoids men who attempt to place her in a passive role or position.

The following material represents selected verbatim excerpts from the longitudinal material on this subject.

Age 3 years, 4 months: Summary of Fels Nursery School Observations. S seems to be able to control and channel her behavior so that she got done just what she wanted to get done. In this activity she was very independent and capable. She was very social but also had a streak of aloof self-sufficiency, and she always made her individuality felt. She was what might be called a strong personality, often very intense, quite stubborn. . . . Her most outstanding characteristic was her consistent independence and integrity. In spite of the fact that she imitated and followed certain boys, she seemed to do this very much from her own choice, and she never lost the flavor of her individuality. She was capable of being social and seemed to enjoy contacts but at all times she was her own master. She would often withdraw from play and go on in her own direction at any time that she wished. . . . She was independent with adults and at times negativistic just to be devilish. She seemed somewhat self-conscious and had some cute little tricks. . . . In all, she could be characterized best by being called "tough minded." She shows determination and will, originality and spark, curiosity and interest in factual detail. She likes to quibble and argue, to verbalize, to construct, to accomplish. She is an individualist, independent and stubborn.

Age 5 years, 4 months: Fels Nursery School Observation. S seems to be vigorous, ruthless, competitive, highly sensual young woman, but one felt quite often that antagonism toward others was simply a direct response to their behavior. . . . She has grown far more social and also popular with an increasingly large crowd of special friends in a gang. She could be, when she chose, quite a successful leader, forging ahead and organizing a group on a hike, directing them and arranging things, and particularly keeping order in a fair sharing of the tools in the carpentry shop. . . . Many of S's conflicts with the adult world seemed a direct imitation of a certain boy. She needed a chance to grumble, would scornfully refuse any adult suggestions or orders, would usually go officially ahead to carry them out. She was quite demanding, often shouting an order to an assistant. . . . With her other work the same drive for strong achievement was also evident, sticking to anything until it was finished, whatever the group stimuli. S still had real trouble in fine motor coordination, would growl as she worked, "I'm doing this as well as I can steer my pencil." For all her teeth gritted effort, the final results would still be relatively crude. She was very skilled in the use of puzzles and interested in the problems of designs and the way things fit together. She scorned any of the ready-made designs for the Christmas tree decorations.

Age 7 years: Observation in Fels Day Camp. S came accompanied by one friend. S did not seem overwhelmed by the large proportion of adults around, but in her sturdy self-sufficient manner went ahead with her own activities. Her friend was at first rather shy and withdrawn and S, with her usual confident bullying and bossing of the adults, tended to take the girl under her wing and make sure she had a good time. S remains an exceptionally eager, imperturbable young woman. On a number of small issues she did insist on her own way, on just how long she would stay in the gym and play before lunch, but was quite reasonable about making compromises. She chose a rather difficult necklace to make and got quite mad when it didn't work out well. She kept doggedly with it, very self-sufficient, and continuing all on her own after getting some initial advice. . . . Her major effort was put on self-appointed tasks, to be able to master jumping over the horse at the gym where she took numerous tumbles until she succeeded. In spite of her distractability and preference for the apparatus she did set herself to learning the new skills required there.

Age 9 years: Report from Teacher. S is one of the most responsible children in the group. . . . She is self-reliant, independent, and knows how to plan her time well. She enters all games with enthusiasm, is very well coordinated, is full of personality and "joie de vivre."

CASE B. Miss B is a 23-year-old, unmarried woman, who is working and living with her parents. She was one of the most overtly dependent women in the sample. During the interview she was very dependent on the interviewer for structure and was rather mild and meek. Her most typical reaction to failure or stressful situations is to deny or to withdraw and she says quite blithely, "I'm not a worrier." She is very sensitive to the opinions of other people and usually conforms with their expectations for her. She accepts her passive-dependent role with authority

people and with love objects. S tends to be very dependent on peers for advice, likes being close to the family, and tends to see herself as inadequate in the face of problem situations.

Following are selected excerpts from her longitudinal records:

Age 2 years, 6 months: Fels Nursery School Observation. At the first day of nursery school, S seemed rather frightened and very reluctant to leave her mother this morning. The mother had to carry her and hold her in the car until the door was shut. For the first few miles she cried and then suddenly stopped and began to take an interest in the various animals and objects. She cried when she reached the nursery school but stopped as soon as she left the other children. On the second day of nursery school she cried again but seemed much less frightened and more angry. During the nursery school she stood watching the other children and at one point ran to another girl and stood beside her. The other little girl paid no attention, and S trailed after her. S wandered around and, when the teacher went to the house, S rushed to follow her and stood around the teacher. S tagged after another little girl all morning. During the nursery school two-week period she was timid and tense.

Age 3 years: Fels Nursery School Summary. At first, S was timid and tense and was gathered under the wing of another peer and her cohorts. From then on she was "at home" with the group. She followed another girl's lead and joined in the activities the other girl organized. On days when this girl was absent she was at loose-ends and tended to return to her original dependence on an adult. Several weeks after her nursery school stay she visited the school one morning for several hours. She was a little apprehensive at first but made no real protest. She stood around not joining in the play until an adult suggested an activity.

Age 4 years: Fels Nursery School Summary. S cried the first day of nursery school after she saw another girl cry. She stayed close to the teacher the first few days and watched the other children with a worried expression on her face. Indoors she chose small blocks or color cubes to play with. In the yard S was very cautious about trying out the apparatus, particularly when there was any balancing involved. She has a high, whining nasal voice, and several letter substitutions made her speech rather difficult to understand. She was quite complying with adult requests. Frequently, she appealed to adults for help in conflicts, such as getting a turn to slide, which is a situation she could have handled for herself.

Age 6 years: Visit to the School. S is retiring, quiet, and shy. She doesn't show the enthusiasm that most of the children in the class do. She seems content. . . . She goes to the teacher for suggestions and skips to her seat jubilantly with a word of approval from the teacher. *S* recites a bit timidly in front of the whole class but accepts the teacher's support and gets through successfully. Her voice is a little soft and her enunciation is not clear. *S* volunteers information a bit tentatively and without enthusiasm. The teacher reports that *S* is about the brightest of the average group. *S* is not a leader but she is very sweet and cooperative and is never any trouble.

Age 6 years, 6 months: Summary of Fels Day Camp Observations. S was outclassed in almost every respect in this group but fluttered happily about after the others doing the best she could. She occasionally withdrew or grew silent but, when encouraged by an adult, she soon recovered. She was not insensitive and did not seem to have her security disturbed more than momentarily. She seems to feel a great confidence and trust in adults and could always be bought off or led along. She lacked initiative in almost every way. She could not go ahead on any craft project nor could she assert herself socially. She needed help and encouragement, hung about the adults, not exposing herself to the center of the group. She is essentially a conformist and wanted only to do what was right. She got into no mischief and had little sense of fun. She was happiest when settled into a situation that was approved and guided by an adult, and at these times she would proddle along very happily. Her main interests lay in conforming to any plans laid by adults and working on simple handcrafts. She was rather unsure in her accomplishments. She was often physically apprehensive.

Age 7 years, 6 months: Summary of Fels Day Camp Observations. The most characteristic as-

pect of *S's* day camp behavior was her ability, high conformity, and social reticence. She did not participate in social activities to any extent and was generally ignored by the other children. She clung to adults, wanted to assist them when possible, and wanted their approval and comforting in all her activities. She seemed to be somewhat apprehensive of physical contacts, especially if they became at all rough. She was apprehensive about almost any physical danger. Her actual physical ability was not particularly poor, and, when she was put into athletic situations, she did surprisingly well. Her general lack of physical participation seems not to be due to poor ability as much as to lack of motivation and apprehension.

Age 8 years: Visit to the School. S is always anxious to do what is right all of the time. She is not a discipline problem. *S* shows no interest in physical activities. Initially, she is lost at school work and takes some time to adjust to new work. *S* was pretty tentative in her first attempt to get the teacher's attention and held up her paper hesitantly. She was very pleased when the teacher came to her. She was uncertain about the problems although they had similar ones before.

Age 8 years, 8 months: Fels Day Camp Summary. S is a small, dark looking girl, bent over, with thick dark hair and a tired face. Her voice is high but with no force; her hands hanging limp at the wrists. Much of this lack of force seemed related to her personality, and at the races she surprised us by doing remarkably well. *S* obeyed adults implicitly and wanted to have their sanction for even small acts which the group had already been given permission for. She has a rather cringing, servile manner. This clinging around adults was particularly marked the first day when she ate her lunch with them.

Age 9 years, 8 months: Fels Day Camp Summary. S is a rather pathetic looking little girl. Rather thin, droopy eyed, clammy handed, somehow reminiscent of an orphan in an old melodrama. She seems nearer to seven or eight than her actual age and with a kind of naivete and unsureness about all she did. She was an exceedingly compliant child in taking the tests, even the reading tests which she obviously disliked, without a murmur.

Summary

This paper summarized some results from a larger investigation of the stability of behavior in a group of subjects who were part of the Fels Research Institute's longitudinal population. This report dealt specifically with the long term stability of passive and dependent behavior from childhood through adulthood.

The Ss were 27 males and 27 females for whom extensive longitudinal information was available from birth through adolescence. One psychologist studied narrative reports based on observations of the child in various settings and rated each child on four variables describing types of passive and dependent behavior for ages 3 to 6 and ages 6 to 10. A second psychologist, who had no knowledge of the childhood data, interviewed each S in adulthood and rated each S on six variables related to aspects of adult passive and dependent behavior. In addition, each adult S was administered a tachistoscopic perception task in which scenes illustrating dependent activity were presented at seven different exposure speeds.

The results revealed that passive and dependent behaviors were quite stable for women, but minimally stable for men. Over 60 per cent of the correlations between the childhood (ages 6 to 10) and adult ratings of dependency were statistically significant for females, while only 9 per cent were significant for men. For example, the correlation between passive withdrawal from problem situations for ages 6 to 10 and adulthood was .52 ($p < .01$) for women and .21 for men. Similarly, the correlation between emotional dependence for ages 6 to 10 and adult dependency on parents was .51 ($p < .01$) for women and .02 for men. The correlations between the ratings for ages 3 to 6 and adulthood were considerably lower and not statistically significant.

It was suggested that environmental disapproval and punishment of dependent behavior in young males led to inhibition of and conflict over dependency in the growing boy. The social acceptance of passive and dependent behavior in females would be expected to result in greater stability for this class of responses for women than for men. The fact that females recognized the tachistoscopically presented dependency scenes earlier than the men was interpreted as support for this explanation.

Case history material for two female subjects was presented to illustrate the type of information utilized in this study.

REFERENCES

CHILD, I. L. POTTER, E. H., & LEVINE, ESTELLE M. Children's textbooks and personality development: an exploration in the social psychology of education. *Psychol. Monogr.*, 1946, *60*, No. 279.

HATTWICK, BERTHA. Sex differences in behavior of nursery school children. *Child Develpm.*, 1937, *8*, 323–355.

KAGAN, J. The stability of TAT fantasy and stimulus ambiguity. *J. consult. Psychol.*, 1959, *23*, 266–271.

SANFORD, R. N., Adkins, M. M., Miller, R. B., & Cobb, E. N. Physique, personality and scholarship: a comprehensive study of school children. *Monogr. Soc. Res. Child Develpm.*, 1943, *8*, No. 1.

TYLER, LEONA E. The development of vocational interests. I. The organization of likes and dislikes in ten year old children. *J. genet. Psychol.*, 1955, *86*, 33–44.

WATSON, R. I. *Psychology of the child.* New York: Wiley, 1959.

WHITEHOUSE, ELIZABETH. Norms for certain aspects of the Thematic Apperception Test on a group of nine and ten year old children. *J. Pers.*, 1949, *1*, 12–15.

Stability and Interrelations of Thematic Test Imagery Over 20 Years

ARLENE SKOLNICK

A comparison of TAT stories written by the same individuals in adolescence and later in adulthood indicated stability for males in power and aggression and for females in achievement and, to some degree, in affiliation.

The use of projective techniques such as the Thematic Apperception Test (TAT) in diagnosis and research rests on the assumption that these tests measure enduring personality traits rather than transistory responses to situational or other influences. As yet, however, little is known about the long-term stability of such responses. The present report, part of a larger study on the relations between fantasy responses and behavior, examines the stability and interrelations over a 20-year period (ages 17–37) of motivational imagery in the TAT responses of Oakland Growth Study (OGS) subjects. (Further information on the methods and purposes of the OGS may be found in Jones [1939]). The motives, selected for theoretical significance, are achievement, aggression, affiliation, and power. Previously, the longest interval over which TAT responses have been compared was 10 years (Moss & Kagan,

1961). Looking at achievement imagery only, these authors found a moderate but significant degree of stability for both sexes. In an earlier report, Kagan (1959) compared several kinds of TAT content categories over a 6-year period (ages approximately 8–14); he found only physical aggression and achievement to have significant stability.

Recently, a number of longitudinal projects have been bearing fruit in the form of reports on the stability of personality traits over time. Comparisons will be drawn between the present findings involving only the TAT, and results of studies using personality data derived in other ways. The general issue of the relation between TAT imagery and behavior will not, however, be discussed in the present paper.

Method

SUBJECTS. Subjects were OGS participants with complete protocols for either or both times, 1938 (age 17–18) and 1958. Forty-four men and 49

This research was supported by Grant M-5300 from the National Institute of Mental Health, U.S. Public Health Service. The author wishes to thank John Clausen, M. Brewster Smith, and Norman Livson for their helpful comments.

women had usable records for both adolescence and adulthood. In addition to this core group were subjects who were tested only once, bringing the total number of subjects available for each period to: 74 boys, 75 girls, 49 men, and 56 women.

PICTURES. The adolescent TAT consisted of 18 pictures, four of which differed for boys and girls. The boys' pictures included nine from the Murray set which is now standard (Cards 1, 5, 6BM, 7BM, 10, 11, 14, 15, 17BM); five from the set generally used in 1938 (a man and woman seated on a park bench; a bearded old man writing in a large book; a dishevelled young man standing behind a well-dressed older one; a tea table and two chairs; a line drawing of two bearded men); and four designed especially for the OGS (the nave of a large church; a madonna and child; a dramatic mountain view; a boy gazing at a cross wreathed in clouds).

Instead of 6BM, 7BM, 17BM, and the two men, the girls were shown 3GF, 18GF, plus a picture of a man and woman standing in a doorway, the man clutching the woman's shoulders, and a picture of a man looking out through a window. Adults of both sexes were shown cards 1, 2, 3BM, 9MF, 12F, 19, plus the picture of two men shown to the boys in 1938.

SCORING METHODS. All protocols were examined for the presence of references to the four motives. For three of the motivational themes—achievement, affiliation and power—the definitions and general approach used by the McClelland–Atkinson group and described in a series of scoring manuals (Atkinson, 1958) were used. Achievement motivation is defined as competition with a standard of excellence, affiliation as concern over maintaining or restoring good interpersonal relationships, and power as concern over controlling the means of influence. In most instances, only the "imagery" category could be scored—that is, presence or absence of imagery relevant to the motive in question. Cards 1, 2, and the picture of the old man and the book in the adolescent set were, however, scored for all categories of achievement imagery.

Aggressive imagery was scored according to a system devised by the author. The subject was given 1 point each time an instance of one of several categories of aggression appeared in a story, except for physical aggression, which received a score of 1–3 points depending on the intensity of the act described. The other categories were: verbal aggression; direct expression of aggressive affect; indirect aggression—accident, sickness, death; antisocial aggression—crime, etc.; hostile description—for example, "He is a nasty man"; suicide and self-injury.

There was also a category called "victimization," which was scored whenever the hero of a story was the object rather than the perpetrator of an aggressive act; this score, however, was not added into the total score for aggression.

RELIABILITY. All scoring was done by the writer and another rater. Rank-order agreement (p) was approximately .85 for achievement, .70 for affiliation, .86 for power, and .85 for aggression. In all instances of disagreement, the divergent ratings were discussed, and stories rerated.

CORRECTION FOR LENGTH. In some previous studies, motivational imagery was found to vary with the length of protocols. While telling longer stories may truly reflect such interpersonal motives as achievement, affiliation, etc., it is generally considered prudent to sacrifice criterion variance to guard against spurious inflation by verbal fluency. In the present data, such a relation between length and motive scores was found in the adolescent but not in the adult protocols. Adolescent motive scores, therefore, were altered to remove this correlation. Corrected scores were obtained by regarding the average score of all four motives as the predicted scores for each length of protocol and subtracting it from the obtained scores. In other words, motive scores of subjects who told very long stories were reduced, while the scores of those who told very short ones were increased.

Results

STABILITY OF TAT IMAGERY. Table 1 presents the relations between adolescent and adult imagery for the four motives. For men, power and aggression show moderate stability, while for women, all kinds of imagery show a positive trend, but

Table 1. Stability of TAT Imagery (Raw Correlations)

	Men (N = 44)	Women (N = 49)
Achievement	.03	.24**
Affiliation	−.11	.21*
Power	.34***	.20
Aggression	.27**	.18

*p < .10, 1 tail; **p < .05, 1 tail; ***p < .01, 1 tail.

only achievement attains significance at the .05 level.

Since aggressive imagery proved stable in men, the components of the aggression score were examined to see which if any categories of this imagery remained stable. As Table 2 indicates, these subcategories as a whole were not notably consistent. Victimization and verbal aggression in women, and direct expression in men, tend to remain stable.

Table 2. Consistency of Aggression (Raw Correlations)

	Men	Women
Physical unweighted	.07	.08
Physical weighted	−.11	.02
Direct expression	.24*	−.05
Verbal	.00	.37***
Indirect	−.05	.12
Antisocial	.05	.01
Hostile description	.07	−.13
Suicide	.10	.00
Victimization	−.05	.28**

*p < .10, 1 tail; **p < .05, 1 tail; ***p < .01, 1 tail.

INTERCORRELATIONS OF TAT IMAGERY. Table 3 presents the relations among the four kinds of imagery for each sex at each period. In both sexes at both times, there is a tendency for affiliation and achievement to be related.

In male at both times, aggression and achievement are inversely related, and aggression and power are directly correlated. In adolescent girls, power and achievement are inversely related, while aggression and affiliation are significantly correlated.

Table 3. Intercorrelations of TAT Imagery Scores (Raw Correlations)

	1	2	3	4
	Adolescent Boys			
1 ACH	. . .	. . .	. . .	. . .
2 AFF	.26*	. . .	. . .	. . .
3 POW	−.11	.02	. . .	. . .
4 AGG	−.22*	−.06	.44**	. . .
	Men			
1 ACH	. . .	. . .	. . .	. . .
2 AFF	.24*	. . .	. . .	. . .
3 POW	−.07	−.03	. . .	. . .
4 AGG	−.25*	.01	.26*	. . .
	Adolescent Girls			
1 ACH	. . .	. . .	. . .	. . .
2 AFF	.20*	. . .	. . .	. . .
3 POW	−.24	−.07	. . .	. . .
4 AGG	−.06	.32*	−.06	. . .
	Women			
1 ACH	. . .	. . .	. . .	. . .
2 AFF	.28*	. . .	. . .	. . .
3 POW	−.17	.15	. . .	. . .
4 AGG	.01	.16	.21	. . .

*p < .10, 2 tails; **p < .05, 2 tails.

Discussion

The finding that aggression and power imagery tend to remain stable in men and that achievement imagery tends to remain stable in women is consistent with other findings about differences in the stability of personality traits according to sex. A strikingly similar finding based on a smaller number of these OGS subjects but comparing drive ratings made by observers at adolescence and adulthood (different observers at each time) was reported by Tuddenham (1959). He found that ratings of "drive for aggression" and "drive for control"—the latter being comparable to the power motive in the present study—were significantly stable in males, while for females drive for achievement approached but fell just short of significance. Reporting on findings from a different longitudinal study, Kagan and Moss (1962) found continuity from the preschool years to adulthood in the aggressive behavior of males and in the passivity and dependency of females. And in a third longitudinal investigation, the Guidance Study, girls again showed a greater consistency than boys on the dependence–independence continuum (Honzik & Macfarlane, 1964).

The above findings have been summed up in the following way by Kagan and Moss: "A behavior will show long term stability if it is congruent with the cultural definition of the sex-role of the individual." *Why* sex-salient behavior should be persistent, however, is an intriguing conundrum. Kagan and Moss assert the findings provide "compelling evidence for the importance of cultural factors," and that "the individual's desire to mold his overt behavior in accordance with the culture's definition of sex appropriate responses is a major determinant of the patterns of continuity and discontinuity in his development."

Flaws in this argument have been pointed out by Honzik (1964; 1965): high correlations mean that individuals are maintaining their places on the sex-salient dimensions; not only are aggressive boys and dependent girls remaining the same, but nonaggressive boys and nondependent girls are doing likewise. Presumably, if everybody were striving to live up to an ideal model, there should be more variability with age and hence low stability coefficients.

One possible response to this argument is: while everybody is maintaining his place relative to everybody else, all boys are nevertheless becoming more aggressive and all girls more dependent. Unfortunately, Kagan and Moss do not supply information as to means. Some doubt, however, is cast upon the concept of large absolute differences between the sexes by data from the present study: there were no significant differences between adult men and women in any of the four kinds of imagery, nor were there differences in variability. (The adolescent male and female TAT cards were not the same, hence no direct comparison is possible. There were, however, no striking differences between the motive scores of the two sexes at adolescence either.) The present results, of course, have to do with projective data, while other findings have been based on behavioral measures. But there is no the-oretical reason to expect that fantasy responses should show a lesser degree of difference between the sexes than overt behavior.

Rather than some biological or cultural factor working in a single direction, the data seem to call for an explanation based upon some differentiating force operating to reinforce whatever behavior relevant to sex role the individual emits, regardless of whether the behavior is at the high or low end of the relevant dimension. How such a process might work is easiest to imagine in the case of aggressiveness in boys; thus, one could speculate that a pecking order gets established very early on the basis of early aggression-relevant responses. Or perhaps there is an early fixation of self concepts based on parental responses to children's behavior; mothers might be quick to characterize children on the salient sex-role dimensions—for, example, they might be more inclined to make remarks like "She's very independent (or dependent)," or "He's very masculine, a real scrapper," than they would be where the child's behavior is not so relevant to sex role.

Another puzzling aspect of the differential stability findings is this: why, if aggression is relevant for the male sex role, is it not relevant for the female role also? A possible answer is that the two roles are not defined in polar opposites; it has been suggested that in learning appropriate sex roles girls are learning how to be like adults and not like babies, while boys are learning how to be masculine and not like girls and women (Emmerich, 1959). This notion seems to explain the salience of dependency for girls and aggression for boys.

The lack of stability in achievement imagery in males in the present study contrasts with the finding by Moss and Kagan (1961) that achievement behavior tends to remain stable for both sexes. This may be because the present adolescent male cards differed from both the adult set and the adolescent female set, or else, that the two populations of subjects were different. Some support for the latter explanation may be found in the fact that achievement drive as measured by observer ratings did not show much stability in the males of this group, while it did in the females (Tuddenham, 1959).

The finding that affiliation and achievement are

associated in both sexes at both times is consistent with a number of other findings linking affiliation and achievement behavior (e.g., Frenkel-Brunswik, 1942; Winterbottom, 1958). The latter study found that parents of achievement-oriented children stressed independence with regard to tasks, but dependence with regard to people. Bandura and Walters (1963) link affiliation and achievement together under the heading of "pro-social behavior."

As for the finding of an inverse correlation between achievement and aggression in males, two explanations suggest themselves: one would be that achievement and aggression represent two alternative modes by which males can express their masculinity. This notion is supported by Kagan and Moss (1962), who similarly found an inverse relationship between achievement behavior and both aggressiveness and athletic interests; they also found fear of bodily harm to be associated with achievement goals. Of course, the idea that athleticism and scholarship are antithetical is not a new idea; it has recently been documented in a sociological study of high-school culture (Coleman, 1961). A second explanation, not necessarily contradictory to the first, would be that aggression and achievement are negatively related because they represent different levels of ego functions: Peskin (1964) found that impulse expression in the form of temper tantrums characterized periods when the IQ's of a group of male subjects were lowest, in contrast to the times when these same subjects had their highest IQ's.

In girls, the inverse relationship between power and achievement also supports a conception of two broad clusters of motives—"pro-social" and self-assertive (Cf. Horney, 1945 and Schutz, 1958). On the other hand, the finding that aggression and affiliation imagery are correlated in adolescent girls contradicts this view. A similar exception was found by Bronson (1966); in pre-adolescent girls she found an association between domineering and dependence, two variables which in males and at other times in females were inversely related. Also, a combination of affiliative and aggressive tendencies has been found to characterize young female schizophrenics, as opposed to young male schizophrenics, who tend to withdraw (Cheek, 1964).

Conclusion

The present findings indicate that motivational imagery on the TAT shows patterns of stability over time comparable to those found by other methods; that is, males tend to remain stable in power and aggression, while females tend to remain stable in achievement and, to some degree, affiliation. Analysis of the interrelationships of motivational imagery suggests a conception of two broad dimensions of behavior — pro-social and antisocial (in the sense of being self-assertive), although a finding of a direct correlation between affiliation and aggression in adolescent girls constitutes an exemption to this scheme.

REFERENCES

ATKINSON, J. W. (Ed.) *Motives in fantasy, action and society.* New York: Van Nostrand, 1958.

BANDURA, A., & WALTERS, R. H. *Social learning and personality development.* New York: Holt, Rinehart & Winston, 1963.

BRONSON, WANDA. Central orientations: A study of behavior organization from childhood to adolescence. *Child Develpm.,* 1966, *37,* 125–156.

CHEEK, FRANCES C. A serendipidous finding: Sex roles & schizophrenia. *J. abnorm. soc. Psychol.,* 1964, *69,* 392–401.

COLEMAN, J. E. *The adolescent society.* Glencoe, Ill.: Free Press, 1961.

EMMERICH, W. Parental identification in young children. *Genet. Psychol. Monogr.,* 1959, *60,* 257–308.

FRENKEL-BRUNSWICK, ELSE. Motivation and behavior. *Genet. Psychol. Monogr.,* 1942, *26,* 121–265.

HONZIK, MARJORIE P. Personality consistency and change: Some comments on papers by Bayley, Macfarlane, Moss and Kagan, and Murphy. *Vita Humana,* 1964, 7, 139–142.

HONZIK, MARJORIE P. Prediction of behavior from birth to maturity. Review of J. Kagan & H. Moss, *Birth to maturity. Merrill-Palmer Quart.,* 1965, *11,* 77–88.

HONZIK, MARJORIE P., & MACFARLANE, JEAN W. Prediction of specific behaviors and personality characteristics from 21 months to 30 years. Unpublished manuscript, Univer. of California, Berkeley, 1964.

HORNEY, KAREN. *Our inner conflicts.* New York: Norton, 1945.

JONES, H. E. Procedures of the adolescent growth study. *J. consult. Psychol.,* 1939, *3,* 177–180.

KAGAN, J. The stability of TAT fantasy and stimulus ambiguity. *J. consult. Psychol.,* 1959, *23,* 266–271.

KAGAN, J., & MOSS, H. *Birth to maturity: a study in psychological development.* New York: Wiley, 1962.

MOSS, H. A., & KAGAN, J. Stability of achievement and recognition seeking behaviors from early child-hood through adulthood. *J. abnorm. soc. Psychol.,* 1961, *62,* 504–513.

PESKIN, H. Intellectual stability, personality structure, and ego autonomy. Paper read at Amer. Psychol. Ass., Los Angeles, September, 1964.

SCHUTZ, W. C. *FIRO: a three-dimensional theory of interpersonal behavior.* New York: Rinehart, 1958.

TUDDENHAM, R. D. The constancy of personality ratings over two decades. *Genet. Psychol. Monogr.,* 1959, *60,* 3–29.

WINTERBOTTOM, M. R. The relation of need for achievement to learning experiences in independence and mastery. In J. W. Atkinson (Ed.), *Motives in fantasy, action, and society.* New York: Van Nostrand, 1958. Pp. 453–478.

Chapter 3: Suggested Additional Readings

BERDIE, R. F.   Personality changes from high school entrance to college matriculation. *Journal of Counseling Psychology*, 1968, *15*(4), 376–380. The Minnesota Counseling Inventory was administered to a group of students when they entered high school and to the same students four years later when they entered college. On the basis of data obtained, the author concluded that both sexes—though men more than women —experience various personality changes in high school and that the changes are mostly for the better.

BRONSON, W. C.   Central orientations: A study of behavior organization from childhood to adolescence. *Child Development*, 1966, *37*, 125–155. This investigation was designed to determine behaviors which are most consistent throughout the developmental span. Measures which proved most predictive and persistent for both sexes were found to fall in three dimensions: withdrawal–expressiveness, reactivity–placidity, and passivity–dominance. However, the meaning and expression of such traits may vary with shifting environmental demands.

CHICKERING, A. W., MC DOWELL, J., & CAMPAGNA, D.   Institutional differences and student development. *Journal of Educational Psychology*, 1969, *60*(4), 315–326. Tests administered to entering freshmen at thirteen small colleges, and again after the students' first and second years, were analyzed in terms of changes in students' personality traits, and according to characteristics of the colleges and of student subgroups.

FRANTZ, T. T.   Student and nonstudent change. *College Student Personnel*, 1971, *12*(1), 49–53. Few differences in areas of personality change were found between college and noncollege individuals. Among both groups young adults changed more in social attitudes than in other areas, in general becoming more gregarious and friendly. They changed least in traditional beliefs, domestic habits, and tendency toward conformity.

JONES, V.   Attitudes of college students and their changes: A 57-year study. *Genetic Psychology Monographs*, 1970, *81*, 3–80. On the basis of longitudinal data, drawn from the same individuals intermittently between the academic years of 1930–31 and 1967–68, the author reports changes in students' attitudes toward war and peace, church and religion.

LONG, B. H., ZILLER, R. C., & HENDERSON, E. H.   Developmental changes in the self-concept during adolescence. *The School Review*, 1968, *76*(2), 210–230. Findings from this study, combined with those from an earlier related study—both involving subjects from grades four through twelve—yielded insights into differential perceptions of self–other relationships during adolescence.

NAWAS, M. M.   Change in efficiency of ego functioning and complexity from adolescence to young adulthood. *Developmental Psychology*, 1971, *4*(3), 412–415. On the basis of an analysis of TAT stories administered to male and female subjects, both as adolescents and as young adults eight years later, the author concluded that human behavior is subject to wide modification in accord with psychosocial and situational demands.

NEWCOMB, T. M., KOENIG, K. E., FLACKS, R., & WARWICK, D. P.   *Persistence and change: Bennington college and its students after 25 years.* New York: Wiley, 1967. This follow-up study of the personality change of a group of Bennington College women who graduated in the late thirties reveals an unusual persistence of the liberal attitude acquired as undergraduates. The book suggests strongly that colleges with special commitments can have a long-term influence on students.

WITKIN, H., GOODENOUGH, D., & KARP, S.   Stability of cognitive style from childhood to young adulthood. *Journal of Personality and Social Psychology,* 1967, 7(3), 291–300. This article reports a study of differential development, as reflected in cognitive style, among two groups, one of individuals aged 8 to 13 years, the other aged 10 to 24 years. Individual consistency in degree of field dependence or independence was determined.

YARROW, L. J. (Ed.)   Symposium on personality, consistency and change: Perspective from longitudinal research. *Vita Humana,* 1964, 7, 65–146. In this issue, representatives of three well-known longitudinal studies (the Berkeley Growth Study, the California Guidance Study, and the Fels Study of Human Development) and of one non-longitudinal study (the Topeka "Coping Project") present selected findings and interpretations. The papers are introduced by Yarrow and discussed by Schaefer and Honzik.

4

Two Related Concepts: Stage Theory and Critical Period Hypothesis

In recent years, psychologists have been paying considerable attention to the related concepts of *stage theory* and *critical period*. Actually, stage theory has a rather venerable history, for among its early proponents were Aristotle and Rousseau (Muuss, 1970). According to the theory, human development progresses by stages, each of which possesses a certain distinctiveness.

In elaborating the theory, Rousseau proposed that teaching should harmonize with the child's development in each of the age-stages. The first period, infancy, included the first four years of life when the child was dominated by feelings of either pleasure or pain. The second, or savage, stage included the years from 5 to 12, and during this stage sensory experience was dominant. The third stage, from ages 12 to 15, was characterized by the awakening of more rational faculties, including self-consciousness and reasoning. The fourth period, adolescence proper, from ages 15 to 20, culminated in the ripening of emotional functions and involved a shift from selfishness to self-esteem and social concern. The fifth stage in development, maturity, was less clearly defined by Rousseau.

There is considerable disagreement among psychologists concerning the discreetness of these stages and the exact duration and particular significance of each. Erikson (1967) points out that the concept of stages will become increasingly fluid—that is, we will no longer be able rigidly to divide the life span into stages and expect each one to remain fixed. Each stage may constitute a different experience for the individual person, depending on various factors, such as his occupational skills. An individual's occupation may in effect become outdated prematurely, relegating him to the status of the older worker whose skills have become obsolete. A particular age-stage may become subdivided—for example, young adulthood may become further subdivided into older and younger adults. The less young adult may become a "principal arbiter"—that is, at least for the limited period of the superiority of his particular specialty, his authority will, as it were, displace the authority formerly reserved to "the older generation." In a sense, then, the so-called younger generation would become divided into the older-young and the younger-young generations. The older young would become the chief directors of the younger young; thus, the power of the parents might decline, and the young adult specialist would become the emerging authority for still younger youth.

The concept of age-stages is often related to developmental tasks, which presumably must be accomplished at particular stages before an individual can satisfactorily transact the responsibilities of higher stages. Thornburg (1970) assigns the following developmental tasks to adolescents: (1) learning appropriate relationships with peers; (2) learning the appropriate masculine and feminine social roles; (3) learning acceptance and use of one's own body; (4) achieving behavioral and emotional independence from parents and other adults; (5) striving toward economic independence; (6) making vocational selection and preparation; (7) preparing and accepting the role of marriage and family life; and (8) developing a social and civic intelligence.

The critical period hypothesis suggests that certain times in life are especially critical for the acquisition of particular sorts of experience. A critical period may span varying lengths of time—hours, days, months, or years—and there may be different critical periods for different functions. If the critical period for acquiring a particular function is missed, presumably a similar experience at a later date will have much less, if any, impact upon the individual's development. Also, learning acquired during a critical period tends to persist. Thus, if childhood be deemed critical for establishing the concept of self as male or female, that feeling when once established is difficult, and perhaps impossible, to change.

Where adolescents are concerned, stage theory involves several issues. Is adolescence a "natural" stage in development, or merely an artifact of modern society? Are experiences during adolescence in any sense critical for what happens later in life? Perhaps infancy and childhood are the truly critical stages, so that by the teens an individual's course is set and is subject to little modification.

Several important questions related to both stage theory and critical periods remain unanswered. Might experiences be so manipulated that children would proceed through life stages at a faster pace than is generally believed possible, or perhaps skip some stages altogether? Also, might experiences in adolescence be so engineered that the period would assume more significance than it presently does? Certainly much research remains to be done concerning life stages to resolve the considerable confusion that surrounds this important topic.

The first of the following selections written by the editor of this volume, relates age-stage theory and critical-period hypothesis to adolescence. The second selection, by Elkind, was chosen for several reasons. For one thing, in his own right, he is one of the most distinguished of developmental psychologists. For another, his research and comments concerning stage theory have been widely recognized. Finally, the study of cognition, with which this article is concerned, is of major interest in contemporary psychology.

REFERENCES

ERIKSON, E. H.   Memorandum on youth. *Daedalus*, 1967, *96*(3), 860–870.
MUUSS, R. E.   Theories of adolescent development—philosophical and historical roots. In E. D. Evans (Ed.) *Adolescence: Readings in behavior and development.* New York: The Dryden Press, 1970.

Stage Theory and Critical Period as Related to Adolescence

The author reviews certain of the better known stage theories, relates them to adolescence, and makes critical observations concerning them, both individually and collectively. She concludes that adolescence may indeed have distinctive features, but much of its significance depends on the way specific individuals experience it.

Among the longer-standing controversies in developmental psychology is whether individuals maintain the same basic sequences in their patterns of development. This question gave rise to the age-stage hypothesis, which suggests that children manifest various behaviors sequentially in the course of their development, and progress through increasingly mature and relatively well-defined stages.

. . . The idea of life stages was pursued in earnest at the University of Vienna in the 1930's. The Vienna writers, especially Charlotte Bühler, postulated five principal stages.[1] During the first stage, childhood, an individual lives at home, and is dependent on his family. From age 12 to about 28, the individual engages in exploratory and preparatory activities, while deciding what to do with his life and establishing his independence. A person performs his major work in life from about age 28 to 50, after which his activities decline. At 65 he retires, gradually restricting his activities and loosening his ties.[2]

Several Well-Known Stage Theories

Some writers concentrate on certain life-stages in particular; others indicate how the various life-stages fit together and attempt to define the special significance of each. Let us now look at certain of the more influential views concerning life-stages viewed developmentally, beginning with Piaget.

Piaget perceived children as progressing through sequential stages of development, for example, in morals.[3] In the first stage, until age 7, the child is a moral realist, and judges deviant acts in terms of damage done. Finally, after certain intermediate stages, the child learns to apply principles differentially and to realize that rules can be altered. At the later stage, intent matters more than damage done. At the early stage, the child who breaks fifteen cups is judged more wicked

---

[1]C. Bühler, *Der Menschliche Lebenslauf als Psychologisches Problem.* Gottingen: Verlag für Psychologie, 1959.

[2]Dorothy Rogers, *Child Psychology* (Belmont, Calif., Brooks-Cole Publishing Co., 1969).
  [3]*Ibid.*

than one who breaks one cup, even though the first child's mishap was completely accidental while the second child's involved disobedience.

Another stage concept, by Harry Stack Sullivan, suggests how adolescence relates to earlier life stages.[4] After infancy, he distinguishes two stages of childhood. The young child has clear interpersonal relations, but is still so young that such experiences are largely confined to the home. Later childhood, roughly what Freud called the latency period, Sullivan refers to as the juvenile era. In this period the child must deal as an individual with strangers, and cope with the gap between his image of himself and others of him, and between what he needs and what they give. When he begins seeing others as competitors, childhood is at an end. Maturity becomes a matter of individual psychodynamics, not biological age. Thus, childhood may end earlier for a lower-class child, who may have to fend for himself almost as soon as he can walk. Adolescence, says Sullivan, is distinguished from earlier stages by the warp of tenderness, but fibers of social experience tie the personality together. Other people come to matter as individuals, and not merely as sources of support or obstructions to impulse. The adolescent learns to love, and to value others for their personalities.

Havighurst's Developmental Task Theory

Havighurst and Erikson base their stage theories on the need for continuous mastery of new tasks, appropriate for successive age-stages. Implicit in such developmental task theories is the idea that an individual must resolve certain conflicts, or acquire certain skills at a given stage if he is to fulfill successfully the obligations of the next age level. Certain developmental tasks, maintains Havighurst, originate chiefly from physical maturation, others primarily from cultural pressures.[5] Learning to write is required by social pressure, while establishing satisfactory heterosexual relationships depends on physical matura-

tion. A third source of developmental tasks is the individual's value system. Whether a girl spends her time learning to knit or to operate a computer may depend on whether she aspires to a domestic or career role in the future.

Erikson's Eight Stages of Man

Erikson defined life tasks in terms of personality characteristics.[6] He portrayed life as consisting of eight periods, ideally beginning with the establishment of *basic trust* in infancy. The quality of the maternal relationship is perceived as crucial for creating in the child a feeling that others can be trusted. In the second stage, the child begins establishing a sense of *autonomy*. In the process of developing basic patterns of eating, sleeping, or toilet training he is permitted certain alternatives and choices, which result in feelings of freedom. In the third stage the child develops *initiative*. At this time, he gains a sense of responsibility, especially through contact with ideal adults. Next comes the stage when the child gains a sense of the technological ethos of his culture. He attends school and gains *respect for industry and its tools*. The fifth stage, adolescence, is a period of *identity* versus role diffusion. Faced with "physiological revolution" within him, and with tangible adults ahead of him, the adolescent becomes preoccupied with how he appears to others compared with what he believes he is, and with how roles and skills cultivated earlier will articulate with "occupational prototypes of the day." The great danger is role confusion; and where such confusion is based on doubt as to one's sexual identity, delinquent and psychotic episodes occur. For most young people, the confusion occurs over the occupational role.

In a strenuous effort to maintain his integrity, the adolescent over-identifies, almost to the point of losing his identity, with cliques and crowds. This involvement of the self with others leads to "falling in love," which is an attempt to define the identity rather than a sexual matter. Clannishness becomes adolescents' defense against identity confusion. They help each other through

[4]Harry Stack Sullivan, *Interpersonal Theory of Psychiatry* (New York, Norton, 1953).

[5]R. J. Havighurst, *Human Development and Education* (New York, Longmans, 1953).

[6]E. H. Erikson, *Childhood and Society* (New York, Norton, 1963).

a period of great discomfort by stereotyping themselves. Nevertheless, the youth searches for social values to guide his identity, and yearns to believe that those who succeed in the adult world also shoulder the obligation of being the best sort of people.[7]

Next comes the sixth stage, adulthood, and with it marriage and the *need for intimacy*. In a culture which subordinates sexuality to duty, work and worship, the sense of intimacy does not come easily. Also involved in marriage is the need for *parental sense*, which may never be acquired if the parent exploits his children. The crisis of development is the last stage—adulthood. In this period, Stage 7, the individual attains *generativity, or accomplishment*—the reverse of stagnation. Finally, in old age, comes ego *integrity*, the culmination of the life stages, and with it fulfillment instead of despair. Only through integrity is an individual capable of defending his own life style.

A special deficit in Erikson's theory is the lumping of males and females together. For instance, adolescent girls may not have the vigorous need for identity that males do. Girls play nurturant, autonomous roles, boys an instrumental one. A vigorous sense of self may actually obstruct or interfere with the girl's subordinating her own needs to those of her husband and the needs of her children.

Criticism of Developmental Task Theory

Theories such as Havighurst's and Erikson's may help to order life's tasks but present certain dangers as well: mastery of specific tasks may indeed be more crucial at certain stages; however, such tasks should not be thought of as discrete and belonging solely to a specific stage. A task can hardly be mastered successfully if the groundwork for its accomplishment is not laid earlier. For example, an adolescent will hardly establish an identity at adolescence unless he has made considerable progress toward that goal earlier. The developmental task theory also encourages

the perception of development as a lock-step process. One performs Task No. 1, then Task No. 2, and so on, in that order. Actually, progress in mastering developmental tasks is overlapping and relatively continuous, though setbacks are normal. Moreover, the identification of such tasks, in so precise a fashion, tends toward crystallizing the life-curriculum prescribed for children, thereby obstructing the sort of critical reexamination and continuous modification needed in a rapidly changing society. For instance, we may assign the goal—to establish satisfactory heterosexual relations—to adolescence. However, if the child society continues its present trend toward embracing both sexes in childhood activities, then tomorrow's child, in order to be well adjusted socially, may need increased interaction with opposite-sex peers at an earlier age.

Finally, the concept of developmental tasks may be wrongly interpreted as implying that each life stage is simply an apprenticeship for what follows. Thus, the child's role would simply be an audition for the role he will play as an adult. Instead, each stage is important for its own sake but should provide a healthy base for later stages.[8]

Psychoanalytic Stage Theory

Traditional psychoanalytic stage theory has been especially significant in determining popular concepts of adolescence. In the Freudian tradition, adolescence is portrayed as the period when sexual interest and activity reawaken in the pubescent boy or girl after a prolonged latency period, during which infantile sexual drives have been repressed or sublimated into other areas. Presumably, the growing individual passes through oral, anal, and genital stages of sexuality, in turn directing erotic impulses toward self, the parent of the same sex, and the parent of the opposite sex. In late infancy, when the boy is between the ages of three and six, his sexual urges are said to be genitalized and are directed toward the mother, representing the so-called Oedipal situation, or the desire for sexual union with the mother and recognition of the father as a rival

[7]E. H. Erikson, *Childhood and Society* (New York, Norton, 1963), pp. 247–274.

[8]Rogers, *op. cit.*

and of a desire for his death. At the same time, the son justifies his hostility toward his father by presuming that his father wishes to castrate him for his incestuous desire for his mother. However, the boy's identification with the father serves to introject within him the father's restrictions and taboos, and bring the Oedipal stage to a close. Sexual feelings toward the mother become sublimated into affection.

Now comes the latency period of late childhood, which is terminated by pubescence. Strong hormonal influences operate to reawaken the sex urges, and heterosexual impulses come to the fore and demand satisfaction. Sex feelings now become so strong that the *ego,* or self, is pictured as constantly in danger of being overcome by *id* (primitive urges) and disregarding the *superego* (conscience). Some writers have advocated imposing strict environmental limits as a means of helping the adolescent hold his sex impulses in check, and of helping him sublimate repressed id drives into art, social life, athletics, or other interests.[9] *Sublimation* refers to substituting for socially disapproved outlets, socially approved ones which satisfy the same need. However, others warn that over-repression may lead to rigidity of the personality disturbances, and stress that the ego should serve as mediator between superego and id.

The psychoanalysts also considered adolescence as the critical period for establishing proper sex-role patterns of male or of female, and for the achievement of normal heterosexuality. Various factors might, however, cause the individual to fixate at an earlier psychosexual level, forever thwarting normal progression to mature heterosexuality. For instance, the young boy might become so attached to his mother that he never marries and continues to live in the maternal home the rest of his life.

There are various criticisms of psychoanalytic stage theory. For one thing, infants lack the hormonal base to support sexual feelings, in the sense that adults interpret them. Moreover, adolescent sexuality is no mere continuation of earlier stages but differs from them in intensity and quality due to the enormously increased hormonal production. When the body attains its distinctive sexual secondary sex characteristics, the adolescent must incorporate a greatly revised physical self-image.

Ausubel questions the psychoanalytic contention that most adolescent interests and activities are merely sublimated products of sex drives.[10] Merely in the process of establishing social status, an individual becomes involved in a host of activities and relationships. Since other motives for such activities are readily apparent, it is simply unnecessary to think of them as being powered by repressed sex needs. Does the boy shoot basketballs into the basket because this activity constitutes a sublimation of the sex act, or merely because he wins applause and a higher social status for so doing, besides gaining a feeling of physical exuberance? Moreover, it is questionable how completely the sex impulses are repressed, especially among males. More or less regular outlets are found in masturbation, petting, and intercourse.

Consider next the psychoanalytic concept of adolescent literary and artistic productions as a means of sublimation of sex drives. Since such activities involve a great deal of symbolism they would seem to qualify very nicely for indirect outlets. However, adolescents' increased emotionality in the broader sense, and not merely sex feeling, may lead to producing such creations. It is difficult to perceive in all the adolescents' creative endeavors evidence of repressed sex feelings. Besides, it is hardly tenable that painting a picture or growing flowers will somehow drain off pent-up sex feelings.

Rankian theory, as stated or interpreted by Otto Rank and his followers, originated in the psychoanalytic tradition, but stressed the individual's conflicting needs for dependence and independence. Society demands of the adolescent that he become independent, but nevertheless makes it very difficult for him to become so.[11] The adolescent fights against his own sexual urges because he fears that to surrender to them will

[9]F. J. Hacker and E. R. Geleerd, "Freedom and Authority in Adolescence," *American Journal of Orthopsychiatry,* Vol. 15 (1945), pp. 621–630.

[10]D. P. Ausubel, *Theory and Problems of Adolescent Development* (New York, Grune & Stratton, 1954), p. 28.

[11]D. Hankins, "The Psychology and Direct Treatment of Adolescence," *Mental Hygiene,* Vol. 27 (1943), pp. 238–247.

threaten his hard-won independence. It becomes a major developmental task of the adolescent to establish a wholesome balance of dependence and independence in dealing with adults and peers. He must acknowledge his dependency on others while not becoming unduly manipulated by them.

Questions Posed by Stage Theory

Stage theory has given rise to many questions, some of them stated or implicit in the foregoing. One question relative to adolescence as a stage is this: *is it a true stage in itself, or is it merely a prolonged transition from childhood to adulthood?* Sorenson calls adolescence "much more than one rung up the ladder from childhood."[12] It is a built-in, necessary transition period for ego development. It is a "leave-taking of the dependencies of childhood and a precocious reach for adulthood." He also calls it "an intermission between earlier freedoms . . . a last hesitation before . . . serious commitments concerning work and love."

If adolescence is to be considered significant in its own right, perhaps it should be institutionalized. *Institutionalization* would imply establishing pretty clear guidelines for adolescents, including definition of responsibilities and privileges. Such a clarification, it is argued, would relieve much of the adolescent's anxiety. As it is, he has difficulty defining himself vis-à-vis an ambiguous situation. Also, institutionalization would assist parents by indicating how the older and younger generations should relate to each other.

Others argue against institutionalization, claiming that it would obstruct regular examination of age-graded tasks, in terms of their functionalism for society or for the individual. For instance, in this culture Americans place a high value on popularity, and it becomes incumbent on the adolescent to learn to get along with his age-mates. But does confronting him with the task of getting along interfere with getting ahead? Does the adolescent sell a bit of himself, at too dear a price, to gain acceptance by others simply because this aspect of adolescence has become confirmed? Also, if adolescence receives too much recognition as a stage, then youth may feel constrained to remain rooted in it. Stone and Church call it a "way station" in development and as such, its most "universal and pervasive feeling is of being out of step."[13] Perhaps feeling out of step may help motivate the adolescent to become adult. If he settled too comfortably into adolescence he might forever remain just partly grown up.

Also implicit in stage theory *is society's task of articulating each stage with what follows.* Should rural youth be trained for city-type living, simply because most of them will eventually live in the city? Or should they simply adjust as well as possible to rural living, on the assumption that what they need most to transfer to adult life is a general way of adjustment rather than specific behaviors? Again, should adolescents be encouraged to substitute serious group endeavors for the many light-hearted pastimes of the youth culture, in order to adapt more easily to the adult responsibilities that follow? Or may the fun culture of youth be an appropriate preparation for an adult world where the work week is shrinking and adults are confronted with increasingly larger chunks of leisure time?

Another question originating in age-stage theory is this: *to what extent are life-stages genetically or socioculturally derived?* If they are genetically based, it would seem that life tasks must somehow be accommodated to them. If they are sociocultural creations, then such tasks might be ordered to fit a particular society or individual. One way to answer this question is to determine factors common to the various life-stages in cultures around the world. Such an examination yields this conclusion: that development in all cultures does indeed proceed by more or less distinctive stages, but that there is very wide variation in the definition and significance of those stages. For one thing, age-stages may be defined differently from one culture to another. Infancy may be prolonged where breast-feeding is lengthened, or accelerated where women must work in the fields. In some backward countries, where there is much illness and malnutrition, old age

[12]R. Sorenson, "Youth's Need for Challenge and Place in Society," *Children*, Vol. 9 (1962), pp. 131–138.

[13]L. J. Stone and J. Church, *Childhood and Adolescence* (New York, Random House, 1957).

begins much earlier than in countries where vigor is maintained longer.

Again, life in some cultures is more rigidly defined in terms of age-stages than others. In primitive cultures, ceremonies mark the end of childhood and adulthood begins, thus bypassing adolescence. Individuals simply glide from childhood into adulthood. There was no moratorium called adolescence, no twilight zone between childhood and adulthood. By contrast, preparation for adult life in complicated societies, requires a distinguishable period with its own rules, customs and relationships. For example, in the British public school, adolescence was more than an interregnum; it was an epoch. Such schools were tough; they defined the content of adolescence, and gave the adolescent something to be adolescent about.[14]

Adolescence as a Critical Period

Cross-cultural comparisons justify another conclusion: that particular life-stages, either universally or within particular societies, become critical, in certain respects, for the stages that follow. This concept, called the *critical period hypothesis,* suggests that similar experiences, either at an earlier or later stage, would have less effect where particular functions are concerned. Unless the infant has established a satisfactory relationship with his mother, perhaps he will be unable to establish satisfactory heterosexual relationships later on.[15] Unless a child has unhampered chances to manipulate objects, perhaps he will forever sacrifice optimal neuromuscular development in later years.[16]

Adolescence itself has been viewed as critical in various ways. Ausubel declares adolescence to be universally a time of extensive personality reorganization. Because of sharp distinctions be-

tween child and adult status, profound changes are required in an individual's attitudes and behaviours.[17] According to Friedenberg, two aspects of growth essential to self-definition are climactic in adolescence.[18] One is a capacity for tenderness, fired by sexuality, which produces a pattern of life not wholly cynical or expedient. Adolescents are passionate, and their passion is no less real when directed toward a hot-rod, a popular singer or the leader of a black jacketed gang. Also, the adolescent acquires a respect for competence both in himself and others. This respect is crucial, because a youngster who does not know what he is good at will not be sure what he is good for.

Many writers, including Friedenberg, believe adolescence critical for establishing identity; but certain forces seem dedicated to destroying identity. For example, America once prided itself on being a land of self-fulfillment; but now Madison Avenue, via Mass Media, is subordinating individuals to social goals. The dominant middle-class individual is "other-directed," unthinkingly obtaining his aspirations and goals from his social class, and concerned only with adjustment and popularity.

If adolescence is critical, is one part of this period more important than the other? Often writers have remarked on the pubertal period as a time of special "storm and stress," but late adolescence may be no less critical, in certain ways. According to Hess, successful performance in the early twenties, as evaluated by occupational commitment, social skill, and psychological health, is more closely related to events and experiences that occur *after* high school than to high school behavior.[19] *Moreover,* these data demonstrate the fluid and unstable nature of adolescent behavior patterns, and provide an empirical basis for the belief that the processes of identity that make for stable   adult behavior and personality behavior and personality continue well past high school.

[14]Edgar Z. Friedenberg, *The Vanishing Adolescent* (Boston, Beacon Press, 1959).

[15]Harry F. Harlow and Margaret F. Harlow, "The Effect of Rearing Conditions on Behavior," *Bulletin of the Menninger Clinic,* Vol. 26 (1962), pp. 213–224.

[16]J. McVicker Hunt, "The Psychological Bases for Using Preschool Enrichment as an Antidote for Cultural Deprivation," *Merrill-Palmer Quarterly,* Vol. 10 (1964), pp. 209–248.

[17]D. P. Ausubel, *Theory and Problems of Adolescent Development* (New York, Grune & Stratton, 1954), pp. 22–23.

[18]E. Z. Friedenberg, *The Vanishing Adolescent* (Boston, Beacon Press, 1959).

[19]Robert D. Hess, "High School Antecedents of Adult Achievement," in Robert E. Grinder (Ed.), *Studies in Adolescence* (New York, Macmillan, 1963), pp. 401–414.

Applications of Stage Theory

Various groups have adapted the stage concept of development to their own needs and goals. The business world has capitalized on life-stages by popularizing the notion that individuals must have distinctively different material goods— clothes, sports equipment, and the like—for each age-stage. The youth must have his collegiate attire; the young business man must put away his college clothes and look the part of an adult.

Educators have attempted to organize the curriculum in terms of stages in cognitive development. For example, Cross emphasizes that educators must consider the "individuality, self-assertiveness, and uniqueness" of adolescents. Adults should consider the way adolescents perceive their own values, and not merely try to get the young person to endorse his own.[20] Unless adults can change their own traditions and policies to accommodate adolescents' characteristics, then youth will initiate change themselves, through rebellious social movements such as the college drug craze and the "hippie movement." In the meantime, considerable talent is lost to the propertied traditionalists. For, as Timothy Leary warns, those youths who have "turned on, tuned in, and dropped out," will make neither soldiers nor executives to carry on middle-class traditions.

Individual Experience with Adolescence

A glaring lack in research concerning age-stage theory is phenomenological evidence. How do individuals differ in their own perceptions of the stages through which they pass? Erikson claims that adolescence is the period, par excellence, for establishment of identity; but is that the way adolescents themselves—or older persons in retrospect—perceive it? In an informal test of this question, the writer asked a group of college students to answer this question: "In your life, in

[20]Herbert J. Gross, "Conceptual Systems Theory— Application to some Problems of Adolescents," *Adolescence*, Vol. 2, No. 6 (Summer 1967), pp. 153–166.

what respects have you found childhood distinctive from adolescence, and adolescence, in turn, different from adulthood—if indeed you feel you have moved beyond adolescence?" There was little conscious awareness of the need to establish identity, except indirectly. Girls often mentioned growing social obligations, boys an awareness of broadening responsibilities and sex consciousness. However, there was a great diversity of replies, pointing up the highly individual ways that different individuals experience adolescence. Here are several replies:

During adolescence I developed independence and this caused friction within my close-knit family. I also developed a self-consciousness because of a complexion problem and braces. During the two years I have been married I have developed a concept of what things are really valuable to me, and what things are simply attractive because they are "in." I have become less fashion-conscious and more academically-oriented. I have learned diplomacy and social graces, and I have acquired many new interests, and I have developed self-confidence and the ability to be aggressive when necessary. (Female)

I don't feel that I suddenly went from childhood to adolescence. As an adolescent, I was more socially conscious—wanting to be popular, wanting approval from my peers. I also became much more sexually aware. Still, this was only a magnification of what I was in childhood—there was no sudden jump from one to the other.

As with childhood, I have gradually reached adulthood—there was no sudden jump between adolescence and adulthood. For me, the main difference is that in adulthood, I am much more self confident and independent in thought. I am also much more socially aware, about world problems, etc. (Female)

Adolescence for me was different from childhood in that I became much more aware of *everything*. Childhood was like a merry-go-round. Nothing had meaning or significance. Adulthood, to me, is an unpleasant step, but a step I know I must take. It encompasses responsibility, something I am not yet sure I can handle. (Male)

In childhood one accepts, in adolescence one criticizes. The distinction is quite apparent for thinking is more dynamic in adolescence. The adolescent makes his own concepts and his parents no longer do his thinking for him. (Male)

The only difference in childhood, adolescence, and adulthood is added responsibilities. More is expected of you at each stage. Also, anti-social behavior among children or adolescents is not judged as hard as if an "adult" did it. I do not feel like an adult because in some situations I am still talked down to and treated like a child. (Male)

From the foregoing several conclusions seem justified. First, all societies appear to be divided according to age-grades and stages, but large variations occur. Adolescence is judged as being significant, even critical in certain ways, but just how is not entirely clear. It is most popularly interpreted as the time for establishing an identity. However, stage theories are too numerous and varied to justify sweeping conclusions, either as to how human development proceeds throughout life, or during adolescence in particular. Badly needed is some theory which ferrets out, synthesizes, and integrates into one overall empirically based theory the major thinking and research that exists on this topic. Such a theory might, in fact, be something completely new, only vaguely resembling the present day formulations of human age-stage progression.

Egocentrism in Adolescence

DAVID ELKIND

The author describes forms of egocentrism for each major stage of cognitive growth outlined by Piaget. Adolescent egocentrism is said to produce two mental constructs, the imaginary audience and the personal fable.

Within the Piagetian theory of intellectual growth, the concept of egocentrism generally refers to a lack of differentiation in some area of subject–object interaction (Piaget, 1962). At each stage of mental development, this lack of differentiation takes a unique form and is manifested in a unique set of behaviors. The transition from one form of egocentrism to another takes place in a dialectic fashion such that the mental structures which free the child from a lower form of egocentrism are the same structures which ensnare him in a higher form of egocentrism. From the developmental point of view, therefore, egocentrism can be regarded as a negative by-product of any emergent mental system in the sense that it corresponds to the fresh cognitive problems engendered by that system.

Although in recent years Piaget has focused his attention more on the positive than on the negative products of mental structures, egocentrism continues to be of interest because of its relation to the affective aspects of child thought and behavior. Indeed, it is possible that the study of egocentrism may provide a bridge between the study of cognitive structure, on the one hand, and the exploration of personality dynamics, on the other (Cowan, 1966; Gourevitch & Feffer, 1962). The purpose of the present paper is to describe, in greater detail than Inhelder and Piaget (1958), what seems to me to be the nature of egocentrism in adolescence and some of its behavioral and experimental correlates. Before doing that, however, it might be well to set the stage for the discussion with a brief review of the forms of egocentrism which precede this mode of thought in adolescence.

Forms of Egocentrism in Infancy and Childhood

In presenting the childhood forms of egocentrism, it is useful to treat each of Piaget's major stages as if it were primarily concerned with resolving one major cognitive task. The egocentrism of a particular stage can then be described with reference to this special problem of cognition. It must be stressed, however, that while the cognitive task characteristic of a particular stage seems to attract the major share of the child's mental energies, it is not the only cognitive problem with which the child is attempting to cope. In mental development there are major battles and minor skirmishes, and if I here ignore the lesser engagements it is for purposes of economy of presentation rather than because I assume that such engagements are insignificant.

SENSORI-MOTOR EGOCENTRISM

The major cognitive task of infancy might be regarded as *the conquest of the object*. In the early months of life, the infant deals with objects as if their existence were dependent upon their being present in immediate perception (Charlesworth, 1966; Piaget, 1954). The egocentrism of this stage corresponds, therefore, to a lack of differentiation between the object and the sense impressions occasioned by it. Toward the end of the first year, however, the infant begins to seek the object even when it is hidden, and thus shows that he can now differentiate between the object and the "experience of the object." This breakdown of egocentrism with respect to objects is brought about by mental representation of the absent object.[1] An internal representation of the absent object is the earliest manifestation of the symbolic function which develops gradually during the second year of life and whose activities dominate the next stage of mental growth.

PRE-OPERATIONAL EGOCENTRISM (2–6 YEARS)

During the preschool period, the child's major cognitive task can be regarded as *the conquest of the symbol*. It is during the preschool period that the symbolic function becomes fully active, as evidenced by the rapid growth in the acquisition and utilization of language, by the appearance of symbolic play, and by the first reports of dreams. Yet this new capacity for representation, which loosed the infant from his egocentrism with respect to objects, now ensnares the preschool children in a new egocentrism with regard to symbols. At the beginning of this period, the child fails to differentiate between words and their referents (Piaget, 1952b) and between his self-created play and dream symbols and reality (Kohlberg, 1966; Piaget, 1951). Children at this stage believe that the name inheres in the thing and that an object cannot have more than one name (Elkind, 1961a, 1962, 1963).

The egocentrism of this period is particularly evident in children's linguistic behavior. When explaining a piece of apparatus to another child, for example, the youngster at this stage uses many indefinite terms and leaves out important information (Piaget, 1952b). Although this observation is sometimes explained by saying that the child fails to take the other person's point of view, it can also be explained by saying that the child assumes words carry much more information than they actually do. This results from his belief that even the indefinite "thing" somehow conveys the properties of the object which it is used to represent. In short, the egocentrism of this period consists in a lack of clear differentiation between symbols and their referents.

Toward the end of the pre-operational period, the differentiation between symbols and their referents is gradually brought about by the emergence of concrete operations (internalized actions which are roughly comparable in their activity to the elementary operations of arithmetic). One consequence of concrete operational thought is that it enables the child to deal with two elements, properties, or relations at the same time. A child with concrete operations can, for example, take account of both the height and width of a glass of colored liquid and recognize that, when the liquid is poured into a differently shaped container, the changes in height and width of the liquid compensate one another so that the total quantity of liquid is conserved (Elkind, 1961b; Piaget, 1952a). This ability, to hold two dimensions in mind at the same time, also enables the child to hold both symbol and referent in mind simultaneously, and thus distinguish between them. Concrete operations are, therefore, instrumental in overcoming the egocentrism of the pre-operational stage.

[1] It is characteristic of the dialectic of mental growth that the capacity to represent internally the absent object also enables the infant to cognize the object as externally existent.

CONCRETE OPERATIONAL EGOCENTRISM (7–11 YEARS)

With the emergence of concrete operations, the major cognitive task of the school-age child becomes that of *mastering classes, relations, and quantities.* While the preschool child forms global notions of classes, relations, and quantities, such notions are imprecise and cannot be combined one with the other. The child with concrete operations, on the other hand, can nest classes, seriate relations, and conserve quantities. In addition, concrete operations enable the school-age child to perform elementary syllogistic reasoning and to formulate hypotheses and explanations about concrete matters. This system of concrete operations, however, which lifts the school-age child to new heights of thought, nonetheless lowers him to new depths of egocentrism.

Operations are essentially mental tools whose products, series, class hierarchies, conservations, etc., are not directly derived from experience. At this stage, however, the child nonetheless regards these mental products as being on a par with perceptual phenomena. It is the inability to differentiate clearly between mental constructions and perceptual givens which constitutes the egocentrism of the school-age child. An example may help to clarify the form which egocentrism takes during the concrete operational stage.

In a study reported by Peel (1960), children and adolescents were read a passage about Stonehenge and then asked questions about it. One of the questions had to do with whether Stonehenge was a place for religious worship or a fort. The children (ages 7–10) answered the question with flat statements, as if they were stating a fact. When they were given evidence that contradicted their statements, they rationalized the evidence to make it conform with their initial position. Adolescents, on the other hand, phrased their replies in probabilistic terms and supported their judgments with material gleaned from the passage. Similar differences between children and adolescents have been found by Elkind (1966) and Weir (1964).

What these studies show is that, when a child constructs a hypothesis or formulates a strategy,

he assumes that this product is imposed by the data rather than derived from his own mental activity. When his position is challenged, he does not change his stance but, on the contrary, reinterprets the data to fit with his assumption. This observation, however, raises a puzzling question. Why, if the child regards both his thought products and the givens of perception as coming from the environment, does he nonetheless give preference to his own mental constructions? The answer probably lies in the fact that the child's mental constructions are the product of reasoning, and hence are experienced as imbued with a (logical) necessity. This "felt" necessity is absent when the child experiences the products of perception. It is not surprising, then, that the child should give priority to what seems permanent and necessary in perception (the products of his own thought, such as conservation) rather than to what seems transitory and arbitrary in perception (products of environmental stimulation). Only in adolescence do young people differentiate between their own mental constructions and the givens of perception. For the child, there are no problems of epistemology.

Toward the end of childhood, the emergence of formal operational thought (which is analogous to propositional logic) gradually frees the child from his egocentrism with respect to his own mental constructions. As Inhelder and Piaget (1958) have shown, formal operational thought enables the young person to deal with all of the possible combinations and permutations of elements within a given set. Provided with four differently colored pieces of plastic, for example, the adolescent can work out all the possible combinations of colors by taking the pieces one, two, three and four, and none, at a time. Children, on the other hand, cannot formulate these combinations in any systematic way. The ability to conceptualize all of the possible combinations in a system allows the adolescent to construct contrary-to-fact hypotheses and to reason about such propositions "as if" they were true. The adolescent, for example, can accept the statement, "Let's suppose coal is white," whereas the child would reply, "But coal is black." This ability to formulate contrary-to-fact hypotheses is crucial to the overcoming of the egocentrism of the concrete operational period. Through the formulation of such contrary-to-fact hypotheses, the young person discovers the arbitrariness of his own mental constructions and learns to differentiate them from perceptual reality.

Adolescent Egocentrism

From the strictly cognitive point of view (as opposed to the psychoanalytic point of view as represented by Blos [1962] and A. Freud [1946] or the ego psychological point of view as represented by Erikson [1959]), the major task of early adolescence can be regarded as having to do with *the conquest of thought*. Formal operations not only permit the young person to construct all the possibilities in a system and construct contrary-to-fact propositions (Inhelder & Piaget, 1958); they also enable him to conceptualize his own thought, to take his mental constructions as objects and reason about them. Only at about the ages of 11–12, for example, do children spontaneously introduce concepts of belief, intelligence, and faith into their definitions of their religious denomination (Elkind, 1961a; 1962; 1963). Once more, however, this new mental system which frees the young person from the egocentrism of childhood entangles him in a new form of egocentrism characteristic of adolescence.

Formal operational thought not only enables the adolescent to conceptualize his thought, it also permits him to conceptualize the thought of other people. It is this capacity to take account of other people's thought, however, which is the crux of adolescent egocentrism. This egocentrism emerges because, while the adolescent can now cognize the thoughts of others, he fails to differentiate between the objects toward which the thoughts of others are directed and those which are the focus of his own concern. Now, it is well known that the young adolescent, because of the physiological metamorphosis he is undergoing, is primarily concerned with himself. Accordingly, since he fails to differentiate between what others are thinking about and his own mental preoccupations, he assumes that other people are as obsessed with his behavior and appearance as he is himself. *It is this belief that others are preoccupied with his appearance and behavior that constitutes the egocentrism of the adolescent.*

One consequence of adolescent egocentrism is that, in actual or impending social situations, the young person anticipates the reactions of other people to himself. These anticipations, however, are based on the premise that others are as admiring or as critical of him as he is of himself. In a sense, then, the adolescent is continually constructing, or reacting to, *an imaginary audience*. It is an audience because the adolescent believes that he will be the focus of attention; and it is imaginary because, in actual social situations, this is not usually the case (unless he contrives to make it so). The construction of imaginary audiences would seem to account, in part at least, for a wide variety of typical adolescent behaviors and experiences.

The imaginary audience, for example, probably plays a role in the self-consciousness which is so characteristic of early adolescence. When the young person is feeling critical of himself, he anticipates that the audience—of which he is necessarily a part—will be critical too. And, since the audience is his construction and privy to his own knowledge of himself, it knows just what to look for in the way of cosmetic and behavioral sensitivities. The adolescent's wish for privacy and his reluctance to reveal himself may, to some extent, be a reaction to the feeling of being under the constant critical scrutiny of other people. The notion of an imaginary audience also helps to explain the observation that the affect which most concerns adolescents is not guilt but, rather, shame, that is, the reaction to an audience (Lynd, 1961).

While the adolescent is often self-critical, he is frequently self-admiring too. At such times, the audience takes on the same affective coloration. A good deal of adolescent boorishness, loudness, and faddish dress is probably provoked, partially in any case, by a failure to differentiate between what the young person believes to be attractive and what others admire. It is for this reason that the young person frequently fails to understand why adults disapprove of the way he dresses and behaves. The same sort of egocentrism is often seen in behavior directed toward the opposite sex. The boy who stands in front of the mirror for 2 hours combing his hair is probably imagining the swooning reactions he will produce in the girls. Likewise, the girl applying her makeup is more likely than not imagining the admiring glances that will come her way. When these young people actually meet, each is more concerned with being the observed than with being the observer. Gatherings of young adolescents are unique in the sense that each young person is simultaneously an actor to himself and an audience to others.

One of the most common admiring audience constructions, in the adolescent, is the anticipation of how others will react to his own demise. A certain bittersweet pleasure is derived from anticipating the belated recognition by others of his positive qualities. As often happens with such universal fantasies, the imaginary anticipation of one's own demise has been realized in fiction. Below, for example, is the passage in *Tom Sawyer* where Tom sneaks back to his home, after having run away with Joe and Huck, to discover that he and his friends are thought to have been drowned:

But this memory was too much for the old lady, and she broke entirely down. Tom was snuffling, now, himself—and more in pity of himself than anybody else. He could hear Mary crying and putting in a kindly word for him from time to time. He began to have a nobler opinion of himself than ever before. Still, he was sufficiently touched by his aunt's grief to long to rush out from under the bed and overwhelm her with joy—and the theatrical gorgeousness of the thing appealed strongly to his nature too—but he resisted and lay still.

Corresponding to the imaginary audience is another mental construction which is its complement. While the adolescent fails to differentiate the concerns of his own thought from those of others, he at the same time over-differentiates his feelings. Perhaps because he believes he is of importance to so many people, the imaginary audience, he comes to regard himself, and particularly his feelings, as something special and unique. Only he can suffer with such agonized intensity, or experience such exquisite rapture. How many parents have been confronted with the typically adolescent phrase, "But you don't know how it feels. . . ." The emotional torments undergone by Goethe's young Werther and by Salinger's Holden Caulfield exemplify the adolescent's belief in the uniqueness of his own emotional experience. At a somewhat different level, this belief in personal uniqueness becomes a conviction that he will not die, that death will happen to others but not to him. This complex of beliefs in the uniqueness of his feelings and of his immortality might be called *a personal fable,* a story which he tells himself and which is not true.

Evidences of the personal fable are particularly prominent in adolescent diaries. Such diaries are often written for posterity in the conviction that the young person's experiences, crushes, and frustrations are of universal significance and importance. Another kind of evidence for the personal fable during this period is the tendency to confide in a personal God. The search for privacy and the belief in personal uniqueness leads to the establishment of an I–Thou relationship with God as a personal confidant to whom one no longer looks for gifts but rather for guidance and support (Long, Elkind, & Spilka, 1967).

The concepts of an imaginary audience and a personal fable have proved useful, at least to the writer, in the understanding and treatment of troubled adolescents. The imaginary audience, for example, seems often to play a role in middle-class delinquency (Elkind, 1967). As a case in point, one young man took $1,000 from a golf tournament purse, hid the money, and then promptly revealed himself. It turned out that much of the motivation for this act was derived from the anticipated response of "the audience" to the guttiness of his action. In a similar vein, many young girls become pregnant because, in part at least, their personal fable convinces them that pregnancy will happen to others but never to them and so they need not take precautions. Such examples could be multiplied but will perhaps suffice to illustrate how adolescent egocentrism, as manifested in the imaginary audience and in the personal fable, can help provide a rationale for some adolescent behavior. These concepts can, moreover, be utilized in the treatment of adolescent offenders. It is often helpful to these young people if they can learn to differentiate between the real and the imaginary audience, which often boils down to a discrimination between the real and the imaginary parents.

The Passing of Adolescent Egocentrism

After the appearance of formal operational thought, no new mental systems develop and the mental structures of adolescence must serve for the rest of the life span. The egocentrism of early adolescence nonetheless tends to diminish by the age of 15 or 16, the age at which formal operations become firmly established. What appears to happen is that the imaginary audience, which is primarily an anticipatory audience, is progressively modified in the direction of the reactions of the real audience. In a way, the imaginary audience can be regarded as hypothesis—or better, as a series of hypotheses—which the young person tests against reality. As a consequence of this testing, he gradually comes to recognize the difference between his own preoccupations and the interests and concerns of others.

The personal fable, on the other hand, is probably overcome (although probably never in its entirety) by the gradual establishment of what Erikson (1959) has called "intimacy." Once the young person sees himself in a more realistic light as a function of having adjusted his imaginary audience to the real one, he can establish true rather than self-interested interpersonal relations. Once relations of mutuality are established and confidences are shared, the young person discovers that others have feelings similar to his own and have suffered and been enraptured in the same way.

Adolescent egocentrism is thus overcome by a twofold transformation. On the cognitive plane, it is overcome by the gradual differentiation between his own preoccupations and the thoughts of others; while on the plane of affectivity, it is overcome by a gradual integration of the feelings of others with his own emotions.

Summary and Conclusions

In this paper I have tried to describe the forms which egocentrism takes and the mechanisms by which it is overcome, in the course of mental development. In infancy, egocentrism corresponds to the impression that objects are identical with the perception of them, and this form of egocentrism is overcome with the appearance of representation. During the prechool period, egocentrism appears in the guise of a belief that symbols contain the same information as is provided by the objects which they represent. With the emergence of concrete operations, the child is able to discriminate between symbol and referent, and so overcome this type of egocentrism. The egocentrism of the school-age period can be characterized as the belief that one's own mental constructions correspond to a superior form of perceptual reality. With the advent of formal operations and the ability to construct contrary-to-fact hypotheses, this kind of egocentrism is dissolved because the young person can now recognize the arbitrariness of his own mental constructions. Finally, during early adolescence, egocentrism appears as the belief that the thoughts of others are directed toward the self. This variety of egocentrism is overcome as a consequence of the conflict between the reactions which the young person anticipates and those which actually occur.

Although egocentrism corresponds to a negative product of mental growth, its usefulness would seem to lie in the light which it throws upon the affective reactions characteristic of any particular stage of mental development. In this paper I have dealt primarily with the affective reactions associated with the egocentrism of adolescence. Much of the material, particularly the discussion of the *imaginary audience* and the *personal fable,* is speculative in the sense that it is based as much upon my clinical experience with young people as it is upon research data. These constructs are offered, not as the final word on adolescent egocentrism, but rather to illustrate how the cognitive structures peculiar to a particular level of development can be related to the affective experience and behavior characteristic of that stage. Although I have here only considered the correspondence between mental structure and affect in adolescence, it is possible that similar correspondences can be found at the earlier levels of development as well. A consideration of egocentrism, then, would seem to be a useful starting point for any attempt to reconcile cognitive structure and the dynamics of personality.

REFERENCES

BLOS, P. *On adolescence.* New York: Free Press, 1962.

CHARLESWORTH, W. R. Development of the object concept in infancy: methodological study. *American Psychologist,* 1966, *21,* 623. (Abstract)

COWAN, P. A. Cognitive egocentrism and social interaction in children. *American Psychologist,* 1966, *21,* 623. (Abstract)

ELKIND, D. The child's conception of his religious denomination, I: The Jewish child. *Journal of Genetic Psychology,* 1961, *99,* 209–225. (a)

ELKIND, D. The development of quantitative thinking. *Journal of Genetic Psychology,* 1961, *98,* 37–46. (b)

ELKIND, D. The child's conception of his religious denomination, II: The Catholic child. *Journal of Genetic Psychology,* 1962, *101,* 185–193.

ELKIND, D. The child's conception of his religious denomination, III: The Protestant child. *Journal of Genetic Psychology,* 1963, *103,* 291–304.

ELKIND, D. Conceptual orientation shifts in children and adolescents. *Child Development,* 1966, *37,* 493–498.

ELKIND, D. Middle-class delinquency. *Mental Hygiene,* 1967, *51,* 80–84.

ERIKSON, E. H. Identity and the life cycle. *Psychological Issues.* Vol. 1, No. 1, New York: International Universities Press, 1959.

FREUD, ANNA. *The ego and the mechanisms of defense.* New York: International Universities Press, 1946.

GOUREVITCH, VIVIAN, & FEFFER, M. H. A study of motivational development. *Journal of Genetic Psychology,* 1962, *100,* 361–375.

INHELDER, BARBEL, & PIAGET, J. *The growth of logical thinking from childhood to adolescence.* New York: Basic Books, 1958.

KOHLBERG, L. Cognitive stages and preschool education. *Human Development,* 1966, *9,* 5–17.

LONG, DIANE, ELKIND, D., & SPILKA, B. The child's conception of prayer. *Journal for the Scientific Study of Religion,* 1967, *6,* 101–109.

LYND, HELEN M. *On shame and the search for identity.* New York: Science Editions, 1961.

PEEL, E. A. *The pupil's thinking.* London: Oldhourne, 1960.

PIAGET, J. *The child's conception of the world.* London: Routledge & Kegan Paul, 1951.

PIAGET, J. *The child's conception of number.* New York: Humanities Press, 1952. (a)

PIAGET, J. *The language and thought of the child.* London: Routledge & Kegan Paul, 1952. (b)

PIAGET, J. *The construction of reality in the child.* New York: Basic Books, 1954.

PIAGET, J. *Comments on Vygotsky's critical remarks concerning "The language and thought of the child" and "Judgment and reasoning in the child."* Cambridge, Mass.: M. I. T. Press, 1962.

WEIR, M. W. Development changes in problem solving strategies. *Psychological Review,* 1964, *71,* 473–490.

Chapter 4: Suggested Additional Readings

CROSS, H. J. Conceptual systems theory—application to some problems of adolescents. *Adolescence,* Summer 1967, *2*(6), 153–165. The author describes how children's behaviors and thinking differ at five stages of conceptual development. He suggests that adolescents vary greatly in their conceptual level, and that learning environments should be adapted accordingly.

LUDWIG, D. J. & MAEHR, M. L. Changes in self-concept and stated behavioral preferences. *Child Development,* 1967, *38*, 453–467. In a study of seventh- and eighth-grade boys, self-concept change proved to be a function of the reaction of significant others. Such changes in self-concept, in turn, effected modifications in the boys' preferences and choices.

MC NASSOR, D. Social structure for identity in adolescence: Western Europe and America. *Adolescence,* Fall 1967, *2*(7), 311–334. This paper compares Western European and American youth with regard to schooling, age of maturity, peer groups, relationship to authority, and identity.

MUUSS, R. E. Jean Piaget's cognitive theory of adolescent development. *Adolescence,* 1967, *2*(7), 285-310. Muuss describes and analyzes Jean Piaget's theories as they apply to the adolescent period, and discusses their implications for education.

MUUSS, R. E. *Theories of adolescence* (2nd ed.) New York: Random House, 1968. Chapter 2. In this chapter, Muuss considers the theories of adolescent development, including their philosophical and historical roots. He traces in some detail historical attitudes toward youth and, in particular, the age-stage theories developed by Rousseau and Aristotle.

PEREZ, J. F., & COHEN, A. I. *Mom and dad are me.* Belmont, California: Brooks-Cole, 1969. This book details a case study of a high school boy who was having difficulty developing his self-concept and was experiencing trouble in school. It focuses on the dialogue between the psychiatrist and the boy, his father and his mother.

REICHART, S. Because we have left love behind. *Journal of Social Issues,* 1969, *25*(2), 137–146. Youth's art and drama reflect their reaction to social change. Their artistic and dramatic productions are creative and dynamic, possessing elements of action, freedom, self-estrangement, absurdity, and desperation.

SULLIVAN, E. V. Political development during the adolescent years. In E. D. Evans, E. D. (Ed.), *Adolescence: Readings in behavior and development.* New York: The Dryden Press, 1970. Pp. 92–107. In this article, Sullivan describes stages in the individual's development of political ideologies, and classifies such development according to classic stage theory. He provides a short theoretical framework, as well as relevant findings concerning children's political socialization.

THORNBURG, H. Adolescence: A re-interpretation. *Adolescence,* 1970, *5*(20), 463–484. On the basis of relevant literature, the writer summarizes the significant developmental tasks to be accomplished during adolescence.

5

Adolescence: A Period of Storm and Stress

Traditionally, adolescence has been portrayed as a state of internal civil war, with the individual's self arrayed against itself. Youth is presumed to be constantly in danger of consumption by his own furies, which are fed from the roots of darkly Freudian hangups reaching deep into his childhood. However, the concept of adolescence as a period of storm and stress raises several questions. Is adolescence particularly stressful, or conspicuously more so than other age periods? If it be conceded that adolescence is stressful, then how stressful is it? Is such stress attributable to physical changes that occur, or to society's failure to adapt to adolescents' needs? How do the sexes differ in degree and type of stress? How does stress vary from early to late adolescence? Finally, what special measures, if any, should be taken to prevent or alleviate such stress?

The concept of adolescence as a period of storm and stress was popularized around the turn of the century by G. Stanley Hall. Hall, often dubbed the Father of Child Study in America, portrayed pubertal changes as so marked, and so catastrophic, as to be seriously upsetting. Since Hall's time, many writers on adolescence have expressed similar views. For example, Stone and Church (1957) call adolescence a "vulnerable period" involving painful problems and the reawakening of past developmental issues only partially resolved. It is during adolescence, they point out, that a true schizophrenic breakdown may first occur. Many normal adolescent traits, in their extreme form, approximate schizophrenic behavior. Such characteristics include persistent feelings of dislocation and estrangement, total docility or exaggerated rebelliousness, emotional volatility, feelings that everybody is against one, talk of suicide, and intense idealism. Breakdowns are most likely to take such forms as schizophrenic delusions, sexual deviations, and psychosomatic disorders. Fortunately, conclude Stone and Church, most adolescents have developed "a tough core of security, and an anchorage in reality, that permit them to withstand and thrive on the stresses of this period [pp. 369-370]."

Traditional psychoanalytic theorists also play up the traumatic features of adolescence. Individuals are said to proceed through certain stages—oral, anal, phallic, latent, and adolescent—and then into adulthood. While individuals at any age may experience an inability to handle impulses, subdue anxieties, or delay gratification, the maturation of sexual impulses makes adolescence especially stressful. According to Blum (1953), sexual maturity "brings in its wake a wave of disturbance, not only in the sexual area, but also in the broader realm of social behavior. [p. 136]" The adolescent, "flooded by his own resurgent impulses, must regroup the defensive forces of his ego in an attempt to meet this new onslaught. [p. 136]"

Similarly, Robert Nixon (1966) speaks of the "shock of puberty" which we all remember as a stage of anxiety. The adolescent spends hours in deep, and usually secret, preoccupation with the physical and psychological changes going on inside him. In time, he accepts himself as a teenager and his anxiety subsides, only to be reawakened in full force, around age 14, when peer groups divide into males and females. Another burst of anxiety, says Nixon, occurs at about age 16, when the adolescent is assailed by doubts concerning all sorts of issues that adults prefer to leave unmentioned.

Many authorities believe that modern society has produced unusual stresses for youth. Templin (1968) declares that since present-day youth have been brought up wholly in an electronic age, they respond differently to adolescent stresses than did earlier generations. They feel without truly understanding, perceive without adequately comprehending. Moreover, they have lived all their lives with the possibility of nuclear holocaust, an endless succession of little wars that threaten to grow big, and the draft. They carry the burden of a profound dissatisfaction with our materialistic, affluent society, which is only deepened with the understanding that one must accept and live with this society [p. 114].

Another writer who identifies societal factors as being responsible for youth's problems is Schonfeld (1967), who portrays modern adolescents as "far from happy." Instead they are "bored, jaded, and disillusioned." Many turn to alcohol, drugs, and narcotics to relieve their anxieties and make them feel more adequate. There are far too many who suffer from feelings of inadequacy, question their own worth, wonder if life is worth living, and too often commit suicide as an escape from reality. Schonfeld also notes increasing incidents of "vandalism, mugging, rape, and burglaries" committed by affluent youth. He attributes this sorry state of affairs to society's affluence in general, and the individual youth's affluence in particular. Having lost any real responsibilities for his society, the youth takes out his frustrations on that society. The best solution, concludes Schonfeld, is to involve youth in meaningful community projects.

However, not all authorities agree that storm and stress are inevitable within our own culture or are to be found among all cultures. Bernard (1957) suggests that emotionality may be heightened at adolescence but hardly enough to justify calling adolescence a period of storm and stress. Jersild (1963, p. 17) notes that every age of life has its problems. Others believe the Sturm and Drang of adolescence to be simply a Western sociocultural creation. They point out that youth in primitive societies glide smoothly from childhood into adulthood. Such cultures are continuous, writes Benedict (1949), in that children's activities often constitute a true apprenticeship for adulthood. By contrast, in Western society, the child is often inadequately prepared to assume adult responsibilities. Many adult activities demand traits forbidden in the child, and adults blame the adolescent when he fails spontaneously to adopt appropriate mature behaviors.

Some writers stress that emotionality is inherent in puberty itself. Buxbaum (1933) states that, unconsciously, first menstruation is experienced as an injury to the genitals, as a castration, and as punishment for masturbation. But another view, that adolescent stress reflects rapid shifts in hormonal balance, is challenged by Garn (1960). Twenty milligrams of testosterone, he observes, is not unsettling except to a few dozen sebaceous glands. Moreover, rebellion occurs in hypogonadal boys as well as in normal boys. Nor does adolescence result in awkwardness. In his opinion, the vicissitudes of adolescence stem from neither genes nor glands but from society's failure to provide a meaningful status for the adolescent.

A review of research suggests that adolescent girls experience more emotional disturbances than do boys (Rogers, 1972). However, Friedenberg (1959) believes boys are more emotional and females less emotional than is commonly believed. Boys are "moodier, more intense, more mystical almost," he says; watch a basketball player's face and you will see reflected in it moments of ecstasy and transfiguration. The female's reputed emotional instability is simply her defense against male domination; in situations where threat of male dominance is not present, the female's emotional stability is normal.

However, if either sex experiences stress, what sort of help is required to combat it? Does society itself need adjustment for its failure to provide a suitable niche for adolescents? Some people believe adolescence is simply a disease to be gotten over. "He—or she—will outgrow it," is their stock reply. Others believe in full-blown guidance programs, designed to anticipate and prevent, as well as to treat, the problems of youth.

In the first of the following selections, Bandura portrays adolescence, at least among boys, as relatively free of trauma. In the second, Weiner reviews research, pro and con, on the subject of youthful turbulence, and concludes that youth may indeed experience certain stresses accruing to their developmental stage. However, in the aggregate, youth's manifestations of stress, including various psychoneuroses and psychoses, do not exceed those of adults.

REFERENCES

BENEDICT, R.   In P. Mullahy (Ed.) *A study of interpersonal relations.* New York: Hermitage Press, 1949.

BERNARD, H.   *Adolescent development in American culture.* New York: Harcourt, Brace & World, 1957.

BLUM, G. S.   *Psychoanalytic theories of personality.* New York: McGraw-Hill, 1953. Pp. 136–155.

BUXBAUM, E.   Angatäusserungen von Schulmädchen in Pubertätsalter. *Z. psa. Padagogik,* 1933, 7.

FRIEDENBERG, E. Z.   *The vanishing adolescent.* Boston: Beacon Press, 1959.

GARN, S. M. Growth and development. In E. Ginsberg (Ed.) *The nation's children.* Vol. 2. New York: Columbia University Press, 1960. Pp. 24–42.

JERSILD, A. T. *The psychology of adolescence.* (2nd ed.) New York: Macmillan, 1963.

NIXON, R. E. Psychological normality in adolescence. *Adolescence,* Fall 1966, *1*(3), 211–223.

ROGERS, D. *The psychology of adolescence.* (2nd ed.) New York: Appleton-Century-Crofts, 1972. Pp. 145–146.

SCHONFELD, W. A. Adolescent turmoil: Socioeconomic affluence as a factor. *New York State Journal of Medicine,* 1967, *67,* 1981–1990.

STONE, L. J., & CHURCH, J. *Childhood and adolescence.* New York: Random House, 1957.

TEMPLIN, L. The pathology of youth. *Journal of Human Relations,* 1968, *16,*(1), 113–127.

The Stormy Decade: Fact or Fiction?

ALBERT BANDURA

The writer first describes the traditional storm-and-stress image of adolescence, then compares this popular version of adolescence with research by himself and Walters. In a study of middle-class families of adolescent boys they found little to support the traditional view. They examine reasons for the faulty image and discuss its unfortunate effects.

If you were to walk up to the average man on the street, grab him by the arm and utter the word "adolescence," it is highly probable—assuming he refrains from punching you in the nose—that his associations to this term will include references to storm and stress, tension, rebellion, dependency conflicts, peer-group conformity, black leather jackets, and the like. If you then abandoned your informal street corner experiment, and consulted the professional and popular literature on adolescence, you would become quickly impressed with the prevalence of the belief that adolescence is, indeed, a unique and stormy developmental period (Gallagher & Harris, 1958; Hurlock, 1955; Josselyn, 1948; Mohr & Despres, 1958; Parsons, 1950; Pearson, 1958).

The adolescent presumably is engaged in a struggle to emancipate himself from his parents. He, therefore, resists any dependence upon them for their guidance, approval or company, and rebels against any restrictions and controls that they impose upon his behavior. To facilitate the process of emancipation, he transfers his dependency to the peer-group whose values are typically in conflict with those of his parents. Since his behavior is now largely under the control of peer-group members, he begins to adopt idiosyncratic clothing, mannerisms, lingo, and other forms of peer-group fad behavior. Because of the conflicting values and pressures to which the adolescent is exposed, he is ambivalent, frightened, unpredictable, and often irresponsible in his behavior. Moreover, since the adolescent finds himself in a transition stage in which he is neither child nor adult, he is highly confused even about his own identity.

The foregoing storm and stress picture of adolescence receives little support from detailed information that Dr. Walters and I obtained in a study of middle class families of adolescent boys (Bandura & Walters, 1959). Let us compare the popular version of adolescence with our research findings.

PARENTAL RESTRICTIVENESS

At adolescence, parents supposedly become more controlling and prohibitive. We found the very opposite to be true. By the time the boys had reached adolescence, they had internalized

Reprinted from *Psychology In The Schools*, 1964, *1*, 224–231, by permission of the author and publisher.

the parents' values and standards of behavior to a large degree; consequently, restrictions and external controls had been lightened as the boys became increasingly capable of assuming responsibility for their own behavior, and in directing their own activities. The parents were highly trustful of their boys' judgment and felt that externally imposed limits were, therefore, largely unnecessary. The following interview excerpts provide some typical parental replies to inquiries concerning the restrictions they placed on their boys:

M. (Mother). I don't have to do anything like that any more. I think he's getting so mature now, he's sort of happy medium. I don't have to do much with him.
I. (Interviewer). What are some of the restrictions you have for him? How about going out at night?
F. (Father). We trust the boy. We never question him.
I. Are there any things you forbid him from doing when he is with his friends?
F. At his age I would hate to keep telling him that he mustn't do this, or mustn't do that. I have very little trouble with him in that regard. Forbidding I don't think creeps into it because he ought to know at 17, right from wrong.
I. Are there any friends with whom you have discouraged him from associating?
F. No, not up to now. They are very lovely boys.
I. How about using bad language?
F. Only once, only once have I; of course I'm a little bit hard of hearing in one ear, and sometimes he gets around the wrong side and takes advantage of that.

The boys' accounts were essentially in agreement with those given by the parents. In response to our questions concerning parental demands and controls, the boys pointed out that at this stage in their development parental restraints were no longer necessary. An illustrative quotation, taken from one of the boys' interviews, is given below:

I. What sort of things does your mother forbid you to do around the house?
B. Forbid me to do? Gee, I don't think there's

ever anything. The house is mine as much as theirs. . . . Oh, can't whistle, can't throw paper up in the air, and can't play the radio and phonograph too loud. Rules of the house; anybody, I mean, it's not just me. . . .
I. Are you expected to stay away from certain places or people?
B. She knows I do. I'm not expected; I mean, she figures I'm old enough to take care of myself now. They never tell me who to stay away from or where. Well, I mean, they don't expect me to sleep down on Skid Row or something like that. . . .

Since the boys adopted their parents' standards of conduct as their own, they did not regard their parents and other authority figures as adversaries, but more as supportive and guiding influences.

DEPENDENCE–INDEPENDENCE CONFLICTS

The view that adolescents are engaged in a struggle to emancipate themselves from their parents also receives little support from our study.

Although the boys' dependency behavior had been fostered and encouraged during their childhood, independence training had begun early and was, therefore, largely accomplished by the time of adolescence. A similar early and gradual decrease in dependency upon adults is reported by Heathers (1955), who compared the dependency behavior of two-year-old and of five-year-old children. He found that, even over this small age range, dependency on adults has declined, whereas dependency on other children had increased.

For most of the boys that we studied, the emancipation from parents had been more or less completed rather than initiated at adolescence. In fact, the development of independence presented more of a conflict for the parents than it did for the boys. Some of the parents, particularly the fathers, regretted the inevitable loss of the rewards that their sons' company had brought them.

I. Do you feel that you spend as much time with Raymond as other fathers do with their sons, or more?
F. I would say about average, but perhaps I

should spend more time with him, because as the years go by, I see that he's growing into manhood and I'm losing a lot of him every year. When he was younger, I think I was with him more than I am now. I think, as he gets older, he's had a tendency to get his pleasures from people his own age, this is fine as long as he makes home his headquarters. That's all I want.

Although the boys devoted an increasing amount of time to peer-group activities, they nevertheless retained close ties to their parents and readily sought out their help, advice, and support when needed.

PARENT—PEER-GROUP CONFLICTS

The boys' primary reference groups were not selected indiscriminately. Since the adolescents tended to choose friends who shared similar value systems and behavioral norms, membership in the peer-group did not generate familial conflicts. In fact, the peer-group often served to reinforce and to uphold the parental norms and standards of behavior that the boys had adopted. Consequently, the parents were generally pleased with their sons' associates because they served as an important source of control in situations where the parents could not be present.

An essentially similar picture of adolescence, based on an intensive study of middle class families, has been presented by Elkin and Westley (1955, Westley & Elkin, 1956). They summarize their findings as follows:

Family ties are close and the degree of basic family consensus is high. The parents are interested in all the activities of their children, and the adolescents, except for the area of sex, frankly discuss their own behavior and problems with them. In many areas of life, there is joint participation between parents and children. . . . In independent discussions by parents and adolescents of the latters' marriage and occupational goals, there was a remarkable level of agreement. The adolescents also acknowledged the right of the parents to guide them, for example, accepting, at least manifestly, the prerogatives of the parents to set

rules for the number of dates, hours of return from dates, and types of parties. The parents express relatively little concern about the socialization problems or peer-group activities of their children (1955, p. 682).

Sources of the Adolescent Mythology

What are the origins of the mythology about adolescence, and why does it persist?

OVERINTERPRETATION OF SUPERFICIAL SIGNS OF NONCONFORMITY

The view that adolescence is a period of rebellion is often supported by references to superficial signs of nonconformity, particularly adolescent fad behavior.

It is certainly true that adolescents frequently display idiosyncratic fashions and interest patterns. Such fads, however, are not confined to adolescent age groups. Several years ago, for example, coon skin caps and Davy Crockett apparel were highly fashionable among pre-adolescent boys. When Davy Crockett began to wane a new fad quickly emerged—every youngster and a sizeable proportion of the adult population were gyrating with hoola-hoops. The hoola-hoop also suffered a quick death by replacement.

If pre-adolescent children display less fad behavior than do adolescents, this difference may be primarily due to the fact that young children do not possess the economic resources with which to purchase distinctive apparel, the latest phonograph records, and discriminative ornaments, rather than a reflection of a sudden heightening of peer-group conformity pressures during adolescence. The pre-adolescent does not purchase his own clothing, he has little voice in how his hair shall be cut and, on a 15-cent a week allowance, he is hardly in a position to create new fads, or to deviate too widely from parental tastes and standards.

How about adult fad behavior? A continental gentleman conducts a fashion show in Paris and almost instantly millions of hemlines move upward or downward; the human figure is sacked, trapezed, chemised, or appareled in some other fantastic creation.

At a recent cocktail party the present writer was cornered by an inquiring lady who expressed considerable puzzlement over adolescents' fascination for unusual and bizarre styles. The lady herself was draped with a sack, wearing a preposterous object on her head, and spiked high heel shoes that are more likely to land one in an orthopedic clinic, than to transport one across the room to the olives.

Fashion-feeders determine the styles, the colors, and the amount of clothing that shall be worn. It would be rare, indeed, to find an adult who would ask a sales clerk for articles of clothing in vogue two or three years ago. As long as social groups contain a status hierarchy, and tolerance for upward mobility within the social hierarchy, one can expect imitation of fads and fashions from below which, in turn, forces inventiveness from the elite in order to preserve the status differentations.

MASS MEDIA SENSATIONALISM

The storm and stress view of adolescence is also continuously reinforced by mass media sensationalism. Since the deviant adolescent excites far more interest than the typical high school student, the adolescent is usually portrayed in literature, television, and in the movies as passing through a neurotic or a semi-delinquent phase of development (Kiell, 1959). These productions, many of which are designed primarily to generate visceral reactions or to sell copy, are generally, viewed as profound and sensitive portrayals of the *typical* adolescent turmoil. Holden Caulfield, the central character in *The Catcher in the Rye* (Salinger, 1945), has thus become the prototypic adolescent.

GENERALIZATION FROM SAMPLES OF DEVIANT ADOLESCENTS

Professional people in the mental health field are apt to have most contact with delinquent adolescents, and are thus prone to base their accounts of adolescence on observations of atypical samples. By and large, the description of the modal pattern of adolescent behavior fits most closely the behavior of the deviant ten per cent of the adolescent population that appears repeatedly in psychiatric clinics, juvenile probation departments, and in the newspaper headlines.

Our study of the family relationships of adolescents also included a sample of antisocially aggressive boys. In the families of these hyper-aggressive adolescents there was indeed a great deal of storm and stress for many years. The boys' belligerence and rebellion, however, was not a unique product of adolescence. The defiant oppositional pattern of behavior was present all along, but because of their greater size and power the parents were able to suppress and to control, through coercive methods, their sons' belligerence during the early childhood years. By the time of adolescence, however, some of the boys had reached the stage where they were almost completely independent of the parents for the satisfaction of their social and physical needs. Moreover, they had developed physically to the point where they were larger and more powerful than their parents. With the achievement of the power reversal and the decrease of the parents' importance as sources of desired rewards, a number of the boys exhibited a blatant indifference to their parents' wishes about which they could now do little or nothing.

I. What sort of things does your mother object to your doing when you are out with your friends?
B. She don't know what I do.
I. What about staying out late at night?
B. She says, "Be home at 11 o'clock." I'll come home at one.
I. How about using the family car?
B. No. I wrecked mine, and my father wrecked his a month before I wrecked mine, and I can't even get near his. And I got a license and everything. I'm going to hot wire it some night and cut out.
I. How honest do you feel you can be to your mother about where you've been and what things you have done?
B. I tell her where I've been, period.
I. How about what you've done?
B. No. I won't tell her what I've done. If we're going out in the hills for a beer bust, I'm not going to tell her. I'll tell her I've been to a show or something.

I. How about your father?

B. I'll tell him where I've been, period.

The heightened aggression exhibited by these boys during adolescence primarily reflected response predispositions that became more evident following the power reversal in the parent-child relationship, rather than an adolescence-induced stress.

INAPPROPRIATE GENERALIZATION FROM CROSS-CULTURAL DATA

It is interesting to note that many writers cite cross-cultural data as supporting evidence for the discontinuity view of child development in the American society. The reader suddenly finds himself in the Trobriand Islands, or among the Arapesh, rather than in the suburbs of Minneapolis or in the town square of Oskaloosa.

In many cultures the transition from child to adult status is very abrupt. Childhood behavior patterns are strongly reinforced, but as soon as the child reaches pubescence he is subjected to an elaborate ceremony which signifies his abrupt transformation into adult status. Following the ceremonial initiation the young initiate acquires new rights and privileges, new responsibilities and, in some cultures, he is even assigned a new name and a new set of parents who undertake his subsequent social training in the skills and habits required to perform the adult role.

In our culture, on the other hand, except for the discontinuities in the socialization of sexual behavior, there is considerable continuity in social training. As was mentioned earlier, independence and responsibility training, for example, are begun in early childhood and adult-role patterns are achieved through a gradual process of successive approximations. This is equally true in the development of many other forms of social behavior.

It should be mentioned in passing, however, that cross-cultural studies have been valuable in demonstrating that stresses and conflicts are not inevitable concomitants of pubescence, but rather products of cultural conditioning. Indeed, in some societies, adolescence is one of the pleasant periods of social development (Mead, 1930).

OVEREMPHASIS OF THE BIOLOGICAL DETERMINATION OF HETEROSEXUAL BEHAVIOR

With the advent of pubescence the adolescent is presumably encumbered by a powerful biologically determined sexual drive that produces a relatively sudden and marked increase in heterosexual behavior. The net result of the clash between strong physiological urges demanding release and even more substantial social prohibitions, is a high degree of conflict, frustration, anxiety and diffuse tension. In contrast to this widely-accepted biological drive theory, evidence from studies of cross-species and cross-cultural sexual behavior reveals that human sexuality is governed primarily by social conditioning, rather than endocrinal stimulation (Ford & Beach, 1951).

The cross-species data demonstrate that hormonal control of sexual behavior decreases with advancing evolutionary status. In lower mammalian species, for example, sexual activities are completely regulated by gonadal hormones; among primates sexual behavior is partially independent of physiological stimulation; while human eroticism is exceedingly variable and essentially independent of hormonal regulation. Humans can be sexually aroused before puberty and long after natural or surgical loss of reproductive glands. Thus, one would induce sexual behavior in a rodent Don Juan by administering androgen, whereas presenting him lascivious pictures of a well-endowed mouse would have no stimulating effects whatsoever. By contrast, one would rely on sexually-balanced social stimuli, rather than on hormonal injections, for producing erotic arousal in human males.

The prominent role of social learning factors in determining the timing, incidence and form of sexual activities of humans is also clearly revealed in the wide cross-cultural variability in patterns of sexual behavior. Sex-arousing properties have been conditioned to an extremely broad range of stimuli, but the cues that are sexually stimulating in one culture would, in many instances, prove sexually repulsive to members of another society. A similar diversity exists in the timing of the emergence of sexual interest and in the choice of sexual objects. In cultures that permit and encourage heterosexual behavior at earlier, or at later, periods of a child's development than is true for American youth, no marked changes in sexual behavior occur during adolescence.

It is evident from the foregoing discussion that "sexual tensions" are not an inevitable concomitant of pubescence. Furthermore, any significant increase in heterosexual activities during adolescence is due more to cultural conditioning and expectations than to endocrinal changes.

STAGE THEORIES OF PERSONALITY DEVELOPMENT

Until recently, most of the theoretical conceptualizations of the developmental process have subscribed to some form of stage theory. According to the Freudian viewpoint (1949), for example, behavioral changes are programmed in an oral–anal–phallic sequence; Erikson (1950) characterizes personality development in terms of an eight-stage sequence; Gesell (Gesell & Ilg, 1943) describes marked predictable cyclical changes in behavior over yearly or even shorter temporal intervals; and Piaget (1948, 1954), delineates numerous different stages for different classes of responses.

Although there appears to be relatively little consensus among these theories concerning the number and the content of stages considered to be crucial, they all share in common the assumption that social behavior can be categorized in terms of a relatively pre-fixed sequence of stages with varying degrees of continuity or discontinuity between successive developmental periods. Typically, the spontaneous emergence of these elaborate age-specific modes of behavior is attributed to ontogenetic factors. The seven-year-old, for example, is supposed to be withdrawn; the eight-year-old turns into an exuberant, expansive and buoyant child; the fifteen-year-old becomes remote and argumentative; parents are finally rewarded at sweet sixteen (Ilg & Ames, 1955). In truth, all seven-year-olds are not withdrawn, all eight-year-olds are not exuberant, expansive and buoyant, nor are all fifteen-year-olds aloof and argumentative. I am also acquainted with sixteen-year-olds who are anything but sweet. The withdrawn five-year-old is likely to remain a relatively withdrawn eight, nine, and sixteen-year-old unless he undergoes social-learning experiences that are effective in fostering more expressive behavior.

Although the traditional stage theories of child development are of questionable validity (Bandura & McDonald, 1963; Bandura & Mischel, 1963; Bandura & Walters, 1963), they have nevertheless been influential in promoting the view that adolescence represents a form of stage behavior that suddenly appears at pubescence, and as suddenly disappears when adulthood is achieved.

SELF-FULFILLING PROPHECY

If a society labels its adolescents as "teenagers," and expects them to be rebellious, unpredictable, sloppy, and wild in their behavior, and if this picture is repeatedly reinforced by the mass media, such cultural expectations may very well force adolescents into the role of rebel. In this way, a false expectation may serve to instigate and maintain certain role behaviors, in turn, then reinforce the originally false belief.

In discussing our research findings with parents' groups I have often been struck by the fact that most parents, who are experiencing positive and rewarding relationships with their pre-adolescent children are, nevertheless, waiting apprehensively and bracing themselves for the stormy adolescent period. Such vigilance can very easily create a small turbulence at least. When the prophesied storm fails to materialize, many parents begin to entertain doubts about the normality of their youngster's social development.

In closing, I do not wish to leave you with the impression that adolescence is a stress- or problem-free period of development. No age group is free from stress or adjustment problems. Our findings suggest, however, that the behavioral characteristics exhibited by children during the so-called adolescent stage are lawfully related to, and consistent with, pre-adolescent social behavior.

REFERENCES

BANDURA, A., & MCDONALD, F. J. The influence of social reinforcement and the behavior of models in shaping children's moral judgments. *J. abnorm. soc. Psychol.*, 1963, 67, 274–281.

BANDURA, A., & MISCHEL, W. The influence of models in modifying delay-of-gratification patterns. Unpublished manuscript, Stanford Univer., 1963.

BANDURA, A., & WALTERS, R. H. *Adolescent aggression.* New York: Ronald, 1959.

BANDURA, A., & WALTERS, R. H. *Social learning and personality development.* New York: Holt, Rinehart & Winston, 1963.

ELKIN, F., & WESTLEY, W. A. The myth of adolescent culture. *Amer. sociol. Rev.*, 1955, 20, 680–684.

ERIKSON, E. H. *Childhood and society.* New York: Norton, 1950.

FORD, C. S., & BEACH, F. A. *Patterns of sexual behavior.* New York: Harper, 1951.

FREUD, S. *An outline of psychoanalysis.* New York: Norton, 1949.

GALLAGHER, J. R., & HARRIS, H. I. *Emotional problems of adolescents.* New York: Oxford Univer. Press, 1958.

GESELL, A., & ILG, FRANCES. *Infant and child in the culture of today.* New York: Harper, 1943.

HEATHERS, G. Emotional dependence and independence in nursery school play. *J. genet. Psychol.*, 1955, 87, 37–57.

HURLOCK, ELIZABETH B. *Adolescent development.* New York: McGraw-Hill, 1955.

ILG, FRANCES L., & AMES, LOUISE B. *Child behavior.* New York: Harper, 1955.

JOSSELYN, IRENE M. *Psychosocial development of children.* New York: Family Service Assoc. of America, 1948.

KIELL, N. *The adolescent through fiction.* New York: International Univer. Press, 1959.

MEAD, MARGARET. Adolescence in primitive and in modern society. In V. F. Calverton & S. D. Schmalhausen (Eds.), *The new generation.* New York: Macauley, 1930.

MOHR, G. S., & DESPRES, MARIAN A. *The stormy decade: adolescence.* New York: Random House, 1958.

PARSONS, T. Psycho-analysis and social structure. *Psychoanal. Quart.*, 1950, 19, 371–384.

PEARSON, G. H. J. *Adolescence and the conflict of generations.* New York: Norton, 1958.

PIAGET, J. *The moral judgment of the child.* New York: Free Press, 1948.

PIAGET, J. *The construction of reality in the child.* New York: Basic Books, 1954.

SALINGER, J. D. *The catcher in the rye.* Boston: Little, Brown, 1945.

WESTLEY, W. A., & ELKIN, F. The protective environment and adolescent socialization. *Social Forces.* 1956, 35, 243–249.

Disruption and Stability in Adolescence

IRVING B. WEINER

The author reviews research, both past and current, relative to the issue: How turbulent is adolescence?

. . . The pioneering contributions of G. Stanley Hall (1904) depicted adolescence as an era of inevitable turmoil in which the major predictable feature of a young person's behavior is his unpredictability:

> The "teens" are emotionally unstable and pathic. It is the age of natural inebriation without the need of intoxicants, which made Plato define youth as spiritual drunkenness. It is a natural impulse to experience hot and perfervid psychic states, and it is characterized by emotionalism. . . . We see here the instability and fluctuations now so characteristic. The emotions develop by contrast and reaction into the opposite (Vol. II, pp. 74–75).

Hall further explicated several antithetical traits that he believed to define normal adolescence: alternations of eagerness, zest, enthusiasm, and intellectual curiosity with apathy, inertia, and cultivated indifference; oscillations between pleasure and pain and euphoria and melancholy; periods of both extreme egoism and abject humility; alternating selfishness and altruism, conservatism and radicalism, and gregariousness and seclusiveness; changes from exquisite sensitiveness to imperturbability, hard-heartedness, and cruelty; vacillations between knowing and doing and between the ascendance of sense and intellect; and the juxtaposition of wisdom and folly (Vol. II, pp. 75–88).

Although subsequent cultural anthropological data challenged the inevitability of adolescent turmoil as described by Hall . . . later psychoanalytic interpretations of adolescence strongly supported his views, at least with respect to Western civilization. Perhaps foremost among psychoanalytic writers in her influence on contemporary thinking about adolescent development is Anna Freud (1936), whose description of normal adolescence is strikingly similar to Hall's:

> Adolescents are excessively egoistic, regarding themselves as the centre of the universe and the sole object of interest, and yet at no time in later life are they capable of so much self-sacrifice and devotion. They form the most passionate love-relations, only to break them off as abruptly as they began them. On the one hand they throw themselves enthusiastically into the life of the community and, on the other, they have an overpowering longing for solitude. They oscillate between blind submis-

sion to some self-chosen leader and defiant rebellion against any and every authority. They are selfish and materially-minded and at the same time full of lofty idealism. They are ascetic but will suddenly plunge into instinctual indulgence of the most primitive character. At times their behaviour to other people is rough and inconsiderate, yet they themselves are extremely touchy. Their moods veer between light-hearted optimism and the blackest pessimism. Sometimes they will work with indefatigable enthusiasm and at other times they are sluggish and apathetic (pp. 149–150).

Elsewhere Anna Freud (1958) affirms her belief that these adolescent upheavals are nothing more than external indications that normal developmental internal adjustments are in progress: "Adolescence constitutes by definition an interruption of peaceful growth which resembles in appearance a variety of other emotional upsets and structural upheavals" (p. 267). Among psychoanalytic writers endorsing Anna Freud's position, Geleerd (1957) considers that, since adolescence is a physiologically troubled state,[1] a certain amount of psychological disturbance is normal: "Personally I would feel greater concern for the adolescent who causes no trouble and feels no disturbance" (p. 267). Geleerd (1961) further maintains that a partial regression to an undifferentiated phase of object relationships, accompanied by increased ego vulnerability and sensitivity to trauma, is not only a normal but a necessary aspect of adolescent maturation.

Spiegel (1951, 1961) comments on the resemblance of adolescence to some psychotic episodes and reports that observations of adolescents over any period of time normally reveal alternating phases of chaos and consolidation. Harley (1961) discusses at length the role in normal adolescent development of the dissolution of psychic structures that have been built up during childhood

and consolidated during latency. According to Eissler (1958, p. 224), "Although puberty may take many courses, we think predominantly of stormy and unpredictable behavior marked by mood swings and melancholy." Fountain (1961) asserts that adolescents can be distinguished from adults by their intensity and volatility of feeling, need for frequent and immediate gratification, ineffective reality testing, and failure of self-criticism.

Other psychoanalytic contributors have focused specifically on the manner in which certain adolescent modes of dealing with conflicts and frustrations normally lead to inconsistent and maladaptive behavior patterns. Bernfeld (1938) categorized adolescents according to their preference for rebellious or compliant modes of responding to environmental demands. The strictly rebellious adolescent, according to Bernfeld, disregards prohibitions, seeks immediate gratification of his needs, and struggles against all obstacles, selfrighteously seeking to overcome them by any means possible. The strictly compliant adolescent, in contrast, settles all problems by repressing them and, at the expense of transient neurotic symptoms and persistently childish affective responses, frequently passes an uneventful adolescence. For Bernfeld various sequential combinations and permutations of these reactive modes define the majority of personality types observed in adolescents.

Ackerman (1958, p. 116) has more recently expressed a similar view of adolescent personality:

The behavior of adolescents today is bipolar. They tend to seek identity at one of two poles: conformity or delinquency. At one extreme occur the weird explosive acts that lean toward crime. At the other extreme emerges a kind of caricature of cautious, monotonous, conforming behavior.

Ackerman (1962) believes that mild and transitory manifestations of many undesirable personality traits normally characterize contemporary adolescents, including the following: antisocial behavior, especially in acts of violence; sexual promiscuity; a quest for kicks but also for a "safe" existence; overconformity with peers;

[1]Although physiological instability in normal adolescents has been inferred by several investigators, Eichorn and McKee (1958) consider available data inadequate to justify such a conclusion. In their study of 100 adolescent boys and girls, on whom physiological measures were taken every six months from age 11.5 to 17.5 years, they found no evidence of a temporary period of heightened physiological variability for girls and only a slight indication for boys.

withdrawal with a loss of faith, disillusionment and despair, lack of adventuresomeness, and loss of spark; disorientation in relations with family and community; and increased vulnerability to mental breakdown. In his opinion all of these difficulties are attributable to the turbulence and instability of the modern family, which he sees as providing the adolescent few of the types of intrafamilial relationships optimal for emotional growth. Pearson (1958) in *Adolescence and the Conflict of Generations* also develops the theme that adolescents today face a serious struggle for maturity because of the older generation's lack of sympathy or understanding and general resistance to their attaining adulthood.

Thus these writers posit either that adolescence is inevitably a period of disruption and maladaptive behavior or that modern civilized environment makes it so. These views have somewhat different implications for individual and social action. To assume that in adolescence disruption is inevitable is to advocate the tolerance, patience, and forebearance in the face of adolescent idiosyncracies originally encouraged by Hall. To trace adolescent turmoil to modifiable environmental circumstances, on the other hand, is to champion a search for social psychological means of redressing the plight of youth.

The latter attitude is implicit in a paper by Hurlock (1966), who attributes a host of negative developments in modal adolescent behavior to increasingly progressive and permissive child-rearing practices. In a sweeping indictment of modern youth she castigates him for his peer conformity; preoccupation with status symbols; irresponsibility; antiwork and anti-intellectual attitudes; disregard for manners, grooming, and virginity; disrespect for older generations; criticism and debunking of those in authority; disregard for rules and laws; and unrealistic levels of aspiration.

The writings of Ackerman, Hurlock, Coleman, and others of a similar persuasion convey a clarion call for a return to the "good old days." This yearning for the way youth used to be bears a disconcerting resemblance to the Socratic plaint. . . . [See p. 27—Ed.] Things seemed little improved in Shakespeare's time:

I would there were no age between ten and three-and-twenty, or that youth would sleep out the rest; for there is nothing in the between but getting wenches with child, wronging the ancientry, stealing, fighting (*The Winter's Tale*, Act III, Scene iii).

More pertinent to the modern era, however, is the following impression of the adolescent dilemma:

Modern life is hard, and in many respects, increasingly so, on youth. Home, school, church, fail to recognize its nature and needs and, perhaps most of all, its perils. . . . Never has youth been exposed to such dangers of both perversion and arrest as in our own land and day. Increasing urban life with its temptations, prematurities, sedentary occupations, and passive stimuli just when an active, objective life is most needed, early emancipations and a lessening sense for both duty and discipline, the haste to know and do all befitting man's estate before its time, the mad rush for sudden wealth and the reckless fashions set by its gilded youth —all these lack some of the regulatives they still have in older lands with more conservative traditions.

These timely views were voiced by Hall in 1904 (Vol. I, pp. xiv–xvi). Their vintage raises the question of how good indeed were the "good old days." Furthermore, if the adolescents of Hall's day exhibited many of the personality characteristics that are viewed with alarm by current writers, is not the idea of progressive adolescent decadence a myth? Kelley (1962, p. 4), for one, writing from many years' experience as an educator, disputes vigorously the belief that youth has gone to the dogs: "The over-all evidence, however, is that youth as a whole behave better than they ever did." And if the decadence idea is after all a myth, is it possible that the whole notion of normative adolescent turmoil and misbehavior, both then and now, is also a myth?

At issue, then, is the oft-stated conviction that adolescence is, or is progressively becoming, an era of disruption during which young people wage undeclared warfare against their parents and other authorities, reject adult values, plunge into sexual promiscuity, pursue transient and superficial interests, and undergo a state of psychological disequilibrium that borders on psycho-

pathology. In fact, a heavy weight of contrary data and opinion argue strongly that these views, whenever generalized to the adolescent population, are indeed a myth.

REFERENCES

ACKERMAN, N. W. *The psychodynamics of family.* New York: Basic Books, 1958.

ACKERMAN, N. W. Adolescent problems: A symptom of family disorder. *Family Process*, 1962, *1*, 202–213.

BERNFELD, S. Die heutige Psychologie der Pubertät (Present-day psychology of puberty). *Imago*, 1927, *13*, 1–56.

EICHORN, D. H., & MCKEE, J. P. Physiological instability during adolescence. *Child Development*, 1958, *29*, 255–268.

EISSLER, K. R. Notes on problems of technique in the psychoanalytic treatment of adolescents. *Psychoanalytic Study of the Child*, 1958, *13*, 223–254.

FOUNTAIN, G. Adolescent into adult: An inquiry. *Journal of the American Psychoanalytic Association*, 1961, *9*, 417–433.

FREUD, A. (1936). *The ego and the mechanisms of defence.* New York: International Universities Press, 1946.

FREUD, A. Adolescence. *Psychoanalytic Study of the Child*, 1958, *13*, 255–278.

GELEERD, E. R. Some aspects of psychoanalytic technique in adolescence. *Psychoanalytic Study of the Child*, 1957, *12*, 263–283.

GELEERD, E. R. Some aspects of ego vicissitudes in adolescence. *Journal of the American Psychoanalytic Association*, 1961, *9*, 394-405.

HALL, G. S. *Adolescence: Its psychology and its relations to physiology, anthropology, sociology, sex, crime, religion, and education.* Vols. I and II. New York: D. Appleton, 1904.

HARLEY, M. Some observations on the relationship between genitality and structural development at adolescence. *Journal of the American Psychoanalytic Association*, 1961, *9*, 434–460.

HURLOCK, E. B. American adolescents today—a new species. *Adolescence*, 1966, *1*, 7–21.

KELLEY, E. C. *In defense of youth.* Englewood Cliffs, N. J.: Prentice-Hall, 1962.

PEARSON, G. H. J. *Adolescence and the conflict of generations.* New York: Norton, 1958.

SPIEGEL, L. A. A review of contributions to a psychoanalytic theory of adolescence. *Psychoanalytic Study of the Child*, 1951, *6*, 375–393.

SPIEGEL, L. A. Disorder and consolidation in adolescence. *Journal of the American Psychoanalytic Association*, 1961, *9*, 406–417.

Chapter 5: Suggested Additional Readings

ALLPORT, G. W. Crises in normal personality development. *Teachers College Record*, 1964, *66*(1), 235–241. The author, an outstanding personality theorist, reports that the role of the teacher is most vivid to middle and late adolescents. Using biographical data obtained from his students, Allport defines the nature of adolescents' crises and outlines the major crisis areas involved. Freudian interpretations seemed to fit well those adolescents who were disturbed, but not the vast majority who were reasonably well adjusted. He suggests that personality theory for guidance not be drawn from the more "lurid" components of Freudian theory.

CROAKE, J. W. Adolescent fears. *Adolescence*, 1967–68, *2*, 459–468. In this study, ninth-grade boys and girls indicated their fears both past and present.

ELKIND, D. Cognitive structure and adolescent experience. *Adolescence*, 1967, *2*(8), 427–434. Elkind emphasizes that adolescent behavioral phenomena relate to and depend upon new cognitive structures which first appear at this age.

MENNINGER, R. What troubles our troubled youth? *Mental Hygiene*, 1968, *52*(3), 323–329. The president of the Menninger Foundation discusses evidence of youth's troubled state, examines the social phenomena underlying this discontent, and challenges readers to do something to improve the situation.

NAKASHIMA, I. I. Adolescence: Rebellion and resolution. *Journal of School Health*, 1965, *35*, 402–406. The author briefly summarizes major developmental problems of adolescents.

NIXON, R. E. Psychological normality in the years of youth. *Teachers College Record*, 1964, *66*(1), 71–79. The writer declares that psychological normality in youth is recognizable and makes it possible to distinguish the abnormals, conformists, and rebels who make up the majority. Few of us, he asserts, had a chance as adolescents to discover our own normality. He describes cases of particular adolescents to make his points.

SCHONFELD, W. A. Adolescent turmoil: socioeconomic affluence as a factor. *New York State Journal of Medicine*, 1967, *67*, 1981-1990. Schonfeld discusses socioeconomic affluence of the family, affluence of the adolescent subculture, and affluence of the individual adolescent. He believes the solution in this regard is to incorporate young people in meaningful projects in both the local community and the larger society.

SCHMUCK, R. Concerns of contemporary adolescents. *Bulletin of the National Association of Secondary School Principals*, 1965, *49*, 19–28. On the basis of extensive research, Schmuck defines adolescents' chief concerns in relating to parents, peers, and teachers. He decides that parents play the chief instrumental role in shaping teenagers' interests.

TEMPLIN, L. The pathology of youth. *Journal of Human Relations*, 1968, *16*(1), 113–127. This essay-review brings together ideas from recent books in examining the symptoms, causes, remedies, and prognoses of adolescent difficulties. The pathology of youth is perceived as the pathology of the culture, which means that genuine solutions must be cultural ones.

6

Influence of Family Life on Adolescents

Throughout the ages, family life has constituted the "social matrix" for the child's development (Clausen, 1956). In both subtle and obvious ways, family experience leaves its imprint on each family member.

The family's influence on its members varies according to many factors. For example, Brantley (1969) found that there is a high correlation between family stress and adolescent social and academic dysfunction. In his study of youths who were failing academically, he learned that two out of every five came from broken homes; the other three came from homes which were still intact but in which family members were subject to special stresses such as alcoholism, inconsistent discipline, unreachable expectations for the children, inflexibility, and outright rejection. In another study, the Gluecks (1968) concluded that the total impact of the societal environment or general culture has less influence on stimulating delinquency than do an individual's biological characteristics and the parental influences during his formative years. In other words, they believe that poverty in itself is not a highly significant factor in adolescent delinquency, nor are the lack of economic and sociocultural opportunity, or residence in a slum, fundamental causes. These popular "explanations" of delinquency simply do not explain it because they do not discriminate between delinquent and nondelinquent youths exposed to the same conditions. Far more important than these as an influence on a child's development, conclude the Gluecks, are the quality of the parent–child relationship and the culture of the home. In fact, a great many delinquents live, not in slums, but in so-called "good" neighborhoods.

Another issue thought to be important to the adolescent's adjustment within the family concerns the effect of the mother's employment. In a study of ninth-grade pupils, boys' adjustment to society proved better when the mother worked full-time than if she worked part-time or not at all (Nelson, 1971). The personality adjustment of girls followed no consistent pattern regarding their mothers' employment status; but girls with nonworking mothers typically made better adjustment scores than did girls with mothers who worked either full- or part-time. However, when all variables are considered, the mother's working seems not to be the deciding factor in determining children's welfare. Besides, no single way of life is best for every situation; apparently it is better for some mothers to work, and for others not to do so (Sears, Maccoby & Levin, 1957).

Teenage boys and girls themselves differ with each other on the question of maternal employment. Adolescent boys apparently look on women's employment as a greater hazard to marriage than do adolescent girls (King, McIntyre, & Axelson, 1968). However, adolescents of relatively high socioeconomic status perceive maternal employment as less threatening to marriage than do lower-class youngsters. In addition, the more their own fathers assist with household tasks, the more accepting of maternal employment are the sons and daughters.

Still another issue concerns teenagers' relations with their parents. Is conflict between the generations as common as is popularly believed? In a study of high school students in different parts of the United States, Herzog and Sudia (1970) found that a large majority deplored their parents' failure to give them full respect, trust, and status as persons. A third of the students believed that their values differed from those of their parents. Most of them were upset about world conditions and blamed adults, including their parents, for these problems. Only about ten percent had no real criticism of the older generation.

Werkman (1966) holds youth themselves responsible for much of their conflict with their parents. He laments youth's consistent demand for immediate gratification of their wants; and he pleads for the restoration of certain past "social rituals" which indicated mutual respect between older and younger family members. He concludes that parents have been excluded from their teenage children's lives, and urges that children be reminded that since they live in their parents' home, they should share more willingly in family life.

Other writers question whether any substantial rift exists between parents and their children. According to Rosenmayr (1968), adolescents may seek boy and girl friends for social life, but they regard their parents as their most intimate reference persons in matters of depth relations. Their parents are closer to them than any other individuals and are a source of support in time of trouble. The mother, in particular, is the central figure in the family in many parts of the world and especially in the lower strata of society. In fact, this mother-centrism is thoroughly documented in studies on all continents. In general, then, believes Rosenmayr, there are no general protests of children against their parents—a fact that may surprise those who have observed youth movements of the twentieth century.

Another broad question concerns family dynamics and how different family members affect each other. In the first reading in this section, Biller and Weiss confirm the belief—widely held and increasingly supported by research—that the father plays a significant role in the growing child's personality development. For some years, it has been recognized that the father plays a key role in his son's development. More recently it has become apparent that he also functions importantly in his daughter's development, especially in the area of sex role. Although this article chiefly concerns the father's influence on his daughter, reference is also made to his relationship to his son. The annotated list of readings, at the conclusion of this section, lists a related article, by Gloria Count Van Manen, which deals with father roles and with adolescent distinctions between the effective role of the father and the nurturant, socializing role of the mother.

One question which might be raised in defense of parents is: When parental roles are being evaluated, should the focus be more on the pragmatic situation than on some elusive ideal? Can any cast of family characters be uniformly excellent? James O. Wilson, a Harvard professor, once said that a Harvard president should have "the temperament of an angel, the physique and stamina of a middle linebacker, and the mind of Galileo." The same is often expected of youth's parents who, after all, are ex-adolescents themselves.

Many other questions about youth-and-family relationships have not been thoroughly researched—for example, do teenagers who have attained a higher educational level than their parents have a correspondingly greater influence on familial decision-making? Do teenagers who work have a greater part in decision-making than those who do not work? How much does children's participation in family councils, regardless of their age or educational status, depend on the equalitarian ideology of the parents? How do siblings influence each other? According to Safilios-Rothschild (1970), existing theories concerning familial power structure do not take into consideration the contribution of any family members except the parents. Nevertheless, children influence each other; they also influence their parents about some decisions, and at least express an opinion about others. Fortunately, the considerable body of research relative to family life around the world helps lend perspective to parent-youth relations in our own country. In our second reading, Elder examines the data on parental authority in five nations: the United States, Great Britain, West Germany, Italy, and Mexico. The overall sociocultural similarities and differences among these countries are reflected in the parents' relationships to their growing children. Except in Mexico, a general trend toward a more democratic parent-youth relationship was apparent—though in varying degree—in all countries.

Despite the vast quantities of research on the family, including cross-cultural studies, Walters and Stinnett (1971) warn against "simplistic explanations concerning the direction of causality in explaining the nature of parent-child relationships [pp. 100–101]." Indeed, few generalizations can be made about family life because nearly every one must be hedged with a long list of contingent considerations.

REFERENCES

BRANTLEY, D.   Family stress and academic failures. *Social Case Work*, 1969, *30*, 287–290.

CLAUSEN, J. A.   Family structure, socialization, and personality. In L. W. Hoffman and M. L. Hoffman (Eds.) *Review of child development.* New York: Russell Sage Foundation, 1956.

GLUECK, S., & GLUECK, E.   *Delinquents and nondelinquents in perspective.* Cambridge, Harvard University Press, 1968.

HERZOG, E., & SUDIA, C. E.   The generation gap in the eyes of youth. *Children*, 1970, *17*, 53–58.

KING, K., MC INTYRE, J., & AXELSON, L. J.   Adolescents' views of maternal employment as a threat to the marital relationship. *Journal of Marriage and the Family*, 1968, *30*, 633–637.

NELSON, D. D.   A study of personality adjustment among adolescent children with working and nonworking mothers. *Journal of Educational Research*, 1971, *64*(7), 328–338.

ROSENMAYR, L.   Towards an overview of youth's sociology. *International Social Science Journal*, 1968, *20*(2), 286–315.

SAFILIOS-ROTHSCHILD, C.   The study of family power structure: A review 1960–69. *Journal of Marriage and the Family*, 1970, *32*(4), 539–552.

SEARS, R. R., MACCOBY, E. E., & LEVIN, H.   *Patterns of child rearing.* Evanston, Ill.: Row, Peterson, 1957.

WALTERS, J., & STINNETT, N.   Parent–child relationships: A decade review of research. *Journal of Marriage and the Family*, 1971, *33*(1), 70–111.

WERKMAN, S. L.   Adolescents: A twentieth century predicament. *American Association of University Women Journal*, 1966, *59*, 185–187.

The Father-Daughter Relationship and the Personality Development of the Female

HENRY B. BILLER   STEPHAN D. WEISS

The writers review research relevant to the father's influence on the daughter's personality development, with incidental reference to his influence on the son as well.

A. Introduction

A variety of factors can influence the personality development of the child, but parent–child relations seem to have a particularly profound significance. Theorists and researchers have long stressed the importance of mothering in the personality development of the child, and more recently there has been a growing interest in the role of the father. The father's impact upon such facets of personality development as identification and sex role has become increasingly recognized by contemporary theorists and researchers (13, 46). However, the focus has been on the father–son relationship with relatively little attention being paid to the father–daughter relationship.

The present paper is an attempt to review ideas and findings from various disciplines which are relevant to understanding what influence the father–daughter relationship may have on the personality development of the female. The role of

the father is emphasized in this review, but it is realized that a fuller understanding of personality development will be achieved only from an analysis of the interaction of a variety of familial, sociocultural, and constitutional factors.

B. Theoretical Background

Deutsch (17, p. 252) describes the traditional psychoanalytic viewpoint in her discussion of Freud's conception (e.g., 20, 21) of the process of feminine development:

> The former psychoanalytic observations of the little girl's development dealt chiefly with her sexual instincts. It was found that with her detachment from her mother, the little girl—already a miniature woman—has an erotic passive attitude toward her father, an attitude that constitutes the kernel of the feminine Oedipus complex.

According to Deutsch (17), the father plays an important function in leading the girl to adopt an

This paper was completed while the first author was a recipient of a Faculty Growth Grant from the Faculty Research Council of the University of Massachusetts.

From H. B. Biller & S. D. Weiss, The father-daughter relationship and the personality development of the female. Reprinted from the *Journal of Genetic Psychology*, 1970, *116*, 79–93, by permission of the publisher and the authors.

erotic passive mode of interacting with males. He showers her with love and tenderness when she acts passive, helpless, and/or femininely seductive, but discourages her masculine and/or aggressive strivings.

The importance of successfully resolving the feminine Oedipal complex is stressed by Leonard, who suggests the need for a girl to "establish a desexualized object relationship to her father" in order for her to be able "later to accept the feminine role without guilt or anxiety and to give love to a young man in her peer group" (38, p. 332). Adequate fathering is assumed to be an essential requirement for the success of this phase of psychosexual development. Without paternal participation the girl may idealize her father and later, as an adolescent, seek a love object similar to this ideal or maintain a preoedipal narcissistic attitude, such as that in adolescence she may be "unable to give love but rather seeks narcissistic gratification in being loved" (38, p. 332).

A restatement of Freud's theory of anaclitic identification, which emphasized the child's fear of loss of parental love and nurturance, has been offered by learning theorists, such as Mowrer (43) and Sears et al. (58). According to these theorists, the child becomes strongly dependent on the parents for supplying nurturance and learns to perform those acts which are rewarded by his parents. In terms of his positive reinforcement and discouragement of other behavior, the father would appear to be a significant influence on his daughter's personality development. The father's reinforcement of the girl's attempts to imitate her mother's behavior would seem particularly important as would the father's general approval of the mother's behavior.

Compared to other theories of identification, Parsons' (14, 19) theory of identification puts more emphasis on the role of the father in the family. A basic assumption of this theory is that a child's learned behavior does not have to be typical of the parent with whom he identifies, but such behavior may be the result of a reciprocal role relationship in which the child and parent participate at various times. There are reciprocal roles which differ for male and female children. Such differential reinforcements as the father carries out in these relationships are re-

sponsible, according to this theory, for the establishment of sex-role learning in the developing child. Parsons considers the father to be the primary transmitter of culturally determined conceptions of masculinity and femininity.

Johnson (33) stresses the importance of fathering when she discusses her interpretation of the Parsonian theory of identification in relation to a number of empirical studies: "We suggest that it is identification with the father, in the sense of internalizing a reciprocal role relationship with the father, which is crucial for producing appropriate sex role orientations in both males and females" (33, p. 319). Especially relevant for the present review are Johnson's remarks about the importance of the father–daughter relationship in personality development:

> The expressive role player is oriented toward the relationships among the actors within a system. He is primarily oriented to the attitudes and feelings of these actors toward each other. . . . The father adds the specifically feminine elements to the female's initial expressiveness by rewarding her, by his appreciative attitude, not simply for being "good" but for being "attractive" (33, p. 320).

C. The Development of Femininity

Feminine development is a process which includes the learning and performance of a complex pattern of behaviors which are consistent with the role expectations of a particular society. A number of studies have added to our information concerning perceptual and cognitive activity involved in feminine development (22, 26, 36). A girl usually seems to develop a feminine self-concept early in life and her sex-role preference and overt behavior often appear related to her view of herself. Typically, definite sex-role expectations are expressed by her parents and are continuously reinforced through subsequent interpersonal relationships. Successive age levels may bring new expectations and demands, but a girl's perception of her sex role at any given age level may help to determine the extent of her particular sex-appropriate and sex-inappropriate activities (26).

It seems relevant at this point to describe briefly what we conceive of as appropriate feminine behavior. Obviously, one has to base any definitions of sex role in relation to a particular society; and subcultural and socioeconomic differences may also be important (12, 13). There has been a marked tendency to define femininity in negative terms and/or as the opposite of masculinity; for instance, stressing passivity and dependency (12, 56). Value judgments are probably involved, to some extent, in most definitions of appropriate sex-role behavior. We believe it is more meaningful to describe feminine behavior in positive terms. A recent study by Vroegh *et al.* (66) suggests that a high degree of femininity in young girls is related to social adjustment, competence, and confidence in her abilities. Other studies (51, 59, 68) have also suggested an association between feminine behavior, adjustment, and confidence in women.

Femininity in social interaction seems to involve expressiveness of warmth and affection and sensitivity to the needs of others. Skill in understanding and communicating feelings and striving to be attractive in appearance also appear relevant. Feminine interests and preferences tend to center around domestic, social, and caretaking activities. Terman and Miles' (64) classic work on the influence of sex differences in personality development offers much relevant discussion of feminine behavior, as does Kagan's (34) excellent review of research related to sex typing.

A fundamental part of the girl's sex-role development seems to be the positive acceptance of herself as a female. The father's particular relationship with his daughter seems very important in her sex-role development. He may foster the establishment of a positive feminine identity by treating her as a female and encouraging her to behave in ways which are considered to be feminine by her society.

Feminine behavior in the girl seems to be much related to how the father defines his role as a male to his daughter and how he differentiates his masculine role from her feminine role. Mussen and Rutherford (45) suggest that "The father's possession of a high degree of masculinity of interests and attitudes and his active encouragement of the girl's participation in appropriate sex-typed activities tend to foster the girl's development of appropriate sex-role preference" (45, p. 603). Thus, whereas the mother behaves in a relatively feminine manner to both her male and female children, if the father differentiates between masculine and feminine roles, his daughter may be more able to establish and maintain a secure sense of femininity. Mussen and Rutherford found that fathers of highly feminine first-grade girls encouraged their daughters more in sex-appropriate activities than did fathers of unfeminine girls. Sears *et al.* (58) reported a significant correlation between girls' femininity and their fathers' expectations of their participation in feminine activities.

Heilbrun (28) studied the content of sex-role-differentiated behavior and concluded that fathers are more proficient than mothers in differentiating sex roles. This researcher states that "fathers are more capable of responding expressively than mothers are of acting instrumentally . . . that fathers systematically vary their sex role as they relate to male and female offspring" (28, p. 796). Participation by the father in a secure and consistent relationship with his daughter, which is emotionally warm, stable, and democratic, seems to provide a highly significant ingredient for feminine development. Such paternal behavior as consistent discipline, for example, seems associated with affiliativeness in young girls (7).

It appears that the more a father participates in constructive interplay with his daughter and the more this interaction involves access for her to learn specific activities defining her feminine role, the more adequate will be her identity. Support of this statement comes from an investigation by Tasch (62, 63). She interviewed fathers of boys and girls in order to learn their conceptions of the paternal role. Such facets of fathering as nurturance and limit setting and father–child activities were studied. The results of this investigation indicated that fathers viewed their daughters as more delicate and sensitive than their sons. Fathers more frequently used physical methods of punishment with their sons than with their daughters. Tasks, too, were differentiated in the home for boys and girls by their fathers. For example, girls ironed and washed clothes, and babysat for siblings; while boys were responsible for taking out the garbage and helping their fathers in certain masculine activities. Aberle and Naegele (1) also report paternal differentiation in expectation and activities as a function of the sex of child considered. Differences in parent–child interactions seem to be both a function of sex of child, as well as sex of parent (53, 54).

Goodenough (22) is another researcher who presented the hypothesis that fathers influence their children's identification more than do mothers because of their differential reinforcements and expectations of sex-typed behavior. This investigator focused upon the influence of the father in terms of the social interests of male and female nursery-school children, and found that the intensity of the fathers' differentiated sex-appropriate behaviors was greater than the mothers'. According to Goodenough, "The evidence suggests that the father has a greater interest in sex differences than the mother, and hence exerts stronger influence in general sex-typing. . . ." (22, p. 321). Of relevance was the finding that there was more paternal stress upon interest in persons for girls than for boys, this interest emerging rather early in terms of social activities (often between two and four years of age). Torgoff and Dreyer (65) also have reported findings which support the importance of the father-daughter relationship in socialization and role orientation. Such findings add sustenance to the views of theorists (33, 49, 71), who stress the significance of the complementary opposite-sex relationship between fathers and daughters.

The implications of the father–daughter relationship with regard to long-term behavior are pointed to in data collected by Winch (69, 70) and White (68). Winch's extensive questionnaire study suggested that the father–daughter relationship was associated with women's courtship patterns in college. Women who were involved in long-term romantic relationships (who appeared near marriage), compared to those who were not, reported closer relationships with their fathers. White studied the parent–child relationships of two groups of women, those pursuing typically feminine roles, such as housewives, and those of women with career interests. White found that the more feminine women tended to show less discrepancy between their self-concepts and -ideals than did career women. The former group was found to be more closely identified with both

parents. However, the career women "tended to come from homes in which the male parent was deceased or in which there was little communication between the girl and her parents" (68, pp. 205–206). In a possibly related study by Levin (39), career women who were unmarried and employed in masculine jobs scored "significantly higher than a comparable group of homemakers (married, with children, and not employed) on a Rorschach measure of degree of the female castration complex" (39, p. 186).

D. Father Absence

The personality development of a child appears much dependent on family milieu. The absence of the father from the home may dramatically upset the dynamics of family life. Aside from economic considerations related to the loss of the father in the family, the mother–child relationship may be adversely affected by the absence of the husband's emotional support.

Considerable research has focused upon the primary effects of this separation on the boy's psychological adjustment (e.g., 13, 46). The specific effects of this absence appear to be much influenced by such factors as the personality of the mother, socioeconomic and subcultural background, and the presence and sex of siblings. However, one may expect that with such factors held constant, the consequences of paternal absence will involve a loss in emotional contacts for the girl, as well as the boy. For example, the daughter's identification may be limited by some imbalance of the mother's influence, such that the daughter receives a less complete view of her sex role (3, 48).

Empirical data supporting the view that father absence can influence the girl's personality development has come from research by Lynn and Sawrey (42), examining the effects of father absence upon Norwegian boys and girls in the second grade. The specific effect of father absence upon the girls in this study consisted of their greater than average dependency upon their mothers. Data from another study (29) suggest that a high degree of dependency on the mother is associated with low peer status for high school girls.

Sears *et al.* (57), on the basis of their findings in projective doll play sessions, report that "there is no indication that the girls are more frustrated when the father is present; on the contrary, his absence is associated with greater aggression, especially self-aggression . . ." (57, p. 240). These writers go on to speculate that such aggressive behavior may be a function of the father-absent girl's conflict with her mother. Heckel (27) reported frequent school maladjustment, excessive sexual interest, and social acting-out behavior in five fatherless preadolescent girls. Such behavior may be a manifestation of intense frustration stemming from unsuccessful attempts to find some adult male figure with whom they can form a meaningful relationship.

Nash (46) notes several studies suggesting that many father-absent children have problems in adjustment, but one difficulty in interpreting most of these studies is that they do not differentiate between boys and girls in data analysis. Father-absent girls often seem to manifest a variety of symptoms which to some degree reflect maladjustment. It appears that these developmental problems are related to a complex interaction of father absence, maternal behavior and preseparation family adjustment.

The growing literature on problems relating to father absence among Negro children has been recently reviewed by Bronfenbrenner (14). There are sociological and psychological data suggesting that many Negro girls (as well as boys) are adversely affected in their social adjustment by father absence. There seems a general lack of interpersonal learning opportunities which are usually associated with the father–child relationship. In addition, Negro girls, in families where the father is absent or ineffectual, develop derogatory attitudes toward males. There is a tendency in lower-class Negro families, and many other lower-class families with somewhat different sociocultural backgrounds, to downgrade males in terms of their seemingly social and economic irresponsibility. These negative attitudes are transmitted by mothers, grandmothers, and other significant females, and unfortunately are often reinforced by observation of, or involvement in, destructive male–female relationships. Such attitudes and experiences seem to contribute to lower-class females' frequent difficulties in interacting with their male relatives, boyfriends, husbands, and children.

We probably would learn much about both effective and ineffective father–child relationships by a careful contemporaneous and historical analysis of different sociocultural patterns. There is a great need for further systematic research to examine the interactive influence of sociocultural and familial variables in personality development.

E. Inadequate and Inappropriate Fathering

Departure in the father-present home from paternal influences that provide family stability and balanced husband–wife complementarity may also make for difficulties in the child's personality development. Problems may result during the child's development from paternal rejection, overdomination, indifference, overindulgence, and/or inconsistent treatment (18, 24, 38, 40, 41).

The importance of the marital relationship upon child development is clearly expressed by Erikson (18): "Children feel the tensions, insecurities, and rages in their parents even if they do not know their causes or witness their most overt manifestations" (18, p. 99). When the environment is experienced in terms of extreme deficits in the father's behavior along with resulting disorganization of the mother's role, the child's personality development may be thwarted. Among the factors which contribute to such deficits in family dynamics is severe marital conflict. Chronic disharmony has been suggested by Baruch and Wilcox (6) to interfere with preschool children's adjustment. It seemed to these investigators that "girls might be more significantly affected by parental tensions than are boys" (6, p. 30), possibly because of their sensitivity and tendency towards intrapunitive behavior.

It appears that the father influences his daughter's personality development in certain direct ways. He may also influence his daughter's personality development indirectly in terms of his relationship with his wife, who acts as a primary model for his daughter in her sex-role development. It seems likely that if the father meets his wife's needs she may, in turn, be able to interact more adequately with her children. Several studies with children (30, 31, 44, 45) have suggested that a warm and nurturant mother–daughter relationship is important in feminine development.

Bartemeier (5) considers the wife's emotional health, self-regard, and capacity for appropriately nurturing her children to be influenced by her husband's attitudes and behavior. Bartemeier believes the father's own history is a significant factor in determining his behavior as a husband and a father. Inadequate fathering may be a reflection of underlying conflicts in the husband which upset his complementary relationship with his wife. Another source of paternal insufficiency may arise from the father's attitudes toward his children as a result of his unresolved problems with his own parents.

The significance of the father's attitudes has been stressed by Peterson *et al.* (50). Studying the family backgrounds of emotionally disturbed children, these investigators found that (a) paternal attitudes were as important as those of the mother in determining maladjustment in their offspring; (b) maladjusted children had experienced the effects of parental emotional disturbance and especially arbitrary discipline by the father; and (c) children with conduct problems had unconcerned and emotionally distant fathers. Such findings are consistent with those of Rubenstein (55) and Hoffman (32), who also discussed the adverse effects of arbitrary power assertion by the father as clashing with childhood autonomy needs.

According to Becker *et al.* (8, 9), conduct problems are generally found in children whose parents show not only arbitrary behavior but who are over-emotional. In some of the cases which they studied, the mother was tense and thwarting, while the father showed inadequate concern with the family. He was found to be a poor enforcer of discipline, particularly of rules established by his wife. Maladjusted and domineering fathers, on the other hand, contributed to shyness and emotional overactivity in their children. This inadequacy of fathering was evident in the husband's lack of an harmonious relationship with his wife, his arbitrary power assertions, and his lack of warmth in dealing with his family.

Poffenberger (52) illustrates further the possible adverse effects of the unaccepting father upon his children by noting that he may directly influence negative self-regard in them. The effects of such an attitude may extend even as far as the outlook of these children toward life in general. Clinical data (60, 67) suggest that fathers who do not accept their daughters' femininity (because they wanted sons and/or are threatened by feminine behavior) can have a very destructive effect on their daughters' personality development.

Other evidence for a connection between inadequate fathering and emotional disorders comes from studies by Sopchak (61) and Lazowick (37). Sopchak (61) studied the effects of poor identification with the father upon college women. He summarizes his results as follows: "Women with tendencies toward abnormality as measured by the MMPI show a lack of identification with their fathers. . . . Masculine women identify with their fathers less than feminine women . . . and identification with the father is more important in producing normal adjustment than is identification with the mother" (61, pp. 164, 165). Lazowick (37) has also studied the influence of inadequate identification with the father and concludes that a high degree of manifest anxiety in undergraduate women is related to the absence of adequate father relations.

A healthy father identification for a daughter seems to us to consist of understanding and empathizing with the father rather than acting masculine or wanting to be masculine like him (as might be the case for the boy). A healthy father identification for a daughter might also include the sharing of certain of the father's values and attitudes as long as these did not interfere with the daughter's development of a feminine self-concept and an expressive mode of social interaction. One possible interpretation and integration of the results of several studies (2, 10, 16, 23, 30, 31, 45) is that when the father plays an active and competent masculine role in the family, his daughter is more likely to imitate his non-sex-typed positive attributes and be more adaptable and less narrow in her behavior repertoire than when he is unmasculine and/or aloof. The probability of the girl's generally imitating the father's masculine behaviors and/or rejecting her femininity seems high in such a situation (i.e., having a masculine competent father who encourages her femininity) *only* if her mother is cold and rejecting or somehow unable to express acceptance, warmth, and nurturance toward her.

Several studies (11, 25, 35, 67) suggest that inappropriate and/or inadequate fathering may be related to the development of homosexuality in females. For instance, Bene (11) reported that female homosexuals felt their fathers were weak and incompetent, and Kaye *et al.* (35) found that fathers of female homosexuals (as compared to control group fathers) tended to be puritanical, exploitive, and feared by their daughters, as well as possessive and infantilizing. Kaye *et al.* also present evidence that suggests that female homosexuality is associated with rejection of femininity early in life. Reviews of case studies of father-absent girls also note many instances of problems in the girls' sexual adjustment (38, 47).

Lidz and Lidz (40) conclude that inadequate fathering is a significant antecedent in the development of schizophrenia; such maladjustment is considered to be associated with a lack of stable paternal involvement in childhood. Research by Hamilton and Wahl (24) revealed that among a population of hospitalized schizophrenic women, almost 75 percent of them experienced some inadequacy of fathering. Baker and Holzworth (4) found that fathers of teenagers in a state mental hospital, compared with fathers of successful adolescents in school, were more likely to have had social histories involving court convictions and excessive drinking.

Lidz *et al.* (41) attempted to specify the nature of insufficient fathering for schizophrenic females. Fathers in severe conflict with their wives, who contradict their wives' decisions, and degrade their wives in front of their daughters, were most notably inadequate in their family relationships. Such men were considered to maintain rigid and unrealistic expectations regarding their wives' conformity to their arbitrary authority. As a result of disappointment in these expectations, such fathers "would like to mould their daughters to fit their needs" (41, p. 128). Such moulding is considered to be more an attempt to win the daughter's allegiance than to seduce her. In conclusion, these researchers state:

In our experience it is the daughter, who sides with the father and seeks his love, who becomes psychotic. She cannot follow the mother in her development and the father's demands are too inconsistent, unrealistic and hostile. In some instances acceptance of the father's tenets would require pathological distortion of reality (40, p. 128).

It thus appears that certain maladjustive tendencies are fostered by distorted expectations and power assertions by the father or his complete passivity. The effects of paternal inadequacy may leave the child generally limited in social experience. Concomitant with limited social experience may be the child's inability to develop fully her interpersonal potential and a narrowing of her perspective regarding her own adequacy as a person.

The available data would seem strongly to warrant attempts to engage fathers in treatment programs if their daughters (as well as their sons) exhibit psychological problems. Techniques of family therapy which include parents and children being observed and treated together seem particularly promising. Fathers' groups and couples' groups may also be excellent vehicles for furthering more positive father–child relationships. Exposure of fathers, and other males who may become fathers and/or be able to play a fathering role to the significance of the father–child relationship through education and the mass media might serve an important preventive community mental health function. Most men seem to want to be good fathers, but many have not had the opportunities to learn about the psychological needs of children and do not seem to be aware of what functions they can perform beyond being providers for their family. If their fathers are absent or hopelessly inadequate, girls (as well as boys) still need opportunities to form meaningful relationships with mature males. Sometimes an older brother, relative, or family friend may serve as an excellent father surrogate. However, it seems crucial for communities to strive to provide manpower sources (both in terms of individuals and organizations) to meet the needs for fathering of many girls (as well as many boys).

F. Research Implications

Hopefully, the ideas and studies reviewed will stimulate further research endeavors. Although there appears to be a considerable amount of data suggesting the importance of the father–daughter relationship, there is much room for methodological refinement and additional studies. Most of the studies mentioned lack adequate procedures for representative subject selection and control groups. Some investigators have relied exclusively on case study and/or retrospective data collection.

Observational process-focused studies of the father–daughter relationship would be helpful as would longitudinal studies assessing changes in the father–daughter relationship as a possible function of developmental stages. Long-term effects of different types of fathering may not be immediately noticeable. Observation of father–daughter and family interaction could take place in clinical, naturalistic, and experimentally devised settings. Such studies could meaningfully complement retrospective-correlational studies.

More careful definition of both relevant independent variables (e.g., degree of both quantitative and qualitative father availability) and dependent variables (e.g., various aspects of sex-role development) should result in more cogent conceptualization, measurement, and data analysis. Studies directed at detecting differences in the fathering of, for instance, neurotics, psychotics, and homosexuals, as well as comparisons of such groups with carefully matched adequately functioning samples, need to be done if we are to delineate specific disturbances in the father–daughter relationships and their effects. Such studies should reveal ways in which fathers can facilitate as well as injure their daughters' psychological functioning. Studies assessing a number of sociocultural, constitutional (e.g., individual differences in temperamental and physique characteristics), cognitive, and familial variables should help put the influence of the father–daughter relationship into a clearer perspective. A reading of critical reviews (e.g., 15, 19) on different areas of child and personality development can contribute to an awareness of relevant variables and possible methodological pitfalls.

Despite the limitations of available research concerning the father–daughter relationship, progress has been made, especially in terms of the growing realization of the general importance of the father's role in female personality development.

G. Summary

The father's role in the family seems to be of great significance in the process of feminine identification and personality adjustment in the female. His influence appears to be expressed in both direct and indirect ways. The relationship which he maintains with his wife affects his children in terms of the balance in parent–child relationships and the emotional climate of the family. Literature cited in this review suggested many ways in which the father's behavior can facilitate or inhibit the girl's personality development. Paternal child-rearing practices, discipline, social attitudes, and personality appear to be important factors. The particular character of the father–daughter relationship appears to affect profoundly feminine development and to have pervasive and lasting effects upon a girl's personality and social adjustment. It is hoped that this review will stimulate further thinking and additional carefully designed research focusing on the father's role in the personality development of the female.

REFERENCES

1. ABERLE, D. F., AND NAEGELE, F. D. Middle class father's occupational role and attitude toward children. *Amer. J. Orthopsychiat.*, 1952, *22*, 366–378.

2. ACKERMAN, N. W. The principle of shared responsibility of child rearing. *Internat. J. Sociol.*, 1957, *12*, 280–291.

3. BACH, G. R. Father fantasies and father typing in father separated children. *Child Devel.*, 1946, *17*, 63–80.

4. BAKER, J. W., & HOLZWORTH, A. Social histories of successful and unsuccessful children. *Child Devel.*, 1961, *32*, 135–149.

5. BARTEMEIER, L. The contribution of the father to the mental health of the family. *Amer. J. Psychiat.*, 1953, *110*, 277–280.

6. BARUCH, D. W., & WILCOX, J. A. A study of sex differences in preschool children's adjustment coexistent with interparental tensions. *J. Genet. Psychol.*, 1944, *61*, 281–303.

7. BAUMRIND, D., & BLACK, A. E. Socialization practices associated with dimensions of competence in preschool boys and girls. *Child Devel.*, 1967, *38*, 291–327.

8. BECKER, W. C., PETERSON, D. R., HELLMER, L. A., SHOEMAKER, D. J., & QUAY, H. C. Factors in parental behavior and personality as related to problem behavior in children. *J. Consult. Psychol.*, 1959, *23*, 107–118.

9. BECKER, W. C., PETERSON, D. R., LURIA, Z., SHOEMAKER, D. S., & HELLMER, L. A. Relations of factors derived from parent-interview ratings to behavior problems of five-year-olds. *Child Devel.*, 1962, *33*, 509–535.

10. BEIER, E. G., & RATZEBURG, F. The parental identifications of male and female college students. *J. Abn. & Soc. Psychol.*, 1953, *48*, 569–572.

11. BENE, E. On the genesis of female homosexuality. *Brit. J. Psychiat.*, 1965, *3*, 815–821.

12. BIELIAUSKAS, V. J. Recent advances in the psychology of masculinity and femininity. *J. of Psychol.*, 1965, *60*, 255–263.

13. BILLER, H. B., & BORSTELMANN, L. J. Masculine development: An integrative review. *Merrill-Palmer Quart.*, 1967, *13*, 253–294.

14. BRONFENBRENNER, U. The psychological cost of equality and quality in education. *Child Devel.*, 1967, *38*, 909–925.

15. CALDWELL, B. M. The effects of infant care. In M. L. Hoffman & L. W. Hoffman (Eds.), *Review of Child Development Research: I.* New York: Russell Sage Found., 1964. Pp. 9–87.

16. CARPENTER, P., & EISENBERG, P. Some relations between family background and personality. *J. of Psychol.*, 1935, *6*, 115–136.

17. DEUTSCH, H. *The Psychology of Women* (vol. 1). New York: Grune & Stratton, 1944.

18. ERIKSON, E. H. Identity and the life cycle. *Psychol. Iss.*, 1959, *1*, Whole No. 1.

19. FRANK, G. H. The role of the family in the development of psychopathology. *Psychol. Bull.*, 1965, *64*, 191–205.

20. FREUD, S. The passing of the Oedipus complex. In *Coll. Papers* (vol. 2). London, England: Hogarth Press, 1924.

21. ———. *New Introductory Lectures in Psychoanalysis.* New York: Norton, 1933.

22. GOODENOUGH, E. W. Interest in persons as an aspect of sex differences in the early years. *Genet. Psychol. Monog.*, 1957, *55*, 287–323.

23. GRAY, S. W. Perceived similarity to parents and adjustment. *Child Devel.*, 1959, *30*, 91–107.

24. HAMILTON, D. M., & WAHL, J. H. The hospital treatment of dementia praecox. *Amer. J. Psychiat.*, 1948, *105*, 346–352.

25. HAMILTON, G. V. *A Research in Marriage.* New York: Boni, 1929.

26. HARTLEY, R. E. Sex role identification: A symposium. A developmental view of female sex role definition and identification. *Merrill-Palmer Quart.*, 1964, *10*, 3–16.

27. HECKEL, R. V. The effects of fatherlessness on the preadolescent female. *Ment. Hyg.*, 1963, *47*, 69–73.

28. HEILBRUN, A. B. An empirical test of the modeling theory of sex-role learning. *Child Devel.*, 1965, *36*, 789–799.

29. HELPER, M. M. Learning theory and the self concept. *J. Abn. & Soc. Psychol.*, 1955, *51*, 184–194.

30. HETHERINGTON, E. M. A developmental study of the effects of sex of the dominant parent on sex-role preference, identification, and imitation in children. *J. Personal. & Soc. Psychol.*, 1965, *2*, 188–194.

31. HETHERINGTON, E. M., & FRANKS, G. Effects of parental dominance, warmth, and conflict on imitation in children. *J. Personal. & Soc. Psychol.*, 1967, *6*, 119–125.

32. HOFFMAN, M. L. Power assertion by the parent and its impact on the child. *Child Devel.*, 1960, *31*, 129–143.

33. JOHNSON, M. M. Sex-role learning in the nuclear family. *Child Devel.*, 1963, *34*, 319–333.

34. KAGAN, J. Acquisition and significance of sex-typing and sex-role identity. In M. L. Hoffman & L. W. Hoffman (Eds.), *Review of Child Development Research: I.* New York: Russell Sage Found., 1964, Pp. 137–167.

35. KAYE, H. E., *et al.* Homosexuality in women. *Arch. Gen. Psychiat.*, 1967, *17*, 626–634.

36. KOHLBERG, L., & ZIGLER, E. The impact of cognitive maturity on the development of sex-role attitudes in the years 4–8. *Genet. Psychol. Monog.*, 1966, *75*, 89–165.

37. LAZOWICK, L. M. On the nature of identification. *J. Abn. & Soc. Psychol.*, 1955, *51*, 175–183.

38. LEONARD, M. R. Fathers and daughters. *Internat. J. Psychoanal.*, 1966, *47*, 325–333.

39. LEVIN, R. B. An empirical test of the female

castration complex. *J. Abn. Psychol.,* 1966, *71,* 181–188.

40. LIDZ, R. W., & LIDZ, T. The family environment of schizophrenic patients. *Amer. J. Psychiat.,* 1949, *106,* 332.

41. LIDZ, T., PARKER, N., & CORNELISON, A. R. The role of the father in the family environment of the schizophrenic patient. *Amer. J. Psychiat.,* 1956, *113,* 126–132.

42. LYNN, D. B., & SAWREY, W. L. The effects of father absence on Norwegian boys and girls. *J. Abn. & Soc. Psychol.,* 1959, *59,* 258–262.

43. MOWRER, O. H. Identification: A link between learning theory and psychotherapy. In *Learning Theory and Personality Dynamics.* New York: Ronald Press, 1950, Pp. 573–516.

44. MUSSEN, P. H., & PARKER, A. L. Mother nurturance and girls' incidental imitative learning. *J. Personal & Soc. Psychol.,* 1965, *2,* 94–97.

45. MUSSEN, P., & RUTHERFORD, E. Parent–child relations and parental personality in relation to young children's sex role preferences. *Child Devel.,* 1963, *34,* 589–607.

46. NASH, J. The father in contemporary culture and current psychological literature. *Child Devel.,* 1965, *56,* 261–297.

47. NEUBAUER, P. B. The one-parent child and his oedipal development. *Psychoanal. Stud. Child.,* 1960, *15,* 286–309.

48. OSTROVSKY, E. S. *Children Without Men.* New York: Collier Books, 1962.

49. PARSONS, T. Family structure and the socialization of the child. In T. Parsons & R. F. Bales (Eds.), *Family, Socialization, and Interaction Process.* Glencoe, Ill.: Free Press, 1955. Pp. 35–131.

50. PETERSON, D. R., BECKER, W. C., HELLMER, L. A., SHOEMAKER, D. J. Parental attitudes and child adjustment. *Child Devel.,* 1959, *30,* 119–130.

51. PINTNER, R., & FORTANO, G. Some measures of dominance in college women. *J. Soc. Psychol.,* 1944, *19,* 303–315.

52. POFFENBERGER, T. A. A research note on father–child relations and father viewed as a negative figure. *Child Devel.,* 1959, *30,* 489–492.

53. ROSENBERG, B. G., & SUTTON-SMITH, B. Family interaction effects on masculinity–femininity. *J. Personal & Soc. Psychol.,* 1968, *8,* 117–120.

54. ROTHBART, M. K., & MACCOBY, E. E. Parents' differential reactions to sons and daughters. *J. Personal & Soc. Psychol.,* 1966, *4,* 237–243.

55. RUBENSTEIN, B. O. Some observations regarding the role of fathers in child psychology. *Bull. Menninger Clin.,* 1957, *21,* 16–27.

56. SALZMAN, L. Psychology of the female—A new look. *Arch. Gen. Psychiat.,* 1967, *17,* 195–203.

57. SEARS, R. R., PINTLER, M., & SEARS, P. Effect of father separation on preschool children's doll play aggression. *Child Devel.,* 1946, *17,* 219–243.

58. SEARS, R. R., RAU, L., & ALPERT, R. *Identification and Child Rearing.* Stanford, Calif.: Stanford Univ. Press, 1965.

59. SEWARD, G. H. Cultural conflict and the feminine role: An experimental study. *J. Soc. Psychol.,* 1945, *22,* 177–194.

60. ————. *Sex and the Social Order.* New York: McGraw-Hill, 1946.

61. SOPCHAK, A. L. Parental "identification" and "tendency toward disorders" as measured by the MMPI. *J. Abn. & Soc. Psychol.,* 1952, *47,* 159–165.

62. TASCH, R. J. The role of the father in the family. *J. Exper. Educ.,* 1952, *20,* 319–361.

63. ————. Interpersonal perceptions of fathers and mothers. *J. Genet. Psychol.,* 1955, *87,* 59–65.

64. TERMAN, L. M., & MILES, C. C. *Sex and Personality.* New York: McGraw-Hill, 1936.

65. TORGOFF, I., & DREYER, A. S. Achievement inducing and independence granting–synergistic parental role components: Relation to daughter's "parental" role orientation and level of aspiration. *Amer. Psychol.,* 1961, *16,* 345 (Abst.).

66. VROEGH, K., JENKINS, N., BLACK, M., & HANDRICH, M. Discriminant analyses of preschool masculinity and femininity. *Multivar. Behav. Res.,* 1967, *2,* 299–313.

67. WEST, D. J. *Homosexuality.* Chicago, Ill.: Aldine, 1968.

68. WHITE, B. The relationship of self-concept and parental identification to women's vocational interests. *J. Counsel. Psychol.,* 1959, *6,* 202–206.

69. WINCH, R. F. Some data bearing and the Oedipus hypothesis. *J. Abn. & Soc. Psychol.,* 1950, *45,* 481–489.

70. ————. Further data and observations on the Oedipus hypothesis: The consequence of an inadequate hypothesis. *Amer. Soc. Rev.,* 1951, *16,* 784–795.

71. WRIGHT, B., & TUSKA, S. The nature and origin of feeling feminine. *Brit. J. Soc. Psychol.,* 1966, *5,* 140–149.

Democratic Parent-Youth Relationships in Cross-National Perspective

GLEN H. ELDER, JR.

A review of data on parental authority in five nations discloses that certain sociocultural similarities and differences among the nations are reflected in parents' relationships to their children. In all but one country, there was a general trend toward more democratic parent–child relations.

An increase in the belief that youth should have a part in making decisions relevant to their lives and a correlated decline in traditional forms of parental authority are significant aspects of social change in the 20th century. These trends appear at least on a rudimentary level in all major regions of the world where the forces of change are at work.[1] Despite resistance from traditional structures, the belief in freedom of choice for youth is spreading rapidly, for it offers them new opportunities[2] and it flourishes in the fertile ground created by the growth of urban-industrial centers, formal systems of education and the mass media. In some areas these changes in family relations are promoted by political regimes—as in Communist China, where an attempt is being made to shift authority from individuals, especially parents, to groups composed of persons similar in age.[3]

In societal change toward an urban-industrial state, the traditional credibility and legitimacy of parental beliefs and practices become vulnerable to the actions of other socialization agents, among which schools and youth groups are especially prominent. The influence of youth groups in socialization is correlated with the formalization of

Research support from the Institute of International Studies, University of California (Berkeley), and the Institute for Research in Social Science at the University of North Carolina is gratefully acknowledged.

[1] William Goode, *World Revolution and Family Patterns* (New York: The Free Press of Glencoe, 1963); John M. Mogey, "A Century of Declining Paternal Authority," *Marriage and Family Living, 19* (Aug., 1957), pp. 234–239; René König, "Family and Authority: The German Father in 1955." *Sociological Review, 5* (July, 1957), pp. 107–125; Robert O. Blood, *Love Match and Arranged Marriages: A Tokyo–Detroit Comparison* (New York: The Free Press of Glencoe, 1967); and C. K. Yang, *The Chinese Family in the Communist Revolution* (Cambridge, Mass.: Harvard University Press, 1959).

[2] Goode, *World Revolution*, p. 369.

[3] Richard H. Solomon, "Communist Patterns and the Chinese Revolution," paper read at the 1967 annual meeting of American Political Science Association, Pick-Congress Hotel, Chicago, September 5–9.

From G. H. Elder, Jr., Democratic parent–youth relations in cross-national perspective. Reprinted from the *Social Science Quarterly, 49* (September 1968), 216–228, by permission of publisher and author.

the educational system, the extension of the preparatory period for youth, and the number of years between the time youth leave their parents and the time they assume full status in families of procreation.[4] Associated with these often diverse sources of influence on youth are the likelihood of conflicting norms between the generations, a competition for the time and loyalty of youth and a lack of shared norms on socialization among parents.[5] Such conditions, coupled with conflict between parents and youth on the issue of freedom of choice, serve to undermine traditional family constraints. In some cases political leaders of victorious revolutions have significantly undermined the authority of the parental generation by giving youth new and better opportunities to serve their countries and themselves. In the Near East, for instance, "the rhetoric of revolution and the ideologies of governments that come to power through it are studded with tributes to youth and criticism of both 'old politicians' and 'old ways'."[6]

The objective of this paper is to assess secular trends in perceived parent–youth patterns since the early 1900's in a secondary analysis of data collected from approximately 1,000 men and women over 17 years old in each of five nations: the United States, West Germany, Great Britain, Italy, and Mexico. These data were originally collected for a study of the antecedents and correlates of political behavior.[7] Though variations in authority patterns by age groups could be partly an indication of age differences in recall of family experiences during the pre-adult years, as well as secular trends, this interpretation is not supported by the subsequent analysis.

Hierarchical relations between parents and youth which provide the latter with little influence in making decisions of personal significance are generally most prevalent among families characterized by one or more of the following attributes: rural residence, working-class background and Catholic religious affiliation.[8] In these families, the adult-centered obedience orientation of parents toward the young portrays an emphasis on external as against internal control, on obedience to authority in contrast to the development of responsible self-direction. Such authority, rooted in the traditional meanings associated with age differences between the generations, is commonly related to a distinctive concept of the child's nature, which is the reciprocal of qualities ascribed to elders. Presumed to lack the judgment, understanding and feelings of an adult, the child is considered irresponsible and untrustworthy. These expectations may not be altered toward adult standards until the child reaches adolescence or until he moves out on his own. Such concepts tend to have a circular, self-reinforcing effect, for they elicit behavior from children which confirms parental expectations. From a study of family patterns in Rangoon, Burma, Hitson describes the Burmese family as a group designed to serve the desires of the father; unquestioned obedience to his wishes is expected from the mother and, especially, from the children.[9] The latter are not considered fully human and thus do not receive the human consideration given to adults. "It is assumed that children will not figure things out for themselves. It is felt that

[4]S. N. Eisenstadt, *From Generation to Generation: Age Groups and the Social Structure* (New York: The Free Press of Glencoe, 1956), p. 177.

[5]Kingsley Davis, "The Sociology of Parent–Youth Conflict," *American Sociological Review, 5* (Aug., (Aug., 1940), pp. 523–535.

[6]Morroe Berger, *The Arab World Today* (London: Weidenfeld and Nicholson, 1962), p. 312.

[7]Gabriel Almond and Sydney Verba, *The Civic Culture* (Princeton, N.J.: Princeton University Press, 1963). I am indebted to the Survey Research Center at the University of California (Berkeley) for the opportunity to analyze these data.

[8]Elizabeth Douvan and Joseph Adelson, *The Adolescent Experience* (New York: John Wiley & Sons, Inc., 1966), p. 316; Leonard J. Pearlin and Melvin L. Kohn, "Social Class, Occupation, and Parental Values: A Cross-National Study," *American Sociological Review, 31,* (Aug., 1966), pp. 466–479; Gerhard Lenski, *The Religious Factor* (New York: Random House, Inc., 1961), Ch. 5; David C. McClelland, *et al.,* "Religious and Other Sources of Parental Attitudes Toward Independence Training," in David C. McClelland, (ed.), *Studies in Motivation* (New York: Appleton-Century-Crofts, Inc., 1955), pp. 389–397; and Urie Bronfenbrenner, "Socialization and Social Class through Time and Space," in Eleanor E. Maccoby, Theodore M. Newcomb and Eugene E. Hartley, (eds.), *Readings in Social Psychology* (New York: Henry Holt, and Company, Inc., 1958), pp. 400–434.

[9]Hazel Marie Hitson, "Family Patterns and Paranoidal Personality Structure in Boston and Burma," unpublished Ph.D. dissertation, Radcliffe College, 1959.

they have to be taught to do everything. It is said that without being told, children will know only how to play and eat."[10] These expectations are generally fulfilled in the behavior of the children.

> Children say that if their parents do not tell them to do anything, they play. They say they do not know why they always wait to be told what to do but they do. . . . It is expected that children will carry out orders given, but that, in the parents' absence, they cannot be trusted in this until girls are eleven, twelve, or thirteen years old and until boys are thirteen, fourteen, or fifteen years old. There is no suggestion that children should anticipate the wishes of their parents by going ahead and doing things without being told.[11]

Elements of this conception of children and its relation to traditional paternal authority are especially evident in rural Mexican, Italian, Puerto Rican and Javanese families.[12]

Accordingly, it was expected that the participation of youth in making decisions would be less prevalent in Mexico and Italy than in other more urbanized and industrialized nations. A review of census statistics shows that most of the population of Mexico and nearly 80 percent of most prov-

inces in southern Italy are rural, in contrast to the largely urban nations of the United States, West Germany and Great Britain. With regard to religion, two of the nations, Italy and Mexico, are almost totally Catholic; the population of West Germany is equally divided between Protestants and Catholics; and the two English-speaking nations are predominantly Protestant. Thus, in Mexico and Italy, Catholicism, agrarianism and a strong male orientation in the culture converge to provide a context especially favorable to parental dominance. For example, a recent comparison of parental treatment received by Mexican and American students found that the Mexican mother was more often viewed as strict, angry when administering discipline, prohibiting disagreements and easily irritated.[13] American mothers were more often characterized as fair, close and supportive. While the Mexican father was more frequently perceived as stern, strict, hard and critical than his American counterpart, he was also more often viewed as understanding, fair and close. Since this affection is expressed in a hierarchical relationship, it does not imply an informal, equalitarian relationship such as may be found in the American family. As might be expected, the combination of strong, unyielding authority and nurturance in the behavior of Mexican parents appears to foster emotional dependence on parents and unquestioned acceptance of parental authority.

Although differences in authority patterns may be negligible at present between the three urban nations, available evidence suggests that democratic parent–youth relations are generally more prevalent in the United States and Great Britain than in West Germany. However, up to the postwar years, English and German families appear to have been more obedience-oriented and adult-

---

[10]*Ibid.*, p. 122.

[11]*Ibid.*

[12]A survey of the limited research on the middle-class Mexican family is provided by Noel F. McGinn, "Marriage and Family in Middle-Class Mexico," *Journal of Marriage and the Family, 28* (Aug., 1966), pp. 305–313. See also Oscar Lewis' series of studies: *Five Families* (New York: Basic Books, 1958); *Life in a Mexican Village: Tepotzlan Restudied* (Urbana: University of Illinois Press, 1963); *The Children of Sanchez* (New York: Random House, Inc., 1961). There appears to be considerable similarity between the Mexican family and the Brazilian family described by Bernard Rosen in "Socialization and Achievement Motivation in Brazil," *American Sociological Review, 27* (Oct., 1962), pp. 612–624. Also relevant to Mexican family patterns is William Madsen's ethnographic study of a Mexican-American community in Texas, *The Mexican-Americans of South Texas* (New York: Holt, Rinehart and Winston, Inc., 1964). Studies of the Italo-American family and of peasant families in southern Italy portray the father as highly domineering over his wife and children. These are cited in Fred L. Strodtbeck, "Family Interaction, Values and Achievement," in David C. McClelland, Alfred Bald-

win, Urie Bronfenbrenner and Fred Strodtbeck, *Talent and Society* (Princeton, N. J.: D. Van Nostrand Company, Inc., 1957), pp. 135–194, and in Herbert J. Gans, *The Urban Villagers* (New York: The Free Press of Glencoe, 1962), Ch. 3. A description of child-rearing in a traditional village in Puerto Rico is provided by David Landy, *Tropical Childhood* (Chapel Hill: The University of North Carolina Press, 1959). On Javanese socialization, see Hildred Geertze, *The Javanese Family* (New York: The Free Press of Glencoe, 1961).

[13]McGinn, *op. cit., pp.* 309–310.

centered in child-rearing than American families of comparable status.[14]

Considering the social, technological and cultural differences among the five nations,[15] it was assumed that the greatest increase in the prevalence of democratic parent–youth relations occurred in the three urban nations followed by Italy and then Mexico. Forces promoting social change generally emanate from urban centers where technology, education and communication systems are most developed. Thus, one probable source of change toward democratic family patterns would be the urbanization of a society: the movement of rural families to the city and the influence of urban-industrial areas on the hinterland. During the last 50 years relatively uniform urbanization was clearly more characteristic of the United States and Great Britain than of Italy and especially of Mexico. Since receptivity to trends in family relations is associated with increased use of mass media, increased education and higher income, a secular trend toward democratic parent–youth relations was expected to be more pronounced among the middle-class than among working-class families.

[14]See Don W. Rapp, "Child rearing attitudes of mothers in Germany and the United States," *Child Development*, 32 (Dec., 1961), pp. 669–678; and Edward C. Devereaux, Jr., "Children of Democracy: On the Consequences for Children of Varying Patterns of Family Authority in the United States and West Germany," summary of a paper presented to the 7th International Seminars on Family Research, Washington, D. C., September, 1962. Similar cross-national differences appear in the relative preference for authority relations between German and American youth immediately after World War II, as reported by Donald V. McGranahan, "A Comparison of Social Attitudes among American and German Youth," *Journal of Abnormal and Social Psychology*, 41 (July, 1946), pp. 245–257. Differences in the prevalence of democratic patterns in American and English families seem likely to be small, although one study found that obedience was more often preferred as a quality in children by English respondents (see Maurice L. Farber, "English and American Values in the Socialization Process," *Journal of Psychology*, 36 [Oct., 1953], p. 245).

[15]For Italy and Mexico, see Margaret Carlyle, *The Awakening of Southern Italy* (New York: Oxford University Press, 1962); Frank Brandenburg, *The Making of Modern Mexico* (New York: Prentice-Hall, Inc., 1964); Charles Erasmus, *Man Takes Control: Cultural Development and American Aid* (Minneapolis: University of Minnesota Press, 1961); and Frederick Harbison and Charles H. Myers, *Education, Manpower, and Economic Growth* (New York: McGraw-Hill Publishing Company, Inc., 1964).

A trend toward family patterns in which children have a role in making decisions relevant to their lives has both developmental and societal significance.[16] During the adolescent years, the opportunity to explore and rehearse current and future roles, to test and evaluate ideas independently and to develop self-confidence as well as skills in independent problem solving provides a socializing experience that is vital to the development of competence and self-reliance. The effective exercise of citizenship responsibilities in a society that is not totalitarian grows out of the prior experience in independent decision-making and problem-solving in the family and school. Moreover, a sense of mastery and self-reliance are instrumental in the learning process, facilitating achievement behavior and making possible effective adaptation to social change. Altogether these qualities represent valuable human resources for modern and developing democracies.

Sample and Methods

The samples in each of the five countries are stratified, multi-stage, probability samples; however, the institutes that designed and executed the surveys varied substantially in the techniques employed and in their field experiences. Though each sample was originally intended to be a representative cross section of the national population, this objective was clearly not achieved in Mexico. In the other four nations, only a rough approximation was realized. Due to cost and technical difficulties, the Mexican sample was drawn from a population of persons living in urban areas of 10,000 or more people. Furthermore, it was necessary to weight the interviews obtained in Mexico City by a factor of 2.5 in order to make this urban stratum of the sample equivalent to its proportion in the national population. These conditions, as well as the high mortality rate in obtaining interviews at assigned addresses (40 percent), seriously weaken any cross-national comparisons between Mexico and the other four na-

[16]Almond and Verba, *The Civic Culture*; David C. McClelland, *The Achieving Society* (Princeton, N.J.: D. Van Nostrand Company, Inc., 1961); and Everett E. Hagan, *On the Theory of Social Change* (Homewood, Ill.: The Dorsey Press, Inc., 1962).

tions. Exclusion of the rural population tends to yield, in effect, an under-estimation of the actual differences between Mexico and the other nations. One indication of the quality of the other four samples is shown by the non-completion rate in interviewing: Germany, 26 percent; Italy, 26 percent; Great Britain, 41 percent; and the United States, 17 percent. In order to remove the effects of race from the analysis, non-white respondents were deleted from the United States sample.

A measure of parental control was constructed from two highly interrelated items (average Gamma coefficient for the five samples is .58) which indicate the respondent's involvement in decision-making at the age of 16 and the extent to which his parents were authoritarian in their control: (1) "As you were growing up, let's say when you were around 16, how much influence do you remember having in family decisions affecting yourself? Did you have much influence, some, or none at all?" "Much influence" was scored as 2; "some," as 1; "none at all," as 0; other and "don't know" responses were not scored. (2) "At around the same time, if a decision were made that you didn't like, did you feel free to complain?" "Felt free" was scored as 2; "felt a little uneasy," as 1; "it was better not to complain," as 0; other and "don't know" were not scored. Scores on the two items were totaled to form the index. In order to obtain a score on all respondents, it was necessary to devise a method for scoring the small number who responded

"other" or "don't know" on the two items. If any subjects in this residual group responded on one item but not on the other, they were scored on the single item. The remainder were classified as having some influence if they indicated that their parents yielded at times to their requests, or if they protested family decisions. Each of these items was highly correlated with the index. Due to the multi-variate nature of the analysis and the relatively small number of cases in each nation, the index was dichotomized with total scores of 0, 1 and 2 representing *authoritarian* control or parental dominance and scores of 3 and 4, a *democratic* type of relationship.

In what follows we shall first compare national trends in democratic parent–youth relations and then assess variations in these secular trends by residence and by social class.

Findings

SECULAR TRENDS IN DEMOCRATIC PARENT–YOUTH RELATIONS BY NATIONS

The percentage of persons who described relations with their parents as democratic during adolescence is shown in Table 1 for each of the five nations. The time span covers approximately 40 years, from persons who were adolescents before World War I to those who reached this age in the 1950's.

Table 1. Percentage Reporting Democratic Parent-Youth Relations by Age, Year at 16, and Nation

Nation	Age and Year at Age 16[a]						
	18-25 (1950-1957)	26-30 (1945-1950)	31-35 (1940-1945)	36-40 (1936-1940)	41-50 (1925-1935)	51-60 (1916-1925)	61+ Before 1916
United States	77(104)	71(77)	63(79)	58(88)	56(153)	48(157)	40(223)
Great Britain	69(82)	68(95)	61(112)	60(139)	58(195)	47(173)	37(169)
West Germany	69(115)	49(80)	47(98)	35(115)	41(177)	34(182)	26(187)
Italy	48(162)	40(121)	39(112)	34(133)	34(168)	33(166)	28(134)
Mexico	31(234)	27(217)	37(177)	34(175)	33(215)	31(172)	26(102)

[a]Total number of cases are given in parentheses.

Democratic parent–youth relations became increasingly more common, except in Mexico, between 1916 and the 1950's. The largest differences between nations occur as predicted between the highly urban-industrial nations with large proportions of Protestants—the United States, Great Britain and West Germany—and the relatively more agrarian, Catholic nations—Italy and Mexico. Not only is the upward trend in the prevalence of democratic patterns less pronounced in Italy and Mexico, but the cross-national comparisons by each group (except 61 years and over) show this type of relationship to be consistently less common in these two nations.

A comparison of persons born before 1900 with those born in the latter part of the 1930's provides a summary of these cross-national differences. The greatest absolute percentage increase in democratic parent–youth patterns appears among Germans (43 percent); this trend is next greatest in the United States (37 percent), then Great Britain (32 percent) and Italy (20 percent), with Mexico (5 percent) showing relatively little consistent change. An examination of relative percentage gain (the percent gain as a proportion of total possible gain) indicates no change in the ordering of the five nations. These trends were similar among both males and females.

The earliest evidence of a decrease in parental dominance appears among the British and Americans born shortly after the turn of the century. Nearly half of those born between 1900 and 1909 indicate that they were permitted considerable freedom to make their own decisions during adolescence. This marked increase in the prevalence of democratic parent–youth relations appears in substantially younger age groups in West Germany. The secular trends in Germany and Italy are suggestive, since the greatest percentage of increase in democratic patterns occurs among post-war adolescents. The data shown in Table 1 tentatively suggest that German youth born just prior to the war were less likely to be dominated by parents than were youth who were born earlier. This may have been due in part to an increase in the prevalence of father-absent households during and after World War II. The greatest change in democratic patterns among Italian respondents likewise occured in the post-war adolescent generation.

Since parent–youth relations in the German family between the two world wars were described as democratic by only one-third of the respondents who were adolescents during these years, it appears that authoritarian parent–youth relations were relatively common in Germany during this period of history, especially when a comparison is made with the United States and the United Kingdom. Prevalent authoritarian parent–child relations in Germany were also noted during these years by Eckstein who, in discussing causes of the instability of the Weimar Republic, claims that this democratic political system was

superimposed upon a society pervaded by authoritarian relationships and obsessed with authoritarianism—German family life, German schools, and German business firms were all exceedingly authoritarian. German families were dominated, more often than not, by tyrannical husbands and fathers, German schools by tyrannical teachers, German firms by tyrannical bosses.[17]

In this period German adolescents were indeed much less likely than their American counterparts to have participated in school discussions and debates (13 vs. 47 percent), and to have had the chance to discuss unfair treatment or disagreements with their teachers (32 vs. 48 percent).[18] On these aspects of adolescent participation and decision-making in school, there was considerable resemblance between Germany and the two Catholic nations in the years between the ends of World Wars I and II. According to these data, the post–World War II years of reconstruction, especially after 1950, brought greater participational democracy to the German classroom. To a lesser extent, this change also occurred in Italy.

Despite considerable social and economic change in Mexico after 1910, hierarchical relations between parents and youth appear to have remained relatively stable; in most age groups

[17]Harry Eckstein, *A Theory of Social Democracy* (Princeton, N.J.: Princeton University Press, 1961), pp. 17–18.
[18]Almond and Verba, *The Civic Culture*, p. 339.

close to 70 per cent of the Mexicans reported parental dominance. Consistent with this finding is the conclusion from a recent survey of research on middle-class Mexican families that changes in "traditional patterns have been slow. Mexico is just now becoming an industrialized nation, and the effects of changes in technology have still to be fully felt."[19] Generally, the Mexican father is still the supreme authority over his wife and children.

In all of the nations except Mexico, the differential trends toward an increasing involvement of youth in decision-making are generally consistent with known societal differences in the degree and form of social change and with the presumed effects of historical events which impinge on the family, such as wars. The pattern of these societal differences suggest that age variations in the ability to recall early family relations accurately is not a major source of error in the results. However, to the extent such variations did occur, one would expect them to be relatively uniform across the five samples.

INTRA-NATIONAL VARIATIONS ON TRENDS IN DEMOCRATIC PATTERNS

Although only the highly urban-industrial nations—the United States, Great Britain and West Germany—show a substantial upward trend in democratic parent–youth relations across age groups, our nationwide perspective may have obscured significant variations in authority trends in Italy, owing to the contrasting social and economic conditions in the north and south. The north, above Rome, is largely urban and prosperous, whereas much of the southern half is rural and impoverished.[20] Though great effort has been made to industrialize the southern provinces, the gains which have been achieved have occurred mainly in the area between Rome and Naples; the foot of Italy (the provinces of Lucania, Calabria, etc.) remains largely agrarian, the landholdings small and relatively unproductive. These regional differences led us to expect greater change in the

prevalence of democratic parent–youth relations in the north than in the south. A comparison of persons 30 years or younger with persons over 50 years of age in two regional groups, defined by birthplace and current residence in the north versus south, did show a greater percentage of increase in democratic patterns in the north than in the south (a difference of 12 percent).

While the usual socioeconomic differentials between urban and rural families, and the fact that rural families lag behind urban families in income and education, would lead us to expect some residential difference in parent–youth patterns in all five nations, the available data on rural–urban residence were not sufficiently precise to permit this analysis, owing to sampling irregularities and the general questions on residence asked in the interviews.

It was assumed that the autonomy of youth in personal decision-making would be associated with social class in both rural and urban areas, with the greatest change toward democratic patterns occurring among persons from middle–class families. In order to obtain a measure of social class, it was necessary to use adult social status since no childhood indexes were available.[21] For the most part, the error involved in this substitution appears to reduce rather than increase the chances of confirming our expectations. If upwardly mobile persons were more likely to have experienced democratic parent–youth relations than downwardly mobile persons, this fact would

[21]The occupation of the respondent or the spouse (if the respondent was female) was used as an indicator of social class. Middle class and working class are indexed by non-manual and manual occupations, respectively. Interviewees who reported farm occupations or who did not report an occupation were classified according to the interviewer's fourpoint rating of social class. Ratings of 1 or 2 were defined as middle-class, 3 or 4 as working-class. Each interviewer was provided with two basic instructions concerning judgments of a respondent's economic level. The respondent was to be classified according to his economic status in the community or area in which he resided. An attempt was made to standardize the proportions of respondents in each area rated one, two, three and four. The one's and two's were equal to the top 16 percent of the community; the three's, the middle 52 percent of the population; and the bottom third were defined as four's. The most common criteria employed in the classification of economic level were housing, occupation, family status and size, income, and comforts and luxuries.

[19]McGinn, *op. cit.,* p. 313.
[20]Carlyle, *The Awakening of Southern Italy.*

minimize age trends in such patterns among members of the working class, if we assume that mobility prospects increased along with educational opportunities during the past 40 years. Comparisons by social class were made in the three nations where democratic patterns increased substantially by age group.

In each of the nations, persons from the middle class were more likely to have had the opportunity to make their own decisions than persons of working-class status, although, contrary to our expectations, the upward trend toward democratic relations is slightly more pronounced in the working class than in the middle class among Americans and Germans. Comparisons within similar age and class groups show that moderate differences remain between the United States and Great Britain, on the one hand, and Germany, on the other, in the prevalence of democratic relations between parents and youth.

Is some of this difference a consequence of the relatively larger proportion of Catholic families in West Germany than in either the United States or Great Britain? The authority of parents, and especially of the father, is firmly supported by Catholic teachings, and, at least in the United States, Catholic parents tend to exercise greater control over their children than Protestant parents of comparable status.[22] Thus, to some extent, the prevalence of authoritarian control in the adolescent experiences of Italians and Mexicans may be due to the strength of the Catholic Church in these countries. An analysis of Protestant–Catholic differences in parent–youth patterns within residence, social class and age groups was possible only among urban-born Americans and Germans. The results, however, showed no consistent difference in the parent–youth relations of Protestant and Catholic persons similar in age and social class. On the other hand, democratic relations remained more prevalent in the experiences of Americans than of Germans with residence, class, religious affiliation and age controlled (an average percentage of difference of 11). Assuming that the items on parent–youth relations possessed similar meaning for persons in the two samples, it appears that cross-national differences between the United States and West Germany are relatively small, especially among the younger generation.

[22]See footnote 9.

Table 2. Percentage Reporting Democratic Parent-Youth Relations by Age, Year at Age 16, Social Class, and Nation

| Nation | Social Class | Age and Year at Age 16[a] | | | Percentage Difference (Youngest minus oldest age group) |
		18-30 (1935-1957)	31-50 (1925-1945)	51+ (1925 or earlier)	
United States	Middle	77(84)	61(149)	50(145)	27
	Working	71(98)	50(171)	37(219)	34
Great Britain	Middle	78(55)	67(131)	50(108)	28
	Working	64(122)	54(105)	38(234)	26
West Germany	Middle	65(66)	55(129)	41(108)	24
	Working	56(129)	32(262)	26(262)	30

[a]Total number of cases are given in parentheses.

Summary and Conclusions

From the data on parental authority in five nations, a pronounced upward secular trend toward democratic parent–youth relations over the past 40 years appears in the urbanized societies of the United States, Great Britain and West Germany. The gradient is flatter among Italians, while no consistent change toward democratic relations was evident in Mexico. Within specific time periods, the five nations are generally in the same ordinal position on the prevalence of democratic parent–youth relations. The post-war period in Germany and Italy seems to have brought considerable change toward democratic relations in the family, as viewed through a comparison of the parent–youth relations experienced by persons who were born before and after 1940. In the three most urban nations, the secular trend varied meaningfully by rural–urban composition, social class and historical events, with democratic relations most frequently reported by persons from middle-class status. The social context defined by regional boundaries differentially influences family change in countries with diverse ecological areas on social and economic development. This is seen in Italy where much of the secular trend toward democratic relations seems to have occurred among persons born in the urban north rather than in the underdeveloped south. All of these findings, however, should be interpreted with recognition of the measurement problems involved in the analysis.

Over the years, European visitors to America have noted that American parents are more permissive than parents in their own homeland, and have related this difference to the greater prevalence of equalitarianism in the United States.[23] There is current evidence of the stronger role of European mothers and fathers in the preceding analysis and in the results of other studies.[24]

This difference may also apply to the child-rearing practices of American and Scandinavian parents. The emphasis on ascriptive authority in the recent past of Germany and Sweden has led one sociologist to suggest that there may be considerable resemblance between socialization patterns in the two countries.[25] However, diversity in the form and complexion of parent–child relations among European nations offers little support for those who make gross comparisons between American and European parents.[26] Danish adolescents, for instance, appear to have more freedom to make their own decisions than their American counterparts, but they also are more reliant on their parents, especially in the relationship with their fathers.[27] A clue to these cross-national differences may be found in the communication and supervisory processes which influence the meaning of authority relations and in the manner in which these relations change as the child moves through the age structure, as well as in the larger sociocultural context of parental authority.

With social and cultural change, the diffusion of a more democratic conception of superordinate–subordinate relations has not been confined to the home, but is manifested as well in work and educational settings. Among the five nations in the present study, some increase in the prevalence of reported participation in formal class discussions appears between the oldest and youngest age groups in each of the samples.[28] Cross-national comparisons of this change between persons who reached adolescence before 1925 and after 1950 show the greatest increase in class participation among Americans (68 vs. 28 percent), the next largest among the Germans and English (40 vs. 7 percent), with the least amount of change among Italians and Mexicans (an average of 19

---

[23]Seymour Martin Lipset, *The First New Nation* (New York: Basic Books, 1963), Ch. 3.

[24]Edward C. Devereaux, Jr., Urie Bronfenbrenner and George Suci, "Patterns of Parent Behavior in the United States and the Federal Republic of Germany: A Cross-National Comparison," *International Social Science Journal*, 14 (1962), pp. 488–506; Rhoda Metraux and Margaret Mead, *Themes in French Culture* (Stanford, Calif.: Stanford University Press, 1954), pp. 27–34.

[25]Lipset, *The First New Nation*, p. 275.

[26]See, for instance, Herbert Hendin, *Suicide and Scandinavia* (New York: Grune & Stratton, Inc., 1964), and Jeanne Block and Bjorn Christensen, "A Test of Hendin's Hypotheses Relating Suicide to Child-Rearing Orientations," *Scandinavian Journal of Psychology*, 7:4 (1966), pp. 267–288.

[27]Denise B. Kandel, Gerald S. Lesser, Gail C. Roberts, and Robert Weiss, *Adolescents in Two Societies: Peers, School, and Family in the United States and Denmark* (Cambridge, Mass.: Laboratory of Human Development, Harvard University, 1968), final report to U.S. Office of Education, Project No. 2139, Ch. 7.

[28]Almond and Verba, *The Civic Culture*, p. 339.

vs. 4 percent). These changes have political significance for those who assume that democracy in the family and school enhances the viability of a democratic form of government. From an ethnographic study of schooling in a small West German village, Warren found evidence of a change toward freer, less formal relations between the teacher and pupil which was generally welcomed by parents. This parental attitude, he suggests, ". . . is a reflection both of a negative reaction to the severe socialization parents themselves experienced and of a general but slow relaxation of restraints in a democratic-industrial society."[29]

This observation illustrates the interdependence of authority relations in different sectors of society in the process of social change by identifying an avenue through which altered family relations may increase the acceptability of similar change in another institution. Change pressures flow in the other direction as well: for instance, when the implementation of democratic relations in schools and in work settings eventually undermines traditional family authority. Political strategies to alter family relations frequently employ schools and youth groups to accomplish this end. In democracies the possibilities of change in the private world of the family are mainly achieved through the consequences of structural modifications in other institutions.

[29]Richard L. Warren, *Education in Rebhausen, A German Village* (New York: Holt, Rinehart and Winston, Inc., 1967), p. 111. In Communist China, changing authority patterns between the teacher and pupil sharply contrast with the formal, unquestioned authority of the teacher in the past, as illustrated by the recollection of a refugee and former school-teacher: "I remember that once when I was a student and didn't understand a mathematics lesson I asked the teacher (for an explanation). But the teacher just got mad at me. This is very wrong. Afterwards I wouldn't dare to ask questions of the teacher" (Solomon, *op. cit.,* pp. 6–7).

Chapter 6: Suggested Additional Readings

BELL, A. P. Role modeling of fathers in adolescence and young adulthood. *Journal of Counseling Psychology*, 1969, *16*, 30–35. In Bell's research, fathers are revealed as their sons' most important role models; however, nonparents become increasingly significant as models in later adolescence.

BRITTAIN, C. V. An exploration of the bases of peer-compliance and parent-compliance in adolescence. *Adolescence*, 1967/68, *2*(8), 445–458. This article deals with the choices adolescents make in relation to conflicting parent-peer relations. The subjects, who were girls from lower-middle and working class families in a small town in the South, tended to be parent-compliant with respect to those choices perceived as relatively more difficult and important.

GNAGEY, W. J. Student attitude learning as a function of parental acceptance and sex of teacher. *Journal of Teacher Education*, 1968, *19*, 313–316. According to Gnagey, those college students who scored high on parental acceptance tended to demonstrate less anxiety that those low on parental acceptance; but they tended more often to be underachievers than overachievers.

KANDEL, D., LESSER, G. S. Parent–adolescent relationships and adolescent independence in the United States and Denmark. *Journal of Marriage and the Family*, 1969, *31*(2), 348–358. Data from a large number of American and Danish adolescents suggest that Danish parents are more democratic than American parents, although the consequences for adolescent socialization follow similar trends in both countries.

KANDEL, D. B., & LESSER, G. S. Parental and peer influences on educational plans of adolescents. *American Sociological Review*, 1969, *34*(2), 213–223. Data on educational plans based on triads of adolescents matched with their mothers and best friends failed to support the notion of a separate adolescent subculture isolated from parental influence. Concordance with mothers is higher than with peers, irrespective of closeness to the parent.

KOPF, K. E. Family variables and school adjustment of eighth grade father-absent boys. *The Family Coordinator*, 1970, *19*(2), 145–150. In this study of father-absent boys, their school adjustment related positively to their participation in household tasks and the mother's positive or neutral attitude to the father. Adjustment proved unrelated to the degree of father absence, age of child at separation, son's ordinal position, sex of siblings, or prior father–son relationship.

PAPANEK, M. L. Authority and sex roles in the family. *Journal of Marriage and the Family*, 1969, *31*(1), 88–96. Questionnaires and interviews, administered to adolescents and their parents, were used to study parental and child roles in families characterized by distinctive marital authority patterns. Where parental roles were highly differentiated, the boy and girl roles and the adult–child roles were correspondingly more differentiated.

REHBERG, R. A., SINCLAIR, J., & SCHAFFER, W. E. Adolescent achievement behavior: Family authority structure and parental socialization practices. *American Journal of Sociology*, 1970, *75*(6), 1012–1034. In an intensive study of male freshmen, Rehberg, Sinclair, and Schaffer disclosed that a democratic parent–son relationship is more conducive to achievement behaviors than is an autocratic relationship, and that child-rearing practices have a significant effect on such behaviors.

SAFILIOS-ROTHSCHILD, C. The study of family power structure: A review, 1960–69. *Journal of Marriage and the Family*, 1970, *32*(4), 539–552. The author reviews the literature concerning family power structure, particularly methodological issues in the study of family decision-making.

STEINER, G. J. Parent–teen education: An exercise in communication. *The Family Coordinator*, 1970, *19*(3), 213–218. Steiner describes a program designed to improve communication between parents and their teenagers who were experiencing conflict within the family. The first effort concerned developmental tasks confronting both adolescents and parents, and how these tasks influence their behavior toward each other.

TEC, N. F. Family and differential involvement with marijuana: A study of suburban teenagers. *Journal of Marriage and the Family*, 1970, *32*(4), 656–664. A study of youths aged 15 to 18 who lived in an affluent suburban community showed that those young people who most often used marijuana came from broken homes or lacked meaningful roles in the family. Marijuana users, more often than nonusers, perceived their families as unfair and lacking in warmth. In addition, fewer users than nonusers felt that they could turn to their families in time of trouble.

VAN MANEN, G. C. Father roles and adolescent socialization. *Adolescence,* 1968, *3*(10), 139–152. The author compares roles of father and mother, and reports a study of their relative effect on socialization and deviant processes.

WALTERS, J., & STINNETT, N. Parent–child relationships: A decade review of research. *Journal of Marriage and the Family*, 1971, *33*(1), 70–111. This comprehensive and scholarly article views research concerning parent–child relationships for the decade of the 1960s, including such topics as parental attitudes, parental supportiveness, child-rearing practices, authority patterns, parental influence on sex roles, family influences on emotional and behavior problems, and family influence on academic performance and creative thinking.

part three

Issues in Self-Actualization

7

Schools for Adolescents

Probably few persons would deny that the school a youth attends has a great influence, whether good or bad, on his development. Indeed, after reviewing relevant research, Thornburg (1971) concludes that education is uppermost among college youth's problems and concerns. Dramatic events and situations such as the Vietnam War, the civil rights crusade, and assassinations of prominent persons have had profound shock effects upon youth in recent years; but the most persistent, pervading influence would seem to be that of the school itself. But is the impact of school or college simply peripheral, or does it have a real influence on youth's basic personality and attitudes? In recent years there has been considerable controversy over this question. One study (Chickering, 1971), involving students on seven college campuses, determined that students' cultural attitudes definitely were modified by their collective college experience, which included their student-faculty contacts, campus friendships, the institutional characteristics, and teaching methods. However, more research is needed on this question.

Those individuals who prescribe for adolescents' education—presumably in order to insure that the education will have a positive effect on youth—usually begin, and sometimes end, by deploring today's educational system as grossly inadequate. Their criticisms take many forms. Patricia Sexton (1961), for example, deplores the schools' failure to discharge their commitment to opportunity and equality. Culturally deprived children, she claims, are unprepared to compete in schools which pursue middle-class goals and reward middle-class values. Frustration, maladjustment, and early dropouts are the inevitable outcomes. On the other hand, Koerner (1963) laments that the schools fail all intellectually capable students. Still other authorities—among them Jules Henry, Paul Goodman, and Edgar Friedenberg—are disturbed about the damage schools do to apparently successful students. What troubles them is the way the school purposefully strives to mold youth to fit passively into the culture. Specifically, Henry (1963) claims that schools are highly efficient in destroying youth's individuality and creative potential. The real offender, he believes, is society, which designs schools in the interests of its own perpetuation. In drawing up their curricula, schools have considered industry's needs and not the child's. Says Henry, ". . . I am not convinced that what is good for General Motors is good for our children. Even less am I convinced that what is good for Missile Dynamics is good for our children, or what is good for the Pentagon is good for them. [p. 144]"

Goodman (1964) also points out that one of the schools' most obvious functions—of which the searching out of students' talents is a part—is to train prospective employees for private enterprise at public expense. Thus, schools teach children "the niceties and not-so-niceties of corporate conduct, and compile dossiers of children's social or antisocial tendencies. Children are not only compelled to attend schools, but to become what the schools want to make them."

Friedenberg (1959) considers the schools' record of success in helping adolescents to clarify their own values to be a poor one. Administrative expediency outweighs human considerations. Confidentiality of students' records is violated, making it dangerous for students to deal honestly with counselors. The schools also act as if America were still a melting pot, says Friedenberg, encouraging uniformity—both external and internal—more than individuality. Standards of excellence are fragmentary and incoherent. The lack of a sound philosophical structure obstructs the development of curricula which will utilize the best cultural resources to help youth make sense out of their lives. Those students who try to "buck the system" and exhibit originality are made to feel anxious and guilty. Nor are schools to be exonerated for these failings; they must bear their share of responsibility for the existing situation because the school, more than any other social institution, is the standard-bearer of the Western liberal tradition (Friedenberg, 1966).

Henry (1966) also points to another problem in the schools—the ubiquitous incompetent teacher who thanks heaven for a system which provides meek students. Such children "permit him to grow old without too much intellectual stir—without making him feel vulnerable [p. 143]." Bright teachers often find intolerable the "embalmed curriculum [p. 138]" and required textbooks which are forced upon them. Only through threatening to fail them does the school manage to motivate children at all. Remove the fear of failure, asserts Henry, and American education "would stop as if its heart had been cut out [p. 137]."

While criticism directed at the educational system is specific and concrete, recommendations as to what schools *should* be are unfortunately often couched in vague, idealistic generalities. "They should inspire moods of wonder and awe at the range of knowledge." "The scope of education is nothing less than the scope of life." "The perceptive teacher perceives her own image in either a lively, or a lifeless, classroom." The banalities go on and on. Controversy begins when the question is raised concerning the schools' role in implementing individuals' personal goals. Undergirding much of the controversy is a persistent issue: Should schools attempt to produce the all-round cultivated man or the specialist (Gusfield & Riesman, 1966)? Should students attend a liberal arts college or a professional school? Within hybrid types of institution, what should be the ratio of academic to professional courses? Some colleges clearly dedicate themselves to one goal or the other. A college producing professionalized specialists is often rigorous, selective, and demanding. A school with a dilettantish concern for liberal arts may be permissive and flexible.

A related controversy is whether schools, in general, should be rigid and exacting, modeled after the British public schools, or should be latter-day offshoots of

Dewey progressivism and permissivism. Also, should the school simply mirror the society it serves or should it attempt to bring about social change? Practically speaking, local school boards insist that the school should reflect the culture of the surrounding community, while various philosophers and critics argue that the schools must become the "pivotal agent of social amelioration and change." According to this latter view, the school should be open around the clock and become a resource for bettering the entire community (Usdan & Nystrand, 1966).

A major problem today is the school's role in dealing with children whose parents differ from the dominant society in terms of culture, economic resources, or values. In this area, questions proliferate like weeds in a tropical garden. How can peer relationships in the school be utilized to modify antisocial group norms? What sorts of reinforcement are needed to produce socially acceptable behaviors? What sort of rapprochement should be made between the child's own cultural norms and the school's middle-class values? Is the child who is hung up between two cultures worse off than the child with a firm foothold in his own minority culture (Henderson, 1967)?

Still another issue in secondary schools and colleges is how much attention should be paid to youth's own reactions. Currently, students have become highly articulate in expressing their views. Many college students, especially, have labeled their educational fare substandard, and much of their disillusionment, writes Mayhew (1968), comes from the discovery that college is not essentially different from high school. Horowitz and Friedland (1970) warn against dismissing such criticism as meaningless, simply because it has become so nearly universal. In fact, to dismiss student protest as merely perennial "griping" is to miss the point entirely. True, students have always revolted against society, and in the past, society largely ignored their criticism. However, as the population increases, the colleges cannot afford simply "to erect higher tuition walls" to keep out disaffected students. Instead, suggest Horowitz and Friedland, if a college should conceive of itself "not as a place, but as a set of functions, a style, a quality, a mode of operation not limited to ivy-covered walls [p. 59]," it might spring itself free from its limiting traditions and become more relevant for the youth of today.

Other writers, however, perceive youth's critical attitude to be more destructive than healthy. Indeed, declares Pitts (1971), youth's new counter-culture has been instrumental in undermining the "post-sputnik" university geared to academic excellence. The counter-culturists endorse a permissive academic atmosphere and commit themselves to their music, drug, and political subcultures without leaving the university. While the older faculty members become somewhat demoralized and grieve over the passing of the traditional university, many younger teachers assist students in their battles with the establishment. Meantime, concludes Pitts, little is done to improve teaching, and the decreasing power of university official-dom makes it less likely that anything constructive will be done. Nor are students likely to seek change in a currently pleasant status which includes soft grading, "Mickey Mouse" courses, and mixed dormitories. At any rate, only the future will reveal what the student's role will be in determining his own educational fare; he remains the lively dark horse in the arena of education.

The first of the following articles, written by a 13-year-old, is typical of many young adolescents' views on education. While this particular adolescent is speaking only for herself, she undoubtedly reflects the views of many of her peers. Most critics of academe are content merely to make negative remarks, detailing only what is wrong about schools. Patty Wirth goes on to tell what she would like in an ideal school.

In the second article, an adult critic of the system tells what he believes should be done to make schools more meaningful and relevant. He believes school instruction should relate to what an individual will need in all aspects of his life role, both currently and in the future, and he outlines in considerable detail the sort of curriculum he believes would meet students' needs better than most curricula do today.

The third article, by Graubard, presents not so much what he feels higher education *should* be as what he believes it *will* be. He boldly predicts sweeping changes in the university, suggesting that present institutions will be displaced by university cities which will shelter a significant number of strong educational institutions cooperating in ways still only dimly discerned. Articles such as this one help us not only to gain better perspective on schools of today but to plan more intelligently for the future.

REFERENCES

CHICKERING, A. W.   Cultural sophistication and college experience. *Educational Record,* 1971, *52*(2), 125–128.

FRIEDENBERG, E. Z.   *The vanishing adolescent.* Boston: Beacon Press, 1959.

FRIEDENBERG, E. Z.   New value conflicts in American education. *School Review,* 1966, *74*(1), 66.

GOODMAN, P.   *Compulsory mis-education.* New York: Horizon Press, 1964.

GUSFIELD, J., & RIESMAN, D.   Academic standards and the two cultures in the context of a new state college. *School Review,* 1966, *74*(1), 95–115.

HENDERSON, G.   Opportunity and alienation in the public schools. *Teachers College Record,* 1967, *69*(2), 151–158.

HENRY, J.   *Culture against man.* New York: Random House, 1963.

HENRY, J.   Vulnerability in education. *Teachers College Record,* 1966, *68*(2), 135–145.

HOROWITZ, I. L., & FRIEDLAND, W. H.   *The knowledge factory: Student power and academic politics in America.* Chicago: Aldine, 1970.

KOERNER, J.   *The miseducation of American teachers.* Boston: Houghton Mifflin, 1963.

MAYHEW, L. B.   Changing the balance of power. *Saturday Review,* August 17, 1968, 48–49, 57–58.

PITTS, J.   The counter culture. *Dissent,* June 1971, 216–229.

SEXTON, P.   *Education and income.* New York: Viking Press, 1961,

THORNBURG, H. D.   Peers: Three distinct groups. *Adolescence,* 1971, *6*(21), 59–76.

USDAN, M. D., & NYSTRAND, R. O.   Towards participative decision-making: The impact of community action programs. *Teachers College Record,* 1966, *68*(2), 95–106.

My Ideal School Wouldn't Be a School

PATTY WIRTH

A midwestern 13-year-old describes her somewhat ambivalent feelings about her school, undoubtedly reflecting the attitudes and emotions of many of her generation.

First of all, to look at me you'd never think I would write anything protesting anything. I look and am middle-class, sheltered, etc., etc., etc. But the main reason I think I am (was?) so oblivious of big issues is because of schools. I am in seventh grade, go to an ultra-"good," modern, junior high school in the suburbs. The teachers there, and the ones at the last year of elementary school, talk about how sad it is that kids today don't have any consciousness of people in the inner city living in slums—but as I said before, it's mostly because of the teachers that I am that way. Not once in school have I had any discussions concerning the draft, Black Panthers, or any controversial issue. Excepting, of course, the stuff I had on drugs—but then I had no opinion to express whatsoever.

I don't have an opinion on anything. I'm being more and more controlled, and I'm not learning anything. I remember a feeling I had in the first grade—like a sponge soaking up knowledge that I'd always be able to use: reading, writing, etc. I haven't had that feeling once this year. It's just taking down what the teacher says, memorizing it, taking the test—and promptly forgetting everything. I'm not getting any impressions, experiences, I'm not interested. For example, some-times when we are reading page 307 in class I feel like jumping up and saying, "Who is really interested in this? Who thinks this is fascinating?"

I "learn" stuff, how to write morpheme strings, how to conjugate Spanish verbs, but will I ever use these when I'm older? There is a pattern: I learn morpheme strings, not necessarily because they'll help later in life, but because how else could I pass to eighth grade? In eighth grade I'll "learn" equally useless stuff so I'll pass to ninth grade, tenth grade, eleventh grade—if I can just make it to college! In college I'll study so I can get some well-paying job, marry some clean-cut guy, and settle down in a house in the suburbs. And anyone who breaks the pattern is looked down upon and given a weird name like—hippie.

I'm getting in a rut, and I'm not having any new experiences. And if I would say this to a teacher, he would probably smile gently, cross his arms and say, "I understand your point, but I'm sorry, you're wrong." Or, "But if you don't get an education . . ." and the unspoken part of the sentence is, "You won't be like us."

And that's what I think is the main problem. *They* consider themselves superior, and either say, "I refuse to discuss such ridiculous trash," or "It's just a phase, you'll grow out of it . . .

From P. Wirth, My ideal school wouldn't be a school. Reprinted from *Teachers College Record,* September 1970, *72*(1), 57–59, by permission of author and publisher.

when you get mature like me, you'll realize how wrong you were." And that's what I think is really sad, because that's what the whole problem, as some call it, "The Generation Gap," or whatever, is about: They think they're superior. I guess I would prefer the first person, he is all but saying he's scared, but the second person is what's really scary because if he "knows" he's better, he'll never understand what anyone ever does. And I know I'm tired of having my life controlled by people who set the pattern down. I think the whole system of values has changed; they grew up during the Depression when money was everything, and to them it's still security. But for me I think the important thing is individuality, independence, I don't know if there is a word for what I want, but I do know that what I'm going through now can't be right.

Everything is narrowing down. In first grade we were encouraged to write stories and read them to the class, and we continued to be encouraged through fourth grade. Then in fifth grade there wasn't really enough time for that, it became less important, and there was more textbook material, more homework. In sixth grade we were introduced to the facts that one-sentence paragraphs were out, and all paragraphs should be about the same length. (God!) But I was saved by "creative writing" where I could still express myself without fear of making (horrors!) a grammatical error. Now in seventh grade the creativity has been dropped out almost entirely. Several people I know who have finished school say that subjects they really liked before junior high, high school, etc., they hated after their "education" because they weren't free to expand on their ideas.

Another thing which I think is wrong with my (the?) school(s) is the textbooks. We have to cover the material we have to cover the material we have to cover the material! I carry a mental picture around of one of my teachers pulling my class through a waist-deep ocean of mud—which in reality is pp. 327–331, Nos. 1–50—saying "Onward, children! We must make it by Tuesday!"

Another example of this: One of my teachers saying to us, "C'mon, if we *can just get through* these last two pages, I'll let you do something fun for the rest of the period." And then there is the teacher who says, "Good afternoon, class. Open your books and turn to page sixty-six. John, would you care to read for us?" Am I learning anything from that?

I mentioned before the lack of discussions. I have never had one discussion in which I was really involved. There is no free exchange, no real communicating. It's just to have the teacher say, "And what do you think?" We all obediently raise our hands. "Johnnie?" And the kid meekly states his answer which is always right or wrong, never just an opinion.

The kids in the schools are one big inconspicuous blob. On the first day of school our principal warned us, "Don't dress in clothes that attract unusual attention or that are conspicuous in any way." And that's the whole thing. Fit into the pattern, the Establishment, or you'll be an outcast, you'll be looked down upon.

Maybe I seem really hostile. But maybe that's because I am. I disagree so completely with everything the school says, and yet I can't disagree. If I would mutter "Oh, Jesus!" when the teacher mentioned hippies, pot, or campuses, there would be a shocked silence; and the teacher would proceed to bawl me out.

I don't want to be controlled. I can feel myself being squashed. Very few of my teachers ever seem to say anything spontaneously. The ground we will cover has already been mapped out. I can't really break away though. Cute clothes and money are too important to me. But I really don't want to be the middle-class-y type of person. I'm kind of two people right now, and I don't like being that way. But the reason I have this big conflict is mainly because of the schools.

My ideal school wouldn't be a school. There should be much more freedom, not this 8:30 to 3:30 bit. You would sign up for different classes and go when you had the time, thus having much more freedom and more experiences. The classes would be much more liberal, and everybody would learn together instead of having the teacher dictate to us what we have to learn. The classes would really be discussions, and the English-math-science-history thing would not exist.

I don't know if the above is really what I want. I do know it would be 1000 percent better than what I'm enduring now. I know I don't want the textbooks. But I also know that the schools can't or won't change for a long time. When and if I would talk to my principal about this, he would probably say, "What about grades? How will we know what learning level you're on? etc., etc., etc."

My sister, who is now teaching a "free school," dropped out of high school in her junior year and went straight to college. My brother also dropped out and took his senior year by correspondence. But what I'm saying is this: Most people get pretty fed up in high school. But I'm in seventh grade! I've got six more years to go! I know I can't learn anything this way, but I really want to learn. And something has got to change because I'm really dead sick of this whole "education."

Reconnection for Relevance: A Proposed New High School Curriculum

JAMES L. FENNER

The author outlines a curriculum which is designed to achieve relevance to real world interests and needs of teenagers.

Before high school can make real sense to teenagers, we have to change it in important ways. We have to find administrators who will be more responsive to students than to bureaucratic higher-ups. We have to decompartmentalize course work, not by dismantling traditional departments of English, secretarial studies, science, and so forth, but instead by offering additional nondepartmental and interdisciplinary courses as electives. We have to tune the high school experience in on the real concerns of young people: self-realization, money, power, the future, sex. And most important, we have to try to relate what we teach in high school to the other things adolescents are learning and to those other sources of experience, information, and understanding that teach them so much so indelibly today.

Any meaningful proposed connection between high school studies and out-of-school learning taking place in our society must presuppose an analysis of just what this out-of-school learning really consists of, what it means to young people, what changes can be made in the schools to relate it to the curriculum, and what effects can be expected to flow from these changes. Fearing[1] has described the great impact and power of the mass media, and Gans[2] has explored the similarities and differences between school and the media as regards their structure, functions, problems, content, and policies. And Newcomb[3] has indicated how tenaciously attitudes formed out of school stick with us (where favorable reinforcements exist) long after their formation.

EXTRA-SCHOOL LEARNINGS

TV is certainly the most productive non-school source of learning today. Even though, as Mac-

[1] Franklin Fearing, "Social Impact of the Mass Media of Communication," in N. B. Henry, Ed., *Mass Media and Education.* NSSE Yearbook. Chicago: University of Chicago Press, 1954.

[2] Herbert Gans, "The Mass Media as an Educational Institution," *The Urban Review,* February, 1967.

[3] Theodore M. Newcomb, "Persistence and Regression of Changed Attitudes: Long-Range Studies," *Journal of Social Issues,* Vol. 19, 1963.

From J. L. Fenner, Reconnection for relevance: A proposed new high school curriculum. Reprinted from *The Teachers College Record,* February 1970, *71*(3), 423–438, by permission of author and publisher.

coby[4] reveals, high school students watch less TV than younger kids do, they still spend more time in front of the bug-box than they do in school and pay closer attention to what it offers than to the school's intellectual menu. Unlike school, TV gives them a sense of involvement which McLuhan[5] has shown to be all the more intense because it is so sketchy, so "cool." It brings them the most expensive and fashionable entertainment talent in the world, "live" from wherever. Witty[6] insists that TV has value: it brings youngsters open-ended talk programs which, with seeming authority, touch upon the most important issues of the day; and it brings documentaries more informative—and certainly more stylish—than anything in their textbooks. With TV, it seems, they live; by comparison, their textbooks seem dead.

Radio is far from dead in the world of today's teenagers. Rock 'n Roll and folk-lore are adolescent-aimed industries now, and they add up to a vast segment of our economy. The "love now" and "student power" action fashions of the day are fed and fertilized by the fare radio purveys: protest lyrics, psychedelic songs, red-hot news, uninhibited talk, and millions of commercial messages that do for the transistorized corner boys what the bug-box does for the stay-at-homes. Rock groups like the Beatles, the Jefferson Airplane, the Mamas and the Papas, and Vanilla Fudge; oddballs like Tiny Tim; folk artists like Odetta and Joan Baez; and folk-rock performers like Bob Dylan and Simon and Garfunkel are true folk heroes among young Americans from 13 to 30.

Film is a rich world for teenagers, and not just because of its role as a medium of individual and social recreation. It is contemporary, style-setting, camp, kitsch, social comment, sex education, philosophical orientation, and escape, all rolled into one, and its appeal is as intense as it is multifarious. Sitting back in the welcoming dark of the movie theater, the youngster learns about love, country, heroism, alienation, politics, business, adulthood, and tragedy. And in the realms of personal appearance, manner, talk, action, gesture, and (especially) motivation, he learns about style.

Students learn more than we sometimes realize from non-verbal sources. Interpersonal distance and the meaning of spatial and kinesthetic relationships between individuals have been explored by Hall[7] and shown to convey important meanings. The symbolism of static visual messages is equally important,[8] especially in such areas as advertising, architecture, and interior decoration. High school teachers have long known the strength of latent messages that seating arrangements convey, and how much more conducive to free discussion some such set-ups are than others. Human spaces and non-verbal communications are consciously used, abused, and learned from, everywhere.

World events teach a youngster much. It hardly matters whether he gets his information from a newspaper, radio, TV, newsweekly, or hearsay: ultimately it comes from the media one way or another. Ellul[9] has shown how much propaganda affects the attitudes of citizens—even young citizens—in a technological society, and how pervasive and powerful they must of necessity be. And today's teenager knows, as perhaps his father never knew, the extent to which events concern him directly: the war, the riots, the black power movement, the draft, the campus protests, the peace marches, the French general strike, the assassinations—everything.

The job market teaches adolescents a great deal. If they work, they learn how the great world works. They learn how to present themselves, how to "make it" with the company, how to play adult, how to save and spend money. If they don't work, they learn about unemployment, about leisure, about discouragement, about job requirements, screening practices, interviews, and questionnaires. They learn about taxes, budgets, the cost of self-support, the difficulty of saving something extra. Or if they don't learn these things, then they

---

[4]Eleanor Maccoby, "Effects of Mass Media," in M. C. Hoffman and Lois W. Hoffman, Eds., *Review of Child Development Research.* New York: Russell Sage Foundation, 1964.

[5]Marshall McLuhan. *Understanding Media.* New York: McGraw-Hill, Inc., 1965.

[6]Paul Witty, "Effects of TV on Attitudes and Behavior," *Education,* October, 1964.

[7]Edward T. Hall. *The Hidden Dimension.* New York: Doubleday and Co., 1966.

[8]Jurgen Ruesch and Weldon Kees. *Non-Verbal Communication.* Berkeley: University of California Press, 1956.

[9]Jacques Ellul. *Propaganda.* New York: Alfred A. Knopf, 1965.

learn about poverty, indignity, idleness, despair, impotence, and futility.

Personal enjoyments teach kids tremendously important learnings. Social and physical relationships with the opposite sex teach them the meaning of love, pleasure, commitment, manipulation, cynicism, and faith in their dealings with others. Cars and drugs provide vehicles for literal and figurative trips away from the confines of home, family, school, neighborhood, or boss, and into a world of adventure and self-discovery. Fashion is a universe of self-expression, originality, conformity, timeliness, self-image-adjustment, consumership, and self-acceptance.

Finally, society's formal, hierarchical structure of power and influence reinforce much that school teaches and provide learnings that go far beyond what school attempts. The changes that Pearl[10] and Bundy[11] propose are intended to be as beneficial to the kids as they are for the adult poor. On the other hand, student power is one thing; civil disorders in the streets are another. Deans of discipline are one thing; police with nightsticks are another. The cop who doesn't see the pusher, the cop who uses tear gas, the cop who accepts a small bribe not to give a ticket for a moving violation, the window clerk at the Bureau of Motor Vehicles who won't lift a finger to help, the bureaucratic supervisor who won't do anything about it—all these represent evils of a credential-ridden and bureaucratic society that a young person finds particularly insufferable. And to him, the flag-wavers that brag about America and seem blind to its emptiness seem contemptible.

WHAT DO NON-SCHOOL LEARNINGS MEAN?

School learnings connect students with the world of the past, with the textbook world of the received wisdom and knowledge of the ages. Non-school learnings connect them with the present and future world around them. Where school shows them how they must see each new ephemeral and maybe "tasteless" fad in the perspec-

tive of a stable tradition, the media show them how necessary it is to change with the changing world in order to be with it, to be in, to swing. Where the former teaches them how to live in the status-ridden world of the "real" power structure, the latter teaches them how to live in whatever enticing dream-world they desire. Where school teaches them required roles, out-of-school experience shows them congenial new ones to try. Where the one gives them information about set subjects, about set authority, about set regulations, etc., the other gives information about new politics, new style, new entertainment, and new issues. Where the one provides inculcation in traditional values, in conservatism, in playing the game, the other propagandizes for current values.

The middle class has found, both in and out of school, an array of indispensable guides of self-realization. The media have given them consumer expertise, a feel for making it, a style for advancement, a fistful of job skills: reading, writing, accounting, organization, and so on. Goodman[12] and Friedenberg[13] demonstrate the extent to which the schools and the media have neglected the potentially-fulfilling road to honest spiritual development in favor of the emptier and more convenient middle-class personal-management skills of thrift, investment, diligence, respect, gratification-postponement, and other forms of hoop-jumping.

For the poor, both school and the media have been powerful inducements to self-hatred and self-contempt. The advertising media have made them hunger for consumer goodies they can never legitimately afford. While Nat Hentoff[14] and Jonathan Kozol[15] on the one hand have shown vividly how they have suffered alienation from self, from middle-class values they don't espouse, from school routines, regulations, and, worst of all, irrelevancies, Martin Deutsch[16] and Frank

[10]Arthur Pearl, "New Careers and the Manpower Crisis in Education." Mimeo, 1968.

[11]McGeorge Bundy, *et al. Reconnection for Learning.* Mayor's Advisory Panel on Decentralization of the New York City Schools. New York, 1967.

[12]Paul Goodman. *Compulsory Mis-education.* New York: Horizon Press, 1964.
and Friedenberg[13] demonstrate the extent to

[13]Edgar Z. Friedenberg. *The Vanishing Adolescent.* Boston: Beacon Press, 1964.

[14]Nat Hentoff. *Our Children Are Dying.* New York: Viking Press, 1966.

[15]Jonathan Kozol. *Death at an Early Age.* Boston: Houghton Mifflin, Inc., 1967.

[16]Martin Deutsch, Ed. *The Disadvantaged Child.* New York: Basic Books, 1967.

Riessman[17] have outlined not only their deprivations but their resources as well. The schools have yet to institutionalize ways of capitalizing on these.

ROADS TO RELEVANCY

There is, of course, more than one road to relevancy in schooling. What is relevant to one aspect of our many-faceted civilization is unrelated to another. What helps one person get a job or get into this or that college prevents someone else from getting anything at all worth knowing out of school. The first attempt to solve this question came in the 1930's after it became apparent that the compulsory education laws were filling up the high schools with students to whom the traditional "academic" course of study—classical and modern languages, mathematics, science, literature, and history—meant little, and who weren't willing or able to get all that stuff into their heads. When these "new" high-school youngsters arrived on the scene and proceeded to fail the traditional courses in droves, to express their hostility at great cost to their teachers' peace of mind, to prevent the "good" students from learning by their disruptions, and to wreak havoc upon the schools' educational statistics, the "general" course was created for them. Because these students were the dumb ones, or "slow" or "disadvantaged," or whatever fashionable euphemism you choose, the "general" course was simply designed as a reduction of the standard course. If the dumb ones couldn't learn as much, then give them less. If some subjects were too hard, then substitute easier ones. So they got—and are getting—a simplified curriculum. However inadequate the traditional courses were in dealing with the problems of the twentieth century, the "general" courses were worse. The high schools had one inadequate (difficult, but outdated) curriculum for the "good" students, and another worse one (empty and outdated) for the "dumb" ones.

In as varied a society as ours, it would be just plain silly to condemn every traditional subject as irrelevant. Some of the old academic and commercial standbys have great value for certain students. One need not be either an adherent of the Bestor-Rickover[18] thesis or an enemy of John Holt[19] to see value in foreign languages, mathematics, science, social studies, literature, music, shop, bookkeeping, stenography, typing, and many other job-oriented, or college-oriented or recreation-oriented or broadening or "skill" subjects—*for some students.* Certainly these should be retained in the high schools, whether as required courses for specialized curricula or as electives for anyone who might be interested. But one need not hark back to the days of Jane Addams and yearn to see the school as a glorified settlement house to know that these old standard traditional courses are not enough today. They are not enough for the college-bound youngster, and they are not enough for the job-bound. They are not enough for the middle class, and they are not enough for the poor. Other subjects —ones that deal with contemporary life and that make use of contemporary issues and media— are required if any youngster is to gain from high school some sense of what his world is like and where it's at and how it hangs together. Probably the naive faith expressed in George S. Counts' *Dare the Schools Build a New Social Order?*[20] is out of place among today's complexities, but certainly reality and reconnection (to borrow a term current in another context) cannot hurt.

The following proposed elective courses for high school are intended to fulfill this requirement. They are intended as electives because I believe students—at least *some* students—would find them —at least *some* of them—intrinsically interesting enough to make them want to take them. This alone would relate them, as far as the nature of their appeal went, to out-of-school interests. They are intended as courses for everybody; and that means a heterogeneous student body. This too would relate them, if only superficially on an organizational basis, to life outside the school.

---

[17]Frank Riessman. *The Culturally Deprived Child.* New York: Harper and Row, 1962.

[18]See Arthur Bestor. *Educational Wastelands.* Urbana: University of Illinois Press, 1953; and Hyman G. Rickover. *Education and Freedom.* New York: Dutton and Co., 1960.

[19]John Holt. *How Children Fail.* New York: Pitman and Co., 1964.

[20]George S. Counts. *Dare the Schools Change the Social Order?* New York: John Day, 1932.

And, most important, they are intended to cut across interdisciplinary boundaries, to bridge some of the gaps between subject and subject or between school and the "real" world, to combine and recombine the world, the media, the person, and the school in new and significant configurations, so that adolescence need not be the nightmare that Jules Henry,[21] John Holt, Paul Goodman, and Edgar Z. Friedenberg assert it to be. It is this feature of the proposals that, I hope, would make these courses valuable for the society (because its youngsters would be able to experience some sense of synthesis), for the school (because students might not feel so hostile to an institution that is giving them an education with a little life in it), and for the young people themselves (because they would be able to see some purpose, some pattern of interrelationships, some relevance to reality, in what the school is offering them). Here are the proposed electives, with brief descriptions of each:

1. ENTERTAINMENT This course would deal with current films, with TV, with radio (very much a source of adolescent entertainment today: "We're portable!" as the "good guys" put it), records, with the theater, and with the entertainment aspects of the mass-circulation magazines. Sebastian De Grazia[22] underlines the hollowness of our leisure. A course like this one wouldn't cure the malaise he describes, but it might be a start, and it would surely be popular. Its purpose would not be primarily to entertain the students; it would be aimed at helping them to understand and assess and respond knowingly to what the entertainment media offer. Materials would be plentiful; they constitute a major part of the out-of-school life of youngsters already, and in class they could be analyzed as to their methods, their craftsmanship, their social implications, their psychological impact, and their visual, verbal, rhetorical, sensory, and kinesthetic structures.

2. PERSONAL RELATIONSHIPS This subject would explore the many levels and values in personal relationships. Carl Rogers[23] insists upon the essential importance of self-discovery. "Psychology" would have been the traditional name for a course like this, and there would still be that aspect to it, but in addition it would deal with the style and content of relationships within the family and the peer-group, and with personal concerns such as love, sex, friendship, ambition, the draft, and perhaps it would touch upon the philosophical as well as the psychological aspects of such matters. Here too, the content of the course would be life as students actually and personally live it outside of school. Although it would deal with these situations in general and in principle instead of attempting to guide pupils in their personal lives directly, it most certainly would bear a direct and magnetic relationship to the reality with which they are in daily contact.

3. MORAL ISSUES This would be a study of ethics as exemplified by the personal relationships of the previous course, or by political questions, or by school or business problems. The course would aim to present issues and analyze them with penetration and clarity rather than to present solutions. Any kind of written or other material could provide the basis for a sequence of discussions: magazine articles, news items, TV, radio, or film shows, excerpts from philosophical writings, the Bible —whatever. These would be grouped into "topics" representing different *kinds* of ethical issues, and presented in discussion as they relate to adolescent concerns both immediate and future. Here the ethics of business, politics, international affairs, child-rearing, sex, and school could be subjected to the kind of analysis that might make even school look relevant.

4. WASHINGTON POLITICS TODAY This would combine the current events that the media inundate us with, the national aspects of what used to be called "Civics," political theory, debates on national programs and/or bills before Congress, biographical and/or political studies of national figures, a little history as the need for it arose in discussion of the day's issues, and perhaps some class predictions of

[21]Jules Henry. *Culture Against Man.* New York: Vintage Books, 1963.
[22]Sebastian De Grazia. *Of Time, Work, and Leisure.* Twentieth Century Fund, 1962.

[23]Carl Rogers. *On Becoming a Person.* Boston: Houghton Mifflin, Inc., 1961.

future political developments. The text for the course would be the daily paper, the news-weeklies, the radio, TV, and perhaps some traditional textbook material on the structure of the Federal government.

5. LOCAL POLITICS TODAY
The emphasis here would be on state and muncipal politics, including education, the police, welfare, the courts, and the tax structure. City and neigh-borhood newspapers would provide the texts. TV and radio coverage of local events would be monitored daily. Local politicians might be asked to address the students. Jury duty would be discussed, possibly in connection with the film *Twelve Angry Men*. Magazine articles on such topics as corruption in politics would cer-tainly be of value and interest. An aspect of such a course that would capture the interest of young people and seem relevant to their real concerns and out-of-school experience is the discovery and discussion of ways of "fighting city hall" effectively: how to mount an effective campaign, when to write letters, when to ob-struct, when to visit whom—how, in other words, to make one's weight felt as a citizen.

6. INTERNATIONAL AFFAIRS TODAY
All the media would provide material for this course. Propaganda analysis would form a con-siderable part of the subject-matter, as would the metaphors of international discourse. The foreign press could be studied for alternative points of view. WNYC has an interesting sup-pertime "Foreign Press Review" several times a week. The course would not try merely to acquaint students with international events, it would seek to help them understand the ri-valries, pressures, aspirations, and other motiva-tions that they reflect. And it would undertake some evaluation of the thoroughness, effective-ness, objectivity, and reliability of the media's presentations of international news.

7. HOW TO THINK STRAIGHT
The tradi-tional name for this course is "Logic," but here a commonsense rather than a technical ap-proach would be stressed. Books like Stuart Chase's *Guides to Straight Thinking*[24] or Robert

Thouless' *How to Think Straight*[25] could be used as texts, and issues and examples for analysis could be found in every news presenta-tion or public document, whether political, so-cial, religious, or whatever, published in Amer-ica. The popularizers of Korzybski[26] have pro-vided interesting case studies in straight and crooked thinking. In this kind of course, the "purely" intellectual enterprise of thinking ac-curately could be given a contemporary applic-ability to social and personal issues that vitally concern young people, thus serving to help integrate in-school and out-of-school learning and experience.

8. THE FUTURE
Nothing concerns teenagers more than the future; probably not even the present. This course, cutting across many sub-ject-matter boundaries, would explore and spec-ulate about the future of technology, or poli-tics, or school, of personal relationships, of sports, of communications, of America, of the Negro, of practically everything. It would draw upon the present as depicted in the media, upon the past as researched out of books for this or that investigation, upon logic, experience, and intention. It might help pupils to feel that they have some realistic possibility of contributing to the shaping of their own futures if they un-derstood more fully the processes and prob-abilities in accordance with which the future tends to unfold.

9. OUTER AND INNER SPACE: A SCI-ENCE SURVEY
In descriptive rather than technical terms, the principles, discoveries, and chief theories of the social and natural sciences would be presented and discussed here. The course, while relying to a degree on historical material about previous discoveries and innova-tions in the sciences, would be kept rigorously up-to-the-minute via regular scrutiny of cur-

[24]Stuart Chase. *Guides to Straight Thinking*. New York: Harper and Row, 1956.

[25]Robert H. Thouless. *How to Think Straight*. New York: Hart Publishing Company, 1939.

[26]See Alfred Korzybski. *Science and Sanity*. Lake-ville, Conn.: Institute of General Semantics, 1958; and the following: Wendell Johnson. *People in Quan-daries*. New York: Harper and Row, 1946; Stuart Chase. *The Power of Words*. New York: Harcourt, Brace and World, 1954; Hugh R. Walpole. *Semantics*. New York: W. W. Norton and Co., 1942; S. I. Hayakawa. *Language in Thought and Action*. New York: Harcourt, Brace, and World, 1964.

rent material presented in the media. Thus, new advances in the technology of space exploration, communications, computerization, automation, or even recent re-evaluations of theoretical systems could be made a part of the course. Biology, psychology, sociology, and anthropology might justify the "inner" part of the title; mechanics, chemistry, sub-atomic physics, and astronomy would be the "outer" space. The point of the course would be not to introduce the technical aspects of the sciences, but to give some pupils some familiarity with underlying concepts of scientific understanding, such as the "reflective thinking" of Dewey,[27] so that they will be better able to follow and comprehend the technological society in which they live.

10. HOW TO USE FIGURES The computational problems of everyday existence stump many pupils because they have learned in school to fear and hate quantitative subject-matter. But computational math and useful arithmetic, if presented afresh in the guise of "tricks" or "speed math" or "mental arithmetic" or "short cuts to accuracy," might grab youngsters and sustain their interest. The Trachtenberg System and other computational devices could be made the basis of a truly useful arithmetic course that would be of value to academic, commercial, vocational, and "general" students. For some, its value would be vocational; for others, academic; for still others, perhaps just recreational or curiosity-satisfying. Certainly it would help relate school to actual student needs.

11. LOCAL RESOURCES: INFORMATION, RECREATION, SERVICE The aim here would be to engage directly in the task of acquainting students with what is real in their surroundings. Particularly among the poor, many students have had limited experiences outside their immediate neighborhoods. In this class, they would have a chance to take the trips their elementary-school teachers never took them on: walking tours through their city's neighborhoods, to the underground cinema, night court, domestic court, the Chinese New Year celebration (if there

are such), and scores of others. It would acquaint them with where and what the tourist attractions are; it would take them to the airport; it would show them how to file for services when they need them; it would give them a sense of their city. Here they would find out how to call an ambulance, how to get psychiatric emergency service, how to apply for these or those benefits, whom to complain to about this or that: the Better Business Bureau, the Rent Control Office, the District Attorney's office, and so on. It would acquaint them with the services offered by the Housing Authority, the Board of Health, adult education programs, the Legal Aid Society, private and public family service organizations, the Department of Hospitals, the Civil Liberties Union, out-patient clinics, the Visiting Nurses' Association.

12. ADVERTISING AND PROPAGANDA Here students would practice analyzing and interpreting the political and economic persuasions that flow around them incessantly. They would deal with local and international propaganda pitches, with the relationship, as Ellul[28] describes it, between technological progress and propaganda, with advertising's protean forms: radio and TV commercials, printed ads, direct mail, billboards, packaging and point-of-sale promotions. They would practice reading between the lines, understanding what is *not* said, understanding the *purposes* of the message-originator, understanding the weaknesses of the receiver. Students would consider the interrelationships inherent in the multiple appeals of advertising: visual, verbal, auditory, etc. A course like this is bound to have practical value and intense interest for adolescents. Chase's *The Power of Words* and Hayakawa's *Language in Thought and Action* might be used as texts with average classes. Even as demanding a work as Ellul's *Propaganda* might be used with superior groups.

13. CHILD DEVELOPMENT AND FAMILY PSYCHOLOGY Here the girls would study family resources, sources of outside help on personal and family problems (medical and

---

[27]John Dewey. *How We Think*. Boston: D. C. Heath, 1933.

[28]Jacques Ellul. *The Technological Society*. New York: Alfred A. Knopf, 1964.

psychiatric clinics, marriage counseling, etc.), principles of child development, cause of family friction, etc. As texts, the class could use not only popular books like Spock's *Baby and Child Care*[29] and Gesell and Ilg's *Child Development*,[30] and the U.S. Government pamphlets, but they could also study popular presentations in the magazines, papers, and on TV to evaluate their worth and seriousness.

14. DO-IT-YOURSELF HOUSEHOLD REPAIRS AND IMPROVEMENTS

This would deal with strictly practical matters that any boy who's going to be a tenant or homeowner would want to know: wiring and rewiring, fuses, circuits, over-loading, circuit-breakers, types of cables and their uses, plumbing, changing washers, fixing valves, carpentry, plastering, painting various types of surfaces for various purposes with various types of paint, waterproofing, insulating, weatherstripping, caulking, air conditioning, fans, circulation, ventilation, floors and their care, fire-hazards and how to prevent them, and appliance repairs. Especially now that the so-called "comprehensive high school" looks as though it is to become a reality in most places, a course like this could well satisfy the requirements of a quite heterogeneous group of boys, including many who might not be interested in any of the regular vocational shop courses.

15. CAR REPAIRS AND IMPROVEMENTS

This would not be a course in auto mechanics. Instead it would provide theory and practice in "little" jobs like polishing, washing, tuneups, tires, minor adjustments, gasolines, oils, checking and replacement of parts, customizing, accessories and their usefulness, sources of supply and advice, how not to get cheated in the service station, how to check things for yourself, and how to judge a used car. Texts might include repair manuals, *Consumer Reports* (the annual car issue) and hot rod and custom car magazines. Or all this material might be incorporated into an expanded "driver education" course.

[29]Benjamin Spock. *Baby and Child Care.* New York: Pocket Books, 1946.
[30]Arnold Gesell and Frances L. Ilg. *Child Development.* New York: Harper and Row, 1949.

16. MEDICAL SCIENCE

This would be designed to acquaint the layman with modern principles and concepts related to medicine and human health. It might include discussion of matters such as sex: its psychology, physiology, and mores; medical hygiene; preventive medicine; medical practices (what to expect your doctor to do for you); sanitation; medical research and recent discoveries; health emergencies and what to do about them; danger signals and symptoms; where and how to get help and treatment. In addition to current medical columns purveyed by the various periodicals, students might study a popular medical "encyclopedia" or the Consumer's Union manual, *The Medicine Show.* Here again, an elective course in school would capitalize on a significant out-of-school interest and use it to convey a useful body of integrated and current information and a sensible set of attitudes.

17. CONSUMER AND LEISURE ENGLISH

Students would discuss and practice how to read labels and other "fine print" intelligently; how to read and understand applications for loans, charge accounts, subscriptions, book clubs, and similar promotional programs; writing letters of inquiry and complaint; reading advertisements between the lines; understanding and appraising TV and radio commercials; getting reliable information on quality and prices; entering promotional "contests": writing last lines for jingles, figuring out rebuses, or telling "Why I like Gloppo in 25 words or less"; doing crossword puzzles; learning teenage etiquette. As texts, the class could use magazines, catalogs, newspapers, and similar materials.

18. GETTING YOUR MONEY'S WORTH

The emphasis here would be on such concerns as comparing supermarket prices (on a cost-per-unit basis, for example); family and personal budgeting; home rents and purchases; charge accounts and their "real" cost; installment purchases and their cost; insurance of various kinds: liability, health, straight life, term, hospitalization, etc.; savings and investment media; where to get reliable information on products and prices; how to save on taxes and compute returns. The thesis expressed by David K. Gast in his article, "Consumer Education and the

Madison Avenue Morality,"[31] would be part of the course; major materials would include *Consumer Reports, Changing Times,* advertisements, and application blanks.

19. HOW TO GET A JOB AND GET AHEAD

This course would survey job resources and requirements in service, communications, manufacturing, white-collar, retail, professional armed-forces, civil-service, and other lines of work. As a career survey, it could be adapted to the "level" and needs of any class. It would acquaint students with job resource manuals available in the library, with job-getting services like the commercial employment agencies and the state employment service, and other similar matters.

20. EVERYDAY LAW

This would be a little like the conventional "business law" courses widely offered in commercial curricula today, but it would not be restricted to commercial applications. In addition to these, it would familiarize students with the ins and outs of negligence suits, leases, contracts, citizens' rights and duties both in court and vis-a-vis the police, and it would acquaint them with the nature of civil suits, family court, small claims court, etc. Trips to the various types of courts would supplement a simple law text. Class discussions would be based on hypothetical and even actual cases representing real situations.

21. PART-TIME AND SUMMER EMPLOYMENT OPPORTUNITIES WORKSHOP

This would be an exploration of job possibilities; instruction in job requirements and duties; a survey of retail, camp, resort, civil-service, library, dining-room, Park Department, ice-cream, post office, even babysitting opportunities, and how to get and make the most of them. The mechanics and legalities of working papers and other school and governmental requirements would be touched upon. Students would be acquainted with school programs such as STEP (School To Employment Program), the Job Corps, co-op educational programs, and others.

22. HOME DECORATION

This would combine features of traditional courses touching upon this area that are currently offered by art, home economics, shop, and merchandising departments. For interior decoration, it would cover color, texture, shape, size, line, pattern, fabric, furniture, accessories, utility, quality, sources, costs. For exterior decoration, topics would include painting, gardening, outdoor design, patios, porches, grills, houseplants, flower-cutting and arranging, landscaping, and bug and pest control.

23. DESIGN CRAFTS

This would correlate art and shop and perhaps even sewing in providing introduction to and practice in the creative crafts of jewelry-making, block printing, ceramics, fabric printing, weaving, knitting, crocheting, gros-point and petit-point embroidery, rug braiding and hooking, quilt-making, sculpture, wall decorations, gift wrapping, toy making, and making ornaments and artificial flowers.

24. MOVIE, TV, AND STILL PHOTOGRAPHY

Going beyond the typical art department course in still photography, this would include color, black and white, film types, film speeds, camera types, shutter speeds and lens openings, camera accessories, filters, darkroom chemicals, processing, and manipulations. In addition, using movie and TV equipment (cameras, sound equipment, monitoring screens, TV tape recorder, etc.) it would correlate the arts of improvision, acting, dramatic writing, continuity, sound background, advertising psychology, and others, in providing students with an opportunity to create commercial and artistic work of all kinds for film and TV. Kohl in *36 Children*[32] has written of how successful ordinary creative writing can be in capable and imaginative hands. A course in creative photography might be even more exciting to adolescents.

25. NUTRITION, DIET, AND PARTY MAKING

This course would cover nutrients and what they do, calorie counting and special diets, expensive vs. inexpensive foods, economy in shopping, planning ahead for meals, budgeting food purchases. In addition, it would deal with problems of entertaining, such as providing hors

[31]David K. Gast. "Consumer Education and the Madison Avenue Morality," *Phi Delta Kappan,* June 1967.

[32]Herbert Kohl. *36 Children.* New York: New American Library, 1967.

d'oeuvres, beverages, dinners, after-dinner noshes, table settings, etc.

26. THE STOCK MARKET Any student, rich or poor, might experience an interest in mediums of investment and speculation. This course could introduce such matters as the mechanics of financial transactions, the stock exchanges, round-lot and odd-lot trading, commissions, margin, analysis of individual companies and industries, sources of information and advice, "technical" (chart) analysis, fundamental economic influences, and other investment and speculative vehicles like bonds, puts and calls, mutual funds, rights, and commodities. Popular and technical publications that could supplement the *Times* and the *Wall Street Journal* as test materials are plentiful.

27. SONGWRITING This course would be taught jointly by a music teacher and an English teacher and would be open to would-be lyricists, tunesmiths, and arrangers. As an elective, it would have appeal for many youngsters because of its concern with the here-and-now world of fads and fashions in popular music. As education, it would make sense because it would help transform a largely passive interest into something approaching craftsmanship and creativity.

28. INTERMEDIA Here students interested in creative enterprises like the theater, film, dance, "happenings," painting, sculpture, or just plain self-expression could experiment with new kinds and combinations of art productions. Some of this material could be developed and polished for public presentation in auditorium or library, or coordinated with the school's regular extracurricular activities, such as the school play or "sing." Combinations of media, like lighting, color, sound, shape, depth, movement, and texture would be organized into new and experimental artforms.

29. CHOREOGRAPHY Open to students interested in dance, this elective would give them an opportunity for creative self-expression, for coping with the problems of organizing movement interestingly and effectively, of filling the stage, of achieving audience involvement, of building a climax, of coordinating and unifying diverse kinds of movement into a viable whole,

etc. The class would involve itself in public performance within and outside the school, both in recital form and as participants in many school theatrical presentations.

30. PROTEST LITERATURE Taught by an English–Social Studies team, this elective would acquaint students with major works of protest literature, from Aristophanes through Swift to the present day. Masterpieces, as well as current ephemera, would be studied both as metaphors of the human condition and as effective reflections of their times and places of origin.

31. SPEED READING Open to any student who wants to increase his reading power, this course would appeal, I believe, primarily to the college-bound or commercial student. The many books available today on better and faster reading, along with tachistoscopic exercises, would provide ample materials for a truly challenging and effective course.

32. SPEEDWRITING As an alternative to standard courses in stenography, an elective in speedwriting might have appeal for students who want a system of fast note-taking for personal use rather than a commercially salable skill. Students might well be attracted by the possibility of mastering a high-speed writing method based on the familiar longhand symbols and therefore more accessible from the start and easier to practice at any time, even when incompletely learned.

33. MEMORY TRAINING Self-help books on this subject are numerous and interesting, but they cannot provide the stimulus or supervision that a teacher and a course can give. Aside from the trivial and superficial appeals that may inhere in this kind of skill-subject, in today's increasingly non-"linear" world it may be more and more important for students to develop methods (even gimmicky ones) for remembering what they see and hear.

34. ROCK AND FOLK SURVEY The history and current state of the rock'n'roll and folk music industries would be the subject matter here. Recordings and dittoed lyrics would be the text. Student research, presentations, symposia, TV tapes, audio tapes, visits to recording and broadcasting studios, and many other activities could form the methodology.

35. INDEPENDENT STUDY With the approval of the appropriate faculty member, a student wanting to pursue studies along lines dictated by his own interests would have the opportunity to consult on the preparation of a study program consisting, perhaps, of suggested readings and an appropriate time schedule. Whether the subject were statistics or psychological novels, the student could proceed at his own pace, consult when necessary with his adviser, and reap the private benefit of having explored a subject himself.

36. WORLD RELIGIONS Comparative study of religious beliefs and practices would acquaint students with the traditions, rituals, and dogmas of the great religions of the East and West. In an age of ecumenism, this kind of factual study would be of interest and of value to students. Parents would approve of it and religious organizations would cooperate in planning and executing it.

37. THE ARTS TODAY A study of the avantgarde in painting, sculpture, film, architecture, multimedia, happenings, dance, theater, poetry, the novel, etc., would capitalize on everything that is happening in the world of the creative arts concurrently with the course. Students would see actual productions and exhibitions throughout the semester and read current materials such as exhibition catalogs, magazines and newspaper criticism, and the Sunday *Times*. Interrelationships between the various art forms and the milieux in which they occur, taboos and conventions observed and broken, and the implications of what a medium is *not* attempting would comprise the substance of the course.

38. VARIETY IN AMERICAN SOCIETY This survey of American sociology would explore varying traditions and customs among segments of America's population drawn from diverse ethnic groups, national origins, ages, socioeconomic classes, and parts of the country. Emphasis would be not on a mere anecdotal account of other groups' funny customs, but on how traditions interact with social, political, ethnic, economic, and geographical background factors as well as with the future. One possible text resource for such a course would be the magazine *Transaction*.

39. EMCEEING, NEWSCASTING AND DISK-JOCKEYING This speech elective would give showbiz-minded students a chance to study and practice the techniques required in the entertainment industry; gagwriting, timing, introducing guests, interviewing, introducing songs, reading commercials, newscasting. Video tape and audio tape would be the standard performance media for classroom sessions. These could culminate in weekly or monthly assembly or P-A system entertainment and public service programs featuring the work of the class.

40. COMPUTER TECHNOLOGY As an elective course this could appeal to a heterogeneous group including those with a philosophical interest in works such as those by Ellul and Weiner, those with a mathematical bent and a possible career interest in programming, and those commercial students who want to learn key punch operation in a realistic setting.

CONCLUSION: SO WHAT?

The foregoing has dealt almost exclusively with the content—as opposed to the methods and hardware—of the relevant high school curriculum. Naturally, much must be done to make the manner as strongly integrative as the matter. TV tapes, programed texts, team-teaching arrangements, individual language-lab style modules, multimedia materials, and the actual commercial media of newspapers, magazines, radio, TV, and film all would play a more prominent role in the new curriculum than they typically do today. The reason for this would be partly that such a school would probably be more interested in relevant methodology by virtue of its commitment to relevant content, and partly because many of the above courses would necessitate the use of out-of-school learnings, both as to substance and as to vehicle. The point here is that although this paper has stressed substance, there can be no doubt that an immensely important feature of the relevant high school will be its style.

A panacea? Hardly, because the out-of-school learnings will stem from the same society that supports the schools, with all its weakness, contradiction, corruption, vulgarity, and short-sightedness. But at least the school will stand a chance of playing an integrative rather than an alienating role. At least it may help students, not to ignore the realities around them while they are in school, but actually to deal with them. At least it may acquaint them with ways in which their surroundings can be useful, threatening, amusing, significant. At least it may help them to find resources within themselves that they can exercise with pride and pleasure. At least it will help them feel that school is for real, that school is "with it," that school is aware that electronic and social revolutions are transforming America. At least it will give them an awareness that controversy can be a source of revelation and illumination, not just repression and discomfort. At least the pupils—even the poor—can feel that school is giving them experiences that count, that they want, that they value, and that connect them with the world instead of isolating them from it. And at least there would be less reason to think of the dropouts as being the smart ones.

How to overcome the inertia and conservatism that paralyze big-system schools, or the local pressures that hound decentralized systems, remains unsolved. But if the problem can be solved, and if the above courses and others like them can be instituted as the elective half of a youngster's high school experience, then adolescence might finally make more sense to kids.

University Cities in the Year 2000

STEPHEN R. GRAUBARD

This imaginative projection of the university of the future lends clearer perspective to our colleges of the present, besides alerting us to the need for intelligent planning ahead.

This, an essay in conjecture, attempts to describe institutions, now existing, whose character may be significantly altered in the next thirty-five years. In the coming decades we can expect to witness the establishment of new kinds of universities (some bearing familiar and even ancient names) in new kinds of urban environments; these I choose to call "university cities." No such city exists now. Residents of Cambridge or Berkeley sometimes imagine that they live in such places; those who inhabit New York or Chicago rarely permit themselves this illusion. In the sense that I use the term *university city*, it is inapplicable to any of these urban centers. Cambridge, Berkeley, Chicago, and New York all harbor major university communities in the same way that Bloomington, Ann Arbor, Madison, and New Haven do, but these are not now (and several may never become) university cities.

What, then, is the university city of the year 2000 to be? Essentially, it will be an urban area of some size and economic importance that will shelter a significant number of strong educational institutions, broadly defined; these institutions will co-operate in ways that are now only dimly perceived. For a university city to develop, there must be a continuing relation among institutions of learning, public and private. Moreover, the collective influence of these bodies must be greater than that of all other corporate groups in the city.

My meaning may be made more precise if I dwell on American cities as they exist today. Many of these would qualify, in my view, as "company towns." Their economy and social organization testify to an overwhelming commitment to some particular activity, usually commercial, but never primarily educational or intellectual. This is most conspicuously evident in our resort cities. While Miami's economy is not solely built on sun and surf, were both suddenly found to be undesirable qualities by vacationers, serious difficulties would ensue for the city. However much Washington, D. C., may imagine itself to be America's London or Paris, it in fact resembles Ottawa and Canberra more than it does the older European capitals. Why? Because it is a "company town"—its business is essentially governmental. The presence of museums, universities, research institutes, and the like cannot alter Washington's fundamental preoccupation with "that man"—his plans and intentions and the op-

From S. R. Graubard, University cities in the year 2000. *Daedalus*, 1967, *96*(3), 817–822. Reprinted by permission of DAEDALUS, Journal of the American Academy of Arts and Sciences, Boston, Mass., Summer 1967, *Toward the Year 2000: Work in Progress.*

position they are calculated to produce. The city's "business" is government in the same way that Detroit's is auto manufacture.

When we look at the larger cities—New York, Los Angeles, Chicago—we encounter economies that are considerably more diversified; these places are indeed redolent of European cities. Would it be a mistake to suggest, however, that all are essentially concerned with commercial and industrial enterprise, with buying and selling, producing and exchanging? These cities take justifiable pride in their outstanding universities; it is in no way a denigration of either the cities or their universities to suggest that educational institutions do not dominate in these great and populous areas. When we say that DuPont dominates Wilmington, the meaning of that statement is clear. It does not express a statistical truth; rather, it suggests a form of influence that cannot be denied. In the same way, New York—immeasurably more complex—is dominated by law, banking, publishing, merchandising, manufacture, advertising, and the like. What do these have in common? They are all essentially business enterprises; their end is profit. There are other institutions in New York—universities, museums, libraries, hospitals—whose reason for being is not primarily commercial, but they do not dominate the city.

By the year 2000, however, the business of certain cities in America will be education, in the broadest sense. These cities will be as different from the commercial, industrial, and governmental cities of today as the latter are from the cathedral towns of an earlier European society. If I am correct in believing that a few cities of this sort will have established themselves in the United States by the year 2000, they must not be seen as displacing existing cities; they will co-exist with them, but will have a different sort of appeal for a growing segment of an increasingly mobile American society.

Why should such a development be anticipated? The easiest answer would be that education, health, and leisure are all becoming "big business." It is as reasonable to expect activity in these matters to center in a few large cities as it was for such concentrations to develop when the manufacture and exchange of specialized industrial products were first undertaken. Those who would point to the dispersal of industry in recent years would find fault with this argument; for them, dispersal offers the "new model" for all institutional development. They would also contend that since health and education needs are universal, one can logically expect high-quality institutions to be established in many places. Those who argue in this way assume that it is not impossible that as many as twenty or twenty-five strong state university systems, each co-operating with other educational institutions, will have established themselves by the year 2000. A new form of "educational equality" among states will have come into being. Since federal funds will undoubtedly exert a large influence on all future educational development—as much on the university as on other levels—this would seem to give support to the idea of a proliferation and dispersal of educational facilities.

If university cities—in the sense that I use the term—could be wished into being by a generous flow of public funds, many would soon exist. But I do not conceive of these cities developing in this manner; rather, I see them as coming about through an increased awareness by many educational institutions, public and private, of their interrelatedness and interdependence. Only when the museum director, the university president, the hospital administrator, the computer technician, the laboratory scientist, and the organizer of a "new industry" recognize their common interests —and understand why no one of them is engaged in a peripheral activity of slight interest to the other—will there be the beginnings of the kind of co-operation that may in time create the university city. It is not a matter of any one of these serving the other, but of each pursuing a set of common objectives that must, for lack of a better term, be defined as broadly educational.

This is more than a call for co-operation among the so-called institutions of higher learning. It goes far beyond the admission that no university, however rich or powerful, can hope to offer instruction in the wide range of subjects now deemed important. So long as universities define co-operation in terms of curricula, imagining that the need is to provide their students with exchange privileges, the implications of the concept of "interdependence" are lost. What is required is not simply that universities co-operate with one another, but that they see how they can relate to other institutions which are not formally constituted as "universities," but which function as such in certain of their activities. Instruction will remain as a central concern of the university; in time, it will be recognized that it has a new dimension.

The present university population mix—overwhelmingly undergraduate and predoctoral or preprofessional—will change dramatically in the next thirty-five years, at least in university cities. There, great numbers of postdoctoral fellows and professional adults of all ages will congregate for longer or shorter periods. They will be seeking something quite different from what is today so quaintly called "continuing education." Long before the year 2000, a businessman will be as apt to spend a sabbatical year at the university as in travel and sport. When men and women no longer deem it unreasonable to pursue two or three different careers in succession, the university city will provide the stimulus (and the instruction) to make such things possible.

University cities will prove attractive to a great variety of industries, but particularly to those that depend heavily on certain kinds of professional competence. The development of light and highly sophisticated industry in Boston along Route 128 —with its proximity to M.I.T. and Harvard—will be seen as a very early prototype of a kind of commercial enterprise that will become increasingly common. Between such industry, educational institutions, research institutes, medical and scientific establishments, and cultural bodies of the greatest variety, close links will exist. The men and women involved in one will recognize their "kin" in the other. The concept of "my university" or "my museum" will seem increasingly foreign. Such institutions will admit to a kind of collective stewardship. Older instruments of control, whether by trustees or corporate owners, may be perpetuated, but they will no longer reflect the administrative, commercial, or aesthetic values that were common when these bodies were more self-consciously independent.

These new relations will serve to instill a new kind of civic pride. University cities will differ markedly; some of the difference will reflect the great variety of co-operative arrangements that will have been worked out to express the inter-

dependence established. Although the idea service will be paramount, it will be commun cated in a very new idiom. The object will n be simply to *serve* the city, in the sense of atten ing to its problems, controlling air pollutio crime, and the like, but rather, to demonstra the primacy and necessity of certain kinds of i tellectual endeavor. Those very institutions th now exist on the periphery of cities—serving f limited times relatively selected elements of t population—will be recognized to be central.

If the university city will scarcely resemble t city of today, so the universities within those citi will show qualities reflecting the new kinds of e perimentation that will be common. Attachme to a particular university for four or more yea will not occur so frequently as it does today. St dents, increasingly mobile, will spend periods several universities and in several university c ies. At one time or another many will choose live in one of the greater university cities. A st dent will begin his higher education in a sm college, leave after a time to spend a period in university city, migrate to another, and purs his profession in a third. It is not improbable th many of the more gifted men and women w have spent some part of their lives in one of t great university cities. The role of student will a more anomalous one than it is presently. many more people of various ages and in vario stages of their professional careers engage in u versity studies, there will be less disposition think of the university as the habitat principal of mature adolescents and young adults.

In university cities, faculty will not exist as corporate group set apart. Their relations wi other professional groups will be more regula At a time when London will be an hour's distan from New York, scholars and teachers will divi their time between several university cities, teac ing and studying regularly both in this count and abroad. This perpetual coming and going w render even more difficult than is now the ca the creation of environments suited to contempl tion and reflection. The bustle of university citi will not be welcome to all scholars; many w seek to pursue their work in greater isolation even in rural retreats. The greatest number wi nevertheless, accept the inconveniences and fi attractive the city's intellectual and social qua ties. The university cities will emerge as principal centers of artistic and creative endeavor. They will support such talents, not least because they will provide an ample market for their product.

How such institutions and cities will relate to those that maintain more traditional separate identities is difficult to know. It is not to be excluded that the new university cities will be viewed with alarm by many who will prefer traditional institutional arrangements. The virtues of "independence" and "smallness" are too powerfully represented in American tradition to be lightly set aside. It is by no means certain that either the Federal Government or many of the state governments will recognize the necessity of such cities or assist in their construction. Some may believe, mistakenly, that "new buildings" are called for, when the object, in fact, is the construction of "new bridges" between existing institutions. The reconceptualizing of the community's interest and the liberating of energies, still too narrowly tied to single institutions, are most urgently required. Unless these are recognized as responses to both an individual and a social need, there is small prospect that university cities will develop. If education, in the broadest sense, is to emerge as the major activity in a number of urban centers, this can be accomplished only by a dramatic reformulation of what is implicit in the idea of education in an advanced industrial society. Where an increasing number of men and women look upon work as a source of income, but also as a condition for personal fulfillment, where the line between leisure and work becomes increasingly indistinct, where definition of a cultural institution is considerably broadened so that it includes many bodies which would not be thought "cultural" today, where the lines between education, health (physical and mental), and leisure are drawn in new ways—there are prospects for a new kind of university in a new kind of urban environment.

Chapter 7: Suggested Additional Readings

BAUMAN, Z. Some problems in contemporary education. *International Social Science Journal*, 1967, *19*(3), 325–337. Education is discussed in terms of its relevance to adolescence, to problems of emotional security, and to the larger society.

CHICKERING, A. W. Cultural sophistication and college experience. *Educational Record*, 1971, *52*(2), 125–128. Studies were undertaken on seven college campuses to determine how, and to what extent, students' cultural attitudes were altered by their total college experiences, including student–faculty contacts, campus friendships, teaching methods, and institutional characteristics.

EURICH, A. High school, 1980. *Bulletin of the National Association of Secondary School Principals*, May 1971, *55*, 42–53. Three prominent educators offer suggestions for supervising schools in the years just ahead.

FELDMAN, K. A., & NEWCOMB, T. M. *The impact of college on students. Vol. 1: An analysis of four decades of research. Vol. 2: Summary tables.* San Francisco: Jossey-Bass, 1969. This two-volume work represents a summary and discussion of what has been learned over the past forty years (from the mid-twenties to the mid-sixties) about the impact of colleges on their students.

GLISSMEYER, C. H. Which school for the sixth grader, the elementary or the middle school? *California Journal of Educational Research*, 1969, *20*, 176–185. The middle school (grades 5–8 or 6–8), a new approach developed around the needs of early adolescents, is recommended as the appropriate avenue to personal and social growth.

HAVIGHURST, R. J. High schools for the future. *Kentucky School Journal*, 1969, *47*(6), 18–19. The author recommends changes in the schools' role in a rapidly changing society.

HITCHCOCK, J. Revolution in the university. *The Yale Review*, 1970, *40*(2), 161–174. The author appraises students' criticisms of the university and suggests what may best be done about them.

HOLLISTER, W. G. Preparing the minds of the future. *Bulletin of the National Association of Secondary School Principals*, 1966, *50*, 30–50. The author suggests ways of educating youth for the much tougher, more stressful intellectual and social life of the society of the future.

KATZ, J., & SANFORD, N. The new student power and needed educational reforms. *Phi Delta Kappan*, 1966, *48*(8), 397–401. Student problems and discontent have reached major proportions and deserve attention. Practical suggestions are made for improving the situation.

MAYHEW, L. B. Changing the balance of power. *Saturday Review*, August 17, 1968. 48–49, 57–58. Campus riots have pointed up the many contradictions and inconsistencies in American higher education today. Suggestions are made for radical revision in university administration.

MC DILL, E. L., MEYERS, E. D., JR., & RIGSBY, L. C. Institutional effects on the academic behavior of high school students. *Sociology of Education*, Summer 1967, *40*(3), 181–199. This study was designed to assess the influence of different pedagogical and social dimensions of school environment on the achievement of students while controlling for relevant personal variables.

PARSONS, T.   The strange case of academic organization. *Journal of Higher Education,* June 1971, *42*(6), 486–498. Parsons and Mayhew discuss the relevance of the college's organization and function to its goal, while detecting significant weaknesses in the system.

RINGWALD, B. E., MANN, R. D., ROSENWEIN, R., & MC KEACHIE, W. J.   Conflict and style in the college classroom—an intimate study. *Psychology Today,* 1971, *4*(9), 45–47, 76–79. The intellectual and emotional interplay between teachers and students was analyzed in four college classes. The data revealed an array of emotional and interpersonal accompaniments to teaching and learning.

SANFORD, N.   Education for individual development. *American Journal of Orthopsychiatry,* 1968, *38,* 858–868. Sanford challenges teachers to concentrate on developing in youth such characteristics as flexibility, creativity, and openness to experience.

STUDER, K. E.   Relevance and responsibility: The academic fulcrum. *Journal of General Education,* 1971, *23*(1), 45–51. The author discusses the plight of the colleges as an ideological battleground, with the possible effects on professors and on the education the youth receives.

SUCHODOLSKI, B.   Civilization—youth—education. *Youth and Society,* 1970, *1*(4), 392–419. An educator discusses what youth are like, what they are becoming, what they will have to be, and the tasks of education in preparing youth for a rapidly changing society.

TROLL, L. E., NEUGARTEN, B. L., & KRAINES, R. J.   Similarities in values and other personality characteristics in college students and their parents. *Merrill-Palmer Quarterly,* 1969, *15*(4), 323–336. A study of resemblances between college students and their parents revealed greater likenesses in values than in other areas.

8

The Adolescent and Creativity

Creativity may be defined in various ways. Some writers differ over whether it is a process or a product. Guilford (1962), a pioneer in the study of creativity, speaks of "originality" as the production of "unusual, farfetched, remote, or clever responses [p. 382]." An idea is novel if it is new so far as the particular individual is concerned. Paulston (1968) sees creativity as "a form of energy of the psyche released when there is a healthy relationship between the conscious and unconscious. This energy, the source of creativity, grows with use and contributes to the health of the psyche, just as the healthy psyche releases energy for creative activity [p. 370]." Developmental studies have typically dealt with creativity as a process. Torrance (1963b), for example, defines creative thinking as "the process of sensing gaps or disturbing missing elements; forming new hypotheses concerning them; testing these hypotheses and communicating the results, possibly modifying and retesting the hypotheses [p. 80]."

Many studies have been conducted to determine what traits characterize the creative individual. However, to date, the characteristics reported have been so numerous that we lack a clear picture of what the creative person is really like. According to Parnes (1971), the creative person possesses sensitivity, synergy, and serendipity. Sensitivity involves "awareness, a keen use of senses, and perception to spot incongruities, deficiencies, and so forth [p. 22]." A cartoon in another book highlights a lack of sensitivity to the environment with this caption: "Dear God, I want to be an inventor but I don't know what to invent." The sensitive individual discovers what to invent. The second characteristic, synergy, might be defined as the ability to conceive a whole greater than the sum of its parts. For example, a Japanese inventor designed a machine that "turns garbage into construction blocks. The steel-clad blocks are odor-free and unbreakable and may be used as foundations in boggy areas, flood control dykes, or as landfill . . .[*The Financial Post,* June 1, 1968, quoted in Parnes, 1971, p. 22]." The third characteristic, serendipity, suggests an awareness of relevancy in accidental happenings. Thus when Duke Ellington was playing a concert in an outdoor festival and a plane flew low over the grandstand, Duke simply modified the tempo to integrate the sounds of the engine; then he directed the plane along with the orchestra.

One way to identify behaviors which may be effective in promoting creativity is to analyze the characteristics of "good copers," and to observe the strategies that such persons use in facing new problems. In this sense, coping behavior involves effective task accomplishment without excessive cost to the individual. In studies by Hammer (1964) and by Parloff and Datta (1965), creative adolescents are described as having a high degree of emotional strength, determination, and ambition, accompanied by sensitivity and intuition. MacKinnon (1965) describes eminent architects as being self-confident, imaginative, nonconforming, and possessing inner ethical and artistic standards; they also score low on various anxiety scales.

Unfortunately, we cannot yet form definitive conclusions about the characteristics of creative individuals because subjects used in such investigations seldom constitute a random sampling of the general population. Besides, such studies are rarely conducted in terms of adequate criterion groups and precise definition of personality measures. However, one helpful byproduct of such studies has been the realization that non-cognitive factors, especially those concerned with motivation and personality, are important correlates of creativity. These factors include nonconformity, freedom of expression, playfulness, and curiosity. Our first reading, by Krippner, is illustrative of the many studies designed to determine what gifted youth are like.

Since all these factors are largely determined by environment, especially the home, researchers have attempted to establish relationships between creative development and patterns of child rearing. In one such study (Nichols, 1964), where creativity was related to dimensions of authoritarian–control, hostility–rejection, and democratic attitudes, only auhoritarian–control factors proved significant. Authoritarian attitudes of the mother related negatively to creativity and originality in the child. Another study, by Getzels and Jackson (1961), demonstrated that the parents of highly creative adolescents were not authoritarian but stressed openness to experience and enthusiasm for life. By contrast, parents of highly intellectual, but uncreative, youths promoted "good" or conforming behavior and studiousness in their children. Indeed, one obstacle each adolescent must overcome, if he is to become involved in creative production, is a long-standing tendency to be conformist. A unique feature of the early years, when the child is primarily exposed to the family and school cultures, is his continuous exposure to conformity training. During these years, when he is being socialized, he is being trained primarily to behave the way others do and to develop attitudes similar to those of others. However, he must attain a high degree of personal autonomy if he is to produce free-hanging, imaginative ideas (Cashdan, 1971).

Creativity also varies by sex and age, even in early grades. By grade 3, reports Torrance (1961), boys score higher than girls on creative tasks, because girls from their earliest years are trained to accept things as they are. Yet if girls have access to scientific toys and other intellectual stimuli usually provided for boys, they too make progress in scientific thinking. As the child matures, generally he becomes more creative. However, the sheer passage of time is not the determining factor here; it is the child's experiences over the years which control his creative growth. The boy who becomes concerned over his masculine image at adolescence may become less creative because he represses sensitive feelings. Both sensitivity and independence are important components of creativity (Torrance, 1963a).

Another major question in the area of creativity is how best to develop it. What sort of educational techniques may prove most effective in stimulating children and adolescents to creative production? One hypothesis suggests that the more ideas an individual generates, the more likely he will be to find good ones—by increasing the likelihood of chance associations that might prove productive (Parnes, 1971).

The teacher's role is especially important in capturing the essence of the creative process. Some teachers are skilled craftsmen of their trade but lack a certain spark; others skillfully encourage youngsters in their quest for fertile moments. However, most teachers classify the creative child who is manifestly bored by classroom routines as a behavior problem. In a study by Torrance (1964), pupils of highly creative teachers, as determined by various objective tests, demonstrated a considerable gain in creative writing ability over a three-month period, while those who had less creative teachers showed no improvement.

Even less able teachers, it is argued, may adapt themselves for creativity and learn how to encourage creativity in students. One method, says Paulston (1968), is to scold conformity and praise disagreement. Students should be taught to question intelligently their own perceptions, their teachers, and their textbooks. "It's so because the textbook says so," should become an obsolete argument. Another authority, Davis, author of the second reading selection in this chapter, portrays creativity as possessing three components. The first, creative attitude, amounts to a favorable attitude toward imaginative problem-solving. The second element consists of certain cognitive abilities, which facilitate use of the relevant mental processes; and the third includes techniques for the systematic production of creative ideas, through which the creative process is engineered. The program he describes for developing creativity in adolescents is itself quite creative, and it incorporates various principles and concepts relating to these three conceptualizations.

Authorities differ somewhat on whether creative potential may be produced, or simply discovered and developed. Are some children born heirs to a creative infinite? Or is it training that makes an intellectual discovery the supreme human thrill? Ausubel (1964) argues that the widespread challenge to teach for creativity is based on several untenable propositions. It assumes that every child has potentialities for creative production, provided they are not stifled by the educational system, and that even if the child has no such potential, inspired teaching may somehow "instill" it. Moreover, all creativity is assumed to be of one piece, instead of diverse and of many sorts. However, says Ausubel, the school can help children who possess unique creative potential by arranging opportunities for spontaneity and individuality, rewarding creative accomplishment, and providing suitable guidance and encouragement.

Unlike Ausubel, Havighurst (1961) believes the production of mentally superior individuals to be a matter of social engineering rather than one of discovery and exploitation of natural resources. On the basis of studies at the University of California, Professor Richard Crutchfield similarly concludes that the attitudes and skills which characterize innovative thinkers can indeed be stimulated by appropriate methods and techniques (Covington, 1967). His point of view, if valid, holds great promise for disadvantaged groups.

REFERENCES

AUSUBEL, D. P.   Creativity, general creative abilities, and the creative individual. *Psychology of the Schools*, 1964, *1*(4), 344–347.

CASHDAN, S.   Social participation and subcultural influences in the study of adolescent creativity. *Adolescence*, 1971, *6*(21), 39–52.

COVINGTON, M. V.   Productive thinking and a cognitive curriculum. Invited Paper Presented at Symposium, *Studies of the Inquiry Process; Problems of Theory Description and Teaching*. American Psychological Association Convention, Washington, D.C., September, 1967.

GETZELS, J. W., & JACKSON, F. W.   Family environment and cognitive style: A study of the sources of highly intelligent and of highly creative adolescents. *American Sociological Review*, 1961, *26*, 351–359.

GUILFORD, J. P.   Factors that hinder and aid creativity. *Teachers College Record*, 1962, *63*, 380–392.

HAMMER, E. F.   Creativity and feminine ingredients in young male artists. *Perceptual and Motor Skills*, 1964, *19*, 414.

HAVIGHURST, R. J.   Conditions productive of superior children. *Teachers College Record*, 1961, *62*, 524–531.

MAC KINNON, D. W.   Personality and the realization of creative potential. *American Psychologist*, 1965, *20*, 273–281.

NICHOLS, R. C.   Parental attitudes of mothers of intelligent adolescents and creativity of their children. *Child Development*, 1964, *35*, 1041–1049.

PARLOFF, M. B., & DATTA, L.   Personality characteristics of the potentially creative scientist. In J. H. Masserman (Ed.), *Science and Psychoanalysis* (Vol. 8), New York: Grune & Stratton, 1965. Pp. 91–106.

PARNES, S. J.   Creativity: Developing human potential. *Journal of Creative Behavior*, 1971, *5*(1), 15–36.

PAULSTON, C. B.   On creativity and teaching. *Teachers College Record*, January 1968, *69*(4), 370–371.

TORRANCE, E. P.   Factors affecting creative thinking in children: An interim research report. *Merrill-Palmer Quarterly*, 1961, *7*, 171–180.

TORRANCE, E. P.   Changing reactions of preadolescent girls to tasks requiring creative scientific thinking. *Journal of Genetic Psychology*, 1963, *102*, 217–223. (a)

TORRANCE, E. P.   *Education and the creative potential*, Minneapolis, Minn.: University of Minnesota Press, 1963, P. 80. (b)

TORRANCE, E. P.   Education and creativity. In C. W. Taylor (Ed.), *Creativity: Progress and potential*. New York: McGraw-Hill, 1964. Pp. 50–128.

Characteristics of Gifted Children

STANLEY KRIPPNER

The author reports recent research concerning the characteristics of gifted children and concludes that many schools fail adequately to cultivate such abilities.

Western culture, throughout history, has been intrigued by the talented individual. In the first chapter of Daniel, the Old Testament chronicler relates how "the king commanded Ashpenaz . . . to bring . . . youths without blemish, handsome, and skillful in all wisdom, endowed with knowledge, understanding, learning, and competent to serve in the king's palace, and to teach them the letters and language of the Chaldeans." Giftedness has not always been so highly respected throughout history. A widely-accepted theory, given alleged scientific credence by Cesare Lombroso (10) and J. F. Nesbit (12) in the latter part of the nineteenth century, held that high mental endowment and creativity were genetically coupled with degeneracy, insanity, and instability.

The first systematic study of gifted youth was published by L. M. Terman in 1925 (21). Terman's data on 1,500 children scoring in the highest one per cent of the population on mental ability tests demonstrated that these children possessed generally superior physical, social, moral, and emotional traits and were markedly superior in the mastery of school subjects. Follow-up studies by Terman and his associates (22) showed that the gifted person was less subject to physical dysfunction and emotional instability than would

be expected of individuals in the general population.

Terman (20) insisted that from the ranks of the children making high scores on intelligence tests, "and from nowhere else, our geniuses in *every* line are recruited." However, recent research (5, 24) has demonstrated that many young people with intelligence test scores in the average range place in the highest categories on tests of originality and creative thinking. Yamamoto (28) stated that if the gifted person is thought of only in terms of high intelligence, almost 70 percent of the most highly creative individuals in our society would be overlooked.

As a result of these data, a broader definition of talent has been accepted by most professional workers in the field; the gifted person is now generally regarded as one who demonstrates consistently remarkable performance in any worthwhile line of endeavor, whether it be academic skills, mechanical skills, music, creative writing, dramatics, or social leadership (27, 25, 26).

A series of studies by M. I. Stein (18) indicates that the creative person is less authoritarian and less anxiety-ridden than the non-creative person. In addition, creative individuals, in general, are more independent, more dynamic, more practical, more utilitarian, and better integrated. They show wiser judgment, a greater degree of self acceptance and self knowledge, and have a better sense of humor than non-creative people. The creative person, according to Stein, tends to work slowly in the initial stages of a problem-solving situation, but rapidly in its final stages. Creative people prefer projects involving complexity, novelty, and decision-making to tasks that are cut and dried. Many creative people do well on mental ability tests, but high intelligence, according to Stein, is not universally found among creative individuals.

Most of Stein's findings resemble those reported by W. W. Purkey (16) in a study of 95 gifted high school students and 63 students of average ability. The gifted students made significantly higher scores than did the average students on measures assessing successful personal and social functioning. However, both groups made similar scores on the measures of self confidence, self insight, and self acceptance.

Dauw (2) studied 319 high school seniors, dividing them into high and low creative thinkers on the basis of Torrance's Minnesota Tests of Creative Thinking. He found that the highly creative students had parents of higher socioeconomic status than the low creative seniors. Furthermore, the parents had better educational backgrounds and took a greater interest in their children. The disciplinary pattern of the highly creative students was consistent, while the low creative group's parents were inconsistent in their discipline. The home backgrounds of creative individuals have been found to differ from those of other persons by several other persons conducting investigations (17, 6).

Project Talent

A comprehensive study of the abilities of American youth was undertaken by the directors of Project Talent in 1960. The project's testing program involved about 440,000 students in the ninth, tenth, eleventh, and twelfth grades in 1,353 public, private, and parochial schools. Administrators of these institutions, which comprised about five percent of all high schools in the United States, completed questionnaires on their aca-

demic offerings and guidance programs. As a result of these two types of data collection, more than 2,000 items of information per student were collected as well as over 1,000 items per school. In 1963, retesting was inaugurated to assess changes occurring over the last three years of high school and several supplementary testing programs were inaugurated. Follow-up studies are planned at five-year intervals (4).

One basic finding of Project Talent's investigators was that about 25 percent of the ninth-grade students had reached a higher level of academic achievement than that attained by the average twelfth-grade student at the time of his graduation from high school (3). It was suggested that this situation "indicates the desirability of adaptng instruction to individual student needs rather than giving them all the same instructional program." The need for greater individualization of instruction was also demonstrated by the finding that the top five percent of the students learn new information at twice the rate of the average student. An optimal instructional program, therefore, should begin at the level the student has already attained and proceed at the rate most appropriate for that student.

Other data indicated that economic factors (such as the beginning salary paid to teachers) were significantly related to the amount of learning by the students. Neither the number of students in a school nor the students' location in an urban rather than a rural area were substantially related to the amount of learning. In other words, large "comprehensive" urban schools are not necessarily the answer to the needs of gifted students; well-paid, competent teachers who can diversify instruction are far more important to the development of students' potentials.

Project Talent's investigation of non-intellectual characteristics (as measured by the Student Activities Inventory and other devices) yielded provocative results when the students' personality traits were compared with their academic achievement (13). For boys, the measures of self confidence, social sensitivity, vigor, calmness, and personal maturity were significantly related to tested achievement in such areas as English, reading skills, and mathematics. For girls, only personal maturity was associated with academic achievement. It was suggested that girls have a somewhat easier time in controlling their emotions and that this factor would reduce the relationships between personality traits and school achievement. Boys have a more difficult time bringing their emotional energy under control; those who are able to handle their impulse life more easily do well academically because they can channel sufficient energy toward learning tasks.

An analysis of specific test responses further demonstrated the connection between emotional control and academic achievement. High-achieving boys typically responded affirmatively to such items as "I am usually self-controlled" and "People consider me level-headed." Also related to high academic achievement for boys were affirmative answers to such items as "I am full of pep and energy" and "I am vigorous," suggesting that there was abundant emotional vigor for the high-achieving boys and that this vigor was capably directed and easily channeled.

Research with Talented College Students

A number of studies have been reported which involved gifted college students. Winners of the National Merit Scholarship Program have been followed up for several years; consistently, they have obtained remarkable scholastic records during their stay in college. In addition, it has been discovered that the National Merit scholars characteristically are first-born children and that they come from small families, their average number of siblings being between one and two (1). In this regard, the National Merit scholars resemble Terman's gifted group, the members of which were frequently first-born children from small families (1947).

In a study of 1,184 National Merit finalists and semifinalists, Nichols and Davis (11) found marked differences between the National Merit group and other college seniors. The National Merit group was less oriented to social and athletic interests, more idealistic and rebellious, and less conventional in their religious beliefs.

I. J. Lehmann (9) studied the attitudes and critical thinking abilities of college students using a number of tests and inventories. He reported that students withdrawing from college were more rigid in their beliefs, tended to think in terms of stereotypes, demonstrated less critical thinking ability, and made lower scores on tests of academic ability than students who completed college. Of those who completed college, positive changes were noted in such attitudinal areas as tolerance, insight, social concern, and responsibility. The changes in critical thinking that were noted by Lehmann, for the most part, occurred by the end of the students' junior year.

Research and the College Protest Movement

Of current interest to many researchers is the college "protest movement." The university population generally includes a sizable minority whose behavior is marked by various types of non-conformity and rebellion. Contemporary protest movements center around opposition to the nation's conduct of the war in Viet Nam, concern with civil rights legislation and its effect on ethnic minorities, and opposition to certain policies enforced by university officials. The use of psychedelic substances such as LSD to induce alterations of consciousness is a more recent expression of student protest; extensive studies to determine the extent of this practice are now in progress at the Chicago Medical School and the New Jersey Neuro-Psychiatric Institute.

Paul Heist (8) investigated students involved in the "Free Speech" movement at the University of California at Berkeley, utilizing the Omnibus Personality Inventory and student background data. He concluded that the movement was predominantly composed of capable students who had left high school with good academic records and who had maintained high grades while at the university. Heist stated that the majority of these students were characterized by "their high mental ability, their autonomy and freedom to choose, their readiness for new ideas and new experiences, their ethical concerns . . . , their interests in a good education, and their strong and intrinsic intellectual orientations." These students "represented the qualities and attitudes which most teachers seek in their best students."

R. E. Peterson (14) distinguished three basic areas of student protest: issues pertaining to instruction, faculty, and freedom of expression; issues bearing on personal freedom and on student participation in a college's administration; issues which were of wider scope than that of the college campus (civil rights, Viet Nam, etc.).

After surveying the administrative deans of nearly 850 colleges, Peterson reported that the civil rights issue was the most frequently cited cause for protest (affecting 38 percent of the campuses) followed by controversy over group living regulations (28 percent), Viet Nam (21 percent), student participation in policy-making (18 percent), university rules regarding controversial speakers (9 percent), alleged curriculum inflexibility (7 percent), and academic freedom (4 percent). The type of institution was a determinant of student activism; the incidence of organized opposition to the nation's policy in Viet Nam ranged from 61 percent at independent universities to 8 percent at church-affiliated institutions to 6 percent in teachers' colleges. Peterson suggested that the students' intellectual aptitudes and interests were also associated with the protest movement:

> There is every indication that the number of student activists has been multiplying in the past five years. How is the rise of this "new student activism" to be explained? Since they are disproportionately enrolled in selective colleges and universities, students actively concerned with broad social and moral issues are undoubtedly concentrated at the high end of the intellectual ability distribution; they are bright enough to detect and comprehend some of what ails American society. In this vein, judging from the relative peace at teachers colleges and technical institutes, it would seem that the intellectual interests of the student activists tend toward the liberal arts and sciences; their commitments are more toward ideas than jobs. Their intellectual bent probably emphasizes comparing and criticizing rather than mastery of facts and skills. In short, because of some combination of genetic and environmental circumstances, these youths have acquired an intellectual style that has lent itself well to critical examination of what is going on around them.

Counterposed against this group of intelligent, independent, critically-minded students, there sometimes stands a college with large classes, intense competition for grades, bureaucratic dealings with students, parent-like control of students' personal lives, and many faculty members disinterested in teaching and unaware of students' needs. For many able young men and women, the encounter with such a college or university is a disappointment; out of frustration, many have looked to the protest movement for sources of commitment that are more fulfilling than that which is available in the classroom.

In the meantime, there is some indication that the number of gifted individuals will increase in future generations. J. R. Platt (15) noted that the brightest 10 percent of young Americans are now being thrown together on college campuses at the most susceptible age for romance and marriage. The genetic consequence of this situation may be a rise in the proportion of gifted children because random matches were more typical in former eras when a greater proportion of talented young people did not go to college. Platt further stated, "Even more spectacular children may be coming out of the intellectual colonies like Oak Ridge or Los Alamos, where one man in six has a Ph.D., and out of the faculty communities of the great universities, where all men and many of the women have advanced degrees." At this rate, concluded Platt, "we may have a dozen Newtons within 20 years."

Nevertheless, society still allows many of its brightest young people to pass unnoticed. In Tulsa, Oklahoma, doctors recently discovered a 17-year-old boy in a school for the mentally handicapped who scored in the very superior range on mental ability tests. As the boy was deaf, he had been sent to a state institution at an early age. His high mental ability was not suspected until an employee left a transistor radio kit on a work table and the boy easily assembled it, after studying the diagrams and instructions.

A few years ago, an army recruit in Virginia was tagged as a "clerk typist" until a university professor intervened and called him "the most outstanding mathematical genius I have encountered in 30 years." A French draftee who dropped out of school to help his father care for the family farm made such a high score on army aptitude tests that the colonel in charge accused him of cheating. He scored even higher on the retests; army records disclosed only one comparable score among 40,000 recruits.

Conclusions

It is apparent that most school systems have not reached a stage where creativity is properly cultivated or where giftedness is widely appreciated. The available research demonstrates the divergency of young people's abilities in high school and college. When an alert, inquisitive individual lacks stimulation from a responsive home, school, or community environment, he often fails to develop his potential fully (24).

The ranks of the gifted contain many underachievers; this inability to maximize one's ability is a more likely factor in emotional disturbance among the talented than the genetic link proposed at one time. The scope of student protest at colleges and universities demonstrates that professors and administrators—the very people who should be most capable of stimulating creativity, individualizing instruction, and meeting students' existential needs—are sometimes inept caretakers of America's most valuable resource, its gifted individuals.

REFERENCES

ABRAHAM, WILLARD. *Common Sense About Gifted Children*. New York: Harper and Brothers, 1958.

DAUW, D. C. "Life Experiences of Original Thinkers and Good Elaborators." *Exceptional Children,* 1966, 32:433–440.

FLANAGAN, J. C. "Project TALENT: Preliminary Findings." A paper presented at the annual meeting of the American Educational Research Association, Atlantic City, N. J., 1962. Mimeographed.

FLANAGAN, J. C., et. al. *The American High School Student*. Technical Report to the U. S. Office of Education, Cooperative Research Project No. 635. Pittsburgh: Project TALENT Office, University of Pittsburgh, 1964.

GETZELS, J. W., AND P. W. JACKSON. "The Meaning of 'Giftedness'," *Education,* 1962, 82:460-464.

GOERTZEL, V., AND M. G. GOERTZEL. *Cradles of Eminence*. Boston: Little, Brown, 1962.

GOWAN, J. C. "Dynamics of the Underachievement of Gifted Students," *Exceptional Children,* 1957, 24: 1–5.

HEIST, PAUL "The Dynamics of Student Discontent and Protest." A paper presented at the annual meeting of the American Psychological Association, New York, 1966. Mimeographed.

LEHMANN, I. J. "Changes in Critical Thinking, Attitudes and Values from Freshman to Senior Year." A paper presented at the annual meeting of the American Educational Research Association, Chicago, 1963. Mimeographed.

LOMBROSO, CESARE. *The Men of Genius*. London: Robert Scott, 1891.

NICHOLS, R. C., AND J. A. DAVIS. "Characteristics of Students of High Academic Aptitude." *Personnel and Guidance Journal,* 1964, 42: 794-800.

NISBET, J. F. *The Insanity of Genius*. London: Kegan Paul, 1891.

ORR, D. B. "Project TALENT: Studies of Non-Intellectual Characteristics." A paper presented at the annual meeting of the American Psychological Association, St. Louis, 1962. Mimeographed.

PETERSON, R. E. *The Scope of Organized Student Protest in 1964–1965*. Princeton, N. J.: Educational Testing Service, 1966.

PLATT, J. R. Quoted in "The Genius Explosion," *Time,* February 21, 1964.

PURKEY, W. W. "Measured and Professed Personality Characteristics of Gifted High School Students and an Analysis of Their Congruence." *Journal of Educational Research,* 1966, 60:99–103.

ROE, A. *The Making of a Scientist*. New York: Dodd, Mead, 1953.

STEIN, M. I. "Social and Psychological Factors Affecting Creativity of Industrial Research Scientists." A paper presented at the Fall meeting of the Industrial Research Institute, Philadelphia, 1957. Mimeographed.

TANNENBAUM, A. J. "History of Interest in the Gifted." In *Education for the Gifted, The Fifty-Seventh Yearbook of the National Society for the Study of Education,* N. B. Henry (Editor). Chicago: University of Chicago Press, 1958. Pages 21–38.

TERMAN, L. M. Introduction to *Gifted Children,*

Their Nature and Nuture. Yonkers-on-Hudson, N.Y.: World Book, 1924.

TERMAN, L. M., et al. *Mental and Physical Traits of a thousand Gifted Children.* Stanford: Stanford University Press, 1925.

TERMAN, L. M., AND M. H. ODEN. *The Gifted Group at Midlife: Thirty-five Years Follow-Up of the Superior Child.* Stanford: Stanford University Press, 1959.

TORRANCE, E. P. *Educational Achievement of the Highly Intelligent and the Highly Creative: Eight Partial Replications of the Getzels–Jackson Study.* Research Memorandum BER-60-18. Minneapolis: Bureau of Educational Research, University of Minnesota, 1960. Mimeographed.

TORRANCE, E. P. *Guiding Creative Talent.* Englewood Cliffs, N. J.: Prentice-Hall, 1962.

WITTY, P. A. *Helping the Gifted Child.* Chicago: Science Research Associates, 1952.

WITTY, P. A. "Recent Publications Concerning the Gifted and Creative Student." *Phi Delta Kappan,* January, 1965, Pages 221–224.

WITTY, P. A. "Some Considerations in the Education of Gifted Children." *Educational Administration and Supervision,* 1940, 26:514.

YAMAMOTO, K. "Creativity and Intellect." A paper delivered at the annual conference of the Minnesota Psychological Association, Minneapolis, 1961. Mimeographed.

Teaching for Creativity: Some Guiding Lights

GARY A. DAVIS

Ways of teaching for creativity are suggested by various authorities in the field, and the author reports on the results of his own research on this topic.

The purpose of this article is to summarize three foundational rules or guidelines for increasing creative potential. Before describing these, however, we first must consider what *being creative* is, and further, what it is we do when we *teach creativity*.

There is no doubt that the shapes and forms of human creativity are without limit. Almost daily we see creative products emerging from the fields of music, entertainment, literary and graphic arts; and from science, medicine, industry and other technologies. We might encounter a creatively planned children's room, an innovative repair of a basement leak, a list of creative Christmas gifts, or some problem solution found by imagination rather than repetition. The commonality in this diversity of creative acts is simply the abstract quality of fanciful resourcefulness itself.

It would seem then, that whatever the specific nature of the problem, a person is more likely to respond creatively if he possesses a particular constellation of attitudes and habits which lead him to consciously seek creative solutions. Indeed, creative individuals often have been characterized by their habitual preference for origi-

nality, their curiosity and flexibility, and their willingness to differ and to take risks. It is these attitudes and habits which are taught by every course or program seeking to foster creative development, from the Torrance and Myers (1970) elementary-level *Idea Books* through Osborn's (1963) and Gordon's (1961) principles for professional group problem solving. The author's research with sixth-, seventh-, and eighth-grade students has shown that, in fact, students can be taught to hunt for new problem approaches and to value original thinking. A student's awareness of the importance of creative innovation in the larger world and in his own life can be increased. The student can be taught some simple techniques for forcing new idea combinations such as modifying product attributes or looking for metaphorically-related solutions (Davis, 1969, 1971; Davis and Scott, 1971). Since the goal of creativity training is to change conscious attitudes and habits in the direction of more creative thinking, the author has developed three guidelines for fostering creative growth, in accord with the goal of creativity training, which concern: (1) using creative teaching tactics, (2) letting students learn creative attitudes and habits by actually creating,

From G. A. Davis, Teaching for creativity: Some guiding lights. Reprinted from *Journal of Research and Development in Education*, 1971, *4*(3), 29-34, by permission of author and publisher.

and (3) providing a psychologically safe atmosphere for creativity.

USE OF CREATIVE TACTICS

Whether one is writing materials for stimulating creativity or teaching creative attitudes and habits directly to the class, imaginative teaching methods are a must. Traditional methods (including such new traditions as team teaching, nongraded schools, and even computer-assisted instruction) have evolved for imparting information—teaching facts and concepts about science or history, or teaching conceptual skills of mathematics or language usage. On the other hand teaching for creativity aims at strengthening flexibility and open-mindedness, teaching some conscious techniques for producing new idea combinations, and all the while reinforcing the use of innate creative abilities. A different end requires a different means.

A much more important reason for using creative teaching methods and creatively prepared materials has been found in the benefits reaped by teaching creativity by example. The teaching-creativity-by-imitation principle cannot be emphasized enough. It is one thing to tell students that creative thinking requires a nimble imagination, as when in college we teach "about creativity"; it is much more effective to demonstrate what "being creative" is like, through creative classroom activities and creatively written and illustrated materials. The actual teaching can and should demonstrate a lively imagination by the teacher, the materials developer, or preferably both.

Teaching creativity by example may be illustrated with two introductory pages from *Saturday Subway Ride* (DiPego, 1970), a professionally written workbook likely to bend the mind of anyone above adolescent age:

Let me tell you about last Saturday.

I took a ride on a new super subway that travels a fast circle from Kansas City to Pittsburgh to Dublin to Tokyo to Santa Monica and back.

What's wrong?

You say there's no such subway, and you're about to close the book and stare out the window.

Well, maybe you're wrong. Maybe I zipped around the world on an underground thought, a daydream, a nightdream, or a 'superfastspecial fivecity' idea.

That's what this book is all about.

Ideas.

You say my subway ride is just a wild idea and pretty silly, and you'd rather pitch pennies?

Well, what about flying? People said that men flying around in machines was a wild idea and pretty silly. Then the Wright brothers took off and ZIP!

People once thought that TV was just a wild idea and probably wouldn't work—and bicycles, too, and life insurance and polio vaccine.

A wild idea is something that people find hard to accept because it's new and sounds strange and looks funny and maybe it's light green suede and smells of paprika. Anyway, it's something people haven't seen before, and that makes them afraid.

Some people only feel safe with old, comfortable, tried-out ideas. I guess those people never learned to stretch their minds.

That's what this book is all about, too—learning to stretch your mind, learning to reach out for big, new, different, and even wild ideas.

Why?

So you can solve problems and create new things and improve old things and have more fun. Ideas are good anywhere, anytime, in any climate and even underwater.

The goal of *Saturday Subway Ride* is to change attitudes and consciously orient students toward using their creative capabilities. It does this by example, as much as by exhortation and exercise.

The various creative thinking materials of Myers and Torrance also demonstrate to the student what "being creative" is like, while asking the student to flex his own inventive muscles. Only writers with imagination, hoping to increase a student's receptiveness to far-fetched idea combinations, would ask, "What could happen if cats could bark when they wanted to?" (Myers & Torrance, 1965a) or "What could a dish made of olives, peanut butter, bread crumbs, and boiled cucumbers be called?" (Myers & Torrance, 1965b).

Still another delightful strategy for altering attitudes and habits is that of Koch, who wanted to ". . . get the gradeschool kids excited about poetry" (Koch, 1970). For example, with his *Class Collaboration Strategy* for creative poetry writing, Koch asked each child to contribute one line, beginning with "I wish" and containing a color, a comic-strip character, and a city or country (e.g., "I wish I were with Charlie Brown in a blue shirt in France"). Later, his very young students wrote entire poems structured by beginning each line with "I wish" ("I wish I had a pony with a tail like hair"); or beginning alternate lines with "I used to" and "But now" ("I used to be a rose, but now I am a leaf"). Other simple patterns asked for comparisons, clang associations, and metaphors. The result of this creative strategy? Students not only found they could write sensitive, colorful poetry, but they wanted to write more and more of it.

In sum then, teaching for creative growth requires innovative teaching methods and materials because: (1) the goal is teaching attitudes and habits conducive to creative behavior, which requires a departure from instructional methods aimed at imparting factual information, and (2) students benefit tremendously from a model—the teacher, the materials, or both—showing what "being creative" is like.

LEARNING CREATIVITY BY DOING CREATIVITY

The second guideline to be emphasized is simply Dewey's time-tested principle of learning by doing. Actively "doing creativity" will stamp in creativity-conscious thinking habits in the same intuitively-sound way that learning-by-doing will improve ice skating, speaking French, or figuring a math problem.

The overall strategy of the Myers and Torrance *Idea Books* evolves around creating conditions which actively elicit creative responses in many forms and in many modes. The examples previously cited bring forth student speculation on the consequences of surprising events (cats barking) and associations to novel idea combinations

("the dish"). Other exercises elicit emphatic metaphorical thinking almost involuntarily: "What would your shoes say to you as you get ready for a bath on the day you come in last in a race at school?" or "Write a letter from the viewpoint of your pet. And be sure it's newsy" (Myers & Torrance, 1966b). Memories, combinatory play, sensory awareness and other facets of creative experience and expression are brought out by asking, "Do you remember when you saw (smelled, touched, tasted) something strange or surprising" (Myers & Torrance, 1966a). Torrance and Myers (1970) further recommend using incompleteness, for example, asking students to project into the future. The teacher (or materials writer) also may pose such thought-provoking questions as: What use can be made of Polar ice formations? or How might an *odor* be used as a communications device?

Saturday Subway Ride also tries to increase creative strength by extracting from every reader some fanciful thoughts and sensations.

Try to avoid responding creatively to these two exercises:

Two astronauts are orbiting their spacecraft around the moon.
   Suddenly, there is a knock on the spaceship door.
Astronaut 1.:
Astronaut 2.:

   Answer one of these questions with a tall tale, a couple of paragraphs just for the fun of it, and just for the brain-stretching exercise:
1. Where were you born?
2. What did you do last Saturday?
3. What does your dad do for a hobby?

Research conducted to evaluate the effectiveness of creative thinking programs has concluded that actual participation in creative thinking is the most critical component of the overall experience. The *Purdue Creativity Program* of Feldhusen, Treffinger, and Bahlke (1970; WBAA, 1966) is a set of 28 audio tapes, with three or four printed exercises to accompany every tape. Each tape consists of two components, a three- to four-minute presentation designed to teach a principle of creative thinking (e.g., being open to new ideas, putting ideas together in new ways, valuing creative problem solving) and a story depicting creative, adventurous behavior by such pioneers as Christopher Columbus, Alexander Bell, John Glenn, and Jonas Salk. A series of experimental studies evaluated the relative contributions of each of three training components, the presentations of the creativity principles, the stories, and the exercises, and all possible two-way combinations of these. Students whose experimental treatments included working through the printed exercises alone, or in combination with the presentations or the stories, typically displayed the greatest improvement in their tested creative thinking abilities.

Our own field research also has pointed to the critical role of active participation in improving creative potential. Our most successful field trial included a teacher and class who, day after day, spent a little time on principles and a lot of time on wild, far-out creative thinking (Davis, Houtman, Warren, & Roweton, 1969). A subsequent study with inner-city students further confirmed that teachers who promoted class and individual activities were more successful in increasing measured creative potential than teachers who felt they could not allow group problem-solving or discussion in fear of losing disciplinary control (Davis, Houtman, Warren, Roweton, Mari, & Belcher, in press).

In sum, the active involvement of the student in thinking of creative ideas and problem solutions is essential in teaching for creativity. Learning by doing acquaints the student first hand with the flexible openness necessary for imaginative problem-solving.

THE CREATIVE ATMOSPHERE

Perhaps the most obvious yet most critical guideline for stimulating creative thinking lies in creating an atmosphere of receptiveness and encouragement for the free expression of ideas. Whether in classroom brainstorming or in creative art, writing, or science projects, the student must be free to create. Or he won't.

Carl Rogers (1962) used the concepts of *psychological safety* and *psychological freedom* to describe the acceptance of both the complete individual and his spontaneous, playful thinking.

Osborn's (1963) fundamental principle of deferred judgment also states in flashing neon that successful brainstorming depends upon a psychologically safe, encouraging atmosphere. In fact, in professional brainstorming the chronic growler or idea-squelcher may be invited to leave an otherwise creative problem-solving session.

New ideas often are funny though, and it is quite consistent with the spirit of group problem-solving to laugh at surprising new ideas so long as this levity is not taken as criticism or punishment. Certainly, the substance of both creativity and humor is new and surprising juxtapositions of ideas; and so it is common for successful brainstorming sessions to be humorous and entertaining.

Humor also may be used deliberately, as the author and others have reported (Davis, 1971; Davis & Houtman, 1968; DiPego, 1970), to contribute to the open and safe creative atmosphere so essential for unrestrained creative functioning. For example, *Saturday Subway Ride* displays a far-fetched, humorous, playful attitude throughout intentionally loosening up the student's conditioned reluctance to challenge strong forces of conformity and tradition. In the *Idea Books* (Myers & Torrance, 1965a, 1966a, 1966b) and in *Sound and Images* (Cunnington & Torrance, 1965) Torrance also cultivates the playful associative behavior which is both the cause and the effect of a creative atmosphere.

Conclusions

In teaching for creative development, both the classroom teacher and the developer of training materials try to increase an individual's capacity for and likelihood of behaving creatively in his personal, educational, and future professional life. If the view is accepted that conscious attitudes and habits related to flexible, imaginative thinking are important and transferable components of creative behavior—common to all forms of creative endeavor—three suggestions should guide teaching for creativity. First, imaginative teaching methods and creatively devised materials must be used since (a) the goal is not the traditional one of transmitting scholarly facts and concepts;

and (b) students may learn what "being creative" is like by using creative teaching activities and creatively prepared materials as models. Second, active participation—learning creativity by doing creativity—is critical. Attitudes and habits of creative thinking must be learned first hand.

Third, the psychologically safe and encouraging creative atmosphere is an obvious yet essential part of any successful effort to train imagination. Humor is one good way to stimulate the playful, associative behavior intrinsic to free idea expression.

REFERENCES

CUNNINGTON, B. F., AND TORRANCE, E. P. *Sounds and Images.* Boston: Ginn & Co., 1965.

DAVIS, G. A. Training creativity in adolescence: A discussion of strategy. In R. E. Grinder (Ed.), *Studies in Adolescence II.* New York: Macmillan, 1969. Pp. 538–545. Reprinted in Davis, G. A., and Scott, J. A. (Eds.) *Training Creative Thinking.* New York: Holt, 1971. Pp. 261–269.

DAVIS, G. A. *It's Your Imagination: Theory and Training of Problem Solving.* New York: Basic Books, in press.

DAVIS, G. A., AND HOUTMAN, S. E. *Thinking Creatively: A Guide to Training Imagination.* Wisconsin Research and Development Center for Cognitive Learning, University of Wisconsin, 1968.

DAVIS, G. A., HOUTMAN, S. E., WARREN, T. F., AND ROWETON, W. E. A program for training creative thinking: I. Preliminary field test. *Technical Report No. 104,* Wisconsin Research and Development Center for Cognitive Learning, University of Wisconsin, 1969.

DAVIS, G. A., HOUTMAN, S. E., WARREN, T. F., ROWETON, W. E., MARI, S., AND BELCHER, T. L. A program for training creative thinking: II. Inner city evaluation. *Technical Report,* Wisconsin Research and Development Center for Cognitive Learning, University of Wisconsin, in press.

DAVIS, G. A., AND SCOTT, J. A. (Eds.) *Training Creative Thinking.* New York: Holt, Rinehart & Winston, 1971.

DIPEGO, G. *Saturday Subway Ride.* Wisconsin Research and Development Center for Cognitive Learning, University of Wisconsin, 1970.

FELDHUSEN, J. F., TREFFINGER, D. J., AND BAHLKE, S. J. Developing creative thinking: The Purdue creativity program. *Journal of Creative Behavior,* 1970, 4, 85–90.

GORDON, W. J. J. *Synectics.* New York: Harper & Row, 1961.

KOCH, K. *Wishes, Lies, and Dreams.* New York: Chelsea House, 1970.

MYERS, R. E., AND TORRANCE, E. P. *Can You Imagine?* Boston: Ginn, 1965. (a)

MYERS, R. E., AND TORRANCE, E. P. *Invitations to Speaking and Writing Creatively.* Boston: Ginn, 1965. (b)

MYERS, R. E., AND TORRANCE, E. P. *For Those Who Wonder.* Boston: Ginn, 1966. (a)

MYERS, R. E., AND TORRANCE, E. P. *Plots, Puzzles and Ploys.* Boston: Ginn, 1966. (b)

OSBORN, A. F. *Applied Imagination.* (3rd Ed.) New York: Scribner's, 1963.

ROGERS, C. Toward a theory of creativity. In S. J. Parnes and H. F. Harding (Eds.), *A Source Book for Creative Thinking.* New York: Scribner's, 1962. Pp. 63–72.

TORRANCE, E. P., AND MYERS, R. E. *Creative Learning and Teaching.* New York: Dodd, Mead, & Co., 1970.

WBAA. *Creative Thinking: The American Pioneers.* (Audio tapes and a manual for teachers.) West Lafayette, Ind.: Purdue University School of the Air, 1966.

Chapter 8: Suggested Additional Readings

DAVIDS, A. Psychological characteristics of high school male and female potential scientists in comparison with academic underachievers. *Psychology in the Schools,* 1966, *3*(1), 79–87. Personal, motivational, and social characteristics of high school students who are talented in science are differentiated from those of low achievers.

CASHDAN, S. Social participation and subcultural influences in the study of adolescent creativity, *Adolescence,* 1971, *6*(21), 39–52. The author summarizes his views concerning creativity as a "multi-dimensional phenomenon" involving cognition, personality, and talent. He also considers the role of culture and of deviant subcultures in the development of creativity.

HAMMER, E. F. Personality patterns in young creative artists. *Adolescence,* Winter 1966–67, *1*(4), 327–350. The author's expressed aim is to formulate hypotheses, based on his research, about which traits, feelings, or attitudes correlate with creativity. In other words, in what personality soil does creativity grow?

HELSON, R. Personality characteristics and developmental history of creative college women. *Genetic Psychology Monographs,* 1967, *76*, 205–256. College senior women who had been adjudged by faculty members to be especially creative were studied in terms of childhood and family background and the period succeeding graduation. All these experiential factors proved important. This monograph is well done, interesting, and the only study of its kind.

JUNGK, R. Imagination and the future. *International Social Science Journal,* 1969, *21*(4), 557–562. The author considers how more creative production may be facilitated if we can escape the bonds of traditional learning research, philosophies, and concepts.

MELEWICZ, M. Don't call us geniuses. *American Education,* 1969, *5*(9), 22–25. The author describes a summer program for bright, creative high school, college, and graduate students, whose average age was 21, which provided experience in applying modern research techniques and scientific methods to the resolution of policy problems. Some of the students' own verbatim reactions to the experience are reported.

NOY, P. The "youth protest" and the "age of creativity." *Journal of Creative Behavior,* 1970, *4*(4), 223–233. Youth's protest is reviewed both historically and currently in terms of the pre-industrial era, the industrial era, and the modern era.

PARLOFF, M. B., DATTA, L., KLEMAN, M., & HANDLON, J. H. Personality characteristics which differentiate creative male adolescents and adults. *Journal of Personality,* 1968, *36*, 315–330. The authors' research was designed to test the claim that creative adults, regardless of field, share certain distinguishing personality characteristics, and to show how such characteristics relate to creative performance.

PARNES, S. J. Creativity: Developing human potential. *Journal of Creative Behavior,* 1971, *5*(1), 15–36. In this broad-ranging article an authority on the subject of creativity appraises various views on stimulating creativity and discusses theoretical questions involved.

SCHAEFER, C. E. The self-concept of creative adolescents. *Journal of Psychology,* 1969, *72*, 233–242. A study of creative high school students indicated little difference by sex in specialty. Creative individuals proved to have open and multifaceted personalities, to be open to impulse expression, and to be independent in thought and action.

SKIPPER, C. E., & DE VELBISS, J. A.   Developing creative abilities in adolescence. *Educational Leadership*, 1969, *27*(2), 191–193. The authors describe a program which influenced students to become more involved in cultural activities, to increase creative sensitivity to problems, and to develop a more significant sense of personal identity.

WALBERG, H. J.   Physics, femininity, and creativity. *Developmental Psychology*, 1969, *1*(1), 47–54. Girls taking high school physics scored higher than boys in verbal aptitude, social values, interpersonal needs, cautiousness, and aesthetic, as opposed to theoretical, valuations. These factors apparently contribute to academic success but inhibit women's later eminence in scientific careers.

WINDHOLZ, G.   The relation of creativity and intelligence constellations to traits of temperament, interest, and value in college students. *Journal of General Psychology*, October 1968, *79*, 291–299. Windholz attempted to determine the relationship between creativity and intelligence, but found no real interdependence between them. The highly intelligent, but not creative, individual was emotionally stable but lacked hypersensitivity. The highly-creative person tended to value people and to desire to help them.

9

Issues Relating to Youth-Versus-Vocation

According to Gold and Douvan (1969), during adolescence an individual first becomes critically aware of the need to choose a vocation, an awareness compounded in magnitude in a highly industrialized technological society. He has many problems of establishing a vocational role—problems originating variously in the home, in the school, in society at large, and within himself.

In the past, a boy frequently learned his occupation directly from his father; today a son often has only a vague idea of his father's work environment, which may be miles from home. Nevertheless, the father may assume an important role in his son's vocational choice, perhaps in ill-advised ways. The father is of another time and does not see the world through the eyes of the new generation. He himself struggled hard to get ahead, and he may have trouble accepting his son's apparently casual attitude about the choice of a career. The son may finally settle on some secure, pleasant sort of work which violates his father's view of what is either masculine or worthwhile. If the father lacks a son, he may project his dreams onto a daughter, only to find that girls of her generation are still more marriage-than career-minded. However, parental training still has a significant, subtle effect, because an individual's work style develops at an early age, often in the home; once it is established, the individual is carried along thereafter by the momentum of his own built-in dynamics.

Vocational problems are also linked with adjustment at school. Ideally, the school should fit the child—the child should not have to adjust to the school. However, children who cannot adapt to an inflexible and uncongenial school setting may simply leave and go to work. The question arises: How may schools readjust to hold such youth? What sort of work-study arrangement may permit continued education, yet at the same time provide for present and future vocational needs?

A partial answer, with advantages for potential dropouts and college-bound youth alike, lies in part-time jobs. Ideally, part-time employment fulfills several requirements: establishment of emotional autonomy from parents, achievement of socially responsible behaviors, additions to one's stockpile of competencies, preparation for future employment, and a source of spending money for current demands.

Most youth do, in fact, indicate that odd jobs and employment during school vacations yield real benefits; however, others fail to find full satisfaction this way. For one thing, child labor laws may make it difficult for a student to obtain the sort of job that lays the foundation for a particular occupation. Indeed, laws relating to adolescent employment are deplorably inconsistent (Folk, 1969). On the one hand, they generally prohibit wage employment to individuals under age 14, while all employment during school hours is prohibited to those under 16, and certain dangerous jobs are banned for anyone under 18. Such restrictions, notes Folk, may prove extremely frustrating to many youths who need spending money. On the other hand, society's solicitude for the safety of 17-year-olds contrasts singularly with its willingness to let them career about in high-powered automobiles and join the Armed Forces, since neither the highway nor the battlefield can be considered a safe place. In practice, young teenagers are largely confined to odd jobs such as mowing lawns, shoveling snow, and babysitting, and older adolescents to waiting on tables at local cafés or summer resorts, or clerking in stores. In some ways, jobs such as these may provide little practical experience for the work role that follows. Typically, they lack the complexity, continuity, or stability of adult work roles. However, such work may prove more functional than it seems. The youth who establishes a satisfactory combination of part-time work and leisure-time pursuits may have an easier time adjusting to a future consisting of ever-increasing leisure and ever-decreasing work than the youth who works full-time.

However, the youth who remains in school does run certain risks. He lingers in a sort of hiatus between youth and adulthood, unable to establish a firm grip on maturity. If he is middle- or upper-class, his parents continue to support him for as long as he remains in school, even after he marries. Although vocational preparation is thus expedited, problems of dependency and emotional entanglements often result.

Meantime, the school's counseling service faces a difficult task in trying to acquaint youth with the range of work open to them. In so diversified a society, the variety is truly bewildering and constantly changing. A type of work may be here today and be altered beyond recognition tomorrow. Certain of the more esoteric, significant occupations are hard to describe in realistic fashion. How does a counselor explain to a student what it is like to do computer programming, social science research, or metallurgical engineering? Also, how early should such counseling begin? Is there a danger of precipitating children into making too early a choice of vocation? Perhaps an early choice helps to focus the individual's interests and to motivate his efforts. However, it is a cliché of vocational guidance, says Sing-Yan Fen(1967), that early adolescence should be a period of exploration, never of decision. Even the gifted should be permitted to "simmer" and weigh the alternatives of becoming a Ph.D. at twenty or a scientist with a poetic vision. For any youth, early choice of vocation may interfere with acquiring the broad background needed for adjustment to a complex, rapidly changing society. Besides, any early decision is based on the adolescent as he now is, and does not take into account his future growth.

In other ways, schools attempt to ease youth's transition to the adult work-world. Somehow, the young worker must be prepared to adapt to long hours, rigid schedules, hierarchical industrial structures, and repetitive routines. Apprenticeships may sometimes be arranged, but often they become overly standardized. Vocational courses help, too, but there is a gap of indefinite proportions between what transpires in the classroom and what occurs in the world of work (Dansereau, 1961). A youth must also be prepared to face the question, "What experience have you had?" No matter how competent he may be, his age becomes a status depressant. Often, the teenager is relegated to the meanest tasks, and even the college graduate may begin on the lowest rung of the occupational ladder.

Many of youth's problems arise from modern man's changing relationship to his work. In earlier generations, society relied for its very survival on each individual's contribution to the economy. Nowadays, many workers suspect that their work could be done as well by machines, and they fear machines will ultimately displace them. In such a climate, it is hardly ego-building to perceive that one's contributions are nonessential. At the same time, the curtailed workday is having a significant effect upon the worker's attitudes. His vocation once was the core of the adult male's existence. Through attaining and advancing in a good job, he validated his masculinity. But now men have far more leisure time, and the world of work has shrunk in their personal universe. Another effect of the shortened work week is the male's return to the family; he now has far more time to spend with his children. As a result, changes are taking place in family patterns as men assume a more active father role.

What effects may such trends have on adolescents? Boys' futures will be drastically altered; girls' lives will be more indirectly, but no less fundamentally, affected. Perhaps a boy's job choice will be less critical than formerly, simply because a smaller portion of his future destiny will depend upon it. He can afford to spend a part of himself each day at a relatively mundane job because many leisure hours remain to him to use as he wishes.

The constructive use of leisure time looms as a major concern in the years ahead. Obviously, vocational and leisure activities are complementary aspects of an individual's life style. Furthermore, as the work week becomes shorter, leisure attains relatively greater significance in one's life plan. Beyond these generalizations, precise conclusions are hard to define. Just how may work and leisure be distinguished from each other? To what extent should youth's leisure activities be guided? Will increased leisure simply convert yesterday's puritan plough-boys into today's space-age playboys, or will it permit man to rise to new heights of self-realization? Is training for leisure time pursuits a basic obligation of the schools? If so, of what should such training consist? What is the proper use of leisure time? Of what special relevance are the above questions to adolescents? More specifically, how do such matters relate differentially to college and non-college youth? In most cases, non-college youth are far more work-oriented than are college youth (Thornburg, 1971). Most of them are already working at middle-income blue-collar jobs, and many already have the responsibilities of maintaining a home and rearing a family. For these youth, learning to use additional leisure time successfully may pose a special challenge.

Changes in the vocation-versus-recreation picture will alter youth's outlook in other areas as well. Since the teenage boy can look forward to having more free time as an adult than his forebears did, he must develop a more complete personality. If he is to handle free time intelligently, so that it contributes to his continuing growth as a person, he needs a broad education. To what extent vocational training might be correspondingly curtailed is debatable. In fact, the amount of vocational training needed by a youth is a basic issue. And what form should the vocational training take?

Can the suggestion that vocational choice has become less critical today go unchallenged? Perhaps the choice is as vital as ever. As machines take over much of the purely routine work, and industry grows more sophisticated, more individuals may have to be trained for new types of creative jobs. Even if the number of hours spent on the job may be less, the work performed may be on a higher level than formerly. Brighter individuals, especially, will be in demand for programming and organizing the projects of a space-age society. On the other hand, there is some question as to just how challenging the average individual's job-of-the-future will be. According to Ferkiss (1969), while certain unskilled jobs are being eliminated, a host of semi-skilled occupations are being created which are almost as unfulfilling and onerous. True, we have more engineers, scientists, and technicians than before, but many of them are engaged in such matters as deciding the "sort of plastic to use in hula hoops" or creating "milkshakes that contain no dairy products." Up to this time, critical decision-making processes remain firmly in the hands of executives. In other words, the new technology seems not to have had any fundamental effect on the capitalist–industrial system. Moreover, future workers may become like automatons or robots as the simpler work problems are solved by computers, with only the more complex issues reserved to highly trained specialists.

The same trends will create problems for less intelligent, less advantaged groups. As machines displace workers in routine tasks, the low-IQ individual becomes superfluous in the job market. What can be done about him? Also, as more jobs require advanced education, what is to be done about school dropouts? Will they become professional rioters, delinquents, and welfare cases?

Another problem related to the rapid change in modern technological society is: How can a youth establish a stable vocational identity in a fluid economy? In the past, it was easy for a youngster to visualize himself as a general practitioner of medicine, as a teacher or lawyer, or whatever. Occupational roles were relatively well defined. But how can the modern youth define himself vis-à-vis a job whose nature is constantly changing and may even disappear in years to come? For example, what may be the effect on the librarian's work of the mechanization and computerization of library services? What sort of teachers will be able to cope with the proliferation of knowledge and with programmed instruction? A current attempt to deal with the future situation is to encourage the adolescent to think of changing self in relation to changing vocation. He projects himself into the future to consider how he may adapt to, and grow with, a changing job.

Many a youth's problems are specific to himself. Perhaps he has physical or mental deficiencies which make him virtually unemployable. He may have personality traits which make it difficult to match him with a congenial job. Besides, he may still be too immature to know if he will like a particular job in later years.

Sometimes a youth may become so wrapped up in the process of decision-making that it is difficult for him to take an objective view of his vocational assets and liabilities. At other times, a combination of sexual maturity and desire for independence may precipitate a youth's leaving school and seeking a job. Society faces a challenge in helping him adjust until he is prepared for the mature role he seeks. Consequently, considerable research nowadays is devoted to assessing the adolescent's ego-involvement in vocational decisions (Bell, 1960).

A related question is: How may adolescents be encouraged to become achievement-oriented — or determined to realize their peak potential? What factors cause an individual to set his sights too high, or too low, or simply off-center? It is commonly assumed that a youth's aspirations will relate closely to his later achievements. However, this question has been relatively neglected. In a follow-up, twenty years later, of young people originally contacted during the spring of 1947, Kuvlesky and Bealer (1967) found that adolescents' aspirations were not especially good predictors of their long-run attainments but that they did play a directional role. However, such sparse research as exists on this question is confusing and often contradictory, suggesting the need for further investigation.

Most of what is written about youth and vocations, including the foregoing, relates more specifically to boys, and somewhat less to girls. Only recently has any considerable attention been paid to the problem of how women may best utilize their potential. Can those women who remain in the home be thought of as utilizing their personalities and abilities to the fullest? Many individuals, especially mothers already confined to this status, argue that this can be so. Others, among them Margaret Mead (1967), contend that we cannot afford to waste women's potential and that we need every individual with creative imagination we can get.

Unfortunately, however, in addition to sharing many of the boy's vocational problems, the girl has special ones of her own. The types of occupations open to her are limited and allow less opportunity for personal growth. Many parents do little to encourage their daughters, who then work out their vocational destinies as best they can. Both the larger society, and the particular families that compose it, make less effort to provide girls with the advanced education required for high-status jobs. Even if a girl attains a good job, she continually encounters subtle, and sometimes open, discrimination. Another problem the girl faces is the uncertainty of what her work role will be. As an adolescent, she does not know whether a vocation will constitute her main role, an auxiliary role, or no part of her role at all. Even as an adult, she may constantly waver between full-time, part-time, or no outside employment.

Actually, the topic of vocation, and its relation to adolescence, involves problems and issues so numerous we can barely touch upon them here. For example, how well have we defined the more subtle, but no less significant, factors affecting a child's vocational attitudes and ultimate vocational choice? How should child training, both at home and school, be modified to assist the child in choosing and preparing for his later vocational role? In addition — as discussed in our first reading, by Osipow — how should the youth's vocational choice relate to his cognitive style, or the characteristic way in which he organizes environmental stimuli in performing various mental tasks? Osipow's theories constitute useful bases for discussing the implications of various issues in the area of vocational guidance. For example, how can the youth be helped to exercise every inch of leverage his potential permits? How can youngsters be helped to blend a desire to earn with a need to create?

The second article, by Seward and Williamson, helps us to appraise the professional goals of our own adolescents by comparing their goals with those of their counterparts in the two Germanies, Chile, Poland, and Turkey. While a great deal has been written about adolescents' professional goals, this study is among the rare ones which permit a cross-cultural view of adolescents as they relate to their future occupations.

REFERENCES

BELL, H. M.   Ego involvement in vocational decisions. *Personnel and Guidance Journal*, 1960, *38*, 732–736.

DANSEREAU, H. K.   Work and the teen-ager. In J. Bernard (Ed.) *Teen-age culture.* Philadelphia: The American Academy of Political and Social Science, November 1961, *338*, 44–52.

FEN, SING-YAN.   Junior high school and the open road. *Teachers College Record*, January 1967, *48*(4), 331.

FERKISS, V. C.   *Technological man: The myth and the reality.* New York: George Braziller, 1969.

FOLK, H.   The over-supply of the young. *Trans-action,* 1969 *6*(10), 27-32.

GOLD, M., & DOUVAN, E. (Eds.)   *Adolescent development.* Boston: Allyn and Bacon, 1969.

KUVLESKY, W. P., & BEALER, R. C.   The relevance of adolescents' occupational aspirations for subsequent job attainments. *Journal of Sociology,* 1967, *32,* 290–301.

MEAD, M.   The life cycle and its variations: The division of roles. *Daedalus,* 1967, *96*(3), 871–875.

THORNBURG, H. A.   Peers: Three distinct groups. *Adolescence,* 1971, *6*(21), 59–76.

Some Cognitive Aspects of Career Development

SAMUEL H. OSIPOW

The author reviews research concerning personality characteristics as they relate to career development, and discusses their implications for the adolescent.

Over the years a great deal of attention has been focused on the study of vocational maturation, the antecedents of good decision-making, and methods of vocational choice implementation through the adolescent period. This attention is understandable, since our educational system is closely tied to vocational choice and training. Many of the educational decisions made and skills acquired during adolescence have significant implications for later vocational choice, attainment, performance, and satisfaction.

A number of perplexing questions have plagued the study of vocational development and implementation. It is troublesome not to be able to identify the early antecedents of good decision-making; it is bothersome not to understand more about the inter-individual differences in information processing for decision-making; it is awkward not to have a handy way to account for the wide tolerance of individual differences exhibited by occupations. A clear need exists for an adequate means to explain the process of vocational development.

Many theoretical descriptions of career development have been put forward (Osipow, 1968). The earliest of these views of vocational devel-

opment were essentially aimed at identifying the individual traits most closely associated with particular occupational preferences, membership, and success. This approach took the point of view that vocational choice is at heart an irreversible decision made at a specific point in time. Thus, an attempt was made to identify the abilities and personality traits that best suited an individual to the pursuit of a particular career in order to reach the objective of matching the individual and occupational traits as closely as possible. A giant matrix of traits could potentially be developed, individual traits could be compared to the matrix associated for an occupation by means of statistical methods, and clients could sort through the matrix to make their decision. This procedure is theoretically feasible within the limits of current tests, inventories, and statistical formulas, since job tasks do draw on abilities differentially. Thus, automobile mechanics are likely to require certain mechanical, spatial, and manual skills and aptitudes; these demands differ substantially from the traits required for success in a medical career.

In the personality realm, however, although occupational differences exist, a considerable and annoying overlap of traits has been observed. Possibly, the overlap occurs because, to some extent, job roles shape personality as well as the reverse. A job role may determine the ideal personality type to enter a given occupation. Once entered, however, "personality" interacts with the occupation. For example, there is a stereotype that depicts accountants to be compulsive. One would expect compulsive people to be highly attracted to careers as accountants. If a relatively uncompulsive individual were attracted to accounting, however, and some undoubtedly are, it may be expected that he would become more compulsive as a result of the nature of the duties involved in being an accountant. The job duties involved in accounting reinforce compulsive, careful behaviors.

Since personality traits significantly moderate the effect of aptitudes on career progress (through their impact on motivation, for example), the accuracy of the aptitude-oriented trait factor model breaks down. As a result, it actually has a limited impact on vocational decision-making despite its wide use by counselors. As the result of disillusionment, possibly premature and overzealous, with the trait factor model, a shift in conceptions about careers has occurred in recent years. It is now popular to see vocational choice as a developmental process. Holders of this point of view suggest that career development is systematic, periodic, and essentially irreversible and cumulative in nature (Ginzberg et al., 1951), with antecedents in early development (Roe, 1957) occurring in clearly demarked stages (Super, 1953). Attention is focused on the compromises that people are required to make between their vocational preferences and their vocational oportunities and possibilities. Super's et al., more recent work (1963) has further enriched the developmental approach by the introduction of the notion of self-concept implementation through emerging career development. This introduction was, at least partially, an attempt to deal with the complexities of personality involvement in career choice.

The simplistic t-f approach has elicited a second type of theoretical reaction; this is, an attempt to devise a more sophisticated trait-factor model. Holland's (1966) work represents such a response. Holland has proposed six occupational environments, each of which demands a different personality style for optimum vocational functioning. According to Holland, people select occupations that represent occupational environments consistent with their personality types. Since people are rarely "pure" types, Holland has devoted considerable attention to personality constellations and their career concomitants, thus avoiding one of the serious shortcomings of the model. Nonetheless, although many studies indicate a relation between personality type and career (Holland, 1966; Osipow, 1968); the relationships are of modest magnitude, and the basis for much career functioning is not clearly established.

PERSONALITY AND CAREER

The notion that personality and career choice are closely intertwined and predictably related is intuitively very attractive. Evidence of this attractiveness lies in the many studies of the relationship between personality and career that have been conducted (Osipow, 1968). Despite the apparent appropriateness of this line of inquiry, most of the research indicates only minimal relationships between personality and career. The lack of stable relationships between personality and vocation is bewildering. The absence of a clear relationship between personality and career is probably partly the result of the wide overlap of personality styles that are possible in implementing certain careers. It also results partly from the deficiencies in instrumentation in the measurement of personality, as well as from the interaction between personality and career mentioned earlier. No adequate theoretical structure exists to explain the particular relationship between personality development and functioning and career choice. Roe's (1957) approach tried to relate some aspects of early personal development to later career entrance, representing one attempt to bridge the personality—career gap, but it met with little empirical success.

It would appear that some important conceptual ingredient is missing that could help explain the wide variance of personality traits, styles, and types tolerated by occupations. It would be helpful if some element were postulated that satisfactorily explained how different types of people function effectively in similar occupational environments and how similar people can be comfortable in a wide range of career activities. How is it that an observer may, for example, find impulsive, outgoing people operating successfully in a wide range of vocations? How is it possible that salesmen can have a wide range of interpersonal styles and personality organizations and yet be able to function successfully, effectively, and with satisfaction?

A partial answer is that effective career performance makes demands on several aspects of human psychological functioning. Among those that come to mind readily are intellective-aptitude requirements. Work involves the adequate performance of a series of tasks. Aptitudes determine the ease with which individuals can develop the skills necessary to become proficient in the performance of these tasks. People differ in the possession of aptitudes, this difference affecting the economy of their acquisition of job-related skills. Since some people are willing and able to practice more than others, aptitudes do not predict performance perfectly. Within limits, however, occupations make significant demands on aptitudes as evidenced in data such as presented by Thorndike and Hagen (1959).

A second type of demand made by careers involves interpersonal behavior. It is likely that people differ in both the inherent behaviors they bring to interpersonal relations as well as in their response to training in interpersonal behaviors. Occupations differ in their tolerance of various interpersonal styles, yet, as has been observed, wide personality style variations within one career are possible. Very little is really known about the antecedents of personal styles and their vocational implications.

A third area of importance to the vocational psychologist lies in the impact of motivation, interests, values, and attitudes on career development. A number of questions can be raised in this regard. What are "interests"? Do they refer to intrinsic subjective gratifications growing out of engagement in circumscribed activities? Are they best conceived as patterns of expressed preferences? Or is it more helpful to think of them as some combination of the two? Implicitly, it is assumed that interests in general are intrinsically related to vocational interests. How valid is that assumption? Are interests merely attitudes in that they predispose individuals to respond to stimulus events in some effective manner?

Do interests serve as motivators to vocationally related activities? Intuitively, it would seem they should, yet much data, often unpublished (for example, Osipow, 1966) indicate that, other things being equal (such as abilities), interests inferred from inventories do not differentially predict vocationally oriented academic performance.

A fourth area of interest to the vocational psychologist has to do with individual perceptual-conceptual organization. Sometimes these events are called cognitive styles. A number of definitions of cognitive style have been proposed. In general, it is an elusive construct. Broverman (1960a; 1960b) has considered cognitive styles to be evident in observed "relationships between abilities within individuals." Murray and Jackson (1964) see cognitive styles as "perceptual attitudes" leading to stable responses to various stimuli. Wallach (1962) seems to use the term to describe the cognitively based generality of responses across situations. Witkin (1965) has defined cognitive styles as "characteristic, self-consistent ways of functioning in their perceptual and intellectual activities." All of these definitions have similar components. They all attempt to use the term to describe the individual's consistency in responding to various stimuli across situations. All the definitions are more concerned with intra-individual characteristics than with inter-individual similarities or differences.

Some operational examples of cognitive styles include creativity (for example, Getzels & Jackson, 1960), automatizing (Broverman, 1964), conceptual versus perceptual motor-dominance (Broverman, 1964), analytic–descriptive, inferential–categorical, and relational (Kagan, Moss, & Sigel, 1963), field dependence and independence (Witkin *et al.*, 1962), and equivalence-range (Sloane, Gorlow, & Jackson, 1963). To Getzels and Jackson, creativity refers to the individual's ability to solve old problems in a unique fashion. The "automatizer" of Broverman is the person who is able to relegate routine perceptual motor functions to the background of his attention and concentrate on higher level conceptual skills. The analytic–descriptive style of Kagan, Moss, and Sigel refers to the tendency of certain individuals to label items in terms of objective attributes they possess; the inferential–categorical person labels or arranges stimuli in terms of their relationship to one another and other elements in the category, while the relational person arranges stimuli in terms of their functional relationships to one another. The field-independent person of Witkin is characterized by a clear self-concept, articulate body-image, and autonomous impulse control. The notion of equivalence-range, as used by Sloane and his associates, refers to the "range of things a person will treat the same"; individuals vary in the degree to which they use broad versus narrow notions of similarity. Many other examples of cognitive styles could be provided, but the above illustrate the concept well.

To summarize: An intellective-abilities focus on career development allows prediction of different levels of vocational proficiency; and interest–attitude–motivational emphasis lends itself to the prediction of job persistence and satisfaction; the interpersonal and cognitive style data suggest individual differences in work organization and emphasis. Little attention has been paid to this last topic.

Cognitive style appears to have some unique features which lend it potential to serve especially well as a unifying construct to integrate observations about careers and personality. The concept can, to some extent, account for the differential functioning of personality types in one occupation while at the same time allow the psychologist to explain the satisfactory functioning of the same personality in many kinds of occupations.

A volume of literature has already accumulated which reveals something about the antecedents of some cognitive styles. The family environment seems to be important. It can be observed from Helson's work (1968) that performance on cognitive tasks related to creativity seems to be correlated among siblings. Creative women seem to encounter more sibling competition with their brothers than with their sisters. Getzels and Jackson (1961) also report familial differences in creative cognitive styles. When comparing the parental environment of high IQ versus high creative children, they found a number of significant differences. Fathers of high IQ's were more likely

to be college graduates than fathers of high creatives; mothers of high IQ's were more likely to have a graduate degree than mothers of high creatives; mothers of high IQ's were more likely to be full-time housewives than mothers of high creatives; parents of high IQ's were more likely to be two or more years apart in age than parents of creative children; mothers of high IQ's were more likely to be concerned with finances than mothers of high creatives; the families of high IQ's subscribed to more magazines than families of high creatives; and, finally, mothers of high IQ's seemed to be more satisfied with their child-rearing procedures than mothers of high creatives.

With respect to familial antecedents of cognitive styles, the work of Anne Roe also seems relevant. Roe (1957) hypothesized that early family environment affects later interpersonal orientation which, in turn, affects later vocational functioning. In her studies of eminent scientists she observed a number of interesting differences in early family experiences according to professional discipline (1951a; 1951b; 1953). Unfortunately, most research with other groups using her concepts has failed to indicate systematic differences related to later vocational entrance. However, the notion that a set of cognitive styles result from various kinds of early childhood experiences and that these styles serve as an intervening variable can be postulated to account for variations in later vocational functioning.

Dauw (1966) found significant differences in the kinds of vocational preferences expressed by high versus low creative thinking boys and girls. The high creative thinkers were more likely to express preferences for work in service organizations, general-cultural, and artistic and entertainment kinds of careers (in Roe's categories), while the low creative boys were more likely to select technological careers disproportionately. For girls, low creative thinkers over-chose organizational careers while high creative over-chose general-cultural and artistic and entertainment careers. Getzels and Jackson (1960), comparing the choices of high and low creative adolescents, found significant differences in both the quantity and quality of the occupational goals expressed by the two groups. Highly creative subjects expressed preferences for more unusual occupations as well as more occupations than low creative thinkers, and had exhibited less concern with the adult world's conventional standards of vocational success.

The work of Kagan, Moss, and Sigel (1963) suggests that children differ in the rate at which their cognitive development occurs and, further, that these differences have an impact on the child's suitability for certain educational experiences at critical developmental periods of discontinuity. This cognitively based differential receptivity to stimuli could very well have a cumulative impact on a youngster's progress through school. It could affect the kind and proportion of success–failure experiences that occur; it could influence an adolescent's developing attitudes toward different types of tests; it could alter his tendency to respond constructively to various educational–vocationally related tasks. For example, a critical style may be useful in the study of literature but troublesome in eighth grade science.

Even such attributes as risk-taking differences may easily be viewed as a cognitive style, one that would have substantial implications for vocational selection and effectiveness. Broverman, Broverman, Vogel, and Palmer (1964) found that physical attributes of strong versus weak male automatizers differ. The strong automatizers had thick, heavy-set hirsute builds, suggesting a high-level male endocrine function which spurred adolescent growth, whereas the low automatizers were not as highly developed physically. It is interesting to speculate about the implications that early physical maturation have for the kind of climate that a young man experiences during his adolescence. The psychological climate resulting from physical differences should substantially affect self-image, and consequently, task preferences, and the general sense of competency in performing educationally and vocationally related tasks.

In another study Broverman (1960a) found that conceptually dominated subjects were less easily distracted while performing a concentration-demanding conceptual task than perceptual motor dominant subjects, that strong automatizers were less easily distracted than weak automatizers on an automatic kind of conceptual task, and that strong automatizers were less distracted than weak automatizers on an automatic perceptual

motor task. Once again, these results have interesting implications. The results suggest that cognitive styles influence the differential functioning and resulting differential environmental feedback to youth about their educational development. In still a third study Broverman (1960b) found that individuals with different cognitive styles vary with respect to their abilities. Conceptually dominated subjects were observed to perform above their own mean level of performance on concentration-demanding tasks and below their own mean level on concentration-demanding perceptual motor tasks. The reverse finding was observed for strong automatizers.

A more molar kind of behavioral style variation associated with different kinds of performance in one occupation is suggested by findings reported by Gough and Woodworth (1960). They examined systematic differences in style among professional research scientists. Through the use of factor analysis, it was possible to identify eight types which highly differentiated the scientists behaviorally even though they performed the same function nominally. Upon close scrutiny it appears that the scientists performed very different work functions under the same vocational label. The eight factor types could represent distinctive syndromes of several cognitive styles of significance in the work environment.

Osipow (1969) observed a number of cognitive similarities and differences in women's functioning across several occupational types. Nursing students, for example, were observed to be relatively receptive to stimuli, field-dependent, uncritical, and narrow in equivalence range. Of interest was the finding that the measures could differentiate the nurses from such similar professionals as dental hygienists, who appeared field-independent, relatively non-supporting, and masculine in their overall cognitive style. Also of interest in Osipow's data was the evidence of considerable variation in the cognitive style that could be observed within an educational field. This suggests the possibility that people entering an occupation who exhibit a very distinctive cognitive style from the modal style for that field will organize their work tasks and occupational objectives in a very distinctive fashion from one another.

IMPLICATIONS FOR CAREER DEVELOPMENT

A number of immediate possible implications come to mind with respect to cognitive styles and careers. First of all, the impact of different cognitive styles on the development of vocational preferences and aversions can be considered. It is possible, for example, that the individual whose cognitive style includes a small equivalence range is likely to find certain kinds of tasks demanding a narrow and intense focus to be more to his liking, more intrinsically satisfying, than tasks that require the collation of broad bands of behavior. Similarly, certain other cognitive styles are likely to support activities that are relatively repetitive as opposed to others that may support activities which include frequent exposure to novel stimuli. The highly creative individual, for example, is likely to blossom under an environment which includes novelty, while the low creative individual is likely to be inhibited by such an environment and, in fact, may function most effectively where he is not frequently exposed to novel events. The interaction between specific cognitive styles and task preference and performance is an empirical question, open to study.

People with different cognitive styles are likely to process information differently (Munsinger & Kessen, 1966). It has been shown that there are systematic differences in preferences for stimulus variability which are associated both with maturation as well as with experience. The Kagan work, dealing with maturation and cognitive style, is also relevant to this respect. Presumably the analytic, reflective youngster is likely to find satisfaction and success in different and more complex tasks than the relational kind of youngster. Furthermore, the experiences these two types of people have are likely to result in cumulative effects on their sense of task success, consequently influencing their sense of self-esteem and self-concepts. This feedback is likely to have long-term and sequential impact on vocationally related decisions.

Of even more interest to counselors concerned with decision-making is the effect of different cognitive styles on the decision-making process itself. One is not hardpressed to imagine that cognitive styles may influence the degree to which individuals are willing to make decisions on limited data versus the degree to which they are able to make decisions at all in the presence of a degree of uncertainty. This is a realm of inquiry which offers considerable potential for investigation.

Still another area that potentially should interest vocational psychologists has to do with the differential management of job tasks associated with various cognitive styles. The individual's perceptual organization should affect the way he chooses to organize daily tasks, the emphasis he gives to certain tasks as opposed to others and the differential job satisfaction that he derives from his vocational activities. All of these aspects of work affect anticipations of potential success, task success, interest performance, and advancement.

Summary

This paper has attempted to illustrate the problem of developing an appropriate conceptual role for the operation of personality in career development. The use of the concept of cognitive style was proposed as a means to integrate personality data into career functioning. Some examples of the way cognitive functioning can influence development in general and educational and vocational development in particular were suggested. The role of cognitive styles remains speculative, however, and is a fresh avenue for research efforts.

REFERENCES

BROVERMAN, D. M. Dimensions of cognitive style. *Journal of Personality*, 1960, *28* 167–185. (a)

BROVERMAN, D. M. Cognitive styles and intra-individual variation in abilities. *Journal of Personality*, 1960, *28, 240–255.* (b)

BROVERMAN, D. M. Generality and behavioral correlates of cognitive styles. *Journal of Consulting Psychology,* 1964, *28,* 487–500.

BROVERMAN, D. M., BROVERMAN, INGE K., VOGEL, W., AND PALMER, R. D. The automatization cognitive style and physical development. *Child Development,* 1964, *35,* 1343–1359.

DAUW, D. C. Career choices of high and low creative thinkers. *Vocational Guidance Quarterly,* 1966, *15,* 135–140.

GETZELS, J. W., AND JACKSON, P. W. Occupational choice and cognitive functioning: Career aspirations of highly intelligent and of highly creative adolescents. *Journal of Abnormal and Social Psychology,* 1960, *61,* 119–123.

GETZELS, J. W., AND JACKSON, P. W. Family environment and cognitive style: a study of the sources of highly intelligent and of highly creative adolescents. *American Sociological Review,* 1961, *26,* 351–359.

GINZBERG, E., GINSBURG, S. W., AXELRAD, S., AND HERMA, J. L. *Occupational Choice: An Approach to a General Theory.* New York: Columbia University Press, 1951.

GOUGH, H. G., AND WOODWORTH, D. G. Stylistic variations among professional research scientists. *Journal of Psychology,* 1960, *49,* 87–98.

HELSON, RAVENNA. Effects of sibling characteristics and parental values on creative interest and achievement. *Journal of Personality,* 1968, *36,* 589–607.

HOLLAND, J. L. *The Psychology of Vocational Choice.* Waltham, Mass.: Blaisdell, 1966.

KAGAN, J., MOSS, H. A., AND SIGEL, I. E. Psychological significance of styles of conceptualization. *Monographs of the Society for Research in Child Development,* 1963, *28,* 73–111.

MUNSINGER, H., AND KESSEN, W. Stimulus variability and cognitive change. *Psychological Review,* 1966 *73,* 164–178.

MURRAY, J. E., AND JACKSON, D. N. Impulsivity and color–form abstraction. *Journal of Consulting Psychology,* 1964, *28,* 518–522.

OSIPOW, S. H. The relationship between interests, aptitudes, and academic achievement. Unpublished data, 1966.

OSIPOW, S. H. *Theories of Career Development.* New York: Appleton-Century-Crofts, 1968.

OSIPOW, S. H. Cognitive styles and educational-vocational preferences and selection. *Journal of Counseling Psychology,* 1969, *16,* 534–446.

ROE, ANNNE, A psychological study of eminent biologists. *Psychological Monographs,* 1951, *65,* No. 14 (whole No. 331). (a)

ROE, ANNE. A psychological study of eminent physical scientists. *Genetic Psychology Monographs,* 1951, *43,* 121–239. (b).

ROE, ANNE. A psychological study of eminent psychologists and anthropologists and a comparison with biological and physical scientists. *Psychological Monographs,* 1953, *67,* No. 2 (whole No. 352).

ROE, ANNE. Early determinants of vocational choice. *Journal of Counseling Psychology,* 1957, *4,* 212–217.

SLOANE, H. N., GORLOW, L., AND JACKSON, D. N. Cognitive styles in equivalent range. *Perceptual Motor Skills,* 1963, *16,* 389–404.

SUPER, D. E. A theory of vocational development. *American Psychologist,* 1953, *8,* 185–190.

SUPER, D. E., STARISHEVSKY, R., MATLIN, N., AND JORDAAN, J. P. *Career Development: Self-Concept Theory.* New York: College Entrance Examination Board Research Monograph No. 4, 1963.

THORNDIKE, R. L., AND HAGEN, ELIZABETH. *Ten Thousand Careers.* New York: John Wiley, 1959.

WALLACH, M. A. Commentary: Active–analytical versus passive–global cognitive functioning. In S. Messick and J. Ross (Eds.) *Measurement in Personality and Cognition.* New York: John Wiley, 1962.

WITKIN, H. A. Psychological differentiation and forms of pathology. *Journal of Abnormal and Social Psychology,* 1965, *70,* 317–336.

WITKIN, H. A., DYK, RUTH B., FATERSON, HANNA F., GOODENOUGH, D. R., AND KARP, S. A. *Psychological Differentiation.* New York: John Wiley, 1962.

A Cross-National Study of Adolescent Professional Goals

G. H. SEWARD   R. C. WILLIAMSON

The author compares the vocational goals of United States adolescents with those of teenagers in five other nations.

PROBLEM

As an extension of a cross-national study of sex-role concepts (Seward and Larson, 1968), the present research is specifically addressed to comparing professional goals of adolescents from the United States, the two Germanies, Chile, Poland, and Turkey. In addition, differences between the sexes and between social-class and ethnic subcultures will be analyzed.

SUBJECTS

Subjects were selected within the age range of 16 and 19 years on the assumption that the problem of goal selection was maximized during the late adolescence identity crisis (Erickson).

Educational level was equalized as well as could be done across the disparate school systems. For the main groups, American junior-college freshman were selected as most comparable with seniors from West German *Gymnasia* and East German *Oberschule;* high school seniors were also chosen to represent the Chilean, Polish, and Turkish populations.

To minimize sample differences in socioeconomic background, subjects for the cross-national comparisons were drawn exclusively from public schools where attendance was relatively independent of parents' income level. Since, however, the West Germans and Americans were found to differ significantly on the basis of father's occupation when total groups were used, the final comparisons were limited to the Los Angeles and Frankfurt/Main samples which, in terms of the same criterion, showed the same stratification.

Within the West German population, over-all social-class effects were analyzed by comparing *Gymnasium* students with those from several private *Länder* boarding schools from different parts of the Federal Republic. Analogous comparisons between public and private schools were carried out for the Chilean groups.

The ethnic variable was represented by a subgroup of American Black students attending the same junior college as the White subjects.

The total number and distribution of the various groups of subjects according to sex, area, and subculture are shown in Table 1.

From G. H. Seward & R. C. Williamson, A cross-national study of adolescent professional goals. Reprinted from *Human Development*, 1969, *12*, 248–254, by permission of author and publisher.

Table 1. Total Number of Subjects, by Area and Subculture

Area		Girls	Boys	Subculture	Girls	Boys
USA:	Los Angeles	68	83	Black	43	28
	Muncie, Ind.	94	40			
GFR:	Frankfurt/Main	100	97	Priv. Sch.	29	43
	Hannover	100	81			
GDR:	Jena	95	94			
Chile:	Santiago	59	79	Priv. Sch.	51	62
Poland:	Paczkow	50	17			
Turkey:	Istanbul	39	17			

MATERIAL

The face sheet of the test booklet, containing the *Semantic Differential* scales used in the original study, provided information concerning birth date, birth place, sex, ethnic grouping, school, father's education, and father's occupation. On the same record blank each participant also indicated the vocational goal to which he or she aspired after graduation. Although the data consisted only of verbal statements unvalidated by behavioral observation, the anonymity of the protocols presumably safeguarded them against deliberate distortion.

PROCEDURE

The goals designated on the face sheets were recorded on separate cards coded in correspondence with the face-sheet identification symbols. After coding, the cards were randomized and 'blind-sorted' by a colleague into four categories: 'major professional', 'minor professional', 'clerical-commercial' and 'undecided'. Distinctions between the first two categories may be illustrated by the following.

Major	Minor
medicine	nursing
dentistry	oral hygiene
architecture	interior decorating
chemistry	pharmacy
physics	photography
engineering	electronics
research	laboratory technique

Since the remaining categories proved too ambiguous to classify, analysis of the results was limited to comparisons between the *major* and *minor professional* goal choices.

RESULTS AND DISCUSSION

The main findings, expressed in terms of chi square, focus on comparisons among the six national groups and the two sexes.

CROSS-NATIONAL COMPARISONS. Table 2 presents the pair-by-pair comparisons among the six national groups. From the data for these comparisons shown in Table 3 it may be noted that the American student groups differed significantly from the corresponding West- and East-German samples in selecting *minor* rather than *major* professional goals. Moreover, the American girls were significantly separated in the same way from those of Chile, Poland, and Turkey. This trend did not characterize the boys' data.

The only other cross-national comparisons deserving comment are those between the Germanies and Poland. A higher proportion of the German Democratic Republic students aspired to top level professions than was true of the Polish youth represented. Differences between the Federal Republic and Poland were in the same direction but failed to reach statistical significance. On the basis of analogous comparisons, the two Germanies proved to be indistinguishable.

Analysis of subcultures within national groups yielded little. It is noteworthy, however, that the Black and White subjects of the American sample, all of whom attended the same school, showed no differences. This finding suggests that exposure to the same values through membership in the same academic community is a more important

Table 2. Cross-National Differences (*p* Values of χ)[1] in Subjects' Choices of Major vs. Minor Professional Goals

Area	GFR	GDR	Chile	Poland	Turkey
			Girls		
USA	<.01	<.001	<.001	<.01	<.001
GFR		n.s.	n.s.	n.s.	n.s.
GDR			n.s.	<.05	n.s.
Chile				n.s.	n.s.
Poland					<.10
			Boys		
USA	<.01	<.001	n.s.	n.s.	n.s.
GFR		n.s.	n.s.	<.10	n.s.
GDR			n.s.	<.10	n.s.
Chile				n.s.	n.s.
Poland					n.s.

[1] In all cases, df = 1, and the values of the chi squares have been corrected for attenuation.

determinant in goal setting than skin color. As for possible social-class effects, in West Germany differences between public *Gymnasium* and private *Länder* school students were non-significant. In Chile, on the other hand, the difference between public and private school boys reached a 0.001 level of significance, indicating that boys attending private schools selected *major* professions to the virtual exclusion of *minor* ones. Perhaps this is a last vestige of the feudalism that in the history of Western culture had set the gentleman and the clergy apart from the peasant (Williamson, 1970). In the case of the Chilean girls, the choices were for the *minor* goals regardless of social class.

SEX DIFFERENCES. Table 3 shows the comparative results for male and female subjects. The sex differences are even more striking than the differences among the national groups. Within each of these groups except Poland and Turkey, whose samples are too small to compare, the boy–girl differences reach high levels of significance. Similar contrasts between the sexes may be noted within the social-class and ethnic subcultures represented. In all cases, the differences point up the greater frequency with which girls, in comparison with boys, elect as goals *minor* rather than *major* professions.

PRESENT INDICATIONS. The high level of professional ambition exhibited by the youth from the two Germanies in comparison with that of the corresponding American subjects is consistent with the previous finding (Seward and Larson, 1968) that higher activity ratings were assigned to the self concepts by both East- and West-German students than was done by the Americans. This striking contrast in goal striving suggests that the Germans are responding to the urgency of rebuilding their societies while the 'affluent Americans' are content to 'rest on their laurels'. Such an interpretation receives special support in the present study from the girls' results, which show that more Americans set lower goals for themselves than did the female subjects from any of the other countries. Thus in the face of vaunted equality of opportunity, these American girls elected *not* to pick up the option.

The marked sex differences in aspiration level that pervade the present findings may be symptomatic of a general inertia in relinquishing the old sex role patterns. Traditionally, girls have been expected to make a career of domestic life. Consequently vocational goals have remained secondary, short-time, stop-gap measures for tiding over the interval between graduation and marriage. (Seward, 1964). With such an orientation, often reinforced by prejudical social practices, it is no wonder that women more frequently than men aim toward the less demanding, comfortable *minor* goals rather than the more strenuous and competitive *major* professions.

Table 3. Sex Differences (p values of χ)[1] for Number of Subjects Choosing Major vs. Minor Professional Goals

Area	Girls Major	Minor	Total	Boys Major	Minor	Total	p
USA	7	117	124	27	43	70	$<.001$
GFR	38	98	136	58	30	88	$<.001$
GFR (Priv.)	4	22	26	14	12	26	$<.01$
GDR	34	54	88	61	31	92	$<.001$
Chile	10	27	37	29	27	56	$<.02$
Chile (Priv.)	4	24	28	51	6	57	$<.001$
Poland	9	38	47	3	7	10	n.s.
Turkey	13	20	33	6	5	11	n.s.
USA	4	43	47	19	30	49	$<.01$
USA (Black)	2	31	33	7	10	17	—

[1] In all cases, df = 1, and the values of the chi squares have been corrected for attenuation.

The problem of the changing social roles of men and women has recently been examined in a number of contemporary societies around the world (Seward and Williamson, 1970). In certain oriental and Mediterranean cultures the old double standard still persists, while more 'progressive' countries are likely to profess an equality between the sexes which in practice amounts to a new kind of double standard according to which woman's 'emancipation' means adding an outside job to an already full-time domestic load. In only a few places like Sweden and the *Kibbutzim* in Israel has there been an effort toward a truly single equalitarian standard for male–female role behavior.

FUTURE DIRECTIONS. Although the present study is admittedly limited in scope, it points the way to further research in a number of directions. One meaningful extension of this work would be to relate the goals expressed by these subjects to their previously determined concepts of male and female social roles, and of themselves. (Seward and Larson, 1968). It would be interesting to discover whether the differences in activity ratings between the American and German girls' self-concepts were specifically correlated with differences in goal levels. Further problems concern the relationships between goals, sex-role concepts, and parental identification. Seward's (1945) early findings that girls deviating from typically feminine patterns of interest reflected atypical home situations, were later confirmed by White (1959) who found that girls with traditional attitudes came from more traditional homes and were more closely identified with their parents than were the career girls. Moreover, congruence between a girl's *self* and *ideal* perceptions and the perceptions her parents had of her were related to her vocational interests. More recent evidence of social change in sex-role concepts has been provided by Steinmann's (1963) study of female college students and their parents. Both generations agreed on a feminine role that integrated nurturing and achieving functions, but the subjects were apparently victims of cultural lag inasmuch as they erroneously assumed that the men preferred the traditional housewife role for women.

New dimensions that invite cross-cultural exploration are suggested by Bergler's (1962) depth study of adolescent goals and Bühler's (Bühler, 1965; Bühler and Massarik, 1968) developmental approach with her *Life Goals Inventory*.

Through these and other channels, all available research resources should be mobilized to increase our understanding of adolescent goal setting, a key problem of today's youth and tomorrow's world.

SUMMARY

In the present study a total of approximately 500 adolescents of each sex were selected from the United States, the two Germanies, Chile, Poland,

and Turkey. They were asked to record their vocational goals which were then sorted into *major* and minor professional levels. Chi Square analyses of the data revealed significant cross-national differences according to which the German subjects showed the greatest ambition. Another main finding was the striking differences between the sexes, with the boys consistently choosing higher professional goals than the girls. The results were attributed to the different motivational pressures to which the various groups had been subjected.

REFERENCES

BERGLER, R. Die Psychologische Struktur der Leitbilder Jugendlicher. *Hum. Develop. 5:* 34–60 (1962).

BUHLER, C. Psychological and psychiatric considerations of a questionnaire study of goals. *Acta psych. scand. 41:* 400–410 (1965).

BUHLER, C., AND MASSARIK, F. (Eds.) *The course of human life* (Springer, New York, 1968).

ERIKSON, E. H. *Identity and the life cycle* (International Universities Press, New York, 1959).

SEWARD, G. H. Cultural conflict and the feminine role: an experimental study. *J. Soc. Psychol. 22:* 177–194 (1945).

SEWARD, G. H. Psychological complications of woman's roles. *Int. Understand. 2:* 1–5 (1964–1965).

SEWARD, G. H., AND LARSON, W. R. Adolescent concepts of social sex roles in the United States and the Two Germanies. *Hum. Develop. 11:* 217–248 (1968).

SEWARD, G. H., AND WILLIAMSON, R. C. (Eds.) *Sex roles in changing society* (Random House, New York, 1970).

STEINMANN, A. A study of the concept of the feminine role of 51 middle-class American families. *Genet. Psychol. Monogr. 67:* 275–352 (1963).

WHITE, B. J. The relationship of self concept and parental identification to women's vocational interests. *J. Couns. Psychol. 6:* 202–206 (1959).

WILLIAMSON, R. C. Role themes in Latin America; in Seward and Williamson: *Sex roles in changing society* (Random House, New York, 1970).

Chapter 9: Suggested Additional Readings

CLAUTOUR, S. E., & MOORE, T. W. Attitudes of twelve-year-old children to present and future life roles. *Human Development,* 1969, *12*(4), 221–238. The particular attitudes of twelve-year-olds toward present and future life roles were determined and then differentiated according to social class, adjustment, sex, and IQ.

DEUTSCHER, M. Adult work and developmental models. *American Journal of Orthopsychiatry,* 1968, *38*(5), 882–892. The significance of an adult's work hinges on how, as child and adolescent, he used learning to develop competence, autonomy, work style, and outlook. This paper surveys the importance of the model of the working father for the development of work competence.

FOLK, H. The oversupply of the young. *Trans-action,* 1969, *6*(10), 27–32. Characteristics of youth employment, types of employer discrimination, and the causes of high youth unemployment are reviewed.

HALL, M. H. A conversation with Peter F. Drucker or the psychology of managing management. *Psychology Today,* 1968, *1*(10), 20–25, 70–72. In an interview, a management consultant discusses a wide range of factors dealing with occupational adjustment in the modern business world.

HIND, R. R., & WIRTH, T. E. The effect of university experience on occupational choice among undergraduates. *Sociology of Education,* 1969, *42*(1), 50–70. This study of male college students indicates that occupational choices undergo considerable change during undergraduate years. The changes are related to factors within the college experience.

HORNER, M. A bright woman is caught in a double bind. In achievement-oriented situations she worries not only about failure but also about success. *Psychology Today,* 1969, *3*(6), 36–38, 62. The author reports a study of the achievement motive in women and the general tendency to avoid excelling. She discusses causes and implications of this situation.

IDEA FORUM: IV. *Bulletin of the National Association of Secondary School Principals,* 1969, *53*(334), entire issue. Significant topics discussed in this issue include the potential of vocational education, the school's role in vocational preparation, an economic analysis of youth's employment, and characteristics of high-ability dropouts.

LITTLE, J. K. The occupations of non-college youth. *American Educational Research Journal,* 1967, *4*(2), 147–153. This study, involving a statewide inquiry among graduating seniors in Wisconsin, answers the questions: What is the occupational destiny of youth with differing levels of education? For what part of the occupational world is attainment dependent upon education beyond high school? What are the characteristics of youth who reach differing levels of occupational attainment?

PICOU, J. S., & COSBY, A. G. Social origins, occupational goals, and Southern youth. *Youth and Society,* 1971, *2*(3), 307–322. A study of sophomore high school students in four southern states revealed that the respondents, in general, had high-level goals, with considerable variation according to social class and residence. Neither race nor family structure seemed especially relevant. Related studies are also reviewed.

PITTS, J.   The counter culture. *Dissent,* June 1971, 216–229. According to Pitts, the counter culture, composed of the alienated youth groups, is displacing the traditional division between work and play with a new synthesis. Its members are attempting to solve the problem of work meaninglessness, and to divorce themselves from unpleasant associations with routine deprivations and personal self-discipline.

RAND, L.   Masculinity or femininity? Differentiating career-oriented and homemaking-oriented college freshman women. *Journal of Counseling Psychology,* 1968, *15*(5), 444–450. Among college freshman women, masculinity-femininity measures differentiated career- and homemaking-oriented women. The career-oriented women had redefined their sex role to include characteristics of both sexes.

WERTS, C. E.   Career choice patterns. *Sociology of Education,* 1967, *40*(4), 348–358. Werts reports on an investigation among college freshmen concerning the relation of the father's education and high school grades to the freshman's own career choice. Career choices were found to vary with the father's education, especially among women with non-traditional careers.

part four

Issues in
Peer Relations

10

Youth Culture — A Myth?

A persistent issue in adolescent psychology in recent years has been the question: Is there a separate youth culture in society today, or is the concept of a teen culture a myth? If such a culture exists but merely reflects the broader culture of society as a whole, can it truly be classified as a "culture" in its own right?

Some writers argue that youth's way of life is a microcosm of the larger society, not sufficiently distinctive to deserve the designation "youth culture." Among these is David Epperson (1964). Ernest Smith (1962) takes the opposite view, declaring that there is a separate adolescent way of life, and he describes the teen culture as it applies to youth who are American, white, urban, middle-class, postpubertal, not yet fulfilling adult roles. Snyder (1966) reviews both positions and concludes that youth indeed have a distinctive culture; however, he believes, this youth culture is no homogeneous entity, but possesses considerable diversity according to socioeconomic, sexual, ethnic, and cross-cultural factors.

Granting the premise that there is indeed a separate youth culture, let us consider first what are the causes of this culture. Some time ago, Murray and Kluckhohn (1948, p. 22) wrote that in all cultures, major discrepancies exist between the ideal patterns for various age groups. This differentiation tends to isolate age groups from each other and to produce characteristic ways of life for each group. Among American adolescents, especially, youth's way of life, or culture, has assumed features distinctive from those of the larger culture — perhaps for several reasons. For one thing, teenagers have been attracted to peer-group activities to offset the discipline and strains imposed by modern schools. Also, in free democratic societies youth are left largely to themselves, and this freedom permits the development of distinctive social groups. In democratic societies, too, the adult is ideally expected to be free-thinking and independent; membership in youth groups helps teenagers overcome the dependency of early childhood and assists them in attaining independent adulthood. In contrast, totalitarian societies attempted to bring youth under centralized control through officially organized, adult-directed youth organizations. A final factor in the growth of a separate teen culture is affluence, for in cultures of poverty, children are too involved in helping with family chores to participate in peer-group activity (Eisenstadt, 1956).

While the aforementioned factors account for youth cultures generally, still others blend to produce particular versions of youth culture. Chickering (1967) has defined four elements as responsible for the special characteristics of recent

American youth cultures. One element was "our peculiar parents"; he cites the wartime American "Oedipal childhood," with the father away or dead and the worried mother seeking affection in her children. Deprived of normal family relationships, the children have tried to find stability in peer groups. A second factor has been the new environment — "signs, billboards, store displays, supermarkets, the traditional media; finally, the new all-consuming substitute environment, television, enveloped us in a cocoon of sensory information [p. 602]." This new "media-envelope" has made them feel like "members of a global village." The third force was the affluent, populous, classless society and the absence of any "tomorrow." Today's youth were the first generation born to widespread affluence. Money was at hand; hence, concern for tomorrow became less pressing. The fourth element, the Bomb, was "the extra-terrestrial dimension, the symbolic Armageddon," a force which made them realize the possibilities of total destruction. The bomb became a reason to live for today rather than for tomorrow. Thus, the youth culture is youth's response to a totally new environment, gaining its strength from youth's united confrontation with institutional America.

In the first of the following readings, Burlingame suggests still other causes of youth culture. One of these, he writes, is the so-called market theory. This theory maintains that youth culture is produced by the salesmanship of the advertising industry; the subculture is thus created by a need stimulated by advertising. Another factor is the automatic groupings created by secondary schools and colleges, which are populated by individuals of the same age; our educational systems are typically based on age grading. Youth continually associating with their peers are encouraged to create their own future.

A second issue to be considered is: What are teen cultures really like, in both material and nonmaterial traits? In present-day Western countries, at least, adolescents have enough money to be consumers on a large scale. This money, in turn, finances the material aspects of their culture, which gives it much of its flavor. Clothes are very important to teenagers; clothing designers, creating specifically for the teen market, constantly introduce new styles, producing continuing obsolescence. Cosmetics, too, are important, and advertisers have begun successfully to tap the male market. Cosmetics and deodorants are being manufactured especially for men, so that boys may use them without forfeiting a self-image of masculinity. The automobile is a staple item in male-adolescent consumption and is also important, though less so, to girls.

Nonmaterial features of the teen culture are no less significant. Teenagers speak their own tongue, a blend of accepted usage and their own special modifications. Their idiom is constantly changing so that even recent alumni of the teen culture may have trouble understanding siblings in the younger set. Youths also have their tribal customs: parking in lovers' lanes and lingering in teen hangouts are among favorite pastimes. The hangout may be a soda fountain, a jukebox joint, or a college snack bar.

A third issue is: What is the composition of the teen culture — does it include all strata of society? Like the larger culture which surrounds it, the teen culture is stratified by social class. Formerly, the youth culture was almost wholly a middle- and upper-class phenomenon, except during the very early teens, for children of the lower classes entered the adult working world almost before they completed puberty. However, a combination of welfare assistance and higher wages for less skilled labor now enables lower-class parents to prolong their children's tenure in school and allows the children to participate in the youth culture. Also, until recently, high-school students were roughly divided into social classes of the college-bound and the vocational–commercial students. Each of these classes had its subtle differences in dress, personal ideals, and sex practices. However, today, many youngsters with lower-class backgrounds are going to college, and some of them are absorbed into the older collegiate version of the youth culture. Other lower-class youth have a strong occupational orientation and are intent on preparing for adult roles.

The youth culture differs somewhat on high school and college levels. In the second reading in this chapter, Schwartz and Merten portray the high school youth culture as a unique, independent subcultural system with its own life-style, world view, argot, status hierarchy, and standards. They depict this adolescent social life as involving a hierarchical status system with its own status symbols, defined by such terms as socie, hoody, snob, and stuck-up. But, although they perceive youths' cultural systems as relatively independent, the authors argue that these systems depend upon and reflect adult values and orientations.

At least four varieties of student culture have been distinguished at the college level (Clark & Trow, 1961). The first, the collegiate culture, is the world of football, Greek letter societies, cars, and drinking, in which courses and professors occupy a dim background role. Adolescents following this culture are not hostile to college; they simply evade its more serious demands. This sort of culture has flourished on the campuses of large state universities. The second, the vocational culture, prevails in urban colleges and universities attended chiefly by children of lower-middle-class families. The students are customers, not in a luxury market, but in a diploma market, says Bernard (1961). Many are married, and working hard — hence, their way of life is not teenage in nature. A third type, the academic culture, has learning as its major value. Practitioners of this culture identify with the faculty and its goals, and shun teen-type cultures. A fourth type is a varied blend of the intellectual, the radical, and the alienated Bohemian students. When these students' intellectual and cultural interests are at odds with those held by their teachers or parents, they become alienated from their own groups. Whereas members of the academic subculture pursue their goals within a formal educational framework, these nonconformists pursue their own goals outside it.

Formerly, the collegiate culture was the dominant one, but now the other three have attained greater significance. The influx of the lower classes into college has accented vocational values; a complex, rapidly changing culture has produced stresses and strains, and with them, nonconformist groups have proliferated.

The discussion so far has related primarily to American youth. Actually, what constitutes youth culture varies from one country to another. For example, in the Israeli kibbutzim, an adolescent's status is defined by character traits such as "honesty, helpfulness, friendliness — these traits being more highly valued than athletic achievement, scholastic achievement, or popularity with the opposite sex [Betensky, 1967, p. 343]." The youth culture in Israeli collectives has other distinctive features as well. Although it is organized by the adult community, it has a formal organization of its own. Moreover, although it operates in harmony with the larger social structure, it has a relatively independent status.

The topic of teen culture subsumes many other issues. What are the culture's more subtle traits? What is youth culture in the process of becoming? Will it spread throughout the world — or will it ultimately disappear? Again, what is the youth culture's overall effect on the youth himself and his society? Is its residual impact beneficial or otherwise? According to Grinder (1969), the youth culture does indeed involve certain hazards. For example, the adolescent may become unduly absorbed by the group's interests and excessively preoccupied with its common goals during a period when he must also be making important life decisions about marriage, vocation, place of residence, and extent of educational attainment. On the other hand, Chickering (1967) concludes that the youth culture affords the "necessary matrix" within which a young person can define an entire, well-integrated identity. Those individuals who do not participate fully in their peer culture suffer relatively acute and prolonged identity crises.

However, not all youth are active members of the current teenage culture; many have preferred to go along with the traditional societal culture. To some onlookers, the teen culture appears shallow, even immoral. It has become associated with a wide range of trappings such as miniskirts, beards, pills, drugs, and campus disruption. The more sympathetic observers lament these trends as the products of a space-and-nuclear-bomb age; the less sympathetic perceive youth as aimless, or as taking great pains to prove they do not care about society. Perhaps only time can provide us with the perspective necessary to determine what the youth culture is really like—and by that time, the whole scene will have changed and will require redefinition!

REFERENCES

BERNARD, J.   Teen-age culture: An overview. In J. Bernard (Ed.) *Teen-age culture.* American Academy of Political and Social Science, November 1961, *338,* 1–12.

BETENSKY, M.   The role of the adolescent in Israeli collectives. *Adolescence,* 1967, *11*(7), 335–344.

CHICKERING, F. B.   How we got that way. *The American Scholar,* 1967, *38,* 602–607.

CLARK, B. R., & TROW, M.   Determinants of college student subculture. In *The study of college peer groups: Problems and prospects for research;* a volume based on the work of a seminar sponsored by the Social Science Research Council, Ann Arbor and Berkeley, 1959-1960 (mimeographed). P. 2.

EISENSTADT, S. N.   *From generation to generation.* Glencoe, Ill.: Free Press, 1956.

EPPERSON, D. C.   A reassessment of indices of parental influence in the adolescent society. *American Sociological Review,* 1964, *29,* 93–96.

GRINDER, R. E.   Distinctiveness and thrust in the American youth culture. *Journal of Social Issues,* 1969, *25*(2), 7–19.

MURRAY, H. A., & KLUCKHOHN, C. (Eds.)   *Personality in nature, society and culture.* New York: Knopf, 1948.

SMITH, E. A.   *American youth culture.* New York: Macmillan, 1962.

SNYDER, E. E.   Socioeconomic variations, values, and social participation among high school students. *Journal of Marriage and the Family,* May 1966, *28*(2), 174–176.

The Youth Culture

WILLIAM V. BURLINGAME

Burlingame defines and analyzes the characteristics of the youth culture in terms of a basic belief system. He also attempts to account for the existence of youth cultures; and, in the process, he cites views of various other authorities.

Introduction

It is scarcely unique for one to observe the obvious discrepancy that exists between certain sentiments and predispositions of young people and those of their elders. Within recent years, it has become increasingly common to hear of these adolescent tastes as constituting a discrete culture which has been alternately referred to as "the adolescent society," "the teenage peer culture," or "the adolescent subculture." More disciplined social scientists would surely take affront. The term "culture" has a technical and restricted usage, and may seem inappropriate to describe the propensities of one peculiar age stratum which exists within a larger cultural matrix. In the same vein, if culture implies a shared base of values and attitudes, it has yet to be demonstrated that young people are not maturing to resemble previous generations. The foci of friction, the areas that approach schism, and the conspicuous dissent of a few may be quite visible, but they do not obscure that which is common and shared among generations. To some extent, then, it is as sensible to examine the given culture, to note the eccentricities of particular groups, and to account for divergence according to the principles of so-cial and economic change or human growth and development. To do so is to pose the following questions: In the maturation of Western culture, what developments have fostered this subset of beliefs and practices among the young? What is their psychological meaning and their utility in promoting growth toward autonomy and maturity? In the present discussion the term "youth culture" is used loosely and advisedly, with greater emphasis placed on the word "youth" with its connotations of growth and development than upon the word "culture."

Documenting the age level separation is not difficult; the following is the colorful if not inflammatory observation of social critic Paul Goodman (1966):

"Teenagers" are not adolescents in a total society of all ages; they are a race with a distinct plumage and music. Their high priests, unlike the movie heroes or athletes of other times who were grownup models, now tend to perform specifically for the teen audience and are hardly (or not yet) out of their teens themselves.

Such a subculture is not a subsociety, like the youth houses of primitive tribes, which were organized around the interests and secrets of adolescents but still took part in community life. Rather, it is a language and mores *against* the adults, or at best excluding them, as if they were a foreign tribe, probably hostile. In principle, every teenager is a delinquent, (pp. 18–19).

Goodman cites plumage and music, although most authorities would view these as peripheral rather than fundamental aspects of culture. There is merit in briefly examining these expressive modes as examples of youth culture adherence.

In the years following World War II, the prototype for male adolescent appearance was the crew-cut collegian, who, in turn, had adopted his garb from the tastes of returning servicemen. The transmission of dress style was orderly, direct, and non-controversial, with the young borrowing in large part from their senior counterparts. By 1955, the process had been decisively interrupted. Such teen heroes as Elvis Presley and James Dean dictated taste; for secondary school boys, this included blue denim (not khaki) trousers which were close fitting, lightened by laundering or bleach, and hung at a precise and controversial point on the hips without benefit of a belt. Closely cropped hair was summarily abandoned in favor of elaborate and massive sideburns combed back to fall in the neck and maintained in place by substantial doses of hair oil. The atmospheric qualities conveyed were rebelliousness, thinly disguised sexuality, and arrogance. In the early 1960s, youthful models continued to prevail, although the form differed. At this time, it was the California surfer whose hair was equally long but fell instead over the forehead. Both hair and denim were now bleached either by sun, salt, or chemical, and pants were severed above the knee in order to enhance mobility in the surf. What had emerged as functional or accidental was rapidly integrated into a carefully specified style which was nearly as common in Michigan as in California. In the late 1960s, a plethora of tastes occurred which differed widely in form but had, in common, their origin in the youth culture. Loose and flowing bell-bottom trousers competed with brief "mini-skirts," while expensive "mod" attire was juxtaposed with the discarded fur coats, uniforms, and work clothing found in thrift shops and rummage sales. The Hippie, mod, and psy-chedelic influences combined to promote a taste that was as ornate, elaborate, flamboyant, and unconventional as anything yet produced in the twentieth century.

Developments in adolescent cult music paralleled. The subdued rhythms of the "big band" sound predominated throughout the 1940s and into the 1950s. The names of Benny Goodman, Glenn Miller, and the Dorsey Brothers were accepted by both young and old; there was Guy Lombardo who produced the "sweetest music this side of heaven" and the crooners of the Crosby tradition, including Frank Sinatra who emerged as a hero of youth but was gradually assimilated as a stock item of middle-class musical taste. By 1955, a dramatic change had occurred as Elvis Presley, among others, drew upon the Negro rhythm and blues, and country and western musical traditions to produce hard-driving "rock and roll." The music of that period was predictable with its four-four beat and banal lyrics: "Who put the bomp in the bomp-ba bomp-a bomp? Who put the ram in the ram-a-lam a-ding-dong?" (*Time Magazine*, 1969). During the early 1960s youthful musicians, in apparent reaction, utilized the heritage of American folk music to produce a sound that had the peaceful, poetic, and soulful qualities previously absent. By 1965, the integration of folk, rock, and Indian raga music together with usage of psychedelic drugs, amplifiers, loud speakers, electrified instruments, and other sorts of electronic paraphernalia had produced music identified variously as "acid rock," "folk rock," or "revolution rock." The lyrics were sexually provocative, preoccupied with drug experiences, or in direct opposition to the usual political and economic institutions. An English group proposed that the time was propitious for "palace revolution" and its recordings were subsequently banned in that country, while American groups sung of "a magic carpet ride" and a "trip" that was "eight miles high."

The content inherent in this revolution in plumage and music is significant, but of greater import is the fact that the form as well as content had been generated from within the youthful constituency itself. Most observers have been inclined to view the decade of the 1950s as a decisive period in which the tastes of adolescents achieved cultural autonomy. This is not to deny the earlier manifestations of a youth culture, such as that noted in the "flaming youth" of the 1920s. Rather, it is to suggest that in the course of evolution a critical threshold has been crossed with youth presently proposing its own tastes, testing these in the adolescent marketplace, accepting some items while rejecting others, and then passing on in fickle fashion to the latest innovation. Not only had custom been generated from within, but there was firm evidence that it was being emulated from above. Adolescents wryly commented to the effect that immediate demise is the fate of any fad adopted by adults. A teenager once informed this writer that a particular dance step had been ". . . killed by middle-aged women in hot pink stretch pants." The homogeneity of youthful taste has since assumed international proportions as well. Without doubt, the mass media have provided national and international coverage, and the message has fallen upon the receptive audience. Youth culture garb and musical taste are common throughout the industrial, urban centers of both Western and Communist nations.

Youth Culture Dimensions

Music and dress have been noted as conspicuous examples of one of the parameters of youth culture practice. Because they are highly visible, it is a comparatively simple matter to illustrate their presence. There remain, however, a number of other features that are more central and pervasive but fall in the ambiguous realm of values and attitudes. The following four categories are intended to encompass the youth culture's core values; the attempt is to provide descriptive clarity, while recognizing that these propositions are at times overlapping or mere extensions of one another.

I. CONSTRUING THE YOUTH CULTURE AS POSSESSING INDEPENDENT CULTURAL EXISTENCE

The presence of this attitude among adults and adolescents underscores a general cultural recognition of the distinct and separate existence of youth. The discontinuity with other generations is emphasized and an aura of uniqueness and desirability is attached. Childhood is disdained; there is abstention from the responsibilities of adulthood; age is the primary criterion for providing distinction. It is no accident that romantic literature has idealized youth to the extent that "youth" and "beauty" have been seen as virtually synonymous. The comparison fiction is that youth exists for its own ends and pleasures but will inevitably be corrupted by age and experience. Youth, then, is viewed as a suspension, a limbo-like state, which denies any organic continuity with childhood and is briefly spared the decay and doldrums inherent in adult status. Although empirical data are sparse, social scientists have not been loath to recognize a subculture of adolescents nor to account for adolescent behavior utilizing such a construct. As early as 1942, Parsons (1958) applied the term "youth culture" and attributed similar qualities to it. More recently, Keniston argued that the youth culture is not simply transitional.

> For the essence of the youth culture is that it is not a rational transitional period—were it one, it would simply combine the values of both childhood and adulthood. Instead it has roles, values, and ways of behaving all its own. (Keniston, 1962).

II. VALUING PEER GROUP SOCIABILITY: A RANGE OF BEHAVIORS FROM CONSTITUTING PEERS AS A REFERENCE GROUP TO SEEKING GROUP ESTEEM AND PARTICIPATING IN SOCIAL RATING PRACTICES.

There are many data that describe the reliance of adolescents on the youth culture and peer group as a reference group for decision-making. When Coleman (1961, pp. 5, 6, 140) asked adolescents to decide whose disapproval would be most difficult to accept, he found a roughly even division between "parents" and "friends," with "teachers" accounting for a very small proportion. Considering that all subjects were secondary school students and resided in the parental home, the figures are somewhat startling. Of even greater significance was the discovery that members of the "leading crowds" (that is, the socially elite) were significantly inclined to regard peer disapproval as more difficult to receive. Thus, those who were considered leaders and pace-setters were oriented toward peers to even greater degree. An additional aspect is the preference for peer group association in contrast to solitary activity. This proliferation of group endeavor, whether formal or loose, whether purposeful or seemingly random, has long been a hallmark of adolescence. In the Coleman (1961, pp. 12–13) research, more than 80 percent of high school students listed choices of preferred ways of spending leisure time which were distinct peer group activities ("organized outdoor sports": 22 percent of boys; "being with the group": 32.5 percent of girls).

Beyond the participation in peer group association rests a higher order value, the search for status, which is somewhat more compelling if not actually coercive. This indulgence in social rating and rank ordering, including the pursuit of group esteem or what is commonly referred to as "popularity," is often one of the most offensive traits of adolescents in adult eyes. On occasion, it appears as if the sense of fair play and democracy so carefully inculcated by middle-class teachers and parents during grammar school years is openly discarded in favor of evaluation based on trivial or superficial criteria. In part, each adolescent's foray into group activity is to expose himself to group judgment regarding his personal adequacy and competence; self-esteem is based on group esteem and the judgment may be painful or inflated. In the Coleman (1961, p. 30) study, high school students were offered choices as to how they would prefer to be remembered at school. The "most popular" item was selected by 25 percent of boys and 35 percent of girls. Equally revealing was the "athletic star" choice of 44 percent of boys and "leader in activities" of 36 percent of girls. These latter activities are usually considered to be direct routes to group esteem. Further manifestations of the drive for social status include the "dating and rating" practice wherein esteem is accorded depending on the prestige of the dating partner, the arranging of social groups ("cliques") into status hierarchies within the social system of the high school, and,

in the absence of other data, granting status to an individual according to the reputation of his group (Hollingshead, 1949).

III. SUBSCRIPTION TO A VARIETY OF PRACTICES AND BELIEFS: THE WILLINGNESS TO ADOPT THESE CUSTOMS IN THE PURSUITS OF AFFILIATION AND ESTEEM

This proposition recognizes that with the advent of culture come artifacts or customs, and that membership requires conformity in various signal aspects of behavior. These constitute a badge of admission and offer a common base for shared activity. Whether these particular adolescent customs are but extensions of present middle-class culture, or operate in the ambiguous or irrelevant interstices, or are truly in conflict with prevailing society is of lesser consequence for present purposes.

The most obvious feature is the adoption of various subcultural trademarks, including approved music, dance, idiosyncratic language, modes of personal adornment, and means of transportation. Since these expressions are particularly conspicuous, they serve not only to differentiate teenagers from others, but offer a visible means of identifying adolescents of kindred sentiment. Of all the characteristics of the youth culture, these alone reveal the greatest flux; although the mode of expression remains, the specific esteemed style may change several times in the course of a year. In the milieu of the junior high school, mastering the current dance step, becoming familiar with this week's favored cult music recordings, adopting the preferred slang or jargon, and dressing to meet the "fad" may possess as much urgency for students as the lessons of their teachers. Due to the rapid exchange of item, these aspects have been less well investigated in formal research. Studying the then current styles of popular music, Coleman (1961, p. 23) discovered near universal agreement as to its acceptance. With popular music, two forms of six accounted for 70 percent of the favored choice; "rock and roll" music (the form most commonly attributed to the youth culture) received 50 percent of the total choice. Dance, idiosyncratic language, dress, and hair style are less well investigated, but equally pervasive. Automobile ownership, however, has been subject to greater study. With one exception, twelfth grade boys owned cars at levels between 40 and 80 percent in all of Coleman's settings. The finding that socially prominent boys were more likely to own cars led Coleman to interpret access to an automobile as contributory to social status (Coleman, 1961, p. 128).

Aside from the attention to symbols, there are other beliefs and practices that have potential for conveying social and self-esteem. Among these are the valuing of athletic prowess for boys, physical beauty and participation in activities for girls, seeking risk, stimulation, action, and excitement, and giving at least lip service to a nonscholarly orientation. Of the several routes to status none is so clearly evident as athletics for the young male. Over the past half century, studies have consistently revealed athletic success to be most strongly linked with social acceptance. Coleman (1961, pp. 30, 194), for example, found that each of the members of the leading freshman clique played either football or basketball. Similarly, almost 50 percent of high school boys would prefer to be remembered as "athletic star" in preference to "brilliant student" or "most popular," and the desire to be a nationally famous athlete led a field of four options. For girls, the analogous attribute appears to be a cluster of qualities best labeled as "glamor" and "personality," which includes physical beauty, a general gregarious quality, and participation in activities. It is not surprising, then, for Coleman (1961, p. 48) to note that the female role most equivalent to athletic star was that of cheerleader. The willingness to undertake activities where there is risk, limited danger, stimulation, and action has often been attributed to youth. Many years ago Kuhlen and Lee (1943) determined that the trait, "willing to take a chance," significantly discriminated between popular and unpopular groups at the sixth, ninth, and twelfth grade levels. Much later, Coleman (1961, p. 124) found that 30 percent of boys and 24 percent of girls checked the item "stirring up a little excitement," as a trait relevant to acceptance within their group. Of note is the finding that socially prominent boys, those most often selected as "friends," and those most often named

as someone to emulate, checked this item more often than did other boys.

The reliance upon scholastic achievement appears to relate negatively to group acceptance and runs counter to youth culture values. It may not be that the culture is hostile to academics, as much as it is that this route rules out other avenues that are esteemed. Sole reliance on study and scholastic achievement suggests the "grind," "brain," or "teacher's pet," stereotypes that effectively eliminate the valued athletic orientation for boys, and the participation in recklessness, thrill-seeking, and risk-taking. This interpretation is less pessimistic but consistent with Coleman who viewed the youth culture as actively antischolastic. His evidence repetitively demonstrated the disadvantages of scholarly achievement as a single path to popularity, to acceptance by the opposite sex, and to being chosen for friendship (Coleman, 1961, pp. 31, 41, 148, 244, 245).

IV. RECOGNITION OF ALIENATION AND CONFLICT BETWEEN GENERATIONS

This general proposition contains a syndrome of attitudes that underscores the separation, mutual lack of understanding, antipathy between generations, and the consequent predisposition of adolescents to withdraw allegiance from adults and societal institutions. At its most benign level, it includes the tendency to view adults as dated, dull, bumbling, awkward, but generally well intentioned. For some 30 years the "Archie" comic strip has promoted the stereotype of adults as rather harmless, ineffectual, impotent creatures who must be indulged because society has delegated greater power to them. At a second level of intensity, there exists an overt and recognized hiatus between generations, emphasizing such qualities as alienation, separation, the inability to communicate, and the lack of bases for understanding. A further step is to acknowledge the previous, and to develop a mild, but critical attitude toward the practices of adults, with the occasional implication that these do not serve as models worthy of imitation. The projection mechanism may define yet another level in which adults are construed as possessing hostile and depreciating motives toward adolescents. With the acceptance of the foregoing, young people may take the final step of renunciation in which they deny allegiance, responsibility, and duty to parents and adults.

The separation between generations is likely a companion piece to the investment in peers. The same citations to research apply, and it would seem redundant to refer to any of the sizable fund of lay and scholarly opinion on this issue. It should be noted that neither the above proposition nor any of the previous intends to suggest that these motives are present in all adolescents. They are present to some degree among many, but their significance inheres in the fact that they are institutionalized within the belief system of the youth culture.

Rationales for the Emergent Youth Culture

To date several distinct explanations have been proposed in attempting to account for the youth culture. As a group, the proposals tend to separate along disciplinary lines and to contain premises that are partially complete rather than mutually exclusive. Most commonly advanced is the "changing social fabric" theory which includes an amalgam of economic and sociological assumptions. In general, these social scientists have stressed industrialization and its manifold effects. As the nation has moved from a rural economy, the locus and unit of production have gradually transcended the home and farm. The wage earner and the means by which one is productive are no longer visible, and young people cannot learn to be productive at the knees of their parents. Nor can children themselves be productive, for there is little for them to produce; in effect, the United States has been the first nation to transform youth from "a family asset as labor to a family liability as student consumer (Denney, 1962). With long preparation being required in order to assume vocational responsibility, and with the adolescent being essentially useless and frequently unwanted on the labor market, an extended period of dependency occurs and learning has been institutionalized. Thus, secondary schools and colleges consist of many individuals of the same age, from whom society can demand little, and provide

little in the way of concrete evidence regarding progress toward maturity. The conditions are se for an independent subculture with goals, tasks and landmarks of its own.

He is "cut off" from the rest of society, force inward upon his own age group, made to carr out his whole social life with others his ow age. With his fellows he comes to constitute small society, one that has most of its impo tant interactions *within* itself, and maintair only a few threads of connection with the ou side adult society. (Coleman, 1961, p. 3).

Although the above rationale is useful in ac counting for age level separation, it does nc contribute particularly to an understanding c youth culture content or its meaning and utili for adolescents.

A second set of interrelated theoretical po tures is entitled the "threshold" and "market explanations. They tend to cite such factors population change, advances in technology, eco omic well being, and the mass media in accoun ing for the youth culture. These writers are a to hold that the youth of today are little differe from adolescents of distant generations, and th the youth culture construct is not particularly a vantageous. The emergence of a so-called adole cent society is, in part, an artifact devolving fro the rapid increase in sheer numbers of adole cents. A visibility threshold has been crossed the extent that a homogenized subculture h emerged, with adolescents now being so conspic ous to one another that their conformity has pr duced a national and international uniformi Census statistics are cited to the effect that t adolescent population is expanding at a rate fo times as great as the national average with t median age of the total population having dropp to the late twenties. Advances in technolog particularly in the mass media, have enhanc the trend toward homogeneity. Radio, with t "disk jockey" who caters to adolescents, has pr duced a cult music and jargon. Television h permitted adolescent music and dance to take national uniformity, while the microgroove reco has allowed adolescents to carry their cult mus beyond the television screen or radio set. The on necessary concomitant is the relative affluen that has occurred since World War II. Akin to the above reasoning is the "market" theory which holds that the youth culture is the product of the acumen and salesmanship of the advertising industry. There is no subculture other than that created by stimulated need, and the behavioristic assumption is made that any product can become a need if packaged and peddled to advantage.

Such contentions have limitations. The very need for conformity remains unexplained as does the apparent need for flux within the conformity pattern. Nor are the constant and repetitious youth culture themes accounted for, nor the failure of certain promotional schemes to succeed. The threshold and market theories suffer from severely simplified assumptions regarding the nature of human motivation.

Several volumes of social criticism have appeared in recent years which point up the plight of adolescents in an organized society. The notion of "alienation" is presented in which society appears to have conspired to deny the promise inherent in adolescence by rewarding mediocrity, conformity, and superficiality, thus preventing the decisive articulation of identity. The youth culture, then, is logically merely an age level manifestation of deteriorating adult values. To the extent that it is in conflict with adults, it may be commendable, but too often, even this reaction is inarticulate and misguided. In *The Vanishing Adolescent*, Friedenberg (1959) held that adolescence is disappearing as a stage when identity can be achieved; the adolescent " . . . merely undergoes puberty and stimulates maturity." Goodman (1956) in *Growing Up Absurd* is also representative of the "alienation" point of view. He contended that society has ceased to make sense for the adolescent. Objective opportunity is lacking, and "security," that is, ". . . the sense of being needed for one's unique contribution . . ." (Goodman, 1956, p. 22) is not easily obtained.

It's hard to grow up when there isn't enough man's work. There is "nearly full employment," but there get to be fewer jobs that are necessary or unquestionably useful; that require energy and draw on some of one's best capabilities; and that can be done keeping one's honor and dignity. In explaining the widespread troubles of adolescents and young men, this simple ob-

jective factor is not much mentioned. (Goodman, 1956, p. 17).

The outcome has been a youth culture which provides a series of eccentric, substitute vehicles toward the achievement of independence and maturity. Goodman suggested by implication that in the proportion to which "objective opportunity" (meaningful activity, in terms of part-time jobs with utility, experiences relating to actual vocational preparation, and significant, engaging academic work) is lacking, adolescents are apt to demonstrate " . . . all the more fierce gang loyalty to their peers." (Goodman, 1956, p. 44).

Both Friedenberg and Goodman have made similar assumptions regarding human motivation. Youth, by being human, strives toward securing meaning, utility, integrity, competence, and the attainment of potential. Society, by virtue of bureaucracy, inefficiency, fear, and stupidity, has succeeded in thwarting youth. By dehumanization and violation of the conditions required for meaningful human existence, identity has been threatened. Goodman stated, "If there is nothing at all, when one does nothing, one is threatened by the question, *is* one nothing?" (Goodman, 1956, p. 41). The result is alienation both from one's own identity and from those individuals and institutions which create the debilitating conditions. The youth culture represents young people's turning in upon themselves in the futile search for meaning, escaping from that which is barren and offensive, and protesting against the absence of promise. Unfortunately, the youth culture seldom approximates much more than adolescent artifices mirroring similar adult practices.

A final position has come from individual psychology and is termed "psycho-social" or "ego process" theory. For these observers, the youth culture offers a sort of "way-station, . . . a temporary stop-over in which one can muster strength for the next harrowing stage on the trip." (Keniston, 1962, p. 161). It is a period of delay during which time a reorganization must be effected before adult responsibilities are assumed. The ego functions of the young person are assaulted from within and without: Full sexual drive is experienced, together with demands for controlled release, impulse management, object choice, and re-evaluation of moral commitments; physical and intellectual growth have occurred, thus requiring a re-assessment of body image and cognitive competency; with the maturation of capacity emerges the necessity to make value choices regarding what it is that is worthwhile; the environment, on viewing impending maturity of adolescents, exerts control on impulse and expects preparation for vocational achievement; by anticipating independence and judgment, the environment also serves as the principal agency which withholds the same, thus creating a task requiring delicate maneuvering on the part of the adolescent; subtly and gradually the capacity for interpersonal relationships of depth which are characterized by mutual and reciprocity has developed, and with it, the necessity to re-test and re-cast social relationships.

Such are the tasks of adolesence and it is the responsibility of the ego to secure synthesis and direction. Achieving "identity" is the term commonly applied to this process and, of several theories, Erik Erikson has likely spoken most directly. The Eriksonian point of view has been summed as follows:

> One of the main psychological functions of a sense of identity is to provide a sense of inner self-sameness and continuity, to bind together the past, the present, and the future into a coherent whole; and the first task of adolescence and early adulthood is the achievement of identity. The word "achieve" is crucial here, for identity is not simply given by the society in which the adolescent lives; in many cases and in varying degrees, he must make his own unique synthesis of the often incompatible models, identifications, and ideals offered by society. The more incompatible the components from which the sense of identity must be built and the more uncertain the future for which one attempts to achieve identity, the more difficult the task becomes. (Keniston, 1962, p. 162).

The peer group and the youth culture provide the medium for securing identity. Because the adolescent must separate himself from the identities of his parents, he must reject their dictates and, occasionally, their values; for "achieving" identity is an active process, rather than one of passive purchase of the achievement of others.

Because society has been deficient in providing clear landmarks and in institutionalizing the steps to autonomy, the adolescent constitutes his own society. It is characteristically non-adult, but, at the same moment, encourages conformity and stereotypy. By demanding this consensus, it provides its own tasks and landmarks and offers a useful series of demarcations to identify. Although a different master, the authority of peers, is constituted, this new master effects a break in the dependency on parents. The youth culture also has its lawful season and must be abandoned as autonomy and selfdirection evolve.

Each of the dimensions of the youth culture can profitably be conceptualized within the psycho-social model. The tendency to idealize the teenage years is clearly the attempt to forestall adult responsibility during which time synthesis may be achieved. A modicum of irresponsibility of flirtation with risk is permitted in order to test possible alternatives. Agemates are billed as authorities and reference groups, not necessarily in the interest of abandoning adult values, but as a means of breaking with adult authority. Conflict may be the possible consequence; however, it may also be initiated by adolescents who are seeking to document their progress to autonomy or to wrest control more abruptly (often in league with peers). The status-seeking and rank-ordering practices offer certainty as to position and self-definition during a time when these matters are ambiguous; in fact, the highly *social* nature of the youth culture permits it to serve as a constant mirror, feeding back data to the emergent and crystallizing identity. The subcultural symbols (language, music, dress) allow protective coloration and temporary comfort to prevent identity diffusion, but also constitute visible and definite tasks. Stereotyping is useful, for if an adolescent cannot remain the child of his parents and is as yet unable to proclaim independence, he can hide within the conventions of his peers. Finally, participation in risk, danger, and physical activity, while possibly serving as sublimations for genital drive, have the function of permitting young people to test the limits of their maturing physical bodies.

The four positions that have been set forth do not conflict as rival theories. In fact, they tend to be complementary. Sociological approaches have paid heed to industrialization, division of labor, the removal of the locus of production from the home and from the observation of the young, and the growth of institutionalized education with its body of age-equals. These foregoing events have created a need for new institutions or sub-cultures to assist in articulating the young to adult status. Psycho-social theory, using the concept of "identity," permits explanation of the psychological meanings of the youth culture, its manifestations, and its utility as a bridge from childhood to adulthood. For individual adolescents, it offers a viable account of growth or blockage. The market and threshold accounts are not first order, but contribute ancillary postulates. They do explain the homogeneity and uniformity but not the reason why it should occur. The alienation concept may offer a rationale to account for the present difficulties in attaining identity and may explain why so many recent encounters between adults and youth are laden with conflict and confrontation.

Since the Coleman study, a substantial research effort has been mounted in the attempt to add further clarity and definition. An attitude scale was derived from the several aspects of youth culture adherence previously described and was subsequently administered to thousands of young people in diverse settings (Burlingame, 1967). A number of propositions were tested to determine whether the existence of the youth culture and the nature of its content could be constructed according to the identity construct. By way of example, if the youth culture were a "way-station," then adherence to it ought to vary according to age, and if it serves as a vehicle in the attainment of identity, then greater or lesser adherence should be related to the abundance or poverty of other forms of environmental provision. The findings were numerous and suggestive. Adherence to youth culture values occurred less among girls than boys of high school age. The peak of adherence for girls occurred in middle or late junior high school, while some boys were still increasing in their sensitivity to its demands through the tenth grade. However, once the apex was achieved, regardless of sex, the larger part of the high school experience was less subject to

its waning effects. Secondary school teachers confirm these results; they routinely observe that conflict with authority and the corresponding idolatry of peers peaks at the thirteenth or fourteenth year for girls and a year or so later for boys. The environmental correlates of youth culture subscription pointed to a triad of associated conditions. Those who adhered to the culture to a greater extent had lesser academic success and more limited educational goals, participated less in adolescent social activities and received lesser social recognition, and came from families of lower socio-economic status. In specific terms, they had lower grade point averages, had lower intelligence quotients, were less likely to attend college, and studied less. Socially, they participated in fewer school and community activities both of task and social nature, spent less time in these activities, and were less likely to be designated for positions of task and social leadership by their peers. Economically, they were more likely to come from settings that contained large lower social class elements, and, in other settings, were likely to represent the more disadvantaged groups. The emergent picture of youth culture adherence very much implies deficit and compensation as causal factors.

It was no surprise to discover that adolescents of different ages and sex employed the youth culture's dimensions differently according to their own needs as well as to society's demands. Factor analytic study revealed that boys, regardless of age, emphasized the risk, action, and danger aspects. Mastery of the physical world and securing an estimate of masculine capacity appeared to be the need, with the youth culture as the means. Linked to this dimension was a preoccupation with authority conflict. Interpretation remains open as to whether the authority issue is an artifact of indulgence in activities disapproved by adults or whether it represents a separate mastery struggle. Boys of all ages relegated group status and popularity concerns to a lesser role. For girls, the situation was reversed. Risk, danger, and physical mastery were insignificant, while social esteem presumed enormous importance. These findings are congruent with the Western cultural expectation that males secure mastery and dominance, particularly in the objective world as providers, while females become specialists in the interpersonal world which reaches culmination in the rearing of children. In an absolute sense, males seem to make greater use of the youth culture. It may not be that their needs are greater so much as that industrial society is impoverished in its opportunities for adolescent boys. If mastery of the physical world and securing an estimate of one's own competencies in relation to it are the vital concerns, it may be that there is no orderly transition to adult male productivity. It could be that boys remain captive in the American secondary school "preparing" for vocation instead of experiencing it, and that their needs are discharged in some counterfeit form into the argot of the youth culture.

Age-level trends support further generalizations regarding the meaning of the youth culture. Among younger adolescents of both sexes were indications of concern regarding impulse control. This finding is consistent with those personality theories which possess well-defined impulse systems and phase systems of growth and development. Early adolescence is often viewed as particularly difficult with the recrudescence of early impulse together with powerful new drives and cathexes. With the ego beset by drive and unable to balance control and drive, the youth culture provides an avenue of controlled expression and, at the same moment, raises new fears as to impulse mastery. Older adolescents arranged dimensions quite differently. Among both boys and girls, factors appeared which suggest personal independence, and, in one case, both adult and peer controls were rejected on the same dimension. The similarity with ego psychological principles is apparent: With maturity comes the installation of autonomy and self-direction in a personality free of compelling internal drive and environmental demand (in the form of dictates from either peers or elders) (Burlingame, 1967).

Summary and Implications

Youth culture features include the tendency to view the adolescent years as idyllic and developmentally distinct, the tendency to constitute age-mates as a reference group for decision making and for the generation of codes of behavior, and the tendency to come into conflict with the usual representatives of societal authority. Within these broad propensities exist a cluster of specific attributes, including the valuing of social status and participation in social ranking practices, the creation of idiosyncratic subcultural expressions for dance, music, dress, and language, the valuing of risk and stimulation, and the devaluing of academic achievement. Judgmentally, the above attitudes reflect a preference for the worldly and the material, the compromise with principle, immediate gratification, and conformity to the mass; these attitudes are taken in favor of deferred gratification, individual integrity and responsibility, social justice and equality, and worthwhile individual achievement. When studied empirically, youth culture adherence is found to be associated with a triad of conditions. Those who subscribed to greater extent had lesser academic success and more limited educational goals, participated less in adolescent social activities and received lesser social recognition, and came from families of lower socio-economic status.

How then may the youth culture be interpreted? Adolescence has been viewed as a time of identity crystallization and synthesis, with bodily growth and sexual drive occurring temporally with increased capacity for interpersonal relationships and increased demand from society for productivity and responsibility. To meet the demand from within and without, the young person must secure balance, direction, and purpose to the end that, at the close of adolescence, he views himself and is viewed by others as self-directing and autonomous. In part, these ego shifts and syntheses must transpire as the young adolescent wrests or takes responsibility for his activities from conspicuous adults and places it under the auspices of his developing ego. Such a process appears to require an additional step—that of constituting the society of his peers as a mediating agent, because he seems less able to acquire the ready-made identities of his parents and not yet able to constitute his own. The youth culture contains elements and fictions that meet the needs of transition. A group ego encourages conformity and provides protective coloration, thus preserving the adolescent ego from risk and extension. Social rating and social exposure offer an arena for role playing and a mirror for self-evaluation. Indulgence in risk-taking and the experimentation with dangerous or forbidden activity allows for needed experience in knowing the limits of newly developed capacity. Conflict with authority serves the whole by providing feedback as to progress toward autonomy and by securing the needed freedom to experiment. As synthesis is achieved, the youth culture and the society of peers is abandoned in favor of the responsibility for production and reproduction.

Such a process cannot be examined without reference to available avenues within the environment that have utility in promoting adolescent ego synthesis. A stable and respectable definition of self seems dependent upon provision within the life space: supportive family relationships, achievement, and social esteem from one's contemporaries. As these are available, the transition is facilitated and the use of the youth culture as an "ego bridge" is decreased. However, when these conditions are absent, the culture of age-mates may remain as the only alternative. The evidence is relatively conclusive. As adolescents have lesser aptitude, lesser achievement, lesser social contact, and lesser economic means, they over-value the youth culture. In short, it is those who are on the perimeter observing and not receiving who believe. Excessive adherence is related to deprivation. In psychodynamic terms, this interpretation is not without precedent. The exaggerated and distorted usage of the youth culture by some adolescents seems to reflect their own deflated and damaged ego capacities. A history of coercive or debilitating conditions coupled with a poverty of supportive feedback from the environment, which is met at adolescence by massive internal drive and external demand, produces disorganization. The behavior of this adolescent is identical to those who respond to the extremes of youth cultism; behavior is characterized by the need for immediate gratification and impulsive outbreak; proving and testing behavior are endless since self-perception is rooted in defeat; conflict with authority serves the twin needs to "get even" and to "get free."

Based on the assumption that the youth culture is a useful growth medium and, in those cases of extreme reliance, the result of deficit conditions, the following implications are suggested. Adolescence seems less a time for the inculcation of society's ways and more a time for the exploration of individual meaning and motivation. Children, in most strata of society, are well aware of what behaviors constitute the "right" and the "wrong" or the "good" and the "bad." By rejecting the earlier means of value transmission (parents and adults) in favor of peers, adolescents are not so much rejecting adult values as they are transferring authority into their own ego systems. This transference calls not for restriction, re-training, or scare and threat tactics, but for freedom and support for investigation. For most adolescents, some temporary adherence to the youth culture seems inevitable and useful for growth. Excessive or prolonged addiction to the society of teenage equals is a diagnostic sign of growth blockage, conflict, or fixation as surely as the signs that can occur at other stages in the life cycle. Further, provisions should be made for the existence of the youth culture, knowing that it will be abandoned with growth. This suggests a measure of privacy for adolescents and the separation of adult and adolescent recreation. A fair proportion of the conflict between generations is generated by "rubbing elbows" as each lives out his own needs. It suggests a policy of toleration for such recreational features as adolescent night clubs, dance halls, and coffee houses. In educational institutions and social agencies the tendency for adolescents to rank and rate should be recognized. Adults should not, in the name of democracy or bad publicity, drive social groups underground. The course of wisdom would be to offer sensitive adult leadership to high school fraternities and sororities, for example, which could curb excesses and remove the attractiveness of a forbidden activity. Conflict with authority appears to be a necessary ingredient for some adolescents and particularly for young males. Conflict in the guise of peer group activity may serve in the articulation of identity by breaking the dependency bond with parents and parent surrogates. All things considered, however, the provision for individual success and self-esteem remain the best guarantees, not against the development of a youth culture, but for the rapid attainment of identity and purpose.

REFERENCES

BURLINGAME, WILLIAM V. An investigation of the correlates of adherence to the adolescent peer culture. Unpublished Doctoral Dissertation, University of Washington, Seattle, 1967.

COLEMAN, JAMES S. *The Adolescent Society.* Glencoe, Ill.: The Free Press, 1961.

DENNEY, REUEL American youth today: a bigger cast, a wider screen. *Daedalus, 1962, 91,* 124–144.

FRIEDENBERG, EDGAR Z. *The Vanishing Adolescent.* New York: Dell, 1959.

GOODMAN, PAUL *Growing Up Absurd.* New York: Alfred A. Knopf, 1956.

GOODMAN, PAUL A social critic on "moral youth in an immoral society." *The Young Americans.* New York: *Time,* 1966, 18–19.

HOLLINGSHEAD, AUGUST B. *Elmtown's Youth.* New York: John Wiley, 1949.

KENISTON, KENNETH Social change and youth in America. *Daedalus,* 1962, *91,* 161.

KUHLEN, RAYMOND G., AND LEE, BEATRICE J. Personality characteristics and social acceptability in adolescence. *Journal of Educational Psychology,* 1943, *34,* 321–340.

PARSONS, TALCOTT Age and sex in the social structure of the United States. In Herman D. Stein and Richard A. Cloward (Eds.) *Social Perspectives on Behavior.* Glencoe, Ill.: The Free Press, 1958, 193.

Time Magazine, August 15, 1969, p. 57.

The Language of Adolesence: An Anthropological Approach to the Youth Culture

GARY SCHWARTZ

The high school youth culture is portrayed as a unique, independent system, possessing its own life style, status hierarchy, argot, and standards, but reflecting adult values and orientations.

For insiders language becomes a chief key to the taste socialization and mood currents that are prevalent in this group at any moment. For outsiders, including adult observers, language becomes a mysterious opacity, constantly carrying peer-group messages which are full of precisions that remain untranslatable.—DAVID RIESMAN, *The Lonely Crowd*)

The Problem

The question of whether there is a relatively self-contained adolescent subculture in this society stimulates recurrent, inconclusive sociological controversy. Contrary to the model of the youth culture as a contraculture, we hold that its reality as a subculture does not rest upon its power to repudiate or undermine basic adult values.

This paper reports on the first part of an on-going anthropological study of the youth culture in an urban community which is supported by the National Institute of Mental Health grant MH 12172-01. Our data are derived from field observation of peer groups operating in their natural habitats and from intensive, free-flowing interviews with selected informants. Initial contacts were made with this youth population through an established youth-serving agency, and subsequent relationships were established by following out friendship networks, i.e, meeting and talking with friends of our initial contacts. We found that these networks seldom bridged the several strata of the status system; thus, it was necessary to establish new contacts and follow out friendship networks in each of the strata. Thus far most of our informants have come from the higher reaches of the adolescent status system (24), rather than its lower levels (10). There are more girls (23) than boys (11) at present in our formal interview sample. Much of our data on the boys came from less structured contexts, such as conversations in cars, etc. Although the number of interviews with each informant varies, we find that some of our more articulate informants have remained with the study for a year on the basis of two or three hour-and-a-half tape-recorded interviews per month. The interviews were usually with individual informants, although occasionally small groups of 2–4 students were interviewed. A considerable portion of our data was gathered in talks with students at dances, parties, hangouts, card games, etc.

We would like to thank Solomon Kobrin and David M. Schneider both for their comments on this paper and their generous advice on the design of this study. We also would like to thank Cal Cottrell, Daniel Scheinfeld, and Henry McKay for their comments on this paper. We alone are responsible for its deficiencies.

From G. Schwartz & D. Merten, The language of adolescence: An anthropological approach to the youth culture. Reprinted from *The American Journal of Sociology*, March 1967, 72(5), pp. 453–468. Copyright © 1967 by the *American Journal of Sociology*. By permission of the authors and the University of Chicago Press.

We shall argue that peer-group interaction is guided by expectations which do not govern the behavior of other members of the community. And we claim that the understandings which transform what might otherwise be transitory encounters into stable peer-group relationships are not fully comprehensible to the rest of the community. More simply, adolescent social relationships are predicated upon premises not completely accessible or intelligible to adults.[1]

From our point of view, the specifically subcultural aspects of adolescent social life reside in those symbolic elements (values, beliefs, and standards) which integrate various concrete norms[2] into a coherent system of action. Later in this paper we will examine some of the symbolic resolutions of adolescent role dilemmas and ambiguities, for example, adolescent beliefs about their own social world which reduce logical and moral inconsistencies between incongruous orientations to various social situations.

As Riesman suggests, the significance of much of adolescent social life is partially hidden from adults by linguistic devices. Consequently, the data which can best reveal the character of the youth culture are linguistic, and the relevant aspect of adolescent language is obviously semantic.

Language and Action

In this paper, we will show that adolescent perceptions and assessments of their own social universe are embodied in a distinctive argot, their status terminology. These status terms refer to moral attributes (those qualities which make some persons admirable, others reprehensible, etc.) and moral dispositions (the kinds of things these people are likely to do and say). The mem-

[1]In a comparatively recent view of the "adolescent society," Bennett Berger, "Adolescence and Beyond," *Social Problems,* Vol. X (1963), asserts that "there is absolutely no good body of data on adolescents, Coleman's included, which indicates the existence of a really deviant system of norms which govern adolescent life" (p. 395).

[2]By concrete norms we mean specific prescriptions and proscriptions which refer to particular types of social contexts (e.g., dating) and which govern or which actors feel ought to govern behavior (e.g., sexual) in these kinds of social settings.

bers of a status category are thought to possess common social virtues and defects. Status terms, then, are not affectively neutral labels for structural positions in the youthful social system. They bestow either negative or positive esteem on those who manifest or exemplify these personal characteristics. Consequently, an individual's rank in the local prestige hierarchy is partly a function of the meanings inherent in those terms his peers use to describe his character and his group affiliations.

Following the logic but not the exact method of componential analysis,[3] the lexical set we call the adolescent status terminology constitutes a semantic domain:[4] a culturally defined and verb-

[3]Componential analysis is a technique for the investigation of semantic domains modeled after descriptive linguistics. It should enable an observer both to describe and predict the ways in which the members of a culture will classify phenomenological reality. Anthony Wallace, "The Psychic Unity of Human Groups," *Studying Personality Cross-culturally,* ed. Bert Kaplan (Evanston, Ill.: Row, Peterson, 1961), succinctly describes this method: "The fundamental and intuitive idea on which the semantic calculus is based is a simple one: that the signification of a 'term' (which may be an extrinsic linguistic symbol, such as a word, or any other overt behavior) is given by a particular pattern of predicates which evoke or are evoked by, that term. A predicate is a symbol for the common property of the members of a class. In the technique of componential analysis, the various criteria (predicates) relevant to the definition of the terms in a lexicon are conceived of as values on dimensions, such that each cell in the space represents a unique combination of values, one from each dimension. Each term can then be mapped onto the space by stating to which combination or combinations of criteria it corresponds. When all the terms have been so mapped, their logico-semantic relationships can be explicitly stated" (p. 143).

[4]There has been a good deal of discussion about replicable, empirical discovery procedures for establishing the boundaries of semantic domains, such as the use of standard control questions which specify the exact level of linguistic contrast. But we rely upon more impressionist techniques for delimiting this semantic domain because we are concerned with the expressive (i.e., the connotational) as well as the referential (i.e., the definitional) meanings of this terminology. This is a more elusive universe of discourse than the usual subjects of componential analysis, e.g., kinship, color, plant, and disease terminologies. Even when componential analysis is applied to purely cognitive domains it experiences some difficulty when these terminologies have an oblique or tangential relationship to observable events or physical objects. Thus, Charles Frake, "The Diagnosis of Disease among the Subanum of Mindanao," *Language in Culture and Society,* ed. Dell Hymes (New York: Harper & Row, 1964), says that "it is difficult, then, to define

ally expressed area of social experience bounded by the existence or occurrence of certain types of objects, events, or behaviors. Although the exact boundaries of this semantic domain are sometimes vague, it comprises an internally consistent system of meanings. At one level of meaning, these terms refer to the kind and the amount of respect the occupants of a status category can claim in the adolescent social system. From the perspective of formal linquistic analysis,[5] the problem concerns the cenceptual (i.e., cultural) criteria which assign particular status terms to larger classes or categories. However, we are not interested in arranging these terms so that their value is specified along these conceptual dimensions and so that the intersection of these values predicts the occurrence of each term in this classificatory scheme. Rather, we want to know how the cognitive and evaluative meanings of this semantic domain are related to social contexts.[6]

The linguistically conditioned ways in which the members of a group perceive and evaluate their social environment have determinant consequences for their behavior. Here we follow Clyde Kluckhohn, who says that "the *vocabularies* of different languages both reflect and perpetuate habitual and distinctive ways of categorizing experience or modes of thought."[7] He goes on to say that "how people behave toward one another is, in part, a function of what they call each other and of *how* they conceive objects, themselves, other people and types of events which enter into their relations."[8] Elucidation of the meanings implicit in the adolescent status terminology will illuminate the complex relationships between the norms of this subculture and the behavior of its members in various social settings.

Stated in functional terms, cultural categories contained in language do not usually determine the particulars (i.e., the who, how much, and when) of any behavioral sequence but, rather, provide the cognitive and evaluative parameters of social interaction in any social setting.[9] These categories identify the appropriate motives, values, roles, and rules which transform the actor's external physical world into what Hallowell calls the

Subanum diagnostic categories in terms or perceptual attributes of the denotata" (p. 201). And Robbins Burling, "How To Choose a Burmese Numeral Classifier," *Context and Meaning in Cultural Anthropology,* ed. Melford Spiro (New York: Free Press, 1965), has found for a clear-cut semantic domain that "the attempt to find pervasive semantic dimensions which unambiguously apportion the entire set of classifiers into clear subjects has hardly been successful" (p. 263). In light of these considerations, our inability to determine the exact boundaries of this semantic domain does not constitute an insuperable obstacle to discovering the meaning of the cognitive distinctions and moral oppositions inherent in this terminology.

[5] Paul Kay in a comment on R. N. Colby's "Ethnographic Semantics: A Preliminary Survey," *Current Anthropology,* Vol. VII (February, 1966), says that "componential analysis is best conceived as an *analytic process* in which the investigator searches for (a) the *dimensions* of meaning underlying the domain and (b) the mapping of the values on these dimensions (*the features of meaning*) onto the set of lexemes. The process of looking for the mappings is not to be confused with particular types of such mappings such as paradigm, taxonomy, and tree" (pp. 20–21, italics in original).

[6] As we have seen, status terms refer to certain kinds of social predicates. In order to elicit these predicates, we rely upon a basic methodological postulate of componential analysis: the contextualization of meaning. Hymes, "A Perspective for Linguistic Anthropology," *Horizons of Anthropology,* ed. Sol Tax (Chicago: Aldine Publishing, 1964), says that "as is widely recognized, a term's meaning depends upon the interaction between its own semantic properties and those recognized in the context in which it occurs. A term can indicate a wide range of meanings, and a context can support a range of meanings. In a given case the term does not so much positively name, as

does the intersection of the term and context eliminates most, or all but one, of the possible meanings" (p. 97). This stress on the intersection of linguistic meaning and social context is particularly applicable to the study of the evaluative aspects of the youth culture. Here there is a complex relationship among the actor's motives, the norms which govern behavior in a social situation, and the ends or goals this subculture defines as worthwhile, i.e., what its members should strive to achieve or become. We hold that the meaning of a particular status term can only be understood after the observer knows the contexts in which it is used and the norms which govern behavior in this situation. Then, for example, he can ask his informants whether "cool" and "mellow" mean the same or different things. Hymes, *ibid.,* claims that the "fact of contrast, and the dimensions, can be determined only by knowing the context of the situation, and discovering what expressions have functional unity through being mutually substitutable for a given end within it" (p. 98).

[7] "Culture and Behavior," *Handbook of Social Psychology,* Vol. XX, ed. Gardner Lindzey (Reading, Mass.: Addison-Wesley Publishing, 1954), p. 938, italics in original.

[8] *Ibid.*

[9] For a persuasive statement of a somewhat different point of view, see Frake, "A Structural Description of Subanum 'Religious Behavior,'" *Explorations in Cultural Anthropology,* ed. Ward Goodenough (New York: McGraw-Hill Book Co., 1964).

behavioral environment of the self. "A *second* function of all cultures is the orientation of the self to a diversified world of objects in its behavioral environment, discriminated, classified, and conceptualized with respect to attributes which are culturally constituted and symbolically mediated through language. The role of language in object-orientation is as vital as in self-orientation."[10] As we shall see in the case of the meaning of the term "cool," these categories tie both the actor's moral orientations and cognitive definitions of social situations to the critical motivational dimensions of the self, that is, his judgments about his own worth—"Any kind of self-depreciation, loss of self-esteem, or threat to the self impairs the complex motivational systems that focus upon the self and its needs. At the same time, self-evaluation through culturally recognized norms is inescapable."[11]

The Structural Origins of the Youth Culture

Considered as a phenomenon indigenous to modern societies, the youth culture can be traced to the problem of socialization in industrial societies.[12] Certainly adolescent norms refer to these structural problems at various levels of meaning. But this does not exhaust the cultural connotations and the behavioral implications of

distinctively adolescent modes of communication. For there is great latitude in the selection of the cultural forms which provide adequate solutions to these structural exigencies and concomitant developmental crises—witness the differences in the content of the peer-group norms in various communities and classes.[13] Therefore, it is not possible to account for the substance and imagery of the youth culture solely in terms of the difficult passage from childhood to adulthood in a highly differentiated society.

The Youth Culture Defined

Part of our society's ideology about the nature of human growth asserts that youth must not prematurely assume adult roles. Thus, it is often said that adolescents need an exemption from the pressures of adult responsibilities in order to discover their individual talents. These ideological sanctions encourage adolescents to transform developmental necessities into aesthetically satisfying as well as socially adaptive modes of behavior. In other words, the efflorescence of adolescent styles results from this license to experiment with the possibilities inherent in adult roles. In turn, the youth culture symbolically affirms and celebrates its freedom from conventional restraints on social behavior which has little or no immediate practical significance. For example, many of our informants lavishly praise what they call "idiot"[14] behavior: actions and attitudes which are childish or foolish from an adult point of view and which sometimes treat situations from seemingly incompatible perspectives, for example, dealing with a love relationship in a manner that is at once flippant and romantic. According to some of our most articulate informants, the ability to engage in any sort of silly col-

[10]A. I. Hallowell, "The Self and Its Behavioral Environment," *Culture and Experience* (Philadelphia: University of Pennsylvania Press, 1955), p. 91, italics in original.
[11]*Ibid.,* p. 106.
[12]S. N. Eisenstadt's classic study, *From Generation to Generation* (Glencoe, Ill.: Free Press, 1956), points out that there is a radical social–psychological transition between childhood and adulthood in industrial societies. Thus, every child in our society must eventually leave his family circle where he is appreciated for *who* rather than *what* he is. According to this theory, the youth culture serves as a "halfway house" between a young person's particularistic and universalistic associations. While youth groups are based upon ascriptive ties, the youth culture enables adolescents to try out roles and form relationships which involve more universalistic considerations: An adolescent must *earn* his status in the peer group. The youth culture, then, allows the adolescent to experiment with objective, universalistic standards without sacrificing the psychological security of highly solidary primary groups.

[13]For a very detailed account of the attitudes and activities of various types of adolescent peer groups, see Muzafer and Carolyn Sherif, *Reference Groups: Exploration into Conformity and Deviation of Adolescents* (New York: Harper & Row, 1964).
[14]Words enclosed by quotation marks (e.g., "cool") are terms used with considerable frequency by our informants. This is not to say, however, that the notions contained in these words are not also expressed by circumlocution. These terms are ordinarily used in reference and rarely in address.

lective action requires a certain amount of inner freedom and *joie de vivre*. In general, these informants tend to associate these sorts of peer-group activities with independence from adult supervision and with actions which demonstrate this autonomy.[15]

Stated more formally, the youth culture consists of those adolescent norms, standards, and values which are discussed in a language particularly intelligible to members of this age-grade. At this point, we should note that members of the youth culture do not deal with or even "talk" about all the concerns which vitally interest or agitate adolescents, and they may even ignore or overlook those concerns which are of enduring significance to the members of this society.[16] Yet the youth culture contains a distinctive vision of social reality. It is embodied in a normative order predicated upon conceptions of those personal qualities which its members believe make a male admirable and a female desirable.

The Youth Culture as a Contraculture

The sociological conception of the youth culture as a contraculture assumes that the cultural and structural aspects of the youth culture are inextricably linked. Thus, evidence which reveals serious structural discontinuities between the generations is also supposed to show a set of youth norms which are opposed to adult values.[17] According to the contraculture model, if adolescents substantially accept core adult roles and values, then the youth culture is essentially epiphenomenal.[18] But if they doubt the legitimacy of societal values, then the youth culture is the appropriate label for this truly rebellious posture. In contrast, our approach to the youth culture holds that the symbolic components of adolescent social life form a relatively coherent subculture *irrespective* of whether its norms eventually subvert, reinforce, or have no lasting effect upon adult values. Our position rests upon a basic theoretical assumption: that the cultural categories which shape adolescent orientations to their own social milieu are largely autonomous inasmuch as they are embodied in systems of meanings whose implications are not immediately apparent to adults.[19]

The structure of advanced societies generates a certain amount of adolescent rebelliousness against adult authority.[20] But this does not mean that opposition to the goals of the older generation is the only, or even the most important, dis-

[15]According to some of our informants, "idiot" should not be equated with childish behavior. We have been told that those persons who are able to act this way are often the same people who appear most sophisticated (i.e., adult-like) in other social contexts. Perhaps, this connection between silly and sophisticated personal styles is a symbolic means of demonstrating what Erving Goffman (*Encounters* [Indianapolis: Bobbs-Merrill, 1961]), calls role distance. They seem to say that we now have mastered the developmental tasks of childhood, and hence these sorts of performances (playing games which have no extrinsic social significance) can now be slightly ridiculed because it no longer constitutes a vital part of our social identities.

[16]This idea was stimulated by James F. Short's remarks on delinquent gangs in "Social Structure and Group Processes in Gang Delinquency," *Problems of Youth: Transition to Adulthood in a Changing World,* ed. Sherif and Sherif (Chicago: Aldine Publishing, 1965), esp. p. 173.

[17]Cf. James Coleman, *The Adolescent Society* (New York: Free Press, 1961), and F. Elkin and W. Westley, "The Myth of Adolescent Culture," *American Sociological Review,* Vol. XX (1955), who have tried to determine whether the norms of the youth culture impede or inhibit the socialization of adolescents into adult occupational roles.

[18]As subordinate and quite powerless members of our society, youth are said to experience social and psychological deprivation because of the conflicting demands which are placed upon them. Viewed as a contraculture, the youth culture evolves out of a normative "reaction-formation" to these pressures. According to Milton Yinger, "Contra-Culture and Subculture," *American Sociological Review,* Vol. XXV (1960), it involves "the creation of a series of inverse or counter values (opposed to those of the surrounding society) in face of serious frustration or conflict" (p. 627).

[19]For example, most adults in this community are aware of, and many approve of, the fraternity and sorority system which operates despite an official school ban on such activity. However, if our adolescent informants are correct, very few adults know why one person is "rushed" and another is not. Though many parents seem to want their children to succeed in this social world, most adults are ignorant of the specific social criteria fraternity and sorority youth use to select certain kinds of persons for their exclusive social circles.

[20]See K. Davis, "The Sociology of Parent–Youth Conflict," *Social Perspectives on Behavior,* ed. H. D. Stein and R. A. Cloward (Glencoe, Ill.: Free Press, 1958).

junction between adolescent and adult views of social reality. Nor is it true that the norms of the youth culture derive their subcultural attributes from intergenerational conflict.

In fact, the traditional cycle of intense intergenerational conflict followed by reconciliation when the younger generation takes its place in society seems less common today than in the past. Instead of direct confrontations over the moral validity, the relevance, and the appropriateness of the other generations' goals and aspirations,[21] both the older and younger members of this society subscribe to a laissez faire ideology. This encourages generational segregation, rather than opposition. Keniston notes that "another salient fact about young people today is a relative lack of *rebelliousness* against their parents or their parents' generation. . . . The result is frequently an unstated 'gentleman's agreement' between the generations that neither will interfere with the other."[22] According to one of our informants, a senior girl:

(Q) Do you know what adults in this community think about various issues?

(A) I'd say there is a very small amount of contact between the teen-agers and the adults because we're self-centered, I think, and the adults are too. We think "I'll leave them alone," and they do too.

Our informants almost instinctively measured their own worth against the standards of the youth culture. And the cardinal concerns of the youth culture are in those domains over which they exercise direct control: friendship, relations with the opposite sex, and various types of expressive activities. This sort of partial cultural isolation is reinforced by the paucity of enduring intergenerational contacts outside of formal socializing agencies, such as the school and family.[23] Thus most of the adolescents we have observed accept a socially imposed hiatus in their life cycle, regardless of whether they are eager, reluctant, or uninterested in becoming an adult; and most of them assume that only their peers can truly understand those kinds of interpersonal accomplishments and failures which make their lives in the adolescent world either gratifying or mortifying.

Open intergenerational conflict in this community revolves around the question of how much control adults rightfully can exercise over adolescents.[24] Both sides in these disputes agree that intrusion into private generational matters is generally unwarranted, for example, adults usually allow adolescents to arrange their own social affairs. The issue, then, concerns the definition of those aspects of adolescent behavior which are legitimately public and hence subject to adult control.

The Relationship Between Adult Values and Youth Norms

In our study of this upper-middle-class urban community,[25] we found that these adolescents

[21]See Walter Laquer, *Young Germany* (New York: Basic Books, 1962), for a description of youth movements which opposed the prevailing ethos of their society in their early stages of development.

[22]K. Keniston, "Social Change and Youth in America," *Daedalus*, XCI (1962), 151–56, italics in original.

[23]See F. Musgrove, *Youth and the Social Order* (Bloomington: University of Indiana Press, 1965), for an interesting historical perspective on the present separation of the generations.

[24]According to the data collected by Henry McKay for the Institute for Juvenile Research, this area, in the 35-year period from 1927 to 1962, had the lowest mean delinquency rate in the city (these rates are based upon official Juvenile Court cases). However, this low rate of delinquency should not be interpreted as evidence of a complete lack of intergenerational conflict. We have observed that behavior which slightly violates adult norms, such as surreptitiously playing poker for high stakes or putting a fraternity picture in the school annual (fraternities and sororities are forbidden), is often sufficient to demonstrate one's autonomy vis-à-vis adult controls. Since the tolerance of deviant youth behavior in the community is small, one can establish one's autonomy through relatively minor acts of defiance of adult authority.

[25]The community we studied is located in a large midwestern city and has a population of approximately 25,000. It has most of the socioeconomic characteristics commonly associated with upper-middle-class residential areas. Since it may be useful to compare this community to the city as a whole, the figures for the latter will be given in parentheses; and the figures for both will be given in approximate percentages. According to data from the 1960 Census, the median family income in this community was $11,000 (6,700). Only 5 per cent (14 per cent) of the families earned less than $3,000 a year, and 58 per cent (21 per cent) had an income of $10,000 a year or more. Eighty-six per cent (24 per cent) of the families lived in single-dwelling units, and of these 82 per cent (33

successfully internalized adult occupational goals. None of our informants questioned the notion that a high school diploma was a minimal requirement for even a half-decent job, and comparatively few students in the local high school dropped out before graduation. Most of these adolescents intended to go to college, and many of them worked reasonably hard to get good grades. They wanted a college degree because they felt it would help them get the professional job or husband which insures a middle-class way of life. However, very few of these adolescents, even the best students, had marked intellectual or scholarly interests. In short, we discovered that adolescent conceptions of the validity of adult roles and values are, at least, largely independent of the standards they use to estimate the relative excellence of their peers.[26]

The youth culture in this area is not completely oblivious to an individual's potential capacity to assume his adult roles. But, as far as his peers are concerned, his success or failure in the academic system of the high school (i.e., his grades) is a relatively minor component of his social identity, although very negative connotations are associated with the status of a "brain"—a person who devotes all his energies to getting high marks. Our informants usually call such a person "twinky," which implies that his demeanor manifests an underlying effeminacy. The choice of term which connotes less-than-manly behavior follows a peculiarly subcultural logic. The standards of

the youth culture are focused on those sorts of behaviors which its members think reflect one's sex-role identity. Their judgments of personal worth are closely linked to general conceptions of those attributes and performances which are thought to reveal a person's masculinity or femininity. For boys, the crucial external signs of inner manhood are physical strength, athletic talent, courage in the face of aggression, a willingness to defend one's honor at all costs, and sexual and drinking prowess. According to girls, the most admirable feminine traits are physical attractiveness, personal vivacity, and the ability to delicately manipulate various sorts of interpersonal relationships.

As a cultural system, the youth culture in this area consists of those norms, life styles, and ideals which are intimately associated with a *variant*, age-graded system of cultural meanings. Of course, the youth culture does not emerge out of a cultural vacuum. Adolescent social patterns obviously are based upon adult conceptions of the desirable types of social relationships and upon adult images of personal virtue. Adolescents, however, do not slavishly copy these general cultural norms. The youth culture experiments with and elaborates on some of the partially unrealized or alternative possibilities in the adult moral order. This is particularly true in the interpersonal realm: Adolescents distinguish various kinds and degrees of trust among friends. Our informants habitually discriminate among "good," "best," and "casual" friends. One informant distinguished among these types of friends in the following terms:

(Q) What are some of the things you expect of a friend?

(A) When you leave [a group], when you walk out, they don't all of a sudden start stabbing knives in your back. It all depends upon the degree of friendship you want [in response to the question].

(Q) What are the various degrees of friendship?

(A) With some girls you just have a casual friendship, and she's got her friends and I've got mine, but we'll sit down and talk. Then like the girls in my club, we are pretty good friends. We know who we

---

per cent) were owned by the occupants. For this population the median number of years of education was almost 13 (10), and 21 per cent (6 per cent) had four years of college or more. Seventy-two per cent (37 per cent) of this population held white-collar jobs.

[26]In "Values and Gang Delinquency: A Study of Street-Corner Groups," *American Journal of Sociology*, Vol. LXIX (1963), R. A. Gordon, J. F. Short, D. S. Cartwright, and F. L. Strodtbeck report that even the most socially disadvantaged, delinquent youth not only evaluate a middle-class way of life very highly but that they also see the conventional path to this end—saving, working at a steady job, and education—as a legitimate, although not always realistic, way to attain a respectable adult status. Yet, as Short, *op. cit.*, points out, these adolescents do not use these values to regulate peer-group life. Similarly, it is wrong to infer that, just because middle-class adolescents are even less ambivalent about adult values, these standards determine the norms of their peer groups.

are going out with. With the casual friend you don't sit and talk about your boyfriend to them. I have one best friend.

(Q) Are there certain things you share with a best friend that you don't share with a fellow club members [i.e., a "pretty good friend"]?

(A) You talk about your boyfriends if you had an argument, but you wouldn't tell them personal things [i.e., to a "pretty good friend"]. I could tell my best friend anything, and she wouldn't think badly of you. You don't have to worry that, will she tell anybody else? While the members of my club, I expect them not to stab knives in my back when I leave, *but my best friend, if someone else does, I expect her to stand up for me. My club members, I wouldn't expect them to stand up for me.*

From a comparative point of view, then, the differences among the cultural categories which shape adult and adolescent orientations to some social situations are admittedly slight. Nevertheless, and this is the important point, the differences between adult standards of personal worth and the meaning of adolescent status terms are great enough to sustain an independent adolescent status system. The multitude of discrete norms which regulate a person's relations with his peers are integrated into a meaningful system of action by distinctively adolescent conceptions of personal worth. The cultural core of the adolescent social system is formed by the meanings of adolescent status terms and prestige categories. An adolescent's estimation of his own interpersonal competence depends, to a great extent, upon whether the particular terms his peers use to describe his status have laudatory or pejorative connotations. These terms indicate whether he is able convincingly to present a "cool" self-image in highly competitive social contexts.

The Meaning of Key Status Terms

The adolescents in this community do not see their status system as a perfectly linear, clearly defined series of hierarchically arranged status po-

sitions. Rather, they perceive it as a set of ranked, slightly ambiguous prestige categories which are internally differentiated. This status system is structured along two dimensions. First, there are horizontal social strata defined by differentially evaluated life styles, that is, modes of dress, speech, and interpersonal demeanor. In general, our informants perceive two salient life styles which they refer to as "hoody" and "socie." However, we see another way of life which lacks an explicit folk designation, though most of our informants distinguish it from "socie" and "hoody" styles. For the lack of a better term, we call this the conventional way of life. It is an essentially residual category which includes all those patterns which are neither clearly "socie" nor "hoody."

The dominant values institutionalized in the status system of the local high school are those held by the majority of the upper-middle-class segment of this youthful population (the high school draws students from a stable working- and lower-middle-class community as well as from our upper-middle-class area).[27] Consequently, most adolescents in this area perceive the "socies" as the top stratum of this prestige system. Since "hoody" and "socie" youth do not agree about who has the most valuable way of life (e.g., our "hoody" informants tell us that "socies" are hypocrites, etc.), an individual's estimation of his own status depends, in part, upon his particular adolescent reference group. From an observer's point of view, the "hoody" adolescents have evolved a truly independent style of life. Nevertheless, our "hoody" informants see their own life style as at least a partly antagonistic response to "socie" values and material advantages. "Hoody" adolescents, by and large, refuse to and often cannot financially afford to compete with "socies" on the latters' terms, and they feel that their mode of life is not accorded general esteem in this system.

[27]In numerical terms, this upper-middle-class group does not constitute a majority of this school population. Yet, through the fraternity and sorority system which it dominates and through less overtly stratified, adult-sponsored youth groups which it co-opts as a recruiting ground, these adolescents control both the formal (e.g., the cheerleaders at this high school are not only restricted to sorority girls but to the members of one sorority) and informal activity systems which emerge out of school associations but which are definitely not confined to this location.

Those who adopt what we have called a conventional way of life gain some social recognition only to the extent to which they can imitate "socie" patterns.

The vertical component of this status system locates an individual's rank within one of these horizontal strata. As far as we can ascertain, a person's rank is a function of how well he is known by the other members of his stratum, and this, in turn, seems closely related to his ability to conspicuously live up to its standards of excellence. This vertical dimension, then, is quantitative rather than qualitative and refers to what our informants mean when they say someone is more or less "popular." Since public renown is a basic value in the "socie" world, those who achieve fame are called "elites." This, however, says nothing about their commitment to one of the various substyles available to the members of this stratum. Although all our informants subscribe to a highly egalitarian social ideology (no one is inherently better than anyone else), "hoody" adolescents take it very seriously. Though many of our "hoody" informants admitted that certain persons in their social circle are more "popular" than others, they have no term which designates high position.

An adolescent's socioeconomic status certainly affects his ability to assimilate "socie" styles. Nevertheless, the decisive factor is his ability to act in terms of these standards whatever his family background. In other words, an adolescent's status identity is created by his overt commitment to an adolescent life style.[28] Some of our lower-middle and stable working-class informants are among the most influential "socies," while a few of our informants from upper-middle-class homes are labeled "hoods" by their peers. "Socies" tend to associate "hoody" life styles with very

stereotyped conceptions of the attitudes and aspirations which distinguish the lower and middle classes. For instance, even those "socie" informants from stable working- and lower-middle-class families repeatedly tell us that "hoods" are the sort of people who do not care about their grades, about school activities, about their personal appearance, about morals, etc. In essence, they believe that the "hoods" incorporate what they think is the critical lower-class social–psychological attribute—a complete lack of interest in "bettering oneself."

At this point, we should note that there are alternate terms for these status categories; for example, the words "socie" and "socialite" are used interchangeably. Also, certain status terms change over time. For instance, many of our informants feel that it is more "in" to use the term "mellow" in those contexts where they formerly used the term "cool," but they also agree that these terms have the same meanings. Status terms also take on special meanings according to the structural position of the speaker. Thus, a "socie" speaker will use the term "hoods" interchangeably with "greasers," "scraggs," etc.; all of these terms have very derogatory implications. Similarly, "hoods" use the terms "snob" and "stuck-up" as synonyms for "socie."

"Hoods" and "socies" very rarely use these terms to describe themselves but almost obsessively use them to describe each other. It is difficult for adults to appreciate the discrepancy between the adolescent meaning of a term like "hoody" and its conventional referents, that is, to delinquents. For example, one of our most articulate informants belongs to the "hoody" stratum, and she accepts this designation insofar as she defines her own personal style as one which consistently opposes "socie" styles. Yet adults would not ordinarily call her "hoody" because she takes a college mathematics course in her spare time and participates in a tutoring project for culturally deprived children.

These status terms do not refer directly to bounded social units which have a clearly demarcated membership. Yet membership in certain cliques, clubs, fraternities, and sororities makes is very likely that a person will be considered a "socie" by his peers. The precise meaning of these terms, however, cannot be understood apart from

---

[28]Most of the adolescents who fall into the conventional category seem more oriented to "socie" than "hoody" dress styles, and some have attempted and failed to join "socie" groups. In contrast to "socies" and "hoods," conventionals have a life style which does not appear to involve a code of honor vis-à-vis other groups. Conventionals, however, tend to define the local social system in terms of what all its members perceive as polar, antagonistic social categories, i.e., "socie" and "hoody." Hence conventionals are difficult to place unambiguously in the status system and lack the definite social identities ascribed to "socies" and "hoods."

the nature of the youth culture in an upper-middle-class community. Here adolescents have a dual orientation to the standards of the youth culture and to the values of the adult world.[29]

The adult world is represented by the achievement orientation of the high school. Our "socie" informants claim that this stratum is divided into the "clean-cut" or "all-around" and the "hoody-socie" segments. The "clean-cut socies" stress role performances which are explicitly linked to the school's activity system. They usually do well in team sports, get fairly good but not necessarily high grades, and most importantly, know how to get along with their teachers and classmates— they are very "sociable."[30] In fact, it seems that part of a non-"socie" social identity involves the belief that one does not have enough social skill and organizational ability to give a "swinging" or "cool" affair, and non-"socie" social gatherings generally reinforce this self-fufilling prophecy.

"Clean-cut socies" must also realize the "cool" patterns of adolescent social life. They must succeed in the intense competition for dates with high-status persons; the social circle from which a person selects his dating partners partially establishes his or her standing in the larger social system. After the second year of high school, "socie" boys must be "conditioned" drinkers, which means not getting prematurely or obnoxiously inebriated in social situations. Sexually, "socie" boys must "make out" and thereby provide some concrete evidence for their frequent and exaggerated boasts about their sexual prowess.

For these boys, drinking and dating are the definitive areas in which one's manhood is tested and proven. They talk a great deal about and admire toughness but studiously avoid situations where they might have to fight. Buying liquor or beer in a store is viewed as a potential threat to their image as autonomous "men," and, conversely, it is seen as a challenge which, if handled properly, can add greatly to one's stature in the group. As our informants perceive it, buying beer in a bar or package store is a battleground reserved only for the courageous: the risks to one's self-esteem are great. If a boy reveals that he is afraid to show a false identification card or otherwise bluff his way through demands that he prove his age, then he loses considerable face within his peer group. But if he stands his ground when accused of being under age and does not give in to his desire to flee the situation, then he proves that he has "guts" regardless of whether the store ultimately sells him the beer. Our informants tell us that it is crucial not to "lose your cool" in these situations, and anyone who fails to rise to the occasion has his claims to "coolness" ruthlessly deflated by his peers.

Girls prove their worth in a more contracted arena. They must attract many high-status boys as dates, and to do so they must occasionally engage in rather intense petting without endangering their "reputations." While their prestige depends partly on the status their presence bestows upon their dating partners, it can be compromised if they give sexual favors to all who request them.

The "socies" (our informants usually employ the term "socie" and qualify it when they want to refer to those who adhere to the "clean-cut" or "hoody" variant) fully realize the adolescent dimensions of this social system. Though a member of the "clean-cut socies" adopts many "cool"

---

[29] N. Riley, J. Riley, and M. More, "Adolescent Values and the Riesman Typology: An Empirical Analysis," *Culture and Social Character,* ed. Seymour M. Lipset and Leo Lowenthal (Glencoe, Ill.: Free Press, 1962), found this same dual orientation to parental and peer-group standards. Also see C. V. Brittian, "Adolescent Choices and Peer Cross Pressures," *American Sociological Review* Vol. XXIII (June, 1963).

[30] Being "sociable" often means that a person is able to articulate previously unconnected persons or cliques into larger and sometimes bounded social networks. This trait, in turn, is closely related to a person's standing in the "socie" world. For example, one of our informants who actively aspired to this stratum told us that part of her lack of success was due to her inability to bring her various, disparate friendship groups together. She sat in the middle of the lunch table between these two groups but could not promote social intercourse between them and felt marginal to both. However, another informant, who lacked the usual physical attributes of a "socie" girl, was an "elite" largely because she could not only integrate separate dyads into larger friendship networks, but could then combine these networks into a named group whose membership was drawn from both the sorority world and from those girls who were by and large sorority "material" but who were excluded by the "blackball" system—one vote against a prospective member was enough to reject her. This girl provided the rationale, the occasions (e.g., "hen parties"), and most importantly, the contacts which enabled some girls to validate their status in the larger social system through membership in this group.

patterns, he never relinquishes his commitment to adult standards of accomplishment. On the other hand, the "hoody-socies" devote themselves wholeheartedly to adolescent conceptions of excellence. They are the most enthusiastic fraternity and sorority members and are not usually very interested in academic pursuits. Instead they spend a good deal of time and energy systematically refining their dating and drinking techniques. And they are the avant-garde leaders in musical tastes, dress styles, etc.

The "hoods" and the "hoody-socies" should not be confused. The latter represent the furthest an adolescent in the "socie" stratum can move away from the adult values without openly rejecting them, that is, they rarely openly defy adult authority in acts of serious delinquency, and, unlike some of the "hoods," they rarely drop out of high school before graduation.

"Socies" have developed a special set of status terms which distinguish various social segments among those who occupy the lower orders of the status system. These terms have depreciatory connotations because they imply that these social types are represented by persons with morally defective or socially underdeveloped personalities. From the "socie" perspective, the "hoods" belong to the more encompassing social category of "out-of-its." One informant described the "out-of-its" as follows: "They're misfits; they're insecure, they don't think they're cute enough, or they're awkward, or they have a lisp or something." This is a heterogeneous category; here one finds the rebels, the retarded or slow learners, the intellectuals, and anyone else who is deviant from the point of view of the prestige criteria which define this status system.

"Socies" also perceive another category of persons who are not attached to or even loosely associated with "socie" cliques and yet who do not fit into the "out-of-its." Some of our "socie" informants call them the "others," and they are just ordinary students who are not distinguished by some success or blatant failure in the adolescent social system. One student described the "others" in this way: "Some of them may not come out of their shell until they get to college, and they may find a group whether it's intellectual or social. These kids will usually gravitate toward getting the higher grades—some don't concentrate on

anything at all. They just go along and get by in school and don't join activities, but just sit home and watch television all the time." The derogatory implications associated with the term "others" do not simply derive from exclusion from "socie" social circles: It means that a person has no definite social identity in this social system. As far as "socies" are concerned, these people are faceless because they are not demonstrably attached to a discernible adolescent style. As one of our informants put it, "others" are people you do not notice or know anything about unless you happened to go to elementary school with them.

As we have seen, the process of status attribution is quite complex and does not result simply from objective talents and characteristics, for example, a boy's athletic ability, a girl's physical attractiveness, etc. Thus, an individual must take the esteem he has gained in a variety of contexts and transform this diffuse prestige into a subculturally validated image of the successful adolescent. He must present himself as "cool," and our informants tell us that if a person truly believes he is "cool" he generally acts "cool." In other words, concrete achievement buttresses the crucial mode of presentation of self in the adolescent subculture, and *it is this self-image and not the concrete role performance which ultimately interests adolescents. Confidence about one's essential masculinity or femininity and the ability to manifest this in smooth performances in many spheres is the essence of high status in this social system.*

One might expect a normative shift toward adult success standards over time in a youthful population largely oriented to college. But as an adolescent progresses through high school he discovers that the tension between adult and adolescent patterns increases rather than decreases. By the final year of high school the social category of the "clean-cut socies" has very few members. Those who cling to "clean-cut" patterns and hence are not trying to be "cool" no longer dominate the status system. In fact, those "clean-cut socies" who do not perceive this shift toward "cool" patterns are called "milk and cookies boys" and rapidly descend in the status system. One informant described what happened to a fraternity which did not make the shift to the "socie" patterns: "The Lambdas aren't well liked now because the Lambdas don't drink, and the other kids are all getting to drink, and they [the Lambdas] are not that well liked anymore because they look down upon it [drinking]. So now if you want social prestige with the kids, you wouldn't dare mention the Lambdas." The former members of the "clean-cut socies" who retain their social supremacy do so by appearing to adhere to responsible adult standards while, at the same time, actively participating in covert adolescent patterns.

Cultural Sources of Integration in the Youth Culture

Every cultural system has internal normative inconsistencies. In this section, we will show how certain cultural categories partially resolve some of the paradoxical or contradictory behavioral implications of the norms which govern dating. "Cute" and "cool" are prestigeful terms in this system, and an "elite" girl should be both. Girls see these as consistent personal attributes when they refer to the norms which regulate the ways in which a person achieves pre-eminence in the prestige system. But when girls talk about the ideal norms which should control relationships between members of the opposite sex, these two terms assume partly antagonistic meanings.

Both our male and female informants define a "cute" girl as a person who exudes a certain kind of sexual attractiveness but who does not demonstrate her sexual superiority in intercourse. In fact, if it is widely known that a high-status girl has had sexual intercourse, she very likely will be dropped from the "elite" circles even if she did not get pregnant. Yet, if she is "cool," a girl must be quite adept in the dating system. This means that she must "make out" with a comparatively large number of boys without, on the other hand, being "made." She must allow herself to reach a relatively high level of sexual excitement and intimacy without giving in to what are described as persistent demands for greater sexual favors. Consequently, if a girl is considered both "cool" and "cute" by her age mates, she must not only be physically attractive but also confidently manage the sexual self-aggrandizement which marks these temporary unions.

So far, "cuteness" and "coolness" are somewhat different but essentially complementary social categories. But girls have their own moral standards which form part of the meaning of these terms. When the social context is restricted to feminine interests and when the norms of proper behavior vis-à-vis males are at issue, "cool" and "cute" become partly contradictory categories.

Adolescent girls in this community discuss the motives and the norms which should govern dating in terms of "good clean fun." A good dating partner should be companionable, have similar interests, and should be a sympathetic and lively person. In this context, the "cute" girl is viewed as the friendly, "all-American girl" whom everyone likes and admires. She is vivacious, attractive, and, above all, not overly interested in the leverage one can obtain over boys through the judicious allocation of her affections. In short, she is a very wholesome girl. However, this category of the "all-American girl" quickly drops out of the picture when the girls talk about the realities of the power struggle which almost invariably accompanies dating. Incidentally, "going steady" is an institutionalized way of emphasizing the solidarity rather than the individualism of dating oriented to the status system. But among "elites" the dominant concern of who is going to control the relationship—all of our informants were convinced that long-term dating was an intrinsically asymmetrical relationship and were afraid that their peers would see them as the subordinate partner[31]—almost inevitably leads to its dissolution in a relatively short time. One girl viewed dating as follows:

(Q) You see this [dating] as pretty much of a game of strategy?
(A) Definitely! It's one of the most fun games around too. Because you never know what's going to happen. . . . It's up to you. There are no rules really. There might be a couple of rules that you take for granted, but basically. . . .
(Q) Like what [rules]?
(A) Well, not to do anything really nasty. Like go out with his best friend—break a date with him and go out with his best friend

[31]Many of our male informants expressed what seemed to us an almost pathological fear of being "pussy whipped," but we shall let psychoanalysts reveal the psychological implications of this term.

or something like that. Nothing really drastic, but aside from that there aren't too many rules, and you've just always got to make sure that you're on top, that you're winning because otherwise if you're not winning you're losing and there's no tie. So you always make sure you're winning.

According to ideal feminine norms, real sex, as distinguished from the "good-night kiss," is out of place, undesirable, and, in some sense, morally wrong on a good date. The feminine vision of a romantic relationship holds that a date should come from mutual concern with the other partner's true or inner qualities. As even a cursory glance at love comics and true romance magazines will attest, female ideology maintains that it is possible to appreciate the true worth of another person only if one is willing to rise above the ordinary trivial absorption in the competitive aspects of cross-sex relations, that is, with the other person's physical appearance, with his or her superficial manners (usually with their sophistication or lack of it), with the other person's prestige value (whether one's peers think he or she is "cool"), etc.

In light of these norms, "coolness," which is manifest in an attachment to "making out," is apparently incompatible with purely feminine conceptions of "cuteness." Thus, when girls talk solely in terms of their own moral standards, the "cute" girl is defined less by reference to her physical attractiveness than by her attractive "personality." Nevertheless, if a "cute" girl is to retain or achieve a position among the "elite" of the adolescent social system, she must attract high-status boys. How, then, does she retain her image of "cuteness" and the esteem that goes with it in the eyes of her girlfriends if she must also engage in a wide range of petting activities with many boys? Or, to phrase this in motivational terms, how does she keep her "cool" orientation toward sex within the moral boundaries of the feminine universe? That is, how can she participate in a rather promiscuous pattern of sexual intimacy with many boys and, at the same time, exercise considerable control over her sexual encounters?

This somewhat contradictory pattern of norma-

tively encouraged sexual promiscuity and restraint is resolved by a higher-order cultural category. This category defines the sexual nature of boys in both cognitive and evaluative terms. Our girl informants tell us that boys "naturally" try to "get all they can" sexually because boys are born with uncontrollable sexual urges.[32] One girl discussed the issue in the following terms:

(Q) Whose responsibility is it [regarding how far things go sexually on a date]?
(A) The girl's. I mean because guys can't help it. I mean they are born that way, but then girls get carried away because guys can't help themselves and girls can. To a point, but once past that point there's no hope.
(Q) Are all guys like this or just particular guys?
(A) Some guys would get as far as they could get, just for kicks, but there are other boys who are just as nice as they can be, but any boy who likes a girl enough . . . I don't think he would do it intentionally to hurt her, but just can't help to get as far as he can get. I don't think even the nicest guy can help being that way.

In terms of dating norms, girls say that it is their responsibility both to satisfy part of this inborn male desire for continual sexual satisfaction and to keep the situation from getting out of hand. Though girls admit that they also have strong sexual feelings, they agree that they and not the boys are capable of rational control, of setting limits.[33] Thus, girls claim that nature has burdened them with the responsibility of keeping petting relationships within the prescribed moral

[32] The Ngulu, by way of contrast, are convinced that women are born sexually insatisfiable (see T. Beidelman, "Pig (Gulwe): An Essay on Ngulu Sexual Symbolism and Ceremony," *Southwestern Journal of Anthropology*, Vol. XX (1964).

[33] For a long time we were puzzled about the reasons why one of our informants was systematically excluded from the girls' group mentioned above. Our other informants in this group told us, at first, that her clinical attitudes toward sex repulsed them, but upon reflection they admitted that they too collectively discussed sex in a similar manner. Upon further investigation, we found that this girl revealed her desire for sex, she "needed it," and hence she violated these norms.

limits. In a basic sense, girls see boys as morally defective—or, if not as morally defective, at least as morally immature. Boys are said to be simply incapable of realistically assessing the negative consequences of giving free rein to sexual impulses in a dating situation. And, from what we have been able to observe, boys often fulfil these cultural expectations which have been phrased in such biological terms.

Although success in dating seems superficially completely tied to ascriptive criteria, there are important performance aspects to dating. Female competence is culturally defined as the ability to manipulate the sexual component of dating relationships to one's own advantage. Some girls have told us about a technique of "dumping" which they use to entice boys and yet keep them in a dependent position, never certain of whether they will be abandoned for a more attractive partner. One girl described her dating relationship in the following way:

Like when Jim and I first started dating, we got along just fine. Then I started to dump on him, being a little snotty once in a while and stuff like this. Then I decided to be nice because it would be nice to be nice for a while, just as a change. Then I figured if he was so nice to me when I was dumping on him, just think if I was nice to him, he would really be nice to me. Well then he decided that wasn't such a hot idea [and] that he would start dumping on me which I didn't think was such a good idea either. So when he started dumping on me, I just decided to give him the shaft.

One of the latent and unintended consequences of this dating system is the widespread fear among "popular" girls that they are being exploited by the boys. A "popular" girl often feels that if she becomes too attached to a boy he may, in reality, be dating her only for the prestige which comes from being in the company of a "cool" and "cute" girl or, what is worse, he may play upon her romantic proclivities to seduce her.

Incidentally, we have found that many of the girls who "fall in love with" a popular entertainer, such as one of the Beatles (an English singing group), are often marginal in a very special way.

They may have all the prerequisites for success in the dating system; they are often physically attractive and personable. But these girls reject the hostility and exploitation inherent in the dating system and prefer an imaginary but romantically perfect relationship with these remote figures.

Conclusion

In conclusion, we do not hold that the youth subculture is a closed normative system. The normative integrity, coherence, and identity of a subculture is not always based upon estrangement from the larger culture nor does it always reside in social organizations which resist integration into the larger society. On the other hand, in a discussion of the reality of the youth culture, Berger declares that subcultures must not only have "relatively distinctive styles of life, but styles of life which are to a great extent self-generated, autonomous, having institutional and territorial resources capable of sustaining it in crisis and insulating it from pressures from without."[34] In our opinion, this limits the concept of a subculture to very special, and possibly almost non-existent, cases of cultural differentiation in this society. The high degree of interdependence of functionally differentiated subsystems in this society makes it unlikely that many subcultures will fulfil all of Berger's stringent prerequisites.

In contrast to Berger's strictures, we propose a more catholic and perhaps more fruitful view of a subculture. Rather, we suggest that the core of the youth culture resides in its distinctive evaluative standards. They endow the adolescent status terminology (and thus the social categories through which the members of this age-grade orient themselves to their peers) with qualities and attributes which do not dominate adult status judgments. Here we follow Anselm Strauss's view of the connection between social categories linked to a person's position in age and other societal structures and the ways in which people perceive social reality:

These changes in conceptual level involve, of course, changes in behavior, since behavior is

[34]Berger, *op. cit.*, p. 396

not separate from classifying. Shifts in concept connote shifts in perceiving, remembering and valuing—in short, radical changes in action and person. . . . Terminology shifts necessitate, but also signalize new evaluations: of self and others, of events, acts and objects; and the transformation of perception is irreversible; once having changed, there is no going back. One can look back, but he can evaluate only from his new status.[35]

From our point of view, then, the members of a subculture can be integrated into basic societal institutions even though their definitions of ordinary social situations are predicated upon a special set of cultural meanings. Consequently, the crucial criterion for the identification of a youth subculture is whether its norms provide its members with a distinctive world view, a style

of life, and the standards against which they can measure their own worth. Here again it is worthwhile to quote Strauss on age-graded perceptions of the world: "But the world is different for persons of different age and generation even if they share in common sex, class, and nationality, and occupation."[36]

Finally, our approach emphasizes the element of free cultural play in the genesis of the youth culture. Of course, we do not deny that the typical psychological and role problems of this age-grade provide the raw materials out of which youth culture is built. But we do point to the ways in which the meanings inherent in this adolescent normative order transcend the requirements of simple adjustment to these exigencies. In other words, these adolescent cultural inventions and innovations impose a discernible order upon the crises and dilemmas of adolescence.

[35] Strauss, *Mirrors and Masks: The Search for Identity* (Glencoe, Ill.: Free Press, 1959), p. 92.

[36] *Ibid.*, p. 138.

Chapter 10: Suggested Additional Readings

BLUM, L. H.   The discothèque and the phenomenon of alone-togetherness: A study of the young person's response to the frug and comparable current dances. *Adolescence,* Winter 1966-67, *1*(4), 351–366. Findings in this study are related to adolescents' self-indulgence and impulse release. Blum concludes that the abandon experienced in such dances as the frug serves as a release for pent-up tension, which might otherwise take some undesirable form.

BURKE, R. S., & GRINDER, R. E.   Personality-oriented themes and listening patterns in teen-age music and their relation to certain academic and peer variables. *School Review,* 1966, *74*(2), 196–211. A review of themes in teenage music suggests that a relatively beneficent view of youth culture is justified. Perhaps youth's participation in youth culture reflects the attractiveness of that culture rather than a rebellion against the adult culture.

GRINDER, R. E.   Disinctiveness and thrust in the American youth culture. *Journal of Social Issues,* 1969, *25*(2), 7–19. Data obtained from 2,220 boys reveals a relationship between high youth culture involvement and low commitment to high school objectives. Some adolescents depend on the youth culture as a reward system and as a support in attaining adulthood.

JENCKS C., & RIESMAN, D.   The role of student sub-cultures, *Teachers College Record.* 1967, *69*(1), 1–21. The role of student subcultures, both historical and current, is analyzed in depth, with considerable insightful comment.

SNYDER, R.   *Young people and their culture.* Nashville: Abingdon Press, 1969. Youth are deemed capable of shaping their own culture, a task which involves fulfillment of certain requisites. Adults who wish to help youth must live in the contemporary world. The discussion is related to fulfillment of Christian ideals.

SUGARMAN, B.   Involvement in youth culture, academic achievement and conformity in school. *British Journal of Sociology,* 1967, *18,* 151–164. A study of secondary-school boys in London indicated a relationship between underachievement in school and high commitment to the youth culture. In America strong youth cultures are represented as operating within the school, in Britain, outside it.

WITTAKER, D., & WATTS, W. A.   Personality characteristics of a nonconformist youth subculture: A study of Berkeley non-students. *Journal of Social Issues,* 1969, *25*(2), 65–88. On the basis of Omnibus Personality Inventory (OPI) scores and biographical data, Berkeley non-students were compared with a random sampling of Berkeley students. The non-students scored higher on Complexity, Impulse Expression, Autonomy, and Estheticism, and lower on Personal Integration and Masculinity-Femininity.

11

Alienated Youth

The term "alienated youth" encompasses those young people who reject normal patterns of growing up in favor of atypical behaviors more congenial to their own needs and temperament. Among such youth, the pattern of behaviors often includes a generalized distrust of others, rejection of socially approved rules of conduct, depression, introversion, and other psychic complaints (Gould, 1969, p. 60). But who are these alienated youth? What are they like? Why are they alienated? What is their effect on society? What, if anything, should be done about them?

Various reasons have been suggested for their alienation. For one thing, a small, static society is generally capable of providing for all its members; but a changing, specialized society, such as exists in most Western nations today, often generates social isolates (Goldman, 1968). For another, present-day society provides little opportunity for children's groups to learn how to get along with each other. Increasingly, children are finding it difficult to be together, as city streets become hazardous and families retreat to the more isolated suburbs. Often, activities which are especially arranged for children lack spontaneity and supress children's natural social qualities. Therefore, young people grow up without having had adequate opportunity to experience comfortable social interaction with other individuals and groups. Also, as society grows more complex and the population more dense, the government exercises greater control over the lives of its citizens, thereby fostering more discontent. Those individuals who fail to fit neatly into the average mold resent the restraints imposed by a conservative, middle-of-the-road majority. Moreover, youth may be overwhelmed by bigness. Society is large-scale, and so are the forces that run it. A few individuals feel frustrated and helpless against this bigness and withdraw into mutually supporting groups. Finally, the schools do their part in producing alienation. Many teachers fail to respect a child's value system, or perhaps to bridge the gap between values of home and school. Often children fail to understand the schools' goals, or how to attain them, and feel isolated and bewildered (Jackson, 1965).

As a result of some or all of these factors, many youth find themselves unwillingly forced into alienation. For example, consider the plight of the poor youth. Gottlieb (1969) portrays poor youths as wanting to be middle-class and to receive their share of the Establishment's pie; but they encounter so many obstacles that few of them can achieve this goal. That is, lower-class and middle-class youths share the same goals and desires, but the lower-class youth lacks the facilities to attain these goals that his middle-class counterpart enjoys. In contrast, middle-class adolescents have become alienated from middle-class life style; they reject the very conditions and advantages that enable them to have the leisure and the intellectual skills to be protesters.

Some writers defend alienated youth, or at least try to explain them; still others praise them or approve certain positions they represent. According to Friedenberg (1959), adolescence is not merely a physical process but a social process, whose fundamental task is helping youth establish self-identification; yet a society hostile to any vividness of self-expression may undermine the self-determination process and alienate the youth fumbling to find his identity. Moreover, says Friedenberg, society errs in labeling as aberrant the fully human adolescent who faces life with love and defiance. Another sympathetic observer, Raywid (1966), insists that behaviors of alienated youth often pose no danger for the community; on the contrary, they may constitute a healthy reaction against conformity. For instance, rebelling groups may express their protest against society by symbolic acts, such as wearing long hair and deviant styles of clothing. How can schools that forbid independent ideas about hair, dress, and grooming succeed in encouraging unorthodox minds, asks Raywid? If blind conformity is dangerous, should we not do what we can to counteract such tendencies, rather than formalize group behaviors? Still others defend patterns of alienation as "natural": youth need their fling and youth without rebellion is not youth. The youthful rebel almost always settles down, they aver, and he is the wiser for having sown his wild oats.

Criticism of alienated youth reflects both the critic and the group under consideration. The conventional person is repelled by anything, however harmless, which is different. Even quite liberal critics may deplore much that is done in the name of individualism. Specific criticisms also depend on the group under consideration. For example, Parkinson (1961) appraises the Beatnik, so named by San Francisco columnist Herb Caen. Beatnik life, says Parkinson, has become "a nexus of jazz, Buddhism, homosexuality, drugs and squalor [p. 276]." It is not easy to estimate the importance of this "extra-official" mode of life. Does it represent "the point of an iceberg," an indication of an underlying, far larger resentment? Or is it only American Bohemia in a new garb? The true rebel, continues Parkinson, does not merely protest the present order but suggests an ideal one. However, the Beatniks manifest little interest in modern society's major concerns —atomic fallout, the population explosion, legal justice, civil rights—except when these concerns somehow impinge on "printing books with taboo words, on problems of dope addicts cut off from their supply, or on rights of poets to slander policemen [p. 276]."

In several respects, the Beatniks are also Bohemian. Both Beatniks and Bohemians are neither true rebels nor revolutionists. Instead, they prefer to follow their own aesthetic pursuits in some congenial atmosphere, manifesting an evasive, rather than a destructive, attitude toward society. Essentially, Bohemians of all decades are cut from the same pattern, and apparent differences between them are merely superficial reflections of the particular times.

Berger (1967) describes another newer, alienated group, the hippies of America in the 1960s, and tells how they adapted eight basic points of Bohemian doctrine outlined by Malcolm Cowley in *Exile's Return*. The first is the Bohemian idea of salvation by the child; analogous to this are the hippies' innocence and belief in "flower power." The Bohemians' second ideal, self-expression, is identical with the hippies' moral injunction to "do your thing." The Bohemian idea of paganism is manifest in the hippies overpowering eroticism—the baring of female flesh, the symbols of male strength (beads, boots, and motorcycles). "The idea of living for the moment" is converted to "being super WOW where the action is in the NOW generation [p. 19]." Point five, the Bohemian's idea of liberty, is revealed in hippie movements to legalize marijuana and to render ecstasy respectable. The idea of female equality means, for the hippies, equality in smoking, drinking, and love-making. Another point in Bohemian doctrine, the idea of psychological adjustment, is sought by hippies through yoga and LSD. The last point, the idea of changing place (they do better things in "you-name-it") emerges in the hippies' fascination with such places as Tahiti, Tangier, and Paris.

Pitts (1971) perceives the hippie movement as having divided itself during early 1970 into four major cultural streams, or organizational patterns: the commune, the drug culture, the music culture, and the political–social movement. Hippie communes take the form of group life without conscious leadership and with a minimum of sex-role differentiation. The second stream of the hippie movement is the drug culture. The third, or music culture, gains its organization from the musicians, disc jockeys, and record industry; and it has its origins in certain types of American popular music, including folk music and rock-and-roll. The final organizational pattern in the hippie movement is the recently familiar phenomenon of active political protest.

In recent years, a great deal has been written about values of alienated youth, and more specifically about the moral status and views of hippies. Some persons brand them teen toughs; other label their criminal capers as mere pranks (boys-will-be-boys). However, most of the expressed public opinion about hippies is just that —opinion without any empirical basis. In our first selection, Levin and Spates examine relevant research on alienated youth by authorities in the field, and also analyze a sampling of periodicals from the Underground Press Syndicate. It becomes evident that no simplistic picture of the hippie is valid, and that his life style and life view are complexly rooted in the broad American societal structure. In the second article, Heath tells why he believes students are becoming increasingly bored, purposeless, and estranged both from themselves and from societal traditions. He suggests how present-day schools have failed to relate to youth's needs.

REFERENCES

BERGER, B. M. Hippie morality—More old than new. *Trans-action,* December 1967, *5*(3), 19–26.

FRIEDENBERG, E. Z. *The vanishing adolescent.* Boston: Beacon Press, 1959.

GOLDMAN, L. Varieties of alienation and educational responses. *Teachers College Record,* January 1968, *69*(4), 331–339.

GOTTLIEB, B.   Poor youth: A study in forced alienation. *Journal of Social Issues,* 1969, *25*(2), 91–119.

GOULD, L. J.   Conformity and marginality: Two faces of alienation. *Journal of Social Issues,* 1969, *25*(2), 39–63.

JACKSON, P. W.   Alienation in the classroom. *Psychology in the Schools,* 1965, *2*(4), 299–308.

PARKINSON, T.   Phenomenon or generation. In T. Parkinson (ed.) *A case book on the beat.* New York: Crowell, 1961, 276–290.

PITTS, J.   The counter culture. *Dissent,* June 1967, 216–229.

RAYWID, M. A.   The great haircut crisis of our time. *Phi Delta Kappan,* December 1966, *48*(4), 155.

Hippie Values: An Analysis of the Underground Press

JACK LEVIN   JAMES L. SPATES

The value structure of the hippie movement is analyzed and evaluated in terms of a sampling of hippie literature from the Underground Press Syndicate.

There is little doubt by this time that the hippie phenomenon of the late 1960s is a social movement of some consequence for American society (see Yablonsky, 1968: 290 ff.). Whatever its greater significance, the movement has already contributed to a revolution in modern dress, hairstyles, music, art, and youth culture.

Since 1966, the mass media have analyzed, scrutinized, supported, and condemned the movement, so that almost all Americans, whether or not they have had direct experience with the hippies, presently hold some opinion regarding the merits of this group of young people.

Why have the hippies attracted so much attention? It is doubtful that the answer lies solely in the number of hippies: percentagewise, they are a very small proportion of the American population—numbering, at high estimate, only 200,000 full-time participants (Yablonsky, 1968: 36). Nor does it seem likely that the concern is a direct product of the much publicized generation gap. Despite ample evidence that most are young (under thirty) and that most of their critics are "old" (over thirty), support for the movement ranges far beyond age lines: many of the hippies' most ardent admirers, if not participants, are over thirty; many of their detractors, under thirty.

After this widespread popularization, social scientists have recently attempted to account for the American reaction to the hippie phenomenon (see Berger, 1967; Davis, 1967; Simon and Trout, 1967; Brown, 1969; Marks, 1969; Yablonsky, 1968). Some have specifically focused upon the value gap between the hippies and the middle-class—a gap which has been characterized as an attempt by the hippie movement to substitute a viable alternative in place of the traditional American value pattern (see Marks, 1969). From this standpoint, the hippie problem becomes distinctly ideological, being directly related to those values or ideals which serve as the most general guidelines for action within society (such as the general American ideal that everyone, in order to be an American in good standing, must achieve individual success through his own occupational efforts).

The value argument raises an important aspect of the problem—that of conflict between different values as an expression of the basic gap between the hippie and middle-class views of life. Values are the most general directives for action in society, in that they are the most generally shared ideas about the correct way to behave. A challenge to the values of a social system is therefore re-

We wish to especially thank Herbert J. Greenwald for his many helpful suggestions. We are also grateful to Stephen R. Marks, Kingsley H. Birge, and William F. Macauley for their critical review of earlier versions of this paper and we gratefully acknowledge the coding assistance of Ann MacConnell, Kenneth Sweezey, and Marilyn Thomas.

"Hippie Values: An Analysis of the Underground Press" by Jack Levin and James L. Spates is reprinted from *Youth and Society*, Volume 2, Number 1, (September 1970), pp. 59–73, by permission of the Publisher, Sage Publications, Inc., and the authors.

garded by the members of that system as a basic threat to the very raison d'être of their social culture. Hence, one might expect the expression of strong concerns regarding the challenging elements of the hippie phenomenon.

The hippie mode of existence cannot be understood apart from the value structure of American society as a whole. More specifically, hippie culture has arisen directly out of the middle-class value system within which the majority of hippies were initially socialized. It has been estimated that over seventy percent of all hippies come from this middle- (or upper-) class orientation (Yablonsky, 1968: 26).

Characteristically, middle-class values tend to specify acts which are oriented to the future and normally require the individual to inhibit emotional expression in order for his resources to be fully directed toward the cognitive or rational solution to life tasks (see Parsons, 1951; Parsons and White, 1964: 196 ff.).

In the American case, the middle-class pattern typically manifests itself in the pursuit of economic concerns—that is, in rationally constructed efforts to increase economic production, profits, and occupational status by means of extended formal education and hard work. The achievement dimension of this pattern cannot be over-emphasized: the middle-class value structure places major demands upon each individual to achieve occupational success, not merely in terms of personal wealth, power, or status, but as a moral obligation to contribute to the building of the good society (Parsons and White, 1964: 196). In other words, middle-class achievement cannot be purely utilitarian: a person cannot use any means to a particular end, but must use instead socially legitimized (normatively sanctioned) means to ends. Basic success, then, is defined in social as well as personal terms, and rewards are commensurate. Thus, from the middle-class perspective, the hard-working businessman who makes $10,000 a year is much more respectable than the gangster who makes ten times that amount, and, all things being equal, it is the businessman who will be given the up-standing position in the society.

These essential features of the middle-class pattern, that is, its economic, cognitive, and achievement dimensions, all of which denote the goal-oriented nature of activity within the sys-tem, can be summarized for convenience under the term "instrumentalism." (see Parsons and White, 1964: 196 ff.; Zelditch, 1955: 309-312).

The Hippie Pattern

The hippies contend that their subculture offers a radical departure from the dominant American value structure which they see as thoroughly materialistic, dehumanizing, inauthentic, and alienating (Yablonsky, 1968: 361-366). This point of view is reflected in the hippies' "almost total rejection of economic individualism and the 'dog eat dog' or 'do unto others before they do unto you' attitude that is seen by them as the driving force behind contemporary American society" (Yablonsky, 1968: 358). The following responses (Yablonsky, 1968: 350, 351, 358, 365) are illustrative of the hippies' rejecting of middle-class values:

[A hippie drop-out since 1960] To me dropping-out means to reject the dominant moral, economic, and social values of one's society. I dropped out because the values in our society have become obsolete. . . . Our society is simply full of internal contradictions between its values and the reality of what people actually think and do. . . . Forty percent of America is terribly poor and yet we have tried to hide this from ourselves and the world because the dominant American middle-class has interests in perpetuating the myth.

[A hippie] In order to act with freedom, one must not be constrained by the oppressive systems of orientation and the selfish meaningless goals that were learned while a member of the uptight, plastic society.

[A 23-year-old hippie] We [America] have reached a high level of material development, many people have become hypnotized and obsessed with a desire for material good. There is a strong feeling of "us" and "them." . . . This is a negative part of contemporary American life and is blocking people from seeing the essence of one another.

In sum, then, it would appear that the hippie views the instrumental values of American society, whatever their original purpose, as presently generating dehumanized life styles, even to the point where human beings themselves, in the active quest for success, have become objects of manipulation to one another.

Such a negative reaction to his own society's dominant values (and to his own original values) has led the hippie to form a life style that is quite at odds with the typical American ideal of the hard-working, self-denying, rational businessman or professional. Yablonsky (1968: 29–31) has set forth what he sees as the basic elements of the ideal hippie: he is a philosopher who claims to be "tuned-in to the cosmic affinity of man"; he thus loves all men (the love ethic); "he has achieved this insight, at least in part, from the use of drugs [marijuana, LSD] as a sacrament"; he is a role model for new hippies to look up to; he is creative; he does not work in the traditional sense of American culture, rather preferring to do his own thing, whatever that may be; he is, in a word, "totally dropped out of the larger society," which he regards as plastic, and is actively engaged in "fostering another mode of existence."

This other mode of existence, for the hippie, an alternative which completely deemphasizes the economic and achievement criteria of American society, and focuses instead upon all objects and actions as ends in themselves, as valuable and necessary foci of immediate gratification and present (rather than future) time orientation. More specifically, rather than attempting to deal with their affairs on a cognitive-rational level, or in terms of economic value, the hippie's ideals (see Greeley, 1969: 14–28) stress nonmaterial or spiritual concerns (such as participation in cosmology, mysticism, and the occult), as well as the search for love and intimacy in human relationships (Yablonsky, 1968: 358, 366). In addition, the achievement aspects of the middle-class pattern are replaced by the quest for self-expression as experienced in the immediate ongoing situation (that is, by grooving on or getting into music, art, psychedelic drugs, and the like). Whereas the middle-class individual is rewarded for following socially legitimized paths to achievement, the hippie is expected to follow his own personal path to wherever it leads him. That is, whatever his thing is, he does it.

The essential components of the hippie value pattern—as indicated by self-expression, affili-

ation, concern for others, and religious philosophical interests—can be conveniently characterized under the term "expressivism" (see Zelditch, 1955: 311).

The value gap between the hippies and the middle class, though often suggested by previous investigations of the hippie phenomenon, has, for the most part, lacked systematic, quantitative substantiation.[1] For this reason, it was the central purpose of the present study to test the hypothesis that, *contrary to the middle class pattern, hippie values stress expressive concerns and deemphasize instrumental concerns.*

Method

To delineate the value structure of the hippie movement, a sample was taken from Underground Press Syndicate (UPS) periodicals published in 1967 and 1968—a recent period during which hippie literature was available. The UPS (1969: 17–18) has an estimated, combined circulation of one million and, as self-described, consists of an "informal association of publications of the 'alternative press' . . . produced in storefronts and basements by feelthy hippies, distributed by unorthodox channels and free-thinking bookstores and from curbs". Ron Thelin, the editor of a representative underground newspaper, has expressed the purpose of his publication in the following manner (1968: 143–144):

[to] provide an organ for the hip community, an evolution of communications consciousness and group consciousness to reflect the universal spirit and the miracles of light in this community [Haight-Ashbury]. . . . To show that LSD provides a profound experience. . . . To provide communication of the historical and ancient discoveries that are coming out of the hip culture, to spread the word, to get everyone to turn on, tune in, and drop out.

[1] See Berger (1967), Davis (1967), Simon and Trout (1967), Brown (1969), Marks (1969), and Yablonsky (1968). One major exception is Yablonsky, whose methods include lengthy participant observation and a questionnaire approach (n=600). However, the study has been severely criticized on methodological grounds, particularly in its participant observations aspect—see, for example, Berger (1969).

Most hippie underground papers appeared in the mid-sixties, many of them after the publicity of 1967, and many of them were short-lived. But their common components were an emphasis on hippie argot, psychedelic lettering and art, the glorification of folk rock, flower power, and love-ins—all, as Thelin says, in an attempt to describe the hip experience to their readers.

To obtain a representative sample of underground newspapers, the following most widely circulated periodicals were selected from major centers of recent hippie activities including both eastern and western regions: *Avatar* (Boston), *Distant Drummer* (Philadelphia), *East Village Other* (New York), *Los Angeles Free Press, San Francisco Oracle,* and *Washington Free Press*. A single issue of each UPS periodical from every second month in the period from September 1967 to August 1968 was selected on a random basis. Every second nonfictional article appearing in this sample of issues, excluding poetry and letters to the editor, was subjected to analysis (n=316).

To provide a comparable sample of articles representative of middle-class values, an analysis was also conducted of concurrently published issues of the *Reader's Digest,* selected for its variety of middle class articles from diverse sources (ese Ginglinger, 1955: 56–61). Excluding fiction and poetry, each article appearing in every other issue of *Reader's Digest* was studied (n=162).

The major value-theme of articles in both samples was coded by means of a modified version of Ralph K. White's *Value Catalogue* (1951). All materials were coded using a detailed set of definitions of the value-themes and appropriate coding sheets.

The central hypothesis regarding expressive and instrumental values was tested in the following manner. On the basis of the theoretical discussion above, the categories Self-Expression, Concern for Others, Affiliation, and Religious–Philosophical were treated as aspects of Expressivism, while the categories Achievement, Cognitive, and Economic became the basis for Instrumentalism. Categories of the value analysis are listed below:

INSTRUMENTAL

(a) Achievement: Values which produce achievement motivation for the individual in terms of hard work, practicality, or economic value are often expressed by means of contributions to society through occupation and high regard for ownership.

(b) Cognitive: These represent the drive for learning as an end in itself as well as the means for achieving success, welfare, or happiness.

(c) Economic: Economic values are at the collective level (such as national, state, industrial), thus differing from individual goals such as achievement.

EXPRESSIVE

(d) Self-expressive: This area includes all the self-expressive values and goals. The main ones are humor, play, and fun in general, relaxation, or exciting new discoveries, and travel. Art and beauty are included as well as other creative–expressive activities.

(e) Affiliative: These may be the product of social conditioning, or a result of the need to belong to a group, to affiliate with another person. This category focuses upon the gregariousness of individuals and the friendships which they develop. These affiliative aims may be expressed as conformity, loyalty to the group, friendship, or other-directedness.

(f) Concern for others: Concern for others does not depend upon a drive to interact. Unlike the affiliative values, this category focuses upon attitudes and feelings toward particular groups or toward humanity in general. Therefore, this category tends to include more abstract objectives than those associated with affiliation.

(g) Religious–philosophical: This category includes goals dealing with ultimate meaning in life, the role of deity, concerns with afterlife, and so on.

OTHER

(h) Individualistic: This category is concerned with values which stress the importance of the individual, the development of his unique personality, individual independence, and the achievement of individualized personal fulfillment including rebellion.

(i) Physiological: These are goals created by simple physiological drives such as hunger, sex, physical health, and physical safety.

(j) Political: This category includes collective goals (such as state, community, national, international objectives) in their central reference to group decision-making processes.

(k) Miscellaneous: Any other goals not covered above (such as hope, honesty, purity, modesty, and manners).

The reliability of the value analysis was tested by having three coders independently code thirty articles from both the UPS and the *Digest* samples. Using a two-out-of-three criterion (that is, where two of three coders agreed), agreement reached 90%. Total agreement was 78%.

Results and Discussion

Results obtained in an analysis of UPS and *Reader's Digest* value-themes suggest that expressivism occupies a central position in the hippie value structure, whereas instrumentalism occurs only peripherally. As shown in Table 1, expressive concerns accounted for 46% of the value-themes in the underground press, while instrumental concerns were the major focus of only

10% of the articles. In sharp contrast, instrumental concerns represented the major value-theme in the *Reader's Digest* sample (42%), while expressive concerns were substantially less important (23%).

Within the expressivism of the hippie sample, the dominant emphasis appeared to be Self-Expression (28%). For example, typical articles in the underground press dealt with the mind-blowing psychedelic properties of drugs, the relationship of early rock and roll music to contemporary rock groups (such as, the Beatles and the Rolling Stones), the influence of such figures as Ken Kesey, Timothy Leary, and Lenny Bruce on the hippie movement.

In the *Reader's Digest* sample, Achievement was the dominant component of instrumentalism, representing 28% of all value-themes. Typically, *Reader's Digest* articles emphasized methods for occupational achievement, including business enterprises created by college students, advice concerning financial investments and taxes, the careers of well-known persons who had achieved occupational success, and so on.

An independent analysis of a random sample of underground press advertisements appearing in our sample yielded the following supportive data: almost 90% of the hippie advertisements

Table 1. Value-Themes in the Underground Press and Reader's Digest[a]

Value-Theme	Underground Press		Reader's Digest	
		%		%
Expressive	46%		23%	
self-expressive		28		9
concern for others		8		6
affiliative		4		3
religious-philosophical		6		5
Instrumental	10		42	
achievement		3		28
cognitive		5		7
economic		2		7
Other	44		35	
individual		20		10
political[b]		19		12
physiological[c]		4		12
miscellaneous		1		1
Total		100		100
(n=478)		(316)		(162)

a. A chi-square analysis was conducted by comparing the Underground Press and Reader's Digest on the two major value-themes, Expressive and Instrumental ($\chi^2 = 61.17$, df=1, p < .001).

b. The distribution of political values reveals an important aspect of the nature of the underground press: a secondary appeal of these newspapers is often to politically radical or New Left types, though most of the material is designed for hippie consumption (see Wolfe, 1968: 135-144)– a group known for its apolitical stance (see Yablonsky, 1968).

c. In the Reader's Digest, this category consisted primarily of health-related topics such as methods of weight reduction, physical diseases such as cancer, and aging. In the Underground Press, it contained references to physiological sex.

focused on expressive-related products, that is, on products which are designed either for expressive behavior or expressive consumption, such as music (rock, folk, blues, soul, and the like), movies, plays, psychedelic shops, clothing (mod), and coffee and tea houses. The most important of these expressive categories contained music-related products such as concerts, records, recording artists, and stereophonic equipment; these products accounted for 25% of all hippie advertisements. These results lend support to the suggestion that expressive concerns are a staple of great magnitude for the readers of the underground and more generally for the hippie movement as a whole.

An examination of the relationship of individualism to the expressive–instrumental dichotomy may shed additional light on the above findings. As is well known, social scientists have long been concerned with the position of individualism in the American value structure. In the middle-class case, individualism has the major task of locating responsibility for contributions to the building of the good society. Thus, each individual must actively strive to accomplish those objectives which society has defined as legitimate concerns.

Similarly, the hippies show a characteristic American concern for the individual. As shown in the present study, 20% of the articles appearing in the underground press contained an individualistic value-orientation. However, the hippie version may indicate an individualism of a different order: an individualism closely tied to the expressive value-orientation. It is here that the hippie phrase, "Do your own thing!" has particular relevance, in that it essentially directs attention to the immediate gratification of needs by means of creative self-expression—an expressive individualism which stands in sharp contrast to the dominant middle-class pattern (Marks, 1969).

The hippies form a unique phenomenon in contemporary America—a large-scale movement which has arisen out of the mainstream of American life to form a contraculture within its societal boundaries. Results obtained in the present study support the contention that the hippies are attempting to stress values of an expressive nature—values which they feel have been neglected by the highly instrumental middle class.

From the sociological point of view, this is where the concern of Americans about the hippies comes home to roost: a way of life is being criticized, and sides are being taken. The ideology of the hip movement attempts to cut to the core of the instrumental view of things. The middle-class ideology, the hippies are saying, neglects the personal needs of the individual to be a human being; it neglects his need to be affective, loving, and trustful of other people; it neglects his need for self-realization by following his own individual needs; in a word, it neglects his need to be expressive.

Yet, how expressive can a social system be? There is increasing evidence that the strongly reactive nature of the hippie value system may in large part account for the general failure of the movement to form viable communities or other social structures.[2] The perceived overemphasis of the middle class on instrumentalism seems to have been matched by a similar overemphasis by the hippies on pure expressivism. In structural terms, extreme expressivism poses a significant problem for long-term stable patterns of interaction—that is, the basic tasks of maintaining the system are not performed on a regular basis, which, in the extreme, can result in social disorganization and decay. Indeed, the literature on the hippies is replete with examples of community and group termination because food was not taken in, rent was not paid, and so on. Clearly, for a stable society, everyone doing his own thing has its limitations.

It is just this system dissolution that the middle-class American intuitively—and, we think, rightly —feels may be a consequence of a purely expressive mode of existence. Knowing this, he, like the hippie, takes a stance in defense of his life style. Though the ideological stance of each group often becomes a battle of ego defenses (that is, "My way of life is right because it is *my* way of

---

[2]Because of harassment by various agencies of the dominant culture, a significant number of hippies have literally taken to the woods to form communes. While some of these social systems have existed for a number of years, their long-term stability has not yet been confirmed. In addition, even if successful, the price of their success may be more instrumentally oriented behavior. Such groups are in the minority if one takes the hippie population as a whole: most hippies still reside in major urban centers and exist in extremely loose confederations. See Brown (1969: 37).

life"), there seems to be objective merit in both positions; extreme instrumentalism does appear to neglect the necessities of personality and organismic expression, while extreme expressivism appears to neglect the requirements of stable systems. For this reason, it may well be that neither the expressive or instrumental value structures may come to be dominant in this ideational conflict. Rather, the solution may be in the form of systems which combine elements of both these systems—systems which are already in the process of formulation.

It already appears that the hippie's purely expressive solution to life is considered too radical as a viable solution for the society as a whole. Very few people completely drop out (which the totally expressive solution necessitates). But there is evidence that fewer and fewer people are taking the straight life in its extreme sense as their life style either. Rather, some sort of balance is apparently being worked out on both sides of the fence.

From a more general perspective, the hippie emphasis on expressive values could be regarded as partially illustrative of a process of widespread balancing in American society as a whole, whereby the social system, being pushed more and more to an instrumental extreme, is reintroducing various modes of expressivism at all levels of its structure. If this is the case, then the societywide trend toward expressivism, exemplified in its most extreme form by the hip movement, could be seen as part and parcel of other strong trends in contemporary America—civil rights, freedom of speech, representation, life style, and the like. Though the end result will most likely not be the extreme expressivism found dominant in many hip subcultures, it may very well be, over time, that an expressivism suitable to all age levels and classes of American society will become part of the American ideology. It is in this sense that the hippie movement may have its most profound influence on the character of the American value system.

REFERENCES

BERGER, B. M. 1969. "Sociologist on a bad trip." *Trans-action* 6(4), (February): 54–56.

——— 1967. "Hippie morality—more old than new." *Trans-action* 5(2), (December): 19–27.

BROWN, M. E. 1969. "The persecution and condemnation of hippies." *Trans-action* 6(10), (September): 33–46.

DAVIS, F. 1967. "Why all of us may be hippies someday." *Trans-action* 5(2), (December): 10–18.

GINGLINGER, G. 1955. "Basic values in *Readers Digest,* selection, and constellation." *Journalism Q.* 32(1), (Winter): 56–61.

GREELEY, A. M. (1969) "There's a new time religion on campus." *New York Times Magazine* (June 1): 14–28.

MARKS, S. R. (1969) "The hippies and the organism: a problem for the general theory of action." Dept. of Sociology, Boston Univ. Unpublished.

PARSONS, T. (1951) *The Social System.* New York: Free Press.

———, AND WHITE, W. (1964) "The link between character and society," pp. 183-235 in T. Parsons. *Social Structure and Personality.* New York: Free Press.

SIMON, G., AND TROUT, G. (1967) "Hippies in college —from teeny-boppers to drug freaks." *Trans-action* 5(2) (December): 27–32.

Underground Press Syndicate (1969) *Directory.* Phoenix: Orpheus.

WHITE, R. K. (1951) *Value-Analysis: The Nature and Use of the Method.* New York: Society for the Psychological Study of Social Issues.

WOLFE, B. H. (1968) *The Hippies.* New York: Signet.

YABLONSKY, L. (1968) *The Hippie Trip.* New York: Pegasus.

ZELDITCH, M., JR. (1955) "Role differentiation in the nuclear family: a comparative study," pp. 309–312 in T. Parsons and R. F. Bales, et al. *Family: Socialization and Interaction Process.* New York: Free Press.

Student Alienation and School

DOUGLAS H. HEATH

Heath discusses students' estrangement from self, from others, and from tradition, and suggests what schools may do about it.

What a paradox! Sputnik spawned a stormy decade of ceaseless educational change and improvement. Billions of dollars have been spent to improve our educational facilities; consolidate our schools; purchase thousands of yellow school buses; expand pupil personnel services; modernize our curricula, particularly in the sciences; offer advanced placement and enrichment courses; provide elaborate language laboratories and other expensive educational technologies; and reeducate and improve the lot of our teachers.

Yet, scarcely a dozen years later, the hurricane of protest, strikes, disaffection, and calumny in our schools makes the Sputnikian days halcyon by comparison. Frightened and bewildered teachers are uncertain about the relevance of what they are doing and resented by their students. Administrators feel trapped between local Birchites attacking sex education programs and seditious

Douglas Heath is professor of psychology at Haverford College, consultant to various educational, religious, and psychiatric groups; and lecturer. This article is based on his experience with students and teachers throughout the country as well as on his research on mental health and the schools. A more detailed discussion of changes in student character and their implication for educational change can also be found in: *Humanizing Schools: New Directions, New Decisions*, Hayden Book Co., 1971.

students fomenting, so it is believed, rebellions against their authority; between parents complaining about school taxes and the breakdown in discipline and teachers now divided not just on issues of curriculum and discipline but on the purposes and worth of education itself.

And our students? Who can make sense of them these days? Certainly, increasing numbers of them are much more knowledgeable, impressively alert to the currents of the world, more morally sensitive and perceptive, less imprisoned by the illusions and myths we adults have long taken for reality. Yet, increasing numbers also seem to be deeply bored and apathetic, even gloomy and despairing, resentful, purposeless, uncommitted and privatistic. Within only a few years, more have come to accept as viable options for their lives the possibilities of becoming addicted to drugs or mentally ill. They speak of suicide more openly now. They increasingly reject the claims of traditional authorities and the way of life of their achieving, puritanistic, but joyless, middle-class parents. The hippie and drug routes do speak to the suppressed needs of more youth than we may wish to admit. Of their schools they think: irrelevant, boring, repressive, joyless. The more articulate students say they are prisoners of a

From D. H. Heath, Student alienation and school. Reprinted from *School Review*, 1970, 78(4), pp. 515–528. Copyright © 1970 by *School Review*, and reprinted by permission of the University of Chicago Press and the author.

dehumanized "system" that makes them feel like "niggers." Increasing numbers repudiate requirements, grades, achievement, and competitiveness. Listen to this poignant comment of a Berkeley senior who has the highest grade-point average of his graduating class:

The first thing I would like to say to you is that it was not worth it . . . [in the pursuit of grades, he had become] subject to a paralyzing mental machinery: if I did not study twelve hours a day, compose at the speed of 1000 words an hour while writing a paper, go through required reading at 33 pages an hour, I was a failure. I pushed myself until I was more enchained than a Russian factory worker in the 1930s. [His longing for human contact, he said] would come at night as I walked home from the library. I would look at the lights in the windows and think to myself: behind those windows are people—real, live, human, fleshy, thinking, feeling, loving, despairing people. I am out here and they are in there. They will never come out here to me, and they would never allow me to come inside to them.

The paradox is that the post-Sputnikian educational changes that brought impressive material improvements to our schools intensified faculty uncertainty about their proper goals and student alienation from the repudiation of their schools. I propose that:

1. Our youth have been undergoing characterological changes that are alienating them from their emotional needs, from each other, and from traditional communal sources of values. Boredom, loneliness, and meaninglessness are the emerging leitmotifs.

2. These changes are caused by an historic and irreversible transition in the power of different social institutions to have educative and maturing effects on the young. Intimate, face-to-face, primary groups like the family, neighborhood, and church are losing their educative power. Increasingly, conforming, impersonal, secondary agencies like the mass media, peer culture, and the school are controlling and shaping the development of young people.

3. Because we educators have been blind to this shift in influence and power and its psycho-social consequences, we have grievously misidentified how our young people need to develop. We have unwittingly supported structural and policy changes in our educational system that have compounded student alienation. We have become only more confused about what our principal educational goals should be.

Characterological Changes

What does it mean that students are becoming increasingly more bored, lonely, and purposeless —signs of a growing estrangement from themselves, others, and their own traditions?

I speak primarily of affluent, white middleclass college-bound suburban and metropolitan high school students, for these are the ones I have been talking with in many parts of the country and on whom I have some psychological test data since the end of World War II. I speak of trends that have been emerging since that time and do not imply that I describe a majority of 17-year-olds—yet.[1] My concern is that such trends may describe the majority in five or ten years.

ESTRANGEMENT FROM SELF

Boredom has several psychological roots: diminished vitality, withdrawal of interest, defensive constriction of the personality because of too severe internal strife, overstimulation, a passive orientation to life. The boredom of contemporary students seems also to be related to a pervasive inhibition of impulsive. It may seem quixotic to speak of a deepening inhibition when one thinks of our long-haired psychedelic young people. Yet, their own words betray their own inhibition: to be cool, hung up, up tight, in a box. My data suggest that for the past two decades there has been an increase in the number of students who overcontrol their impulses, who are serious and conscientious, who feel under some strain to meet the increased expectations of society and their schools. To be "cool" is to maintain self-control

[1] Those interested in the basic studies and actual data may wish to read my *Growing Up in College: Liberal Education and Maturity* (San Francisco: Jossey-Bass, Inc., 1968).

in order not to give the appearance of being emotional, nostalgic, sentimental, dependent, weak, tender, affectionate, enthusiastic, or committed. A youth cannot afford to allow himself to be "vulnerable" and risk being rejected and hurt. The consequence is that he shies away from childish self-abandon, adolescent pranks and playful humor, party stunts, informal group singing, and other activities in which he risks "blowing his cool." Young people talk of being separated intellectually from their emotional needs, of being empty inside.

Of course, we humans are not built to cut ourselves off from our feelings, to feel dead inside. If we cannot be spontaneous and express emotion, then out of frustration and restlessness we turn to more intensive external events that will "turn us on." So how does a youth nowadays get his kicks? He retreats to his room to immerse himself in the deafening road of folk rock. Or he seeks out a band whose music is so loud and encompassing that he actually feels physical, perhaps erotic, vibrations in his groin. Or he turns to drugs that help him "blow his mind," that is, his inhibitions, in order to make him feel alive again, to experience a range and intensity of feelings he cannot experience on his own, to come to know that life can be "beautiful." Sensitivity, marathon, or encounter groups have become enormously popular with young people in our culture, and variants of these procedures are beginning to flood the schools and colleges. Our youth now need institutionalized ways by which to learn how to feel like children again, how to communicate emotionally with another, how to recover a primitive emotional wholeness that has been "cooled" out of them. Folk rock, drugs, and *T* groups are ways to recover a sense of integration or wholeness in which feeling becomes re-fused in awareness with thought. Is it any wonder that teachers from all parts of the country say they have to work harder to keep their students with them, that English teachers have been forced to teach more bizarre and "way out" literature, that many of us are forced to use more dramatic, vivid current materials?

I do not fear that student activists or their errant aggressiveness will "destroy" our schools and colleges. At least they are alive and kicking, though I do not enjoy being kicked. I fear, instead, that a much larger number of our students are becoming turned off, overly inhibited, tight, passive, the walking dead. Our problem as educators is to help them become actively and emotionally involved with their lives, to help them learn not to be so passively dependent upon something "out there" for entertainment, to help them learn how to tolerate the pain of frustration and boredom without fleeing into drugs or intellectual stupor.

ESTRANGEMENT FROM OTHERS

All of us have been lonely at times, though some much more so than others. But this younger generation is a lonelier one. Perhaps they are more aware of their isolation than their parents have been, for they do not have to preoccupy themselves with long hours of work to survive. Our affluence guarantees the satisfaction of their survival needs. My data suggest that the trend is for 17-year-olds to feel less tied to other persons, groups, and even their own country. Some statistics may be helpful at this point to illustrate my observations [See Table 1]. I report the percentage of "true" replies for every fourth year of 17-year-olds entering my own college since the end of World War II.

It is not that young people do not value close friendships. They do—perhaps more than their parents ever did. They dare not risk initiating such relationships because many do not have the social skills and confidence to be able to get close to someone else. Thirty-seven percent of the senior men graduating from Berkeley in one class said they had never made a close friend in college; almost a third of the men and 25 percent of the women at Stanford said they had never had a "date" while at the university. Forty percent of our own entering freshmen have said they feel very lonely.

But we are not built to be isolated individualists, not to be touched or to touch, despite those young people who hide their loneliness behind slogans of self-sufficiency and "do your own thing" or who escape into a Simon and Garfunkel lyric like

Hiding in my room, safe within my womb
I touch no one and no one touches me.
I am a rock

Table 1.

	Students Entering in					
	'48-'49	'52	'56	'60	'64	'68
When I was a child I didn't care to be a member of a crowd or gang.	33	35	35	38	49	47
I could be happy living all alone in a cabin in the woods or mountains.	23	28	31	38	33	45
My worries seem to disappear when I get into a crowd of lively friends.	71	69	73	68	58	55
I am a good mixer.	77	49	48	63	60	43

I am an island
And a rock feels no pain
And an island never cries.

The "in" words are openness, trust, love, and community—words that express need for the intimacy and belongingness that so many report their lives now lack.

How are our youth seeking to overcome their strangement from others? The hippie commune, the conspiratorial drug group, the mass confrontation that, ironically, provides for many their first meaningful experience of human solidarity and community, create some transitory experiences of acceptance and belongingness. Again, the attraction of the encounter or sensitivity group is that it too provides a glimpse of what intimacy could be. Despite their artificiality, some of these groups prove difficult to terminate. But it is primarily through sexual relations that increasing numbers of our young people will seek to escape loneliness and to learn interpersonal intimacy. It is not that they pursue sexual experiences just for hedonistic or erotic pleasure. Sex is becoming the means of learning how to relate more openly and trustingly with another.

Now if it is true, as my studies and those of other researchers suggest, that the quality of interpersonal relationships, particularly with peers, in adolescence is the primary determinant of maturing, including intellectual growth, then we need to reexamine our educational practices and structures to discover how they accentuate our students' isolation and estrangement from each other. Is it really healthy for private schools and colleges to build new dormitories that provide single rooms to which students can too readily retreat when faced by a crisis in their personal relationships? As educational technology gives us the opportunity to individualize instruction for each child, do we risk separating him even further from cooperative social learning experiences? Should we not also reemphasize team study or research projects in order to help a youth learn how to listen, cooperate, and share with another? Perhaps by working with someone else on a common task he will learn how to communicate with and care for another person.

ESTRANGEMENT FROM TRADITION

The intellectual, religious, and political assumptions that served as the core of our adult identities provided us with some certainty and assured us that our lives were meaningful and purposeful. These assumptions are but myths for growing numbers of young people. And they are less willing to commit themselves to myths or illusions. No longer is disciplined intelligence, apotheosized in science and technology, viewed as a means of salvation by many of our brightest youngsters. Increasingly, they reject the rationalistic academicism and scientism that have produced hydrogen bombs, destroyed the beauty of their earth, and automated them. Nor do our traditional religious beliefs and practices appeal to the many young people who find God, miracles, heaven and hell, prayer, and the Bible irrelevant to this secular world.[2] Nor is there any real conviction that there is some divine plan, purpose, or absolutistic principle to discover. The Puritanistic ethic has lost its hold for a pleasure-seeking "now" generation. Our black and Vietnamese tragedies and the unresponsiveness of our government to the heightened moral consciousness of many of this generation have unmasked the hollowness of our democratic myths.

The consequences of this profound change in value have been a deepening gloom and hopelessness. For the first time a generation confronts a world in which there seems to be no viable alternatives to uncertainty, purposelessness, and meaninglessness.

But, again, human beings are not built psychologically to live absurdly or contingently. We are built to believe, to seek meaning and purpose, and to create order. To find some certainty and truth, more and more are turning inward, a process accentuated by drugs and the failure of adult leaders to provide channels through which the moral idealism of our youth can be expressed. "If I can no longer trust any authority—that of our intellectual, religious, and political traditions and leaders—then at least I can trust myself and my judgment." Thus, it is not surprising to learn that whereas after World War II 25 percent of 17-year-olds entering college thought they were important persons, nowadays 56 percent believe so. Nor is it surprising that large numbers of our young people now organize their values around psychedelia and the aesthetic way of life; the criteria for the true, right, or good become one's own feelings and inner life. If an experience is beautiful—even a drug-induced hallucination—that is the only justification it needs. Truth has no objective basis. Nor is a teacher's competence any longer compelling to a youth who finds his own truth in subjective reactions. The Woodstock festival tells us that the emerging sacraments of the new subjectivism are folk rock and drugs.

These trends challenge us to discover how to help our youth learn to live with uncertainty, how to nurture faith and hope, how to develop more mature values. Is not the real meaning of

[2]D. H. Heath, "Secularization and Maturity of Religious Beliefs," *Journal of Religion and Health,* 8, no. 4 (1969):335–58.

the generation gap our failure as adults to be models of hope and vision that speak to the 1984 world into which young people are moving?

What do our youth need to become more mature and educable? They certainly do not just need to learn more information or to sharpen their abstract verbal skills. By overemphasizing narrow academicism we risk making many of our more sensitive and intelligent youths even more unamenable to further intellectual growth. What I have learned from the hippies, the drug devotees, and the activists is that we educators have failed to speak to the needs of young people to grow more wholely. They need to learn to spontaneously express their affectionate and appreciative feelings. They need to learn to develop more intimate cooperative relationships. They need to learn to act responsibly in actual encounters with the meaningful problems in order to test their emerging values and, in Van Doren's words, their "skills of being." They need to learn to reflect upon experiences in which they have had to integrate their knowledge and intellectual capacities, emotional needs, social ideals, and interpersonal skills. To provide only traditional academic training for this generation of students is to risk estranging it even more from itself and souring it to the potential beauty of life as well as to the pressing human needs of our society.

Societal Causes of Alienation

The trends I've described are obviously the product of many complex societal factors. We are in the midst of a historic transition in the power of different societal institutions to have maturing effects on young people. The family, neighborhood, and church are rapidly losing their power to nurture emotional spontaneity, cooperative, intimate, and caring attitudes and skills, and stable integrative values. The mass media, peer culture, and school increasingly dominate the life space of our youth and are inducing passivity and emotional inhibition, conformity and impersonalization, and conflicting and unstable values.

The decline in the power of the traditional neighborhood and the church to further the growth of youngsters has already been well described by Bronfenbrenner[3] and others. Despite the widespread conviction that there have been marked changes in the atmosphere and child-rearing practices of white middle-class families in the past decades, remarkably little information is available to document such a trend. My own meager data suggest there have been no dramatic changes in either permissiveness of affective tone during the past two decades. What may have happened is that the typical family is now no longer as protected or guarded from the influences of other forces in our society. The consequence is that our children may watch on television as other people fight, kill each other, decide what to buy, live in excessive splendor, make love, disobey parents, and so on. They become aware very early of every adult secret, our perversities and weaknesses, our conflicting ways of life. They see every disaster, relive the assassinations of their heroes, and suffer their funeral marches along Pennsylvania Avenue. Since we adults also are now uncertain about what we believe, our children no longer encounter many stable, convincing models of values.

The mass media, peer culture, and the schools have also been encroaching on the family by usurping more and more hours of a youth's time. If it is true that the average child looks at television some thousand hours a year, we must ask from where that time comes. The answer is that it is taken from family activities, from play with friends, from hobbies, and from other emotional and social experiences in which a child formerly learned how to develop communicative, interpersonal, and coping skills. How many hours does it take to learn how to argue without turning off, to listen to others, to cooperate in setting rules and then accommodate to them, to empathize, sympathize, and care for another? Surely we are not born with such skills. Instead, television teaches a child to watch passively, experience vicariously, and perceive impressionistically. Whereas a child used to learn playful skills and attitudes with which to cope with boredom later in life, now television prepares the child to be a bored adolescent. Why? Human experience

is finite. There are only so many human emotions, crises, and ways of coping with them. To keep our attention, the media must present us with novelty. What happens to a child who too early has been to the moon, Biafra, or Vietnam? The second and third trips become dreadfully routine. So television must go way out—to the more intense, perverse, or bizarre—in order to stay "in." Now, each of us knows that when we see violence, for example, we become tense and perhaps even a little angry ourselves. Since most middle-class families do not permit children to hit each other, they have few ways by which to express their aroused tensions. They learn to inhibit their feelings. After thousands of hours of this conditioning does not one become insensitive to the massacres at Pinkville and does not one need the release of marijuana?

Any adult who is close to adolescents knows how powerfully the peer culture affects their values and attitudes. When Bob Dylan says everyone must get stoned, the Beatles visit a guru, and Mick Jagger gets a girl pregnant outside of marriage, then millions of young people get the message. It does not take more than a few weeks for a new idea or behavior or mode of dress to spread around the world. An ethos, an expectancy, even a mystique, evolves of what an "in" adolescent should do and believe. I have visited schools in rural New Hampshire, suburban Texas, metropolitan Chicago, and the backwoods of British Columbia. The students read the same "in" authors, assert the same slogans and opinions, wear the same pins, and talk the same language, whether about pot or sex or authority. We have a truly national but homogenized and conforming culture nowadays in which the real educators of our adolescents' values are our Dylans and Jaggers. The persistent attack on convention, tradition, and the authority of those over thirty leaves a vacuum into which our charismatic hard-rock anti-heroes stride.

Because most of us do not understand the hidden needs of our students or the effects that the mass media and their peer culture have upon them, we institute innovations in our schools that only accentuate the alienation of students. Have we educators asked ourselves just what is our responsibility for the increasing boredom, social

[3] U. Bronfenbrenner, "The Split Society: Children versus Adults," *Cornell Alumnus News* (September 1968).

alienation, accentuated intellectual narcissism, and indiscriminate repudiation of tradition?

THE EFFECTS OF THE SCHOOLS

The advent of Sputnik, James Conant's recommendations, and collegiate competition profoundly affected the direction and structure of our school system. One principal effect was the improvement of the academic quality of our schools. Academic excellence became the rallying slogan and sole criterion against which the quality of the school was to be judged. Human excellence,[4] the historic goal of all major educational philosophers since Socrates, was eclipsed. Central to academic improvement was the belief that excellence required a major structural change in the size of the school. To provide comprehensive education that included diverse and specialized courses, better facilities, and guidance services, many states mandated the consolidation of small schools into large schools. In Pennsylvania, for example, small high schools of 400–600 students that unquestionably offered high-quality education were forced to merge to create high schools of several thousand students.

What has been the effect of such large, superbly equipped schools upon their students? First, there is remarkably little evidence that the alleged benefits of a large school, like better science facilities or more language courses, make any noticeable contribution to any educational outcome.[5] Neither the school's holding power, students' scholastic achievement, subsequent performance in college, satisfaction with their school experience, nor students' self-esteem and competence have been improved significantly.[6] Second, recent evidence suggests that the crucial educational determinants of a student's development are the humanistic climate or atmosphere of the school, the student's sense of participant involvement, and the student's identification with the purposes of the faculty.[7] Third, there seems to be an inverse relation between the school's size and any of these atmospheric and motivational determinants.[8] That is, the larger the school, the more impersonal and bureaucratic its atmosphere becomes, the less students are involved in activities, and the less they identify with the academic purposes of the faculty. Fourth, in contrast to so much educational research that frequently produces contradictory results, the evidence about the psychological effects of a large school is impressively consistent. For example, it is clear that as a school grows, the number of its extracurricular organizations does not increase proportionately. Students in large schools participate in fewer activities and hold fewer positions of leadership and responsibility than students in smaller schools. They encounter their friends less often and have less contact with the adults of their school.[9] There is a direct relation between the size of the school and the frequency of cheating by its students. Interestingly, students in large schools take more specialized courses and so do not have the same intellectual breadth as do students in smaller schools. Students in large schools tend to be more competitive and develop a narrower conception of their own worth. Teachers in large schools do not talk about students with other teachers as frequently; they give less personal help. Their faculty meetings are concerned more with administrative than with educational policy questions. Finally, guidance personnel are found to be less effective in large schools, primarily because they do not know their students within the full context of their activities in the school.[10]

The evidence is highly suggestive that we educators have misidentified the crucial determinants of a student's growth. Our singular pursuit of aca-

---

[4] I have tried to define this vague goal more precisely in *Growing Up in College.*

[5] J. S. Coleman, *Equality of Educational Opportunity* (Washington, D.C.: Office of Education, 1966); A. W. Tamminen and G. D. Miller *Guidance Programs and Their Impact on Students* (Saint Paul Office of Education and Pupil Personnel Services Section, Minnesota Department of Education, 1968).

[6] Tamminen and Miller.

[7] Coleman; Tamminen and Miller; Heath, *Growing Up in College.*

[8] Tamminen and Miller; Heath, *Growing Up in College;* R. G. Barker and P. V. Gump, *Big School, Small School: High School Size and Student Behavior* (Stanford, Calif.: Stanford University Press, 1964); A. Chickering, *Project on Student Development at Selected Small Colleges,* National Institute of Mental Health, 3d Annual Report (Chevy Chase, Md.: National Institute of Mental Health, 1968).

[9] D. H. Heath, "School Size: The Effect on Adjustment and Social Contact of High School Seniors" (in preparation).

[10] Tamminen and Miller.

demic excellence, defined by narrow academic considerations, may have improved the academic preparation of some students but may also have narrowed their sense of competence, limited their self-esteem, and made increasing numbers of them closed to subsequent intellectual growth.[11] Our large schools with their associated impersonality, rigidities, and bureaucratic, frequently authoritarian atmospheres fail to provide the opportunities for young persons to know many other persons well and to be known in any more than a few roles within the school. The large school is, indeed, a "system" and does become the model of the Establishment against which to develop antisystem and, perhaps, by extension, antisocietal attitudes. The large school is the one system young people *do* know well. Obviously, many other characteristics of a school may also contribute to the student's estrangement from his own emotional life, from other students, and from his traditional sources of values, like democratic assumptions. Authoritarian attitudes of teachers; domination of teachers in the classroom; the lecture style of dispensing information; the restriction of the teacher to a specialty, particularly in the elementary school where no one person now knows a child all the way around as a person; accelerated courses, particularly in the sciences; the failure of the schools to deal with value conflicts; and a host of other factors may also fuel the trend toward greater boredom, belonginglessness, and purposelessness.

[11] D. H. Heath, "Better Educated: Less Educable?" in *The Time Has Come Today,* ed. S. Letter (New York: Teachers College Press, in press).

How shall we react to the growing educational crises we face, to the confusion and gloom that pervade faculty meetings, to the resignation that seems to be on the rise? We could seize the opportunity that despair always presents to begin to reorder our educational priorities. We could reaffirm our historic commitment to the goal of promoting maturing and educability. If human excellence is our commitment, then we will not use academic achievement, frequently too narrowly defined, as the only measure of the effectiveness of our schools. We will not introduce new educational technologies like television or computer-assisted instruction solely on the basis of their claims that they will increase the amount of information learned; we will also ask what their emotionally inhibiting and impersonalizing effects might be. We will not build larger schools or educational parks and fail to assess their effects on the quality of our students' personal relationships, their sense of belonging to the school, and their feelings of self-worth. We will not continue to lecture at our students, reinforce their pervasive passivity and suppress their spontaneity, and rob them of the opportunity to learn to initiate and direct their own educational growth. I would urge all educators to consider the effects of what they do within the context of our youths' needs to become more accepting of their own emotional needs, more open, trusting, and skillful in their relations with others, and more aware of how to develop mature values. Apathy, loneliness, and meaninglessness challenge us to develop an educational environment that helps each youth to develop more integratively and so more humanly.

Chapter 11: Suggested Additional Readings

Anti-American generation. *Trans-action,* 1969, *48,* 6(10). This special issue concerns various forms of youth's alienation, including hippies, gangs, and deserters from military service.

BROWN, M. E. The condemnation and persecution of hippies. *Trans-action,* 1969, *6*(10), 33–46. The author sharply criticizes current means of social control, especially as they relate to hippies, and suggests that all forms of deviance have been forced into the status of heresy.

BROWN, W. N. Alienated youth. *Mental Hygiene,* 1968, *52*(3), 330–336. The author defines and identifies the various categories of alienated youth, and analyzes the causes and results of alienation.

COHEN, M., & HALE, D. *The new student life.* Boston: Beacon Press, 1967. This excellent collection of papers discusses reasons for the unrest of present-day youth. Whether factors such as poverty and living conditions may give rise to another leftist movement is discussed.

FREDENBURGH, F. A. An apologia for the hippie generation. *Mental Hygiene,* 1968, *52*(3), 341–348. The author traces historical trends which have a bearing on understanding today's youth, as well as current factors which help shape their behavior. In spite of, or to a large extent because of, its malaise, the current generation offers hope.

GOTTLIEB, D. Poor youth: A study in forced alienation. *Journal of Social Issues,* 1969, *25*(2), 91–119. The poor youth "want in but can't make it." They lack resources for goal attainment.

GOULD, L. J. Conformity and marginality: Two faces of alienation. *Journal of Social Issues,* 1969, *25*(2), 39–63. In his study of male undergraduates, Gould discovered an alienation syndrome, or a generalized distrust of others, a rejection of socially approved rules of interpersonal conduct, social introversion, psychic and somatic complaints, depression, and yeasaying, as well as impulse control and ambivalence.

HENDERSON, G. Opportunity and alienation in public schools. *Teachers College Record,* 1967, *69*(2), 151–157. The problem of alienation is defined and related to the programs of the schools. Recommendations are made for curtailing the problems of student alienation.

JOHNSON, J. J. The hippy as a developmental task. *Adolescence,* 1969, *4*(13), 35–42. This brief, perceptive essay portrays the hippie stage in terms of normal adolescent needs. The focus is on understanding hippie behavior as a natural outgrowth of the situation in which many adolescents find themselves.

KARR, S. D., & DENT, O. B. In search of meaning. The generalized rebellion of the hippie. *Adolescence,* 1970, *5*(18), 187–195. The author distinguishes between the hippie-prone, or drop-out from society, and the activitists. The hippie rejects middle-class values and finds in the hippie group a vehicle for rebellion and search for meaning.

KENISTON, K.   *The uncommitted: Alienated youth in American society.* New York: Harcourt, Brace and World, 1965. Keniston's thesis is that American society encourages the alienation of middle-class boys and that boys who are vulnerable become alienated. The first part of the book reports an intensive study of twelve Harvard students; the second offers an analysis of American life with emphasis on the writings of Parsons, Erikson, and Riesman.

KULIK, J. A, STEIN, K. B., & SARBIN, T. R.   Dimensions and patterns of adolescent antisocial behavior. *Journal of Consulting and Clinical Psychology,* 1968, *32*(4), 375–382. Delinquent and non-delinquent boys were found to differ significantly on a self-report checklist of antisocial activities. On the basis of these data, the delinquent boys were divided into four empirical types, who in turn differed in racial composition and other social and personal variables.

NEWMAN, C.   The making of a hippie. *American Journal of Psychotherapy,* 1969, *23*(3), 463–472. This article reports psychotherapeutic observations of a seventeen-year-old boy who was in the process of becoming a hippie. Changes in his behavior and fantasy life are evaluated.

PITTS, J.   The counter culture. *Dissent,* June 1971, 216–229. The author analyzes and evaluates four major cultural forms in the hippie culture: the commune, the drug culture, the music culture, and the political youth movement.

POLK, K.   A reassessment of middle-class delinquency. *Youth and Society,* 1971, *2*(3), 333–353. On the basis of relevant research and his own studies, Polk concludes that middle-class delinquency does not differ in context or style from working-class delinquency.

PROPPER, M. M., & CLARK, E. T.   Alienation: Another dimension of underachievement. *The Journal of Psychology,* 1970, *75,* 13–18. This study related the various levels of academic achievement to the conceptualization of alienation. The dimensions of Davids' alienation syndrome, pessimism, distrust, anxiety, egocentricity, and resentment significantly distinguished high from low academic achievement of upper-middle-class male adolescents.

RODE, A.   Perceptions of parental behavior among alienated adolescents. *Adolescence,* 1971, *6*(21), 19–38. After reviewing relevant literature, the author describes a study among high school youths, grades 10 to 12, which differentiated the attitudes of alienated and non-alienated individuals toward their parents.

ROSZAK, T.   *The making of a counter culture: Reflections on the technocratic society and its youthful opposition.* New York: Doubleday, 1969. "Technocracy" is critically analyzed and its young people are perceived as the only serious opposition to the consolidation of the military-expert complex. "Technocracy's children" have not been content to oppose, but have been trying, against all odds, to build enclaves of peace and usefulness within its mad walls. Drugs, prophetic poetry, and life styles represent fragile attempts to recover the self and redeem the world.

SHELLOW, R., SCHAMP, J. R., LIEBOW, E., & UNGER, E.   Suburban runaways of the 1960's. *Monographs of the Society for Research in Child Development,* 1967, *32,* 28–33. An investigation of youths, aged 10 to 17, who had run away from home, revealed only a small minority to be disturbed. The majority simply sought to escape unpleasant pressures.

SMITH, D. E., & STERNFIELD, J.   The hippie communal movement: Effcts on child birth and development. *American Journal of Orthopsychiatry,* 1970, *40*(3), 527–530. The author describes the characteristics of the hippie psychedelic communes and speculates about their future.

WARNER, R. W. JR., & HANSEN, J. C.   Alienated youth: The counselor's task. *Personnel and Guidance Journal,* 1970, *48,* 443–448. To cope with the problem of youth's alienation, the writers suggest a thorough examination of the schools' goals and structure.

12

Dating

Dating is not to be confused with courtship, though both are integral aspects of heterosexual relationships in the Western world. Dating is present-oriented and can be an end in itself, without commitment to a lasting bond or affiliation, while courtship is adult-oriented, with marriage as its goal. In the recent past, research on the subject of dating usually was the province of sociologists; but it has now become apparent to many psychologists that dating is very significant in the personal and psychological development of youth, and that an analysis of the practice can help us understand youth both as individuals and as an age group.

Adolescents live in a world largely insulated from adults, and the adult observer may be entirely ignorant of the dater's world. The adult assumes that the same rules of the dating game apply as did in his own youth; but do they? Apparently, modifications in dating do occur, often reflecting larger sociocultural change. Today, girls play a more aggressive, and boys a more defensive, role than formerly. Perhaps this change helps account for the increased incidence of going steady, pinning, short engagements, and early marriages among contemporary youth.

Various factors affect teenagers' dating patterns, and parental influence is particularly important. For example, the adolescent who feels unusually obligated to his parents dates less often than one who does not share this feeling. Girls date at an earlier age than boys do, and marriage-oriented adolescents date more frequently than career-directed ones. There is also a minority of boys and girls who do not date, for various reasons. In one study (Wittman, 1971), approximately 26 percent of the males and 24 percent of the females of dating age in a rural school had not started dating, while in an urban school in the same area 16 percent of each sex were nondaters. Whether or not these nondaters are considered as being rejected by their peers depends upon the local dating practices.

Critics of dating differ in their evaluation of it. Dating is considered by some as wasting time that could better be spent at other pursuits. The practice is criticized as being too expensive; boys may drop out of school and go to work in order to finance their dates. Moreover, adolescents are considered too immature to handle the intense sexual feelings aroused on dates. In contrast, defenders of the practice claim that dating constitutes a desirable preparation for marriage. In the dating situation, adolescents receive heterosexual experience of a more intimate nature than is provided in larger social groups. According to Davan (1969), the young adolescent who does not date will lack adequate experience, in later years, for adjusting to varied personalities and for making frank expressions of friendship. Such a youth either goes through a delayed period of dating or else enters marriage without the dating experience which ordinarily constitutes part of the marital-preparation process in the United States.

Dating is especially crucial for the female. The male's adult role is firmly anchored in his occupation, but the dominant female role is still that of housewife and mother. The girl's adult security depends largely on her relationship to the particular man she marries, and dating therefore becomes a deadly serious business for her. In general, women have higher aspirations for their dating partners than do men (Coombs & Kenkel, 1966).

Considerable controversy rages over the issue of whether "going steady" should be encouraged or deplored. The "going steady" system is a social–erotic relationship that may be considered a limited-period engagement. However, it differs from the true engagement in this respect: the engagement, at least traditionally, indicates a publicly recognized social relationship with controlled erotic impulses and an implicit intent of getting married. By contrast, the going-steady relationship in principle excludes sexual relations but makes no claim on the ultimate decision to marry (Rosenmayr, 1968).

When unchaperoned dating first gained headway in the early part of the twentieth century, dating partners were changed more often than today. By World War II, steady dating had taken hold, and today most students have had such an experience. Nevertheless, as Wittman (1971) points out, teenagers should not be treated as a homogeneous quality in this respect. While most teenagers apparently sometimes go steady, students at two Kentucky high schools studied by Wittman were exceptions. These boys and girls dated many individuals, and when they did go steady, it was simply for companionship, not for status or prestige.

Authorities disagree sharply in evaluating the pros and cons of steady dating. The defenders of the practice argue that while casual dating encourages shallow relationships, steady dating permits the simultaneous development of appropriate sexual behavior and mutual affection which is important training for a later marital relationship. Also, adolescents gain security from having a sure date for peer-group functions, and the social graces are more easily acquired in the company of a regular partner. Finally, since permissiveness-with-affection is an accepted current social pattern, the girl who goes steady may have sexual experience without jeopardizing her reputation.

Opponents of steady dating say that teenagers need a more varied heterosexual experience. Before they settle down in marriage they should learn to relate to various types of the other sex. Also, regular dating often merges prematurely into courtship. Moreover, the isolation granted teen daters projects them into situations they are too immature to control. Steady daters, in particular, are likely to risk premarital sex experience by rationalizing that they are in love.

Criticism of the going-steady practice is not confined to adults. In one study, Martinson (1968) concluded that as youth grow older they look on going steady in high school as having been a mistake. Also, on looking back, young adults realize that their experiments with sexual intercourse were foolhardy, for if a pregnancy had resulted, the consequences would have been very serious. Martinson also found that youths are at once confused and searching in their sexual attitudes and they need help to attain a healthy, mature sexuality.

Still other studies relate dating to other areas of adjustment, without specifically attempting to evaluate the practice as good or bad. On the basis of data obtained from a group of women while they were in college and again twelve years later, Klemer (1971) tentatively concluded that women with high self-esteem dated more often but went steady less often in college than did their peers with lower self-regard. Both those individuals with very high and very low self-esteem tended to be less happily married. While it is easy to conjecture about the causes of this phenomenon, the lack of data prevents hard and fast conclusions.

How promiscuous are teenagers on dates? It is commonly assumed that teenagers are a wild lot sexually, but Reiss (1961) disagrees. The coitus rate for females doubles between the ages of 20 and 25. On the basis of available evidence, notes Reiss, teenagers show greater conservatism and responsibility in sexual codes and behavior than is commonly believed.

Other questions about dating are, How early should parents permit dating? To what extent should parents regulate choice of dating partners? What sex standards should prevail on dates? Where can adolescents gain healthy guidelines for their dating behaviors? So far, researchers have failed adequately to answer these questions. Especially needed are phenomenological studies of what dating means for individual adolescents' development.

In the first of the following articles, McDaniel discusses the girl's dating role and her reasons for dating. He considers the basic issues of socialization involved and helps to place the practice of dating in proper perspective in relation to the whole growing-up process. In the second selection, Weiss presents a picture of interracial dating between Caucasian and Chinese youth.

REFERENCES

COOMBS, R. H., & KENKEL, W. F.   Sex differences in dating aspirations and satisfaction with computer-selected partners. *Journal of Marriage and the Family*, 1966, *28*(1), 62–66.

DAVAN, R. S.   *The American family*. New York: Crowell, 1969.

KLEMER, R. H.   Self esteem and college dating experience as factors in mate selection and marital happiness: A longitudinal study. *Journal of Marriage and the Family*, 1971, *33*(1), 183–187.

MARTINSON, F. M.   Sexual knowledge, values, and behavior patterns of adolescents. *Child Welfare*, 1968, *47*(7), 405–410, 426.

REISS, I. L.   Sexual codes in teenage culture. In J. Bernard (Ed.), *Teenage culture*.

Philadelphia: The American Academy of Political Science, November 1961 *338,* 53–62.

ROSENMAYR, L.   Towards an interview of youth's sociology, *International Social Science Journal,* 1968, *20*(2), 286–315.

WITTMAN, J. S., JR.   Dating patterns of rural and urban Kentucky teenagers. *Family Coordinator,* 1971, *20*(1), 63–66.

Dating Roles and Reasons for Dating

CLYDE O. McDANIEL, JR.

This article reports the results of a study designed to explore the relationship between the college girl's dating role and her reasons for dating.

There is a large inconsistency within the literature on female dating behavior. On the one hand, the female is characterized as assertive and unmindful of the marriage-oriented reasons for dating.[1] Bowman declares that

> The woman plays a role and has a vital part in making choices and in developing the [dating] relationship. . . . There are indications that women are losing their traditional reserve and are more direct and aggressive in their approach to men.[2]

Herman's 1955 study shows that dating represents, for many girls, merely doing as others do

and a means for lessening competition.[3] He labels this type of dating "dalliance."

On the other hand, the female is characterized as receptive and very much aware of the marriage-oriented reasons for dating.[4] Tyler declares that

> [While dating] women assume the role of the pursued. Women respond favorably to pursuit by men. . . . It is worth keeping in mind that there is a feminine as well as a masculine role in dating. We have not yet reached the stage where both sexes widely accept the principle of 'dutch dating'. An open display of aggression on the part of a woman makes men avoid her.[5]

Cameron and Kenkel's 1960 study shows that 70 percent of the students in their sample were thinking of marriage,[6] and Hewitt's 1958 study

This paper is based on the author's doctoral dissertation, "Relationships between Female Dating Roles and Reasons for Dating" (unpublished Ph.D. dissertation, University of Pittsburgh, 1967). The author is grateful for the advice of Robert W. Avery, Jiri Nehnevajsa, Morris Berkowitz, Ray Elling, Howard Rowland, and Jacquelyn A. Alford in preparing the dissertation. Data for the study were gathered from December, 1966, through February, 1967.

[1] An aggressive girl is one who takes the initiative or acts as aggressor in most dating activities.

[2] Henry A. Bowman, *Marriage for Moderns* (New York: McGraw Hill Book Company, Inc., 1960), pp. 9 and 128.

[3] Robert D. Herman, "The Going Steady Complex: A Re-Examination," *Marriage and Family Living*, 17 (1955), pp. 92–98.

[4] A receptive girl is one who is responsive in most dating activities to male initiative.

[5] Leona E. Tyler, *The Psychology of Human Differences* (2nd ed.; New York: Appleton-Century-Crofts, Inc., 1956), p. 310.

[6] William J. Cameron and William F. Kenkel, "High School Dating: A Study in Variation," *Marriage and Family Living*, 22 (1960), pp. 74–76.

C. O. McDaniel, Jr., "Dating roles and reasons for dating," *Journal of Marriage and the Family*, February 1969, 31(1); 97–107. By permission of the author, reprinted from the *Journal of Marriage and the Family*.

shows that most of the traits his sample desired in a date were also desired in a marriage partner.[7]

One of the reasons for such inconsistence is the failure, on the part of current dating theorists, to specify which stage of courtship is being used as a reference point. While studies have been done to assert that courtship is a progressive phenomenon and that girls do assume different roles for different reasons, no one has related stages and reasons for dating, or stages and dating role. This study was aimed at answering a set of questions which inquire about some of the relationships between the female's role in dating and her reasons for dating (in each stage of courtship). Since these questions also inquire about the conditions under which the relationships obtain, their answers aid in placing dating–courtship firmly within the boundaries of socialization.

This study was designed essentially to discover what impact stages of courtship have on the relationship between female dating role and reasons for dating by answering the following specific questions:

1. In what sequence do stages of courtship occur?[8]
2. What is the relationship between stages of courtship and dating roles?[9]
3. What other factors influence dating roles?[10]
4. What is the relationship between stages of courtship and reasons for dating?[11]
5. What is the relationship between dating roles and reasons for dating?
6. Is a penalty paid by girls if their dating roles

do not change as they move through the stages of courtship?
7. What impact do the perceptions of males have on facilitating change in female dating behavior?

Methodology

Survey methodology was employed to execute the study. Of the 600 questionnaires which were distributed to undergraduate students at the University of Pittsburgh, 396 were returned from single females while 181 were returned from single males.

Determining adequate sample sizes and selecting respondents were not done arbitrarily. In order to determine the sample size for single females the author used the following criterion as a guideline: select a sample size which is practical and manageable and yet which is large enough to allow for subgroup analyses. This criterion was buffered by the awareness that the aim of the study was not to generalize to any particular population, but to test relationships. The author consequently decided on a sample size of 400. Since the major intent of the study was to discover the impact of stages of courtship (a trichotomized variable) on the relationships between two sets of dichotomized variables—role behavior (assertiveness and receptivity) and reasons for dating (recreation, mate selection, and anticipatory socialization)—a sample size of 400 allowed the possibility of simultaneously analyzing these relationships. Such a cross-tabulation scheme would result in forty-eight subgroups with a chance possibility of eight to nine cases in each.

In order to place female "subjects" on a sample list, simple random sampling was employed: random sampling, not for the purpose of facilitating accurate generalization to the parent population, but for the purpose of making sure all categories in the antecedent and independent variables would be substantially represented. Since there were about 5,000 single dormitory females in the population from which the sample of 400 was to be drawn, from a list of all the single females in the population, every eighth one was designated as a respondent for the study.

[7] Lester Hewitt, "Student Perceptions of Traits Desired," *Marriage and Family Living*, 20 (1958), pp. 344–349.

[8] Only three stages of courtship were used in this study: random dating, going steady, and pinned/engaged.

[9] Three types of dating roles were used in this study: assertive, assertive–receptive, and receptive. The assertive–receptive role type is manifest when the girl alternates about evenly between assertiveness and receptivity.

[10] Other factors used in this study were three types of reference sources (original family, peer group, and personal–boyfriend), degree of dissatisfaction with dating role, commitment to boyfriend, and complementarity of girl's and boyfriend's personality traits.

[11] Three reasons for dating were used in this study: recreation, mate selection, and anticipatory socialization (training to become good marriage mates).

A sample size of 200 for single males was arrived at in much the same way. Since there were 9,000 single male students at the University from which a sample of 200 was to be drawn, from a list of all the single male students, every forty-fifth one was designated as a respondent. The reason for using the smaller sample was to make simple comparative analyses of females who were actually dating (and had not completed progress through the courtship system) with males' perceptions of how females should act while dating. The smaller sample facilitated the testing of implicit hypotheses such as the following: "dating males, at certain stages of courtship, expect their girl friends to be assertive (or receptive)."

Summarily, the entire sample can be described in a few statements. It was composed predominantly of young single female students. Further, being undergraduates, they were principally freshmen and sophomores. They were overwhelmingly democratic, upper middle-class, and white. Most of them began dating at or around junior-high-school age. The girls, in a typical middle-class fashion, were somewhat sensitive about revealing their ages or anything connected with age. Most of them had had the experience of the first two stages of courtship—random dating and going steady—but few had been pinned or engaged. Finally, most of the sample presently were either random dating or going steady.

It was impractical to observe directly the behavior which constituted the data for this study. However, indirect observation was practical. Among the many methods available which would facilitate indirect observation, the self-administered questionnaire seemed most appropriate. The foregoing was especially true because the self-administered questionnaire lent itself to simultaneously questioning members of the respondent group with a minimum of inter-action among them. The method, which did not require an interviewer because each respondent read the questions herself (himself) and filled in her (his) own answers, took the following form: After each of the potential respondents had been identified and placed on a sample list, each of them was contacted via campus mail. Upon such contact, they were notified that they had been selected and were asked to be available on a specified date in order to fill in the questionnaires. Then, with the aid of the Dean of Men, and Dean of Women, and relevant dormitory heads, the questionnaires were distributed and promptly returned via campus mail.

The contents of the questionnaire were based on a list of items which are characteristic of dating behavior. These were categorized and judiciously assigned to each variable (see the next section for conceptual and operational definitions of each variable). Where feasible, the items were incorporated in the critical-incident technique form.[12] Furthermore, most of the questions incorporating the items were either phrased normatively or hypothetically in order to allow the respondents to answer the questions freely and nonthreateningly.[13] The items came from published results of research and from observations of the author and referred to both attitudinal sets and to behavior, such as engaging in sex. In assigning items to variables, the author employed the Guttman Scalogram model. Adherence to this measurement model made it possible to construe each variable along a unidimensional scale and to make no measurement assumptions which exceeded ordinality.

The questionnaire was pretested with small samples of graduate and undergraduate students at the New Kensington branch of the University of Pennsylvania, at Carnegie Institute of Technology, and at Chatham College. In analyzing the data, all zero-order relationships were assessed through the use of Spearman's Rho along with a conservative level of significance (.05). All higher-than-zero-order relationships were assessed through the use of elaboration and percentaging with no level of significance being chosen. That is, where it was necessary to tease out subgroup relationships, percents were employed with modal differences being indications of the patterns of relationships. One essential feature of elaboration

[12] John C. Flanagan, *The Critical Incident Technique* (Pittsburgh: The American Institutes for Research, July, 1954).
[13] There is clear evidence that expressed value positions do provide insight into behavior. See, for example, Winston Ehrmann, *Premarital Dating Behavior* (New York: Henry Holt and Co., 1959), pp. 213–276. In this section of his book, Ehrmann provides convincing evidence that girls' most intimate courtship behavior correlates quite well with their expressed personal codes about intimate courtship behavior.

is that it allows no single hypothesis to be viewed independently of others. Instead, there is a series of hypotheses which must be looked at in combination. Consequently, the tactic here was to captalize on *patterns* of percentage differences.

Data Analysis and Discussion

1. STAGES OF COURTSHIP

Since it was postulated that significant changes take place among females within certain stages of courtship, it was necessary to hypothesize the sequence in which the changes were expected to occur. Dating is known to manifest itself in at least three stages: random dating, going steady, and pinned/engaged. Random dating occurs when the female is dating but not with any special person; going steady occurs when she is dating a special person but has not made any commitment to marry; and being pinned/engaged occurs when she is dating a special person and has made a commitment to marry.

Hypothesis I: It was expected that these three stages were progressive, i.e., that girls randomly date before they go steady, and randomly date and go steady before they become pinned/ engaged.

The rationale for the progression is based on the assumption that girls must scout around a bit before they learn that society expects them to choose special persons who are suitable for marriage mates. When they find such persons, they must test their compatibility by dating them steadily. If compatibility cannot be attained, the girls revert back to random dating, and the process starts again. If and when compatibility is attained, the girls commit themselves to marriage and become engaged.

In order to discover whether or not occupancy in one stage of courtship presupposes occupancy in other stages, the three stages were incorporated as items in the questionnaire. Table I shows that, among single females, all the items scaled and yielded a very high Coefficient of Reproducibility (.972) and Minimal Marginal Reproducibility (.820). In the order of their decreasing attractiveness, the stages arranged themselves in

Table 1. Stages of Courtship Participated in

Scale Scores		Single Females	
		F	%
Random dating, going steady, engaged	1	103	26
Random dating, going steady	2	186	47
Random dating	3	107	27
Total		396	100

Coefficient of Reproducibility = .972; Minimal Marginal Responsibility = .820; no non-scalable questions.

the following manner: (1) random dating (2) going steady, and (3) pinned/engaged. One can be sure, with such a high Coefficient of Reproducibility, that if a girl is going steady, she has random dated; and if she is pinned/engaged, she has random dated and gone steady; and any variable which correlates fairly well with stages of courtship participated in can, to that extent, be used in the same manner in which the latter can be used. While it must be remembered that stage of courtship participated in is not syonymous with present stage of courtship, it appears that Hypothesis I was not disconfirmed.

2. ROLE BEHAVIOR

Robert Winch, *et al.,* while empirically elaborating the Winch theory of the complementarity of needs in mate selection, suggested an excellent analytical role scheme which was used in assessing role behavior in this study.[14] The scheme was suggested when, through cluster analysis, Winch and his associates arrived at the general hypothesis that "an important dimension of dating for both sexes is the assertive–receptive dimension."[15] They found, on the one hand, that the *assertive* dater was achievement–oriented,

[14]Robert F. Winch, Thomas Ktsanes, and Virginia Ktsanes, "Empirical Elaboration of the Theory of Complementary Needs in Mate Selection," *Journal of Abnormal and Social Psychology, 51* (1955), pp. 508–518.

[15]*Ibid.,* p. 513.

autonomous, dominant, hostile, a status aspirant, and a status striver; they found, on the other hand, that the *receptive* dater was abasive, deferential, succorous, prone to vicariousness, an approacher, and anxious.[16] The behavioral indicants of these were used in this study as assertive and receptive roles respectively.[17] The assertive-receptive role was a combination.

Although eighteen items were included in the questionnaire to measure assertiveness, only nine scaled such that an acceptable Coefficient of Reproducibility (.90) and Minimal Marginal Reproducibility (.76) were produced. The items which scaled acceptably—in the order of their decreasing attractiveness—were the ones dealing with girl's (1) always being in control on dates, (2) wishing to marry only a potential success, (3) not being dependent on her date, (4) reprimanding her date for misbehavior, (5) being cautious on dates, (6) staying at least one step ahead of her date, (7) wishing to stay at least one step ahead of her date, (8) subtly manipulating her date, and (9) making all the decisions on dates.

As was the case in measuring assertiveness, eighteen items were used to measure receptivity. Again, in order to achieve an acceptable Coeffi-

[16] *Ibid.*, pp. 509–513. Winch and his associates defined each need (n) and each trait (t) behaviorally as follows: a. *achievement* (n)—to work diligently to create something and/or to emulate others; b. *autonomy* (n)—to get rid of constraint of other persons or to be unattached and independent; c. *dominance* (n)—to influence and control the behavior of others; d. *hostility* (n)—to fight, injure, or kill others; e. *status aspiration* (n)—to desire a socioeconomic status considerably higher than one has; f. *status striving* (n)—to work diligently to alter one's socioeconomic status; g. *abasement* (n)—to accept or invite blame, criticism, or punishment or to blame or harm the self; h. *deference* (n)—to admire and praise another; i. *succorance* (n)—to help sympathetically; to nurse, to love, to protect, to indulge; j. *vicariousness* (t)—the gratification of a need derived from the perception that another person is deriving gratification; k. *approach* (n)—to draw near and enjoy interaction with another person or persons; and l. *anxiety* (n)—fear, conscious or unconscious, of harm or misfortune arising from the hostility of others and/or social reactions to one's behavior.

[17] From a strict role standpoint, these two concepts may appear to be polar extremes of a single continuum and thus analytically inseparable. From a behavioral and empirical standpoint, however, the two concepts comprise two separate continua, because a given act can only be either assertive or receptive. Since a role is manifest by acts, by modal definition it may be either of the three role types.

cient of Reproducibility (.90) and an acceptable Minimal Marginal Reproducibility (.819), nine of the items had to be discarded. The items which conformed to an acceptable scale—in the order of their decreasing attractiveness—were those dealing with a girl's (1) rejoicing when her date rejoices, (2) enjoying being near her date, (3) admiring her date, (4) wanting to be tenderly cared for by her date, (5) dressing to suit her date, (6) being disturbed if her date is disturbed with her, (7) allowing her date to make the decisions on dates, (8) accepting her date's criticisms, and (9) never going stag to a party.

Hypothesis II: It was expected that the girls in this study would be assertive in the first stage of courtship, assertive–receptive in the second stage, and receptive in the last stage.

The rationale for such a progression is as follows: Girls, in the early stage of courtship are inexperienced and unsophisticated with regard to appropriate role behavior. They are assertive initially because they view their right to act as aggressors in social interaction as identical with boys' right to act as aggressors. In heterosexual interaction on dates, however, they are made aware of their inappropriate role behavior through negative reinforcement from boys. In this way, they learn that receptivity is more frequently approved than assertiveness. At the same time, they are beginning to place a premium on attaining a mate. Both of these are seen as significant features in the definition of their adult status. They resort to receptivity, then, because it enables them to obtain a mate, and because it is consistent with their adult status definition.

To test Hypothesis II, present stage of courtship was related to assertiveness and to receptivity. The first stage, of course, is random dating and was assigned a lower weight than the later stages—going steady and pinned/engaged.

The first column in Table 2 shows that (1) *there is a tendency for girls in the early stage of courtship to be assertive,* and (2) *there is a tendency for girls in the later stages of the courtship to be receptive.* Although the correlations are small, they are significant, indicating that a fairly high degree of confidence can be placed in them. Since stages of courtship scale, there is reason to believe that girls in the early stage of

Table 2. The Relationships among Other Factors and Assertiveness, Receptivity among Single Females

Role Behavior	Stages of Courtship	Other Factors						
		Original Family Orientation	Peer-Group Orientation	Personal Orientation	Degree of Dissatisfaction	Commit-ment to Date	Traits Desired in a Date	Actual Traits of Date
Assertive	−.35	.13	.18	−.12	––	.20	−.16	.14
Receptive	.24	.26	.12	.12	.23	.29	−.13	.17

N = 396, P ≤ .05.

courtship approach heterosexual relationships with the belief that they have just as much right, power, and authority as boys. Their immediate goal is to initiate cross-sexual relationships, and the data indicate that they do so with straight-forwardness. However, something happens between early dating and later dating, because female role behavior tends to shift toward receptivity. Whatever the influence is, it is difficult to say, but an attempt is made in the succeeding sections to tease out much of it.

It is interesting to note that the two correlations in the first column of Table 2 differ not only in direction (or sign) but also in magnitude. This seems to imply that there is a stronger tendency for girls to be assertive in the first stage than there is for them to be receptive in the last stage, or that fewer girls have changed to receptivity in the later stages. The differences in the sizes of the correlations are probably due to the fact that those girls who have not changed cluster in the second, or transitional, stage of courtship—going steady— wherein they are becoming receptive while not actually relinquishing assertiveness. If this is true, it can be said that the girls in the second stage of courtship are assertive–receptive. Furthermore, it means that a certain amount of credence is accorded to Hypothesis II.

3. THE INFLUENCE OF REFERENCE SYSTEMS, DEGREE OF DISSATISFACTION, COMMITMENT, AND COMPLEMENTARITY ON ROLE BEHAVIOR[18]

[18] *Original-family orientation*—From among the ten items used to measure the extent of orientation to the original family, only one proved non-scalable. The ten items were hypothetical activities wherein the respondents were asked to indicate how they would be affected if their parents (or parent substitutes) disapproved of their participation in the activities. The nine remaining items yielded a Coefficient of Reproducibility of .911 and a Minimal Marginal Reproducibility of .669. The nine items—arranged in the order of their decreasing attractiveness—were the ones concerning the respondents' (1) becoming engaged, (2) dating a particular person, (3) dating, (4) petting on dates, (5) going to the movies with a date, (6) attending a football or basketball game with a date, (7) talking to strange boys, (8) studying alone with a boy, and (9) having lunch with a boy.

Peer Orientation—The extent of peer-group orientation was measured by asking respondents to indicate how they would be affected if their age-association sex group (peer group) disapproved of their participation in the same ten hypothetical activities used in measuring the extent of original-family orientation. Again, only one item proved non-scalable. In this case, the Coefficient of Reproducibility was .925 and the Minimal Marginal Reproducibility was .753. The nine scalable items—in the order of their decreasing impact on the respondents assuming their peer groups' disapproval—were the ones concerning their (1) becoming engaged, (2) dating a particular person, (3) dating, (4) petting on dates, (5) talking to strange boys, (6) going to the movies with a date, (7) attending a football or basketball game with a date, (8) having lunch with a boy, and (9) studying alone with a boy.

Personal Orientation—Ten items were used to measure the extent to which the respondents evaluate and determine their own dating behavior. All of the items scaled except two. With a Coefficient of Reproducibility of .915 and a Minimal Margin Reproducibility of .832, the eight scalable items—in the order of their decreasing attractiveness—were concerned with whether the respondents (1) would prefer to be the sole determinator of whether or not to pet on dates, (2) would enjoy having interesting experiences on dates in spite of whether or not they could be related to friends, (3) would prefer not to discuss with friends the fact of their having sexual intercourse on dates, (4) would disregard her friends' opinions if she wished to hold hands on dates, (5) would prefer to be the sole determiner of whether her dating conduct was rewarding to her, (6) would prefer not to have her friends around when she is with her date, (7) would rather go to the movies alone with her date,

Many other factors can be hypothesized to account for the girls' being assertive in the first stage of courtship and receptive in the last stage. The author thought that if some of these other

and (8) would prefer going to games alone with her date.

The Extent of Satisfaction with Dating Role—Ten items were used to measure the extent of satisfaction-dissatisfaction with the dating situation. Only five of them did not scale. Those which did scale yielded a Coefficient of Reproducibility of .900 and a Minimal Marginal Reproducibility of .666. The five items included in the scale—in the order of their decreasing attractiveness—concerned whether the respondent would be disturbed if she found it necessary to (1) ask her date to talk to her when he is obviously preoccupied in conversation with someone else, (2) ask her date for another date, (3) "pay the tab" for her and her date's dinners, (4) tell her date where the two of them are to go on a date, and (5) straighten her date's tie, hat, hair, etc.

Commitment to Dating Partner—Twenty-one items were used to measure the extent of commitment to dating partner. Ten of these did not scale. With a Coefficient of Reproducibility of .918 and a Minimal Marginal Reproducibility of .774, the eleven items which did scale—in the order of their decreasing attractiveness—were those concerned with whether the respondent would comply if her dating partner wished her to (1) run an errand for him, (2) correct her general, apparently disorderly conduct, (3) raise her scholastic average, (4) travel a long distance to visit his parents, (5) help him pass a test, (6) "pay the tab" for their dinners, (7) give him expensive presents, (8) defy her parents, (9) change her religious preference, (10) change her political preference, and (11) ostracize a long-time friend.

Complementarity of Traits—Complementarity of traits was measured by combining a scale of traits desired in a date with a scale of perceived traits of respondent's date. *Traits Desired in a Date*—Ten items were used to measure traits desired in a date. These were incorporated in the questionnaire as a list of traits, and respondents were asked to indicate whether or not they desired each one in an ideal date. Five of them did not scale. Yielding a Coefficient of Reproducibility of .900 and a Minimal Marginal Reproducibility of .690, the five traits which did scale —in the order of their decreasing attractiveness— were—(1) emotional maturity, (2) stability and dependability, (3) affection, (4) industriousness, and (5) family-mindedness. *Perceived Traits of Respondent's Date*—The same ten traits used in measuring traits desired in a date were used to measure perceived traits of date. The only difference is that this time the respondents were asked to indicate whether or not they thought their dates actually possessed the traits. None of the traits proved non-scalable, and at the outset a Coefficient of Reproducibility of .900 and a Minimal Marginal Reproducibility of .730 were obtained. In the order of their decreasing attractiveness, the traits were as follows: (1) neat appearance and good manners, (2) pleasantness of disposition, (3) physical attractiveness, (4) considerateness, (5) affection, (6) industriousness, (7) poise and confidence, (8) stability and dependability, (9) emotional maturity, and (10) family-mindedness.

factors related significantly with role behavior, then confidence could be placed in the assumption that they influence assertiveness initially and receptivity later. The last seven columns in Table 2 show the relationships among some of the other factors and role behavior.

A number of facts become apparent when these columns are perused. It seems that as the girls make the shift from assertiveness to receptivity, they simultaneously become: (1) more original-family oriented, (2) less peer-group oriented, (3) much more personally oriented, (4) much more dissatisfied with their dating role (5) more committed to their dates, and (6) relatively unchanged in terms of complementarity (both assertive and receptive girls desire fewer traits in their dates than they actually get).

In view of the foregoing, it is believed that a series of events occur in the process of girls' changing from assertiveness in the first stage of courtship to receptivity in the last stage. Some of the events cause assertiveness, some of them result from assertiveness and cause receptivity, and some of them result from receptivity.

It is believed that achievement is prescribed by the peer group and the original family dominates the first stage of courtship. The girls are much more aware of peer-group norms than they are of original-family norms, but they are unaware of their own ability to prescribe the content of their dating behavior. First, the peer group demands that they initiate cross-sexual relationships; and later the original family demands that they select particular dates and exclude others. Concurrently, the girls in the first stage have not learned that they have less power than the males in initiating cross-sexual relationships, since they were socialized, in the past, on the same generational plane as the males.[19] As a result, they feel that they have just as much right and power to act as aggressors in attaining their goals—heterosexual though they may be—as the males. This causes them to be assertive in their dating behavior and to be fairly satisfied with their dating role, since it conforms with the expectations of their most important reference

---

[19] See Talcott Parsons and Robert F. Bales, *The Family, Socialization, and the Interaction Process* (Glencoe, Illinois: The Free Press, 1955).

groups (at that time) and is consistent with their past socialization.[20]

Continuing, the early daters are not nearly as much "in love" with their dates as are their "sisters" in the later stages of courtship. But it appears that many of them are sometimes inclined to indicate that they are committed to their dates. They have a fairly high evaluation of their dates (even though they do not necessarily desire many traits in their dates). It is quite likely that some of the early daters are "falling in love" with their dates. If this is true, it means that their reference source is shifting to themselves and their boyfriends. When these two phenomena occur, the girls move into the later stages of courtship wherein their boyfriends more seriously reject assertiveness among girls. With emotional investment in boyfriends, the girls are forced to become receptive, because now it conforms to the expectations of their new reference source.

Receptivity, however, is not consistent with past socialization,[21] and one of the interesting findings in this study is that the receptive girls are dissatisfied with having to play their receptive role. The girls in the later stages play the receptive role, but this does not mean that they have accepted the role. This, indeed, seems to provid a built-in conflict for newlyweds, especially since it is known from a separate finding that married females are more avant-garde than single females and that they advocate assertiveness in some of the more crucial areas of dating behavior much more strongly than single females.[22]

As a summary, it may be well to speculate on the order in which the dating roles are probably subscribed to by the girls in this study. It appears that the girls are assertive first; that is, they enter the courtship process feeling themselves equal to boys in rights, power, and authority, and they express themselves accordingly while random dating. At a second stage—going steady—the girls are assertive–receptive; that is, receptivity is gradually being learned and is gradually supplanting assertiveness. And finally, at the third stage—pinned/engaged—when the girls are ready to be married, they are receptive.

4. REASONS FOR DATING

The findings from a study done by Lowrie in 1951 were applicable here.[23] Lowrie's study was designed to discover why students date. Four reasons were identified: (1) mate selection, (2) recreation, (3) anticipatory socialization, and (4) adult role clarification. Because of ambiguity of definition, adult role clarification was not used in this study. Mate selection is the conscious searching for compatible dating and/or marriage partners. Recreation is dating solely for the purpose of enjoying heterosexual interaction. Anticipatory socialization is learning, through dating, the knowledges and skills which are prerequisite to assuming specific marital roles.

In the present study, ten items were incorporated in the questionnaire to measure the extent to which mate selection was used as a reason for dating. All ten items scaled and yielded a Coefficient of Reproducibility of .911 and a Minimal Marginal Reproducibility of .818. In the order of their decreasing attractiveness, the ten items were concerned with a girl's (1) making herself as attractive as possible to attract the boy of her choice, (2) *incidentally* dating to choose the right husband, (3) dating, prior to engagement, enough boys to make a choice from a wide range of potential husbands, (4) being provided, through dating, with opportunities to refine her standards for good husbands, (5) not thinking of incompatible dates as good husbands, (6) comparing, in the dating situation, her ideal mate choice with reality, (7) *not just incidentally* considering mate selection while dating, (8) considering "romantic love" as secondary to her other standards for a good husband, (9) dating only those boys whom she considers potentially good husbands, and (10) *primarily* dating to choose the right husband.

Again, ten items were used to measure the extent to which recreation was used as a reason for dating. Only one of these proved non-scalable.

[20] *Ibid.*

[21] *Ibid.*

[22] Clyde O. McDaniel, Jr., "Relationships among Female Dating Roles and Reasons for Dating" (unpublished Ph.D. dissertation, University of Pittsburgh, 1967), p. 135.

[23] Robert H. Lowrie, "Dating Theories and Student Responses," *American Sociological Review*, 16 (1951), pp. 334–340.

With a Coefficient of Reproducibility of .916 and a Minimal Marginal Reproducibility of .820, the remaining nine scalable items—in the order of their decreasing attractiveness—were those concerning a girl's (1) *incidentally* dating to have lots of fun, (2) considering dating as a pleasant opportunity for companionship with the opposite sex without the responsibility of marriage, (3) having fun while dating in order not to miss a large portion of the beauty of youth, (4) considering enjoying herself as a major issue when contemplating going out on a date, (5) dating only those boys with whom she feels most comfortable, (6) obtaining sexual enjoyment while dating, (7) not worrying about marriage while on dates, (8) *primarily* dating to have lots of fun, and (9) not worrying about pleasing her date, just herself.

From among the ten items used to measure anticipatory socialization, only one proved nonscalable. The Coefficient of Reproducibility and the Minimal Marginal Reproducibility were quite satisfactory, being .917 and .800, respectively. In the order of their decreasing attractiveness, the remaining nine scalable items are those concerning a girl's (1) not being marriagable to a particular boy until he has seen her assuming a variety of different roles (2) learning, through dating, the general attitudes and behaviors of boys in order to facilitate initial marital adjustment, (3) *incidentally* dating in order to learn what behavior is necessary for being a good wife, (4) learning how to please a date in order to learn how to please a husband, (5) testing sexual compatibility with a potential mate while dating, (6) allowing engagement to serve as a trial marriage, (7) not seeing anything "wrong" with trial marriages, (8) *primarily* dating in order to learn what behavior is necessary for being a good wife, and (9) dating only those boys who can teach her something about marital roles.

Hypothesis III: It was expected that the girls in this study date for the purpose of recreation in the early stage of courtship, mate selection in the second stage, and anticipatory socialization in the last stage.

The rationale for the progression is based on the assumption that girls are either not aware of or not interested in the maritally oriented functions of dating in the early stage. They learn soon that, women, to be socially acceptable, must be married. As a result, a conscious mate selection process ensues; this is done in a sequence of tests while going steady. Once a mate has been selected and tested, girls' emphases shift to the more immediate future wherein they begin actively to anticipate some of their perceptions of their roles as wives.

While these three reasons for dating are isomorphic with the implicit deductions of each of three theoretical schools of thought (see next section), Lowrie failed to cash in on a major theoretical contribution by not relating them with certain types of dating roles, stages of courtship, or with any of the variables involved in courtship. However, Lowrie's study does indicate that young people do not date solely for the purpose of having fun. Many are seriously concerned with other functions, particularly the marital and socialization functions.

The first three cells in the first three columns of Table 3 show the relationships among present stage of courtship and the three reasons for dating among single females. The data indicate that anticipatory socialization is positively correlated with the engagement stage of courtship; recreation is positively correlated with the random dating stage of courtship; and mate selection is positively correlated with all three stages of courtship, but the highest correlation obtains with the going-steady stage of courtship. This makes it highly probable that the following relational pattern obtains: (1) in the early stage of courtship, there is a tendency for the girls to justify their dating on the basis of mate selection and recreation (however, recreation dominates); (2) in the interim stage of courtship, there is a tendency for them to justify their dating on the basis of mate selection; and (3) in the last stage of courtship, there is a tendency for the girls to justify their dating on the basis of mate selection and anticipatory socialization (however, anticipatory socialization dominates). If such a pattern obtains, a certain amount of credibility is accorded to Hypothesis III and to the assumptions underlying it.

Table 3. Some of the Relationships among Stages of Courtship, Female Reasons for Dating, Female Role Behavior, and Male Attitudes toward Female Assertiveness and Receptivity

Female Reasons for Dating	Present Stage of Courtship			Female Role Behavior	
	Random Dating	Going Steady	Engagement	Assertiveness	Receptivity
Anticipatory Socialization	−.28**	−.15**	.30**	——**	.16**
Recreation	.24**	−.17**	−.30**	.23**	——**
Mate selection	.15**	.32**	.12**	.29**	.32**
Male Attitudes					
Toward Female Assertiveness	.10*	−.12*	−.24*		
Toward Female Receptivity	.16*	.20*	.30*		

*N = 181 (Number of Males).
**N = 396 (Number of Females).
P ≤ .05.

5. RELATIONSHIPS AMONG ROLE BEHAVIOR AND REASONS FOR DATING

From the foregoing it follows that role behavior and reasons for dating among single females are related to each other in the following manner:

Hypothesis IV: The females who date primarily for the purpose of recreation are very likely to be assertive.

Hypothesis V: The females who date primarily for the purpose of mate selection are very likely to be assertive-receptive.

Hypothesis VI: The females who date primarily for the purpose of anticipatory socialization are very likely to be receptive.

The main focus of Hypotheses IV, V, and VI is: "Exactly what do assertive and/or receptive girls get out of courtship?" As seen in the last two columns of Table 3, this question was answered by relating types of role behavior to reasons for dating. The data indicate that (1) *the assertive girls date for the purposes of mate selection and recreation;* (2) *the receptive girls date for the purposes of mate selection and anticipatory socialization*; and, since both assertive and receptive girls justify their dating on the basis of mate selection, (3) *the assertive–receptive girls date for the purpose of mate selection.*

It seems that if girls were continually assertive throughout courtship, two of the functions uncovered by Lowrie would go lacking, but if they were continually receptive, they would get no fun out of dating. If they were sometimes assertive and sometimes receptive, they would be continually searching for mates. Assertiveness does not undermine the functions of courtship; it merely contributes to specialized aspects of them. Since it is known that the girls shift from assertiveness to receptivity as they move through courtship and that their dating emphases also shift, the findings in the last two columns of Table 3 were expected. However, the findings indicate that Hypotheses IV, V, and VI are not disconfirmed.

The data show that at least three schools of thought can be used to summarize the role behavior of modern-day females.[24] Waller and

[24] Those three schools can be abstracted from a careful reading of the following sources: Willard Waller, *The Family: A Dynamic Interpretation* (New York: Holt, Rinehart, and Winston, 1938); Geoffrey Gorer, *The American People* (New York): W. W. Norton and Company, 1948); Ernest Burgess and Harvey Locke, *The Family: From Institution to Companionship* (New York: American Book Company, 1945); and Samuel H. Lowrie, "Dating Theories and Student Responses," *American Sociological Review,* 16 (1951), pp. 334–340.

Gorer's school (an Assertive school) seems to present a neat characterization of early female daters as assertive and motivated by hedonistic considerations.[25] Burgess and Locke's school (an Assertive–Receptive school) seems to give a fairly accurate presentation of females who are in transit from the early stage (random dating) to the last stage (pinned/engaged).[26] Their girls are pictured as sometimes assertive and sometimes receptive and motivated by desires to select mates. The stage of courtship which best describes this school is going steady. Lowrie's school (a Receptive school) more properly portrays later daters, wherein the girls are receptive and motivated by desires to attain anticipatory socialization benefits.[27] The stage of courtship which best describes this school is pinned/engaged.

Each of the schools is valuable as far as it goes. Each characterizes a part of the dating process. When the three schools are combined, however, a much clearer picture of dating roles and functions is presented, wherein one can see that dating roles and functions change as the girls move through courtship. The question immediately arises as to what would happen if the roles and functions do not change. Apparently, some penalty is paid by the girls if they do not change their role behavior from one stage to another. The next section presents insight into the nature of this penalty.

6. ASSERTIVENESS, RECEPTIVITY, AND SOCIALIZATION

If the girls do not change from assertiveness to receptivity while moving through courtship, one wonders what happens. The data, in this study, show that two things happen: (1) society imposes negative sanctions, and (2) the girls do not progress to later stages of courtship, or if they do progress, they soon regress to earlier stages. The first finding is presented in the last two cells of the first three columns of Table 3. These six cells show that "society" (in the form of the male) does not, in fact, like females who are assertive.

And more significantly, they dislike them most in the last stages of courtship.[28] The more advanced the men are in the stages of courtship, the more they de-emphasize female assertiveness and the more they emphasize female receptivity. It can be assumed, then, that with such an attitude toward the female role in dating, the males impose serious negative sanctions on the expression of female assertiveness during the later stages of courtship. Credibility is added to this statement when one remembers (from Table 2) that girls become, during the later stages, more personally and boyfriend oriented. This means that they are, indeed, aware of the types of sanctions imposed by their boyfriends and that they are more concerned with learning the proper role behavior for an adult woman and wife.

The second finding is presented in Table 4 which shows that a significant number of girls do, in fact, regress or fail to progress to further stages of courtship. This is evidenced by the fact that the correlation between present stage of courtship and stage of courtship participated in is −.60, indicating that (1) most of the girls who presently reside in later stages of courtship are quite likely to have participated in earlier stages, and (2) *many of those who have participated in later stages are quite likely to be presently residing in earlier stages.* The negative exchange which is implied by the second statement seems to take place between random dating and going steady, pinned/engaged. More girls are presently random dating than have *only* random dated in the past. And fewer girls are presently going steady or are pinned/engaged than have gone steady or have been pinned/engaged in the past. The residue of present random daters is accounted for in the two succeeding categories under "Stages of Courtship Participated In" ("Random Dated, Gone Steady" and "Random Dated, Gone Steady, Pinned/Engaged"). This means that some of the

---

[25] Waller, *The Family*; and Gorer, *The American People*.
[26] Burgess and Locke, *The Family*.
[27] Lowrie, "Dating Theories and Student Responses."

[28] The attitudes of males toward female assertiveness and female receptivity were assessed by asking the 181 single males in the study to respond to the same items which were used to measure assertiveness and receptivity among females. For both attitudes toward female assertiveness and attitude toward female receptivity, about half of the items had to be discarded in order to obtain Coefficients of Reproducibility of .90. The items which were retained were identical with those included in the scales of assertive and receptive dating behavior among females.

Table 4. The Relationship between Present Stage of Courtship and Stage of Courtship Participated in

Present Stage of Courtship	%	Stage of Courtship Participated in	%
Random dating	55	Random dated	26
Going steady	30	Random dated, gone steady	47
Pinned/engaged	15	Random dated, gone steady, pinned/engaged	27
Total	100(396)		100(396)

$r_s = -.60, P \leqslant .05$.

girls who are presently random dating were once going steady and were once pinned/engaged.

Since it is known that the early daters (random daters) are assertive and the later daters (pinned/engaged) are receptive, one would guess that one of the main reasons for the negative exchange is the failure, on the part of some later daters, to shift from assertiveness to receptivity. One can visualize a learning cycle wherein girls learn through trial and error to become receptive. If they do not become receptive, they never get married. Admittedly, the foregoing is a very strong statement, but the evidence in Table 2 shows that most of the later daters are not assertive, and most of the early daters are not receptive in spite of the fact that many of them were once residents of later stages of courtship. Presumably, the later daters who are still assertive will repeat the cycle until they become receptive.

Summary

In order to provide a picture of the foregoing findings, elaborate cross-tabulation procedures (contingency analyses) were performed, the results of which are reported in Figure 1. The cross-tabulation involved: (1) dichotomizing each of the variables in the paradigm (except stages of courtship and commitment which were trichotomized); (2) cross-tabulating role behavior with reasons for dating among single females (modal categories were pulled out and placed in column 2); and (3) sequentially cross-tabulating the results in column 2 with present stage of courtship, reference groups, complementarity, commitment, and degree of dissatisfaction. The modal categories were pulled out and placed in column 1, 3, 4, 5, and 6.

Such a picture makes it quite clear that the six hypotheses raised at the outset are credible. Now it is possible to summarize the major findings of this study. The findings are as follows:

1. There is a tendency for the girls in this study to random date first, to go steady second, and to become pinned/engaged third or last.
2. There is a tendency for girls in this study to be assertive in the first stage (random dating) and receptive in the last stage (pinned/engaged). They are assertive–receptive in the second stage (going steady).
3. There is a tendency for girls in this study who are assertive to be original-family and peer-group oriented, complementary plus, low-medium in commitment, and mostly satisfied-dissatisfied with their dating roles.
4. There is a tendency for girls in this study who are receptive to be original-family and personally and boyfriend oriented, complementary plus, medium–high in commitment, and mostly dissatisfied with their dating roles.

It is believed that some of the intervening variables cause assertiveness, some result from assertiveness and cause receptivity, and some result from receptivity. However, further research is needed to assess the exact causal status of the intervening variable set.

5. There is a tendency for girls in this study who are in the first, second, and third stages of courtship to give recreation, mate selection, and anticipatory socialization, respectively, as their primary reasons for dating.

Figure 1. Summary

Socialization Sequence: Stages of Courtship	Relationship Between Role Behavior— Reasons for Dating	Reference Group Orientation	Degree of Complementarity	Degree of Commit- ment	Degree of Satis- faction with Dating Role
1. Random dating	assertive-recreation	original family, peer group	complementary plus	low/ medium	satisfied
2. Going steady	assertive receptive— mate selection	original family, peer group	complementary plus	medium	satisfied/ dissatisfied
3. Pinned/ engaged	receptive—anticipatory socialization	self and boyfriend	complementary plus	medium/ high	dissatisfied

6. There is a tendency for the girls in this study who give recreation as their primary reason for dating to be assertive. They are probably participating in the first stage of the courtship socialization sequence (random dating). This is consistent with Waller and Gorer's Assertive school with regard to reason for dating and role behavior.

7. There is a tendency for the girls in this study who give mate selection as their primary reason for dating to be assertive–receptive. They are probably participating in the second stage of the courtship socialization sequence (going steady). This is consistent with Burgess and Locke's Assertive–Receptive school with regard to reason for dating and role behavior.

8. There is a tendency for the girls in this study who give anticipatory socialization as their primary reasons for dating to be receptive. They are probably participating in the third stage of the courtship socialization sequence (pinned/ engaged). This is consistent with Lowrie's Receptive school with regard to reason for dating and role behavior.

Assertive dating behavior does not undermine the functions of courtship, but contributes to specialized aspects of them, i.e., recreation and mate selection.

9. Tentatively, evidence is offered to the effect that girls in this study do learn to be receptive. If they are not receptive in the early stages, they probably have a lot of fun while dating. If they are not receptive in the later stages, they either regress to earlier stages, or at least they fail to progress to more advanced stages. Such a phenomenon is enhanced by the males' strong dislike for girls who are assertive in the later stages.

A single testing of a theory is never definitive. Each hypothesis included in a theory is always threatened by the possibility of its rejection. Such a possibility is allowable only through an appeal to more research. A single testing only heightens the awareness that further research, to be useful, should be conducted with different and more sophisticated methods. In the present study, a college population, the use of the questionnaire technique, the use of percentages, and the use of ordinal statistics may have presented impediments to the validity of the findings. Further testing of the theory in this study must attempt to avoid these limitations.

The Patterning of Chinese-Caucasian Interracial Dating

MELFORD S. WEISS

Divergent expectations and dating behaviors are related to such factors as racial stereotyping, sex-linked psychological profiles, and socialization practices and characteristics of the Chinese community.

The initial expectation of this study was that Chinese dating standards and patterns would be modernistic, reflecting the acculturation of Chinese into today's American youth culture. But it was also expected that a sense of Chinese ethnic solidarity would produce a preference to date within the Chinese group. Most Chinese males clearly expressed their preference for a Chinese dating partner. However, while almost all of the females admitted they would prefer to marry a Chinese man, their descriptions of typical Chinese-American male dating behavior were not all complimentary. For the purpose of this paper, Chinese-American refers to the first generation native born American of Chinese descent. The females continually compared Chinese and Caucasian counterparts and concluded that Chinese finesse at the dating game left much to be desired.

Dating attitudes are a product of the socialization process and have their roots in cultural institutions and ideologies. This paper is primarily directed at exploring the positive attitudes toward interracial Caucasian dating expressed by Chinese females. Because the informants in this study were all American born Chinese youth they are influenced by American social institutions.

This study suggests: (1) That the dating attitude of young Chinese-American males and females, influenced by their differential treatment by white American society, is both a consequence and result of, continuous exposure to, and partial Chinese acceptance of, American racial stereotyping; (2) that the interracial dating success and failure of Chinese-Americans is linked to their involvement in American social life, and that males and females participate disproportionately in social activities; (3) that Chinese-American males and females demonstrate different psychological attitudes towards social–sexual situations and that these sex-linked attitudes are related to both Chinese *socialization* patterns and acculturation and structural assimilation into American life, and (4) that the social structure of the Chinese community may inadvertently encourage some interracial dating practices.

This paper was presented at the 67th Annual Meeting of the American Anthropological Association, November 1968, Seattle, Washington.

From M. S. Weiss, The patterning of Chinese–Caucasian interracial dating. Reprinted from the *Journal of Marriage and the Family,* May 1970, *32*(2), 273–278, by permission of author and publisher.

This paper is an initial attempt to explore these social–psychological factors responsible for divergent interracial dating patterns of Chinese-American males and females.

Methodology

This paper is based upon anthropological fieldwork in a West Coast Chinese-American community (1967–1968). Fieldwork methodology included individual and group in-depth interviews in both synchronic and diachronic perspective with Chinese-American boys and girls and their families, attendance and participation at Oriental and mixed dances, parties, organizational meetings, and other social events as well as visiting Chinese-American homes and attending numerous Chinese community celebrations and dinners.

Supplementing traditional techniques of participant observation, questionnaires were administered to 80 of the 400 Chinese students at a local junior college. Twenty-five Chinese-American students (13 females, 12 males) completing the questionnaire were subsequently interviewed about their dating attitudes and behavior.

Conclusions substantiated and/or suggested by this study are applicable to the teen-agers and young adults (14–21) presently living in the Chinese-American community in which this research was conducted. It may, however, have general applicability to other Chinese-American communities.

BACKGROUND: THE CHINESE EXPERIENCE IN AMERICA

The early Chinese communities in America (1850–1900) have previously been characterized by the dominance of traditional family and district associations in Chinese economic and political life, the acknowledged unchallenged superiority of the male elders, the subservient position of women in the family, and the acceptance by the younger generation of parental controls in matters of courtship and mate selection (Kung, 1962; Lee, 1960).

By contrast, Chinese-American communities of the 1960's are intensely involved in the processes of urban sociocultural changes and acculturation and assimilation, both resulting in the divergence from traditional practices. With the decentralization of the community and the dispersion of its members, the family associations are declining in importance because they can no longer meet all the needs of contemporary community life (Willmott, 1964; Lee, 1949). Male elders are rapidly losing the ability to control inappropriate behavior of the younger generation—a generation more responsive to the nuances of American life than bonds of family and community (Lee, 1956). As women gain a more equal footing in the financial, recreational and socializational practices of the family, the dominant position of the father is weakened (Barnett, 1958).

One of the more dramatic departures from traditional Chinese-American life is evidenced by Chinese-Caucasian dating patterns—patterns which emphasize Chinese youth's new found independence from familial restrictions and increasing adherence to western romantic demands; resulting in an eager attempt on the part of the Chinese-American female to embrace Caucasian courtship rituals and the concomitant social dictums that accompany them.

THE GENERAL PATTERNING OF INTERRACIAL DATING

The results of the questionnaire and interviews indicated that Chinese-American females have internalized the dominant dating values of the Caucasian teenager, have better adjusted to American social custom, and are better accepted by the Caucasian community as dating partners and potential mates than the young Chinese-American male. Consequently Chinese-American girls expect to be treated like their Caucasian contemporaries. Many Chinese-American boys cannot meet these expectations and as a result, the girls may seek romance, companionship and adventure in Caucasian arms.

Chinese-American males have experienced many successes in American society. They have proven themselves as scholars in our educational system, enterprising enterpreneurs in their business ventures, and as professionals (Kwoh, 1947:113). Yet in the area of interracial social relationships, dating and marriage, many Chinese-American males fail to exhibit the successes achieved by the female—and it is specifically in these interpersonal arenas that the future of assimilation of ethnic and racial minorities into American life will be determined (Gordon, 1964).

THE NATURE OF CHINESE STEREOTYPES

American society has historically been given to negative stereotypes of the Chinese male. In early years male Chinese arrivals to America have been characterized as "bestial celestials," "atheistic heathens," "opium smokers," "gamblers," and "gangsters" (Barth, 1964:129–156; Farwell, 1885: 97–114). More recent Chinese character profiles include the evil and cunning Dr. Fu Manchu, the inscrutable Charlie Chan, and the agreeable but puzzled and simple proprietor of a hand-laundry shop (Sung, 1967). Although the Chinese male has also been popularly characterized as "clever, honest, industrious and studious," "a paragon of family virtue," "respectfully obedient to his elders" (traits acceptable in business and family success), he is still identified as "shy," "introverted," "withdrawing" and "tongue-tied" (traits unacceptable to current ideas of romanticism) (Sung, 1967). Furthermore, the Occidental stage, screen and television image of the "hero" and the "he-man," emphasizing virility and sexual attraction—a prime factor in the courtship game—includes too few physical or cultural features of Oriental men. Chinese males are rarely mentioned as "heroic" and "adventuresome" and have never been popularized in American fiction as "dashing impulsive lovers."

The Chinese female image, on the other hand, has been better accepted by the American public. "Suzi Wong" is portrayed as slim, sexy and loveable in a tight cheong-sam. The "Oriental dishes" of Flower Drum Song and the well publicized Miss Chinatown beauty pageants have particularly emphasized Chinese feminine beauty and charm. Chinese women have appeared in Playboy's center-fold and lend support to the exaggerated romantic tales of servicemen returning from Far Eastern duty ports. As a result, Chinese girls with Caucasian escorts receive few disparaging public stares, while Chinese men walking hand-in-hand with white women are often the subject of malicious gossip.

American stereotypes of "Chinese"—although based upon much fictitious characterization— accept the Chinese female as a satisfactory sexual and dating companion but reject the Chinese male in a similar category. Caucasian "social indices" reflecting an unfavorable Chinese male image discourage the Chinese-American male from seeking dates with Caucasian girls. With little confidence as a romantic competitor, he is often unsuccessful with Chinese-American girls as well. Perhaps the most illustrative example of the Chinese-American females' acceptance of American sex-linked discrimination is the Chinese-American girl dining with her Caucasian date who can't help staring at the Chinese boy and his white girlfriend and wondering what in the world she sees in him.

IMAGE AND IDENTITY: THE CHINESE-AMERICAN MALE

Perhaps the most damaging indictment of Chinese-American male "dating ineptness" comes from the dating age Chinese-American female. Girls who regularly date Caucasians can be quite vehement in their denunciation and disapproval of Chinese-American males as dating partners. But even the foreign-born Chinese girls—who do not usually inter-date—also willingly support a demeaning courtship image of the Chinese-American male. Moreover, "Chinese inadequacies" and "failures" are contrasted with Caucasian "confidence" and "success" in similar situations. Chinese-American girls report that getting-to-know-you chatter with most Chinese-American boys is basically shallow and tends to revolve around common experiences as Chinese. Males are often considered to be egocentric and to rarely consider the girl as an equal partner in a common dating activity. Conversation is less likely to contain introspective elements. Questions relating to personal identity ("Who am I") and social meaning ("what is it all about") are usually excluded from Chinese-American male repertoire. The boys tend to joke about such matters ("you must be kidding") and to further ridicule the girl ("you're sick in the head").

Chinese-American dating activities are often limited to evening hours and to private or predominately Chinese settings with the drive-in movie a favorite—leading one Chinese-American girl to sarcastically remark: "One more Chinese date this month and I'll have seen every drive-in movie in town." Chinese-American boys are often accused of behaving "childishly" at dances and parties, embarrassing their dates by not displaying "mature" and "sophisticated" mannerisms. Hurried, clumsy love-making attempts in parked cars do not meet the girls' romantic expectations, leading them to characterize Chinese-American boys as sexually inept. More often what they complain about is "lack of advances," but one Chinese-American girl reports: "It's easy to get pregnant with a Chinese boy; he never knows how to take precautions."

The aforementioned comments on Chinese-American male dating behavior are less the observations of this researcher than the reporting of Chinese-American girls. Furthermore, current American dating ideology makes it fashionable to belittle and demean "traditional" role-type behavior. When presented with these "stories" Chinese-American males deny the more derogatory accusations yet basically agree that they are more inhibited and less aggressive than Caucasian males, and admit to feeling uncomfortable, if not insecure, in racially mixed company and in predominantly Caucasion settings. Caucasian males, on the other hand, express more confidence in interracial dating procedures and in the absence of a shared "identity" with girls of Chinese descent, give the appearance of broadening their conversational horizons. When comparing Caucasian to Chinese-American males, the former are easily accorded more social and sexual maturity, and are often referred to as "suave," "cool," "sophisticated," "swinging" and "sexy"—adjectives rarely associated with Chinese-American males.

In order to elicit more definitive information about attitudes towards Caucasian and Chinese-American dating partners, Chinese-American females were asked to specifically describe their reasons for dating Chinese and Caucasian boys. Those who preferred to date Chinese-Americans constantly indicated "parental coercion," "Chinese and Caucasian community pressures," "respect for tradition," "the sharing of a common heritage with other Chinese," "race consciousness" and "the many problems associated with interracial marital unions." Responses for Caucasian dating preferences are of an entirely different nature: "Caucasians know better dating places," "more fun on dates," "more considerate," "sexy and good looking," "easy-going personality" and "they are the fun part of American culture."

These differing "preference typologies" for Chinese-American and for Caucasian dates suggest that the girls prefer the adventure, romance and easy familiarity associated with Caucasian life, and by accepting these "wants" have accepted many of the mores of "Americana." Although they may prefer Caucasian-style dates as best representative of the individuality and free-expression of this society, the realities of family life and a future within this community channel their marital choice to a Chinese mate.

Thus, Chinese-American boys who demonstrate proficiency in the "Caucasian-style" dating game are in much demand as friends, dates and eventually husbands. One Chinese-American girl neatly summarized her dating desires by posting on her dormitory door: "WANTED . . . A NON-CHINESE AMERICAN—OF CHINESE DESCENT."

The Chinese in America cannot help but be influenced by the nature of Caucasian stereotypes of Orientals. The reader should not be left with the impression that most Chinese-American males are either inept or inadequate. My contention is that Chinese-American females, born and reared in a predominately Caucasian society and subject to the propagandizing influences of American mass media, either consciously or subconsciously accept many American racial stereotypes and furthermore act upon the assumption that they have some validity. Thus, when a "Chinese date" turns out to be a disappointment, the Chinese male stereotype images are further reinforced.

SOCIAL INTERACTION AND DATING EXPECTATIONS

The results of the questionnaire indicated that Chinese-American college males usually carry a full-time course load (fifteen or more credits), demonstrate an intense commitment to their academic study program (predominantly science, math, and engineering) and spend many after-class hours at the school library. Many of these students hold part-time jobs in Chinese-owned restaurants and grocery markets as clerks, checkers, busboys and waiters. Their on-the-job relationships with both Chinese and Caucasian clientele are subordinate and superficial.

Chinese-American female students, however, take fewer courses (twelve hours or less) in more non-academic subjects (cosmetology, home economics, typing) and spend less time in library confines than Chinese-American males. Most females are not employed after school, and many with part-time jobs are more likely to work for Caucasian employers. Chinese-American females spend many "leisure" hours in snack bars and on campus grounds in the company of their Chinese-American and Caucasian peers. The girls "tune in" to social conventions concerning heterosexual activities and quickly learn the expectations and frustrations of American teen-age dating styles. Although Chinese-American extra-curricular organizational life is largely spent with other Chinese-Americans, females are more likely to be escorted to Caucasian dances, invited to Caucasian parties and attend predominately Caucasian churches than are males.

Chinese-American males do participate in "Caucasian" school organizations but these activities do not demand the same social sophistication as parties and dances. Chinese-American boys rarely join the predominately Caucasian fraternities, while Chinese-American females are better represented in woman's social associations. Females declare they are usually "at ease" in the company of Caucasian peers; males often indicate insecurity and anxiety in competitive interracial situations. The females consider themselves "more Americanized" than the males.

As Chinese-American females continue to participate in interracial activities, they learn the current fads and fashions associated with Caucasian courtship rituals and come to expect similar considerations. Chinese-American males, whose participation in the non-Chinese world is limited, are either unaware or more commonly uncertain of these "social graces." Since the males must take the initiative for arranging dates, Chinese-American males find themselves at a distinct disadvantage when compared with their Caucasian peers.

Our data suggests that the nature and degree of interracial social participation significantly affects dating expectations, and that Chinese-American females spend more time in "mixed" activities than Chinese-American males; thus, hastening the females' incorporation into American social life.

Perhaps a major factor affecting the dating attitudes of Chinese-American males and females is not so much in the rate of acculturation but the sphere in which acculturation takes place. Chinese-American women become integrated primarily in the expressive sphere of interpersonal relationships while Chinese-American men appear to be acculturated in the instrumental sphere of work (their dedication towards their studies including part-time work suggests a real commitment to the American dream of *social mobility*). The strong motivation of Chinese-American men to achieve social status through educational means also suggests that the striving for occupational success takes precedence over and may actually impair their ability to "socialize" with other people.

PSYCHOLOGICAL PROFILES AND SEX-RELATED DIFFERENCES

Abel and Hsu (1949:286) support differential sex-linked attitudes when reporting the responses for American born Chinese males and females. Rorschach protocols suggest that Chinese-American females approach the American response pattern to a greater degree than do Chinese-American males. The males seem insecure about their sex roles, their acceptance in relation to Americans as people, and their relationship to girls in general. Although the females expressed adjustment difficulties, they marshalled their resources, faced their conflicts squarely, and handled sexual preoccupations more directly. Hsu further suggests that because Chinese-American males are more responsible for carrying on the family name and following in their "ancestors' footsteps," their exposure to Chinese and western ideals often involves conflicting emotions. They are less sure of the roles they should or could lead. In attempting to break away from tradition and better fit into the American patterns, they encounter many difficulties within both the Chinese and American community. Their protocols suggest that many may be emotionally disturbed since they show frequent anxiety signs, repressed feelings of rebellion, a dilemma in the sexual sphere, and the inability to work out sexual difficulties.

Chinese-American females have a less rigid role to maintain than their male counterparts. They are not as responsible for carrying on family "tradition" and are less subjected to parental pressures to conform. They, therefore, find it less challenging to adjust to contemporary American life. Male feelings of inadequacy are not complemented by female "adjustments" to acculturation. It takes but little imagination to project these suggested sex-role discrepancies directly into the dating situation.

COMMUNITY GRAPEVINE AND CLOSED SYSTEM

Most Chinese parents (native and foreign born) disapprove of interracial dating, yet certain features of social life in this Chinese-American community not only encourage Chinese-American females to date non-Chinese men, but even discourage casual and/or consistent dating within the Chinese-American group.

The Chinese are dispersed throughout the city, yet a "sense of community" is nevertheless consciously maintained in part by an efficient yet informal information exchange system which unites the community by cutting across age, sex, and generational barriers. This Chinese "grapevine," strengthened by long-standing friendships and cross-cutting organizational and social activities, functions through the spreading of news and rumor to maintain a running commentary upon the activities of its younger members. "Grapevine" gossip exposes dating activities to "Chinese public view" by rapidly relaying dating stories to parents, relatives, dating partners and potential mates.

While foreign-born Chinese parents consider "dating" a direct prelude towards serious intentions, and see consecutive and/or consistent dates with one individual as swiftly leading to a future marital commitment, Chinese-American youth (particularly females) consider "dating" as a pleasant end in itself. Thus, non-serious Chinese dating may lead to unwanted gossip. Caucasians more readily approve of casual courtship prac-

tices (particularly those of an interracial nature) and because they are unable to directly contribute to Chinese gossip sessions, a "Caucasian date" may spare the girl from a "double-pronged" feedback into the Chinese community, allowing the girl multiple and varied dating experiences without necessarily endangering her reputation. The grapevine functions most successfully with spicy and risque episodes. Rebuffed and jealous Chinese-American males have been known to tell "tall tales" to enhance their social reputations—tales which add little to the girl's reputation, as scandal is appreciated neither by parents nor potential mates. In any event Chinese–Chinese "heavy dates" rarely remain secret affairs. Although Caucasian males are also prone to ego building "stories"—because they are not plugged into the Chinese network—their fictional and/or factual adventures are unlikely to reach Chinese ears.

Chinese parents opposed to interracial marriages may not seriously view a Caucasian escort as a possible choice, and are sometimes less concerned with multiple Caucasian outings than would be the case with a Chinese suitor. Chinese parents are concerned with all of their daughter's dating partners. However, Chinese dates are particularly scrutinized because Chinese males are indeed potential mates. A casual date with a Caucasian, although often disapproved of, is, in many cases tolerated because he is not considered as a potential marriage partner by the parents.

Two important structural features in this Chinese community are a relatively stable population for persons under twenty-five and the tendency for the Chinese to split into "foreign-born" and "native-born" social groups. Because the total community population is under 10,000 scattered throughout the city, and further split into separate groups, eligible dates can be a considerable problem, particularly for American-born Chinese females who rarely date foreign-born Chinese boys. Moreover, close childhood and school ties continue with age-mates within groups and friendship does not easily become romance. Thus, Chinese-Americans must frequently go outside the Chinese community in search of dating companions. Caucasians, whose life-style already appeals to the Chinese-American female, are able to furnish an immediate identity and find it easy to meet "date searching" Chinese-American girls.

The Chinese-American male, finding it difficult to date Caucasian girls, remains frustrated.

Summary

The social and cultural orientations and sentiments of the Chinese in America are gradually shifting from the ethnic subculture to the larger American society. As Caucasian society continues to become a positive reference group, its norms and values begin to guide as well as modify the behavior and perspectives of the Chinese (Fong, 1965:271).

Yet, cultural and structural assimilation of the Chinese-American into white America have not always resulted in a similar acceptance of both Chinese-American males and females. Sex-linked American discriminatory practices have contributed to a male-negative/female-positive dichotomy. The effects of this "stereotyping" are further validated and reinforced by the Chinese-American female successs in interracial social activities and personality adjustment to American life. The social structure of the Chinese community, its restrictive nature and differential sex-linked demands upon its youngsters also share in the responsibility for the continuance of the females success in interracial dating.

Further Suggestions

Although the focus of this study is dating, with an obvious emphasis upon the cross-sex relationship, Chinese-American males still remain ill at ease with Caucasians of *both* sexes. The lack of successful interracial personal relationships in social activities carry over into adult lives where the inability of the Chinese-American male to relate positively to mixed ethnic and racial social/sexual situations continues.

American sex-linked discriminatory practices and "poor" social interaction experiences combine to isolate the Chinese-American male from active participation in many community wide organizational activities. When Chinese-American males do join in extra-Chinese city events, they often do so as members of all Chinese groups rather than as individuals. Moreover these activities are usually limited to business or "Chinese community" functions and rarely to specifically "social" events (Weiss, 1969).

REFERENCES

ABEL, THEODORA M. AND FRANCIS L. K. HSU 1959. "Some aspects of personality of Chinese as revealed by the Rorschach tests." *Research Exchange and Journal of Projective Techniques XIII:* 285–301.

BARNETT, MILTON L. 1958. "Some Cantonese-American problems of status adjustment." *Phylon XVIII:* 420–427.

BARTH, GUNTHER 1964. *Bitter Strength: A History of the Chinese in the United States 1850–1870.* Cambridge: Harvard University Press.

FARWELL, WILLARD B. 1885. *The Chinese at Home and Abroad.* San Francisco. A. L. Bancroft and Company.

FONG, STANLEY 1965. "Assimiliation of Chinese in America: changes in orientation and social perception." *American Journal of Sociology LXIII* (3):265–273.

GORDON, MILTON M. 1964. *Assimiliation in American Life.* New York: Oxford University Press.

KUNG, S. W. 1962. *Chinese in American Life: Some Aspects of Their History, Status, Problems and Contributions.* Seattle: University of Washington Press.

KWOH, BEULAH ONG 1947. "Occupational Status of the American-Born Chinese College Graduate." Unpublished Doctoral dissertation, University of Chicago.

LEE, ROSE HUM 1949. "The decline of Chinatown in the United States." *American Journal of Sociology LIV* (5):422–432.

———, 1956. "The recent immigrant Chinese families of the San Francisco–Oakland area." *Marriage and Family Living* 18:14-24.

———, 1960. *The Chinese in the United States of America.* New York: Oxford University Press.

SUNG, BETTY LEE 1967. *Mountain of Gold: The Story of the Chinese in America.* New York: The Macmillan Company.

WEISS, MELFORD S. 1969. "Conflict and compromise: the structuring of a Chinese community in America." *Clearing house for Sociological Literature. CFSL* No. 69-6.

WILLMOTT, W. L. 1964. "Chinese Clan associations in Vancouver." *Man* 49:33-36.

Chapter 12: Suggested Additional Readings

BALSWICK, J. O., & ANDERSON, J. A.   Role definition in the unarranged date. *Journal of Marriage and the Family,* 1969, *31*(4), 776–778. A study of college students found that both sexes believed the other sex to be more permissive than it actually was, and that this misconception was based on the "line" that both sexes use.

COOMBS, R. H.   Value consensus and partner satisfaction among dating couples. *Journal of Marriage and the Family,* 1966, *28*(2), 166–173. An empirical study of dating couples found support for the following hypothesis: satisfaction with one's partner increases with an increase in objective value consensus, perceived partner's valuing of self, and ease of communication; ease of communication increases with an increase in objective value consensus and perceived partner's valuing of self.

COOMBS, R. H., & KENKEL, W. F.   Sex differences in dating aspirations and satisfaction with computer-selected partners. *Journal of Marriage and the Family,* 1966, *28*(1), 62–66. When blind dates were arranged by computer, it was found that females had higher expectations of their first date than did men.

HUDSON, A. W., & HENZE, L. F.   Campus values and mate selection: A replication. *Journal of Marriage and the Family,* 1969, *31*(4), 772–775. In this study, which compared campus values and mate selection from 1939 to 1967, it was concluded that college students have not shifted significantly in ideals of mate selection from half a generation ago. In fact, the values of the two generations appear to be remarkably consistent.

KLEMER, R. H.   Self esteem and college dating experience as factors in mate selection and marital happiness: A longitudinal study. *Journal of Marriage and the Family,* 1971, *33*(1), 183–187. On the basis of longitudinal data collected from college women in 1956 and again in 1968, Klemer tentatively concluded that women with high self-esteem had dated more frequently and gone steady less often while in college than had women with lower self-regard. In addition, the women who had dated more often had married earlier; and both those women with very high and very low self-esteem had achieved less marital happiness than those with average self-regard.

POLLIS, C. A.   Dating involvement in patterns of idealization: A test of Waller's hypothesis. *Journal of Marriage and the Family,* 1969, *31*(4), 64–69. Data are presented which fail to support either Waller's contention that idealization is minimal or absent at the beginning of a dating relationship or his theory of increasing idealization with increasing involvement. Relevant research is also cited and discussed.

SKIPPER, J. K. PR., & NASS, G.   Dating behavior: A framework for analysis and an illustration. *Journal of Marriage and the Family,* 1966, *28*(4), 412–413. The writers summarize several researchers' analyses of the functions of dating, and indicate the common elements that seem to exist.

STRONG, E., & WILSON, W.   Three-filter date selection by computer–phase II. *Family Co-ordinator,* 1969, *18*(3), 256–259. A campus computer service gave each participating student three dates—a "similar" date, a "compatible" date, and a "complementary" date. Post-date feedback determined relative preference for each type of date.

WITTMAN, J. S. JR. Dating patterns of rural and urban Kentucky teenagers. *Family Coordinator,* 1971, *20*(1), 63–66. This study concerns the status of high school students in two high schools relative to the practice of "going steady".

13

Biological Sex Role

Unresolved questions about human psychosexual development abound. What is the origin of sexual feelings? Do sexual feelings and problems affect males and females differently? Is the double standard of morality fair and reasonable? How much sexual expression does a teenager need? Common beliefs about such matters are shot through with fallacies. It has been generally assumed, even by psychoanalytic theorists, that individuals' psychosexual development progresses smoothly by some natural process, with masculinity and femininity somehow emerging differently according to an innate, instinctive sexuality. However, the origin and steps in the development of psychosexual differentiation are still unclear. Morphologically, in the prenatal period, sexual differentiation passes from an original plastic stage to one of fixed immutability. Postnatally, psychosexual differentiation proceeds rapidly during infancy, and becomes fixed about the same time that language is acquired. "By school age," asserts Money (1965), "psychosexual differentiation is so complete that sex reassignment is out of the question, save for the rare instances of ambiguous psychosexual differentiation [p. 13].

At adolescence, therefore, an individual's psychosexual self-perceptions apparently have already become fixed and must be dealt with as they are. The question then arises as to what should be done about adolescents who have habituated patterns at odds with the approved patterns of society. A boy's erotic feelings may be directed solely to members of his own sex; or he may feel like a girl in a boy's skin, a condition called transsexualism. Some authorities believe such an individual should simply be helped to accept himself and to accommodate to societal standards as best he can. Others believe that society's tolerance in the area of sexuality is too narrow and should be expanded. Still others insist that distortions in psychosexuality are susceptible to modification, under skilled psychiatry.

The first article that follows, by Brown and Lynn, provides a conceptual framework within which such questions may be viewed. These writers, both authorities in this area, clarify certain concepts and terms about which much confusion exists.

Other issues in psychosexual development relate not so much to basic theory as to sexual practices and their implications. Such questions become crucial for adolescents who ordinarily must cope with newly acquired sexual feelings without having adequate sexual outlets. But how much sexuality is "adequate," and what is the boundary line between "permissable" and "promiscuous" behaviors? College women, asserts Walters (1956), no longer deem premarital chastity a necessary virtue — an attitude which appears to set a new standard. But have youth's sexual standards really declined? Or are youth simply the perennial scapegoats of parents who have conveniently "forgotten" their own sexual escapades? Are youth's sexual encounters casual and lacking in ethics, and has the pill extracted all sin, sensuality, and hazard from sex?

According to Smigel and Seiden (1968), in the 1920s the sexual behaviors of youth underwent dramatic changes. This period was followed by a plateau, with very slight further changes in sexual mores occuring until the 1960s. If indeed there has been a recent sexual revolution similar to that of the 1920s, it is largely in terms of youths' frankness about sex and their freedom to discuss it. Women, in particular, have sought and been accorded broader educational and social rights in this area. One of these is the right to choose a sex partner and to determine one's own standard relative to sex. For their part, males have begun to modify their erstwhile so-called male prerogatives — for instance, their formerly common demand that the wife be a virgin. However, young males themselves are probably more monogamous and less promiscuous today than formerly, and their sexual relationships are also more stable. The double standard of sexual behavior, which implies a dual moral sexual code (one for men and one for women) has not yet fallen, but it has been declining as young people are mutually establishing a single standard based on sexual affection.

For better perspective on the status of youth's sex practices in America, we should consider the cross-cultural data. According to research by Christensen and Gregg (1970) comparing sexual norms in America and Scandinavia, the trend in America is toward the traditional Danish norm of premarital sex justified by commitment, while the emerging Danish pattern is away from both commitment and restriction and toward more free and promiscuous sex. Meantime, with the greater liberalization of females in both countries, the attitudes and behaviors of the sexes have tended to converge.

In our second reading selection, Luckey and Nass provide data concerning the sexual attitudes and behaviors of college students in five countries, including the United States. The results of their study indicated that students in Canada and the United States had more conservative views than did their counterparts in Europe, and that women in all five countries held more conservative views than men. On the other hand, some writers believe the gap between masculine and feminine sexual expression is closing. After reviewing the research, Rosenmayr (1968) concludes that more boys than girls have intercourse; but when incidence and frequency are combined, the total "sexual outlet" is very similar. In other words, fewer girls have intercourse but those who do so indulge more often. Boys have more sexual partners while girls prefer more enduring relationships. Initially, girls are more reluctant to have intercourse; but once they have agreed, they are more active sexually than boys.

Another and growing issue in the area of youth-and-sex is: How much and what sort of sex education is needed? Are most youths functional illiterates in sex or sophisticated practitioners of the art? When sex instruction is given, should both sexes receive it simultaneously? Family life educators almost universally recommend that the sexes be mixed for family life courses. However, in a study designed to test this assumption, it was found that equally successful instruction may take place in mixed and nonmixed groups (Adams, 1971).

REFERENCES

ADAMS, W. J.   Sex composition in family life courses: How important is this? *Family Coordinator,* 1971, *20*(1), 55–62.

CHRISTENSEN, H. T., & GREGG, C. F.   Changing sex norms in America and Scandinavia. *Journal of Marriage and the Family,* 1970, *32*(4), 616–627.

MONEY, J.   Psychosexual differentiation. In J. Money (Ed.) *Sex research: New developments.* New York: Holt, Rinehart and Winston, 1965.

ROSENMAYR, L.   Towards an overview of youth's sociology. *International Social Science Journal,* 1968, *20*(2), 286–315.

SMIGEL, E. O., & SEIDEN, R.   The decline and fall of the double standard. *Annals of the American Academy of Political and Social Science,* 1968, *376,* 6–17.

WALTERS, P. A.   Promiscuity in adolescence. *American Journal of Orthopsychiatry,* 1965, *35,* 670–675.

Human Sexual Development: An Outline of Components and Concepts

DANIEL G. BROWN   DAVID B. LYNN

The authors analyze human sexual development in terms of sexual structures and functions, his sex-role identification and behavior, and genital arousal and behavior relative to source, direction, aim, and object of gratification. They suggest a conceptual framework within which problems relating to human sexuality may be viewed.

This paper is an attempt to clarify the terminology and present a conceptual schema relative to human sexuality. The term *sexual* has been used so broadly as to include everything from biological differentiation of male and female, to orgasm, masculine or feminine role behavior, parental behavior, and even the pervasive psychic energy implied in the Freudian usage of the term libido. The boundaries of human sexuality are, in short, unclear. The terms and concepts in this area often lack precise meaning and not infrequently lead to conceptual confusion. Examples of this ambiguity may be seen in the fact that the following terms are used more or less synonymously: male and masculine; female and feminine; hermaphroditism, transvestism, transsexualism, homosexuality, and sexual inversion; and sexual drive, libido, and eroticism.

In recent years there has been an accumulation of research concerned with human sexuality indicating that the notion of an innate, predetermined psychologic sexuality does not correspond with existing evidence.[1]

Rather, recent investigations suggest that the psychosexual status of the individual is undifferentiated at birth. The individual begins life psychosexually plastic, capable of developing along a variety of lines depending upon the definition of sex roles in his particular culture as well as his unique learning experiences in the first few years of life especially. This psychosexual plasticity has been convincingly demonstrated by research showing that hermaphroditic children, i.e., those with a mixture or inconsistency of male and female components, usually grow up as masculine *or* feminine depending on the sex assigned them and the sex role in which they are reared. Research also suggests, however, that at

[1] J. Money, "Psychosexual Development in Man," in *The Encyclopedia of Mental Health*, ed. by A. Deutsch, New York: Franklin Watts, 1963, pp. 1678–1709.

From Daniel G. Brown and David B. Lynn, Human Sexual Development: An Outline of Components and Concepts, Reprinted from the *Journal of Marriage and the Family*, May 1966, *28*(2) 155–162. By permission of author and publisher.

least as far as sex role identity is concerned, this plasticity does not persist beyond early childhood; once a masculine or feminine sex role is established, it may be extremely difficult for this basic pattern to be changed or reversed later in life.[2]

The research with hermaphrodites blends well with recent research and theoretical developments concerning sex-role identification, indicating that masculinity or femininity does not emerge as an automatic unfolding, but rather result from familial and other influences as the individual develops.[3]

The following outline is an attempt to provide clarity and a basis for integrating recent findings in the field into a systematic framework. Three major independently varying components of human sexual development and behavior will be differentiated. These are 1. *the biological–constitutional* component, i.e., hereditary, congenital, and maturational factors; 2 *sex role,* the individual's identification of himself with one sex or the other; and 3. *genital–sex object preference,* the source, aim, and direction of sexual stimulation, desire, activity, and satisfaction. These major components will be reviewed in terms of hypothesized primary determinants, basic terminology, operational definitions, general manifestations, standard developmental outcome or norm, and nonstandard developmental outcome or deviation.

Biological–Constitutional Component

DETERMINANTS
HYPOTHESIZED PRIMARY

The hypothesized determinants of the biological–constitutional component are hereditary, congenital, and maturational.

[2] J. L. Hampson and J. G. Hampson, "The Ontogenesis of Sexual Behavior in Man," in *Sex and Internal Secretions,* ed. by W. C. Young, Baltimore: Williams & Williams, 1961, pp. 1401–1432; and J. Money, "Sex Hormones and Other Variables in Human Eroticism," in *Sex and Internal Secretions,* ed. by W. C. Young, Baltimore: Williams & Williams, 1961, pp. 1383–1400.

[3] See, for example, D. G. Brown, "Psychosexual Disturbances: Transvestism and Sex-Role Inversion," *Marriage and Family Living, 22*:3 (August 1960), pp. 218–226; R. E. Hartley, "A Developmental View of Female Sex-Role Definition and Identification," *Merrill-Palmer Quarterly, 10*:1 (January 1964), pp. 3–16; and D. B. Lynn, "Sex-Role and Parental Identification," *Child Development 33*:3 (September 1962), pp. 555–564.

BASIC TERMS

The basic terms are male–maleness and female–femaleness. These terms should be used to refer only to the biological aspects of sexuality and should be distinguished from masculine–masculinity and feminine–femininity, which refer to the psychological characteristics and behavior patterns typical of one sex in contrast to the other.

OPERATIONAL DEFINITIONS

Here the concern is with the relationship between male and female factors in the physiology of the individual, specifically the degree of male and female factors in the following structures and functions: 1. chromosomal composition (XX or XY); 2. gonadal composition (ovarian or testicular tissue); 3. hormonal composition (estrogen-androgen balance); 4. internal accessory structure (vagina, uterus, and fallopian tubes or seminal vesicles and prostate); and 5. external genitalia (clitoris and labia majora and labia minora or penis and scrotum).

GENERAL MANIFESTATIONS

In addition to the overall anatomical and physiological differences in genitalia between the sexes, there are also differences in general physique, body shape, physical dimensions, and other similar manifestations. Even in preschool years there are marked sex differences in body composition in that girls have more fatty tissue, while boys, although only slightly heavier, have more muscle tissue.[4] In adulthood a layer of subcutaneous fat develops, rounding and softening the contours of the face and body of women. The greater growth of the larnyx in males results in a deeper voice than that of women. Females develop enlarged breasts, an enlarged bony pelvic basin, and relatively wide hips; whereas males have a widening of shoulders. In addition to differences in pubic hair distribution, males are

[4] S. M. Garn, "Roentgenogrammetric Determinations of Body Composition," *Human Biology, 29* (1957), pp. 337–353; and S. M. Garn, "Fat, Body Size, and Growth in the Newborn," *Human Biology, 30* (1958), pp. 256–280.

characterized by a heavy growth of facial and body hair; whereas females develop a light down on the upper lip, forearms, and lower legs.

STANDARD DEVELOPMENTAL OUTCOME OR NORM

The standard outcome in the biological development of the individual is a predominance of anatomical and physiological structures and functions that are the basis of either maleness or femaleness; that is, the chromosomal, gonadal, internal accessory structures, external genitalia, and general manifestations are consistently male or female at maturity.

NON-STANDARD DEVELOPMENTAL OUTCOME OR DEVIATION

One of the more significant deviations in the biological sexual composition of the individual is that of hermaphroditism. There are other atypical forms of development, such as precocious puberty in which appropriate sex hormones function prematurely. However, hermaphroditism, sometimes referred to as intersexuality, is a biological anomaly of special interest in the behavioral sciences because it provides a basis for studying the interaction of physiological, social, and psychological variables in the sexual development of the individual. Hermaphroditism is a condition in which there is inconsistency in or among one or more of the following factors in the biological composition of the individual: chromosomal, gonadal, hormonal, internal accessory structures, and external genitalia. Examples include an individual showing ambiguity in external genitalia, a person having ovaries and a penis, or one who is chromosomally male but has a vagina and female accessory organs. Androgyny refers to the condition in which a male has female biological traits; gynandry involves a female with male biological traits.

Money, Hampson, and Hampson list the following varieties of hermaphrodites:[5]

1. Congenital hyperadrenocortical females—externally hermaphroditic; normal internal reproductive organs and sex chromatin pattern. Without cortisone therapy, growth and development is precocious and virilizing.

2. Hermaphrodites with ambiguous or masculinized external genitals—normal functional female internal reproductive structures and ovaries and female sex chromatin pattern. Unlike females with hyperadrenocorticism, this group does not show progressive virilization; secondary feminization at puberty is the rule with reproduction possible.

3. Classical true hermaphroditism—testicular and ovarian tissue both present; enlarged phallus; variable development of the genital ducts; male or female sex chromatin pattern.

4. Cryptorchid hermaphrodites with relatively complete Müllerian differentiation—penis, hypospadic or normal; possible virilizing at puberty; male sex chromatin pattern.

5. Cryptorchid hermaphrodites with relatively incomplete Müllerian differentiation—hypospadic or clitoral phallus; possible virilizing at puberty; male sex chromatin pattern.

6. Simulant females with feminizing inguinal testes and vestigial Müllerian differentiation—blind vaginal pouch; male sex chromatin pattern.

Sex-Role Component

HYPOTHESIZED PRIMARY DETERMINANTS

The determinants hypothesized for the sex-role component are environmental conditioning and the social learning experiences of the individual.

BASIC TERMS

Masculine–masculinity and feminine–femininity are the basic terms, in contrast to male–maleness and female–femaleness, which, as previously indicated, refer to the biological composition of the individual.

[5] J. Money, J. G. Hampson, and J. L. Hampson, "Hermaphroditism: Recommendations Concerning Assignment of Sex, Change of Sex, and Psychological Management," *Bulletin of Johns Hopkins Hospital,* 97 (1955), pp. 284–300.

OPERATIONAL DEFINITIONS

Here the concern is with the extent that a person's behavioral patterns and psychological traits are typical of one sex in contrast to the other in a given culture and social environment. In this connection sex-role identification may be distinguished from sex-role preference.[6] Sex-role preference refers to the desire to adopt the behavior associated with one sex or the perception of such behavior as preferable or more desirable. Identification may also be contrasted to sex-role adoption, the latter referring to the actual adoption of behavior characteristic of one sex or the other, not simply the desire to adopt such behavior.[7]

The fact that a woman on appropriate occasions wears trousers or short hair does not necessarily mean that she is identified with the masculine role even though she is adopting certain aspects characteristics of that role. Sex-role identification is reserved for reference to the introjection and incorporation of the role of a given sex and to the basic, underlying reactions characteristic of that role.

Thus, a person may identify with the opposite sex but for expediency adopt much of the behavior characteristic of his own sex. In some respects he may prefer the role of his own sex, although there is considerable identification with the opposite-sex role. One would expect such a person, having identified substantially with the opposite sex, to have a number of underlying reactions characteristic of the opposite-sex role despite his adopting much of the behavior characteristic of the same-sex role. On the other hand, the woman who on appropriate occasions adopts aspects characteristic of the opposite-sex role, such as wearing trousers or wearing short hair, is certainly not necessarily identified with the masculine role. Thus, sex-role adoption refers to overt behavior characteristic of a given sex, while sex-role identification refers to a more basic, internalized process in which behavioral characteristics of one sex role or the other are incorporated.

[6] D. G. Brown, "Sex-Role Preference in Young Children," *Psychological Monographs, 70*:14 (1956), (Whole No. 421).
[7] D. B. Lynn, "A Note of Sex Differences in the Development of Masculine and Feminine Identification," *Psychological Review, 66*:2 (1959), pp. 126–135.

GENERAL MANIFESTATIONS

Certain attitudes, preferences, social motives, fantasies, dreams, and feelings; gestures, gait, and other expressive movements and postures; general demeanor; communicative qualities such as spontaneous topic of conversation and casual commitment, enunciation, word associations, and word choices; some patterns associated with paternal or maternal behavior; and various everyday habits and mannerisms typical of the masculine or feminine role constitute the general manifestations.

STANDARD DEVELOPMENTAL OUTCOME OR NORM

The standard outcome is identification with, preference for, and adoption of the sex role that is consistent with a person's biological constitutional composition, i.e., the acquisition of a masculine role in males and a feminine role in females.

There has been an increasing amount of research and theoretical formulations in recent years concerning sex-role behavior.[8] In general, there is considerable agreement as to the importance of learning in the individual's attaining the role appropriate to his or her sex, i.e., there is a consensus that the individual learns to identify with a given sex role, to prefer one role or the other, and to adopt aspects of one role or the other. Emphasis on the learned aspect of sex or gender role acquisition has been given much support by recent research on hermaphroditism. As previously indicated, individuals of comparable anatomical and physiological deviation in

[8] See, for example, A. Bandura and A. C. Huston, "Identification as a Process of Incidental Learning," *Journal of Abnormal and Social Psychology, 63*:2 (September 1961), pp. 311–318; U. Bronfenbrenner, "Freudian Theories of Identification and Their Derivatives," *Child Development, 31*:1 (March 1960), pp. 15–40; Brown, "Psychosexual Disturbances: Transvestism and Sex-Role Inversion," *op. cit.*; Hartley, *op. cit.*; J. Kagan, "The Concept of Identification," *Psychological Review, 65* (1958), pp. 296–305; R. R. Sears, "Identification as a Form of Behavior Development," in *The Concept of Development*, ed. by D. B. Harris, Minneapolis: University of Minnesota Press, 1957, pp. 149–161; B. Sutton-Smith, J. M. Roberts, and B. G. Rosenberg, "Sibling Associations and Role Involvement," *Merrill-Palmer Quarterly, 10*:1 (January 1964), pp. 25–38; and R. F. Winch, *Identification and Its Familial Determinants*, Indianapolis: Bobbs-Merrill, 1962.

composition have been reared successfully as either boys or girls. These studies show that chromosomal sex and gonadal sex can be overridden by learning experiences. That hormonal sex can also be overridden is demonstrated by female hermaphrodites with an androgenital syndrome, but who are raised and living as women. Before the recent advent of cortisone therapy to suppress adrenal androgens, these women were heavily virilized and totally lacking in female secondary sexual characteristics; they sometimes had a very enlarged clitoris, and sometimes a fused, empty scrotal sac. Nevertheless, their assigned sex as women generally dominated their hormonal sex. In reference to the singular importance of sex-role assignment and rearing, Money points out that it is possible for psychosexual differentiation in a person to be contradictory of chromosomal, gonadal, hormonal, or external genital and internal sex and to agree instead with assigned sex.[9] The crucial significance of learning in the acquisition of gender role is clearly indicated.

Workers concerned with hermaphroditism have suggested a parallel between the acquisition of sex or gender role in humans and imprinting in lower animals. Thus, there may be a critical period within which the gender role of an individual is established.[10] In a review of the factor of age in psychosexual development in children, Brown suggests that sex-role differentiation is a gradual process beginning between the first and second year of life and becoming definitely established by or during the fifth year.[11] On the basis of hermaphroditic cases of sex reassignment, Money concludes that the critical period for "gender imprinting" is between eighteen months and three years of age, beginning with the onset of mastery

of language.[12] He considers the die to be well cast by the age of six with major realignment of gender role and sexual identity rare after that.

NON-STANDARD DEVELOPMENTAL OUTCOME OR DEVIATION

The non-standard outcome is the acquisition of a sex role or certain aspects of a sex role not consistent with a person's biological composition.[13] Several examples are discussed below.

1. *Transvestism* involves the desire for, act of, and emotional satisfactions connected with wearing the apparel of the opposite sex. Apart from their cross-sex dress, transvestites may otherwise establish a heterosexual adjustment. This points up the necessity of clearly distinguishing between transvestism and other concepts, such as homosexuality and sex-role inversion.[14] One factor often found in the life histories of transvestites is that during the first two or three years of life, the child intentionally or otherwise often wears and fondles clothes of the opposite sex and in some instances is praised for his appearance in the clothes of the opposite sex. In childhood some male transvestites have long hair that is curled as a girl's; in the background of still others is a mother who wanted a girl rather than a boy.

2. *Sex-role inversion* is the phenomenon in which a person of one biological sex learns to think, feel, and act like the opposite sex. This involves the acceptance and adoption of the sex role of the other sex. Although transvestism is a component of inversion, it is *not* unique to inverts. Transvestism will almost always be found in cases of inversion since desiring and wearing the clothes of the other sex is one of many aspects of adopting the role of that sex; however, the converse is not true—inversion is *not* necessarily found in transvestites. Thus, a transvestite may be atypical in his sex-role functioning *only* with

[9] J. Money, "Developmental Differentiation of Femininity and Masculinity Compared," in *Man and Civilization: The Potential of Women,"* ed. by S. M. Farber and R. H. L. Wilson, New York: McGraw-Hill, 1963, p. 56.
[10] See, for example, Brown, "Psychosexual Disturbances: Transvestism and Sex-Role Inversion," *op. cit.;* D. G. Brown, Homosexuality and Family Dynamics," *Bulletin of the Menninger Clinic,* 27:5 (September 1963), pp. 227–232; Hampson and Hampson, *op. cit.;* and Money, "Sex Hormones and Other Variables in Human Eroticism," *op. cit.*
[11] D. G. Brown, "Sex-Role Development in a Changing Culture," *Psychological Bulletin, 54* (1958), pp. 232–242.

[12] Money, "Sex Hormones and Other Variables in Human Eroticism," *op cit.*
[13] Actually, the hermaphrodite who has a consistent sex role is, by definition, non-standard in that his role must be at variance with some aspect of his ambiguous biological composition.
[14] D. G. Brown, "Inversion and Homosexuality," *American Journal of Orthopsychiatry, 28* (1958), 424–429.

respect to this lifelong but relatively isolated, compulsive behavioral pattern.

Various incongruous combinations of sex-role behavior may occur in a given person. For instance, a boy may dislike playing with girls, but show an interest in domestic activities, such as cooking, sewing, housekeeping, and using make-up, as well as a liking for mechanical toys, tools, and building materials.[15]

Instances in which a male child has a relatively positive attachment to the father, or at least a relationship which is free of basic rejection or hostility, and at the same time has a mother who allows, encourages, or forces him to wear feminine dress and to develop other feminine patterns are likely to result in some degree of confusion or duality in sex-role development. The person may show some uncertainty as to his sex role, or he may actually develop *two relatively dichotomous selves* one of which is masculine and one feminine. An individual may describe himself as "ruggedly masculine and aggressive" when dressed in masculine clothes but "passive, gentle and submissive" when attired in feminine clothes. It is evident in such a case that two sex roles coexist in the same personality. A variation of this pattern is seen in the case of a person who reported that he often felt "like two people in one, male and female" and "never completely male and never completely female."[16] This individual during his childhood showed a mixture of feminine interests—dolls, cooking, sewing—as well as masculine pursuits—mechanical tasks, tools, playing cowboys. As an adult he alternated between muscle-building exercises and efforts to be "more of a man" and wearing feminine clothing, using cosmetics, and trying to appear more like a woman. Still another person reported that when he was in his feminine phase he tried to approximate the ideal-image of women whom he admired when he was in his masculine role. He attempted to become the kind of woman that his masculine self found most attractive. While in his masculine role his whole personality would change, and he

would become thoroughly masculine in interests, dress, and behavior.[17]

It is interesting to note that cases such as those described above bear some resemblance to instances of dual or multiple personality in that there is an alternation between different roles of sex, rather than between roles of "good" and "bad." Part of the time the person is masculine in appearance and behavior; at other times the same person is feminine. Instead of a Dr. Jekyll and Mr. Hyde or an Eve White and Eve Black, there is a "Mr." Doe and a "Miss" Doe. However, there is an important difference between individuals with dual sex roles and those with dual personalities. In contrast to cases of dual personality, in which one of the two selves is amnesic for the other, individuals who develop two sex roles are aware of the existence of both roles. Thus, when such a person is in the feminine role, he will dress, talk, and act like a woman; although he is quite aware of his other self in which he dresses, talks, and acts like a man.

In addition to transvestism, homosexuality should be differentiated from sex-role inversion. While homosexuality typically occurs in individuals who show sex-role inversion, there is considerable evidence that a number of other factors may predispose the individual to the development of homosexuality as well. The homosexual is an individual who desires and/or obtains predominant or exclusive sexual satisfaction with members of his own sex; the invert is one whose thoughts, perceptions, attitudes, fantasies, feelings, preferences, interests, and behavioral tendencies are typical of the opposite sex.[18]

With reference to the determinants of sex-role identification, it might be predicted that a male displaying gender role inversion would have a father who, during the individual's early childhood, had been physically absent most of the time, psychologically ineffective and socially distant, or chronically abusive and cruel to the boy and, in addition, a mother who is "idolized" by the

---

[15] Brown, "Psychosexual Disturbances: Transvestism and Sex-Role Inversion," *op. cit.*

[16] B. Karpman, "Dream Life in a Case of Transvestism," *Journal of Nervous and Mental Disease*, 106 (1947), pp. 292–337.

[17] C. V. Prince, "Homosexuality, transvestism and transsexualism," *American Journal of Psychotherapy*, 11 (1957), pp. 80–8.

[18] D. G. Brown, "The Development of Sex-Role Inversion and Homosexuality," *Journal of Pediatrics*, 50:5 (May 1957), p. 614.

boy, emotionally "smothers" him, or to whom the boy is excessively close and attached. For girls inversion would be expected to develop only in cases in which there is a serious disruption in the mother–daughter relationship and early abnormal attachment to the father that prevents the little girl from identifying with the mother or where the mother herself denies or despises her own femininity and thus exposes the daughter to a distorted feminine model. Another predisposing family pattern, which might function in isolation or in conjunction with those already mentioned, is one in which the parent or parents actually encourage and rear a child of one sex to feel, think, and behave like that of the other.

3. *Transsexualism* involves sex-role inversion and also the desire for surgical sexual transformation, such as the case of George (Christine) Jorgensen. As in most other psychosexual disturbances, transsexualism is primarily associated with men rather than women. For example, following the publicity concerning the "change of sex" case of Jorgensen in Denmark, the endocrinologist who supervised the changeover received three times as many letters from men as from women expressing a desire for medical change of sexual identity.[19] This differential might partially be explained by the fact that the particular operation given the publicity was one involving a change from male to female. Perhaps the apparently greater feasibility of surgical procedures involved in amputating the penis than in constructing male genitalia may also have been a factor. However, it is probable that the suggested predominance of transsexualism among men has more deeply rooted origins than the above explanations. Among the factors which predispose males more readily than females to sex-role inversion may be the fact that, since all infants are attached to the mother or mother-substitute in earliest life, it is the boy, not the girl, who must shift from an initial identification with the feminine model to masculne role identification with the father or father-substitute. In addition, because fathers in this culture are usually away from home much of the time, the girl typically has her model

for identification, the mother, with her more often than the boy has his model, the father, with him.

Genital–Sex Object Preference

HYPOTHESIZED PRIMARY DETERMINANTS

Environmental conditioning and social learning experiences are hypothesized as the primary determinants for the third component of sexual development, genital–sex object preference.

BASIC TERMS

Genital sex desire, drive, and gratification are the basic terms. The Freudian term *libido,* although defined variously during the many years of Freud's writing, always encompassed more than genital sex desire, drive, and gratification.

OPERATIONAL DEFINITIONS

Genital–sex object preference is defined as the source of genital sex arousal, the aim and direction of genital sex drive, and the nature of the object and situation with which genital gratification or orgasm occur.

GENERAL MANIFESTATIONS

This component is manifested in genital sex arousal, excitement, and behavior either directly observable or covertly present at the level of fantasy, dreams, and imagination.

The male orgasm is a relatively simple and easily observable reaction. However, the orgasm in women has been less well understood until the recent highly significant research of Masters and Johnson.[20] These investigators furnish evi-

---

[19] D. G. Brown, "Inversion and Homosexuality," *op. cit.*

[20] W. H. Masters and V. C. Johnson, "The Physiology of the Vaginal Reproductive Function," *Western Journal of Surgery, Obstetrics and Gynecology,* 69 (1961), pp. 105–120; and W. H. Masters and V. C. Johnson, "The Sexual Response Cycle of the Human Female. III. The Clitoris: Anatomic and Clinical Considerations," *Western Journal of Surgery, Obstetrics and Gynecology,* 70 (1962), pp. 248–257. All of the major research and significant findings of Masters and Johnson will be published in a book now in press.

dence that the muscular spasms of ejaculation in the male have their counterpart in the female. Photographic documentation indicates the tumescence of a cylindrical orgasmic platform immediately inside the vagina and extending along the vaginal barrel for about one third of its length. The orgasmic platform and adjacent tissues outside the vaginal orifice throb and contract spasmodically during the time orgasm is reported. Meanwhile, the innermost end of the vagina has ballooned out and the cervix has somewhat retracted. The manifestations of orgasm are identical whether stimulation is masturbatory and clitoral or produced by artificial coitus with a hollow, clear-plastic object simulating the phallus.

Although the focus of this section is on genital sexual arousal, extremely intense sexual experience is possible independent of genitopelvic happenings. The paraplegic has no neural connections between the upper and lower parts of the nervous system. Nevertheless, some paraplegic patients describe vivid orgastic experiences in erotic dreams which simulate true genital orgasm. These "orgastic" dreams, of course, lack erection or ejaculation, because no neural connections exist between the brain and the genital region.[21]

STANDARD DEVELOPMENTAL OUTCOME OR NORM

The standard outcome is heterosexuality. More specifically, the prescribed outcome in our society is monogamous heterosexuality. Heterosexuality has been so taken for granted that until recently it was assumed to be completely biologically determined and any deviation therefrom, the result of some biological defect. The previously mentioned studies, showing that hermaphroditic children with the same anomaly grow up as masculine or feminine in agreement with the assigned sex and acquire the genital–sex object preference appropriate to that sex, make it evident that environmental conditioning and social learning experiences are of crucial importance. In addition, since the male hormone androgen apparently functions as the erotic hormone for

women as well as men, an increase in the androgen level may very well increase the erotic drive of a woman yet not result in a shift of her sex object preference nor motivate her to take a masculine role in erotic activity. In other words, a heterosexual woman given androgen may become more strongly erotically motivated, but she does not become homosexual in her desires.

Those investigators who have studied hermaphroditism conclude that genital-sex object choice may be the result of appropriate imprinting at the critical period in the child's development. In this regard Money suggests that a person may engage in a homosexual act when past the critical period without becoming a chronic homosexual. Money reports that, in general, imprinted eroticism appears to be permanent and ineradicable.[22]

NON-STANDARD DEVELOPMENTAL OUTCOME OR DEVIATION

The following are examples of deviations in the genital component:

1. *Autosexuality* (masturbation) is the genital stimulation and gratification of a person by himself. The sexual outlet is statistically so common, occurring in practically all males and the majority of females, it is considered non-standard only when it is the exclusive or nearly exclusive erotic preference of an individual. It is also recognized that when masturbation occurs it is often in connection with fantasied heterosexual or homosexual situations.

2. *Homosexuality* refers to the phenomenon in which an individual predominantly or exclusively desires and/or obtains genital sexual stimulation and gratification with a person of the same biological sex.[23] In a previous section of this paper, sex-role or sexual inversion was differentiated from homosexuality. Almost invariably the individual with inverted gender identification desires

---

[21] J. Money, "Phantom Orgasm in the Dreams of Paraplegic Men and Women," *Archives of General Psychiatry*, 3 (1960), 373–382.

[22] Money, "Sex Hormones and Other Variables in Human Eroticism," *op. cit.*

[23] This concept of homosexuality becomes extremely blurred when dealing with the erotic life of a hermaphroditic individual since his biological sex is ambiguous.

sexual activity with a person of the same anatomic sex, and when this is the case can be regarded as homosexual. However, there are many homosexuals who are not inverted in their sex or gender role. Homosexuals have in common only their preference for sexual partners of the same biological sex. Often the inverted male homosexual corresponds to what has traditionally been called the passive male homosexual, who takes the role of the opposite sex in homosexual activity. The non-inverted homosexual corresponds to the active male homosexual, the one taking the role appropriate to his own biological sex. Similarly, the inverted female homosexual often corresponds to what has been called the active female homosexual, the one taking the masculine role in homosexual activity; and the noninverted female homosexual, the passive female homosexual, often corresponds to the one taking the feminine role in homosexual activity. However, homosexuals sometimes "switch roles" in their sexual activity; the one who is the passive partner on one occasion acts as the active partner on the next occasion. It is very unlikely that they switch sex-role identification in the sense of their basic personality structure, showing role inversion one day and normal role behavior the next, unless there is involved also the dual sex-role phenomenon mentioned previously. Inversion, therefore, should refer to the individual's total personality structure. The invert may be described as a psycho-somatic misfit with the physical characteristics of one sex, such as being anatomically male, but the personality characteristic of the other sex, being psychologically feminine.

One would predict that the etiology of homosexuality in cases which are inverted would be quite dissimilar from those which are not inverted. In a previous section the hypothesized determinants of inversion were conditioning experiences. Money considers imprinting an important part in homosexuality, but he does not distinguish between homosexuals who are or are not inverted. "Effectively imprinted at the critical period to respond to homosexual stimuli—a person becomes a chronic homosexual. Effective stimuli may be extremely specific and variable from person to person, which may account for the varieties of homosexual preference."[24] However, Money does not elaborate on the nature of the experiences occurring between the age of eighteen months and three years—the critical period— which may lead to chronic homosexuality.

3. *Other deviations* include bisexuality, zo-oerasty, pederasty, exhibitionism, fetishism, sadism, and masochism, all of which involve genital desire, stimulation, and gratification that deviate from the normal heterosexual, interpersonal relationship.

[24] Money, "Sex Hormones and Other Variables in Human Eroticism," *op. cit.,* p. 1397.

A Comparison of Sexual Attitudes and Behavior in an International Sample

ELEANORE B. LUCKEY   **GILBERT D. NASS**

Data regarding attitudes and behavior in the areas of sex role and courtship were obtained from male and female college students in the United States, Canada, England, Norway, and Germany.

Sexual attitudes and practices of college and university youth have recently been surveyed and reported by numerous investigators. The present study includes data from the United States, Canada, England, Norway, and Germany. It should be stressed at the outset that this research was not designed to pinpoint such facts as how many men and women were having sexual outlets and how many times per week and what kind of outlets these were. The investigation purports rather to be a comparative study that suggests existing sexual attitudes and behaviors and reports similarities and differences which seem to exist between the sampled national populations.

This study was done in collaboration with Vance Packard, who has used the findings as a basis for his book *The Sexual Wilderness,* David McKay, New York, 1968, and was presented at the Groves Conference on Marriage and the Family, Boston, 1968. The computational part of this work was carried out in the Computer Center, University of Connecticut, which is supported in part by grants GP-1819 and GJ-9 of the National Science Foundation.

The Sample

Unmarried undergraduate university students from five countries were included in the sample. The United States was represented by 21 colleges and universities. These were selected with the aim of geographical distribution that would insure adequate representation of the entire country. Seven were in eastern states: a New England men's college, a private university in New York City, an Ivy League university, a state university in New England, a state college in New England, a private women's college in the northeast, and a private women's college known to have liberal parietal rules. Five were in middlewestern states: a state university, a Catholic university in a metropolitan area, a Protestant university in a non-metropolitan area, a private coed university in a metropolitan area, and one in a non-metropolitan area. Three were in southern states: a state university, a state university in the upper south, and a private university in a metropolitan area. Finally, six were in western states: a state

From E. B. Luckey & G. D. Nass. A comparison of sexual attitudes and behavior in an international sample. Reprinted from the *Journal of Marriage and the Family,* May 1969, *31*(2), 364–379. By permission of authors and publisher.

university in the Rocky Mountain area, a state university in the southwest and one in the northwest, a state university in California and a private one there, and a state college in the southwest.

Contained in the American sample were two all-male colleges and two all-female colleges; two were specifically church-related. Public and private, metropolitan and non-metropolitan, secular and non-secular, coeducational and sexually segregated schools were included. The varied sample was chosen to provide data suggestive of a national picture. In each school 100 students were contacted in schools that were coeducational; the population was half male and half female.

A major university was selected from each of the other countries. An equal number of men and women were chosen from each population. From the German university information was solicited from 450 individuals; each of the other foreign populations was 300. The 150 additional subjects in the German sample were included in order to compensate for using a mailed questionnaire rather than one personally handed to the subjects; it was assumed that the response would be lower. Choosing one university that is "typical" of any country's student population is difficult if not impossible—this being especially true in England because of the variety of university types. However, in each country the choice of a large university was made because of its diversified population both geographically and demographically.

The number of respondents was gratifying; out of a total of 3,450 solicitations there were 2,230 subjects (64.6 percent) who responded,

representing a 66.8 percent return from the United States sample and 61.6 percent from the foreign universities. The return was considered generally higher than can be expected from a study of this kind and implies an adequate sample from which to generalize. It is interesting that in the North American samples more women responded than men, but in all the European samples the reverse was true. This suggests that European women may be more reluctant to discuss sexual matters than the American and that American men are more reticent than European.

In the United States only third- and fourth-year students were included in the study, but because foreign universities are not structurally comparable with American universities, the subjects were selected according to age; those between 20 and 22 were included. In all samples the ages were *very* similar; the mean for men being 21.1 years and for women, 20.9 years.

Procedure

An inventory composed of 42 questions was designed so that answers could be solicited by checking or circling appropriate responses. In some instances explanatory or further comments were invited. The questionnaire was headed simply "College Checklist" and included questions on social sex roles including career roles for women, attitudes toward marriage especially with regard to sexual behavior, general views on affectional and sexual relationships, affectional and sexual experience of the respondent, and age.

Table 1. Questionnaire Distribution and Response

Sample Category	Number Distributed	Number Returned			Percent Returned
		Male	Female	Total	
21 United States universities	2,100	670	728	1,398	66.6
Canada	300	89	91	180	60.0
England	300	142	103	245	81.6
Germany	450	134	121	255	56.7*
Norway	300	86	66	152	50.6
Totals	3,450	1,121	1,109	2,230	64.6

*Because some of these respondents were married, they were considered not eligible for the study and were discarded. The response rate of the unmarried students was 62 percent, and it was this number which was included in all further analyses.

The questionnaire along with a cover letter of explanation was distributed on each of the campuses, except the German, by student distributors who were supervised by a reliable assistant. Confidentiality and anonymity were assured, and stamped, addressed envelopes provided for direct return to the investigators. The German questionnaire which is the only one translated from English to the native language was *mailed* to a random sample of students. In all cases a randomly selected sample was attempted; although in schools where a goodly number of students were known to fit into a special category (for example, students living in their own apartments off campus), a special attempt was made to include some of these subjects.

There were some minor differences in questionnaires in order to keep them appropriate to the population with which they were being used. The German translation modified some of the questions, and therefore the data are not comparable; this will account for lack of German data in some categories.

Results

(1) SEX ROLE DIFFERENCES

Sex roles of the male and female and whether the differences between the sexes should or should not be encouraged give clues to the attitudes youth hold with regard to their own sex and the other, whether "equality" and "sameness" is the current mode or whether sex differentiation is emphasized. Several questions were designed to approach this answer from different angles.

When asked if they thought individuals and society functioned best if male and female roles in life were different though equal, Canadian students provided the strongest approval; Norwegian students were by a considerable margin the least enthusiastic.

Coeducational living arrangements—with men and women occupying separate rooms but in the same dormitories, on the same floors, and in the same wings—were looked on with much more favor in the European schools than in those in Canada and the United States. In all cases men were more disposed to these living arrangements than were women.

At all universities there was little support for separating the sexes in the classroom. Fifteen percent of the males and 10 percent of the females in the United States sample indicated that they believed such separation "would produce a better environment for study." The Canadian and English response was similar, but only five percent of the Norway students held such a belief.

The subjects were asked, "Is a four-year college education generally as essential for the personal fulfillment and life satisfaction of girls as it is for men of comparable intelligence?" As

Table 2. Percentage *Yes* Responses to: "Do you support the idea that individuals and society function best if male and female roles in life remain essentially different though equal?"

	Male	Female
United States	84.7	88.3
(N)	(645)	(691)
Canada	88.1	94.2
	(84)	(86)
England	68.4	65.6
	(133)	(96)
Germany	63.8	51.9
	(116)	(108)
Norway	49.4	41.9
	(77)	(62)

Table 3. Percentage Responses Favoring Coe< Living Arrangements (No Separation of Sex b Floors or Wings) in Dormitories

	Male	Female
United States	35.7	26.1
(N)	(655)	(713)
Canada	36.4	20.0
	(88)	(90)
England	66.9	62.4
	(139)	(101)
Germany	65.0	54.1
	(117)	(109)
Norway	Item not included because of prevailir dormitory practices.	

might be expected, there were decidedly more women than men who replied affirmatively. In Norway 91.8 percent of the women and 81 percent of the men replied affirmatively. Only two-thirds of the American men were sure. European men and women were much closer in their agreement than were the North American, and more were sure that there should be equal education. The widest discrepancy between male and female subjects was found in the United States.

Female subjects were asked if they had seriously in mind an occupational career that they would like to pursue most of the next 20 years. Many more of the English and Norwegian women had such careers in mind than those of other countries. Half or fewer of the Canadian, German, and American women planned careers, but more than three-fourths of English and Norwegian. The dilemma posed by career–marriage decisions for women was seen to exist to a considerable degree in all countries. When they were asked if they believed a good many bright girls consciously downgraded their ambitions for a career because of fear that it might hurt their chances of marriage, 71 percent of the Canadian agreed as compared to 57 percent of those in the United States; although about 60 percent of the men in each of the two countries held this position. In all countries except the United States, more women than men believed this to be true. There was a marked difference between opinions of European men, of whom only about a third thought women had to play down their ambitions in contrast with those in North America. Although the percentage of assenting women ranged from 71 to 38, the greatest difference existed between American and Canadian women. There is no ready explanation of this difference, which is inconsistent with practically all the other findings indicating the United States and Canadian populations hold similar views.

Sex role differences were generally emphasized to a greater extent in the North American countries than in the English and Scandinavian sample where men and women expect more equalization and less differentiation. European students, to a greater extent than American students, preferred both mixed-sex dormitory arrangements and classrooms. The European women planned to have careers, saw it as not interfering with marital

roles, and recognized need for education. Their men agreed. Americans and Canadians tended more to see the woman's place in the home.

(2) PARENTAL INDEPENDENCE

Interesting ambiguities with regard to notions of parental independence were presented by the variation in opinions as to whether or not a strong society would be produced if social arrangements could be made that would enable all young people to be financially independent of their parents by age 21 regardless of whether they pursued higher education or not. England and Norway gave this idea the greatest support with about half of them agreeing to it. Germany gave it the least. Men generally favored the idea to a greater extent than women.

A related dimension, that of the parentally financed undergraduate marriage, was supported by two-fifths of the English students, both men and women. About a fourth of the Canadian and United States students supported the position; less than a fifth of Norwegian men did.

The view that young people under 21 desire more guidelines and limits received the greatest support from Canadian and United States students (men 36 percent, women 54 percent). Only about 20 percent of the English supported the position, and in all countries women indicated a greater desire for guidelines than men.

Each national sample provided a different pattern in picking the category of people who should set male–female intimacy guidelines. Among persons who felt there was a need for more clearly defined standards, Canadian and American students most frequently designated "parents" and "adults" should be those to set the standards. English students favored "youthful peers" and "adults," and Norwegian students cited "parents" and "schools." "Churches" were virtually ignored by all males and were not much more frequently cited by the females.

Although no clear-cut or well-defined pattern emerged from these findings, it can be generally concluded that the English and Scandinavian youth favored greater financial and moral independence from the parental generation than the North American. However, the majority of young people in all countries rejected social arrange-

Table 4. Percentage Responses to: "If you feel there is a need for more clearly-defined standards who, under modern conditions, should have the main responsibility for setting them?"

	United States		Canada		England		Norway	
	Male	Female	Male	Female	Male	Female	Male	Female
Youthful peers	21.8	17.8	11.4	18.9	31.4	34.8	6.7	13.5
Parents	37.4	43.1	41.8	25.1	25.7	15.2	47.3	36.5
Schools	6.8	5.8	12.3	18.1	12.9	17.9	27.1	27.0
Churches	5.1	3.9	2.1	7.8	2.9	8.9	—	9.5
Adults	28.9	29.4	32.4	30.1	27.1	23.2	18.9	13.5
	100%	100%	100%	100%	100%	100%	100%	100%
(N)	(412)	(466)	(48)	(58)	(70)	(56)	(37)	(37)

ments which would make them financially independent of parents by age 21. They also rejected parentally financed education–marriage. Decidedly more North American than European students, and women more than men, felt guidelines and limits were needed for sexual standards, and only in England were "youthful peers" favored over adults for determining such standards.

(3) ATTITUDES TOWARD MARRIAGE AND SEXUAL BEHAVIOR

Marriage was given a strong vote of confidence by all the samples, as the majority responded negatively to the question, "Can you visualize a happy, satisfying life for yourself that might not include marriage?" About 20 percent more Canadian and American youth responded "no" than European. Ten percent more of the Norwegian men than women replied negatively; this is the only response where the male percentage was higher than the female. Some of the subjects were not sure; English men more frequently indicated the "uncertain" response (31.6 percent) than any other group. Canadian females (15.7 percent) were less often in doubt than any other group. Twenty-nine percent of the Norwegian females and 26.2 percent of English females responded that they *could* be happy though unmarried, but only about 15 percent of Canadian and American women replied in the affirmative. About a fourth of the male subjects in the United States, Norway, and England believed they could live happily though unmarried. Few Canadian subjects—either men or women—indicated they fancied an unmarried life. Again it is the European samples that have indicated a greater break with the traditional pattern.

Table 5. Percentage of Affirmative Responses Indicating that Ideally a Man and Woman Who Marry Should Have Their First Full Sexual Experience Together

	Affirmative Responses		Only After Marriage	
	Male	Female	Male	Female
United States	50.5	51.1	35.5	46.9
(N)	(646)	(709)	(600)	(657)
Canada	49.4	65.5	23.7	51.2
	(85)	(87)	(80)	(84)
England	37.3	29.3	20.0	28.1
	(134)	(99)	(125)	(89)
Norway	46.3	60.0	20.5	28.3
	(82)	(60)	(73)	(60)

Table 6. Percentage Male and Female Responses to: "Do you think it is reasonable for a male who has experienced coitus elsewhere to expect that the girl he hopes to marry be chaste at the time of marriage?"

	United States		*Canada*		*England*		*Norway*	
	Male	*Female*	*Male*	*Female*	*Male*	*Female*	*Male*	*Female*
Yes	21.3	35.9	20.5	32.6	15.1	10.9	1.2	6.5
No	68.4	53.4	71.1	56.2	59.7	54.5	71.8	66.1
Preposterous Anachronism	10.3	10.7	8.4	11.2	24.5	34.7	27.1	27.4
	100%	100%	100%	100%	100%	100%	100%	100%
(*N*)	(643)	(716)	(83)	(89)	(139)	(101)	(85)	(62)

The ideal age of marriage was fairly uniform among the universities. Males at all schools indicated about 25 as the modal choice. American women most frequently indicated an age between 21 and 23; all other national groups indicated a year or two older. In general, both men and women in all samples indicated a preference for the man to be slightly older than the woman.

The idea that a couple who marry should have their first full sexual experience together found greatest support among Canadian and Norwegian females. The least support was by English females. The range of difference was greater between female samples. The greatest congruence between the sexes was found in the United States sample, where about one-half thought this true.

An additional specification that the sexual experience should be "only after marriage" was preferred by all female subjects when compared to male and was marked by subjects of both sexes more frequently in American universities. English men and women, and then Norwegian, marked this qualification least frequently.

In an attempt to appraise attitudes toward the double standard sex code, the question was asked:

Do you think it is reasonable for a male who has experienced coitus elsewhere to expect that the girl he hopes to marry be chaste at the time of marriage?

A "yes" response was interpreted as potential support for the double standard. Virtually no support was given the idea by Norwegian students. American and Canadian females most strongly supported the double standard position with approximately a third of them agreeing; a fifth

of the men from these same two countries held this view.

The German questionnaire was modified to read:

One often hears the opinion that it is better for a marriage if the girl is still a virgin before marriage but the man has had sexual experience beforehand. Other people say a man with sexual experience cannot expect to marry a virgin girl. With which opinion do you agree most?

Only 13.2 percent of the men and 18.9 percent of the women supported the double standard position. About a fourth of the women and a fifth of the men believed neither partner should have experience before marriage; two-thirds of the men and slightly more than half the women believed that both partners should have premarital experience. In all samples subjects rejected the double standard—European students more than North American. Interestingly, in all countries except England, women more frequently than men *supported* the double standard.

Also related to attitudes held toward the double standard was the inquiry (See Table 7):

Would it trouble you to marry a person who had experienced premarital coitus with someone else before becoming seriously involved with you?

The percentage of women answering "No" was highest in the United States and lowest in Canada; the greatest percentage of men was in Norway and the lowest, in Canada. Twice as many

Table 7. Percentage Responses to: "Would it trouble you to marry a person who had experienced coitus with someone else before becoming involved with you?"

	United States		Canada		England		Norway	
	Male	Female	Male	Female	Male	Female	Male	Female
Yes, seriously	16.7	9.0	15.0	12.4	10.1	6.9	2.4	6.5
Some, but not seriously	53.5	29.8	54.0	41.6	43.5	34.7	50.6	35.5
No	29.8	61.2	31.0	46.0	46.4	58.4	47.0	58.0
	100%	100%	100%	100%	100%	100%	100%	100%
(*N*)	(658)	(722)	(87)	(89)	(138)	(101)	(85)	(62)

women as men in the United States answered "No," and this represented by far the greatest discrepancy between the sexes in any one sample. As was expected, in all cases men indicated more concern than women about the chastity of their marital partner. This suggests that some male students, also primarily American and Canadian, encourage the double standard.

In all the samples both men and women subjects were approximately equally divided between those who held the opinion that an individual might have had numerous sexual affairs before marriage and still bring a deep and enduring commitment to the person he marries and those who either did not think so or were uncertain about it. Certainly it can be said that numerous premarriage sexual partners were not seen as a serious deterrent to the marriage relationship by the majority of students in each of the samples. Sexual activity prior to marriage was viewed negatively by more females than males, and Norwegian women were the most skeptical. Except for the American sample, the difference between countries was not so great as between the two sexes of specific countries. In the United States

men and women showed remarkable agreement (Table 8). It's interesting that in the United States and Canada, where there is considerably less premarital coitus (see Table 14), there are almost as many students who believe numerous sexual affairs would not interfere with marriage as in those countries where there is more premarital coitus. This would indicate that it is not fear that the experience would destroy some quality in the marriage that acts as a deterrent to premarital intercourse.

When asked the following question, "Yes" responses were high in the English and Norwegian samples; low in the American and German (see Table 9):

Regardless of age (after 16) or the stage of formal commitment, do you feel that full intimacy is appropriate if both persons desire it and they have a sense of trust, loyalty, protectiveness, and love?

In general, women subjects consistently were more reluctant to sanction such intimacy. The category receiving the greatest number of re-

Table 8. Percentage Responses to: "Do you feel a person can have numerous sexual affairs and still bring a deep, enduring emotional commitment to the person he or she marries?"

	United States		Canada		England		Norway	
	Male	Female	Male	Female	Male	Female	Male	Female
Yes	52.1	52.9	63.2	46.7	55.7	51.0	58.8	43.5
No	14.1	18.4	13.8	20.0	9.3	18.0	15.3	24.2
Am not sure	33.8	28.7	23.0	33.3	35.0	31.0	25.9	32.3
	100%	100%	100%	100%	100%	100%	100%	100%
(*N*)	(657)	(717)	(87)	(90)	(140)	(100)	(85)	(62)

Table 9. Percentage Responses to: "Regardless of age (after 16) or the stage of formal commitment, do you feel that full intimacy is appropriate if both persons desire it and they feel a sense of trust, loyalty, protectiveness, and love?"

	United States		Canada		England		Germany		Norway	
	Male	Female	Male	Female	Male	Female	Male	Female	Male	Female
Yes	31.6	19.4	36.2	23.6	55.3	43.9	28.0	25.9	42.9	50.0
Only if mature	38.4	40.9	46.8	34.6	33.4	41.9	61.9	57.1	41.0	27.8
Doubt	12.1	10.6	6.4	21.8	5.2	6.0	—*	—*	12.5	5.6
Definitely not a sufficient basis	17.9	29.3	10.6	20.0	6.1	8.2	10.1	17.0	3.6	16.6
(N)	100% (190)	100% (284)	100% (47)	100% (55)	100% (132)	100% (98)	100% (118)	100% (112)	100% (56)	100% (36)

* "Doubt" alternative was not on Germany queationnaire.

sponses from all subjects in all countries was "Only if mature."

The following question was answered most frequently by all students in all countries by "Only if married" for ages prior to 18. However, generally marriage is seen as less important as the age of the individual increases.

What kind of relationship should prevail before a male and female should consider coitus as personally and socially reasonable?

Both English men and women, more than any other nationality, indicated that "going steady" and being "casually attracted" between ages 14-17 were appropriate conditions for intercourse; English women checked the response indicating coitus was appropriate *only* in marriage substantially less frequently than did women of any other country in all age categories from 14 to 24 and over (Tables 10 and 11).

The widest gap between categories for both men and women, in all age groups, and among all nationalities was between "going steady" and "good friends." In many instances but without a discernible pattern, more male subjects considered it appropriate to have coitus with one to whom he was casually attracted than with a good friend. Women seemed to favor slightly the friend

Table 10. Age Level and Type of Relationship Viewed by *Males* as Appropriate for Considering Coitus

Type of Relationship	Ages 14-17				18-20				21-23				24 and Over			
	U.S.	Can.	Eng.	Nor.	U.S.	Can.	Eng.	Nor.	U.S.	Can.	Eng.	Nor.	U.S.	Can.	Eng.	Nor.
Only if married	67.6	80.3	28.7	55.7	33.5	38.6	9.6	17.6	23.4	16.0	11.0	7.2	18.9	12.1	13.1	7.5
Officially engaged	10.7	5.3	13.9	27.9	14.8	15.7	15.8	17.6	15.0	18.7	8.4	13.0	13.9	12.1	7.6	9.0
Tentatively engaged	6.7	3.6	7.9	6.6	15.5	15.7	15.8	35.1	16.1	21.3	12.8	20.3	11.5	16.7	11.2	16.4
Going steady	8.5	3.6	26.8	6.6	20.5	15.7	28.1	16.2	19.0	20.0	32.1	31.9	18.1	22.7	25.2	23.8
Good friends	2.1	3.6	5.9	1.6	8.1	8.6	9.6	5.4	14.3	12.0	12.8	8.8	13.9	16.7	9.3	17.9
Casually attracted	4.4	3.6	16.8	1.6	7.6	5.7	21.1	8.1	12.2	12.0	22.9	18.8	23.7	19.7	33.6	25.4
(N)	100% (469)	100% (56)	100% (101)	100% (61)	100% (540)	100% (70)	100% (114)	100% (74)	100% (566)	100% (75)	100% (109)	100% (69)	100% (501)	100% (66)	100% (107)	100% (67)

Table 11. Age Level and Type of Relationship Viewed by *Females* as Appropriate for Considering Coitus

Type of Relationship	Ages 14-17				18-20				21-23				24 and Over			
	U.S.	Can.	Eng.	Nor.	U.S.	Can.	Eng.	Nor.	U.S.	Can.	Eng.	Nor.	U.S.	Can.	Eng.	No
Only if married	86.5	94.6	43.1	78.4	58.6	62.0	16.4	40.0	46.0	45.8	13.7	26.0	38.3	39.7	13.5	24.
Officially engaged	7.7	3.6	13.8	10.8	16.7	15.5	17.8	13.3	19.2	22.3	12.3	10.0	17.4	20.6	9.5	11.
Tenatively engaged	2.1	1.8	13.8	5.4	11.7	14.1	9.6	22.3	15.4	23.6	8.2	24.0	14.0	12.7	10.8	13.
Going steady	2.5	0	12.3	2.7	9.7	5.6	35.6	20.0	13.6	6.9	31.5	30.0	19.2	17.5	24.3	37.
Good friends	0.8	0	9.2	0	1.2	2.8	9.6	0	3.2	1.4	19.2	4.0	6.1	6.3	16.2	2.
Casually attracted	0.4	0	7.8	2.7	2.1	0	11.0	4.4	2.6	0	15.1	6.0	5.0	3.2	25.7	11.
	100%	100%	100%	100%	100%	100%	100%	100%	100%	100%	100%	100%	100%	100%	100	
(N)	(530)	(56)	(65)	(37)	(580)	(71)	(73)	(45)	(624)	(72)	(73)	(50)	(557)	(63)	(74)	(4

over the casual attraction. These findings undoubtedly reflect the romantic concept that being in love and being physically attracted to a sexual partner is more appropriate than is a basis of friendship.

The English were generally more acceptant than other nationalities of premarital intercourse under a variety of conditions and at younger ages. Females in all samples generally expressed considerably greater support than did the males for consideration of coitus "only if married." Canadian females, the most conservative group, gave no support for coitus outside the married or engaged relationship for ages 14-17, but 27 percent approved when the age was 24 or over. Chronological age, which probably was judged to reflect personal maturity, was held by all subjects as an important factor in determining under what conditions coitus was appropriate.

When questioned about the opinion that a good lovemaking relationship was "almost always consummated by" mutual, simultaneous orgasm, respondents showed no national differences and no differences within the sexes. About half of the men thought it was true, about a third of the women.

By studying the opinions that were expressed toward marriage and sexual behavior, one can generally conclude that although traditional values are held to some extent in all countries, what may be called "liberal views" are also to be found in each of the national samples. European countries are more liberal than those on the North American continent. Men are less invested in marriage and less restricted in sex than women. Marriage is still an overwhelmingly popular way of life, and the age of marriage is ideally the early twenties. Indicative of a swing away from the traditional was the evidence that the double standard of sexual morals is definitely on its way out, and students are not greatly concerned about the first sexual experience being in marriage or being with the partner who eventually becomes the spouse. Even having several sexual partners before marriage was not judged particularly detrimental to the marriage. Age was viewed as a very important factor determining under what conditions coitus was appropriate; the older the individual the more freedom he had.

The English in general were seen to have the least restrictive attitudes toward sexual behavior. Norwegian women, although liberal, tended to be a good deal less liberal than their men. The Canadian sample held somewhat more conservative attitudes than the United States, but in most instances the two samples resembled each other and could be contrasted with the European samples.

(4) SEXUAL EXPERIENCE AND BEHAVIOR

When women were asked to classify the men whom they had dated in the past year into those they thought (a) would be frightened by real intimacy; (b) those who seemed content with gestures of intimacy such as a farewell embrace; (c) those who were happy enough if their hands were allowed to wander; and (d) those who were disappointed if they couldn't persuade the girl to go all the way, more American and Canadian girls marked b than any other response. English and Norwegian marked d and German marked c (Table 12). The contrast between Canadian and American women when compared to English women is particularly noticeable on response d. The North American women indicated that men were decidedly less demanding than English women reported men to be.

Canadian and United States men give a very congruent picture of their dates during the past year (Table 13). Both indicated most of their dates usually went along for fun up to the point of light petting. English male students most frequently suggested the partner resisted real intimacies unless there had been talk of love. German students most frequently indicated their dates were pretty conservative beyond perhaps a goodnight kiss, and Norwegian men most frequently described their dates as "happy to go as far as I want to go, short of coitus."

The description that "They seem to want to go all the way if we have a chance" was marked most frequently by Norwegian students and least frequently by Canadian students. Specific behaviors of dating partners cannot be determined with any reliability by the responses of either women or men subjects or by comparing the two (Tables 12 and 13). The multiple responses of male students are especially difficult to interpret; however the composite picture of dating behavior that does appear from the data is one of conservativism in Canada and the United States, where men and women agree that gestures of affection and light petting are modal. In contrast more European women (especially English and Norwegian) reported that men are disappointed if "you don't want to go all the way," and more European men reported that women want to go all the way! The fact that European students do indeed engage in more sexual activity on dates was confirmed when subjects reported on their own sexual behavior.

Subjects were asked to indicate their participation in a spectrum of sexual behaviors from light embracing and holding hands to coitus (Tables 14 and 15). Among the males, Canadian students generally indicated the highest frequencies of participation in the casual and light

Table 12. Percentage Female Responses to: "Review in your mind briefly the men you have dated in the past year. How would you classify most of them in regard to interest in intimacy?"

	United States	Canada	England	Germany	Norway
a) I think real intimacy would frighten most of them.	13.8	11.1	13.6	15.7	14.2
b) They seem content with gestures of intimacy such as the farewell embrace.	41.5	44.4	22.2	9.6	26.2
c) If their hands can wander, that seems to keep them happy.	25.0	31.7	18.5	50.6*	28.6
d) They are disappointed if you don't want to go all the way.	16.0	12.8	44.4	24.1	31.0
e) Only dated one.	3.7	0.0	1.3	0.0	0.0
(N)	100% (581)	100% (63)	100% (81)	100% (81)	100% (42)

*German reworded as follows: "Most are satisfied with necking."

Table 13. Percentage Male Responses to: "Review in your mind the girls you have dated this past year. How would you classify most of them in regard to interest in intimacy?"

	United States	Canada	England	Germany	Norway
They are pretty conservative beyond perhaps a goodnight kiss.	22.2	16.7	16.3	45.2	19.7
They will usually go along for fun up to a point of light petting.	46.6	50.6	35.0	8.9	42.1
They resist real intimacies unless there has been talk of love.	43.5	36.4	39.0	22.8	32.9
They seem happy to go as far as I want to go, short of coitus.	27.4	28.6	33.0	31.7	46.1
They seem to want to go all the way if we have a chance.	14.9	24.7	34.1	37.0	40.8
(N)	(609)	(77)	(123)	(101)	(76)

*Multiple responses were suggested in the questionnaire; therefore each figure reports the percent of the total N of each respective sample which agreed with that specific response.

petting behavior categories, and the English students the highest in general petting, nude embrace, and coitus. German men consistently reported the lowest rate of involvement in all categories. The pattern of behaviors reported by American and Canadian men was strikingly similar in all categories, with Canadian men consistently reporting somewhat more conservative behavior.

As would be expected, there is a decided drop

Table 14. Percent of Males Reporting Experiencing Respective Sexual Behaviors

Type of Sexual Behavior	United States	Canada	England	Germany	Norway
Light embracing or fond holding of hands	98.6	98.9	93.5	93.8	93.7
Casual goodnight kissing	96.7	97.7	93.5	78.6	86.1
Deep kissing	96.0	97.7	91.9	91.1	96.2
Horizontal embrace with some petting but not undressed	89.9	92.0	85.4	68.8	93.6
Petting of girl's breast area from outside her clothing	89.9	93.2	87.0	80.4	83.5
Petting of girl's breast area without clotnes intervening	83.4	92.0	82.8	69.6	83.5
Petting below the waist of the girl under her clothing	81.1	85.2	84.6	70.5	83.5
Petting below the waist of both man and girl, under clothing	62.9	64.8	68.3	52.7	55.1
Nude embrace	65.6	69.3	70.5	50.0	69.6
Coitus	58.2	56.8	74.8	54.5	66.7
One-night affair involving coitus; didn't date person again	29.9	21.6	43.1	17.0	32.9
Whipping or spanking before petting or other intimacy	8.2	5.7	17.1	.9	5.1
Sex on pay-as-you-go basis	4.2	4.5	13.8	9.8	2.5
(N)	(644)	(88)	(123)	(112)	(79)

in the number of subjects who report petting below the waist of the girl and petting below the waist of *both* the man and the girl. Mutual genital petting behavior is reported only slightly more frequently than coitus by men subjects of all countries and by women in European countries; however, 15 percent more American and Canadian girls report mutual genital petting than report coitus. Apparently a crucial point in determining whether most subjects continue to coitus or not is mutual genital petting. This is *less* true for girls in Canada and the United States than for any other group.

The reported coital participation among males in order of frequency was: England highest, followed by Norway, then the United States and Canada, and lowest Germany (Table 14). The pattern indicated by German and Norwegian men is that coitus is more frequent than mutual genital petting. All the other samples reported that for some five to eight percent of the men, genital petting does not continue to coitus.

Men who reported involvement in whipping and spanking together with sexual intimacy were most frequently English. The second highest frequency for men was the United States sample which reported less than half the incidence of the English. German men reported the least.

English men reported the greatest patronage of prostitutes; then the German; and lowest were the Norwegian. A little more than four percent of United States and Canadian men reported they had had sex on a pay-as-you-go-basis. It is especially interesting to note that Germany, which had the lowest coital percentage, had the second highest percentage of prostitution, and Norway which has the second highest coital involvement has the lowest prostitution reported. This leads one to conclude that quite a different set of values operate in the two countries, and that Germany maintains more of the traditional point of view and condones the double standard to a greater extent.

Women subjects in general reported less participation in all categories of sexual behavior than men did (Table 15). The highest rates for sexual behavior except for light embraces were reported by English women. Canadian, American, and

Table 15. Percent of Females Reporting Experiencing Respective Sexual Behaviors

Types of Sexual Behavior	United States	Canada	England	Germany	Norway
Light embracing or fond holding of hands	97.5	96.5	91.9	94.8	89.3
Casual goodnight kissing	96.8	91.8	93.0	74.0	75.0
Deep kissing	96.5	91.8	93.0	90.6	89.3
Horizontal embrace with some petting but not undressed	83.3	81.2	79.1	77.1	75.0
Petting of girl's breast area from outside her clothing	78.3	78.8	82.6	76.0	64.3
Petting of girl's breast area without clothes intervening	67.8	64.7	70.9	66.7	58.9
Petting below the waist of the girl under her clothing	61.2	64.7	70.9	63.5	53.6
Petting below the waist of both man and girl, under clothing	57.8	50.6	61.6	56.3	42.9
Nude embrace	49.6	47.6	64.0	62.1	51.8
Coitus	43.2	35.3	62.8	59.4	53.6
One-night affair involving coitus; didn't date person again	7.2	5.9	33.7	4.2	12.5
Whipping or spanking before petting or other intimacy	4.5	5.9	17.4	1.0	7.1
(*N*)	(688)	(85)	(86)	(96)	(56)

German females showed similar and slightly less participation through the less intimate and the petting behaviors to the nude embrace; in these same categories the Norwegian females consistently reported the least participation. However, with the nude embrace and coitus, the international female pattern changed; a greater proportion of German and Norwegian women reported involvement and a lesser proportion of Canadian and American women. It can be assumed that petting as a prelude to coitus is more frequently the practice with European women, but with American and Canadian women it is either an end in itself or is the cut-off point of sexual activity. The order of coital frequency as indicated by women subjects is: highest, English; then Germany; Norway; and finally the United States and Canada. These data would tend to confirm the male responses which followed the same pattern except for Germany.

A third of the English women reported "one-night stands"; and although more than 20 percent less frequently reported, the Norwegian females ranked second highest. The United States, Canada, and Germany followed in that order. Although the percentages reported by men subjects were considerably higher, the order of frequency was the same.

The one behavior category in which the female subjects reported in both a similar pattern and a similar percentage as the males within their respective sample was that of "whipping and spanking." The generally low percentage may account somewhat for this finding. Both England and Norway, which report a proportionately greater number of students engaged in these sado-masochistic practices, also rank high in coital frequency. The positive correlation of the two factors can be speculated upon, but accounting for the relationship remains for further investigation.

The ages at first petting and first coital experience are given in Table 16. The mean age for males at first petting was lowest (15.6 years) in England and Norway, eight months older in the United States, and a year older for both Canada and Germany. English females began petting earliest at age 15.6; Norwegian females almost a year later; German females at age 17; and finally

Table 16. Mean Ages of Males and Females at Age of First Petting Experience and of the First Coitus

Universities	First Petting Mean Age		First Coitus Mean Age	
	Males	Females	Males	Females
United States	16.3	17.3	17.9	18.7
(N)	(608)	(612)	(374)	(297)
Canada	16.6	17.3	18.5	18.4
	(85)	(76)	(50)	(29)
England	15.6	15.8	17.5	17.5
	(117)	(81)	(90)	(57)
Germany	16.6	17.0	19.0	19.5
	(107)	(90)	(61)	(57)
Norway	15.6	16.5	18.4	18.8
	(73)	(50)	(53)	(29)

Canadian and American females still four months later. English students who began petting youngest also had intercourse youngest. German and Norwegian students who were the oldest at first intercourse began petting experiences at approximately the same ages as men in other samples. United States and Canadian men and women report the shortest interval between the age at which they began petting and the age at which it was consummated in intercourse. In all cases men reported first petting at an age younger than women; except for Canadian and English men who reported first coitus at nearly the same age as Canadian and English women, men were also younger at age of first coitus.

It is interesting to note the pattern of delay between first petting and first coitus for each sample. The shortest interval is demonstrated by the Canadian and American girl. This is followed by the American man and the English man and woman. Norwegian and German men and women delay coitus for the longest intervals —all over two years—and Norwegian men wait nearly three years.

Considerable variation exists in the sample in the reported number of coital partners (Table 17). The greatest promiscuity was reported by English students, with almost three-fourths of the males reporting "several" and "many" partners, and two-thirds of the females reported in

Table 17. Percentage Coitus-Experiencing Males and Females, by Designation of Number of Partners

Number of Partners Engaged in Coitus	United States		Canada		England		Germany		Norway	
	Male	Female	Male	Female	Male	Female	Male	Female	Male	Female
One	24.3	46.6	36.7	44.8	17.6	22.4	41.7	47.4	32.1	32.1
Two	17.9	18.8	10.2	34.5	8.8	12.1	25.0	28.1	17.0	21.4
Several	40.4	26.5	34.7	17.3	47.3	44.8	30.0	24.5	37.7	39.3
Many	17.4	8.1	18.4	3.4	26.3	20.7	3.3	0.0	13.2	7.2
(N)	100% (374)	100% (298)	100% (49)	100% (29)	100% (91)	100% (58)	100% (60)	100% (57)	100% (53)	100% (28)

these same categories. About 58 percent of the American male students reported "several" and "many" partners; about half the Norwegian males reported "several" and "many" partners; only a third of the German men reported in those categories. As is to be expected, women students in all samples were less promiscuous. Nearly half of the German, American, and Canadian women reported only "one partner," and congruently, fewer of them indicated "many" and "several." Fewer than a fourth of the Canadian and German women marked these combined categories. About a third of the American women and nearly half of the Norwegian women marked these. Nearly two-thirds of the English women marked one or the other of these categories.

Alcohol was not reported as a major factor in first coital experience by many of the subjects. More English females reported they were under the influence of alcohol when they first had intercourse than any other group in the sample; even so, more than half indicated, "I and my partner had not had anything alcoholic to drink." The English had the highest rate reporting "both under the influence of alcohol"; and the German the lowest except for Norwegian women, none of whom reported the couple had been under the influence of alcohol. More Canadian youth than any other reported *no* involvement with alcohol and first coitus—about three-fourths; 68 percent of the Norwegian men and women reported in that same category and about two-thirds of the American men and women. More English men and women reported alcohol was involved with one or the other or both partners than any other nationality.

Although there are some irregularities and unevenness of pattern, the total picture that one gains from looking at these data is a consistent one presented by the agreement of each sex and by congruent findings in each category of behavior. The English student has more sexual activity, begins younger, has more partners, has more one-night stands, more sadomasochistic experiences, and is more likely to have been influenced by alcohol at the time of the first coital experience.

North American students are less experienced and generally more conservative; the Canadian youth is somewhat less liberal than his counterpart in the United States. The Norwegian student tends to be less the "swinger" than the English. Premarital sexual experience does not start so early and is restricted to fewer partners. Although the picture of German students is not so clear, they generally occupy a place between the liberal English and Norwegian samples and the North American.

Summary and Discussion

(1) SEX ROLE DIFFERENCES

Some interesting consistencies and inconsistencies are presented by the findings with regard to sex role differences when the various countries are compared. Although in the United States and Canada more students agreed that men and women were indeed different though equal, and fewer than half of the Norwegian students took this position, it was the Norwegian students who in the largest percentage indicated that a four-year college education was generally as essential for women as men. English students tended to agree with the Norwegian; and consistent with this both Norwegian and English female students expressed in greater numbers an intent to follow a career over most of the first 20 years of their out-of-college life.

The Canadian and United States students presented a different picture from the European in that more of them stressed "equality but difference," and fewer of them believed a four-year college education is necessary for women. The North American women tended to be less interested in a career. Canadian men and women more than those of any other country believed women consciously downgraded career ambitions in favor of marriage potential. The European students generally felt this was less true.

European schools favored coed living arrangements much more than North American students, but all students favored mixed classes in the classroom.

Making a broad generalization from these statistics, we could say with reliability that the European students—both men and women—indicated a greater acceptance of sexual equality of opportunity, both in the academic world and in the professional. Canadian men and women expressed ideas which to a greater extent indicated that the female's role and her preparation for it was marital rather than professional. They denied, however, that this marital role was not "equal" with the male role.

(2) PARENTAL INDEPENDENCE

English students favored independence from parents and early marriage with financial support from parents to a greater extent than students of any other nation and rejected the idea that more definite guidelines and limits for youth were needed. Both American and Canadian students were less inclined to want either earlier independence or subsidized marriages and were more inclined to think adult guidelines would be a good idea. There was virtually no support given to religious agencies as a crucial molder of guidelines or limits for youth in the realm of sexual intimacy.

One might conclude from these responses that English youth felt more competent to start and manage life on their own, given the freedom to do so.

(3) ATTITUDES TOWARD MARRIAGE AND SEXUAL BEHAVIOR

That the majority of youth the world around (or at least in this sample) still believe a satisfying life includes marriage is indicated; however, North American students were more sure of this than European. It was surprising to the investigators, however, that nearly a quarter of the samples said marriage was *not* necessary. All samples agreed that men should marry ideally at about age 25 and women at about 23.

Except in England, women more than men favored the idea that the man and woman who marry should have their first sexual experience together. Again the more conservative answers were expressed by the North American students, who preferred coital partners to be marriage partners and were more skeptical of promiscuity and its influence in marriage than were the European students.

Women students in general were more conservative (even in liberal countries) than were men. The women, as much as or more than the men, seem to perpetuate the double standard, and it was perpetuated by North American youth more generally than European. Women are willing to accept lack of chastity on the part of the male more readily than the male accepted the lack of chastity of the female; although Norwegian students did not seem to value premarital chastity, they rejected promiscuity and the double standard of behavior. English students seem to operate most nearly on the single sex standard, and that standard was described as liberal. Again, United States and Canadian students were more conservative; they were more caught in the traditional double standard.

The majority of students in all samples agree that "maturity" should be a major criteria on which decision and choice of coital partners should be determined; English students, when compared with students from other countries, indicated that this choice can be made at an earlier age.

(4) SEXUAL EXPERIENCE AND BEHAVIOR

Reports by both men and women subjects of their sexual behavior was consistent with their attitudes. More European than North American women reported that men wanted to "go farther on dates"; more European than American men said that women were willing to go farther! Canadian and American men and women were more conservative—content with petting and necking.

North American women, contrary to European women, indicated their dates were generally content with a moderate degree of intimacy instead of disappointment if they would not go all the way. European men, contrary to North American men, indicated women dates seemed to want to go all the way when the opportunity was available.

While the investigators tried to construct patterns of sexual behavior from the responses of men and women students indicating their degree of involvement in activities which range from light embracing to coitus, it became obvious that English men and women more freely participate in a gamut of sexual activities including more genital petting, more frequent coitus, more patronage of prostitution, more sadomasochistic practices, more one-night stands. They start both petting and coitus at a younger age, have more sexual partners, and report alcohol has been a factor in initial coital experience. The general ranking of male student coital rates by countries provides the following descending order: England, Norway, United States, Canada, Germany. The order for female student coital rates was: England, Germany, Norway, United States, and Canada.

Canadian and American youth report patterns of behavior very similar to each other and are in general to be considered conservative regarding sexual behavior. German students hold the most conservative attitudes and exhibit the most restricted behavior among the European samples; Norwegian students were more liberal, and the English consistently the most liberal. Females, as one would expect, are more conservative in all countries than are the males. English women, however, hold views and behave very similarly to English men.

It can be generally concluded from looking at this mass of data that both attitudes and behavior of North American students are more conservative than those of the European. On the background of other studies done earlier, it is evident that there is an increasingly liberal attitude toward sex and generally more premarital participation.

The study gives a reliable report on sexual attitudes and behaviors held by university students in the participating countries, but it fails in that it gives little clue to the meaning of motivation associated with these. Meaning can perhaps be projected into the statistics, but so much of interpretation lies in the eye of the interpreter, that these investigators prefer to let the statistics speak for themselves as they can. The cross-cultural aspects of these data have provided a sound basis on which a comparative assessment of general trends in university students' sexual attitudes and behavior can be made. The variations that have been found suggest the need for further study to explicate and inquire into the meaning of the differential findings, as well as to continue the incorporation of research controls through cross-cultural analysis.

REFERENCES
Research on Premarital Sexual Attitudes, Standards, and Behavior

CHRISTENSEN, HAROLD T. "Scandinavian and American Sex Norms: Some Comparisons with Sociological Implications," *Journal of Social Issues* (April, 1966), 60–75.

COLEMAN, JAMES Female Status and Premarital Sexual Codes," *American Journal of Sociology*, 72 (September, 1966).

DEDMAN, JEAN "The Relationship Between Religious Attitude and Attitudes Toward Premarital Sex Relations," *Marriage and Family Living* (May, 1959), 171–176.

EHRMAN, WINSTON W. *Premarital Dating Behavior*, New York: Bantam Books, 1959.

FREEMAN, HARROP A., AND FREEMAN, RUTH S. "Senior

College Women: Their Sexual Standards and Activity," *Journal of National Association of Women Deans and Counselors* (Winter and Spring, 1966).

KINSEY, ALFRED et al. *Sexual Bebavior in the Human Male*. Wm. Saunders Co., 1948.

———, *Sexual Behavior in the Human Female*. Wm. Saunders Co., 1953.

KIRKENDALL, LESTER A. *Premarital Intercourse and Interpersonal Relationships*. New York: Julian Press, 1961.

MANN, W. E. "Canadian Trends in Premarital Behavior," *The Bulletin for Social Service* (December, 1967) whole issue.

REISS, IRA L. *Premarital Sexual Standards in America*. New York: Free Press, 1960.

ROBINSON, IRA, et al. Changes in Sexual Behavior and Attitudes of College Students," *Family Life Coordinator*, (April, 1968), 119–124.

ROSS, ROBERT T. "Measures of the Sex Behavior of College Males Compared with Kinsey's Results," *Journal of Abnormal and Social Psychology, 45* (1960), 753–755.

RUBIN, ISADORE "Changing College Sex: New Kinsey Report," *Sexology*. (June, 1968), 780–782.

SCHOFIELD, MICHAEL *The Sexual Behavior of Young People*. Boston: Little, Brown and Co., 1965.

Chapter 13: Suggested Additional Readings

ADAMS, W. J. Sex composition in family life courses: How important is this? *Family Coordinator,* 1971, *20*(1), 55–62. In a study designed to test the common assumption that sex education should occur in mixed sex groups, it was found that progress was not significantly different in mixed and non-mixed groups.

BEACH, F. It's all in your mind. *Psychology Today,* 1969, *3*(2), 33–35; 60. An authority on sex research considers the biological bases of sex behavior and how such behaviors differ for each sex.

BRODERICK, C. B., & ROWER, G. P. A scale of preadolescent heterosexual development. *Journal of Marriage and the Family,* 1968, *30*(1), 97–101. Data are provided to support the thesis that most pre-adolescent boys and girls undergo an orderly pattern of progression in heterosexual development. The specific stages in such development are tentatively described.

CAREY, J. T. Changing courtship patterns in the popular song. *American Journal of Sociology,* 1969, *74*(6), 720–731. A content analysis of popular lyrics indicates a change in boy–girl relationships over the past 11 years. Fewer lyrics deal with boy–girl relations now, and the tunes of these songs are less romantic and more physically oriented. The lyrics evidence a wider range of concerns among youth, and raise questions about the individual's relation to the social order.

CHRISTENSEN, H. T., & GREGG, C. F. Changing sex norms in America and Scandinavia. *Journal of Marriage and the Family,* 1970, *32*(4), 616–627. On the basis of questionnaires administered to comparable university groups in Denmark and America in 1958 and again in 1968, the authors conclude that sex norms have been changing rapidly, and that attitudes and behaviors of the sexes have converged, partly in consequence of increasing liberalization of females.

KEPHART, W. M. Some correlates of romantic love. *Journal of Marriage and the Family,* 1967, *29*(3), 470–474. Questionnaires submitted to white college students reveal differences in the romantic orientation of males and females. However, the female becomes more realistic as she approaches marriage.

KUNZ, P. R. Romantic love and reciprocity. *Family Coordinator,* 1969, *18*(2), 111–116. College students were asked to supply endings to a short story. From their replies, the author concluded that males and married students were more inclined than females and unmarried students to take a realistic view of marriage. However, most college students had an emphatically romantic orientation. Apparently, the romantic complex in the mate selection process leads to unrealistic expectations in marriage.

LA BARRE, M. Pregnancy experiences among married adolescents. *American Journal of Orthopsychiatry,* 1968, *38*(1), 47–55. This paper discusses the experiences and problems of pregnant married teenagers and calls attention to the need for studies of the life-situational and dynamic factors involved in such cases.

MARTINSON, F. M. Sexual knowledge values and behavior patterns of adolescents. *Child Welfare,* 1968, *47*(7), 405–410, 426. Martinson reports a study of the sexual tudes and behaviors of a population of unmarried high school adolescents in Minnesota.

PAUKER, J. D. Fathers of children conceived out of wedlock: Prepregnancy, high school, psychological test results. *Developmental Psychology,* 1971, *4*(2), 215–218. Data for fathers of children born out of wedlock, as compared with controls, indicated few significant differences.

REISS, I. L.   *The social context of premarital sexual permissiveness.* New York: Holt, Rinehart & Winston, 1967. This monograph focuses on attitudes toward the appropriateness of different kinds of sociosexual activity within certain kinds of relationships. The author's research questions related attitudes toward particular sexual behaviors to various factors, including socioeconomic background, family characteristics, and dating behavior. The study involved college and high school students as well as adults.

ROESSLER, R. T.   Sexuality and identity: Masculine differentiation and feminine constancy. *Adolescence,* 1971, *6*(22), 156–196. The author outlines differences in masculine and feminine sociosexual development and indicates how each hinges on the other. He cites research to support his main hypothesis that the female's increasing awareness of her career potential may disturb the erstwhile equilibrium of male–female relations.

SAGARIN, E. (Ed.)   Sex and the contemporary American scene. *Annals of the American Academy of Political and Social Science,* 1968, No. 376, entire issue. Major issues discussed in this 14-article analysis of human sexuality are sex within our society, the double standard, the role of home, school, and church in human sexuality, and attitudes toward sex.

SCHWARTZ, M. S.   A report on sex information knowledge of 87 lower-class ninth grade boys. *Family Coordinator,* 1969, *18*(4), 361–371. This article reports a study of the sex knowledge of 87 ninth-grade lower-class boys from different ethnic groups.

SHIPMAN, G.   The psychodynamics of sex education. *Family Coordinator* (Journal of Education, Counseling and Services), 1968, *17*(1), 3–12. An exploratory study of 400 university students confirmed the absence of sex training of children by their parents. The author analyzed factors associated with the role of parents, including the incest taboo, the need for privacy, and mutual denial of personal sexuality of both parents and children.

SIMON, W.   Sex. *Psychology Today,* 1969, *3*(2), 23–27. This article is concerned with changes in sexual definition and practice in America in the past few decades. These changes are related to concurrent modifications in American life styles and values.

VOGEL, S. R., BROVERMAN, I. K., BROVERMAN, D. M., CLARKSON, F. E., & ROSENKRANTZ, P. S.   Maternal employment and perception of sex roles among college students. *Developmental Psychology,* 1970, *3*(3), 384–391. Perceptions of sex roles held by college students were analyzed with regard to the employment history of the students' mothers.

14

Social-Sex Role

Only in recent years have psychologists accorded much attention to social-sex role—that is, to the part an individual plays as girl or boy, woman or man. Formerly, growing individuals were discussed under a blanket designation as "children" or "adolescents" but were rarely differentiated by sex. Today, however, writers and researchers have come to treat sex role as a significant factor in human development, especially in cultures where sex roles are highly polarized.

Generally, sex roles are thought to be rooted in biology. Boys are believed inherently to make better leaders, and girls better babysitters. Boys are deemed more logical, and girls more intuitive. These ideas receive some support from research. Among monkeys, male youngsters engage in rougher play and make more threats than their sisters (Harlow, 1962). Biological correlates of characteristic sex behaviors also exist among humans. Periods of the ovarian cycle have been found to correspond to irritability, flightiness, and introversion–extroversion in females (Benedek & Rubenstein, 1939). Castrated males report reduced aggressiveness and lowered energy level. A study by Gray and Buffery (1971) found that the male's more aggressive behaviors stem from a fundamental difference between the reproductive functions of the sexes, a difference practically universal among animal species and quite marked among mammals. The authors concluded that "the sex differences in emotional and cognitive behavior among mammalian species . . . are all remote but necessary consequences of the same overriding fact: the division of labor between the sexes in reproductive behavior. Conversely, we would argue that those features of human social organization—the mother–infant nuclear unit and the generally greater role played by males in competitive social interaction . . . are of essentially biological origin, that is to say, they are specified in the gene pool of our species [pp. 106-107].

Nevertheless, it is improbable the psychosexual differentiation, at least for humans, is genetically determined. In cases of hermaphroditism, where the individual has external primary sex characteristics of both sexes, a child may simply be designated as a boy or as a girl (Money, 1963). Even if the sex assigned him be directly contrary to his gender, his psychosexual identity becomes that of the assigned sex. The critical period in the acquisition of psychosexual role, believes

Money (1965, p. 12), is about the same time as the establishment of native language.

Apparently, the processes of identification, canalization, and reinforcement all are involved in the acquisition of sex role. A child may identify with his like-sex parent. Also, the stage is set (canalization) so that it comes easier to behave as one sex or the other. Meantime, society rewards children for following the prescribed sex role (positive reinforcement) and punishes those who do not (negative reinforcement). However, these processes are applied somewhat differently for girls and boys. In childhood, girls are granted greater latitude than boys, for reasons not entirely clear, but girls themselves may not exceed certain limits. However, the girls' freedom to depart from the norms lessens somewhat in the teens. In its sex-role development, each sex depends on the other (Roessler, 1971). Any attempt to understand the male's identity formation must also take into consideration "the subtleties" of the female role. For example, explains Roessler, as women gain more freedom in modern society, the increased options open to them may have serious implications for men; as the woman attempts to work out a "balance between her female constancy and her human potential," she can only maintain the balance by "casting the male in the role of a modern king." However, as the woman becomes increasingly aware of her career potential, she no longer needs to cast the male in his traditional role of provider and king. Therefore, suggests Roessler, "one wonders what effect these unclear female expectations will have on masculine identity formation [p. 196]."

These same processes operate in quite subtle ways to influence an individual's behavior, wherever matters of sex role are involved. For example, on tests introduced as measures of masculine, feminine, and neutral skills, sixth-grade boys performed distinctly better on sex-appropriate tests, intermediately well on neutral tests, and least well on sex-inappropriate tests (Stein, Pohly, Mueller, 1971). Girls performed equally well on feminine and neutral tests, but less well on masculine tests. The fact that boys were affected more than girls reflects the greater societal pressures on boys to behave in a sex-appropriate manner. Probably because his sex status is higher, the boy adheres to his sex-role more closely. In short, sex-typed labels are sufficient to influence a child's motivation for activities, and they importantly modify his success in performance.

The current status of sex roles is unclear. It has been suggested that the roles are gradually less differentiated. Reasons for this sex-role depolarization are not hard to find. For one thing, machines have taken over most of the brute-strength jobs once performed by males, and most jobs today can be done by both sexes. For another, the emphasis on personal compatibility in marriage encourages the possession of congenial or at least complementary, instead of opposite, traits by husband and wife. Moreover, parents treat boys and girls more alike than formerly; however, this trend is more prominent among the well-educated and upper classes than among lower classes (Bronfenbrenner, 1961).

Figures which indicate increasing employment of women outside the home are often cited to prove that women are tending to reject their traditional sex role. However, sheer numbers constitute a shaky basis for formulating hypotheses.

Actually, most women still view homemaking and child-rearing as their primary role. Women generally seek employment to provide a better life for the children rather than to establish a career (Hartley, 1960). Changes in the female role as homemaker appear to be in peripheral rather than basic areas of behavior.

What the sex roles ideally should be, or how active a part society should play in altering them, is debatable. As Mead (1967) points out, the present-day relationships between men and women have fairly clearcut characteristics, including "early marriage, marriage as a principal form of relationship between men and women, parenthood for all couples immediately following on or even preceding marriage, a separate domicile for each nuclear family . . . [p. 871]." However, changing conditions could lead to the practice of artificial insemination, and perhaps to extra-uterine gestation (p. 872). As a result, new styles of family living might develop, including special approval of very small families and even childless marriages, or a new social style in which parenthood might be restricted to a smaller number of families, whose main function would be child-rearing, while the rest of the population would function, for the first time in history, simply as individuals.

From these changes, certain alternative sex relationships might develop, the first being a growing disregard for sex as the basic form of differentiation. That is, both sexes would receive the same sort of education and upbringing. Men and women would be differentiated, not by sex-typed personality characteristics, but simply by temperament. Alternately, personality typing according to sex would continue as the basic criterion for differentiation. Woman's historical role would continue, despite her many activities outside the home. In either case, declares Mead, males should learn new ways of achieving masculine identity, and females should learn to function as complete, independent, creative individuals.

To date, little conscious effort has been directed toward sex-role modification. Several factors operate to obstruct change in this area. For one, males enjoy various sex advantages and possess the power to preserve their preferred status. Also, females are taught from birth to be passive; hence, they are unlikely to protest the secondary role assigned them. Both sexes ordinarily believe the characteristics of their role to be natural and therefore unsusceptible to fundamental change. Indeed, such changes in sex roles as do take place typically evolve slowly and without social planning. For example, college attendance may, in effect, defeminize girls to some extent. In a study of personality change as a result of college attendance, Nichols (1967) reported that girls tend to become more masculine in the more masculine college environments.

Teenagers face various problems related to sex role, partly because adolescence highlights differences between boys and girls. Teen activities are polarized—in dancing the boy leads, the girl follows. Such polarization may arouse jealousies and hostility, often unconsciously. Moreover, when an individual matures sexually, he is expected simultaneously to adopt mature behaviors appropriate to his sex. Since these behaviors vary widely from those of childhood, considerable adaptation may be required. An individual who adjusted very well to the more neutral sex role of childhood may have a greater problem in adolescence. The homely girl who never has dates feels lonely among peers who boast of their conquests. The boy from a lower-class home may lack the graces required for mixed social functions at school.

Adaptations to each sex role pose certain problems. The boy's role is more discontinuous than the girls—that is, his role as a child makes less provision than hers for what the corresponding adult role will be. When a girl assists her mother in the home or plays with her doll, she is engaged in activities directly related to the domestically oriented role of the woman. However, the boy's pursuits may vary widely from his later roles as worker and father. Also, the boy, more than the girl, is driven by societal pressures to achieve and to prove himself sexually.

The girl has her special problems, too. Often, she is uncertain what her own role should be. Perhaps the difficulty is in integrating the complex factors involved in the modern girl's self-image. To a considerable extent, this involves harmonizing the contradictory demands to be both feminine and modern. The two roles, says Komarovsky (1946), are mutually exclusive, carrying contrasting sets of personality traits. Each role involves certain attitudes toward work, men, love, and self. Moreover, society ordinarily fails to discriminate between active and aggressive women. Many active women are quite feminine, and have no interest in encroaching upon male territory. Nevertheless, they wish to strive for some purpose, not in competition with men, but solely in pursuit of worthwhile goals. An active girl—the more so because she is feminine—may feel anxious—whenever she departs from the traditionally passive female role (Bettelheim, 1962). As a result, in the process of moving from adolescence to adulthood, the female experiences greater damage to her ego than does the male during the same period (Nawas, 1971). The girl is strait-jacketed, both as youth and adult, in a sheltered role fashioned by society and reinforced by its agent, the family. By contrast, whatever stresses the boy may feel in later adolescence are counterbalanced by the anticipated privileges of male adulthood.

In general, boys accept the roles assigned them more easily than do girls. For one thing, they are pressured by parents and peers to do so (Hartley, 1959). Males are also accorded higher status, especially as they grow older. In consequence, notes Ausubel (1958), "the male counterpart of a 'tomboy' who relishes sewing and reads girls' books is indeed a rarity [p. 367]." In contrast, many girls may be discontented with at least certain aspects of their role. Our age does not value the role of housewife, states Korner (1956); instead, there is a "thorough indoctrination that being a housewife is a fate, not a call [p. 544]." In like vein, Steinemann (1963) says that the traditional role of the woman is other-oriented in the sense that she achieves personal fulfillment by proxy—that is; by fulfilling the needs of others.

Actually, adaptation to sex role is a highly personal matter, dependent upon the particular individual's traits and experience. The twelve-year-old tomboy may have trouble evolving into a demure young lady. A shy, insecure boy may find that the adolescent male role requires a degree of dominance he does not possess. Another boy may enjoy adolescence but dread the responsibilities associated with full manhood. A girl who has achieved prominence in high school activities may resist accepting a secondary role in marriage.

Implicit in the foregoing discussion are many complex issues relating to sex role. Should teachers and parents attempt to make less masculine boys more so, and masculine girls less so? Should society undertake deliberate attempts to modify less desirable features of sex role? To what extent, if any, might adaptation to sex role be facilitated by hormonal injection, perhaps during the prenatal period? What sorts of sex roles are needed for modern society? Are less differentiated roles actually more functional nowadays? Certainly, many assumptions relating to sex role warrant reexamination. Traditionally, departures from sex-typical behaviors are assumed to be abnormal and undesirable; however, a broader interpretation of sex role is more congruent with full personal development (Minuchin, 1965)

The following two articles provide a helpful background for considering these issues. The first, by Lynn, provides a comprehensive theory concerning sex-role identification; Lynn has written widely on the subject and here proposes various provocative hypotheses. In the second article, Angrist considers the topic of sex role in depth, first reviewing various definitions of the concept, then discussing its usefulness in the study of heterosexual relationships and suggesting approaches for future research on the topic. She indicates special difficulties in dealing with the sex-role concept in a changing, complex society where a great many variables, such as age-stage in the life cycle, and familial and occupational status, must be considered.

REFERENCES

AUSUBEL, D. P.   Ego development among segregated Negro children. *Mental Hygiene,* 1958, *42,* 362–369.

BENEDEK, T., & RUBENSTEIN, B. B.   Correlations between ovarian activity and psychodynamic processes: The ovarian phase. *Psychosomatic Medicine,* 1939, *1,* 245–270.

BETTELHEIM, B.   The problem of generations. *Daedalus,* 1962, *91,* 95.

BRONFENBRENNER, U.   The changing American child—A speculative analysis. *Journal of Social Issues,* 1961, *17,* 1.

GRAY, J. A., & BUFFERY, A. W. H.   Sex differences in emotional and cognitive behavior in mammals, including man: Adaptive and neural bases. *Acta Psychologica,* 1971, *35,* 89–111.

HARLOW, H. F.   The heterosexual affectional system in monkeys. *American Psychologist,* 1962, *17,* 1–9.

HARTLEY, R. E.   Sex-role pressure and the socialization of the male child. *Psychological Reports,* 1959, *5,* 457–468.

HARTLEY, R.   Current changes in sex role patterns. *Merrill-Palmer Quarterly,* 1960, *6,* 153–164.

KOMAROVSKY, M.   Cultural contradictions and sex roles. *American Journal of Sociology,* November 1946, *52,* 184–189.

KORNER, I. N.   Of values, value lag, and mental health. *American Psychologist,* 1956, *11,* 543–546.

MEAD, M.   The life cycle and its variations: The division of roles. *Daedalus,* 1967, *96*(3), 871–875.

MINUCHIN, P.   Sex-role concepts and sex typing in childhood as a function of school and home environments. *Child Development,* December 1965, *36*(4), 1032–1048.

MONEY, J.   Developmental differentiation of femininity and masculinity compared. In S. M. Farber and R. H. L. Wilson (Eds.) *Potential of Women.* New York: McGraw-Hill, 1963, pp. 52–56.

MONEY, J.   Psychosexual differentiation. In J. Money (Ed.) *Sex research: New developments.* New York: Holt, Rinehart and Winston, 1965.

NAWAS, M. M.   Change in efficiency of ego functioning and complexity from adolescent to young adulthood. *Developmental Psychology,* 1971, *4*(3), 412–415.

NICHOLS, R. C.   Personality change and the college. *American Educational Research Journal,* 1967, *4*(3), 173–190.

ROESSLER, R. T.   Sexuality and identity: Masculine differentiation and feminine constancy. *Adolescence,* 1971, *6*(22), 156–196.

STEIN, A. H., POHLY, S. R., & MUELLER, E.   The influence of masculine, feminine, and neutral tasks on children's achievement behavior expectancies of success and attainment values. *Child Development,* 1971, *42*(1), 195–208.

STEINEMANN, A.   A study of the concept of the feminine role of 51 middle-class American families. *Genetic Psychology Monographs,* 1963, *67*, 275–352.

The Process of Learning Parental and Sex-Role Identification

DAVID B. LYNN

This paper summarizes Lynn's theoretical formulations concerning sex-role identification, and attempts a more comprehensive, coherent clarification of concepts. Research is quoted in support of the newer hypotheses.

The purpose of this paper is to summarize the writer's theoretical formulation concerning identification, much of which has been published piecemeal in various journals. Research relevant to new hypotheses is cited, and references are given to previous publications of this writer in which the reader can find evidence concerning the earlier hypotheses. Some of the previously published hypotheses are considerably revised in this paper and, it is hoped, placed in a more comprehensive and coherent framework.

Theoretical Formulation

Before developing specific hypotheses, one must briefly define identification as it is used here. *Parental identification* refers to the internalization of personality characteristics of one's own parent and to unconscious reactions similar to that parent. This is to be contrasted with *sex-role identification*, which refers to the internalization of the role typical of a given sex in a particular culture and to the unconscious reactions characteristic of that role. Thus, theoretically, an individual might be thoroughly identified with the role typical of his own sex generally and yet poorly identified with his same-sex parent specifically. This differentiation also allows for the converse circumstances wherein a person is well identified with his same-sex parent specifically and yet poorly identified with the typical same-sex role generally. In such an instance the parent with whom the individual is well identified is himself poorly identified with the typical sex role. An example might be a girl who is closely identified with her mother, who herself is more strongly identified with the masculine than the feminine role. Therefore, such a girl, through her identification with her mother, is poorly identified with the feminine role.[1]

FORMULATION OF HYPOTHESES

It is postulated that the initial parental identification of both male and female infants is with the mother. Boys, but not girls, must shift from this initial mother identification and establish mascu-

Presented at the Annual Meeting of the American Orthopsychiatric Association, 1966.

[1]D. B. Lynn, "Sex-Role and Parental Identification," *Child Development, 33*:3 (1962), pp. 555–564.

From David B. Lynn, The Process of Learning Parental and Sex-Role Identification. Reprinted from the *Journal of Marriage and the Family,* November 1966, *28*(4), 466–470, by permission of the author and publisher.

line-role identification. Typically in this culture the girl has the same-sex parental model for identification (the mother) with her for more hours per day than the boy has his same-sex model (the father) with him. Moreover, even when home, the father does not usually participate in as many intimate activities with the child as does the mother, e.g., preparation for bed, toileting. The time spent with the child and the intimacy and intensity of the contact are thought to be pertinent to the process of learning parental identification.[2] The boy is seldom if ever with the father as he engages in his daily vocational activities, although both boy and girl are often with the mother as she goes through her household activities. Consequently, the father, as a model for the boy, is analogous to a map showing the major outline but lacking most details, whereas the mother, as a model for the girl, might be thought of as a detailed map.

However, despite the shortage of male models, a somewhat stereotyped and conventional masculine role is nonetheless spelled out for the boy, often by his mother and women teachers in the absence of his father and male models. Through the reinforcement of the culture's highly developed system of rewards for typical masculine-role behavior and punishment for signs of femininity, the boy's early learned identification with the mother weakens. Upon this weakened mother identification is welded the later learned identification with a culturally defined, stereotyped masculine role.

(1)* Consequently, males tend to identify with a culturally defined masculine role, whereas females tend to identify with their mothers.[3]

Although one must recognize the contribution of the father in the identification of males and the general cultural influences in the identification of females, it nevertheless seems meaningful, for simplicity in developing this formulation, to refer frequently to *masculine-role identification* in

males as distinguished from *mother-identification* in females.

Some evidence is accumulating suggesting that *(2) both males and females identify more closely with the mother than with the father.* Evidence is found in support of this hypothesis in a study by Lazowick[4] in which the subjects were 30 college students. These subjects and their mothers and fathers were required to rate concepts, e.g., "myself," "father," "mother," etc. The degree of semantic similarity as rated by the subjects and their parents was determined. The degree of similarity between fathers and their own children was not significantly greater than that found between fathers and children randomly matched. However, children did share a greater semantic similarity with their own mothers than they did when matched at random with other maternal figures. Mothers and daughters did not share a significantly greater semantic similarity than did mothers and sons.

Evidence is also found in support of Hypothesis 2 in a study by Adams and Sarason[5] using anxiety scales with male and female high school students and their mothers and fathers. They found that anxiety scores of both boys and girls were much more related to mothers' than to fathers' anxiety scores.

Support for this hypothesis comes from a study in which Aldous and Kell[6] interviewed 50 middle-class college students and their mothers concerning childrearing values. They found, contrary to their expectation, that a slightly higher proportion of boys than girls shared their mothers' childrearing values.

Partial support for Hypothesis 2 is provided in a study by Gray and Klaus[7] using the Allport-Vernon-Lindzey Study of Values completed by 34 female and 28 male college students and by their parents. They found that the men were not sig-

[2]B. A. Goodfield, "A Preliminary Paper on the Development of the Time Intensity Compensation Hypothesis in Masculine Identification," paper read at the San Francisco State Psychological Convention, April, 1965.

*Specific hypotheses are numbered and in italics.

[3]D. B. Lynn, "A Note on Sex Differences in the Development of Masculine and Feminine Identification," *Psychological Review,* 66:2 (1959), pp. 126–135.

[4]L. M. Lazowick, "On the Nature of Identification," *Journal of Abnormal and Social Psychology,* 51 (1955), pp. 175–183.

[5]E. B. Adams and I. G. Sarason, "Relation Between Anxiety in Children and Their Parents," *Child Development,* 34:1 (1963), pp. 237–246.

[6]J. Aldous and L. Kell, "A Partial Test of Some Theories of Identification," *Marriage and Family Living,* 23:1 (1961), pp. 15–19.

[7]S. W. Gray and R. Klaus, "The Assessment of Parental Identification," *Genetic Psychology Monographs,* 54 (1956), pp. 87–114.

nificantly closer to their fathers than to their mothers and also that the men were not significantly closer to their fathers than were the women. However, the women were closer to their mothers than were the men and closer to their mothers than to their fathers.

Note that, in reporting research relevant to Hypothesis 2, only studies of *tested similarity*, not *perceived similarity*, were reviewed. To test this hypothesis, one must measure tested similarity, i.e., measure both the child and the parent on the same variable and compare the similarity between these two measures. This paper is not concerned with perceived similarity, i.e., testing the child on a given variable and then comparing that finding with a measure taken as to how the child thinks his parent would respond. It is this writer's opinion that much confusion has arisen by considering perceived similarity as a measure of parental identification. It seems obvious that, especially for the male, perceived similarity between father and son would usually be closer than tested similarity, in that it is socially desirable for a man to be similar to his father, especially as contrasted to his similarity to his mother. Indeed, Gray and Klaus[8] found the males' perceived similarity with the father to be closer than tested similarity.

It is hypothesized that the closer identification of males with the mother than with the father will be revealed more clearly on some measures than on others. *(3) The closer identification of males with their mothers than with their fathers will be revealed most frequently in personality variables which are not clearly sex-typed.* In other words, males are more likely to be more similar to their mothers than to their fathers in variables in which masculine and feminine role behavior is not especially relevant in the culture.

There has been too little research on tested similarity between males and their parents to presume an adequate test of Hypothesis 3. In order to test it, one would first have to judge personality variables as to how typically masculine or feminine they seem. One could then test to determine whether a higher proportion of males are more similar to their mothers than to their fathers on those variables which are not clearly sex-typed, rather than on those which are judged

clearly to be either masculine or feminine. To this writer's knowledge, this has not been done.

It is postulated that the task of achieving these kinds of identification (masculine role for males and mother identification for females) requires separate methods of learning for each sex. These separate methods of learning to identify seem to be problem-solving for boys and lesson-learning for girls. Woodworth and Schlosberg differentiate between the task of solving problems and that of learning lessons in the following way:

> With a problem to master the learner must explore the situation and find the goal before his task is fully presented. In the case of a lesson, the problem-solving phase is omitted or at least minimized, as we see when the human subject is instructed to memorize this poem or that list of nonsense syllables, to examine these pictures with a view to recognizing them later.[9]

Since the girl is not required to shift from the mother in learning her identification, she is expected mainly to learn the mother-identification lesson as it is presented to her, partly through imitation and through the mother's selective reinforcement of mother-similar behavior. She need not abstract principles defining the feminine role to the extent that the boy must in defining the masculine role. Any bit of behavior on the mother's part may be modeled by the girl in learning the mother-identification lesson.

However, finding the appropriate identification goal does constitute a major problem for the boy in solving the masculine-role identification problem. When the boy discovers that he does not belong in the same sex category as the mother, he must then find the proper sex-role identification goal. Masculine-role behavior is defined for him through admonishments, often negatively given, e.g., the mother's and teachers' telling him that he should not be a sissy without precisely indicating what he *should* be. Moreover, these negative admonishments are made in the early grades in the absence of male teachers to serve as models and with the father himself often unavailable as a model. The boy must restructure these admonishments in order to abstract principles defining

[8]*Ibid.*

[9]R. S. Woodworth and H. Schlosberg, *Experimental Psychology*, New York: Holt, 1954, p. 529.

the masculine role. It is this process of defining the masculine-role goal which is involved in solving the masculine-role identification problem.

One of the basic steps in this formulation can now be taken. *(4) In learning the sex-typical identification, each sex is thereby acquiring separate methods of learning which are subsequently applied to learning tasks generally.*[10]

The little girl acquires a learning method which primarily involves (a) a personal relationship and (b) imitation rather than restructuring the field and abstracting principles. On the other hand, the little boy acquires a different learning method which primarily involves (a) defining the goal (b) restructuring the field, and (c) abstracting principles. There are a number of findings which are consistent with Hypothesis 4, such as the frequently reported greater problem-solving skill of males and the greater field dependence of females.[11]

The shift of the little boy from mother identification to masculine-role identification is assumed to be frequently a crisis. It has been observed that demands for typical sex-role behavior come at an earlier age for boys than for girls. These demands are made at an age when boys are least able to understand them. As was pointed out above, demands for masculine sex-role behavior are often made by women in the absence of readily available male models to demonstrate typical sex-role behavior. Such demands are often presented in the form of punishing, *negative* admonishments, i.e., telling the boy what not to do rather than what to do and backing up the demands with punishment. These are thought to be very different conditions from those in which the girl learns her mother-identification lesson. Such methods of demanding typical sex-role behavior of boys are very poor methods for inducing learning.

(5) Therefore, males tend to have greater difficulty in achieving same-sex identification than females.[12]

(6) Furthermore, more males than females fail more or less completely in achieving same-sex identification, but they rather make an opposite-sex identification.[13]

Negative admonishments given at an age when the child is least able to understand them and supported by punishment are thought to produce anxiety concerning sex-role behavior. In Hartley's words:

> This situation gives us practically a perfect combination for inducing anxiety—the demand that the child do something which is not clearly defined to him, based on reasons he cannot possibly appreciate, and enforced with threats, punishments and anger by those who are close to him.[14]

(7) Consequently, males are more anxious regarding sex-role identification than females.[15] It is postulated that punishment often leads to dislike of the activity that led to punishment.[16] Since it is "girl-like" activities that provoked the punishment administered in an effort to induce sex-typical behavior in boys, then, in developing dislike for the activity which led to such punishment, boys should develop hostility toward "girl-like" activities. Also, boys should be expected to generalize and consequently develop hostility toward all females as representatives of this disliked role. There is not thought to be as much pressure on girls as on boys to avoid opposite-sex activities. It is assumed that girls are punished neither so early nor so severely for adopting masculine sex-role behavior.

(8) Therefore, males tend to hold stronger feelings of hostility toward females than females toward males.[17] The young boy's same-sex identification is at first not very firm because of the shift from mother to masculine identification. On the other hand, the young girl, because she need make no shift in identification, remains relatively firm in her mother identification. However, the

[10]D. B. Lynn, "Sex-Role and Parental Identification," *op. cit.*
[11]*Ibid.*
[12]D. B. Lynn, "Divergent Feedback and Sex-Role Identification in Boys and Men," *Merrill-Palmer Quarterly, 10*:1 (1964), pp. 17–23.

[13]D. B. Lynn, "Sex Differences in Identification Development," *Sociometry, 24*:4 (1961), pp. 372-383.
[14]R. E. Hartley, "Sex-Role Pressures and the Socialization of the Male Child," *Psychological Reports, 5* (1959), p. 458.
[15]D. B. Lynn, "Divergent Feedback and Sex-Role Identification in Boys and Men," *op. cit.*
[16]E. R. Hilgard, *Introduction to Psychology*, New York: Harcourt, Brace, and World, 1962.
[17]D. B. Lynn, "Divergent Feedback and Sex-Role Identification in Boys and Men," *op. cit.*

culture, which is male-dominant in orientation, reinforces the boy's developing masculine-role identification much more thoroughly than it does the girl's developing feminine identification. He is rewarded simply for having been born masculine through countless privileges accorded males but not females. As Brown pointed out:

> The superior position and privileged status of the male permeates nearly every aspect, minor and major, of our social life. The gadgets and prizes in boxes of breakfast cereal, for example, commonly have strong masculine rather than feminine appeal. And the most basic social institutions perpetuate this pattern of masculine aggrandizement. Thus, the Judeo-Christian faiths involve worshipping God, a "Father," rather than a "Mother," and Christ, a "Son," rather than a "Daughter."[18]

(9) Consequently, with increasing age, males become relatively more firmly identified with the masculine role.[19]

Since psychological disturbances should, theoretically, be associated with inadequate same-sex identification and since males are postulated to be gaining in masculine identification, the following is predicted: *(10) With increasing age males develop psychological disturbances at a more slowly accelerating rate than females.*[20]

It is postulated that as girls grow older, they become increasingly disenchanted with the feminine role because of the prejudices against their sex and privileges and prestige offered the male rather than the female. Even the women with whom they come in contact are likely to share the prejudices prevailing in this culture against their own sex.[21] Smith[22] found that with increasing age girls have a progressively better opinion

of boys and a progressively poorer opinion of themselves. *(11) Consequently, a larger proportion of females than males show preference for the role of the opposite sex.*[23]

Note that in Hypothesis 11 the term "preference" rather than "identification" was used. It is *not* hypothesized that a larger proportion of females than males *identify* with the opposite sex (Hypothesis 6 predicted the reverse) but rather that they will show *preference* for the role of the opposite sex. *Sex-role preference* refers to the desire to adopt the behavior associated with one sex or the other or the perception of such behavior as preferable or more desirable. *Sex-role preference* should be contrasted with *sex-role identification,* which, as stated previously, refers to the actual incorporation of the role of a given sex and to the unconscious reactions characteristic of that role.

Punishment may suppress behavior without causing its unlearning.[24] Because of the postulated punishment administered to males for adopting opposite-sex role behavior, it is predicted that males will repress atypical sex-role behavior rather than unlearn it. One might predict, then, a discrepancy between the underlying sex-role identification and the overt sex-role behavior of males. For females, on the other hand, no comparable punishment for adopting many aspects of the opposite-sex role is postulated. *(12) Consequently, where a discrepancy exists between sex-roles preference and identification, it will tend to be as follows: Males will tend to show same-sex role preference with underlying opposite-sex identification. Females will tend to show opposite-sex role preference with underlying same-sex identification.*[25] Stated in another way, where a discrepancy occurs both males and females will tend to show masculine-role preference with underlying feminine identification.

Not only is the masculine role accorded more prestige than the feminine role, but males are more likely than females to be ridiculed or punished for adopting aspects of the opposite-sex role. For a girl to be a tomboy does not involve the

[18]D. G. Brown, "Sex-Role Development in a Changing Culture," *Psychological Bulletin, 55* (1958), p. 235
[19]D. B. Lynn, "A Note on Sex Differences in the Development of Masculine and Feminine Identification," *op. cit.*
[20]D. B. Lynn, "Sex Differences in Identification Development," *op. cit.*
[21]P. M. Kitay, "A Comparison of the Sexes in Their Attitudes and Beliefs About Women: A Study of Prestige Groups," *Sociometry, 3* (1940), pp. 399–407.
[22]S. Smith, "Age and Sex Differences in Children's Opinion Concerning Sex Differences," *Journal of Genetic Psychology, 54* (1939), pp. 17–25.

[23]D. B. Lynn, "A Note on Sex Differences in the Development of Masculine and Feminine Identification," *op. cit.*
[24]Hilgard, *op. cit.*
[25]D. B. Lynn, "Divergent Feedback and Sex-Role Identification in Boys and Men," *op. cit.*

censure that results when a boy is a sissy. Girls may wear masculine clothing (shirts and trousers), but boys may not wear feminine clothing (skirts and dresses). Girls may play with toys typically associated with boys (cars, trucks, erector sets, and guns), but boys are discouraged from playing with feminine toys (dolls and tea sets). *(13) Therefore, a higher proportion of females than males adopt aspects of the role of the opposite sex.*[26]

Note that Hypothesis 13 refers to *sex-role adoption* rather than *sex-role identification* or *preference. Sex-role adoption* refers to the overt behavior characteristic of a given sex. An example contrasting sex-role adoption with preference and identification is an individual who *adopts* behavior characteristics of his own sex because it is expedient, not because he *prefers* it nor because he is so *identified.*

Summary

The purpose of this paper has been to summarize the writer's theoretical formulation and to place it in a more comprehensive and coherent framework. The following hypotheses were presented and discussed:

1. Males tend to identify with a culturally defined masculine role, whereas females tend to identify with their mothers.

2. Both males and females identify more closely with the mother than with the father.

[26]D. B. Lynn, "A Note on Sex Differences in the Development of Masculine and Feminine Identification," *op. cit.*

3. The closer identification of males with their mothers than with their fathers will be revealed most frequently in personality variables which are not clearly sex-typed.

4. In learning the sex-typical identification, each sex is thereby acquiring separate methods of learning which are subsequently applied to learning tasks generally.

5. Males tend to have greater difficulty in achieving same-sex identification than females.

6. More males than females fail more or less completely in achieving same-sex identification but rather make an opposite-sex identification.

7. Males are more anxious regarding sex-role identification than females.

8. Males tend to hold stronger feelings of hostility toward females than females toward males.

9. With increasing age, males become relatively more firmly identified with the masculine role.

10. With increasing age, males develop psychological disturbances at a more slowly accelerating rate than females.

11. A larger proportion of females than males show preference for the role of the opposite sex.

12. Where a discrepancy exists between sex-role preference and identification, it will tend to be as follows: Males will tend to show same-sex role preference with underlying opposite-sex identification. Females will tend to show opposite-sex role preference with underlying same-sex identification.

13. A higher proportion of females than males adopt aspects of the role of the opposite-sex.

The Study of Sex Roles

SHIRLEY S. ANGRIST

The concept of sex role is defined and related to the way the sexes learn their respective roles. Particular approaches for studying sex role are then suggested.

For some years, behavioral scientists have played an ambivalent love affair with role theories. As a way of describing patterned behavior, they find role concepts relevant, useful, and handy—but also inadequate, muddled, and overly simple. As Levinson (1959) said: "The concept of role remains one of the most overworked and underdeveloped in the social sciences." Discussions of this ambivalence about role theories are well documented in the literature and I will not dwell on them here. The key dilemmas in role analysis research could be summarized as follows:

The terminology is various, inconsistent and only partly overlapping in usage. It is true that the core ideas have involved three elements: (a) role behavior based on role expectations of relevant others; (b) expectations keyed to a specific role; (c) a social location or interaction system for role expectations and behavior (Gross, 1958). However, the term role itself has been taken to mean different things: observable behavior, expectations for behavior (typically required for the role incumbent), norms for behavior (what incumbent's behavior ought to be), or even some combinations of these.

The context in which roles can be located ranges widely from the whole society to the narrowly *dyadic* group. Models of actors in their social location as role incumbents typically indicate reciprocity of the structural relationship between: man-woman, mother-child, teacher-pupil. In so doing, the interaction and influence between sets of role actors and their reciprocals is assumed to occur in a shared arena for the relationship. Thus, research has tended to concentrate on roles easily locatable, e.g., within the nuclear family or work settings. The society-wide role types, such as "male," "adult," "intellectual," have been notably more difficult to study in role theory terms.

In this paper, the focus is on one role type—sex role. The aim is to review definitions of it and to discuss its usefulness in studying how men and women learn to enact sex related roles. The above-mentioned dilemmas will reappear in the attempt to isolate definitions of sex role. Finally, two approaches for studying sex roles will be suggested.

Definitions of Sex Role

It has been proposed that role has three separate foci according to the main fields utilizing the construct. Gordon (1966) suggests that the

From S. S. Angrist, The study of sex roles. Reprinted from *Journal of Social Issues*, Vol. XXV, No. 1, (1969), pp. 215–232, by permission of the author and publisher.

anthropological, psychological and sociological core meanings are respectively: position, behavior and relationship. Supposing we take this three-pronged look beyond generic role to ask: what is meant by sex role? The prime conclusions which emerge from such an inquiry are that sex role is rarely defined, the attempt definitions vary widely, the construct lacks clarity, and the three fields reveal overlap in usage. Still there is some differential emphasis as suggested in Table 1.

When sex role refers to a position, it *de facto* stresses the position's location in a highly structural social context. Indeed strongly tied to Linton's (1945) classical definitive formulation, and utilized widely in anthropological field studies, the positional meaning dwells on sex as ascribed and tied to age groups. The ascriptive quality is elaborated in definitions of sex roles as "recruitment roles" and "non-relational" (Nadel, 1957; Banton, 1965). The prescriptions for appropriate behavior are assumed to be widely held and agreed upon. Further, the whole society is used for locating sex role; this jibes with the gestalt-type descriptive analyses of primitive societies. The main content thrust of this approach is the division of labor in society, with standards of appropriateness for the apportioning and fulfillment of tasks by sex and age (Mead, 1935; Murdock 1966; Southall, 1959).

THE OVERLAP IS EVIDENT

However, the aforementioned overlap in utilization of the sex role construct is also evident. Thus, in sociological studies, the positional meaning of sex role is apparent in groups smaller than whole societies: e.g., in small groups, involving

study of the sorting out of tasks and special behaviors (Bales, 1958), in large-scale organizations, like legislatures and school systems (Gehlen, 1967; Gross, 1958), and in the American nuclear family division of tasks between husband and wife (Blood, 1960; Nye, 1963). It may be concluded that the sex role-as-position meaning is difficult to apply, if not irrelevant, to less structured settings where expectations are not largely consensual and organized, and behavior is not normatively based (Gross, 1958; Newcomb, 1950).

The view common in social psychological approaches assumes the universality of sex differences—their respective biological characteristics, however culturally elaborated, are the basis for polar behavior and attribute models. Stress is on behavior as measured by variables like school achievement, occupational choices, play object preferences, and on behavior-related attributes of the individual—personality, adjustment, need achievement, aspirations. Girls perform better on verbal tests, achieve higher grades; boys excel in science, mathematics and mechanical ability. Girls are more fearful and nervous, while boys have greater achievement needs and higher aspirations (see Brown, 1965, and Wigney, 1965, for summaries of relevant research). The behavioral focus is operationally tidy. The resultant dichotomies seem to reinforce the clusters of sex-related characteristics: women are women and men are men wherever they may live, eat, play, work or interact. However, developmental features of sex-related behaviors are accounted for as some researches emphasize age or stage as a factor (Emmerich, 1961; Wallace, 1966). The issue raised then is the validity of universal sex role behavior

Table 1.   Meanings and Usage of Sex Role

Meaning of Sex Role	Core Definition	Emphasis	Social Location
Position	Normatively appropriate expectations for M & F	Division of labor of group or societal tasks	Structured settings
Behavior	What M and F do and are like	Personality, abilities, preferences	Setting need not be relevant
Relationship	The process of role taking	Socialization and interaction	Dyad or larger groups with varying structure

measures without regard to the delineations of other impinging characteristics or to the pertinent social location.

For Sociology Role Theory Is Relevant

For the sociological approach, the setting for role-taking is indeed relevant and specified. Sex role grows out of self-development during the socialization process. The individual interacting with others learns his own and others' roles. He discovers and interprets behavior, revising temporarily fixed roles (Cottrell, 1942; Parsons, 1955; Mead, 1934; Sarbin, 1954; Turner, 1962). The difficulty lies in defining all the features pertinent to comprehension of the relationship between the role-taker and the others in the context. Group size and degree of structure immediately must be considered. Theoretically, any group can be studied, ranging from dyad to whole society. In practice, research on relationships has been most feasible in highly defined social locations (Angrist, 1968; Farber, 1959; Stryker, 1962). As Stryker pointed out, one cannot assume as Mead did that all social groups have rational orientations, utilitarian goals and highly organized structure. To specify daughter-in-law or ex-patient wife seems sufficiently concrete indication of the role-taker and the relevant others. But perhaps it is more accurate to zero in on the social specifics: e.g., a Polish Catholic first generation urban American young newly married couple as the nuclear family type in which the wife is being studied.

Thus, the deficiencies of role theories burden the sex role construct no less. Indeed, sex role epitomizes some difficulties: the many definitional stances, fuzzy empirical referents, and overemphasis on delimited social arenas for studying roles. Sex role singularly suffers from absence of specific definition—its meaning is connotative instead of denotative. As several observers note concerning American society, there exists little consensus on the content of sex roles, especially for women (Goode, 1960a; Gross, 1958; Parsons, 1942). The definitional weakness may mirror the hardship of specifying and studying that which is rapidly changing, blurred and high-

ly variant in form. In that sense, the social location problem is tied to the definitional one: How to pinpoint what is vaguely describable? How to describe what is vaguely locatable?

To deal with such variability, sex role may be seen as involving four elements: label, behavior, expectations and location. The label "male" or "female" refers to the biologically-determined phenomenological fact that the labeled individual probably has or probably will enact organized sets of behaviors open to persons with that label. He (or she) will probably himself expect to evidence, or others will expect him to evidence, what are sex-related attributes and behaviors. The expectations may be generically normative—what men-in-general should be or do, or concretely normative—what you, Man X, with your special characteristics in this particular situation, should be or do. The closer the relationship between actor and relevant other, the less generic and the more specific the norms that apply. No priority is given to expectations as evocative or determinative of behavior. Although that may be the case, equally likely is the evocation of expectations on the basis of specific behaviors or cues (Angrist, 1968). The label itself can activate both behaviors and expectations from others, but always in relation to a social location.

Sex Role Involves Multiple Roles

To delineate the exact context for sex role is to encompass the whole set of roles an actor is heir to. Reference here is to a role constellation: th combination of roles one individual can play at a given stage in his life vis-a-vis other individuals and groups (Angrist, 1967). The point has to be underscored that no single role is feasibly isolated except conceptually. In reality, individuals judge and are judged by multiple criteria. They react and are reacted to as complex bundles of characteristics. Even in the encounter between strangers, the "personal front" is conveyed through vehicles such as clothing, age, sex, racial features, size, looks, posture, bodily gestures (Goffman, 1959). No single such label or vehicle, but their combinations, composes the front. Students of role behavior have amply documented the idea that a person participates in a complex society as a many-faceted actor, an incumbent of many roles, carrier of many labels, performer of different sets of behaviors, subject to multiple kinds of expectations.

HOW IS A ROLE ENACTED?

How then is a given role enacted? Both from the actor's viewpoint (and usually the relevant others') and from the observer's view, the individual, through group- or self-determined priorities, features one role above his other ones. Bates (1956) described this as a "dominant role," which temporarily and in appropriate context supersedes "latent roles." In this framework, age and sex-roles are dominant ones. Thus, father in the family is husband, sex partner, son-in-law, worker; influencing all these is his dominant role of male. The articulated system of role relationships put forth by Gross (1958) provides for the "focal position" of the role sector, and counter positions which relate to the focal one. For any given analysis, the researcher indicates which position is focal for his purposes.

So central is the multiple role dimension to Sarbin's (1954) theory, that he incorporates it *ipso facto* as a dimension in role enactment. The "number-of-roles" dimension is implicated in social adjustment so that, other things being equal, "the more roles in a person's behavior repertory, the 'better' his social adjustment." Lack of role-taking skills thus can be characteristic of psychopathology.

With somewhat different stress, Goffman (1961) distinguishes focused from unfocused roles. Sex roles are then to be viewed as unfocused or diffuse in the larger society. A focused role occurs within a "situated activity system," activity which occurs entirely within the walls of single social establishments. The individual holds a key role around which other roles intrude inevitably. Age–sex roles are such intruders: they introduce modulations ". . . in the performance of other roles" but have no principal jurisdiction in a social establishment or any set of tasks allocated to the performer . . . "Even while the local scene establishes what the individual will mainly be, many of his other affiliations will be simultaneously given little bits of credit" (Goffman, 1961).

Life Cycle Aspects of Sex Role

While these conceptions deal with multiple roles, they stress the temporal, contextual or structural dominance of one role over others. Another kind of view is embodied in the life-cycle concept. Perhaps the strongest embodiment of the role constellation idea appears in the life-cycle framework of some family studies (Glick, 1965; Hill, 1964). The individual is seen in a natural history of social development through life stages from child-in-the-family to single adult, to husband, father, grandfather; or to wife, mother, grandmother. The stages comprise elements of sex and age, marital, familial, school and work roles so that, actually, some roles overlap others (e.g., child, schoolgirl, teenager), some endure (e.g., female, even "mother" is relatively long term), others change (e.g., college students). A given individual's life-cycle may be cut into, so to speak, in order to observe the combination of roles in that stage or time slice (Angrist, 1967; Axelson, 1960). Or the family as a group may be studied in terms of its stage, whose definition stems from such matters as the length of time the couple is married, the presence or absence of children, and school stages and ages of the children, husband's work status, health of family members (Farber, 1961; Montz, 1950).

THE LIFE CYCLE TIME SLICE

Implicit use of the life cycle time slice in family literature has led to the elision of sex role into family role: female, then, means wife-and-mother; male means husband-and-father. Although this seems a logical emphasis in the family field, some consequences derive from this highlighting: (a) the study of sex role has tended to concentrate on conjugal or marital roles especially for women; (b) the family is seen primarily in the stage of *procreation* rather than at *orientation*, thus families with adult children, especially unmarried ones, are rarely studied; (c) role constellations of the unmarried do not fit the familial life cycle model and tend to be either ignored—e.g., working divorcee with young children, single career girl, wealthy bachelor business executive—or defined as deviant. However, it is true that recently the divorced have come in for specific study and with some life-cycle analysis. See, for example, Hunt (1966).

The life-cycle approach assumes progression or development so that in the family, any one stage has a high probability of being followed by others in a predictable order. Each stage has its developmental tasks (Kenkel, 1960), and individual family members have careers, that is, they progress through a series of roles; in this sense the family is a system of careers (Farber, 1961). Further, adult roles are said to have a cycle with stages, each with unique tasks and adjustment problems. This role-cycling analysis provides a kind of microscopic look at the structure content and continuity of a given role (Rossi, 1968).

It can be seen from the preceding illustrations that the features of role constellation (the natural history of the life span, the time slice, the role multiplicity of any single individual at any time in a given location) are already an explicit part of family studies.

Sex Role Constellation

What value has the role constellation approach to studying sex role?

First, it provides a workable solution to the location problem in studying sex roles. By close delineation of the several labels operative at a given time, relatively precise measurement of behavior and expectations vis-a-vis relevant others within the exact location becomes manageable and meaningful. The social location may be the household (composed of wife, husband, three children, maid) or the nuclear family (composed of wife, husband, three children).

Second, the normalcy of dealing with numerous and changing demands, expectations, and performing a wide repertoire of behaviors becomes apparent. The individual family member or school teacher is "many things to many people" as the colloquialism goes. Instead of struggling to unravel the threads of role conflict, the research task becomes to analyze the methods for meshing sets of individual behaviors and expectations. The idea that people manage to juggle, avoid, manipulate, interpret, the scope of their roles seems closer to empirical reality than that individuals act in terms of a single role blueprint at any

given time or place. In fact, some mechanisms for behavior under potentially conflict-ridden conditions have been described as "role-segregation," the scheduling of role enactments so that their audiences are segregated (Goffman, 1961), and ordinary role relations as a sequence of "role bargains" in which each individual seeks to reduce his role strain (or felt difficulty) in fulfilling his role (Goode, 1960b).

To summarize, the utility of a role constellation approach to the study of sex roles rests on the fact that the individual rarely, if ever, behaves just as a man or woman. Rather, sex modifies, sometimes strongly, sometimes weakly, whatever social interactions or relationships he is engaged in.

Role Flexibility

The issue may be turned differently to show that a given actor in his several roles is not constantly subject to view by members of his several role sets. By role set, Merton (1957) means "that complemental role relationship which persons have by virtue of occupying a particular social status." Indeed, for many roles, the audience may be quite distant at least some of the time—the husband's breadwinner specific role activities cannot readily be gauged by the wife (as when he decides to "work late") nor can huband judge the wife's homemaking activities for most of each day (nor count how many hours she spends on the phone). This lack of visibility includes elements of (a) distance from the audience, (b) temporal discreteness, (c) spatial discreteness (Preiss and Ehrlich, 1966). But as Goffman (1961) suggests, even when the actor is highly visible in a role, he typically shows "role distance" from it. A certain objectivity, making light of the role, intrusion of other peripheral roles into the situation, all reflect the actor's manifestation of role distance. This may be considered a means for avoiding conflict or for dealing with unavoidable conflict. It is the normalcy of an actor's multiple role involvements that permits him to exercise perspective on any single role.

Two other factors operate to foster flexibility in roles—(a) the frequent vagueness of, or disagreement in, expectations, and (b) the ability of role behaviors and labels themselves to generate expectations.

The vagueness or indeterminacy of sex role expectations is well documented as evidence that men's and women's dress, family and work lives are increasingly less dichotomous in industrialized urban societies, and even polar personality differences hold less consistently (Silverman, 1967; Vincent, 1966). In marital roles this vagueness has been considered responsible for conflict—for example, women more often prefer a companionate type marital role, while their husbands expect them to perform in more traditional domestic patterns (Rodgers, 1959). Women, in one study, emphasized an "ideal self" as modern but a "real self" as traditional female sex role (McKee, 1959). And young girls held quite traditional conceptions of sex roles although these differ from what characterizes their own primary social groups (Hartley, 1959). This kind of discrepancy between sets of women's role expectations, or between male and female expectations for women, may be interpreted as evidence of confusion about sex roles—indeed, most observers have done so. But it also represents a range of maneuverability —as some students of role conflict suggest, the very multiplicity of choices coupled with absence of sharply-defined expectations can foster flexibility for the actor (Parsons, 1942).

THE FLEXIBILITY ALLOWANCE

It is important to underscore this oft-observed phenomenon that all roles or realms of behavior have a stretch about them, or flexibility allowance. The notion of role constellation highlights the typicality of multiple involvements, identifications, expectations, locations and labels. Constructs like role distance, focused roles, role dominance suggest that perceived role conflict may be rare and manageable rather than common and disruptive. Of course, one may see the potentially negative consequences of such flexibility: confusion to the point of inaction where action is required or ineffectiveness in implementing one's role (Getzels, 1954).

The capacity for role labels behavior to elicit expectations suggests that flexibility also operates so that the actor can influence or determine others' expectations. Instead of assuming the unidirectional flow of behavior from expectations, the latter may be evoked from "personal front" cues and from behavior. Others react initially to the person's appearance, to what he seems to be in terms of labels, such as Negro, man, handsome, hippie, by expecting him to behave according to those labels. The actor can try to generate responses from others by the way he presents himself in appearance and behavior in a situation. Although others' perception of the actor may not jibe with his own, more or less accurate labels are quickly attributed to him and utilized until interaction alters these preconceptions. This evocative power of labels and behavior involves role perception in Sarbin's (1954) sense of silent naming or locating the position of the other and then responding to it. It is an implicit ingredient of Meadian social psychology focusing on the processual interplay between the role-taker and relevant others. It is in role-as-ascribed-qualities —what one is or appears to be—that the evocative function of labels and behavior is observable. Still, this idea has been latent rather than manifest in role theories—as Preiss and Ehrlich (1966) assert, determinism based on expectations has been the predominant assumption.

Again, the negative consequences of role labeling should be considered. As many studies of deviant behavior show, the label (self-imposed or endowed) continues to evoke expectations for deviant behavior, and perhaps stigmatized status, even when individuals would like to be rid of their negative cast (Mechanic, 1962; Phillips, 1964)—the label has a life of its own. As if recognizing this, families or relevant others of deviants may cling to acceptable, normal, healthy labels or substitute false, though less damning, ones (Schwartz, 1957).

CONTINGENCY ORIENTATION

The learning of adult sex roles, as indicated earlier, is seen primarily as occupation-directed for males and family-directed for females. While man's strait jacket during socialization is occupational choice and achievement, woman's strait jacket is marriage. This bifurcated picture is accurate in the sense of separate key goals for each sex, but it is inadequate to describe the flexibility phenomenon in sex role behavior. At this point, I am unprepared to substantiate such a hypothesis for males (although I submit that male role flexibility exists also) but the picture for females should emerge firmly.

My hypothesis is that flexibility in future fulfillment of women's roles is built into socialization both early and late as contingency training. In other words, woman lives by adjusting to and preparing for contingencies. The degree varies by social class, so that the lower the class the higher the contingency orientation. Indeed, women in lower socioeconomic groups have characteristically faced greater unpredictability in life style and greater acceptance of life's hazards as inevitable than higher class women (Rainwater, 1960). Lower class women may not only be more practical in this respect, but also more realistic (Lefton, 1962). The present discussion centers on middle and upper class college-educated women. This contingency orientation is reflected in personality development, in belief systems and in choices.

THE GIRL LEARNS TO BE "FEMININE"

The girl learns to be "feminine"—with all the adjectival subscales that term connotes—relative passivity, deference, low intellectuality, cooperativeness. That is to say, she learns to fit in, "to know her place," to take cues from authoritative males (Bem, in press). Catering to people's palates, to their moods, to their needs—these are feminine skills considered necessary to being wife and mother.

Beliefs and expectations about suitable behavior for a girl dwell primarily on the domestic realm of adult women's roles. Given that central theme for girls, an elaborate set of "ifs" surrounds it. For example:

(a) Douvan (1960) refers to the fact that a girl cannot commit herself to anything but marriage; she must remain malleable enough to fit the value system of her potential future spouse. One contingency element, then, is preparation to fit an unknown spousal relationship.

(b) A second contingency is lack of guarantee that she will marry. Although all but a few women hope and plan to marry, remaining single is both a fear and a possibility—ability to be financially self-supporting is a motivation for vocational training in case one does not marry.

(c) The economic necessity to work is considered a likely eventuality at some time in the women's life. She may need to support herself and husband while he completes his education, she may have to supplement or temporarily supply the family income, or earn money for special purposes—a car, vacation, or college costs for children.

(d) After marriage, temporary or permanent childlessness becomes a possibility, whether by accident or design. Leisure activities or gainful employment, either to fill free time or to provide content to life, may be viewed as resources for filling such a gap.

(e) When children grow up and leave home, the woman faces a drastic decline, even elimination, of her mothering functions. The need or freedom to fill this void may re-open work or leisure pursuits as realistic options.

(f) Exmarriage like nonmarriage is a contingency to be prepared for with "security" or "insurance." Divorce or widowhood can require the woman to become a breadwinner. Hence, a common rationale among girls is to be able to work, "just in case."

THE CONTINGENCIES ARE REAL

Obviously, the contingencies are real. This does not mean that all growing girls perceive and deliberately plan for them. The research task would be to determine how much rational accounting and preparation for the adult woman's contingencies occurs, how categories of women differ in degree of preparation, and whether some contingencies are more directly prepared for than others.

Not all the possible contingencies are given equal weight. In fact, one contingency takes priority during late adolescence and early adulthood rendering others subordinate. It is preparation for, even overstress on, marriage and the marital role. Epitomizing as it does the essence of American conceptions of feminity, this marital role emphasis masks the multiplicity of functions which family life entails for the woman. As the key contingency, preparation to fit the unknown spouse leads girls to tailor their behavior for maximum eligibility. This means acting feminine (passive, cooperative, non-intellectual), in dating situations(Komarovsky, 1946) and high school girls' acceptance of traditional but disliked domestic responsibilities for their married lives (Hartley, 1959). It means perception of limited options in the occupational world. The inability of occupational choice theories to handle women's patterns reflects women's contingency orientations (Psathas, 1968). Women's expectations for adult roles have been dubbed unrealistic (Rose, 1951); on the contrary, one could argue that they are concretely realistic. While a boy enters college considering types and conditions of work, the girl's primary focus is on marriage. Work is peripheral. College then becomes important—as broadening social experience, for self-development, for mate-finding. Whereas during the preteen years boys and girls tentatively consider occupations, only boys consistently pass into the reality stages of exploring, crystallizing and specifying an occupation. Ginzberg (1963) notes that " . . . major adjustments must be made in the general (occupational) theory before it can be applied to girls. . . ."

LONGITUDINAL RESEARCH ON ROLE ASPIRATIONS

In my current longitudinal research on college women's role aspirations, there is evidence for the extent to which a contingency orientation operates. Study subjects initially consisted of the 188 freshmen entering the women's college of a larger coeducational university. Students were asked to complete a questionnaire each fall and to be interviewed twice during the four years. Attrition over four years left 108 seniors; complete questionnaire data were obtained for 87 of this cohort.

Occupational preferences during freshman and sophomore years show extensive shifting: 37% shifted preferences within the first month of freshman year, fully 70% had changed by September of sophomore year (Cf. Davis, 1965, and Wal-

lace, 1966).[1] Not only did choices change, but early in sophomore year 42% still reported feeling undecided about their occupational choice compared with 58% who had said so as freshmen. Indecision about or disinterest in occupation is reflected in the low proportion of the cohort of 87 who as freshmen were career salient— 30%.[2] This percentage is especially noteworthy since the college in which the research was done is reputed as vocationally–professionally oriented. Indeed, by senior year, 43% were career salient, perhaps suggestive of the school's influence. But panel analysis of the choice patterns shows radical vacillation between career and non-career interests. Of the 37 who were career salient seniors, only 6 had been so consistently over the four years. The others had arrived there via one or more changes in salience. By contrast, girls who are not career salient predominated in all four years and showed considerably less shifting.

MARRIAGE IS THE KEY CONTINGENCY

The extent to which marriage is a key contingency is suggested from my analysis of single women's responses to questions about home versus career preferences. In a study of educated women's life styles, five and fifteen year alumnae of the women's college referred to above completed questionnaires on their leisure and work activities. Details on the sample and procedures are in Searls (1966) and Angrist (1967). Of the 318 respondents, 85% were married and mainly homemakers. Of 90 women employed at least part-time, roughly one-third each were single, married without children, or married with children. For the single working women (average age of 27 years) 48% said they would most want to concentrate on home and family if they were to marry; only 24% and 12% of childless working women and working mothers, respectively,

---

[1] These percentages are based on 125 freshmen of the 143 who became sophomores and for whom complete questionnaire data were obtained.

[2] Career salient is defined in terms of answers to two questions about adult roles. Career salient are girls who 15 years from now would like to be career women (either single, married or with children) and who would work full-time or part time even if their husbands earned enough so that they would never have to work.

picked that option.[3] However, when preferred occupations are compared with actual ones, there is some indication that they now realistically confront the non-marriage contingency—compared with married working women, the single ones prefer substantially higher level occupations than those they have: 47% had professional jobs but 65% desired them. This discrepancy was highest for the single women.

Among the small group of 34 alumnae with a median age of 36, who were mothers and working part-time, only 44% reported working in fields which they preferred. The actual jobs held were generally related to their college major, but often unrelated to jobs they desired. In answer to the question: "What one occupation or field would you most like to work in if you had the necessary training?"—only one person preferred a sales, secretarial or clerical job, but 5 held such jobs, 7 preferred semi-professional jobs but only 3 had chosen such. In general, the older the woman, the less likely her preferred job resembled her actual one. Thus, while marriage was an explicitly anticipated contingency, work appears to have been only vaguely prepared for. Although college major is reflected in later work choices, the major itself was probably chosen with the criteria reported by contemporary women in the same college: "to be practical," "to be able to work in case I ever have to."[4]

AND AFTER MARRIAGE

After marriage the contingency orientation shows up in new ways. While marriage was an

[3]The question was: assume that you are trained for the occupation of your choice, that you are married and have children, and that your husband earns enough so that you will never have to work unless you want to. Under these conditions, which of the following would you prefer? (Check one) (1) to participate in clubs or volunteer work, (2) to spend time on hobbies, sports or other activities, (3) to work part-time in your chosen occupation, (4) to work full-time in your chosen occupation, (5) to concentrate on home and family, (6) other (explain briefly).

[4]Lotte Bailyn (1964) describes women's occupational choice process as revokable, irrational and discontinued. Of course, the ideas and data reported above need to be tempered with the work world conditions impinging on women's occupational choice, for example, the difficulties of finding high level part-time work.

explicit contingency one prepared for, others remained only implicit. Again, drawing on the alumnae data mentioned, one sees the married women's accommodation to stages and features of family life. For example, among full-time homemakers the type of leisure activities pursued varies according to ages of children—women with preschoolers tended to follow recreational and self-enrichment activities which are largely home-centered; women with school age children pursued predominantly community activities (Angrist, 1967). Similarly, the older homemakers found less enjoyment and mastery in homemaking than the younger women—perhaps they reflected boredom with domesticity, or else their late-found option to like homemaking less as it is less needed by older children (Searls, 1966).

Statistics on women in the labor force also show this contingency orientation. A pattern of phasing in and out of the work world represents married women's reactions to the family life cycle. Women's lowest participation in the labor force is between the ages of 25 to 34 when family responsibilities are greatest. The peak comes at 45 to 54 years of age when 42% of the married woman population is in the labor force. Whereas one quarter of women workers in 1940 came from the 45–54 age group, 50% did so in 1962; for the 35–44 age group, the figure rose from 29% in 1940 to 45% in 1962. These new peaks reflect younger ages at which women complete child-bearing and become freer of family responsibilities (U.S. Dept. of Labor, 1963).

Concern over women's work force trends and the compressed parental years manifests itself in the "re-tread" phenomenon. Continuing education programs have arisen to deal explicitly with the presumed crisis of the later years, to help women take a kind of second look at life (Center for Continuing Education, 1965). Marriage becomes a past or minor contingency and others like filling time, or economic self sufficiency loom large.

In Conclusion

In this paper, several themes were discussed. (a) Sex role definitions and usages were reviewed in terms of their predominant meanings of role either as position, behavior, or relationship. Each meaning tends to be associated with a topical emphasis and social location assumptions. Sex role as positional usually involves the division of labor by sex in structured groups; as behavior, sex role tends to be defined in terms of personality, abilities, preferences without regard to context; as relationship sex role learning in socialization is the focus in varied social settings. Each meaning of sex role contributes something to another conception suggested in this paper of sex role as having four elements: label, behavior, expectations, and social location.

(b) The special vagueness of changing sex role norms in contemporary society justifies looking at the multiplicity of actual role involvement by actors, rather than isolating single roles. Study of role constellations is suggested as a way of dealing with the time-tied nature of roles based on characteristics such as age, stage in the life cycle, familial and occupational status. This approach de-emphasizes role conflict and implies the normalcy of multiple relationships with differing temporal and spatial priorities.

(c) The extent of role flexibility is illustrated from studies of women's roles. To some degree women perceive themselves and are seen as having options in their adult roles. These options are considered as contingencies around which women's sex role learning occurs. Socialization for contingencies is hypothesized to be a key theme in women's lives and manifest both in early and adult socialization. The primary contingency is marriage, but several others impinge on women and either implicitly or overtly influence their role constellations.

REFERENCES

ANGRIST, SHIRLEY S. Role constellation as a variable in women's leisure activities. *Social Forces*, 1967, *45*, 423–431.

ANGRIST, SHIRLEY S., LEFTON, MARK, DINITZ, SIMON, AND PASAMANICK, BENJAMIN. *Women after treatment*. New York: Appleton-Century-Crofts, 1968, ch. 8.

AXELSON, L. J. Personal adjustments in the post-parental period. *Marriage and Family Living*, 1960, *22*, 66–68.

BAILYN, LOTTE. Notes on the role of choice in the psychology of professional women. *Daedalus*, 1964, *93*, 700–710.

BALES, R. F. Task roles and social roles in problem-solving groups. In E. E. Maccoby, T. M. Newcomb and E. L. Hartley (Eds.) *Readings in social psychology*. New York: Holt, 1958, 437–447.

BANTON, MICHAEL. *Roles: an introduction to the study of social relations*. New York: Basic Books, 1965.

BATES, FREDERICK L. Position, role, and status: a reformulation of concepts. *Social Forces*, 1956, *34*, 313–321.

BEM, DARYL J., AND BEM, SANDRA L. Training the woman to know her place. In Daryl Bem, *The psychological foundation of beliefs and attitudes*. In press.

BLOOD, ROBERT O., JR., AND WOLFE, DONALD. M. *Husbands and wives*. New York: Free Press, 1960.

BROWN, ROGER. *Social psychology*. New York: Free Press, 1965, 161–172.

CENTER FOR CONTINUING EDUCATION. *Opportunities for women through education*. Ann Arbor: University of Michigan, 1965.

COTTRELL, L. S. The adjustment of the individual to his age and sex roles. *American Sociological Review*, 1942, *7*, 617–620.

DAVIS, JAMES A. *Undergraduate career decisions*. Chicago: Aldine, 1965.

DOUVAN, ELIZABETH. Sex differences in adolescent character process. *Merrill-Palmer Quarterly*, 1960, *6*, 203–211.

EMMERICH, WALTER. Family role concepts of children ages six to ten. *Child Development*, 1961, *32*, 609–624.

FARBER, BERNARD. Effects of a severely mentally retarded child on family integration. *Monographs of Society for Research in Child Development*, 1959, *24*, No. 2.

FARBER, BERNARD. The family as a set of mutually contingent careers. In Nelson N. Foote (Ed.) *Household decision-making*. New York: New York University Press, 1961, 276–297.

GEHLEN, FRIEDA FOOTE. *Women members of the U.S. House of Representatives and role expectations*. Paper presented at Ohio Valley Sociological Society Annual Meeting, South Bend, Indiana, April 1967.

GETZELS, J. W., AND GUBA, E. G. Role conflict, and effectiveness: an empirical study. *American Sociological Review,* 1954, *19,* 164–175.

GINZBERG, ELI, GINSBERG, SOL W., AXELRAD, SIDNEY, AND HERMA, JOHN L. *Occupational choice: an approach to a general theory.* New York: Columbia University Press, 1963, 160–176.

GLICK, PAUL C., AND PARKE, ROBERT. New approaches in studying the life cycle of the family. *Demography,* 1965, *2,* 187–202.

GOFFMAN, ERVING. *The presentation of self in everyday life.* New York: Doubleday, 1959, ch. 1.

GOFFMAN, ERVING. Role distance. In *Encounters.* Indianapolis: Bobbs-Merrill, 1961, 85–152.

GOODE, WILLIAM J. Norm commitment and conformity to role-status obligations. *American Journal of Sociology,* 1960, *66,* 246–258. (a)

GOODE, WILLIAM J. A theory of role strain. *American Sociological Review,* 1960, *25,* 383–396. (b)

GORDON, GERALD. *Role theory and illness.* New Haven: College and University Press, 1966, ch. 1.

GROSS, NEAL, MASON, WARD S., AND MC EACHERN, ALEXANDER W. *Explorations in role analysis.* New York: Wiley, 1958, ch. 1–5.

HARTLEY, RUTH E., AND KLEIN, ARMIN. Sex role concepts among elementary-school girls. *Marriage and Family Living,* 1959, *21,* 59–64.

HILL, REUBEN, AND RODGERS, ROY H. The developmental approach. In Harold T. Christensen (Ed.) *Handbook of marriage and the family.* Chicago: Rand McNally, 1964, 171–211.

HUNT, M. M. *World of the formerly married.* New York: McGraw-Hill, 1966.

KENKEL, WILLIAM F. *The family in perspective.* New York: Appleton-Century-Crofts, 1960, ch. 14.

KOMAROVSKY, MIRRA. Cultural contradictions and sex roles. *American Journal of Sociology,* 1946, *52,* 184–189.

LEFTON, MARK, ANGRIST, SHIRLEY, DINITZ, SIMON, AND PASAMANICK, BENJAMIN. Social class, expectations, and performance of mental patients. *American Journal of Sociology,* 1962, *68,* 79–87.

LEVINSON, DANIEL J. Role, personality, and social structure in the organizational setting. *Journal of Abnormal and Social Psychology,* 1959, *58,* 170–180.

LINTON, RALPH. *The cultural background of personality.* New York: Appleton-Century-Crofts, 1945.

MC KEE, JOHN P. AND SHERRIFFS, ALEX C. Men's and women's beliefs, ideals, and self-concepts. *American Journal of Sociology,* 1959, *54,* 356–363.

MEAD, GEORGE H. *Mind, self and society.* Chicago: University of Chicago Press, 1934, 354–378.

MEAD, MARGARET. *Sex and temperament in three primitive societies.* New York: William Morrow, 1935.

MECHANIC, DAVID. Some factors in identifying and defining mental illness. *Mental Hygiene,* 1962, *46,* 66–74.

MERTON, ROBERT K. *Social theory and social structure.* Glencoe, Illinois: Free Press, 1957, 368–379.

MOTZ, ANNABELLE BENDER. Concepts of marital roles by status groups. *Marriage and Family Living,* 1950, *12,* 136 and 162.

MURDOCK, GEORGE P. Comparative data on the division of labor by sex. In Bruce J. Biddle and Edwin J. Thomas (Eds.) *Role theory.* New York: Wiley, 1966, 263–264.

NADEL, S. F. *The theory of social structure.* Glencoe, Illinois: Free Press, 1957.

NEWCOMB, T. M. *Social psychology.* New York: Dryden Press, 1950.

NYE, F. IVAN, AND HOFFMAN, LOIS. *The employed mother in America.* Chicago: Rand McNally, 1963, ch. 27.

PARSONS, TALCOTT. Age and sex in the social structure of the United States. *American Sociological Review,* 1942, *7,* 604–616.

PARSONS, TALCOTT, AND BALES, R. F. *Family, socialization, and interaction process.* Glencoe, Illinois: Free Press, 1955.

PHILLIPS, DEREK L. Rejection of the mentally ill. *American Sociological Review,* 1964, *29,* 679–687.

PREISS, JACK J. AND EHRLICH, HOWARD J. *An examination of role theory.* Nebraska: University of Nebraska Press, 1966.

PSATHAS, GEORGE. Toward a theory of occupational choice for women. *Sociology and Social Research,* 1968, *52,* 253–268.

RAINWATER, LEE. *And the poor get children.* Chicago: Quadrangle Books, 1960.

RODGERS, DAVID A. Spontaneity and specificity in social role relationships. *Journal of Personality,* 1959, *27,* 300–310.

ROSE, ARNOLD. The adequacy of women's expectations for adult roles. *Social Forces,* 1951, *30,* 69–77.

ROSSI, ALICE S. Transition to parenthood. *Journal of Marriage and the Family,* 1968, *30,* 26–39.

SARBIN, THEODORE R. Role theory. In Gardner Lindzey (Ed.) *Handbook of social psychology.* Cambridge: Addison-Wesley, 1954, *1,* 223–258.

SCHWARTZ, CHARLOTTE. Perspectives on deviance—wives' definitions of their husbands' mental illness. *Psychiatry,* 1957, *20,* 275–291.

SEARLS, LAURA. College major and the tasks of homemaking. *Journal of Home Economics,* 1966, 58, 708–714.

SILVERMAN, WILLIAM, AND HILL, REUBEN. Task allocation in marriage in the United States and and Belgium. *Journal of Marriage and the Family,* 1967, 29, 353–359.

SOUTHALL, A. An operational theory of role. *Human Relations,* 1959, 12, 17–34.

STRYKER, SHELDON. Conditions of accurate role-taking: a test of Mead's theory. In Arnold M. Rose (Ed.) *Human behavior and social processes.* Boston: Houghton-Mifflin, 1962, 41–62.

TURNER, RALPH. Role taking: process versus con-
formity. In Arnold M. Rose (Ed.) *Human behavior and social processes.* Boston: Houghton-Mifflin, 1962, 20–40.

U.S. DEPARTMENT OF LABOR. *Handbook on women workers.* Washington, D.C.: Women's Bureau Bulletin No. 285, 1963.

VINCENT, CLARK. Implications of changes in male-female role expectations for interpreting M-F scores. *Journal of Marriage and the Family,* 1966, 28, 196–199.

WALLACE, WALTER L. *Student culture.* Chicago: Aldine, 1966.

WIGNEY, TREVOR. *The education of women and girls.* Toronto: University of Toronto, 1965.

Chapter 14: Suggested Additional Readings

BEZDEK, W., & STRODTBECK, F. L.   Sex-role identity and pragmatic action. *American Sociological Review*, 1970, *35*(3), 491–502. The authors evaluate the proposition that to be means-oriented is parallel with male sex-role requirements while to be goal-oriented is congruent with female role requirement. Sex-role theory in general is appraised.

BILLER, H. B., & LIEBMAN, D. A.   Body build, sex-role preference, and sex-role adoption in junior high school boys. *The Journal of Genetic Psychology*, 1971, *118* (1st half), 81–86. The relationship between body build and two aspects of sex role (preference and adoption) was investigated among ninth-grade boys.

BRODERICK, C. B., & WEAVER, J.   The perceptual context of boy–girl communication. *Journal of Marriage and the Family*, 1968, *30*(4), 618–627. Responses of boys and girls (age 10–17) to cartoons depicting various boy–girl situations are presented and discussed.

BRUCE, V.   The expression of femininity in the male. *Journal of Sex Research*, 1967, *3*(2), 129–139. The author indicates various ways that behaving in a so-called feminine fashion may meet healthy needs in the male. She cites, in particular, research with transvestites.

HARFORD, T. C., WILLIS, C. H., & DEABLER, H. L.   Personality correlates of masculinity–femininity. *Psychological Reports*, 1967, *21*, 881–884. Among male volunteers, aged 20 to 60, ten measures of masculinity–femininity were related to personality traits. Quite different characteristics were associated with high or low masculinity.

HEILBRUN, A. B., JR.   Sex-role identity in adolescent females: A theoretical paradox. *Adolescence*, 1968, *3*(9), 79–88. Studies of the female's identification and sex-role identity underscore the father's part in his daughter's developing femininity.

HEILBRUN, A. B., JR.   Sex role instrumental–expressive behavior, and psychopathology in females. *Journal of Abnormal Psychology*, 1968, *73*(2), 131–136. An investigation into the relationship between sex-role identity (masculinity–femininity) in late adolescent females and their adjustment. A comparison of the personality attributes of masculine and feminine girls with their maladjusted counterparts revealed little difference between the feminine groups.

HELLER, A.   On the future of relations between the sexes. *International Social Science Journal*, 1969, *21*(4), 535–544. After examining certain of the biological and historic bases for the relations between the sexes, the writer conjectures what shape this relationship may take in the future.

KAGAN, J.   Check one: Male, female. *Psychology Today*, 1969, *3*(2), 39–41. Kagan discusses the significance of sex-role identity; how sex-role standards are learned; the content of such standards; and the cross-cultural extensiveness of sex-role standards.

KAMMEYER, K.   Sibling position and the feminine role. *Journal of Marriage and the Family*, 1967, *29*(3), 494–499. College girls' sibling positions are related to appropriate feminine role behavior and beliefs about female personality.

ROSENKRANTZ, P., VOGEL, S., BEA, H., BROVERMAN, I., BROVERMAN, D. M.   Sex-role stereotypes and self-concept in college students. *Journal of Consulting and Counseling*

Psychology, 1968, *32*, 287–295. After analyzing opinions of youths in their late teens and early twenties, the authors conclude that males' behaviors are more socially acceptable than females', and that males have higher feelings of self-worth than females.

SEBALD, H.   Parent–peer control and masculine–marital role perceptions of adolescent boys. *Social Science Quarterly*, 1968, *49*(2), 229–236. The findings here reported partially support the hypothesis that father absence tends to result in dependency in the son. Father-controlled boys proved to be relatively masculine, and mother-controlled boys more feminine and equalitarian, in their perception of the marital role.

SEWARD, G. H., & LARSON, W. R.   Adolescent concepts of social sex roles in the United States and the two Germanies. *Human Development*, 1968, *11*(4), 217–248. This study compared concepts of adult social sex role held by adolescents in the United States and the two Germanies. Contemporary youth in America and the Germanies believed themselves capable of wiser future leadership than they perceived as demonstrated by their elders.

SEXTON, P.   How the American boy is feminized. *Psychology Today*, 1970, *3*(8), 23–29, 66–67. The feminized boy does well in school, is neat, and rarely fights. But, claims Sexton, he resorts to drugs, withdrawal and deviance because of a masculinity crisis.

SMIGEL, E. O., & SEIDEN, R.   The decline and fall of the double standard. *Annals of the American Academy of Science*, 1968, *376*, 6–17. After surveying sex research of the past few decades the authors conclude that the double sex standard is declining but has not fallen.

STEIN, A. H., POHLY, S. R., & MUELLER, E.   The influence of masculine, feminine, and neutral tasks on children's achievement behavior, expectancies of success, and attainment values. *Child Development*, 1971, *42*(1), 195–208. In a study of sixth graders, boys performed best on the sex-appropriate tests, intermediately well on neutral tasks, and least well on sex-inappropriate problems. Girls performed equally well on the feminine and neutral tests, but significantly lower on the masculine tasks. The results reflect the stronger expectations laid upon boys that they will adhere closely to their sex roles.

STEINMANN, A., & FOX, D. J.   Specific areas of agreement and conflict in women's self-perception and their perception of men's ideal woman in two South American urban communities and an urban community in the United States. *Journal of Marriage and the Family*, 1969, *31*(2), 281–289. An inventory was designed and administered to determine how women perceived themselves in their home and family, as compared with their achievement-oriented roles, and also how they felt men's ideal woman would perceive herself in these roles. North American, as compared with South American, women felt careers could be integrated with family life. Both groups believed that men prefer family-oriented, submissive women.

STEINMANN, A., & FOX, D. J.   Attitudes toward women's family role among black and white undergraduates. *Family Coordinator*, 1970, *19*(4), 363–368. An "Inventory of Female Values" was administered to white and black undergraduates of both sexes to determine how concepts of the ideal woman vary according to race and sex.

STERRETT, J. E., & BOLLMAN, S. R.   Factors related to adolescents' expectations of marital roles. *Family Coordinator*, 1970, *19*(4), 353–356. Senior high school students indicate expectations of their future marital role. The findings are related to the subjects' age, social status, and grade average.

VROEGH, K.   Masculinity and femininity in the elementary and junior high school years. *Developmental Psychology*, 1971, *4*(2), 254–261. The correlates of masculinity and femininity, in terms of traits associated with masculine and feminine roles, were determined for children in grades 1–3, 4–6, and 7–8.

part five

Issues in Developing Values and Social Consciousness

15

Youth's Values and Religion

A discussion of youth's values and religion must begin with the basic issues of how moral development proceeds and upon what influences it depends. Lawrence Kohlberg (1970), an authority on moral education, describes moral development as a gradual but continuous growth process by which an individual progresses through a sequence of increasingly more sophisticated moral stages. Kohlberg portrays moral character as emerging from the interaction of maturation and socialization, rather than from characteristics fixed by early childhood experience. Although character education, in direct form, has had little success and hence has fallen into some disrepute, Kohlberg advocates that conscious effort be made to mold adolescents' values and morals.

Authorities agree that family experience is primary in determining children's moral development. Only recently, however, has the father's role been accorded proper recognition. Among the considerable body of research now available, Hoffman's (1971) work clearly indicates that father absence has adverse effects on a boy's development. These effects may be produced, at least in part, by changes in the mother's attitudes toward the boy, since women without husbands are apparently less affectionate toward their sons than are women with husbands. In contrast, paternal absence has no special effect on a girl's conscience development. For one thing, girls ordinarily identify more with the mother than with the father; in addition, the mother may compensate for the husband's absence by showing increased affection for the daughter.

It is not only persons actually living in the home who influence an individual's moral development; other adults may also serve as ideals or "identification figures." During adolescence, youth do not become completely independent in their assessment of values (Rosenmayr, 1968). They are relatively open to influence with regard to their values, require an attachment to ideal figures, and, to satisfy unrest, may seek feelings of security from symbols, models, and cultish images.

The adolescent subculture, too, with its own values, ideals, and beliefs, is a primary influence on adolescents' moral growth (Cawelti, 1968). A complex of issues relates to the definition and evaluation of youth's own values. For the young, did the old-fashioned virtues and standards perish in the holocaust of Hiroshima? Do the current "cool" codes of youth have a core of morality? And just what are these codes? How good are they? What sort of values does youth need?

Some critics assume the role of youth's defenders, others that of youth's detractors. A well-known developmental psychologist, Elizabeth Hurlock (1966), deplores youth's shoddy values. Adolescents dismiss decent appearance as nonessential, she says, and care little for good grooming. They live by the motto, "Eat, drink, and be merry," and take no thought for the future: "Uncle Sam will take care of you." Virginity is rejected as mid-Victorian. She feels that this unfortunate attitude arises from the peer group itself and is fed by the mass media which glamorize extravagance.

In another much-quoted study, of students at ten midwestern high schools, Coleman (1961) concluded that adolescents are chiefly interested in frivolous matters. He reported that the image of the athletic star is most attractive for boys; the images of activities leader and most popular date are more attractive to girls than the role of the brilliant student. However, on the basis of a later, but similar, study among American and Canadian students, Friesen (1968) concluded that those high school students who choose athletic stardom as something for which they wish to be remembered are quite well aware of what they are doing. The youth recognizes that such a role holds immediate value for him, especially in determining his status among his peers, but he realizes also that it has little value for future years.

Though he does not pass judgment on young people or prescribe what their values should be ideally, Bernard (1961) believes that teen magazines portray faithfully what youth care about: beauty, fun, and popularity are the values most frequently encountered in these publications. While scholarship is more valued than formerly, it still excites less interest than athletics. However, Bernard finds that athletic prowess is growing less important, at least on the college level.

Other writers come out strongly in support of youth. They portray an honest, no-nonsense generation as recognizing and opposing the shoddy values of Big Business, Establishmentarianism, and Middle-Class Self-Righteousness. Young people face a difficult task, says Parsons (1962), in preparing themselves for a nuclear age. Society is changing so rapidly that the older generation cannot supply adequate role models—they are constantly out of date. Hence, young people must grope their way and chart their own course as best they can, and they are meeting the challenge this dilemma imposes. They recognize the importance of academic achievement for their future. Indeed, concludes Parsons, the most significant fact about current youth culture is its concern for meaningfulness. The exception is in the lowest sector, where truancy and delinquency are common; and this is understandable, because youth's generally heightened expectancies have placed these lower-class young people at a correspondingly greater disadvantage.

Parsons also discerns certain changes taking place in youth's values, among them a decreased respect for sheer male physical prowess, especially in athletics, except among delinquent groups. He finds youth's attitudes toward alcohol and sex changing, as well. Formerly, youth often expressed rebellion through these media. Nowadays they continue to indulge, but for different reasons. Drinking is more widespread, but generally moderate in amount; sexual relationships are taken seriously. Youth have simply become more integrated into the adult culture and reflect society's growing acceptance of sexual activity and of alcohol.

Who is to judge youth's judges and determine whose views are right? And on what will such judgments be based? What kinds of questions can we pose to elicit values? Can we trust youth's verbalizations of their beliefs? A view of the difficulties inherent in any attempts to answer these questions—and an interesting example of the interplay of youth's defenders and detractors—is provided by Jacob (1957), who prepared a summary critique of youth's values and then reported the comments that this critique elicited from W. C. H. Prentice and James C. Coles. Jacob reports students to be self-centered. What would he have them be, asks Prentice? Church-centered? Government-centered? Youth are said to accept the business culture of society. Should they reject it? What alternatives to youth's current values exist, given the constraints of present-day society? Youth are also labeled conformist. How may conformity be differentiated from convergent values accruing to common experience?

Coles also questions Jacob's conclusions, but on less theoretical grounds than Prentice (Jacob, 1957). The studies from which Jacob's conclusions are drawn, Coles points out, date back two decades; in addition, they involve data-collecting procedures, such as objective or multiple-choice type instruments, of questionable validity. Coles also criticizes Jacob's report that students failed to name religion as one of three life activities affording greatest satisfaction. On this basis, Coles asks, are we to assume that religion plays but a small part in students' lives? Possibly some students define "satisfaction" in hedonistic terms, and if so, they would hardly report religion as "satisfying." Besides, adds Coles, most individuals may have no need for sophisticated values in a complex, science-oriented, big-system kind of society such as is envisioned for the future. Such a society will require a highly educated elite to direct it, while other individuals, with their roles defined by computers, will be measured and conditioned to fit into the slots considered best for them.

If youth do indeed need values, what form should these values take? Wirth (1967) detects in youth themselves a yearning for real-life substance. Youth resent the isolation of education from life, a situation which Dewey warned against. They are hungry for genuine participation in the off-campus community. Therefore, Wirth believes, we should help youth relate meaningfully to the out-of-school world. They could help with reclamation projects in mountain areas, clean up urban slums or, following the Russians' example, work in industrial laboratories or experimental gardens without having to wait until they receive their Ph.D.s.

By looking at youth in quite different cultures, we gain perspective on our youths' values (Betensky, 1967). For example, in the Israeli collective, the youth culture serves as an instrument for social control and gives the youth a sense of purpose and a feeling of social continuity. In these mini-societies of the kibbutzim, the youth prepares for his adult role through sharing the common values of the larger group. He is also close to his family and reflects its values as well as those of the community.

In sum, the picture of youth's values is confusing, with little agreement among authorities as to what those values are or how worthwhile they are. One of the most frequently quoted of these authorities, Gordon W. Allport, has contributed the first reading selection. Allport sees young people as somehow missing the mark in their moral codes. He blames educators for their failure to help youth develop appropriate values, and challenges the schools to remedy their inadequacy in guiding young people.

Equally confusing is the picture of youth's religious beliefs and practices. No real consensus of opinion exists on just how the individual develops religious views, and no recent research either confirms or refutes Hirschberg's (1956) portrayal of religious stages. According to his study, written some years ago, the very young child perceives God as vividly alive and relates religious views to personal experience and family. In late childhood, religion becomes less egocentric and assists in impulse control. However, in adolescence, many individuals, especially college students, reevaluate their religious views and often experience considerable conflict. The conclusions they reach by early adulthood tend to persist throughout their lives.

What part does religion play, or should it play, in youth's development? According to Harvey Cox (Harris, 1970), the influence of conventional religion has declined and the reason is imbedded in our total society. Our "tight bureaucratic and instrumental society—the only model we've known since the industrial revolution—renders us incapable of experiencing the nonrational dimensions of existence—the absurd, the inspiring, the uncanny, the awesome, the terrifying, the ecstatic—none of these fits into a production- and efficiency-oriented society. They waste time, aren't dependable [p. 47]." Cox believes that everyone, including youth, should keep sight of the larger environment, including "the cosmic phenomena open to us through intuition, awe, and ecstasy—because of our enormous self-consciousness about the events of the past, present, and future [p. 62]." To be fully human, he feels, we must be in touch both with history as defined by time, and with the "cosmic circle," which connotes eternity.

In the second reading selection, Bealer and Willets summarize recent research concerning the religious attitudes and interests of American highschool youth. It has been asked whether youth's religion is "for real" or whether it is simply a Sunday affair of no relevance to everyday life. This article helps to resolve this question concerning American youth generally and youth of different denominations. Apparently there is no modal American youth, religiously speaking. Some are pious, some are pagan, a few are religious fanatics, another few are atheists—most are somewhere in between. Such a study might well be undertaken again in a few years, especially since data such as these swiftly become outdated. It becomes evident that American adolescents' religious views and behaviors are highly varied and that no one view can be considered definitive.

REFERENCES

BERNARD, J.   Teen-age culture: An overview. In J. Bernard (Ed.) *Teen-age culture.* Philadelphia: The American Academy of Political and Social Science, November 1961, *338*, 5.

BETENSKY, M.   The role of the adolescent in Israeli collectives. *Adolescence,* 1967, *11*(7), 335–344.

CAWELTI, G.   Youth assesses the American high school. *PTA Magazine,* 1968, *62,* 16–19.

COLEMAN, J. S.   *The adolescent society.* New York: Free Press, 1961.

FRIESEN, D.   Academic–athletic–popularity syndrome in the Canadian high-school society. *Adolescence,* 1968, *3*(9), 39–52.

HARRIS, T. G.   Religion in the Age of Aquarius: A conversation with theologian Harvey Cox: *Psychology Today,* 1970, *3*(11), 45–47, 62–67.

HIRSCHBERG, J. C.   Religion and childhood. *Menninger Quarterly,* 1956, *10,* 22–44.

HOFFMAN, M. L.   Father absence and conscience development. *Developmental Psychology,* 1971, *4*(3), 400–406.

HURLOCK, E.   American adolescence today—a new species. *Adolescence,* 1966, *1*(4), 7–21.

JACOB, P. E.   *Changing values in college.* New York: Harper and Row, 1957, pp. 1–11.

KOHLBERG, L.   Moral development and the education of adolescents. In E. D. Evans (Ed.) *Adolescence: Readings in behavior and development.* Hinsdale, Illinois: The Dryden Press, 1970, pp. 178–196.

PARSONS, T.   Youth in the context of American society. *Daedalus,* 1962, *91,* 97–123.

ROSENMAYR, L.   Towards an overview of youth's sociology. *International Social Science Journal,* 1968, *20*(2), 286–315.

WIRTH, A. G.   The Deweyan tradition revisited: Any relevance for our time? *Teachers College Record,* December 1967, *69*(3), 68.

Values and Our Youth

GORDON W. ALLPORT

Dr. Allport first reviews the somewhat disturbing research relating to youth's values, and then calls on the schools to do a more adequate job in this area. He feels that the teacher should pay special attention to the incidental learnings that pupils acquire along with prescribed curricula. Also, experiences should be arranged so that questions of value relate to the child's own needs and become functional in his own life. Values to be encouraged include not only those embraced in the Judeo-Christian ethic but others, often neglected, such as intellectual curiosity and human brotherhood.

One aim of education is to make available the wisdom of the past and present so that youth may be equipped to solve the problems of the future. If this is so, then we have good grounds for a feeling of consternation concerning the adequacy of our present educational procedures. The reason is that in the immediate future, the youth of today will have to live in a world very unlike the world of the past from which our store of wisdom has been drawn.

Some Prospects

Think of the vastly changed nature of life in the future, for which we have little relevant wisdom from the past to call upon:

1. The new generation of students will have to face an ever increasing domination of life by

Adapted from an address delivered during the 1961 Summer Lecture Series at the Western Washington College of Education, Bellingham, Washington.

From Gordon W. Allport, Values and Our Youth. Reprinted from the *Teachers College Record, 63,* 1961, 211–219, by permission.

science, by technology, and by automation. (One thinks of the story of two cows grazing along the roadside. An immense milk truck passes with the painted legend: Pasteurized, Homogenized, Vitamin B Added. One cow turns to the other and says, "Makes you feel inadequate, doesn't it?")

2. The new generation will have to recognize the impossibility of living any longer in a state of condescension toward the colored peoples of the world (about three-quarters of the world's population). Centuries of comfortable caste discrimination and segregation are from here on impossible to maintain.

3. The coming generation will have to deal with a population explosion whose predicted magnitude staggers our imagination.

4. It will need a completer understanding of world societies and their marked differences in values. In the past, we could be politely ignorant of such places as Africa, Latin America, and Asia in a way that is no longer possible.

5. It will have to create a world government or,

at least, an effective confederation to forestall the threat of thermonuclear war.

6. As if a planetary world view were not difficult enough to achieve, the coming generation may have to develop an interplanetary point of view. (I find this prospect especially alarming because we seem to be solving the problems of outer space before those of the inner space of mind, character, and values.)

It is no wonder that this preview of problems confronting our youth throws us educators into a state of self-scrutiny bordering sometimes on panic. Where can youth find the needed equipment? Are they sound enough in mind and morale?

Sometimes our dismay finds an outlet in gallows humor. They tell of the benevolent lady who saw a depressing specimen of the very young generation sprawled on the curb of a city street, swilling down cans of beer. Greatly shocked, she asked, "Little boy, why aren't you in school?" "Cripes, lady," he replied, "I'm only four years old."

And they tell the story of the London bobby. London police, we know, are well trained for social work, even for psychotherapy. This bobby's beat was Waterloo Bridge. He spotted a man about to jump over and intercepted him. "Come now," he said, "Tell me what the matter is. Is it money?" The man shook his head. "Your wife perhaps?" Another shake of the head. "Well, what is it then?" The would-be suicide replied, "I'm worried about the state of the world." "Oh, come now," said the bobby. "It can't be so bad. Let's walk up and down the bridge here and talk it over." Whereupon they strolled for about an hour discussing the state of the world, and then they *both* jumped over.

Humor helps us put our dilemma into sane perspective, but it does not solve the problem. The vague apprehension we feel has led to certain empirical studies of the values of today's youth, with results, alas, that are not reassuring.

Assessing Values

Not long ago, Professor Phillip Jacob undertook to survey (5) all available studies concerning the values held by college students. He found a marked uniformity among them. Fully three-quarters of the students were "gloriously contented, both in regard to their present day-to-day activity and their outlook for the future." Their aspirations were primarily for material gratifications for themselves and their families. They "fully accepted the conventions of the contemporary business society as the context within which they will realize their personal desires." While they will not crusade against segregation and racial injustice, they will accept nondiscrimination when it comes as a "necessary convention in a homogenized culture." They subscribe to the traditional virtues of sincerity, honesty, and loyalty, but are indulgent concerning laxity in moral standards. They normally express a need for religion, but there is a hollow quality in their beliefs. They do not desire to have an influential voice in public policy or government. Their sense of civic duty stops at the elementary obligation of voting. They predict another major war within a dozen years, but they say that international problems give them little concern and that they spend no time on them. Only a minority value their college education primarily in terms of its intellectual gains. They regard it as good because it gives them vocational preparation, social status, and a good time. Such is the flabby value-fibre that Jacob discovers among college students of today.

The picture becomes more vivid in cross-national perspective. James Gillespie and I, in a comparative study (3) of the values of college youth in 10 nations, asked students to write their autobiographies of the future ("My life from now until the year 2000") and also gave them an extensive questionnaire. The instrument was translated into nine different languages.

In comparison with youth of other nations, young Americans are delightfully frank and open, unsuspicious and cooperative. Their documents had no literary affectation (and, may I add, little literary quality). But the most important finding was that within these 10 nations, American students were the most self-centered, the most "privatistic" in values. They desired above all else a rich, full life for themselves, and showed little concern for national welfare or for the fate of mankind at large. The context of their outlook was private rather than public, passive rather than pioneer. The essential point is made clear by two excerpts, the first drawn from the autobiography of a Mexican girl, 18 years of age, and the second from a Radcliffe student of the same age:

Since I like psychology very much, I wish, on leaving this school, to study it, specializing in it, and exercising it as a profession. I shouldn't like to get married right away, although like any woman I am desirous of getting married before realizing all my aspirations. In addition, I should like to do something for my country —as a teacher, as a psychologist, or as a mother. As a teacher, to guide my pupils in the best path, for at the present time they need solid bases in childhood in order in their future lives not to have so many frustrations as the youth of the present. As a psychologist, to make studies which in some way will serve humanity and my beloved country. As a mother, to make my children creatures who are useful to both their country and all humanity.

Now follows the Radcliffe document. Its flavor of privatism is unmistakable:

Our summers will be spent lobster fishing on the Cape. Later we'll take a look at the rest of the country—California, the Southwest, and the Chicago Stockyards. I want the children, when they get past the age of ten, to spend part of the summer away from home, either at camp or as apprentices to whatever profession they may show an interest in. Finally, I hope we will all be able to take a trip to Europe, especially to Russia, to see what can be done about Communism.

Many critics have called attention to the same American value predicament. Our current social pattern, they say, is almost completely geared to one objective alone, namely a profitable, expanding production. To insure expanding production, there must be more and more consumption. Hence comes the expensive glamor of our advertising and its control of our mass media. The sole objective seems to be to stimulate the accretion of goods. Self-respect and status, as well as comfort, are acquired in this way. Someone has called our national disease "galloping consumption." Half a century ago, William James saw the peril and was much worried by what he called "the American terror of poverty." He saw there was truth in the jibes that other countries direct at our "materialism."

Hope in Uneasiness

Now a high standard of living is not in itself an evil thing. All the world wants what we already have. But the single-minded pursuit of production and consumption has brought a dulling of other values. One consequence is symbolized by the scandal of rigged quiz programs. These were in the service of advertising, which in turn was in the service of a profitable expanding economy. Another consequence is the accumulated froth of our TV, radio, and movies. Another is the widely discussed conformity of the organization man, as well as the futile rebellion of the beats. An especially peppery critic, Paul Goodman (4), has shown that the starved lives of juvenile delinquents and of young people caught in the organizational grind are at bottom much alike. Both are attracted to the cult of easiness and aspire to nothing more than amiable mediocrity. Both styles of living fail to prepare youth for the problems that lie ahead for themselves and for the nation.

A somewhat vulgar story seems to me to summarize all this mordant criticism. Moses, a stalwart leader of the old school, said to the Israelites in Egypt, "Load up your camels, bring along your asses, and I'll lead you to the promised land." By contrast, the modern American prophet seems to urge, "Light up your Camels, sit on your asses, and I'll bring you the promised land."

All this familiar criticism is irritating; yet the fact that it flourishes is a hopeful sign. We suspect it may be too harsh. I am inclined to think so. It is rash indeed to indict a whole generation. At worst, Jacob's gloomy picture held for three-quarters of the college students studied, but not at all for a vital and far from negligible minority. And even though the gloomy generalizations have some truth in them, are the assets given fair attention? I myself have some favorable impressions, although one man's view is not reliable. But youth today appears to enjoy a certain freedom and flexibility that was not common in the more rigid days of our parents and grandparents. I even have the impression that there is less neuroticism among students now than among those of a generation ago. What is more, young people, I find, are not blind to the world changes that are occurring. Their apparent repression of the challenge is due largely to their bewilderment concerning proper paths to take. (And one has the feeling that our own statesmen in Washington are no less bewildered.) All in all, these are hopeful signs that should not be overlooked.

Values and the School

Another hopeful sign is the fact that many teachers are asking, "What can we do to be helpful?" They know, and we all know, that the ability of the school to give training in values is limited. For one thing, the home is vastly more important. A home that infects the child with galloping consumption, that encourages only canned recreation and has no creative outlets, can only with difficulty be offset by the school. Another limitation lies in the fact that the school is ordinarily expected to mirror current social values and to prepare the child to live within the existing frame. It is an unusual school system and an unusual teacher who even *wish* to transcend the current fashions of value.

But assuming that we have an unusual school system and an unusual teacher, what values shall they elect to teach? If they do not choose to follow the prevailing fashions, what standards shall they follow? The ancient Romans were fond of asking, "Who will judge the judges?" and "Who will guard the guardians?" Can the guardians turn perhaps to standard discussions of "the aims of education?" Such discussions are numerous, abstract, and often dull. Their weakness, I feel, is their effort to formulate absolute goals, vistas of abstract perfection. The result is often a series of platitudes or generalizations so broad as to be unhelpful. Of course we want to develop "good citizenship"; we certainly want to "free the child's intellect." These and all other absolutes need to be reduced to concrete, stepwise processes before they can guide us in the strategy of teaching values.

The teacher must start with the situation as he

or she finds it and in concrete instances sharpen the value-attributes of the lesson being taught. To a considerable extent, these value-attributes can be drawn from the codified wisdom of our nation. We cannot neglect the value of profitable production and high living standards, for all our vocational and professional education contribute to this end. But the codified wisdom of our unique society extends far beyond the obsession of today. Our values include also such matters as respect for civil liberties. Does the school accent this value? They include approval for individual initiative, for philanthropy, for compassion. And they imply much concerning civic duties that are the reciprocal of civic rights. What must we do to deserve our precious cornucopia of freedom? Vote? Yes. But voting does no good unless the voter is informed above the stereotyped level of the mass media. He must also pay taxes willingly. Do schools and colleges teach the young to pay a glad tax? I wonder. To me the most disturbing finding in *Youth's Outlook on the Future* lay in the elaborate talk about one's right to a rich, full life and in the almost total silence regarding one's duties.

I am saying that in the first instance teachers should choose the values they teach from the whole (not from a part) of our American ethos. Deep in our hearts we know, and most of the world knows, that our national values, derived, of course, from Judeo-Christian ethics, are about the finest mankind has yet formulated. In no sense are these values out of date, nor will they go out of date in the world of tomorrow. Yet many of them are badly rusted. Unless they are revitalized, however, our youth may not have the personal fortitude and moral implements that the future will require.

The Larger Anchor

Excellent as the American Creed is as a fountainhead of values, it does not contain them all. It says nothing explicitly, for example, about intellectual curiosity. And yet surely schools exist to augment this value. The most severe indictment of our educational procedures I have ever encountered is the discovery that a sizeable percentage of graduates of our colleges after completing their formal education never afterward read a single book.

There are other important values that are not spelled out in our American Creed. I am thinking of those details of human relationships that make all the difference between boorishness and brotherhood in the human family. As our population increases, it becomes more and more important to teach the elements of the new science of human relations which go far toward smoothing the roughness of common life by leading us to respect effectively the integrity of the other fellow. I recall a teacher of English whose class was studying *The Merchant of Venice*. She turned a wave of incipient anti-Semitism in her class to a sound lesson in values. Shylock, she explained, was like the resentful, self-seeking portion of every person's nature. We are all potential Shylocks. But while self-love is prominent in all of us, we are so constructed that it need not be sovereign in our natures.

To return for a moment to the relation between home and school—the former, as I have said, is far more important. Recognizing this fact, some people say, "Well, let's leave the teaching of values to the home and to the church. Schools can't do much of anything about the matter."

This position is untenable. If the school does not teach values, it will have the effect of denying them. If the child at school never hears a mention of honesty, modesty, charity, or reverence, he will be persuaded that, like many of his parents' ideas, they are simply old hat. As they grow toward adolescence, children become critical of the teaching of both parents and the church. They are in a questioning stage. If the school, which to the child represents the larger outside world, is silent on values, the child will repudiate more quickly the lessons learned at home. He will also be thrown onto peer values more completely, with their emphasis on the hedonism of teen-age parties or on the destructiveness of gangs. He will also be more at the mercy of the sensate values peddled by movies, TV, and disk jockeys. What is more, some homes, as we have said, give no fundamental value training. In such a case, it is *only* in the school that the child has any chance at all of finding ethical anchorage.

This brings us to the hardest question: How does the teacher, the instructor, the professor,

handle his assignment in the classroom? How is it possible to teach values, including the value of intellectual curiosity?

The Meaning of Value

Before tackling this question, we must pause to define what we mean by value. You will recognize that I am using the term psychologically, not in its objective philosophical sense. Values, as I use the term, are simply *meanings perceived as related to self*. The child experiences values whenever he knows that a meaning is warm and central to himself. Values, to borrow Whitehead's term, are "matters of importance" as distinct from mere matters of fact.

So much for definition. Now the hard-pressed teacher is given a solid substantive curriculum to teach. The curriculum in its original state consists of mere matters of fact. And on the number of facts absorbed the pupil's standing depends. It takes virtually all of a teacher's time to convey factual information and grade the pupil on his achievement. There is little time left to transmute these matters of fact into matters of importance, let alone teach all of the moral and social values we have thus far been discussing.

The curriculum itself is not, and should not be, a direct aid. Prescribed instruction in values would be laughed out of court. We have recently been bumped by Sputnik headforemost into core subjects. Get on with science, mathematics, language! Away with courses in folk-dancing, personal adjustment, and fudge-making! I agree that value-study has no place in curriculum planning, but not because it is a frivolous subject—rather, because it is a subject too hard and too subtle for curriculum makers.

Education for values occurs only when teachers teach what they themselves stand for, no matter what their subject is. If I were to write a treatise on the teaching of values, I would give most of my emphasis to the moral pedagogy that lies in a teacher's incidental comments, to the *obiter dicta*. The hard core is central, but the hard core has a penumbra of moral significance. I mentioned the teacher of English who made a value-lesson out of Shylock. I recall also my college professor of geology who paused in his lecture on diatom ooze to say to us, "Others would not agree with me, but I confess that whenever I study diatoms, I don't see how anyone can doubt the existence of God because the design and behavior of these protozoa are so marvelous." Is it not interesting how we all recall the *obiter dicta* of our teachers, the penumbra of value they point out to us, surrounding the hard-core data? We remember them better than the subject matter itself.

Why does the student remember them so well? No current theory of learning seem able to tell us. I suspect it is because values, being matters of importance to the self, are always warm and central and ego-involved and therefore claim priority on our attention. The child, being value-ripe, cannot help being impressed when the teacher betrays excitement and enthusiasm for a mode of thought or for the content of the subject being studied. True, the youngster does not, and should not, adopt the teacher's values ready-made; but the teacher's self-disclosure leads the student to self-discovery.

What wouldn't we give if we could develop intellectual ardor in every child for hard core subjects? Why is it that for most pupils arithmetic, spelling, physics, remain forever dull matters of fact and never become a meaning perceived as related to the self? One reason, I think, is that the weary teacher fails to convey his own sense of the importance of the subject to the student. If he did so, he would, as I have said, at least fix attention upon the value-potentiality of the subject.

Another reason perhaps is that not all of a teacher's *obiter dicta* are wholesome. Some, indeed, may be deeply damaging, though the teacher may be innocent of any such intent. Sometimes we hear incidental (but still attitude-forming) remarks like this one: "All right now, children. You have had a good time playing at recess; now settle down to your English lesson." Play is recognized as a matter of joyful importance. English, the teacher is saying in effect, is a mere routine matter of fact.

Values and Learning

I think our educational psychology has been mostly wrong about the process of learning—or perhaps not so much wrong as woefully incomplete. At the beginning of his learning career, a young child cannot, of course, be expected to feel adult enthusiasm for the intellectual content of his studies. He does his work in the first instance to avoid a scolding or because he has a habit of obeying instructions. Soon he finds added incentive. The teacher—really in the role of mother—gives praise and love ("Susan, I am proud of you"). There is a great deal of such dependency in the learning situation. Love and social reward (as well as some fear of punishment) sustain the processes of attention and retention. When the child puts forth intellectual effort, he does so in order to obtain a gold star, commendation, or other symbols of love.

All these incentives are extraneous to the subject matter. The youngster does not learn it because it is a matter of importance. When he leaves school or college, he loses these extraneous supports. He finds his love relations directly; they are no longer a reward for intellectual effort. Hence, intellectual apathy sets in, and, distressing to say, no further books are read.

In such a case as this, intellectual curiosity was never tied to independence, only to extraneous supports. At some point in the schooling—and the earlier the better—intellectual activity should become not a second-hand but a first-hand fitting to the sense of self. At the beginning, all learning must be tied, perhaps, to specific reinforcements; but if the dependency is long continued, authentic curiosity fails to develop.

It would be going too far to put the blame for intellectual apathy onto our current teaching of educational psychology. Yet I am inclined to feel somewhat punitive about this matter. Psychology has not yet settled down to the problem of transforming matters of fact—whose acquisition current learning theories explain fairly well—into autonomous matters of importance—which they do not explain at all.

Our emphasis has been on learning by drill and reinforcement. Such "habit acquisition" receives all the emphasis. But the learning theory involved postulates a continuing dependency relation (extraneous reinforcement). When the relation terminates, the habits of study simply extinguish themselves. I am surprised, therefore, that stimulus–response psychologists do not see this consequence of their own theory. Insofar as teachers employ an educational psychology of this order, they are not likely to break the dependency relation, which belongs properly only to the earlier stages of schooling.

Matters of importance, I strongly believe, are not acquired by drill or by reinforcement. They are transformations of habits and skills from the "opportunistic" layer of personality into the ego-system itself (1). Once inside the ego-system, these habits and skills turn into true interests and utilize the basic energy, the basic spontaneity, that the organism itself possesses. They are no longer sustained as "operant conditionings" by outside rewards. The interest, now being the very stuff of life itself, needs no outer supports.

Functional Autonomy

I have called this process of transforming means into ends, of changing extrinsic values into intrinsic values, *functional autonomy*. Concerning this concept, I am often asked two questions: How do you define "functional autonomy," and how does functional autonomy come about?

For a definition, I offer the following: Functional autonomy refers to any acquired system of motivation in which the tensions involved are no longer of the same kind as the antecedent tensions from which the acquired system developed.[1] To answer the question of how functional autonomy comes about requires a more extended and technical discussion. I can only hint at the direction of my answer. Neurologists are gradually discovering a basis for what I would call "perseverative functional autonomy." I refer to the "self-sustaining circuits," "feedback mechanisms," and "central motive states" that are now commonly recognized to exist in the nervous system. This line of discovery, I find, provides a partial answer to the question. But I believe we have to go further and call on the concept of self. Values, we have said, are meanings perceived as related to the self. Functional autonomy is not a mere perseverative phenomenon; it is, above all, an ego-involved phenomenon. Besides admitting an opportunistic layer

---

[1]If this definition seems too technical to be immediately helpful, see Ch. 10 of *Pattern and Growth in Personality* (2) for a more extended treatment of functional autonomy.

to personality, which is the exclusive concern of most current theories of learning, we have no choice but to admit also a "propriate" layer. It is in this layer that all matters of importance reside.

The goal of the educator, then is to shift the content of the subject he teaches from the opportunistic (matter of fact) layer to the propriate. But there is no sure-fire, mechanical strategy to use. The best general rule, one that John Dewey saw clearly, is to strive ceaselessly to integrate routine matters of fact into the growing experience system of the child himself. It would take a long treatise to specify various detailed strategies of teaching that would help achieve this goal.

Let me focus on only one aspect of this topic, upon a common mistake that teachers make. I myself am a continual offender. It is to present students with our own carefully thought out conclusions when they themselves lack the raw experience from which these conclusions are fashioned.

This particular error is inherent, for example, in the lecture system. Instead of lecturing on comparative religion, for instance, it would be much better to require all students to attend services of worship that are unfamiliar to them. If raw experience is present, then perhaps a lecture may be effective. Much of the intellectual apathy we complain about is due to our fault of presenting conclusions in lieu of first-hand experience. To us, our well-chiseled conclusion, summing up a long intellectual struggle with a problem of knowledge or of value, seems like a beautiful sonnet. To the student, it may be gibberish.

The fallacy of giving conclusions holds both for subject matter and for values. A lad of 15 cannot profit from the fully fashioned philosophy of life of a man of 50. To register at all, a statement about values must fall precisely on his present growing edge.

Teaching, then, is not the art of offering conclusions, however hard won and valid they may be. No teacher can forcibly enter the students' proprium and plant a functionally autonomous motive. He can at best open channels of experience and, by his *obiter dicta*, sometimes lead the student to see the value-potential in the experience.

The theory of personality that we need to guide a more fully developed educational psychology will teach us something important about our basic verb "to educate." It will show us that only at the outset of learning is it a transitive verb. By drill, by reward, by reinforcement, the teacher does indeed educate the child—in matters of fact. But true maturity comes only when the verb is reflexive. For in matters of importance, where values lie, the growing individual alone can educate himself.

REFERENCES

1. ALLPORT, G. *Becoming*. New Haven: Yale University Press, 1955.
2. ALLPORT, G. *Pattern and growth in personality*. New York: Holt, Rinehart, and Winston, 1961.
3. GILLESPIE, J. AND ALLPORT, G. *Youth's outlook on the future*. New York: Random House, 1955.
4. GOODMAN, P. *Growing up absurd*. New York: Random House, 1960.
5. JACOB, P. *Changing values in college*. New York: Harper, 1957.

The Religious Interests of American High School Youth

ROBERT C. BEALER   FERN K. WILLITS

The authors summarize recent research, and draw certain conclusions, about the religious concerns of American high school youth.

Introduction

Knowledge of one's clientele is a prerequisite to any effective action program. Without adequate information about the interests, attitudes, and related social dimensions of an intended audience, even the best conceived programs can fail. Today's young people are the target of many efforts in religious education. Nonetheless, very little organized information about adolescent religious interests is available to people concerned with reaching our youth. Another writer has noted in this regard that:

With each year we know more about when the adolescent enters cliques, whom he admires among his peers, what affects his performance in school, which occupations he aspires to, why he becomes delinquent . . . to name just a few

areas in which research has been undertaken. But what he thinks about his religion and the degree to which he observes its rules, and why, is possibly one of the least researched areas in contemporary American life (28, p. 2).

But this does not mean that the research record is completely bare.[1] Some few studies have been done. Their conclusions, unfortunately, are neither systematic nor unitary. It is the task of this paper to try and bring some order to the diversity of ideas that have been addressed and, hopefully, to draw some tentative conclusions regarding the

[1]Because the paper is concerned with summarizing the scientific evidence regarding the religious interests of adolescents, we have excluded from consideration the large number of tracts which have commented on the presumed state of affairs or presented simply the author's intuitions or personal perceptions of the religious scene. We have also limited our attention to those studies which have been conducted in the last decade or so, feeling that the fervor and possible flux of recent activity in American religious institutions casts doubt on the current descriptive relevancy of studies conducted prior to the early 1950's. Furthermore, as sociologists, we have tended to most thoroughly explore the sociological literature, although we have not confined our efforts here. Even so, significant omissions may have occurred.

The authors wish to acknowledge the aid of Orville E. Lanham in helping compile the research information on which this paper is based. The paper was prepared for a conference on "Religion in the Public Domain" sponsored by the Penn State University Department of Religious Studies and held at University Park, Pennsylvania, May 1–3, 1966.

From R. C. Bealer & F. K. Willits. The religious interests of American high school youth. Reprinted from the September–October 1967 issue of *Religious Education* by permission of the authors and the publisher, The Religious Education Association, New York City.

religious concerns and interests of American high school youth.[2]

In addressing the relevant research, we need, first of all, to establish what we mean by religiousness and delineate the different ways in which individuals *can* be religious. It is not a startling matter to note that there are different aspects to religious orientations. Yet past research, in general, has curiously avoided this recognition.

One noteworthy exception is the conceptualization of religious commitment offered by Charles Glock and Rodney Stark in their recent book *Religion and Society in Tension*. They distinguish the following five dimensions of religion:

(1) The *ritualistic dimension* encompasses the specifically religious practices expected of religious adherents. It comprises such activities as worship, prayer, participation in special sacraments, fasting, and the like.

(2) The *experiental dimension* gives recognition to the fact that all religions have certain expectations, however imprecisely they may be stated, that the religious person will at one time or another [and in one way or another] achieve direct knowledge of ultimate reality or will experience religious emotion. . . . Every religion places some value on subjective religious experience as a sign of individual religiosity.

(3) The *ideological dimension* is constituted . . . by expectations that the religious person will hold to certain beliefs. The content and scope of beliefs will vary not only between religions but often within the same religious tradition. However, every religion sets forth some set of beliefs to which its followers are expected to adhere.

(4) The *intellectual dimension* has to do with the expectation that the religious person will be informed and knowledgeable about the basic tenets of his faith and its sacred scriptures.

(5) The *consequential dimension* . . . encompasses the secular effects of religious belief, experience, and knowledge on the individual (14, pp. 20–21, *passim*).

Glock and Stark suggest that persons who are highly religious in regard to one dimension are not necessarily equally religious in regard to the other aspects and any consideration of the nature of religious commitment needs to consider each of the various dimensions.[3] In addressing the question of the religiousness of youth this paper uses the Glock and Stark conceptualization as a framework for organizing some of the research materials that have been reported.

I. The Ritualistic Dimension

Undoubtedly the most studied facet of adolescent religious behavior is religious practice— what Glock and Stark have termed the *ritualistic* dimension. In a sample of approximately 1300 high school students surveyed in 1961 by George Gallup, more than 85% indicated that they were members of a church or temple, and more than 60% of the boys and almost ¾ of the girls indicated that they attended religious services "regularly" (10). Information derived from the Purdue University Opinion Polls in 1957 and 1962 is more precise concerning the frequency of attendance. In both time periods, almost 70% of the youngsters indicated that they attended religious services once a week or oftener. In fact, ¼ reported that they attended *more* than once a week. Catholics were most likely to attend once a week or oftener, with more than 80% of the youth reporting in this way compared with slightly less than 70% of the Protestants and fewer than 40% of the Jews (24, 25).

In addition, more than half of the respondents indicated that they prayed one or more times a day. Only 20% said that they never or only occasionally prayed (25, p. 174). These figures are

[2]We have excluded research studies of college students because it is quite clear that such persons are a rather select element and probably not representative of the more general population of adolescents. The exclusion is, of course, not made without cost. College students are an extremely well researched grouping in our society. As captive, readily cooperative respondents, they are the subjects of a large part of the research literature. And, what is true for social science inquiry generally is no less so for studies of religion (see particularly, 37).

[3]For systematic research supporting this suggestion see (7, 17). These studies did not, however, use adolescent subjects.

about the same as those found in national samples of Lutheran youth (35) and Presbyterian adolescents (39). As with church attendance, girls were more "religious" in regard to frequency of prayer than were boys.

Over-all, if we consider the question of religious commitment only in terms of frequency of participation in or attendance of ritualistic services, we must conclude that American youth are not irreligious. However, this dimension focuses "on what people do rather than on the meaning of the activity to them" (14, p. 28). This information is of limited utility for in itself it says nothing about the *reasons* for participation.[4] Some adolescents go to church for "non-religious" reasons. They may go out of a secular deference to or an identification with either parents' or peers' wishes, or for a number of other reasons taken singly or in combination.[5]

The notion that attendance at religious services is not always identical with other facets of religious orientation is to emphasize the need to look beyond the "ritualistic." Unfortunately, the other dimensions have not been as extensively assessed by research studies. However, some questions bearing on most of the dimensions have been utilized in various investigations, and it is from these items that we can hopefully gain some additional insights into the religiousness of youth.

---

[4]Even with the limited data so far collected, most published studies *could* provide more insight into the meaning of ritual behavior than they have so far done by using only slightly altered analysis techniques. That is, if one has answers to how often a young person prays and data also on whether or not he feels that his prayers have been answered—as for example in the Purdue studies—the answer to the second question could be used to see whether rates of prayer being perceived as harkened to is related, at least, to the rate of praying. In this limited way, the possible meaning of ritual behavior could be extended. Incidentally, we should point out that, while extant studies could give us more insights along this line, one cannot make such comparisons from the published data. One would need access to the distributions upon which the published tables are based in order to make the necessary cross-tabulations.

[5]Rosen's study (28) found all of these factors operating. His study is the rare exception in that he has tried to get at the motives involved in religious practices. However, there are sufficient belief and faith differences between the Christian majority and the Jewish minority to suggest that it would be hazardous to try and generalize Rosen's findings to Catholics and Protestants. Nonetheless, note particularly pp. 73–80; 92–104; 125–137; 152–160.

II. The Experimental Dimension

The experimental variable refers to "religious feeling" or the experiencing of religious emotion. At least two types of such religious experiences can be differentiated: (1) simple concern, a seeking after a purpose in life or a wish to believe in a transcendentally based ideology; and (2) a subjective awareness of a divine presence and "interpersonal" encounters with God.

1. CONCERN

The degree to which youth are subjectively concerned about religion and the transcendental is unclear. One of the Purdue studies asked their respondents whether they "would like to know more about religion." If we can assume that one cares to have more knowledge about a phenomenon only if there is at least some interest in it, their responses are revealing. Youth gave an overwhelming "yes" reply to the question. Over-all, 89% of the young people responded in this way and the figure was approximately the same regardless of the person's age, sex, place of residence, family income, region of the country or degree of parental education. The only exception to the extremely high "yes" response rate was for Jewish children where only 68% answered affirmatively (25, p. 168). This may reflect the fact that the question taps an intellectual as well as an experiential aspect and that, with the traditional tendency of Jewish children to be schooled in their cultural and religious heritage, these respondents were merely saying that they were already knowledgeable and felt less of a need for further information. The same confounding of personal religious concern and simple interest in obtaining more knowledge may be present in the answers of other respondents and this probably results in an *overstatement* of the level of concern of the average adolescent.

A somewhat different means of assessing concern was utilized in a national poll conducted by Elmo Roper. A sample of adolescents and young adults was asked: "Try to think back to a couple of years ago. What was your most important problem or thing you were most worried about then—the thing that bothered you most *then*, whether you'd call it important or unimportant today?" The same question was repeated to get at "the most important problem or thing worried about *now*" and, again, as "what in the *next* couple of years ahead" would be a worry. The responses centered largely around education, job aspirations, sex, and interpersonal relationships generally. Concern over religious matters was evidenced by only 1% or 2% of the respondents (27, p. 145). This figure, however, may considerably *underestimate* the level of concern because the question appeared at the very end of the interview following a battery of items specifically eliciting the respondent's information and worry about education, jobs, social relationships, and sex.

Some insight into the apparently conflicting findings regarding the level of youthful "concern" over religion can perhaps be gained by turning to several other empirical studies. Unfortunately, none of these utilized representative cross-sectional samples of American adolescents. Consequently, the data cannot be directly generalized to the total teenage population. However, the findings may be at least suggestive.

A nationwide sample of nearly 3,000 Lutheran adolescents was asked to indicate their level of concern over 240 different "problem items." Factor analysis reduced the 240 items to seven families or areas of highly intercorrelated concern items. Here religious matters, called in the study "personal faith," clearly emerged as a topic of youth's interest. Sixty-six per cent of the sample marked items of personal faith as being at least to some degree "disturbing." Like the Roper study, interpersonal relations, sex, and education were found to be significant areas of concern (35, pp. 90–93).

It is also instructive to note the kinds of items in the Lutheran "personal faith" measure. The most prominent one was the register of much or quite a bit of worry over an inability to "find a deep faith in God." Fully 60% of the Lutheran youth expressed this response; 24% expressed "some" concern. Only 16% registered no misgivings about their orientation. Similarly, 86% of the youngsters had "much" or "some" concern over their feelings that they were not living up to their professed Christian convictions; 14% were unconcerned over this matter (35, p. 328).

Furthermore, when those youth who participated most in the ritualistic aspects of religion were compared with those who participated least, more than half of *both* groupings indicated that they desired help regarding matters of personal faith (35, p. 193).

Another study, using a national (but again probably non-representative) sample of pre-adolescents and adolescents, found that, in response to a request to indicate things about which they "wondered," there was considerable interest expressed in religious items. Over half of the sample "wondered" about religion, and this form of wonder increased as the youngsters grew older. Furthermore, the wondering about matters classed as "religion and philosophy" shared the number one rank with items classed as "science and technology" (9).

In yet another study, this one utilizing high school students in Lexington, Kentucky, religious values, as measured by the Allport, Vernon, and Lindzey scale ranked first with all the respondents. This was true irrespective of sex, race, and whether or not the person was college bound or non-college oriented in plans (18, p. 39).

If we can generalize from these studies, it appears that, while American adolescents may see other problem areas as more pressing or crucial, they are not religiously unconcerned. While we do not have the data to precisely gauge this aspect of the experiential dimension, and while it may not be uniform for all types of adolescents, it does seem safe to assert a level of religious concern clearly above that which one might garner from the more popular notions that teenage interests are somehow limited to cars; pizza, pimples, and personality; or sex, sports, songs, and school (4, 15, 31, 33, 36).

2. FAITH

Thus, American adolescents appear to have some religious concerns. To what extent does this concern find expression in *faith*, the second aspect of the experiential dimension?

Faith, as an aspect of the experiential dimension of religion is taken here to refer to a feeling of closeness, and of personal interaction with the divine. This interpersonal encounter between man and God, has been suggested by Glock and Stark as having an ordered progression of intimacy:

> By conceiving of the divinity and the individual undergoing the religious experience as a pair of actors involved in a social encounter, we may specify some general configurations of relations between them which can be ordered in terms of social distance. . . . We may sketch four such possible configurations of inter-actor relations:
>
> 1. The human actor simply notes . . . the existence or presence of the divine actor;
> 2. Mutual presence is acknowledged, the divine actor is perceived as noting the presence of the human actor;
> 3. The awareness of mutual presence is replaced by an affective relationship akin to love or friendship;
> 4. The human actor perceives himself as a confidant of or a fellow participant in action with the divine actor (14, pp. 42–43).

While we have no data that systematically assesses the degree of religious commitment in terms of the level of intimacy of the relationship between youth and God, some information drawn from the Gallup study and the Purdue Polls allows some insight here. To acknowledge the presence of God is the least intimate and least entangling of the man–God relationships. Nearly all teenagers do report that they believe in God. Less than 5% indicated that they "have some doubts" or don't believe at all (10). The next level of intimacy is to admit that God knows one's behavior. Somewhat over 80% of the respondents in the Purdue Polls said they believed that "God knows our every thought and movement." However, while the respondents may have a sense of being *watched,* they were considerably less certain of being *cared for* by the Divine. Just 60% fully agreed that "God controls everything that happens everywhere." To act *in trust* on the control of the other is to admit the highest level of entwinement and faith. Asked if they believed religious faith was better than logic for solving life's important problems, only 38% responded "yes" in 1962 (24, pp.4–5). It should be noted that, the proportion of the over-all adolescent population that expressed agreement with the reality of the varying levels of religious com-

mitment *decreased* as the level of commitment or intimacy increased, with more than 95% acknowledging the existence of God, but less than 40% willing to entrust their lives completely to divine power.[6]

Jewish youth were less likely to report that they felt on "intimate" terms with God than was the Christian adolescent. Only 38% of the Jewish young people agreed that God knows one's every thought and action; 31% agreed that God controls everything, and but 23% agreed that religion is better than logic for solving the important problems of life (25, pp. 171–172).

Catholic students in this study answered approximately like the Protestants with a somewhat greater tendency to affirm God as controlling the universe and a somewhat greater willingness to agree that life's important problems are best solved on the basis of faith (24, pp. 171–172).

From these data, it would seem that unswerving trust and faith is *not* the norm for American adolescents. The overwhelming majority are quite willing to agree that the Almighty exists, watches, and perhaps controls the world. But there is marked reluctance to really trust this control and count solely upon it. They are not at all sure that "God will take care of them." One gets the impression that many youth are "playing it cool"— unwilling to fully accept the implications of divine control but also unwilling to deny its existence. In this regard, it is interesting to note that a lack of faith in others is not taken as villainous. Over 60% of the teenagers polled in the Purdue Study disagreed with the statement that: "Most people who don't believe in God are bad people." Another 20% indicated that they were uncertain (25, p. 172). Thus, for most teenagers, rejection of the Almighty is not seen as catastrophic. But, the youth were not quite willing to leave God out either. Asked whether "Men working

---

[6]Based only on the availability of table marginals we cannot be certain that Glock and Stark's model of intimacy with the Transcendental is accurate. They suggest that persons at more intimate levels of involvement should have gone through earlier, less intimate stages. For this to be demonstrated in our data the 38% of youth in 1962 who answered "yes" to a willingness to take faith over logic in solving life's important problems should also have said "yes" to the two earlier questions about a knowing and a controlling God. We do not know whether, in fact, they did.

and thinking together can build a good society without any divine or super-natural help," only one-third of the sample could agree to this (25, p. 172). Uncertain whether God is necessary or not, the American teenager apparently "hedges" the matter.[7] He seems to be saying: we cannot have a good society without God but people who deny God are not bad. What is true for the whole, does not hold for the parts!

III. The Ideological Dimension

The third dimension of religiousness, ideology or "belief," addresses the extent to which individuals differ in regard to their acceptance of church doctrine. Every religion sets forth some set of beliefs to which its followers are expected to adhere. Of course, there is a vast array of such beliefs associated with the Judaeo-Christian heritage that might conceivably be examined here. We have neither the space, nor, more important, the data to do this. Therefore, we shall examine only those beliefs on which some information is available and which seem to be common to the dominant religious groups in American society.

Some beliefs warranting the existence of the divine and defining its character have already been noted in the previous discussion in terms of the nature of man's relationship with God. Let it suffice to recall here that almost all teenagers acknowledged the existence of God, and conceptualize the Almighty as all-knowing. In addition, more than 80% (in the Gallup Poll) reported that they believed God to be their judge who observes their actions and will reward or punish them for what they do. These are all highly traditional and "orthodox" views.

Moreover, more than 80% of the adolescents surveyed indicated that they believed that there is a life after death (10). The Lutheran study, cited earlier, found a slightly higher percentage (90%) who asserted belief in life after death.

Going beyond belief in after-life, the Purdue study also asked whether our fate in the hereafter

depends upon how we behave on earth. Sixty-nine percent of the total sample affirmed a belief that such was the case. Only 9% registered a negative response. The remainder (22%) failed to answer the question or recorded a "don't know" reply. Catholic youth were somewhat more convinced, with 77% answering "yes." Jewish youth were more skeptical, with only 23% saying "yes," and 46% registering a doubting "don't know" answer (25, p. 172).

A similar tendency for a clustering of "don't know" answers was found when the youth were asked about the sacredness of the scriptures. While the majority (57%) of young people indicated they agreed that "the first writing of the Bible was done under the guidance of God," fully ¼ of the sample indicated a "don't know" response. As on most of the other belief items, Catholics had the highest rate of agreement (64%) and Jews the lowest (42%) (25, p. 173). Finally, we can note the Gallup data showed that, although roughly 90% of American youth felt the Bible to be "true," about ⅓ of the adolescents qualified their response and indicated that it was "mostly" rather than "completely" true. However, less than 2% of the sample was willing to answer that the Bible is "just a fable" (10).

What can be concluded from these data? Strommen has nicely summarized the over-all picture of youth's beliefs when he writes of his Lutheran adolescents:

> Searching minds and disquieted hearts often doubt what is taught. . . . A few upwards to many doubters are seen for every belief [surveyed]. . . . Yet the percentage of these doubters is less than might be expected for this scientific age. Only 17 percent, for example, doubt that "miracles take place today" . . . only one-third disbelieve in the existence of a devil . . . and only one-third doubt that the Bible is historically accurate (35, p. 54).

Whatever may be said, then, of the quality of today's adolescents, the evidence presented here certainly suggests that they are not untraditional. At least in the basic ideological factors assessed here, American teenagers either overwhelmingly accept the orthodox point of view or, at the very most, they express some doubts about it. Almost none, however, *reject* the traditional positions.

[7]This kind of hedging does not appear to diminish with age. While high school seniors were more accepting of non-believer than were freshmen, the percentage seeing divine help as necessary *increased* with increasing age from 37% for the ninth grades to 51% for seniors. (25, p. 172).

IV. The Intellectual Dimension

The fourth dimension of religion delineated by Glock and Stark refers to the degree of knowledge that the individual possesses of church dogma, doctrine, and history. This is a cognitive aspect. It asks not what the individual feels, or believes, but what he "knows" intellectually. As with the ideological dimension a wide range of ideas could be assessed to determine the level of knowledge of adolescents concerning their religious heritage. Unfortunately, while there is evidence that at least some such studies have been carried out, the results have not found their way into published literature readily available to the general reader. A study dealing with college sophomores may be suggestive (20). However, if such persons were at least as knowledgeable as the average adolescent, then the typical teenager in American society is quite ignorant of basic church tenets. In a test of 100 items (50 questions covering various aspects of the Old Testament and 50 dealing with the New Testament), the range of scores was between 0 and 80—But, the *median* score was only 17! Thus, while the adolescent overtly supports both the established church *and* the basic tenets of Judaeo–Christian belief, he may very well know little of the "factual" information concerning his religion.

V. The Consequential Dimension

The final dimension of religiousness differs from the preceding four. It refers, not to the *internal* aspects of religion, such as faith, belief, and knowledge, but rather raises the question of how religious commitment, as measured by the other dimensions, conditions or influences the behavior or feelings of the individual.

Research has not been unconcerned with this aspect. However, certain methodological shortcomings mar the work and make it of limited worth. There has been a general failure in these studies to differentiate the various dimensions of religiousness, and, unfortunately,

research on religious effects cannot be done in isolation from [careful] research on other as-

pects of religiosity. How religious a person is on these other dimensions provides the warrant for asserting that a given act is, in fact, a religious effect. By definition, an act can be a religious effect only if it flows from religiosity (14, p. 35).

Most of the work done assessing the importance of religious effects, whether using adult or adolescent populations, has tended to use ritualistic practices—usually church attendance or membership—as the measure of religiousness. While this is a convenient index, easily measured and readily obtainable, it is probably among the least satisfactory indicators (1). This is true if for no other reason than that it fails to differentiate within the population. The overwhelming majority of people apparently regard themselves as church members and "regular" attenders.

Even in those few instances where more adequate indicators of religious commitment have been employed, the insights gained from the research are limited because almost all of these studies are cross-sectional. "Done at one point in time, they do not allow warranted conclusions as to the causal direction of the associations they find" (14, p. 37). Simply because two factors are empirically related does *not* necessarily mean that they are causally linked, nor is the direction of cause and effect always obvious. Thus, in one study, based on the observed relationship between church attendance and civil liberties, it was concluded that church attendance *leads* people to be less civil libertarian. However, the opposite conclusion could be equally plausible. That is, being less supportive of civil liberties may lead people to more church attendance. Similarly, while the research is by no means consistent and conclusive in this regard, some studies have found a negative association between religiousness (as indicated by church participation and/or beliefs) and delinquency (30, 32, 35). But, we cannot be sure that religious values are in fact the causal agent. The relationship could easily result from the linkage of both delinquency and religiousness with another causal factor such as social class. Unless one has longitudinal data to carefully trace the influence of religion, we must remain essentially ignorant of its consequence.

While we know very little about the effects of

various religious orientations, this does not mean that beliefs and interests are necessarily unimportant or causally impotent. Undoubtedly they can be and sometimes are crucial conditioners of action.[8] To what extent this occurs, however, is not clear.

Some Concluding Remarks

How religious are the youth of America? We have suggested that the answer to this question is not a simple one. To arrive at any evaluation at all, we need to consider all of the various dimensions of religion. In the brief review of research just presented, we have suggested that typically the adolescent embraces both a traditional belief system and a not immodest degree of participation in the ritualistic aspects of religion. His level of knowledge has not been systematically assessed but probably is low. In terms of the experiential dimension, his concern and interest in religion, while not clearly measured, appear to be quite high. The development of concern into deep, orthodox faith is not, however, apparently typical. The American adolescent seems reluctant to deny the idea of a supernatural, but, at the same time, is unwilling or unable to yield himself with firm conviction to the hands of the Divine. Perhaps the best label we can apply to the teenager's religious orientation is "hedging." He appears to embrace neither nihilism nor firm commitment.

Of course, it should be clear that the picture we have drawn from the meager data available is for the "average" or "typical" teenager. While we have given some brief indications of diversity within the adolescent grouping, we obviously could not fully explore it within the limited scope of this paper. Yet, clearly, the recognition of the point is vital. *There are* some youth who have deep religious commitment and act upon it[9] and

some few who show almost no religiosity. Moreover there is considerable variability not only in degree, but also in content. As Strommen has noted regarding his sample of Lutheran youth:

> [They] . . . are astonishingly heterogeneous in their beliefs. Some embrace concepts which identify them as distinctively Lutheran, whereas others hold beliefs that are indistinguishable from those of other Protestants. Almost half hold a mixture of beliefs which include tenets that are neither Christian nor distinctive. . . . This great variety constantly qualified any generalizations about Lutheran youth (35, pp. 69 and 233).

When this consideration of *within* denomination variability is superimposed on the contention and research findings of Glock and Stark that the differences *among* Protestant denominations, as seen in adult members, are considerably greater than some recent ecumenical movements and desires would lead one to expect, the dangers in making sweeping generalization are highlighted.

It also needs emphasis that, while we have limited our survey to adolescents, this should *not* be taken to mean that adolescents are unique. On the contrary, the characterization of the average American teenager may be equally applicable to the average American adult. Adults too may exhibit the same "hedging stance" as the youth— unwilling to deny the existence of God, yet reluctant to totally trust divine power to guide them. We do know, from careful analysis of the research record that, popular mythology to the contrary, the adolescent tends strongly to accept rather than reject parental values (2, 41). What is true in other areas is probably equally true for religion. Thus, for example, in the Purdue studies, 78% of the youth felt their beliefs agreed with the orientation of both parents (25, p. 168). This supposition of generational agreement has been confirmed in other studies (22). Thus, whether

---

[8]Max Weber's analysis and documentation of the significant role of the particular religious orientations he called the Protestant Ethic in the development of Western societies is well known (38).

[9]P. A. Riffel (26) has pointed to what he calls "scrupulosity" as one style of adolescent self identity in which there is meticulous adherence to religious and moral precepts. This pattern of rigid conformity to traditional beliefs and practices seems to occur most frequently among youth attending parochial schools and appears to be a transitory

(though not necessarily a short-lived) phase. In the scrupulosity pattern there can be little doubt about the importance of religious motives. However, the extent of this style of adolescent identity is not clear. David Matza has estimated that, "scrupulosity seems of roughly the same order of magnitude as that youthful style at the other end of the spectrum which nowadays attracts so much public attention—juvenile delinquency" (19, p. 200).

one takes the religious orientations of American adolescents to be "good" or "bad," it is vital to recognize that the dispositions do not exist in a vacuum, but in a socially supporting milieu.

Is there anything then about the adolescent's beliefs and religious behavior that is distinctively "adolescent?" We do not have data to make firm conclusions in this area, but we can speculate from what we know of the "teen" years. Adolescence is typically a time in which the youth is seeking his own self identity (6, 16, 21). Unsure of the kind of person he is and wishes to be, he is often beset by a sense of insecurity in relating himself to others, and to the world in general (35). An important aspect of concern is likely to be the matter of resolving one's relationship to the supernatural. Most adolescents are unwilling to simply accept their families' faith without question (only slightly over ¼ of the youth assessed in the Purdue study indicated that one should do this). At the same time the youth is vitally concerned over the quality of his interpersonal relations with others. Given the context of American society where religious commitment is given at least overt endorsement as "good" by old and young alike, the individual adolescent may be unwilling to risk social rejection by making public the doubts he has over religion. Consequently, his behavior is likely to reflect, for the most part, a ritualistic performance of church attendance and an overt subscription to at least basic Judaeo–Christian dogma. In fact, this involvement in such activities may be more intense than the participation of his parents or the general adult population.[10] In a paradoxical way his concerns about the sacred gets caught in a web where to communicate about the concern becomes a sacred breach against one's self. It is perhaps revealing that, in the Purdue study, when asked if they enjoyed "arguing about religion," less than one in five of the youth said "yes" (25, p. 168). But religious doubts may still exist and the adolescent's uncertainty concerning the "correctness" of his beliefs may make him unwilling to rely wholly upon his faith to guide his actions. And so he hedges. Whether we are correct in this interpretation is, of course, an open matter and one which, like so many areas of adolescent religious behavior, obviously needs more insightful research.

[10]Directly comparable data for youth and adults is sketchy, but suggestive. The Purdue survey found that, while 69% of the teenagers said they attend formal worship services, "about once a week" or oftener, only 40% reported that their fathers and 57% that their mothers attend at least two or more times a month (25, p. 167). Furthermore, the Gallup Poll found that both college students and young adults were less likely to be "regular" attenders than were high school students (10).

REFERENCES

1. ALTSHULER, NATHAN. "Religion and Mental Health: Demographic and Personal Variables," in Richard V. McCann, *The Churches and Mental Health.* New York: Basic Books, 1962, Chapter 12, pp. 209–227.
2. BEALER, ROBERT C., WILLETS, FERN K., AND MAIDA, PETER R. "Rebellious Youth Subculture — A Myth," *Children*, Vol. 11 (1964), pp. 43–48.
3. ———— "The Myth of a Rebellious Adolescent Subculture: Its Detrimental Effects for Understanding Rural Youth," in Lee G. Burchinal, ed., *Rural Youth in Crisis: Facts, Myths, and Social Change.* Washington, D.C.: Department of Health, Education, and Welfare, 1965, pp. 45–61.
4. BERNARD, JESSIE, ED. "Teen-Age Culture." *The Annals*, Vol. 338 (1961).
5. ELKIND, DAVID AND SALLY. "Varieties of Religious Experience in Young Adolescents," *Journal for the Scientific Study of Religion*, Vol. 2 (1962), pp. 102–112.
6. ERIKSON, ERIK H., ED. *Youth: Change and Challenge.* New York: Basic Books, Inc., 1963.
7. FAULKNER, JOSEPH E., AND DEJONG, GORDON F. "Religiosity in 5-D: An Empirical Analysis," paper read at the American Sociological Association, Chicago, Illinois, September, 1965.
8. FICHTER, JOSEPH H. *Dynamics of a City Church: Southern Parish.* Chicago: University of Chicago Press, 1951.
9. FUKUYAMA, YOSHIO. "Wonder Letters: An Experimental Study of the Religious Sensitivities of Children," *Religious Education*, Vol. 58 (1963), pp. 377–383.
10. GALLUP, GEORGE, AND HILL, EVAN. *Religious Beliefs of Youth*, 1961. Unpublished data.

11. ———, "Youth: The Cool Generation," *Saturday Evening Post*, Vol 234 (1961), pp. 63–80.

12. GESELL, ARNOLD, AND AMES, L. B. *Youth: The Years From Ten to Sixteen.* New York: Harpers, 1956.

13. GLOCK, CHARLES Y., AND STARK, RODNEY. "Is There an American Protestantism?" *Transaction*, Vol. 3 (1965), pp. 8–13; 48–49.

14. GLOCK, CHARLES Y. *Religion and Society in Tension.* Chicago: Rand McNally & Company, 1965.

15. GOTTLIEB, DAVID, AND RAMSEY, CHARLES. *The American Adolescent.* Homewood, Illinois: The Dorsey Press, 1964.

16. JERSILD, ARTHUR T. *The Psychology of Adolescence.* New York: The Macmillan Company, 1963, 2nd ed.

17. LENSKI, GERHARD. *The Religious Factor.* Garden City, New York: Doubleday, 1961.

18. LOTT, ALBERT J., AND LOTT, BERNICE E. *Negro and White Youth.* New York, Holt, Rinehart, and Winston, Inc., 1963.

19. MATZA, DAVID. "Position and Behavior Patterns of Youth," in Robert E. L. Faris, ed., *Handbook of Modern Sociology.* Chicago: Rand McNally and Company, 1964, pp. 191–216.

20. PAYNE, RAYMOND. "Knowledge of the Bible Among Protestant and Jewish University Students: An Exploratory Study," *Religious Education*, Vol. 58 (1963), pp. 289–294.

21. PECK, ROBERT F., AND HAVIGHURST, ROBERT J. *The Psychology of Character Development.* New York: John Wiley, 1960.

22. PUTNEY, SNELL, AND MIDDLETON, RUSSELL. "Rebellion, Conformity, and Parental Religious Ideologies," *Sociometry*, Vol. 24 (1961), pp. 125–135.

23. REISMAN, DAVID, GLAZER, NATHAN, AND DENNEY, REUEL. *The Lonely Crowd: A Study of the Changing American Character.* New York: Doubleday, 1953.

24. REMMERS, H. H. "Teenagers' Attitudes Toward Study Habits, Vocational Plans, Religious Beliefs, and Luck," Report of Poll No. 67, The Purdue Opinion Panel. Lafayette, Indiana: Division of Educational Reference, December, 1962.

25. REMMERS, H. H., AND RADLER, D. H. *The American Teenager.* Indianapolis: Bobbs-Merrill Company, Charter Books, 1962.

26. RIFFEL, P. A. "Sex and Scrupulosity," in W. C. Bier, ed., *The Adolescent: His Search for Understanding.* New York: Fordham University Press, 1963, pp. 39–51.

27. ROPER, ELMO, AND ASSOCIATES. *A Study of the Problems, Attitudes and Aspirations of Rural Youth.* Unpublished report prepared for the Rockefeller Brothers Fund, October, 1963.

28. ROSEN, BERNARD C. *Adolescence and Religion: The Jewish Teenager in American Society.* Cambridge, Mass.: Schenkman Publishing Company, Inc., 1965.

29. ROSS, MURRAY. *Religious Beliefs of Youth.* New York: Association Press, 1950.

30. SCHOLL, MASON E., AND BEKER, JEROME. "A Comparison of the Religious Beliefs of Delinquent and Non-Delinquent Protestant Adolescent Boys," *Religious Education*, Vol. 59 (1964), pp. 250–253.

31. SEVENTEEN MAGAZINE. *The Teen-age Girl:* 1960. New York: Seventeen Magazine, 1960.

32. SHOEBEN, EDWARD J., JR. "Moral Behavior and Moral Learning," *Religious Education*, Vol. 58 (1963), pp. 137–145.

33. SMITH, ERNEST A., *American Youth Culture.* Glencoe, Illinois: The Free Press, 1962.

34. STOUFFER, SAMUEL. *Communism, Conformity, and Civil Liberties.* Garden City, New York: Doubleday and Co., 1955.

35. STROMMEN, MERTON P. *Profiles of Church Youth.* St. Louis, Missouri: Concordia Publishing House, 1963.

36. "The Teen-agers," *Newsweek*, March 21, 1966, pp. 57–75.

37. VAN DYKE, PAUL, II, AND PIERCE-JONES, JOHN. "The Psychology of Religion of Middle and Late Adolescence: A Review of Empirical Research, 1950-1960," *Religious Education*, Vol. 58 (1963), pp. 529–537.

38. WEBER, MAX. *The Protestant Ethic and the Spirit of Capitalism*, trans. by Talcott Parsons. London: Allen and Unwin, 1930.

39. WHITMAN, LAURIS B., KEATING, BARRY J., AND MATTHEWS, ROBERT W. *The Presbyterian National Education Survey*, Vol. 3. New York: Board of Christian Education of the United Presbyterian Church in the United States of America, 1965.

40. WILLIAMS, ROBIN M. *American Society: A Sociological Interpretation.* New York: Knopf, 1960, 2nd ed.

41. WITHEY, STEPHEN B. "The Influence of the Peer Group on the Values of Youth," in Cook, Stuart W., ed., *Review of Recent Research Bearing on Religious and Character Formation*, supplement to *Religious Education*, Vol. 57 (1962), pp. s-34–s-44.

42. YINGER, J. MILTON. *Religion, Society, and the Individual: An Introduction to the Sociology of Religion.* New York: Macmillan, 1957.

Chapter 15: Suggested Additional Readings

ADELSON, J., GREEN, B., & O'NEIL, R. Growth of the idea of law in adolescence. *Developmental Psychology,* 1969, *1*(4), 327–332. To trace the growth of concepts about law during adolescence, depth interviews were conducted with subjects aged 11, 13, 15, and 18. The authors found that adolescents' concept of law becomes increasingly functional and less absolutistic as they mature.

GREENE, M. Moral education and dissenting youth. *Teachers College Record,* 1969, *71*(2), 287–291. Greene suggests that today's young rebels need help in discerning what they want and how to secure it. Youth need to be moral, to learn responsibility, to be liberated, and to discover acceptable ways of dealing with current ambiguities in society.

HADDEN, J. K. The private generation. *Psychology Today,* 1969, *3*(5), 32–35, 68–69. This comprehensive survey of college seniors yielded various significant conclusions, the principal one being that present-day college youth are "private." The article reports student views on a wide range of topics.

HOFFMAN, M. L. Father absence and conscience development. *Developmental Psychology,* 1971, *4*(3), 400–406. Among father-absent and father-present seventh grade children, father-absent boys obtained lower scores on various moral indexes than father-present boys, and were rated as more aggressive. However, no differences were detected between father-absent and father-present girls.

KAVANAUGH, R. E. The grim generation. *Psychology Today,* 1968, *2*(5), 50–55. A college counselor comments on types of present-day college students, their interests, and their values.

KOHLBERG, L., & KRAMER, R. Continuities and discontinuities in childhood and adult moral development. *Human Development,* 1969, *12*(2), 93–120. The authors discuss longitudinal data involving a group of subjects from ages 6 to 25, and their middle-aged fathers. They treat moral development as an evolving process, and enumerate some of its variations.

LAWSON, D. The hero, youth, and values. *Educational Theory,* 1969, *19*(2), 174–184. This interesting discussion, liberally illustrated, concerns youth's heroes, or models, in terms of values and the social context.

MYERHOFF, B. G. New styles of humanism. *Youth and Society,* 1969, *1*(2), 151–177. The writer establishes a historical context for comprehending the youthful minority, whom she calls the new humanists. She considers the quality of life these young people accept and reject, and examines the possible impact on modern society of their search for a meaningful existence.

ROSCOE, J. T., RITTER, C. E., TEGLOVIC, S., JR., & THAYER, J. D. American college student values. *Colorado Journal of Educational Research,* 1968, *8*(1), 3–26. Students (whose mean age was 20.8) from seventeen universities across the country were administered the Polyphasic Values Inventory. The results are summarized in this article, both for the subjects as a whole and also according to certain variables, including sex, age, college class, college majors, and political, religious, and philosophic preferences.

THOMPSON, O. E. Student values in transition. *California Journal of Educational Re-*

search, 1968, *19,* 77–86. The author reports the results of a study which was designed to provide information about the values of high school students and those of their teachers.

WILLIAMSON, E. G.   Youth's dilemma: To be or to become. *Personnel and Guidance Journal,* 1967, *46*(2), 1731–1777. This paper portrays youth as engaged in three basic moral or intellectual activities: selecting life purposes, limiting their concern for immediate satisfaction, and striving to become their highest and best potentiality. Educators and counselors are challenged to assist youth to grow through successfully resolving the dilemmas inherent in these problems.

16

Youth and Drugs

Drugs may be classified in various ways. Smith (1969) groups drugs in these categories: sedative–hypnotic drugs, such as barbiturates, alcohol, and marijuana; narcotics, including morphine, heroin, opium, and codeine; central nervous system stimulants, embracing everything from caffeine and nicotine to the amphetamines; and finally, the psychedelic drugs such as STP, LSD, PCP, and a cannabis ingredient known as THC.

Marijuana is the most easily obtainable and also the most commonly used drug (Suchman, 1968). It is known variously as grass, pot, tea, maryjane, weed, hemp, gage, boo, and broccoli. While some individuals insist that it is harmless, most narcotic addiction begins with its use. Marijuana ordinarily produces in the user an ecstatic, euphoric condition and a distortion in time and space perception (Chilnick, 1969).

The amphetamines and barbiturates are considered the softer drugs; they are often prescribed for legitimate medical reasons and are quite readily available. Amphetamine users may begin by taking diet or pep pills, perhaps for "kicks" or to remain awake, for amphetamines, in stimulating the central nervous system, increase alertness and lift the mood. In time, however, regular users may acquire a dependency upon these drugs. While the normal dosage prescribed for a diet pill is from five to fifteen milligrams of amphetamines, "pill-heads" may take from 1,000 to 5,000 milligrams a day. These dosages may produce behavioral disorganization, paranoia, and perhaps psychosis.

Although amphetamines are not often fatal, they can produce a high depression cycle known as the upper-downer syndrome, a cycle produced when use of amphetamines is followed by that of barbiturates (Strack, 1968). For three or four days the individual may be excitable; however, after his supply of pills runs out he may simply collapse from physical exhaustion, sleep for 24 to 48 hours, awaken with an enormous appetite, and then sink into a mood of depression. In order to obtain a maximum "high," some persons take amphetamines intravenously, although oral consumption is more common (*U. S. News and World Report, 1969*).

The most commonly used of the hallucinogenic drugs is LSD, which can produce dramatic shifts in thought, mood, and perception. It also distorts intellectual functioning and plays tricks with the senses. According to Smith (1969), LSD users often reject society and seem to be looking for a new outlook on life that will give them the courage to go on living. LSD is not addictive; however, it can apparently produce a chromosomal breakdown and geneticists are unsure about its other effects (Johnson & Westman, 1968). Among adolescent LSD users, "turning on" may lead to a severe psychic disorder which can produce psychotic effects for a long period after the drug wears off. Indeed, drugs may induce such behaviors among persons who have hitherto displayed quite stable emotions and personalities (Strack, 1968). Richards, Joffe, Smith, and Spratto (1969) conclude that LSD has produced more psychological damage than any other drug.

Of course, it is fair to add that certain drugs, properly used, have clinical value. Under careful supervision, LSD can safely be used for medical or psychiatric treatment. Other medication has been used to calm disturbed children. For example, Witter (1971) notes the case of the child with minimal brain dysfunction (MBD), one of at least 38 terms associated with a subset of learning disabilities. Such a child is often hyperactive, loud, and demanding—the model of the uncontrollable student. About 200,000 children in the United States are receiving amphetamine and stimulant therapy, and for perhaps another 100,000 tranquilizers and antidepressants are being prescribed. According to testimony of experts at a Department of Health, Education, and Welfare hearing, reports Suchman (1968), such use of medication to modify the behavior of grade school children can be expected to increase radically. The same experts generally dismiss any connection between children's reliance on drugs in grammar school and their possible later drug habits as adolescents. Nevertheless, research on the topic is still in its infancy, and hard-and-fast conclusions cannot yet be drawn.

In an investigation of the incidence of use of various drugs, Kohn and Mercer (1971) found that the most widely taken drug is marijuana (97.96 percent of the persons in their sample had used it); psychedelic drugs are somewhat less used (35.71 percent); and amphetamines less still (21.43 percent). The presumed harmfulness of marijuana is still highly controversial, even among scientists. Authorities do agree quite well on the dangers of indiscriminate use of common psychedelics, notably LSD, and on the harmfulness of amphetamines.

Let us now consider some of the issues involved in drug use by adolescents. Just how important is the problem? Are most youth groping their way through life darkly, their world view shrouded in a drug-induced haze? Has the drift to drugs degenerated into a stampede? Are youth indifferent to the potential dangers of drugs?

According to Lindesmith (1965), the student's use of marijuana satisfies much the same need for him as social drinking does for his parents; and just as social drinking is not the same as alcoholism, neither is smoking marijuana the same as narcotic addiction. That is, Junior smokes marijuana casually, for the same reasons that Dad sips a martini, just as casually. Marijuana smoking is a social problem only because it conflicts with the accepted norms of the larger society, whereas social drinking, which is generally acceptable, is not considered a problem.

However, simply to conclude that youth are no worse than their elders cannot erase the fact that a problem exists. In a study of West Coast students, Suchman (1968) found that 21 percent had used drugs, and of these, all had used marijuana. Even the hard drugs such as LSD have spread throughout our society (Lindesmith, 1965). They are used by high school and even grade school students and by all social classes.

Why do adolescents use drugs? According to Hollister (1969), they do it for varied reasons: to get thrills, to relieve feelings of inadequacy, to reduce boredom, to escape responsibility, to compensate for doubts and fears, and to demonstrate against their parents. A youth seeking to shed his outer mask, or public face, in order to be his inner, authentic "self," may use drugs to bolster his courage. Drug use may be related to peer group pressures; a student is far more inclined to use marijuana when his friends also use it. According to Suchman (1968), the use of drugs is part of a subcultural group way of life, in particular a subculture characterized by the "hang-loose" ethic—so-called because it represents a cutting loose from the traditional establishment to escape from conformity and to gain access to new experiences. More specifically, it repudiates, or at least questions, the cornerstones of conventional society, such as "christianity, 'my country right or wrong,' the sanctity of marriage and premarital chastity, civil disobedience, the accumulation of wealth, the right and even the competence of parents, the school, and the government to lead and make decisions for everyone—in sum, the Establishment [Simmons & Winograd, 1966, p. 12]." The hang-loose ethic is related to marijuana use, and males more frequently smoke marijuana and follow this ethic than do females.

Perhaps one reason youth use drugs is simply that they are there. Keniston (1969), for one, blames society itself for the magnitude of the drug problem; because of society's ineptness and leniency in handling drug pushers, drugs are easy to obtain. Moreover, according to Simmons (1967), the marijuana problem "seems to be the pivot around which [deep] conflicts and confrontations are raging—oldsters versus youngsters, hippies versus straight society, administered morality versus personal freedom [p. 11]."

What characteristics distinguish youthful drug users from nonusers? In a study of affluent suburban youths, ages 15 to 18, the individuals more deeply involved with marijuana were those who lacked adequate parental models, who received little recognition in the family, and who perceived the family as rigidly controlling and indifferent (Tec, 1970). The more frequent users also tended to be more cynical, rebellious, apathetic, and anti-establishment.

In another study (Hogan, Conway, Fox & Mankin, 1970), drug users, as compared with nonusers, proved to be socially poised, open to experience, and interested in the feelings of others. On the other hand, they were also pleasure-seeking, somewhat rebellious, and impulsive. The nonusers were rule-abiding and responsible; nevertheless, they were somewhat inflexible, conventional, and narrow in their interests. Still another study (Kohn & Mercer, 1971), found that the college student who indulges in illicit drug use and develops permissive attitudes toward it is likely to be a third- or fourth-year student who "professes atheism, agnosticism, or some atypical religious preference; does not attend organized religious services; and, most to the point here, has a markedly left-wing, rebellious socio-political outlook [p. 130]."

Smith (1969) classifies drug users in four categories: experimental, periodic or recreational, compulsive, and ritualistic. The experimental user does so out of curiosity, or because of group pressure. He is usually quite unsophisticated and disposed to try anything once. The recreational, or periodic, user takes drugs chiefly for excitement and fun, yet he may develop a pattern of drug use, especially when in a group. The compulsive user has become psychologically and physically dependent upon drugs as a means of escaping from the boredom and routine of his life. Finally, the ritualistic drug user believes that drugs open the door to religious and spiritual experience. Such an individual is not a drug abuser but a cultist seeking some sort of special revelation via drug use.

What should be done about youth's use (and abuse) of drugs? Stricter laws prohibiting the use of drugs will not necessarily provide the answer. Concerning marijuana, in particular, present laws and law enforcement have proved ineffective. Among persons arrested for possession of marijuana, only about one in 100 is brought to trial and convicted, simply because the present laws are almost impossible to interpret (*Time,* 1969). Many laymen support the opinion that marijuana should be legalized, but the majority of physicians, psychologists, and legal officers oppose this, partly because they still do not know what health hazards prolonged use of marijuana may present (*Modern Medicine* Poll, 1969).

What sort of drug education should be directed to adolescents today? Weissman (1969) believes that the emphasis should be on the drug users, rather than on the drugs themselves; if adolescents knew why they used drugs, they could more easily be persuaded to dispense with them. Similarly, Thornburg (1971) concludes that drug education must be made relevant to each individual's needs. It must (1) inform adolescents about drugs; (2) help them identify social and personal factors which may contribute to drug use; and (3) make them aware of their personal responsibilities relative to drugs. Without a basic understanding of why they resort to narcotics, users unreform with amazing alacrity.

It is indeed important, but difficult, to get youth to take an objective view of drugs. True, most of them have gotten the message that speed can kill and LSD can deform, but they remain skeptical about reported ill effects of marijuana. Ordinarily, they are interested in talking about any drug and its effects, but they do not respond well to statistics concerning drug use. Nor do they want to be lectured. They are generally self-educated concerning drugs and tend to question the Establishment's statements about them (Kohn & Mercer, 1971). They rarely read the scientific literature on the subject but form their impressions from first-hand observations of drug users and discussions with their peers.

Our first selection, by Suchman, chosen from the veritable deluge of recent articles about youth and drugs, relates students' values and self-image to their use of drugs. Although some differences appeared with regard to their behaviors, attitudes, and values, the youthful drug users and nonusers could also be distinguished from each other on the basis of demographic factors related to sex, socioeconomic status, and religion. Marijuana proved to be the recreational drug of choice and its use formed the central core of the youthful subculture. In the second article, Akers discusses drinking and drug use by teenagers in terms of the most currently available research. He defines the important sociological and social issues associated with drinking and the taking of drugs and suggests ways to deal effectively with the problems relating to both practices.

REFERENCES

CHILNICK, L.   Pot on the campus. *Sooner Magazine,* 1969, *41*(4), 12–13, 19–20.

HOGAN, R., CONWAY, J., FOX, S., & MANKIN, D.   Personality correlates of undergraduate marijuana use. *Journal of Consulting and Clinical Psychology,* 1970, *35*(1), 58–63.

HOLLISTER, W. G.   Why adolescents drink and use drugs. *PTA Magazine,* 1969, *63,* 2–5.

JOHNSON, F. K., & WESTMAN, J. C.   The teenager and drug abuse. *Journal of School Health,* 1968, *38,* 646–654.

KENISTON, K.   Students, drugs, and protests. *Current,* 1969, No. 104, 5–25.

KOHN, P. H., & MERCER, G. W.   Drug use, drug use attitudes and the authoritarianism-rebellion dimension. *Journal of Health and Social Behavior,* 1971, *12*(2), 125–131.

LINDESMITH, A. R.   *The addict and the law.* Bloomington, Indiana: University Press, 1965.

Modern Medicine Poll on Sociomedical Issues: Abortion–homosexual practices–marijuana. *Modern Medicine,* 1969, *37*(22), 18–25.

RICHARDS, L. G., JOFFE, M. H., SMITH, J. P., & SPRATTO, G. R.   *LSD-25: A factual account.* Washington, D. C.: U.S. Department of Justice, 1969.

SIMMONS, J. L. (Ed.)   *Marijuana: Myths and realities.* Hollywood, California: Brandon House, 1967.

SIMMONS, J. L., & WINOGRAD, E.   *It's happening: A portrait of the youth scene today.* Santa Barbara, Calif.: Marc-Laird, 1966.

SMITH, D.   The trip there and back. *Emergency Medicine,* 1969, *1*(1), 26–41.

STRACK, A. E.   Drug use and abuse among youth. *Journal of Health, Physical Education and Recreation,* 1968, *39,* 26–28, 55–57.

SUCHMAN, P. A.   The "hang-loose" ethic and the spirit of drug use. *Journal of Health and Social Behavior,* 1968, *9,* 146–155.

TEC, N. F.   Family and differential involvement with marijuana: A study of suburban teenagers. *Journal of Marriage and the Family,* 1970, *32*(4), 656–664.

THORNBURG, H. D.   *Contemporary adolescents: Readings.* Belmont, California: Brooks-Cole Publishing Company, 1971.

Time.   Pop drugs: The high as a way of life. 1969, *94*(13), 68–78.

U. S. News and World Report.   Two doctors warn against the use of amphetamines. 1969, *57*(26), 24–25.

WEISSMAN, R.   Teen and drugs: Monkey on our backs. *Arizona Teacher,* 1969, *57,* 10–13.

WITTER, C.   Drugging and schooling. *Trans-action,* July–August 1971, Whole No. 69, *8*(9–10), 31–34.

The "Hang-Loose" Ethic and the Spirit of Drug Use

EDWARD A. SUCHMAN

A cross-sectional sampling survey of drug use on a college campus reveals the close association between the use of drugs (overwhelmingly marijuana) and adherence to what might be characterized as a "hang-loose" ethic. Use of drugs was more likely to occur among those students whose behavior, attitudes or values, and self-image were indicative of opposition to the traditional, established order. Such differences occurred regardless of those demographic characteristics of the students also related to drug use, such as sex, socio-economic status, and religion. For these students, marijuana was the recreational drug of choice and its use became a central core of their subculture.

Studies of college students made about 15 years ago found that generation of youth to be "politically disinterested, apathetic, and conservative." (Goldsen, et al., 1960:199; Jacob, 1957). To an increasing degree, the college student of the current generation is striving to overcome this image of passive conformity and conservatism in order to evolve a new and more meaningful role for himself, both on campus and in the larger community. Reflecting the many social, political, and economic forces that have widened the generational gap between young people and those "over 30," this youth movement is seeking to develop new values and behavior patterns, often in defiance and opposition to those of the established order.

Central to this new world of youth is a whole new range of recreational and psychedelic drugs. Studies of college students in the last generation found alcohol to be the major campus "vice" and alarming reports were published about the "drinking problem of college students." (Straus and Bacon, 1953). No mention was made of other drugs. In this respect, the students displayed one more sign of their conformity—drinking was also the favorite social pastime, and problem, of their parents. Almost as if rejection of the establishment also demanded the development of a different form of "high," the new generation of college students is increasingly turning to other drugs for the relaxation and "kicks" their parents found in alcohol. As described by Simmons and Winograd (1966:86), "The drug scene is the central plaza of happening America . . . it is here, in the drug scene that generational change in America most vividly thrusts itself forward. . . ." And perhaps forgetting their own bouts with the law in the days of prohibition and repressing the serious

From E. A. Suchman, The "hang-loose" ethic and the spirit of drug use. Reprinted from the *Journal of Health and Social Behavior,* June 1968, *9*(2), 146–155, by permission of the author and the American Sociological Association.

threat of alcoholism as a major health problem today (Suchman, 1963; Plaut, 1967), adults have been almost unanimous in their condemnation of this new and strange intoxicant. As one "over 30" judge recently opined, alcohol is the socially approved drug of choice for the well-adjusted, responsible, hard-working member of society seeking sociability and pleasant relaxation, while the use of marijuana represents the neurotic and antisocial behavior of the juvenile delinquent.

Unfortunately, there is little empirical data about what is taking place in the colleges today. The present study represents an initial attempt to ascertain basic facts about the use of drugs by one college population and to examine those factors, both causes and consequences, associated with the use of drugs. The major assumption is that drug use on the campuses today is largely limited to the occasional smoking of marijuana cigarettes and represents a social form of recreation far removed in nature from the traditional problem of narcotics addiction and, for that matter, alcoholism. (McGlothlin, 1967) Furthermore, the set of hypotheses to be tested is that the use of marijuana will be highly associated with other expressions of a new breed of youth characterized by a hang-loose ethic. As described by Simmons and Winograd (1966:12), "One of the fundamental characteristics of the hang-loose ethic is that it is irreverent. It repudiates, or at least questions, such cornerstones of conventional society as Christianity, 'my country right or wrong,' the sanctity of marriage and premarital chastity, civil disobedience, the accumulation of wealth, the right and even competence of parents, the schools, and the government to head and make decisions for everyone—in sum, the Establishment."

Method of Procedure

This study was conducted in November, 1967, at a West Coast university. A representative sample of 600 students out of a student body of 12,200 was selected at random from the registration lists of undergraduate and graduate students. A questionnaire dealing with drug use and various aspects of college life, educational and political values, and current social issues was prepared on the basis of detailed interviews of students, especially so-called "hippies," and observation of student activities, especially so-called "happenings." Interviews and observation were carried out by 125 students enrolled in a course on social research methods.

The questionnaire was administered in two parts of almost equal length. The first part was a personal interview, while the second, which sought information on more sensitive topics, such as sex, drug use and the draft, was filled out by the respondent and placed with the first part in a sealed envelope without identification. The questionnaires were thus kept anonymous to increase the probability of truthful answers. The completion rate of interviews was 81 percent. The remaining 19 percent were not interviewed largely because the assigned respondent could not be reached during the week allotted to field work, rather than the refusal to be interviewed (less than 5 percent). A comparison of the sample obtained with available demographic characteristics for the entire population shows no characteristic with a difference beyond what might be expected by chance.

CONCEPTUAL AND OPERATIONAL MODEL

Our dependent variable is frequency of drug use as reported by the respondent. Our major independent variable is degree of adherence to the "hang-loose" ethic as determined by a series of questions designed to tap (1) behavioral patterns, (2) attitudes and values, and (3) self-image and personality. The behavioral patterns refer to such acts as taking part in "happenings" and mass protests, and reading underground newspapers. We view such behaviors as indicative of a rejection of traditional society on the part of the student and subject to disapproval by the representatives of that society. The attitudes and values studied are drawn from the educational area (i.e., worthwhileness of college education, student power), the political area (i.e., Vietnam war, the draft), and the social area (i.e., hippies," the law, sex and life goals). Finally, we study the student's self-image in such respects as conformity, cynicism, anti-establishment and rebellion in an effort to index his own portrait of himself vis-a-vis the established order.

In all three aspects of behavior, attitudes, and self-image, our major hypothesis is that the more the student embraces the "hang-loose" ethic (as opposed to the so-called "Protestant ethic") the more frequently will he make use of drugs.

Findings

PREVALENCE OF DRUG USE

The following proportions of students reported taking some drug (Question: "How frequently do you take drugs (marijuana, LSD, etc.)?"):

About every day	2.0
Once or twice a week	6.6
Once or twice a month	6.6
Less than once a month	6.0
Do not use drugs	78.8
Total	100.0% (N=497)

Of the drugs used, marijuana was listed by *all* students taking drugs, with occasional use of LSD mentioned by 18 percent of those taking drugs (2.2 % of the entire population). A wide variety of other drugs (i.e., "speed," Methadrine, peyote) also was listed, none by more than 10 per cent. There can be little question concerning marijuana's being the recreational drug of choice among this college population, one of five admitting its use, despite its illegality. The word "drugs" as used in this report may therefore be equated largely with marijuana.

This figure of 21.1 percent use is quite similar to the results of surveys at UCLA (33%) (Santa Barbara News-Press, 1967), Harvard (25%), Yale (20%), and Princeton (15%) (Time, 1967), although a Gallup Poll of 426 college campuses reports only about 6 percent as having smoked marijuana (Reader's Digest, 1967). While this "numbers game" is largely unproductive in the absence of any reliable and valid data, it does seem apparent that marijuana use on the campus is high enough to warrant serious attention.

Most of the students using drugs began in college, 40 per cent in their freshman year, although 22 percent had smoked marijuana before coming to college. Almost all began to use drugs through the personal influence of a friend who was already smoking marijuana (Becker, 1953). Drug use usually took place at night as a social activity with other people in the student's or a friend's room.

Overwhelmingly, the reaction of the students smoking marijuana is positive. Four out of five report that they have never gotten sick, although one out of four does mention having experienced a bad "trip." Less than 10 percent want to stop or have ever tried to stop, although 20 percent report being "somewhat" worried.

There is no evidence in these findings to support the claims that smoking marijuana is a predecessor to the use of other, more than dangerous drugs. Marijuana users may occasionally "cross over" to try other drugs, but this is more of a search for new experiences than "progressive degeneration."

ALCOHOL AND MARIJUANA

In addition to the question about their own use of drugs, the students were asked, "How frequently do most of the students you know do the following: smoke marijuana, take LSD, drink alcoholic beverages?" They were also asked in relation to these three recreational drugs, "How strongly do you approve or disapprove doing each of the following?" and "How much pressure do you feel to engage in any of the following?" A comparison of their responses to these three aspects of use, attitude, and pressure for marijuana, LSD, and alcohol is given in Table 1.

First, we note the higher perception of marijuana use as compared to actual use. While 4 out of 5 students (78.8%) report that they do not use marijuana themselves, only 1 out of 3 (30.7%) estimates that most of the students they know do not smoke marijuana. Almost 2 out of 5 (38.6%) report that most of the students they know smoke marijuana frequently or occasionally.

Second, we see that alcohol continues by far to be most frequently used, with an overwhelming majority of students (84.1%) reporting that most of the students they know drink alcohol frequently or occasionally, as compared to 38.9 percent for marijuana and 10.0 percent for LSD.

Third, we note that approval parallels use, with most of the students (70.6%) approving alcohol,

Table 1. Comparison of Drugs According to Use, Attitudes, and Pressures

Questions	Type-Drug		
	Alcoholic Beverages	Marijuana	LSD
Use[a]			
Frequently	47.2	14.1	1.2
Occasionally	36.9	24.5	8.8
Seldom	10.0	18.9	16.9
Never	2.4	30.7	53.8
Don't know	3.5	11.8	19.3
Attitude[b]			
Strongly approve	11.4	5.6	1.2
Approve	59.2	29.5	3.6
Undecided	22.2	31.5	20.9
Disapprove	5.2	20.1	25.7
Strongly disapprove	2.0	13.3	48.6
Pressure[c]			
A great deal	12.9	3.0	2.8
Some, but not much	38.2	16.5	2.0
Very little	47.0	78.1	92.6
No answer	1.9	2.4	2.6
Total per cent	100.0	100.0	100.0
Total cases	497	497	497

[a]Question: "How frequently do most of the students you know do the following:"
[b]Question: "How strongly do you approve or disapprove of students doing each of the following:"
[c]Question: "How much pressure do you feel to engage in any of the following:"

some approving marijuana (35.4%), and few approving LSD (4.8%). The ratio of approval to disapproval is 10.1 in favor for alcohol, 1:1 for marijuana and 1:20 against LSD. It would appear that the campus is split on the use of marijuana, but overwhelmingly in favor of alcohol and against LSD.

Fourth, the pressure to use each of these drugs also parallels attitudes and practices. Most students report pressure to drink alcohol beverages (51.1%), but only 19.5 percent report feeling any pressure to smoke marijuana, with 4.9 per cent feeling some pressure to use LSD. These findings underscore the highly personal and voluntary nature of marijuana or LSD use. If anything, students are being more highly pressured toward possible alcoholism than drug addiction. The major recreational drug on the college campuses is still alcohol.

The relationship between pressure toward use of drugs and the actual frequency of use is quite high. An individual who reports feeling pressure to smoke marijuana is twice as likely to be a frequent user of marijuana (at least once a week) than one who reports little or no pressure (15.7% vs. 7.2%). A similar relationship exists between pressure to use LSD and actual use (16.6% vs. 8.5%). This finding is supported by the much more frequent use of marijuana among those students who report that most of the students they know also smoke marijuana. As many as 68.6 percent of those students who report that most of the students they know smoke marijuana frequently do so themselves, as compared to only 0.7 percent among those whose friends do not smoke marijuana.

A significant reversal between alcohol and drug use occurs in these data. The more the individual knows other students who drink alcohol, and the more pressure he feels to drink himself, the *less* likely is he to use marijuana. This finding would indicate that marijuana is more of a substitute for alcohol than a supplement. For many students it would appear that the use of marijuana represents a preference over alcohol as a source of "high."

The relationship of attitudes toward use and actual use is, not unexpectedly, extremely high. Approval is much more likely to mean use (45.7%), with only a small minority (0.6%) disapproving of smoking marijuana at the same time that they do it. This finding once again attests to the voluntary nature of this act. It is also interesting to note that half of the students who approve of smoking marijuana still do not do so themselves. Most of the students (66.6%) do not feel that "anyone smoking marijuana is foolish" although only a minority agree that "the use of psychedelic drugs should be a matter of conscience and not legal restriction" (34.7%) and that "the university should not cooperate with legal authorities in the enforcement of drug use laws" (23.2%). In all cases, those students having positive attitudes towards marijuana, either in the wisdom of its use or in its freedom from legal restrictions, are much more likely to be users of marijuana.

DEMOGRAPHIC COMPARISONS

The use of drugs varies significantly by sex, social class, marital status, and religion. No differences were found by age, year in college, birthplace or current marital status of parents. Males are almost three times as likely as females to be using drugs (e.g., smoking marijuana) at least once a week (13.9% vs. 4.6%), upper income groups twice as likely as lower income groups (14.1% vs. 7.3%), single students four times as likely as married students (8.9% vs. 2.1%) (but engaged students show greatest use—10.7%), and Atheists and "other religious affiliations reporting much more use (25.0%) than Protestants (4.9%), Catholics (4.8%, and Jews (4.0%). Similar differences occur in the category "less than once a week."

Social class differences are much more pronounced among the females than male students. Among coeds, the proportion smoking marijuana at least once a week rises rapidly from 1.5 per cent among those who come from families with annual incomes under $12,000 to 13.1 per cent from families with incomes of $20,000 or more. No statistically significant social class differences are found among the male students. In general, our analysis by demographic characteristics would support the findings of others that marijuana smoking is not, like the use of narcotics, linked to a lower income sub-culture.

THE "HANG-LOOSE" ETHIC:
BEHAVIORAL CORRELATES

Our primary hypothesis has been that drug use is only one aspect of the more general "happening" scene and reflects a broad range of other "anti-establishment" behaviors. Support for this hypothesis comes from our finding that drug use varies considerably according to such activities as participating in "happenings" (34.3% drug

users among those who participate frequently vs. 17.0% among those who do so rarely), reading "underground" newspapers (42.0% users among frequent readers vs. 3.7% among non-readers), and participating in mass protests (45.9% among those who have done so more than twice vs. 15.2% for non-participators). It appears from these results that drug use in the form of smoking marijuana is highly associated with "non-conformist" behavior.

If we look at the student's cumulative grade as an index of his academic behavior, we see that drug use is more likely to occur among the poorer than the better students. Among those with an average grade of 3.0 or higher, only 15.3 per cent report the use of drugs as compared to 31.0 per cent among those with an average of 2.5 or less. The difference in grade probably represents one more manifestation of the rejection of the "hard work–success" ethic of conventional society.

THE "HANG-LOOSE" ETHIC:
ATTITUDINAL CORRELATES

Similar differences in frequency of drug use are found in relation to a wide range of educational, political, and social attitudes and values indicative of a rejection of the established order. Drug use is more likely to be reported by those students who are relatively antagonistic to the educational system and who are dissatisfied with the education they are receiving. For example, among those students who disagree with the statement, "American colleges today should place more emphasis on teaching American ideals and values," more than seven times as many are frequent smokers of marijuana than among those who agree (13.8% vs. 1.8%). Similarly, whereas 30.2 per cent of those students who "often" feel that what they are learning is a waste of time smoke marijuana, only 12.9 per cent of those who don't feel this way do so. However drug use does not mean "apathy" toward academic life—more smokers of marijuana are to be found among those students who believe that students should have a more active role in making decisions about student life than among those who do not (28.4% vs 11.1%).

On the political scene, drug use is much more likely to occur if the student is opposed to the Vietnam war (37.5% among those favoring immediate military withdrawal vs. 3.0% among those supporting President Johnson's policy). Drug users are also more frequent among those who believe that "human lives are too important to be sacrificed for any form of government" (32.0% vs. 12.6%). Opposition to the draft is another political view associated with drug use. Among those who are opposed to military service, 35.2 per cent use drugs as compared to 15.0 per cent among those who are not opposed, and, in fact, for those male students whose decision to attend college was affected by the possibility of being drafted, 41.7 per cent are drug users as compared to 25.2 per cent among those for whom this was not a consideration.

Social attitudes also reflect this "hang-loose" ethic on the part of drug users. Drug users are more likely to be found among those who feel it is all right to get around the law if you don't actually break it (34.6% vs. 13.8%) and who feel that the "hippie" way of life represents a desire for serious change as opposed to an unproductive expression of non-conformism (26.6% vs. 10.5%). The student who reports that he expects to get the most satisfaction out of life by means of his leisure time recreational activities is a much more frequent user of marijuana than the student who values participation in civic affairs or family relations (45.2% vs. 12.5% and 17.0%). An indication of possible family conflict among drug users is given by the higher proportion of drug users among those students who feel that their parents don't respect their opinions (29.2% vs. 15.3%).

One finding in regard to social attitudes appears contrary to many claims made about drug use. A series of four questions designed to index "alienation" (i.e., "These days a person does not really know whom he can count on"; "If you don't watch yourself, people will take advantage of you") showed no statistically significant relationships to smoking marijuana, despite the claim of Halleck (Time, 1967) that "Smoking marijuana has become almost an emblem of alienation." Given the large number of significant differences found, this lack of any association between drug use and alienation is impressive. The "hang-loose" ethic, while it may represent antagonism to the conventional world, does not appear to create apathy and withdrawal. Subscribers to this ethic are not so much "anomic" in regard to society in general as critical of the existing "Establishment" in specific.

THE "HANG-LOOSE" ETHIC: PERSONALITY CORRELATES

The more the student's self-image tends to be rebellious, cynical, anti-establishment, "hippie," and apathetic, the more likely he is to smoke marijuana. Conversely, the more his self-image tends to be conformist, well-behaved, moral, and "square," the less likely is he to make use of marijuana. The greatest differences are to be found between those students who regard themselves as "hippies" (39% difference in favor of use) or well-behaved (37% difference against use). The smallest differences occur in relation to apathy (8% difference in favor of use) and cynicism (10% difference in favor of use).

These contrasts in self-image between users and non-users are congruent with the previous findings in relation to behavioral and attitudinal correlates. Such attitudes as disrespect for the law and skepticism about the worthwhileness of college, coupled with such behaviors as participating in mass protests and "happenings," match the self-portrait of the marijuana smoker as anti-establishment, cynical, and rebellious. If we view these traits as indicative of an underlying value system, we can quite readily see the contrast in "Protestant" vs. "hang-loose" ethic between marijuana smokers and non-smokers. These self-characterizations do lend face validity to the general public stereotyping of the marijuana smoker as "deviant" and the marijuana's own stereotyping of those who do not use marijuana as "square."

DEMOGRAPHIC CONTROLS

Each of the major differences in behavior, attitudes, and personality between users and non-users of marijuana was examined separately by sex, income, and religious group. Since, for example, males are more likely than females to smoke marijuana and also to subscribe to the "hang-loose" ethic, the possibility exists that both ethic and drug use are reflections of sex and are not really associated in and of themselves.

Analysis of the demographic control tables shows that this, by and large, is not the case. In almost every instance, the differences in marijuana use occur independently for both the demographic control and the behavioral, attitudinal, and personality correlates of the "hang-loose" ethic. In other words, the "hang-loose" ethic continues to be related to marijuana smoking regardless of the sub-group of the student population being studied.

This is illustrated in Table 2, which presents the relationship between several different indices of the "hang-loose" ethic and marijuana use separately for males and females. First, we note that males are more likely than females both to subscribe to the "hang-loose" ethic and to smoke marijuana. Second, we see that for males and females separately, the more the student adheres to the "hang-loose" ethic, either in his or her behavior, attitudes, or personality, the more likely he or she is to smoke marijuana. Thus, we conclude that both sex and ethic contribute independently to marijuana use. This same conclusion appears in general for other demographic variables and for other indices of the "hang-loose" ethic.

We can also see from Table 2, in general, that the relationship between the "hang-loose" ethic and marijuana use is somewhat higher among the males. Also, the differences due to sex are much smaller than those due to variations in behavior, attitudes, or personality. It would thus appear that one's ethic is a more important determinant of marijuana use than one's sex. For example, in all cases, those females who subscribe to the "hang-loose" ethic are much more likely to use marijuana than those males who do not.

ATTITUDE TOWARD USE AND FREQUENCY OF USE BY OTHER STUDENTS

In the same way that we have analyzed the student's use of marijuana according to various correlates of the "hang-loose" ethic, we can also examine his attitudes toward such use and his

Table 2. Relationship between "Hang-Loose" Ethic and Marijuana Use, According to Sex

"Hang-loose" Ethic	*(Per Cent Smoking Marijuana)*			
	Male		Female	
Behavioral				
Participate in mass protests				
No	9.9	(141)	3.8	(212)
Once or twice	12.5	(48)	5.9	(51)
More than twice	40.0	(25)	16.7	(12)
Attend a "happening"				
Rarely	8.6	(116)	2.4	(168)
Occasionally	15.5	(58)	3.7	(82)
Frequently	33.3	(33)	20.8	(24)
Attitudinal				
"It is all right to get around the law, if you don't actually break it."				
Disagree	18.2	(99)	11.3	(168)
Undecided	34.0	(47)	19.0	(63)
Agree	40.3	(62)	26.7	(45)
"How strongly do you approve or disapprove of students having premarital sexual intercourse?"				
Disapprove	0.0	(18)	1.2	(81)
Undecided	26.8	(56)	11.1	(90)
Approve	33.8	(136)	33.3	(102)
Personality				
"Anti-establishment"				
Not at all well	18.0	(111)	12.1	(182)
A little	32.4	(34)	13.2	(38)
Undecided and well	46.9	(64)	32.7	(55)
"Well-behaved"				
Very well	15.6	(32)	4.6	(65)
Fairly well	21.4	(131)	17.8	(185)
Undecided and not well	56.2	(48)	27.6	(29)

reports about how many of the students he knows also smoke marijuana. (Since so few students report feeling any pressure to smoke marijuana, this aspect is omitted from the following analysis.) We present the results of this analysis in a summary fashion in Table 3. With only one exception—the relationship of family income to attitudes to marijuana use—all of the variables listed are significantly related (chi square $p<.05$) to attitudes to use and frequency of use by other students in the same direction as the student's own use of marijuana. That is, the behavioral, attitudinal, and personality correlates of the "hang-loose" ethic also relate to one's attitude toward smoking marijuana and the frequency of marijuana use among the students one knows. These three aspects of attitudes toward use, use by one's friends, and use by oneself, then, all become part of the general picture of marijuana use as such use reflects adherence to the "hang-loose" ethic.

The relative size of the associations (keeping in mind the variations from question to question of the number of answer categories) can be determined in an approximate way from the size of Cramer's V, a coefficient of association (Blalock, 1960:230). Self-image tends to be more highly related than either attitudes or behavior. Sex atti-

Table 3. Relationship Between Attitude to Use of Marijuana, Frequency of Use by Other Students and Selected Characteristics

Student Characteristics[a]	Attitude to Use of Marijuana[b]	Frequency of Use by Other Students[c]	Student Characteristics[a]	Attitude to Use of Marijuana[b]	Frequency of Use by Other Students[c]
Demographic			Social values		
Sex	.14[d]	.19	Approval of pre-marital		
Income	n.s.	.14	sex, if consent	.32	.28
Behavior patterns			Approval of abortion	.22	.20
Attend "happening"	.17	.30	Approval of birth control	.22	.17
Read "underground"			Approval of law-breaking	.15	.14
newspaper	.30	.26	Frequency of other student		
Participate in mass			behaviors		
protest	.16	.20	Drink alcoholic beverages	.15	.19
Self-image			Smoke marijuana	.42	—
"Hippie"	.28	.30	Take LSD	.29	.41
Anti-establishment	.23	.19	Have sexual intercourse	.30	.37
Well-behaved	.23	.22	Attitude to student behaviors		
Educational values			Drink alcoholic beverages	.25	.14
College a waste of time	.16	.16	Smoke marijuana	—	.42
Students active in stu-			Take LSD	.33	.30
dent affairs	.14	.13	Have sexual intercourse	.42	.31
Political values					
Vietnam a mistake	.19	.20			
Human lives not to be					
sacrificed in war	.12	.12			
Conscientious objection					
a loophole	.19	.17			

[a]See previous text for question wording used to determine student characteristics.
[b]Question: "How strongly do you approve or disapprove of students smoking marijuana?" (Strongly Approve, Approve, Undecided, Disapprove, Strongly Disapprove).
[c]Question: "How frequently do most of the students you know smoke marijuana?" (Frequently, Occasionally, Seldom, Never, Don't Know).
[d]Coefficients of association as determined by Cramer's V.

tudes are, in general, more highly related than either political or educational values. Very high associations are to be found among attitudes and behaviors in regard to smoking marijuana, taking LSD, having sexual intercourse, and drinking alcoholic beverages, in about that order.

In summary, this table of associations underscores the interrelationships between attitudes and use, and between the various correlates of the "hang-loose" ethic and such attitudes and use. It is quite clear that the more one's behaviors, attitudes, and personality conform to the "hang-loose" ethic, the more likely one will be to approve of smoking marijuana and the more likely is it that one will associate with other students who smoke marijuana.

Finally, in Table 4, we show the mutual effects of attitude toward smoking marijuana and several aspects of the "hang-loose" ethic upon the use of marijuana. By and large, similar differences are found for all other aspects of the "hang-loose" ethic. As hypothesized, these two variables are independently related to drug use with the most

Table 4. Relationship between "Hang-Loose" Ethic, Attitude Toward Marijuana Use, and Use of Marijuana.

"Hang-Loose" Ethic	*(Per Cent Smoking Marijuana)*	
	Attitude to Use of Marijuana	
	Favorable	*Unfavorable*
Attend a "happening"		
Rarely	31.3 (83)	4.5 (201)
Occasionally	51.9 (54)	11.8 (84)
Frequently	73.5 (34)	25.6 (19)
"It's all right to get around the law, if you don't actually break it."		
Disagree	37.3 (75)	4.7 (191)
Undecided	42.2 (45)	14.3 (61)
Agree	60.4 (48)	14.6 (55)
"Anti-establishment"		
No	39.8 (103)	6.6 (260)
Yes	54.9 (71)	19.3 (47)

frequent use occurring among those students who have both a favorable attitude toward the use of marijuana and an adherence to the "hang-loose" ethic. In general, an unfavorable attitude toward the use of marijuana will be equated with the absence of marijuana smoking. However, even among those with an unfavorable attitude, use will be higher with adherence to the "hang-loose" ethic. Similarly, given a favorable attitude toward use of marijuana, actual use is much more likely to take place among those students displaying "hang-loose" attitudes, behavior, and personality.

On the basis of these interrelationships of demographic characteristics, attitudes, behavior, and personality to drug use, the following sequence or chain of events appears quite probable (although it would require a prospective study to test it); adherence to the "hang-loose" ethic is more likely to occur among certain predisposed personality types (i.e., rebellious, cynical) and in certain social sub-groups (i.e., males, non-religious); such adherence is likely to lead to a favorable attitude toward smoking marijuana both for its "high" effects and its symbolism of rebellion against authority; this favorable attitude will be supported by other students who also embrace the "hang-loose" ethic and engage in similar overt and covert expressions of rejection of the established order. Finally, given this climate of opinion and behavior, the smoking of marijuana becomes almost a "natural" act for many students far removed from the public's current efforts to define it either as a legal or a health problem.

Summary and Discussion

The data presented in this report strongly support the major hypothesis that the more the student embraces the "hang-loose" ethic, the more frequently will he make use of marijuana. Also supported is the further hypothesis that certain social sub-groups such as males will more frequently both smoke marijuana and adhere to the "hang-loose" ethic, but that regardless of group membership, the "hang-loose" ethic will be related to marijuana use. In regard to attitudes toward use, we find, as hypothesized, that the more the student subscribes to the "hang-loose" ethic, the more favorable will he be toward marijuana use; and the more favorable he is, the more will he actually use marijuana. These attitudes toward use and the "hang-loose" ethic become independent factors in marijuana smoking, reinforcing each other with the greatest use occurring among those students with a favorable attitude who also believe in the "hang-loose" ethic. Finally, the student's use of marijuana is strongly supported when his friends also smoke marijuana.

These findings have significance for both sociological theory and social action. From a theoretical point of view, they support the interpretation of drug use as a part of a sub-cultural group way of life. Among students, this sub-culture is strongly characterized by a "hang-loose" ethic which attempts to cut itself loose from the traditional "establishment" and to develop freedom from conformity and the search for new experiences. This culture becomes expressed in such behaviors as attending "happenings," reading underground newspapers, participating in mass protests, avoiding the draft, engaging in sexual intercourse and, very much to the point of this report, smoking marijuana. Such use of marijuana constitutes an important means both of attaining "freedom" from the pressures of society and of expressing antagonism toward the "unfair" laws and restrictions of that society. For such students, marijuana serves much the same function as "social drinking" does for their parents, and their "law breaking" has the same social sanctions as drinking did during Prohibition. And just as "social drinking" is a far cry from "alcoholism," so is smoking marijuana far removed from "narcotics addiction."

The relationship of both social drinking to alcoholism and smoking marijuana to narcotics addiction illustrates a significant interaction between social problems, health problems, and legal problems (Suchman, 1963:58–64). A social act (e.g. one carried out by members of a group as part of the sub-cultural norm of that group) will be labelled a social problem when it conflicts with the accepted norms of the larger society. In this sense, marijuana smoking among students has become a social problem, whereas drinking alcohol has not. The type of corrective action "legitimatized" by the larger society to meet this problem will then determine whether it is viewed as a health or a legal problem. The more the social problem threatens the "value system" of the society, the more likely is it to be labelled a legal as opposed to a health problem and to be assigned to the police rather than the doctor. Restriction and punishment become the means for handling the problem rather than understanding and treatment.

In the absence of any clear-act evidence that (1) marijuana smoking is physiologically addictive or has serious health effects, and (2) use of marijuana leads to crime and delinquency or use of other drugs, it seems premature to view it as either a health or a legal problem. (Mayor's Committee on Marijuana, 1944). Our data would strongly suggest that use of marijuana is predominantly a social act favored by a sub-group in our society which happens to be disenchanted with the established order and for whom such use has become simply a normal preference for their own particular recreational drug. (Simmons, 1967). To crack down on these youth with all of the powerful forces of law and order and to justify such a restriction of freedom in the name of preventing crime or disease seems more an uncontrolled expression of adult moral indignation and righteousness than of human concern or social justice—and, sadly, an ineffective and destructive expression at that. (Lindesmith, 1965). While there can be little question that the "hang-loose" ethic is contrary to the Protestant ethic and the spirit of capitalism, and may be socially disapproved for that and other reasons, the issue, it seems to us, should be openly faced and debated as one of conflicting social values and not of crime or health. As formulated by Simmons (1967:11), "It [the marijuana issue] seems to be the pivot around which far deeper conflicts and confrontations are raging—oldsters versus youngsters, hippies versus straight society, administered morality versus personal freedom."

Surely, it should be possible to express one's disapproval of marijuana and to seek its control without making its use a crime against society.

REFERENCES

BECKER, H. S. 1953. "Becoming a marijuana user." *American Journal of Sociology 59* (November): 235–242.

BLALOCK, HUBERT M. 1960. *Social Statistics.* New York: McGraw-Hill.

GOLDSEN, ROSE K., ET AL. 1960. *What College Students Think.* Princeton: D. Van Nostrand.

JACOB, PHILLIP E. 1957. *Changing Values in College.* New York: Harper and Bros.

LINDESMITH, ALFRED R. 1965. *The Addict and the Law.* Bloomington: The Indiana University Press.

MAYOR'S COMMITTEE ON MARIJUANA. 1944. "The marijuana problem in the City of New York," pp. 233–360 in David Solomon (ed.), *The Marijuana Papers.* Indianapolis: The Bobbs-Merrill Co., 1966. For an excellent analysis of this report see David Arnold, "The meaning of the La Guardia report," pp. 111–135 in Jerry Simmons (ed.), *Marijuana Myths and Realities.* North Hollywood, Calif.: Brandon House, 1967.

MCGLOTHLIN, W. H. 1967. "Toward a rational view of marijuana," pp. 163–214 in Jerry Simmons (ed.), *Marijuana: Myths and Realities.* North Hollywood, Calif.: Brandon House.

PLAUT, THOMAS F. 1967. *Alcohol Problems: A Report of the Nation.* New York: Oxford University Press.

Reader's Digest. 1967. November, 1967.

SIMMONS, JERRY L. (ED.). 1967. *Marijuana: Myths and Realities.* North Hollywood, Calif.: Brandon House.

SIMMONS, JERRY L., AND WINOGRAD, BARRY. 1966. *It's Happening: A Portrait of the Youth Scene Today.* Santa Barbara, Calif.: Marc-Laird Publications.

STRAUS, ROBERT, AND BACON, SELDEN D. 1953. *Drinking in College.* New Haven: Yale University Press.

SUCHMAN, EDWARD A. 1963. *Sociology and the Field of Public Health.* New York: Russell Sage Foundation.

SUCHMAN, E. 1963. "The addictive diseases as socio-environmental health problems," pp. 123–143 in H. Freeman, et al. (eds.), *Handbook of Medical Sociology.* Englewood Cliffs, N. J.: Prentice-Hall, Inc.

Time. 1967. May 19, 1967.

Teenage Drinking and Drug Use

RONALD L. AKERS

The author presents data concerning trends and variations in the use of alcohol and drugs by adolescents. He discusses current theories regarding the causes and significance of youths' drug and drinking habits and the social problems related to this behavior.

Introduction

Whether some set of circumstances or the behavior of some members of society constitute social problems depends upon from whose perspective they are viewed. For somewhat different reasons, drinking alcohol and taking drugs are among the kinds of behavior of adolescents that the adult community and authorities define as deviant. Young people may not define doing things proscribed by adult authority as major social problems. However, in American society, adolescence is a relatively powerless social status, and it is the adult's view that prevails. Drinking by teenagers is deviant only because such behavior is reserved for adults in our society; drug use is deviant because it is prohibited for the young and old alike.

This difference notwithstanding, both adolescent drug use and drinking continue to occupy top positions in the list of adult concerns about their children, and many of the same questions continue to be asked about both problems. How much is there? Who is doing it? Why do they do it? Are those who drink alcohol or use drugs more likely to commit other delinquent acts? What changes have taken place through the years? Is the situation getting worse or better? What can be done about the problem? The purpose here is to examine empirical evidence on and theoretical explanations of teenage drinking and drug use in an attempt to furnish some answers to these questions. The first section summarizes some data on the epidemiology, extent, trends, and variations in these two types of adolescent behavior. The second section points to some questions deserving further research and offers some comments and suggestions on public policy relating to use of alcohol and drugs by adolescents.

Epidemiology of Teenage Drinking and Drug Use

DRUG USE

The various substances that are included in the drug problem fall into five major categories. The two major types are: the *opiates*, including principally heroin and morphine and opiate-like synthetics such as demerol and dolophine, and *hallucinogens,* including primarily marihuana and LSD. Others are: *depressants,* such as barbiturates, *stimulants,* such as the amphetamines and cocaine; and *deliriants,* such as airplane glue and aerosol sprays. Of these, the opiates invariably and the depressants sometimes produce physiological addiction. The others may be used habitually, but they do not produce physiological dependence. The epidemiological information presented here related basically to the opiates and hallucinogens.

Adolescent drug use in this century was very small until after World War II. In the nineteenth century, opiate users and addicts were most likely to be rural, white, middle-class females, and the average age at first addiction was between 35 and 40 (Brown, 1966; Marshall, 1966). In the twentieth century, thanks largely to a changed enforcement policy which made the major source of drug supply through illegal channels, opiate use began to be concentrated among urban, lower-class, non-white, and delinquent or criminal males (Lindesmith, 1967, pp. 130–132; Lindesmith & Gagnon, 1964, pp. 163–167). The average age of first use and addiction remained well above adolescence, however, throughout the 1930s (Winick, 1965, pp. 7–9). Until this time marihuana use was virtually unknown in this country; it was confined to lower-class Mexican-Americans in the Southwest. In the 1930s marihuana use began to spread among young adult men, mainly lower-class Negroes and jazz musicians, and then began to trickle down to younger groups. Starting after World War II and continuing into the early 1950s, marihuana and heroin spread through the ghettoes and slums of northern large cities. During this time, official statistics and hospital admissions reflected a dramatic drop in the ages of users and addicts. Adolescense became a common age at which drug use began. But the youthful drug users of both heroin and marihuana were almost exclusively lower-class slum dwellers, although even in these areas the majority of the teenagers did not smoke marihuana and probably no more than 10 percent used heroin. Moreover, the trend toward increased drug use among adolescents began to taper off in the mid-fifties; in the late 1950s, the average age of drug users began to rise again (Winick, 1965, pp. 7–9; Ausubel, 1958, pp.

63, 93–94; Kobrin & Finestone, 1968; Bates, 1966, p. 66; Blum, 1967, p. 48; Lindesmith, 1967, pp. 237–239).

The increased number of adolescent opiate users was never enough to bring the average age of addicts down to the teenage years; it was enough to ensure that the typical opiate addict became and remains today a young adult. Opiate use has been and remains concentrated in the large urban centers of population (Ball & Cottrell, 1965, p. 473; Ball & Bates, 1966, p. 59; O'Donnell & Ball, 1966, p. 9). Further, it is concentrated in the slums, in the poorest, most deprived, most crowded, and unstable neighborhoods, and among members of minority ethnic groups and others at the bottom of the socioeconomic scale (Blum, 1967, pp. 49–50; Chein, 1965, pp. 109–112; Chein, 1966, pp. 123–125; Chein et al., 1964, pp. 45–74; Winick, 1965, pp. 10–16; Kobrin & Finestone, 1968, pp. 114–115).

Marihuana use developed differently. Although it continues to be done in the same slum environment with heroin, marihuana smoking has become increasingly an activity of young, middle-class and upper-class whites. Starting in the early 1960s marihuana became the chief drug, along with LSD, in the psychedelic drug movement. The "classic" hippie groups were comprised mainly of young adults, but they were recruited from the college-aged and college-oriented children of the affluent. Subsequently, marihuana use appears to have spread among these well-to-do older adolescents and young adults, and then to have moved from college to high school to junior high school. In addition to marihuana and LSD, a variety of other drugs and combinations are used; speed and other amphetamines (stimulants), barbiturates (depressants), and a range of hallucinogenic drugs.

That drug use has increased among adolescents in recent years is evident; but just what proportions it has reached is virtually unknown. Arrests of persons under 21 for possession of marihuana have gone up at a rate far in excess of adult drug arrests, and most of the increase is accounted for by arrests of whites (Carey, 1968, pp. 44–46). Estimates in 1965 placed the number of college students who had experimented with marihuana at 10 to 11 percent (Blum, 1967, p. 24; Young & Hixson, 1966, p. 76). In a study of five California campuses, it was found that 21 percent of the students in 1967 and 57 percent in 1968 had smoked marihuana at least once; 4 percent in 1967 and 14 percent in 1968 reported themselves as regular smokers (*Newsweek*, 1969). Informal surveys on various college campuses during 1967 and 1968 found from about 6 percent to 30 percent of the undergraduates smoked marihuana at least once and 1 percent to 15 percent had tried LSD. A 1967 Gallup Poll among a representative sample of college students found only 6 percent reporting one or more marihuana experiences (Louria, 1968, pp. 8–12). This does not constitute very full knowledge of drug use among college-age people, but even less is known about drug use among high school-aged youth; the estimates of the percentage of high school and junior high school students who have smoked marihuana or taken LSD range all the way from 5 percent to 90 percent, depending upon whether one asks school officials or the students. A survey taken in Long Island, New York schools found 8 percent of the students had used marihuana and 2 percent had used LSD. A study in San Francisco high schools reported 20 percent of the students had smoked marihuana one or more times (Louria, 1968, p. 10). In another study of marihuana use among high school seniors in three California schools only about 10 percent (16 percent of the boys and 4 percent of the girls) reported having ever smoked marihuana (Mauss, 1969).

DRINKING

The research evidence on teenage drinking is much clearer and leaves little doubt that most people in this country will have had alcoholic beverages by the time they are adults. It is also evident that the vast majority of the drinkers, both as adolescents and as adults, are moderate, social drinkers. Neither adult nor underage drinking is a matter of random individual variation; both vary in socially patterned ways by age, sex, religion, region, community, and social class.

Until the first part of this century, drinking was a pastime of the minority of the population; the overwhelming majority of drinkers were men who typically consumed relatively large quantities of hard liquor and did most of their drinking in public saloons. In the past 60 years, however, the quantity taken at any one sitting and the per capita consumption of absolute alcohol have decreased; beer has taken the place of spirit alcohol as the most popular beverage alcohol. A larger portion of the drinkers are women. More of the drinking is now done in private homes. A greater proportion of the population drink, but the typical pattern is now social drinking in moderation. Only about 6 percent of the drinkers are alcoholics (McCarthy, 1964). Studies of adults have consistently found that about 75 percent of the men and 60 percent of the women drink alcohol to some extent. About 20 percent of the males and 5 percent of the females are frequent or heavy drinkers. The highest proportions in all categories of drinkers, from light to heavy, occur in the early 20's to late 30's age range (Riley & Marden, 1959; Mulford, 1964; Cahalan *et al.*, 1967).

The place of underage drinking in this picture was not known until the 1940s. Questionnaire survey studies done at that time found that a little over 40 percent of the adolescent boys and less than 30 percent of the girls were drinking at least sometimes (McCarthy, 1959). Although there are regional variations (ranging from around 25 percent in the South to 90 percent in the Northeast), studies since then have consistently found that the majority of high school students have had alcohol to drink at least once, and an average of about half of the boys and about one-fourth of the girls have established at least an occasional pattern of drinking (Baur & McCluggage, 1958; Maddox & McCall, 1964; Maddox, 1964; MacKay *et al.*, 1967; Slater, 1952; McCarthy, 1959; Windham *et al.*, 1967).

These studies agree that as one passes through the teenage years, the probability that he will drink continues to increase. The majority of the boys and a sizeable minority of the girls will have had drinking experience by the time of high school graduation; by late adolescence the proportion of drinkers equals or exceeds the overall adult rate (Straus & Bacon, 1962). The proportion of teenage users increases with community size. Those from Protestant families are less likely to be drinkers than those from Catholic or Jewish families. The findings on the relationship between social class and teenage drinking are not entirely consistent, but probably the most accurate picture is that the lowest rates of use are found in the middle-level status groups and the higher rates in the upper and lower strata (Baur & McCluggage, 1958; Maddox, 1964; Maddox & McCall, 1964).

DRUGS, DRINKING, AND DELINQUENCY

Besides drinking of alcohol being one traditional reason why juveniles are taken into custody, the evidence is fairly clear that there is a connection between drinking and other delinquent behavior. Comparisons of high school students and institutionalized delinquents have invariably shown that a higher proportion of the officially adjudicated delinquents are drinkers; moreover, although the percentages are relatively small in either case, institutionalized adolescents are more likely to be heavy and problem drinkers. The delinquent youths start drinking at an early age, their parents are more likely to be drinkers, and they are more likely to have friends who drink (Nelson, 1968; MacKay, Phillips, & Bryce, 1967; MacKay, 1963; Blacker *et al.*, 1965). These findings are confirmed when abstainers, drinkers, and problem drinkers are compared on unofficial, self-reported delinquency involvement; the highest percentage of those scoring high in delinquency involvement is among "problem" drinkers and the lowest percentage is among those who do not drink (Globetti & Windham, 1967, pp. 150–155).

The relationship between drug use and the commission of other delinquent and illegal acts by adolescents has not been subject to the same systematic attention as that between drinking and delinquency. Research has shown that opiate addiction in adults is related to commission of income-producing crimes (but not violent crimes), and presumably this would hold for juveniles (O'Donnell, 1966). One study done in Chicago in the early 1950s supports this contention, finding most adolescent drug users to engage in other forms of delinquency, although the delinquent acts both preceded and followed drug use (Kobrin & Finestone, 1968). There are no substantial relationships between use of other drugs and commission of delinquent acts.

SUMMARY OF EPIDEMIOLOGY OF DRINKING AND DRUG USE

Opiate use among young people is still disproportionately a phenomenon of the urban slums and ghettoes where it is part of a drug-oriented subculture. The rate of opiate use among the whole adolescent population is relatively small and appears to have leveled off and remained relatively stable for the past 15 years. On the other hand, alcohol is the most frequently used intoxicating substance among teenagers; although its use is subject to systematic variations, it is known to some extent throughout all regions, communities, social classes, and ethnic groups. Hallucinogenic and other non-opiate drugs occupy an intermediate position between opiates and alcohol. They are used in the same slum subculture as opiates, but are certainly not confined to this setting. In fact, the increased prevalence of their use has come about as a result of the upsurge among affluent, middle and upper status youth. Marihuana use has not yet reached the proportions of drinking; its increase is largely confined to affluent, college-oriented teenagers in the metropolitan areas of the north and the east and west coasts and is virtually unknown in some areas. But if present trends continue, marihuana will come to compete with alcohol as the favorite intoxicant of teenagers.

The positive relationship between drinking and delinquency has been fairly well-established; property offenses are related to opiate addiction, but the relationship between use of other drugs and delinquency is unknown at this time.

Sociological Theories of Alcohol and Drug Behavior among Adolescents

GENERAL SOCIOLOGICAL ORIENTATION

The general sociological view of drinking and drug behavior is that they are responses to sociocultural and group influences. Both conforming the deviant use of alcohol and drugs are social phenomena, products of the general culture, and the more specific groups and social situations with which individuals are confronted. There are systematic variations in cultural traditions and systems of social control with regard to drugs and alcohol from one society to another and over time. The extent and nature of drug use and addiction, drinking and alcoholism in different societies around the world and through history reflect variations in customs and laws. Within the same society one will be subject to differential group and cultural influence depending upon his social status-roles and group memberships as defined by his location in the age, sex, socio-economic, religious, occupational, ethnic, and other systems in society. Thus, the differences in the functions served by alcohol, the way it is used and integrated into eating, ceremonial, social, and other contexts, and the rates of alcoholism reflect different cultural traditions. The community in which one lives, his location within that community, his family, class, religion, and other membership and reference groups all expose him to certain cultural and subcultural orientations toward drugs and alcohol. What he does with and thinks about these substances then will be affected by these orientations. (The best introductory overview of this general sociological perspective on *alcohol* is in Pittman (1967), Clinard (1968, pp. 388–444), Pittman and Snyder (1962), and Straus (1966). As applied to *drugs* in a general way see Ausubel (1958, pp. 57–67).)

NORM QUALITIES

One factor in the impact that the socio-cultural milieu has on alcohol and drug related behavior is the *quality or type* of norms to which one is exposed by his reference groups (groups with which he identified whether or not he is a member). Early studies of religious norms and drinking practices found that those who identified with religions that strongly prohibited drinking were less likely to start drinking, but those who did begin were more likely to become problem drinkers than were those identified with religions that permitted moderate imbibing (Mizruchi & Perruci, 1962; Skolnick, 1958).

Building upon these studies, Larsen and Abu-Laban identified three types of drinking norms: *proscriptive,* abstinence norms that prohibit any drinking; *prescriptive,* norms that permit drinking, but that provide definite guidelines and limits

on acceptable drinking; and *nonscriptive,* vague, incomplete, permissive norms that neither prohibit nor provide adequate guidelines for proper drinking. They found that regardless of the reference group (parents, family, friends, religion, and co-workers) the highest percentage of drinkers was found among those who had been exposed to prescriptive norms, and the highest percentage of heavy drinkers were found among those who had been exposed to vague, nonscriptive drinking standards (Larsen & Abu-Laban, 1968).

These studies have been on adult drinking patterns, and their implication for teenage drinking or drug use has not been made clear. It would seem, however, that the norm-quality explanation would predict that teenagers whose reference groups carry proscriptive or nonscriptive norms concerning alcohol or drugs are not apt to use either, but if they do the probability is higher than for those from prescriptive milieux that they will become heavy drinkers or habitual drug users. Unfortunately, no one has yet examined this proposition in the context of drug use. There is research relevant to norm-qualities and teenage drinking, but the findings have not been entirely consistent (see Preston, 1969; Globetti, 1967; Alexander, 1967).

TEENAGE DRINKING AND DRUG USE: ADOLESCENT REBELLION OR IMITATION

Perhaps the most common explanation of teenage drinking or drug use is that they are forms of "adolescent rebellion" and alienation from adult patterns; this view is countered by that which sees them as the result of adolescent "imitation" of adult patterns. Sometimes both explanations are presented together. For instance, Straus notes that some young people drink to symbolize a negative break with family and religion, but that most teenage drinking is simply the outcome of positive identification with family, peers, and other groups supportive of drinking. Adolescents tend both to press for adult status and to reject restrictions against their drinking (Straus, 1966, pp. 253–255). As long as the argument is presented in this way, that some teenage behavior is rebellion and some is imitation, the two explanations are not necessarily contradictory. However, insofar as claims are made that *most* teenage drinking and drug taking results from one and not the other, the two theories can be seen as competing explanations.

The "rebellion" theory is that adolescents resent adult authority which proscribes drugs and alcohol for them. They get alienated from and rebel against the conventional system represented by their parents, the law, religion and the school system. Alcohol and drugs then are turned to as ways of expressing that rebellion; in so doing they are supported by peer group pressures and norms which are contrary to the expectations of the adult system. Thus, using drugs or alcohol are right by peer group standards because they are wrong by adult standards.

The "imitations" argument is that alcohol and/ or drugs are an integral part of our society and their use by teenagers is just one way of attempting to behave as adults do and become incorporated into society. Thus, they do not reject so much as they emulate or imitate adult patterns. It is an exercise in anticipatory socialization into adult status and runs counter to adult expectations only in that it is done at an inappropriate or premature age.

The rebellion versus imitation views with regard to drinking are obviously related to the studies on norm qualities. The finding that those whose drinking is positively sanctioned by prescriptive norms are more likely to drink, and in some cases to drink more frequently, suggests that drinking in this context is the natural outcome of socialization into adult normative drinking patterns. On the other hand, the finding that proscriptive injunctions are related to heavy drinking suggests that faced with total abstinence norms, some will rebel, break the traces of prohibition, and become alienated from the groups that are the sources of these norms.

Thus, Globetti (1967) and Alexander (1967), both of whom conducted studies of teenage drinking in abstinence settings, support the adolescent rebellion theory. Alexander maintains that drinking "may represent an expression of hostility toward the normative authority of the total society," or against an individual who has authority (1967, p. 543).

Globetti's study did not reveal any relationship between parent–child relations and drinking, but it did show that:

. . . drinkers may be characterized as higher in deviance than non-drinkers as indicated by their participation in mild forms of deviant behavior, by their pessimism and by their rejection of middle-class values. In addition, they appear to be estranged from such important socialization groups as the family, the school, the church, and the community. The users identified in this study, so the data suggest, seem to be teenagers with problems. Their drinking appears to be an expression of rebellion or hostility toward the normative authority of the community. (Globetti, 1967, p. 132).

This notion of rebellious youth engaging in anti-authority activities supported by a peer-group culture has also been applied to teenage drug taking. Ausubel, for instance, labels adolescent drug use "reactive addiction" and places it in the same category as truancy, use of alcohol and tobacco, and reckless driving in that:

. . . it is expressive of a general anti-adult orientation characterized by defiance of traditional norms and conventions and flouting of adult-imposed taboos and authority.

Like other forms of adolescent rebellion, reactive addiction is generated and propagated through peer groups. (Ausubel, 1958, p. 51).

Louria, likewise, pictures drug taking by young people as a reaction against what they perceive to be an inept, self-serving system; the estrangement takes the forms of both open rebellion and alienation and is characteristic of the hippies, ghetto minorities, and affluent youth alike (Louria, 1968, pp. 24–27). On the basis of research in the Berkeley, college-related drug scene, Carey argues that the first step into drug use is a strong sense of disillusionment and alienation from conventional society which is seen as basically hypocritical (Carey, 1968, pp. 48–49).

The distinctive dress and grooming styles that many young people display today, the problems of inter-generational conflict, the discontinuities wrought by rapid social change in the cultural atmosphere in which parents were reared and that in which they attempt to rear their own children, the flouting of adult rules, and many other matters of differences between generations would seem to underscore the rebellion of youth against the adult system in general and parents in particular. This impression has become particularly salient with the insertion into the rhetoric of youthful protesters of phrases indicating the corruption, hypocrisy, and inequities of the "establishment" manned by adults. Using proscribed substances may be one way of showing they want no part of it. At the same time, it is clear that the majority of adolescents are not in open revolt against either their parents or adult authority, and some theorists have argued that the youngster's indulgence or abstinence may simply reflect the interplay of various positive influences, with authority rejection playing little or no part.

For instance, Maddox and McCall, while not denying that peer group settings are the occasions for much drinking, label as a myth the notion that the "youth culture" of peers places irresistible pressure on the abstaining youth to drink. Furthermore, even peer-group drinking is more an emulation rather than rejection of adult patterns (Maddox & McCall, 1964, pp. 3–8; see also McKay, 1965, pp. 3–4). Their major contention, supported by their research findings, is that, in general, teenage drinking is expressive of identification with an anticipatory socialization into adult behavior (Maddox & McCall, 1965, pp. 77–98).

> . . . Drinking may be used as a test of loyalty to peer groups precisely because it is discouraged by adults. The contrary evidence, however, is compelling. The probability of alcohol use increases with age, i.e., as assumption of adult roles is approached. There is a demonstrated relationship between the drinking behavior of parents and their offspring . . . a majority of adolescents in our society would in all probability come to use beverage alcohol eventually even if there were no peer group experience at all since young people tend to perceive some drinking as an integral part of normal adult behavior. The emphasis of this evidence overwhelmingly favors adolescent identification with adulthood, rather than hostility to adult goals or authority. (Maddox & McCall, 1964, p. 7).

The idea that drug use like alcohol use by teenagers may also be more in the nature of modeling behavior after, rather than rejecting, convention-

al society is presented succintly by Simon and Gagnon:

> These new patterns of marijuana use . . . must be seen in terms of their continuity with general trends in contemporary American culture. One of these trends . . . is the fact that we have become as a nation, a population of pill-takers. Both the actual miracle and the myth of modern medicine have made the use of drugs highly legitimate, as something to be taken casually and not only during moments of acute and certified distress. Our children, in being casual about drugs . . . far from being in revolt against an older generation, may in fact be acknowledging how influential a model that generation was. (Simon & Gagnon, 1968, p. 60).

Or as Louria says, "If young persons see their parents egregiously misusing and overusing drugs is it any wonder that they should become part of the youthful drug cult?" (Louria, 1968, p. 17).

As Maddox and McCall point out, the evidence with regard to drinking beverage alcohol is that the bulk of teenage drinking is very much a matter of copying adult models. Peer groups are also important influences, but they function to undergird and support parental models.

In general, the variations in frequency, amount, and type of teenage drinking patterns by sex, religion, region, and community reflect fairly faithfully the pattern variations of the adult community. More specifically, the most accurate predictor of what the teenager does with and thinks about alcohol, is the attitudes and behavior of his parents. The abstainer is most likely to come from an abstaining home; the moderate drinker from a home in which the parents drink moderately; and the heavy drinker from homes in which heavy drinking has been the pattern (Maddox, 1964). Moreover, a sizeable portion of the drinking teenagers report that their first drinking experience and some current drinking occurs at home with parental approval. Maddox and McCall found that among those who have tasted alcohol, more than half the boys and two-thirds of the girls report that the occasion for this tasting included parents or other adult relatives. Next to parents, adolescent peer group influences are most important. But they appear not to function as counter-normative groups forcing the abstainer to drink; they do provide the occasions and setting for unsupervised drinking without parental approval. Peer group settings for drinking are more important for boys than for girls; the girls who drink at all tend more frequently than boys to drink at home and less frequently than boys to drink in clandestine, peer-only groups. The salience of drinking as a mark of "coming of age," symbolization of and rite of passage into adult status, and the general association of drinking with adult status is evidenced by the frequency with which adolescents attribute drinking by their peers to be for reasons of trying to act "smart" or "grown-up." (Maddox & McCall, 1964; Maddox, 1963; Ullman, 1962; Slater, 1952).

Unfortunately, the studies of drug use by adolescents have not investigated the impact of parental and adult influence in the same way that studies of drinking have. Some general and tentative observations can be made, however, concerning the extent to which teenage drug use is rebellion against or reflects positive adult influence in the way in which teenage drinking does.

There can be little question that we live in both a "cocktail" and a "pill-taking" culture; it is possible then that teenage drug use as well as teenage drinking is due to the positive identification of adolescents with the model provided by society. However, there are some essential differences at this point in history in the way in which American society is alcohol-oriented and the way in which it is drug-oriented. These differences would argue that the imitation of adult model explanation seems at this time to fit drinking better than it does drug use.

Alcohol is widely available to and used openly by adults. It is openly advertised, sold, and regularly stocked in many homes. Drinking for social, pleasurable, and recreational purposes is integrally incorporated as a nondeviant part of our culture. With adults, only its misuse or abuse is uniformly condemned. Its moderate use is denied only to minors, and even then, only the law is uniform on this point; many adults do not vigorously object to adolescent's drinking although they may consider it premature. Since it is associated primarily with adult role behavior, drinking alcohol serves well to symbolize the aspiration and attainment of adulthood. One does not reject a pattern by copying it. Only in completely abstinent family–religion settings does drinking serve well as an expression of adolescent rebellion.

On the other hand, the drugs that the teenagers are using are not legal nor socially approved even for adults. In fact, adults of the generation who are parents of teenagers typically know less about drugs, are more convinced of their undesirability, and are less likely to use drugs than their children. They are supported in the general negative connotations attached to drugs and those who use them by established religion, schools, and law enforcement. In a sense, most teenagers find themselves in the same sort of abstinent milieu with respect to drugs that some find themselves in with respect to alcohol.

It is true that youngsters see adults taking drugs. But the example of drug use among adults must be qualified by the fact that it is nearly always done, at least justified, within a medical context, either under medical supervision or self-medication. Adults do not normally use drugs solely for non-medical purposes; mood-changing drugs are used, but their use purely for sociability, recreation, or pleasure is not accepted nor regularly praticed. Non-medicinal use of drugs is not incorporated as a non-deviant practice in our society; their medicinal use is acceptable for adult and child alike. For these reasons, drugs would seem to serve poorly as symbols of adult status, but serve well as symbolic of "our thing" and rebellion against the adult establishment among adolescents.

It may be, however, that teenage drug taking is learned from adult models in different ways. The alienating shortcomings of the system which are often cited were not perceived by some sort of magic by the youth; rather they have been cataloged and broadcast by adults. Today's youth were not born with greater knowledge and insight into the true nature of drugs than their parents: rather they have had the benefit of years of serious research and study by medical and social scientists, who have pointed up the misrepresentations, hoaxes, and outright lies about drugs propagated for so many years by law enforcement and the mass media. Moreover, the psychedelic drug movement is not now and never has been confined to college and high school youth. Middle-class adults also are and have been involved; in fact, have been leaders in the movement. The praises of LSD, marihuana, mescaline, and other drugs were first sung by adults, ably abetted by the same mass media that earlier had propagandized against drugs, long before adolescents took up the cry. Some of these adults have been middle-aged, but by and large, they have been adults of a generation somewhat younger than the parents of teenagers. They have nonetheless proven able mentors and models for the young to emulate. (For two excellent discussions of the influence of adults on young people in this sense see Simon and Gagnon (1968) and Louria (1968, pp. 38–45).)

There is already some evidence that marihuana use among high school students is in part a function of anticipatory socialization into college life style (Mauss, 1969). It would seem that in the future, adult users will more and more simply be those who continue the social use of drugs such as marihuana learned in high school and college today in much the same way that persons have learned to use alcohol. The major differences in social acceptability of marihuana and alcohol in society as a whole today can be expected gradually to lessen and disappear as the current adolescents and young adults come to be the definers of morality. Thus, marihuana (and perhaps other drugs) may come to find a place in society analogous to alcohol—social-pleasurable use acceptable for adults and legally denied to minors who will nonetheless engage in drug practices learned primarily from parents and peers.

Differential Association-Reinforcement

The author previously has collaborated on the formulation of a general social learning theory of deviant behavior to which the label "differential association-reinforcement" has been given (Burgess & Akers, 1966). It has been used to analyze opiate use, addiction, and relapse, and use of hallucinogenic drugs (Akers *et al.,* 1968; Akers, 1969). Space precludes a full explanation of this theory as applied to the combined problem of teenage drinking and drug use. Therefore, what follows should be seen as a suggestive outline, rather than a fully documented and tightly reasoned analysis.

The basic contention is that use or non-use of alcohol and drugs is a normally learned (conditioned) response which is shaped by the patterns of (primarily social) reinforcements and involves exposure to normative definitions favorable or unfavorable to use through association with both users and non-users. All of the theories discussed above are consistent with this approach for each implicitly or explicitly assumes that social learning is the basic process in teenagers coming to drink or use drugs. The quality of norms, reference groups, and the rules and authority of the adult community against which an anti-adult teenage culture may be opposed or which teenage behavior imitates, all constitute various conditions and contingencies comprising the environment in which drug and drinking behavior is learned. The differential association-reinforcement theory attempts to indicate the learning process that one undergoes in this environment in becoming a user.

This explanation of pre- and non-addictive drug use has been summarized as follows:

. . . before one will first try a drug he must: (1) find the drug available or learn how to obtain it, and (2) learn and apply either positive or neutralizing definitions to its use. He will not continue beyond the first experimental experience unless he (3) learns to take the drug properly for optimal effect, (4) either finds the effects intrinsically rewarding or learns to define the effects as desirable, and/or (5) obtains other social rewards contingent upon taking the drug . . . such that rewards for use are frequent and great enough to offset the negative consequences of use and the rewards for alternative behavior. (Akers, 1969, p. 79).

It is contended here that such a process, although the substance of what is learned is different, is also operative in non-pathological drinking. Addictive drug behavior is "escape–avoidance" behavior which develops with opiate (and sometimes barbiturates) when one learns that he must take the drug to alleviate or avoid withdrawal distress. Addictive drinking would seem to be the same kind of escape behavior.

Availability and acquisition of ability to take drugs or drink alcohol are fairly obvious steps.

For most adolescents availability of alcohol presents no real problems; it abounds in our society. Certain kinds of drugs, marihuana and mild hallucinogens, are becoming more readily available, although through illegal channels. Drinking or taking pills require no special ability; one need only swallow. But smoking marihuana properly and the effective use of the hypodermic and related apparatus do require some ability. The other steps in the process require fuller comment.

Even if drugs or alcohol are available, one is not likely to avail himself of them if he does not see drinking or drug use as a permissible, desirable, or positively rewarding experience that he would want to undergo or if he does not see it as relatively safe, not as bad as some say, worth the risk, or justifiable on some ground. Teenagers raised in a prescriptive drinking environment learn from parents, peers, and other groups that social drinking is an acceptable, positive experience for adults and that within limits it is permissible for minors. Or they may learn essentially neutral definitions of alcohol; it is something that one may try or not as he pleases. The situation is similar for those whose initial introduction to drugs is through a drug-oriented subculture of one kind or another; they may learn positive definitions of drugs as cool or exciting. By the time they reach adolescence, then, these people have few moral or personal obstacles to overcome in taking the first drink, pill, or fix.

For most, though, the first thing that is learned about drugs is that they are dangerous and that their non-medical use is morally abhorrent. Even in a prescriptive environment, one is also apt to first encounter negative definitions of underage drinking; it is all right for adults, but kids should leave it alone. In proscriptive religious, family, and community settings, he learns that drinking alcohol is bad for everybody. Before one who learns these views will try drugs or alcohol he must neutralize or replace them with definitions favorable to use; that is, drinking (or using drugs) is bad only if you get a habit and I can control it; they lied about it; lots of people do it and it doesn't hurt them; and so on. The teenager may learn these counter definitions through association or identification with groups other than those in which he received his initial socialization. These may be adults or they may be groups of peers and friends who provide him with rationales for rejecting his earlier learning.

Through the application of such positive, permissive, or rationalizing definitions one gets to the point of experimenting with drugs or alcohol. Whether he will continue to use them depends upon the consequences of his drinking or drug experiences. If the drug or alcohol effects one experiences and/or the reactions of others who are present or know about his taking them are rewarding, he will continue; if they are unpleasant or unrewarding, he will not.

For the majority of adolescents the actual or expected sanctions from parents, friends, and law enforcement in reaction to their drug taking are most likely to be negative; for many this is also the most likely reaction to their drinking. They are not, therefore, apt to try or to continue using drugs or alcohol. For the others, using one or the other of these substances is a way of gaining acceptance, approval, recognition, and other social rewards. In neither case is the non-user aggressively enticed or forced to become a user, but the positive social sanctions of peer groups of friends are very important social reinforcers for both drinking and taking of drugs. In addition to this peer group support, the adolescent reared in a prescriptive or permissive drinking environment may receive various overt and subtle signs of approval (or lack of disapproval) from adults for his drinking. It is through such social reinforcement that one learns to find the use itself rewarding. The initial effects of alcohol or drugs may be intrinsically enjoyable, but for the most part enjoyment of either is a socially acquired taste. Typically one has received prior socialization into what he is supposed to experience; thus, if he has learned to expect what he takes to taste good or produce enjoyable effects, any intrinsic pleasure is likely to be heightened or he will interpret the effects, whatever they are, as pleasurable. For many, however, initial effects are anything but pleasant; the beverage or the smoke may taste or smell bad; he may get sick; the intoxication or high may be frightening. Some will keep up use, nonetheless, sustained entirely by the social rewards contingent upon continuation. But most of those who continue will become conditioned to enjoy the effects and the pleasurable reactions to taking drugs or alcohol will be combined with social reinforcement to sustain further use. As long as these rewards are forthcoming to a greater extent than they would be for alternative behavior and are not offset by current or expected aversive consequences, use will continue.

Concluding Remarks: Teenage Drinking and Drug Use as Sociological and Social Problems

It should be noted here that further research needs to be done to determine to what extent the foregoing analysis is capable of accuracy accounting for adolescent behavior of this kind. In general, more research needs to be done on drugs of the type that has been conducted on teenage drinking among representative samples of the adolescent population. Research on both drinking and drugs should pay more attention to securing out-of-school samples. It is also important that further analysis and research attempt to study the two problems together. Despite the fact that similar questions are asked about and similar explanations are given for the two, they are most often considered separately. (One instance in which the two are at least discussed within the same article is Pollack (1966).) For this reason, there are some significant questions concerning the relationship between the use of drugs and the use of alcohol by adolescents for which good answers are unavailable and to which future research should be directed. What are the differences and similarities in the way drugs and alcohol are viewed by the same sample of persons of this age group? How similar or different are the social and physical settings and occasions in which alcohol and drugs are used? Is the current prevalence of drug use the same as, greater than, or less than alcohol use among adolescents? Does more drug use mean less, more, or no change in the teenage consumption of alcohol? Does the introduction of drugs in a significant way in recent years mean that the teenage population can be divided into identifiable social types with regard to their use or non-use of alcohol and drugs—the "straights" or "squares" who use neither; the "mixers" who use both; the "boozers" or drinkers who use only alcohol; and the "druggies" or "heads" who use only drugs? What are the relative numbers in each of these categories? To what extent are the motivations and learning patterns similar for consumption of alcohol and drugs?

To this point, we have been mainly concerned with this kind of adolescent behavior as a sociological problem—something to be described, explained, and researched. In conclusion, some comments will be offered on teenage drinking and drug use as social problems—something about which there is social concern and for which legal and social policies have evolved.

In constructing a social policy to deal with the problem of teenage drinking in this country a strongly proscriptive stance seems to have been the one most often represented. Every state has laws against underage drinking, most stating absolute prohibitions against the use, purchase, or possession of alcoholic beverages by anyone under the arbitrary age of 21. Most states also have some sort of official, in-school or out-of-school, programs on teenage drinking. Many of these still carry strongly moralistic messages that condemn drinking in unqualified terms and carry exaggerated warnings of the personal and legal problems which it can entail. But the notion of drinking as an unmitigated evil has clearly lost out in this country. Only a minority continue to view it with unqualified disapproval. Most see teenage drinking as only mildly deviant, wrong only because it is done prematurely. Under some circumstances, especially for older adolescents, even this premature use is all right. The outcome of this normative conflict has been a history of ineffective educational programs and widespread violation of the law by both juveniles and adults. There would seem to be some consensus on the undesirability of excessive drinking, whether by adolescents or adults. It would seem advisable then to be less concerned with keeping adolescents totally abstinent and more with promoting a prescriptive atmosphere of responsible drinking.

The goals should not be to reduce drinking of any kind, but to increase the proportion that is responsible and moderate drinking—which is not likely to lead to abuse, accidents, delinquencies and other problems. This seems to be the direction in which expert opinion in the field of alcohol education is headed . . .

A slight modification in the nature or form of drinking habits is possible—a reduction in the number of drinkers probably is not. (Akers, 1968, pp. 8–9).

One way in which to do this is to lower what is now an unrealistically high minimum age for drinking which forces many adolescents to drink furtively in clandestine settings that are not especially conducive to learning responsible drinking. Another is educational programs that provide accurate and realistic information on the consequences of drinking.

Drinking probably never has been viewed by the majority of adults with the same horror as have drugs. Non-medical use of drugs continues to be viewed with moral repugnance, even for adults. Consequently, the legal prohibitions against drug use have consistently been more punitive than those against drinking. Illegal purchase of alcohol by teenagers, while clearly prohibited, is at most a delinquent charge, but illegal possession of drugs is a crime even for adults; it can be charged as a felony, carrying not just delinquent but criminal penalties. The reaction to the drug problem, to an even greater extent than the alcohol problem, has been an increasingly punitive law enforcement response. This was the case when drug use was confined to a relatively small group in the urban lower class. Now the increased use of a variety of drugs among affluent teenagers is being recognized with headline dismay, and again the reaction has been mainly a cry for more law enforcement. Although some are thereby deterred from taking drugs, the past history of such a response shows that it also results in the creation of a lucrative black market (Lindesmith, 1967; Schur, 1965).

Realistic laws are needed for drugs, just as for alcohol. Although they present special problems, reform in the laws and public policy relating to opiates and other strong drugs is needed (President's Commission, 1967). But such reform would seem to be especially relevant with regard to marihuana. It was predicted above that the differences in the societal situations of marihuana and alcohol will gradually diminish. My personal opinion is that this would be desirable and should alleviate some of the problems currently revolving around marihuana; I would recommend that marihuana be regulated in much the same manner as alcohol (including a legal age limit lower than 21).

There is just as much or more need for accurate information and education about drugs as about alcohol. The history of publicly disseminated information and education about drugs has been replete with wildly exaggerated claims and horror stories about the degenerating and crime producing effects of drug use. The vast majority of adults, law-makers, and law-enforcers still believe that marihuana is extremely more dangerous than alcohol. Younger people have learned that much of what they have heard from adults about marihuana is not true and tend to believe that marihuana is not dangerous. (See the 1969 Gallup Poll results in Gunther (1969, p. 29).) The tendency then is to discount all adult-initiated information about drugs and thus increase the probability of trying more harmful drugs. Realistic, substantial knowledge about the real problems that use of alcohol or drugs engender can be effective in curtailing the abuse of both. However, the more exaggerated, unreal, and hypocritical definitions of drugs and alcohol, the more likely they are to be neutralized and discounted by youth. Such a "scare" approach to the problem, far from effectively reducing drug and alcohol abuse among adolescents would seem to serve only to widen whatever credibility gap already exists between generations.

This critique of current policy does not deny that in addition to being troublesome for the community, many young people experience real personal problems with drugs and alcohol; some who partake do so to excess and others suffer ill effects in any case. The argument is simply that those with such problems are probably better helped by some alternative policy, such as community-based agencies and programs which dispense realistic information and aid. An excessively punitive policy may not help, and simply result in presenting both society and adolescents with problems above and beyond whatever difficulties are engendered by the effects of the drugs and alcohol.

REFERENCES

AKERS, RONALD L. Teenage drinking: A survey of action programs and research. *Journal of Alcohol Education*, 1968, *13*, 1–10.

AKERS, RONALD L. Deviant drug use. Unpublished manuscript, University of Washington, 1969.

AKERS, RONALD L., BURGESS, ROBERT L., AND JOHNSON, WELDON T. Opiate use, addiction, and relapse. *Social Problems*, 1968, *15, 459*–469.

ALEXANDER, C. NORMAN, JR. Alcohol and adolescent rebellion. *Social Forces*, 1966, *46*, 542–550.

AUSUBEL, D. P. *Drug Addiction: Physiological, Psychological, and Sociological Aspects*. New York: Random House, 1958.

BALL, JOHN C., AND BATES, WILLIAM M. Migration and residential mobility of narcotic drug addicts. *Social Problems*, 1966, *14*, 56–69.

BALL, JOHN C., AND COTTRELL, EMILY S. Admissions of narcotic drug addicts to public health service hospitals, 1935–63. *Public Health Reports*, 1965, *80*, 471–475.

BATES, WILLIAM M. Narcotics, Negroes and the South. *Social Forces*, 1966, *45*, 61–67.

BAUR, E. JACKSON, & MC CLUGGAGE, MARSTON Drinking patterns of Kansas high school students. *Social Problems*, 1958, *5*, 347–356.

BLACKER, EDWARD, *et al.* Drinking behavior of delinquent boys. *Quarterly Journal of Studies on Alcohol*, 1965, *26*, 223–237.

BLUM, RICHARD. Mind-altering drugs and dangerous behavior. In President's Commission, Task Force Report: *Narcotics and Drug Abuse*. Washington, D.C.: U.S. Government Printing Office, 1967, 21–66.

BROWN, LUCIUS P. Enforcement of the Tennessee anti-narcotics law. In John O'Donnelly and John C. Ball, (Eds.) *Narcotic Addiction*. New York: Harper and Row, 1966, 34–35.

BURGESS, ROBERT L., & AKERS, RONALD L. A differential association-reinforcement theory of criminal behavior. *Social Problems*, 1966, *14*, 128–147.

CAHALAN, DON, CISIN, IRA H., & CROSSLEY, HELEN M. *American Drinking Practices*. Washington, D.C.: Social Research Report #3, George Washington University, 1967.

CAREY, JAMES T. *The College Drug Scene*. Englewood Cliffs, N.J.: Prentice-Hall, 1968.

CHEIN, ISIDOR The use of narcotics as a personal and social problem. In Daniel Wilner and Gene Kassebaum (Eds.) *Narcotics*. New York: McGraw-Hill, 1965, 103–117.

CHEIN, ISIDOR Narcotics use among juveniles. In John A. O'Donnell and John C. Ball (Eds.) *Narcotic Addiction*. New York: Harper and Row, 1966, 123–141.

CHEIN, ISIDOR *et al.* *The Road to H: Narcotics, Delinquency, and Social Policy*. New York: Basic Books, 1964.

CLINARD, MARSHALL B. *Sociology of Deviant Behavior*, 3rd ed. New York: Holt, Rinehart and Winston, 1968.

GLOBETTI, GERALD Teenage drinking in an abstinence setting. *Kansas Journal of Sociology*, 1967, *3*, 124–134.

GLOBETTI, GERALD, & WINDHAM, GERALD O. The social adjustment of high school students and the use of beverage alcohol. *Sociology and Social Research*, 1967, *51*, 148–157.

GUNTHER, MAX Will the U.S. ever legalize pot? *True*, 1969, 28ff.

KOBRIN, SOLOMON, & FINESTONE, HAROLD Drug addiction among young persons in Chicago. In James F. Short, Jr. (Ed.) *Gang Delinquency and Delinquent Subcultures*. New York: Harper and Row, 1968, 110–130.

LARSEN, DONALD E., & ABU-LABAN, BAHA Norm qualities and deviant drinking behavior. *Social Problems*, 1968, *15*, 441–449.

LINDESMITH, ALFRED R. *The Addict and the Law*. New York: Vintage Books, 1967.

LINDESMITH, ALFRED R., & GAGNON, JOHN Anomie and drug addiction. In Marshall B. Clinard (Ed.) *Anomie and Deviant Behavior*. New York: Free Press, 1964, 158–188.

LOURIA, DONALD B. *The Drug Scene*. New York: McGraw-Hill, 1968.

MC CARTHY, RAYMOND G. High school drinking studies. In Raymond G. McCarthy (Ed.) *Drinking and Intoxication*. New Haven: College and University Press, 1959, 205–211.

MC CARTHY, RAYMOND G. Consumption rates and trends from 1850 to 1962 in the U.S. and other countries: Alcoholism rates. In Raymond G. McCarthy (Ed.) *Alcohol Education for Classroom and Community*. New York: McGraw-Hill, 1964, 132–142.

MAC KAY, JAMES R. Problem drinking among juvenile delinquents. *Crime and Delinquency*, 1963, *9*, 29–38.

MAC KAY, JAMES R. Alcohol, alcoholism, and youth. *New Hampshire Bulletin on Alcoholism*, 1965, *14*, 1–6.

MAC KAY, JAMES R., PHILLIPS, DEREK L., & BRYCE,

FORBES O. Drinking behavior among teenagers: A comparison of institutionalized and non-institutionalized youth in New Hampshire. *Journal of Alcohol Education,* 1967, *13,* 20–22.

MAC KAY, JAMES R. *et al.* Teenage drinking in New Hampshire. *New Hampshire Bulletin on Alcoholism,* 1967, *3,* 1–11.

MADDOX, GEORGE L. Teenage drinking in the United States. In David Putnam and Charles R. Snyder (Eds.) *Society, Culture and Drinking Patterns.* New York: John Wiley, 1962, 23–245.

MADDOX, GEORGE L. Adolescence and alcohol. In Raymond G. McCarthy (Ed.) *Alcohol Education for Classroom and Community.* New York: McGraw-Hill, 1964, 32–47.

MADDOX, GEORGE L. High school student drinking behavior: Incidental information from two national surveys. *Quarterly Journal on Alcohol,* 1964, *25,* 339–347.

MADDOX, GEORGE L., AND MC CALL, BEVODE C. *Drinking among Teenagers.* New Brunswick: Rutgers Center of Alcohol Studies, 1964.

MARSHALL, O. The opium habit in Michigan. In John O'Donnell and John C. Ball (Eds.) *Narcotic Addiction.* New York: Harper and Row, 1966, 45–54.

MAUSS, ARMAND L. Anticipatory socialization toward college as a factor in adolescent marijuana use. *Social Problems,* 1969, *16,* 357–364.

MIZRUCHI, EPHRAIM H., AND PERRUCI, ROBERT Norm qualities and differential effects of deviant behavior. *American Sociological Review,* 1962, *27,* 391–399.

MULFORD, HAROLD A. Drinking and deviant drinking, U. S. A., 1963. *Quarterly Journal of Studies on Alcohol,* 1964, *25,* 634–650.

NELSON, DALE O. A comparison of drinking and understanding of alcohol and alcoholism between students in selected high schools of Utah and in the Utah State Industrial School. *Journal of Alcohol Education,* 1968, *13,* 17–25.

Newsweek. The drug generation: Growing younger. *Newsweek,* 1969, April 21, 107–108.

O'DONNELL, JOHN A. Narcotic addiction and crime. *Social Problems,* 1966, *13,* 374–385.

O'DONNELL, JOHN A., AND BALL, JOHN C. (Eds.). *Narcotic Addiction.* New York: Harper and Row, 1966.

PITTMAN, DAVID J. International overview: social and cultural factors in drinking patterns, pathological and nonpathological. In David J. Pittman (Ed.) *Alcoholism.* New York: Harper and Row, 1967, 3–20.

PITTMAN, DAVID J., AND SNYDER, CHARLES R. (Eds.) *Society, Culture, and Drinking Patterns.* New York: John Wiley, 1962.

POLLACK, JACK H. Teenage drinking and drug addiction. *NEA Journal,* 1966, *55,* 8–12.

President's Commission on Law Enforcement and Administration of Justice Task Force Report: *Narcotics and Drug Abuse.* Washington, D. C.: United States Government Printing Office, 1967.

PRESTON, JAMES. On norm qualities and deviant drinking behavior. *Social Problems,* 1969, *16,* 534–537.

RILEY, JOHN W., AND MARDEN, CHARLES F. The social pattern of alcoholic drinking. In Raymond G. McCarthy (Ed.) *Drinking and Intoxication.* New Haven: College and University Press, 1959, 182–189.

SCHUR, EDWIN M. *Crimes without Victims.* Englewood Cliffs, N. J.: Prentice-Hall, 1965.

SIMON, WILLIAM, AND GAGNON, JOHN H. Children of the drug age. *Saturday Review,* 1968, September 21, 60–63, 75–78.

SKOLNICK, JEROME Religious affiliations and drinking behavior. *Quarterly Journal of Studies on Alcohol,* 1958, *19,* 452–470.

SLATER, A. D. A study of use of alcoholic beverages among high school students in Utah. *Quarterly Journal of Studies on Alcohol,* 1952, *13,* 78–86.

STRAUS, ROBERT Alcohol. In Robert Merton and Robert Nisbet (Eds.) *Contemporary Social Problems,* 2d. ed. New York: Harcourt, Brace, and World, 1966, 236–280.

STRAUS, ROBERT, AND BACON, SELDON The problem of drinking in college. In David J. Pittman and Charles R. Snyder (Eds.) *Society, Culture, and Drinking Patterns.* New York: John Wiley, 1962, 246–258.

ULLMAN, ALBERT D. First drinking experience as related to age and sex. In David J. Pittman and Charles R. Snyder (Eds.) *Society, Culture, and Drinking Patterns.* New York: John Wiley, 1962, 259–266.

WINDHAM, GERALD, PRESTON, JAMES D., AND ARMSTRONG, HAROLD B. The high school student of Mississippi and beverage alcohol. *Journal of Alcohol Education,* 1967, *13,* 1–12.

WINICK, CHARLES Epidemiology of narcotics use. In Daniel Wilner and Gene Kassebaum (Eds.) *Narcotics.* New York: McGraw-Hill, 1965, 3–18.

YOUNG, WARREN, AND HIXSON, JOSEPH *LSD on Campus.* New York: Dell Publishing Co., 1966.

Chapter 16: Suggested Additional Readings

AUSTER, S. L. Adolescent drug use. *Educational Leadership,* 1969, *27*(3), 281–286. The author discusses several different drugs, with particular reference to their physical and psychological effects on adolescents.

CAREY, J. T. *The college drug scene.* Englewood Cliffs, N. J.: Prentice-Hall, 1968. Written from the college user's perspective, this book portrays aspects of the drug scene, specifically the drug-using subculture at Berkeley.

DEMOS, G. D. Drug abuse and the new generation. *Phi Delta Kappan,* 1968, *50*(4), 214–217. A dean of students offers suggestions to educators, such as: know the problem, let drug users level with you, avoid rigid policies, give accurate information and learn to listen.

HOGAN, R., CONWAY, J., FOX, S., & MANKIN, D. Personality correlates of undergraduate marijuana use. *Journal of Consulting and Clinical Psychology,* 1970, *35*(1), 58–63. In a study of university students, drug users, as compared with nonusers, proved to be more socially poised, open to experience, and interested in the feelings of others. They also appeared to be more pleasure-seeking, impulsive, and rebellious. By contrast, nonusers were rule-abiding and responsible; however, they were also more inflexible, conventional, and narrow in their interests.

KOHN, P. M., & MERCER, G. W. Drug use, drug use attitudes and the authoritarianism–rebellion dimension. *Journal of Health and Social Behavior,* 1971, *12*(2), 125–131. This study reports that more rebellious respondents were generally more permissive about drugs—especially marijuana—and more likely to use them than were their more authoritarian peers.

LINDESMITH, A. R. Drug use as a divisive influence. *Phi Delta Kappan,* 1968, *50*(4), 218–221. This essay reviewing a book, *The Poisoned Ivy,* compares the current status of drug law enforcement with the situation that prevailed before repeal of alcohol prohibition.

MC GLOTHLIN, W. H., & WEST, L. J. The marihuana problem: an overview. *American Journal of Psychiatry,* 1968, *125,* 126–134. The writers briefly review what is known about the effects of marijuana use, and report preliminary data which tends to differentiate the characteristics of users and nonusers.

MESSER, M. The predictive value of marijuana use: A note to researchers of student culture. *Sociology of Education,* 1969, *42*(1), 91–97. Data on drug use by college students (62% of whom had smoked marijuana) suggested that the use of drugs is associated with a subcultural system which attracts many students to a radically defined world view. Data on drug use, therefore, serves as an operational indicator of this subculture.

PRESTON, J. D. Community norms and adolescent drinking behavior: A comparative study. *Social Science Quarterly,* 1968, *49*(2), 350–359. This paper reports the relationship between several sociocultural variables and the use of beverage alcohol among adolescents in two southern communities. Local norms were especially significant in helping explain observed differences.

SEBALD, H. Drinking and the use of drugs. *Adolescence: A sociological analysis.* New

York: Appleton-Century-Crofts, 1969. Chaper 17. In this chapter Sebald discusses the effects of various chemicals on youth and the characteristics common among youthful chemical users, and provides various statistical data relating to them. He is chiefly concerned with alcohol and LSD; but he also discusses opium and the so-called hard drugs.

WEIL, A. T., ZINBERG, N. E., & NELSEN, J. M.   Clinical and psychological effects of marijuana in man. *Science,* 1968, *162,* 1234–1242. On the basis of pilot experiments the authors describe the primitive state of knowledge about marijuana, the research problems encountered in designing such research, and the results of their investigations.

WITTER, C.   Drugging and schooling. *Trans-action,* July–August 1971, *8*(9/10), Whole No. 69, 31–34. This article concerns the question of giving drugs to school children to relieve certain academic and emotional problems. After reviewing the literature, the author concludes that research is yet too indecisive to justify hard and fast opinions on the issue.

17

Conflict Between the Generations

The conflict between the generations (or "generation gap"), which has received considerable attention recently, is hardly a new phenomenon. It has been written about and commented upon for many years, and the causes of the gap have been variously defined. Much of the conflict apparently derives from the process of cultural change, which may even overshadow cross-cultural differences. The gap between age-groups within a culture is often greater than that existing between cultures (Berrien, Arkoff, & Iwahara, 1967).

Friedenberg (1959) sees the conflict as originating with adults. Their hostility, he asserts, derives from their anxiety about adolescents. Many older persons are frightened or enraged by teenagers' spontaneity. Resentful and fearful of aging, they find youth's youthfulness an affront and fail to realize that those who love youth stay young the longest. Another cause of conflict is prolonged education, which often forces youth to be dependent upon their parents for an unusually long time. The parents project their own dreams, expectations, and rules onto the children they support; some pressure their children to enter prestigious colleges and to choose high-status occupations.

Coleman (1961) points out that with the prolonging of formal education, parents find themselves confronted not with a set of individuals to be trained for adulthood, but with small social systems. These teen groups present a united front to the overtures made by the adult society. Moreover, the massing together of large numbers of adolescents in high schools and colleges has produced an atmosphere in which the legitimacy of adult authority has been called into question. This situation has developed in the twentieth century; in the nineteenth century, youth rarely challenged their elders' basic right to authority. Even the riots which marked nineteenth-century college life were more like peasant revolts against tyranny than like revolutionary movements.

In any discussion of the conflict between the generations, it is important to distinguish between college and noncollege youth. Noncollege youth so closely resemble their parents that for them the generation gap is a myth. It is the college youth who have created the concept of the generation gap by challenging traditional values and modes of life. Away from home, the students find that the credibility gap widens between parents' preaching and peer pronouncements. Indeed, both high school and college peer groups are largely insulated from their elders.

Bettelheim (1962) sees the generations conflict as arising when a parent considers the child's main task is to obey the parent's will; if the youth fights back, a psychological impasse is reached. At other times, a generation gap exists because adults fail to fulfill their role as exemplars and counselors of youth. Having lost their own social and ethical bearings, they provide nothing to which the youth can cling. Adults' experience, once the cornerstone of their authoritative status, has lost much of its value. Hence, youth suffers a confusion of possible goals and lacks a clear program for reaching any of them.

The generation conflict has taken special forms in recent times, for specific reasons. For one thing, according to Mead (1969), today's rebellious young people resemble "the first generation born in a new country listening to their parents' tales of the old country—and watching their parents struggling, often clumsily, often unsuccessfully, with new conditions [p. 135]." Nowhere in the world do members of the older generation really understand what their children themselves know; and no longer do older children know more than younger ones. Modern children lack guides, for their parents are "immigrants in time, immigrants from an earlier world, living in an age essentially different from anything we knew before [p. 135]." In consequence, the older generation is completely estranged from the younger one—more so than at any other period in history, because of the very rapid pace of change today. By the very nature of this situation, youth have necessarily rejected, as being completely nonfunctional for the present, all the lessons their parents learned from the past. The conflict has been joined, as ideologies of youth and their elders meet in collision course.

Today, youth's revolt against the older generation often brings apparent victory, but the young cannot afford to go their own way. They continue to be dependent upon adults and must accept the fact that adults control the assignment of status within the society (Jencks & Riesman, 1967). Indeed, after youth's unprecedented revolt in the 1960s, many young people have begun to realize that "society still holds the upper hand." Especially when jobs are hard to come by, youth begins to face up to the serious side of life. As one coed college graduate said, "It was quite a party, a real binge, and it left quite a hangover. Now the time has come to straighten up and do the dishes [U.S. News and World Report, 1971, p. 27]."

Others doubt that the generation gap, if it still exists, is of any great dimension. According to Templin (1968), the conflict is subsiding. Adults' permissiveness and their growing understanding of youth culture have lessened the tensions. Where formerly, indiscriminate criticism of youth was an accepted, even approved, adult practice, now adults find themselves expected to be accepting of youth. (Parsons, 1962).

Also, rebellion assumes that the target of one's hostility is an active threat. But when the adult world seems terribly remote, as it does at present, youth is not threatened by it. Besides, a youth feels so distant from his parents, in generational if not affectional terms, that he can afford to understand them and "even to show a touching sympathy for their hesitant efforts to guide and advise him [Keniston, 1962, p. 156]." For their part, parents realize they are out of date, and they hesitate to impose their values and preferences on their children. The result is a sort of gentlemen's agreement between the generations that neither will interfere with the other. However, this attitude does create certain problems. When they are denied adequate parental models, young people feel cheated; and often, nowadays, youth feel they have never really had parents.

Some writers deplore the narrowing of the gap between generations. Adult–adolescent conflict, says Friedenberg (1959), is inherent in the personality development of Western man. In certain primitive societies, such as Samoa, the young "pass delicately as Ariel through puberty into adulthood." But, when mature, these primitive people, though charming, seem insufficiently characterized, hardly like adults. In competitive Western societies, conflict is the instrument by which an individual learns "the complex, subtle differences between himself and his environment [pp. 14–15]." In this sense, conflict is not war—it is dialectical, and leads to a higher synthesis, to the youth's critical participation in adult society.

Bettelheim (1962) agrees with Friedenberg that something is irreparably lost in the diminution of adult–youth conflict. How can youth test his worth, he asks, or his own strength and vitality—the things he feels most dubious about—if he finds himself pushing against a vacuum? Youth benefits from testing himself against an established order, because nothing else is so safe a testing ground.

Rosenmayr (1968) observes that the matter of rebelling against authority is a crucial aspect of changing age roles. If an adolescent is to grow up, he must cease simply to subordinate himself and learn to exercise authority. Therefore, it is not simply that he capriciously desires to be independent; it is essential that he become so in order to fill his new role as adult. Thus, the generation gap becomes a positive force in society, for such a gap must be expected if each generation is to improve upon, and not merely reflect, the older generation's experience (Haan, 1971). Moreover, since the younger generation have experiences quite different from those of their elders, they perceive themselves as different also in their relation to society.

Youth's revolt is also portrayed as necessary for their own development as individuals (Erikson, 1968). For one thing, the gap serves to protect the youth from premature commitment to a particular adult identity (Weiner, 1971). The process of his identity formation can remain fluid while the youth tries out various roles, to determine which he can play most effectively. Nevertheless, to protect themselves during this transitional period which is characterized by so much uncertainty and ambiguity, adolescents cling together. This togetherness, in turn, serves as a buffer against the sort of adult demands which would result in premature definition of youths' goals. Manufacturers, entertainers, and others further accentuate youths' togetherness by fostering special adolescent fashions in clothing, speech, and entertainment. However, conflict of the generations is not to be considered as identical with the pretense of "toughening up" the adolescent. Conflict does mean resisting authority, when the authority makes no sense. The polar opposite to this healthy concept of conflict is the fawning acceptance of authority. Nor is this sort of conflict expressed in delinquency, which essentially is conflict-gone-wrong.

Most discussion of the generations conflict applies, at least implicitly, to males;

certainly the matter affects the sexes differently. For boys, says Bettelheim (1962), conflict is more crucial. Young men expect eventually to displace their elders in running their country's affairs. In days when vigor and strength were essential in a head of a household, it was accepted as natural that a young man, at his physical peak, should take over that role. Today, when experience counts more than brute strength, the young man can no longer be sure that his elders will move over and give him a place and sometimes he must challenge them with force.

The girl's situation is somewhat different, since biology brings an end to the mother's role of childbearing and, as a consequence, child-rearing. If the daughter's perception of her own role is the same as her mother's, there is no essential conflict. Her mother has been prepared by nature to move over.

In the first of the following readings, Bengtson considers both historical and current approaches to the problem of the generation gap. He cites relevant research, identifies special issues involved in arriving at conclusions on this question, and makes positive suggestions by which schools may bridge the gap between the generations. In the second article, Schiamberg reviews theories relevant to generational conflict in both technological and nontechnological societies and discusses their implications for education. It becomes apparent that the generation gap is neither new nor localized, and that it is found among both primitives and moderns, in times past and present.

REFERENCES

BERRIEN, F. K., ARKOFF, A., & IWAHARA, S.   Generation difference in values: Americans, Japanese-Americans and Japanese. *Journal of Social Psychology*, 1967, *71*, 169–175.

BETTELHEIM, B.   The problem of generations. *Daedalus*, 1962, *91*, 68–96.

COLEMAN, J. S.   *The adolescent society.* New York: Free Press, 1961.

ERIKSON, E. H.   *Identity: Youth and crisis.* New York: Norton, 1968.

FRIEDENBERG, E. Z.   *The vanishing adolescent.* Boston, Beacon Press, 1959, 14–15, 117.

HAAN, N.   Moral redefinition in families as a critical aspect of the generational gap. *Youth and Society*, 1971, *2*(3), 259–283.

JENCKS, C., & RIESMAN, D.   The war between the generations. *Teachers College Record*, October 1967, *69*(1), 1–21.

KENISTON, K.   Social change and youth in America. *Daedalus*, 1962, *91*, 156.

MEAD, M.   The generation gap. *Science*, 1969, *164*(3876), 135.

PARSONS, T.   Youth in the context of American society. *Daedalus*, 1962, *91*, 115–116.

ROSENMAYR, L.   Towards an overview of youth's sociology. *International Social Science Journal*, 1968, *20*(2), 286–315.

TEMPLIN, L.   The pathology of youth. *Journal of Human Relations*, 1968, *16*(1), 113–127.

U. S. News and World Report, 1971, *71*(6), 27.

WEINER, I. B.   The generation gap—fact and fancy. *Adolescence*, 1971, *6*(22), 155–166.

The Generation Gap

VERN L. BENGTSON

The author reviews both classical and current approaches to the problem of the conflict between generations and considers certain of the issues involved in investigating this question.

Of these phenomena on which social scientists gather data and write analyses, there are few of more popular relevance today than discussions of the "generation gap." It is of course true that the problem of generations is one of the older issues in modern sociology; despite this, very few thorough studies have yet been made to illuminate the nature and extent of continuity or differences between age groups today. Even more importantly, there have been no empirical attempts to analyze the effect on social structure of such differences between generations. Indeed, all too often the discussion of such issues has been impressionistic, speculative, and even apocalyptic—not only in the popular press, but also in the pages of scholarly books and journals.

Author's note: With the collaboration of William C. Martin, Chico State College.

The preparation of this paper was made possible in part by a grant from the Andrew Normal Foundation and from the Biomedical Sciences Research Grant FR-07012-02 to the University of Southern California. Support also came from the Gerontology Center of USC. The author is indebted to Sol Kobrin, LaMar Empey, and Marijo Walsh of USC, to Joseph Kuypers of the University of California, Berkeley, and to Reuben Hill of the University of Minnesota, for helpful suggestions in the preparation of this paper.

The purpose of this paper is to review some classical and some contemporary approaches to the problem of generations, and to order these perspectives in a typology reflecting some underlying dimensions of the social-psychological investigation of generations.

The term generation gap should be read as in quotation marks throughout this paper; for the phenomenon to which it refers is undoubtedly neither strictly generational nor is it a gap, using any reasonable definition of those terms. Be that as it may, the term has worldwide usage and a sort of connotative reality. The man on the street knows, in his own way, what the generation gap refers to, and social scientists have, rightly or wrongly, followed his lead in using the term.

The Generation Gap and Mass Culture Today

A fruitful way to begin this analysis is through a brief survey of the evidence of generational differences as portrayed in such everyday chronicles as the mass media and political rhetoric. For in the characterization of social movements and the

"The Generation Gap: A Review and Typology of Social-Psychological Perspectives" by Vern L. Bengtson is reprinted from *Youth and Society*, Volume 2, Number 1 (September 1970), pp. 7–32, by permission of the Publisher, Sage Publications, Inc., and the author.

identification of social problems, mass culture often antecedes social scientists by several years.

The message from the media is that differences between age groups are becoming a serious social problem, not only in America but in most Western industrialized countries (see Neugarten, 1970). Concern over the youth problem turns very often into outright hostility; and discrimination against the aged, more subtle but no less pervasive (see Butler, 1969), has serious implications in nations where increasing longevity swells the ranks of the aged. One might say that *age-ism* has become a common theme in mass culture today, just as racism finally became acknowledged a decade ago in American society. Defined as prejudice by members of one age group against another age group(s), age-ism implies stereotyping, interpersonal distance, and often, conflict of interest. It describes the subjective experience implied in the popular definition of the generation gap (Butler, 1969; Neugarten, 1970).

Evidence for age-ism is found in almost any newspaper or mass distribution magazine picked at random during the past few months or years. For example, in one three-day period in the spring of 1970, the Los Angeles *Times* printed a variety of news items, editorials, and cartoons—and several advertisements—that portrayed relations between generations as cause for serious concern. One article explored the international ties of student protest movements; another reported the "get tough" reactions of several public officials toward campus demonstrations. A feature reporting the rapidly expanding commune movement and hippie subculture was presented on the same page as a brief article reporting on increasing drug arrests in an affluent suburb of Los Angeles. On the editorial page, a syndicated columnist described the immorality of student demonstrations, while the editorial urged that taxpayers not take out their grievances against student demonstrators at the polls by voting down school bond elections. One cartoon showed the President making a clumsy attempt to "rap" with youthful constituents, while another portrayed student protestors riding roughshod over Law, Order, and Justice. On the front page was a report of working class men assaulting student protestors; it was continued on an inside page next to a large adver-

tisement suggesting that the purchase of a Mustang would "bridge the generation gap." Thus, in many ways, some humorous but most pensive, the mass-distribution newspaper reports substantial differences between youth and the mature generation today. The implication of most of this portrayal is that these differences lead to social disorganization: the nation is "coming apart at the seams" and an elite group of youth is doing most of the tearing.

Or to take another example, the alleged disorganization of the family by intergenerational tension is reflected in the titles of articles in American mass-distribution magazines between 1968 and 1970. *Life* discusses "The Gulf Between Parents and Their Kids (Wider than Ever Before)"; *Look* analyzes "The Way Between Mother and Daughter"; *Saturday Review* wonders "What Are Our Young People Telling Us?" while the *Ladies Home Journal* suggests, somewhat tentatively, that "We Can Close the Generation Gap—IF."

A third example of generational relations as seen in popular culture is in the political arena. Not only has the gap become a political issue, it has been elevated to the level of a national problem. In one of his first addresses to the nation following his election in 1968, President Nixon characterized differences between youth and adults in our society as "a yawning gulf . . . between the two halves of our people, a great divide and misunderstanding that weakens our body politic" (Dougherty, 1968). He proposed and later implemented a National Youth Agency to "bring us together again in this area." Since then, the charge of discrimination against youth, or at least youthful protestors, has been leveled against the administration with growing fury. In the California gubernatorial campaign of 1970, an important campaign issue has been the warning of Governor Reagan that "there will be a bloodbath on our campuses" if protestors do not subside (Los Angeles Times, 1970). In the spring of 1970 thousands of campuses across the nation responded, in one way or another, to the deployment of U.S. troops in Cambodia, protesting not only on moral grounds but on the basis of discrimination against youth. The violence that has ensued is literally without precedent in American history; and the traditional ploy of "nothing but the best for our kids" has become unpopular. As the *Wall Street Journal* (1968) editorialized,

> Many middle-aged Americans are likely to feel that youth rebels not because it feels deep grievances, but because it has never felt any. What troubles the older generation is the nagging thought that this ill-mannered rebellion is reward not for its failures but for its success.

From the evidence available in the mass media, then, differences between age groups today are seen as an extensive social problem in contemporary society. Relations between the generations are seen as tenuous and often outright hostile. And the result of the differences and tensions between the generations is seen as an alarming disruption of present social organization.

When one turns to an analysis of the earlier sociological formulations of the problem of generations, however, an entirely different perspective is seen. In a tradition of research that was for the most part ignored in the United States, European sociologists made analyses of the cycle of generations to account for the inevitable ebb and flow of historical events.

Classical Sociology and the Problem of Generations

Concern with discontinuity between generations dates as far back as recorded history goes (see Feuer, 1969, for an excellent review). Egyptian and Hebrew sages defined wisdom in terms that implied dire consequences for youth who forsook the way of their elders. The Maxims of Ptahhotep—the first document on ethics of which there is record—was, as Feuer notes, already concerned with the problem of generations. Plato and Aristotle incorporated generational struggle in their theories of political change. Aristotle suggested the cause of political struggle could be found in the conflict of fathers and sons.

In the late nineteenth century, Continental social historians—for the most part followers of Hegel—began to systematically explore generations as a dimension of social organization and political change. As summarized by Mannheim

(1952), Heberle (1951), and Marias (1968), the thesis they attempted to document was that the rhythm of changes in ideas and political institutions is associated with the emergence of new biological generations.

As Mannheim describes it, the goal of these early sociologists was to deal with the problem of social time to account for change in the nature of the social fabric from period to period. He contrasted the "positivist" with the "romantic–metaphysical" definition of generations—a distinction which is still useful when applied to current perspectives of generations. The early positivist school tied the movement of history to the fact that persons growing in an identifiable span of time under[-went] basically the same set of social events—wars, economic conditions, political movements—as they came of age. A new generation, arising with predictable regularity every 25 to 30 years, produces an identifiable historical era and serves as a link in the chain of progress. By contrast, the romanticists defined generations, not in terms of time span, but in terms of common sharing of experiences of a purely qualitative sort. A generation is defined by the shared *geist* of an era which colors all its products and is in a sense, independent of historical time. Thus the classical period in art lasted for three calendar generations, while the expressionism of the late nineteenth century only one; yet both can be seen as a generation of definite perspective in expressing artistic perception. From this viewpoint, then, a generation lasts as long as a single art form or mode of expression prevails.

The problem with both these positions is that they both fail to account for the "noncontemporaneity of the contemporaneous." This was Pinder's (1926) figure of speech referring to the contrasts in outlook that exist between two or three generational cohorts who live together as the same point in time. Mannheim proposes that the concept of generation be used as nothing more than a kind of identity of location in time, embracing related age groups who are embedded in a historical–social process. There is a "trigger action" of social and historical events which determine whether a new generation emerges every year, or every thirty or one hundred years, or whether it emerges at all. Thus during some periods, generations do not appear as social change agents because there has not been a catalyst to produce their consciousness as a generation: that is, a group differentiated from other generations and a unity despite the distinctions that usually occur within any age group (see the excellent discussions by Berger (1960) and Troll (1970) for contemporary perspectives of the Mannheim theme and the problems in generational analysis).

The classical sociological analysis of generations has been most often employed to explain political movements. Mentre (1920), Heberle (1951), and most recently Feuer (1969) have applied the concept to the rise of national parties and to political revolutions. Heberle suggested the concept of "decisive politically relevant experiences" to explain why succeeding generations may be oriented to interpret the institutions of society in different ways. However, he emphasizes that the entire generation will not have identical objective experiences, and a generation will include many subdivisions (social classes, for example) that create differences within them. Intragenerational divisions are still less pronounced than differences between generations. Such contrasts between generations will be greater in periods of rapid social change, and the longer a generation stays in power politically, the sharper will be the clash with the youngest generation (as in Germany in 1918 when the elderly leaders of old political parties blocked the rise of younger men). Feuer (1916), a contemporary writer in the classical sociological tradition, suggests that the "moral deauthorization of the older generation" is a principal component of revolutionary change based on generational distinctions.

A final position in the classical tradition of sociology is that suggested by Davis (1940) in analyzing "the sociology of parent-youth conflict." Whereas Mannheim, Pinder, and Heberle focus principally on historical and structural conditions producing differences between generations, Davis focuses more on interpersonal and developmental issues. Whereas Mannheim considers conflict between age groups usual but not inevitable, Davis suggests that it is unavoidable, without commenting on the ultimate social gain or loss to be derived from such changes between generations.

For Davis, conflict between generations is the result of three universals in human development, modified by four variables having to do with the modern condition. The three universal factors leading to parent–child conflict are: (1) the basic birth cycle difference between parent and child; (2) the decreasing rate of socialization with the coming of maturity (that is, youth changes rapidly in personal orientations, while their parents change more slowly); and (3) the resulting intrinsic differences between parents and children in the physiological, sociological, and psychosocial planes of behavior.

These factors, according to Davis, may lead to conflict; but whether they do so, and to what degree, depends on the variables of: (1) the rate of social change; (2) the extent of the complexity of the social structure; (3) the degree of integration of the culture; and (4) the velocity of movement within the culture.

A review of the classical sociological analysis of generations, then, reveals many ideas that are relevant to the current social concern about the generation gap. How do these ideas compare with contemporary scholarly analyses of the nature of differences between age groups, and the effect of such differences on the stability and change of the social order? The next section presents a review of current perspectives in the scholarly literature to allow such a comparison.

Current Perspectives on Generational Differences and Social Change

In the past few years there has been a renaissance of scholarly interest in the problem of generations. The author has compiled a bibliography of over one hundred references to generational differences, though the number of empirical papers in this list is very small. To attempt to summarize these many orientations is difficult; however, one can posit some underlying issues which form dimensions useful in categorizing the current perspectives.

First, there is the issue of the *extent* of differences between age groups. Is there a very wide gap, a little gap, or none really at all? Is the gap serious and disruptive of the social order, or is it the natural mechanism of social change? In what dimensions of human behavior, values, or attitudes is the gap most manifest; in which areas is continuity the greatest?

Second is the question of the *novelty* of the current character of relations between generations. Has the gap always been there; has it always been as wide as it is today? What factors lead to the conflict being more pervasive at some periods in history than in others? Is such conflict the result, or the cause, of rapid social change?

Third, there is the issue of the *permanence* of difference between generations, in the life history of both the individual and the society. Will the differences so evident between today's youth and their elders dissolve as a natural correlate of achieving maturity; will youth grow out of it? Or will the currently observed difference in attitudes and behaviors become part of a mature personality, leading to decided change in the society when today's youth become the command generation? And, finally, is such change predictive and perhaps cyclical over long periods of time, or is it random? Is it true as in the old proverb, that what one generation builds the second rejects, leading the third generation to build the same sort of social mores as the first?

Such questions reflect the nature of the problem facing social scientists attempting to deal with generational differences, their correlates and consequences (see Aldous, 1965; Adelson, 1970; Troll, 1970). Using such issues as guides, one can organize the many current opinions regarding this problem in several ways. The simplest way is to proceed using one dimension to organize the literature, and then add another to form a more complete typology.

The dimension to be used first here is that of the extent of differences between age groups. Three rough categories of theorists and data appear: those that point to a "Great Gap" between age groups; those at the other end of the spectrum who suggest that the "Gap is an Illusion"; and those in between who infer "Selective Continuity and Difference" between age groups in today's society. All three positions are well represented in the current literature, and all three have some antecedents in classical treatment of the problem.

THE "GREAT GAP" POSITION

Some sociologists, anthropologists, and educators have published data and impressionistic essays that indicate profound differences between youth and adults today regarding value system, orientations toward social institutions, interpersonal relations and communication, and locus of control and authority. In its extreme, the message is that a social revolution along generational lines is sweeping the world, toppling established adult social structures. Richman (1968) suggests that the "bona fide generation gap, qualitatively different from those that have occurred before," finds its focus on overthrowing outdated political systems. Seeley (1969) views the present youth movements as the beginning of a transformation of society analogous to the Renaissance or Reformation—if they are not crushed by the Establishment. One psychologist, educator Walter Angel (1968), summarizes his position with this quote: "the whole glacier of tradition is breaking up, and . . . a generation gap wider than we suspect has opened up under us." The gap appears, Angel adds, not at the extreme edges of society—the hippies and radicals—but throughout America where "a new madness, a new social but not necessarily ephemeral fad, a new psychological disease has gripped our nation." He labels the malignancy "gaposis" and suggests four strains: affluence, values, education, and communication as forces which are pulling apart age groups in our society.

Margaret Mead (1970) explains the pulling apart in terms of differential environmental experiences while young. It is no longer possible for the middle-aged parent to tell his son, "I was once a youth like you." The father never was just like him. Being twenty years old in 1970 is different from being the same age in the 1930s. Youth grow up in an environment of instant visual news, a threat of mass annihilation, and a growing concern with the credibility of establishment leadership.

Perhaps the most eloquent exponent of this perspective of youth–adult relations is Edgar Friedenberg (1959, 1965, 1969a, 1969b). He has argued prolifically that adult institutions have failed to listen to, let alone understand, a youth group which is progressively alienated. In his epigrammatic way he suggests that "young people aren't rebelling against their parents; they're abandoning them." Most recently, he has argued that the generation gap reflects "a real and serious conflict of interest" rather than mutual misunderstanding: youth is a discriminated minority, he says, and the "genuine class conflict between a dominant and exploitive older generation and youth who are slowly becoming more aware of what is happening to them will escalate into open conflict before long" (Friedenberg, 1969).

Certain analyses of popular culture by social scientists substantiate the notion of significant differences between youth and the over-thirty group. A number of current films (*The Graduate; Wild in the Streets; Goodbye, Columbus*) portray variously exploitation, conflict, or simply difference in interpretation across generational lines. Herbert Goldberg (1968), a clinical psychologist as well as songwriter, has documented the revolution in popular music since 1962 in terms of the style and media employed, the youthfulness of the performers, and the thematic portrayal through lyrics of revolt, parent–child differences, humanistic values, and sensory stimulation. Korngold (1968) has similarly analyzed the burgeoning underground press movement as a new social institution serving the particular interests and needs of a youth subculture. These developments have led some sociologists to suggest that the culture gap between young and old is progressively widening (see Simmons and Winograd, 1967; Seeley, 1969) or at least that youth are fashioning a new, humanistic ethic to replace the protestant ethic of their elders (Myerhoff, 1969). Such cultural innovations may someday fulfill the prophesies of some current writers of an entirely new social order. (It is interesting to note, however, as Goldberg points out, how rapidly some cultural innovations of youth have been adopted by Establishment fashion—witness mod clothing and sideburned junior executives—and how easily youthful performers like the Beatles become sophisticated capitalists and behave in some respects much like the Jet Set their songs decry.)

From a psychodynamic perspective comes additional confirmation for the "Great Gap" view of relations between age groups. Freudians have long accepted the proposition that rebellion (challenging the power of an autocratic, authoritarian father-figure) is an essential step in the achievement of the power and independence essential to the masculine identity role. Bettelheim (1965) has observed that factors that traditionally have mitigated generational conflict even in this country have become feeble or inoperative. The family plays a decreasing role in the socialization of the young; the elder generation is no longer the resource it was for coping with the world. The result is that one simply has to rebel if one is to become socially as well as psychologically an adult.

In short, regardless of the many roots of generational difference, the "Great Gap" position emphasizes that there are basic and, in some sense, irreconcilable differences in behavioral predispositions between age groups in American society, and the force of these differences is resulting in rapid cultural transformation. Many would add that such transformations are all for the best. Margaret Mead (1970) has suggested that, in societies where there is rapid social change, generational discontinuity is more adaptive than is substantial similarity between cohorts, since old responses become inappropriate to radically new situations, and parents must learn from their children. Or, as Friedenberg (1969b: 42) has put it:

> If the confrontation between the generations does pose, as many portentous civic leaders and upper-case Educators fear, a lethal threat to the integrity of the American social system, that threat may perhaps be accepted with graceful irony. Is there, after all, so must to lose? The American social system has never been noted for its integrity. In fact, it would be rather like depriving the Swiss of their surfing.

THE "GAP IS AN ILLUSION" POSITION

At the opposite end of the spectrum, a second position emphasizes the continuities between generations, arguing that contemporary anxiety over the differences between age groups is greatly overplayed; it also draws on historical analysis to indicate the seemingly inevitable recurrence of periods of heightened conflict between age groups. In this sense, "the more things change, the more

more they stay the same" can be applied to relations between age groups as well as to political changes. Several contemporary analyses suggest that, though there are inevitably behavioral differences between age groups, the continuities in various aspects of behavior between one generation and the next, and the substantial solidarity between youth and their parents, take precedence over these differences (see Campbell, 1969, pp. 827–833, for an excellent review of the evidence for this position).

Four examples can be given. In the most comprehensive analysis to date of student protest movements, Feuer (1969) has presented voluminous historical documentation to the effect that the conflict of generations can be seen as both inevitable and recurrent. The intensity of the conflict varies, however, under such conditions as gerontocratic power structures and the obvious failure ("de-authorization") of the older generation to solve the problems facing the era. Current student movements are not to be considered simply as a manifestation of generational conflict: they have a more psychological base and end in failure unless attached to larger groups, defined not only on the basis of age. In short, youthful assault on the established structure is no more characteristic, nor revolutionary, in America in the 1960s than at other times and places within the modern era.

Similar findings are suggested in a second area, that of the so-called "sexual revolution," by Bell (1966) and Reiss (1968). The data of these studies may be interpreted to suggest that the greatest generational change in sexual behavior, at least with regard to premarital sex, occurred following World War I between the cohort born before, or after, 1900, and not between today's youth and their parents. A survey by Walsh (1970) suggests that patterns of sexual behavior before marriage among current college students are remarkably similar to those characterizing their parents' generation.

Or, to give a third example, there are several studies which have touched on influence, sentiment, and interaction patterns between parents and youth. Some of these suggest that most adolescents and their parents perceive a decidedly satisfactory relationship in terms of communication, understanding, and closeness (Douvan and Adelson, 1966; Larson and Myerhoff, 1965;

Adelson, 1968; Lubell, 1968; Bengston, 1969). Others indicated that parents are more important referent persons than peers for some aspects of decision-making in adolescence (Kandel and Lesser, 1969). Musgrove (1965) has suggested an interesting variation on this theme: in his samples, adolescents have generally favorable orientations toward adults, while the adults in his sample displayed decidedly less favorable descriptions of young people in general.

The fourth perspective comes from the research or political attitudes of students and their parents. In the main, such intergenerational research has indicated substantial continuity among both activists and nonactivists. For example, Thomas (1970), in a study of sixty politically active parents (thirty liberal and thirty conservative) and their college-age children, found that "children of highly politicized parents tend to be like their parents both in their political attitudes and their political behavior." Westby and Braungart (1968) found considerable similarity between members of the Young Americans for Freedom and their parents' political identification, and slightly less for SDS members; their conclusion is that a stratification theory explains political activism better than a generational hypothesis (the young are rebelling from the parents, and that's why they demonstrate). Gamson, Goodman, and Gurin (1967) studied radicals, bystanders, and moderates during the 1966 University of Michigan uprising and concluded that "discontinuity between background and present beliefs is an inhibiting factor, making action *less* rather than more likely. . . . Freed from the cost of sharply breaking with their background, the activists are willing to go further in support of their beliefs." Such examples could be used to argue that "the gap is an illusion."

There are, of course, several factors at work that make generational conflict more visible today, and perhaps different in nature—factors such as rapid social change (Davis, 1940); technological advances which decrease the span between generations (Berger, 1960); the revolutionary effects of the mass media on socialization experiences (Hayakawa, 1968); the changing population distribution with the "pinching" in the middle-age range (Birren and Bengtson, 1969); and, finally, greater sensitization to differences between age groups brought about in part by the popular press. Despite factors such as the above, those who come down on the side of continuity in intergenerational behavior would hold that today's social conflict is not basically generational in nature at all. Perhaps, as Adelson (1968) has suggested:

What we have tended to do is to translate ideological conflict into generational conflict; it may be easier to contemplate a rift between the generations than to confront the depth and extent of our current social discord. . . . The feverish politics of the day do not align the young against the old, not in any significant way. Rather they reflect . . . the ideological differences in a deeply divided nation.

THE "SELECTIVE CONTINUITY AND DIFFERENCE" POSITION

A possible position can be suggested as intermediate between these two extremes. Like the second position, it maintains that in most respects, conflict between the generations is peripheral; solidarity, and continuity of values are substantial across generational lines within the family and across cohort lines in the broad social order. However, like the first perspective, it emphasizes that the rapid pace of social change has created new modes of behavioral expressions that may be quite different from those of the preceding generation.

Selective continuity from one arena of behavior to another is seen in the three-generational studies of Aldous and Hill (1965) and Hill and Aldous (1969). This is probably the most extensive study to date of intergenerational continuity and difference. Among the 84 three-generational lineages in their research (all adults and all living in separate households), the greatest continuity of behavior appeared in the transmission of religious affiliation. Less transmission from generation to generation appeared in the pattern of dividing marital household tasks, educational achievement, and the making of decisions within the family.

An interesting side note of this research, in the context of social change, is the suggestion of greater similarity between middle-aged parents and their married children than between the parents and the grandparents. Hill and Aldous comment that the historical period of the 1930s may have represented a watershed between generations in family decision-making behavior—a comment consistent with other observations about the "sexual revolution" and changes in religious patterns between generations (see Birren and Bengtson, 1968).

Additionally, Aldous has made some analyses of the *consequences* of continuity between generations. For example, continuity in religious affiliation over three generations is associated with less marital tension for the youngest generation; continuity in occupation (for white-collar groups) appears to have consequences in higher income for the younger generation than lack of such a tradition.

Such evidence of generational continuity in some aspects of behavior, and of differences in others, points to a contrast that may be made between overt behavior and covert value systems. Behavior as outwardly manifest may vary substantially from generation to generation, while values or personal philosophy may in fact be similar. Taking this as a hypothesis, the literature suggests some confirming evidence.

For example, Keniston (1968) has suggested a distinction between "core" and "formal" values in his sample of young radicals. He emphasizes that the young radicals come from liberal or radical families, but denies that what has been called the "red diaper baby" hypothesis adequately explains the radical differences in means displayed by them. The accumulating literature of student activists supports this notion: rather than rebelling from parental values, many activists, both of right and left, are in fact carrying them to their logical conclusion (Flacks, 1967; Keniston, 1968; Thomas, 1970; Block et al., 1970). For example, Troll, Neugarten, and Kraines (1969: 333) present data that shows considerable similarity between young adults and their parents in the domain of values:

If one member of a family is dedicated to righting wrongs and changing the world (dedication to causes), it is likely that so will the others, even though the particular causes they espouse may not be the same; if one member values achievement (achievement need), probably so do the others, and so on. The salient values of this group of college students, whether they are activists or not, tend to be the salient values of their parents.

Troll's families exhibited greater similarity in the area of values than in other domains of personality—consistent with the "Selective Continuity" orientation.

Another way to look at the selective continuity is through the traditional value–norm differentiation proposed by Merton: specific values of the two cohorts—freedom, democracy, responsibility—may indeed be similar, but the norms, and therefore the behaviors, used by each age group to achieve the value ends may differ greatly (Bengtson, 1969). Or, to propose another perspective, differences in the structure and experiences of primary socialization agencies may account for the variability of the behavioral continuities present (see Larson and Myerhoff, 1967; Moriwaki and Bengtson, 1969). Block has recently presented data to substantiate the hypothesis that family patterns may account for this determined rebellion and selective continuity, at least as perceived by the child. Larson and Myerhoff suggested that continuity in socialization techniques lead to continuity in value patterns; these in turn were predictive of school adjustment patterns of adolescent boys (Larson, 1967).

The problem with the selective continuity is that it doesn't say much that is useful unless further specification is added, as in Troll's distinction between similarity in personality and similarity in values and the Hill–Aldous differentiation among family behaviors. That some things change, and some things stay the same, is simply irrefutable; and to say that there is neither a great gap nor a complete congruence between generations may be points worth emphasizing in order to allay anxieties of parents and taxpayers. But, unless researchers will specify more clearly what the points of difference are, how extensive they may be, and propose models to demonstrate what the consequences of intergenerational differences are, this field of investigation may continue to add a sea of interesting facts gathered from ad hoc studies of campus demonstrations to our already entrenched speculations.

In concluding this review, one is struck with the value-laden flavor of many of these positions. The three perspectives presented above, one or the other of which seem to crop up in the conclusion section of almost every paper in this field, come close to being value statements, reflecting either radical or conservative or mixed preferences on the part of the investigator. As such, much of this scholarly debate has added little to the development of predictive knowledge in the area of intergenerational relations.

Perspectives for Future Research: A Typology of the Nature and Extent of Generational Differences

In the search for more scientifically useful analyses of social problems, the course of events usually goes from the review of past work on the issue to the creation of typologies that allow for the identification of ideal types, and thence to the gathering of data suggesting the analytic utility of these constructs. In the analysis thus far, reviews of contemporary and traditional approaches to the problem of generational differences have been made, and the contemporary approaches have been organized around a dimension derived from mass culture approach to the problem: the extent of generational difference.

But to analyze the extent of differences between age groups is not a particularly productive enterprise when taken alone. More profitable, from a scientific perspective, is to add to this dimension some of the others discussed which have much broader sociological implications. When one considers the implication of social change in the light of the nature and the effect of generational difference, a number of interesting possibilities arise in terms of the effect of generational contrasts on the social structure.

Figure 1 presents a typology that combines an identification of the extent, nature, and effect of differences between generational cohorts. The vertical dimensions, used to order the preceding section, has already been discussed. The horizontal dimension dichotomizes the predominant nature of differences into structural factors which lead therefore to permanent social change, and

Nature and Effect of Generational Differences

		Structural Factors; permanent change	Developmental Factors; temporary change
	1. "Great Gap"	A. Social revolution	B. Normal rebellion
Extent of Generational Difference	2. "Selective Gap"	C. Social evolution	D. Nothing really new
	3. "Illusory Gap"	E. Social change, but not by generations	F. Solidarity will prevail

Figure 1. The Types of Consequences from Various Perspectives of Generational Differences.

developmental or maturational factors whose effect is thus temporary in the life of the society. Individual cells represent various views on the effect of generational differences. The bivariate possibilities may be characterized thus:

TYPE A: Social revolution. There are substantial differences between age groups; the differences are induced by primarily structural factors, such as age–status inequities or adherence to an outmoded ethic. Major social change will be the result as youth move into adulthood, permanently imprinted by the inequities they have experienced (Friedenberg; Mead; Seeley; Mannheim).

TYPE B: Normal rebellion. There are substantial differences between age groups in norms, values, and behaviors; but these differences are primarily due to maturational factors. When children grow up and assume adult responsibilities, the great differences will disappear. Social change, therefore, will be minor, and the rebellion largely individual (Freud; Bettelheim; Reiss; Davis).

TYPE C: Social evolution. There are major differences between age groups in some areas, and major continuity in others. Behaviors and norms are different, while values are not. The normative differences and the acting out lead to new styles of life and thus social change. A selective gap between generations will result in major changes on issues, such as sexual mores, racism, and the like, but the changes will be gradual and selective, rather than sudden and revolutionary,

because the value system is transmitted more or less continuously (Keniston, Block et al).

TYPE D: Nothing really new. There are major differences in some areas because of normative contrasts, but continuity in others because the value system that youth will assume in adulthood is constant: responsibility, protection of home and family, necessary materialism. For example, youth become less permissive of premarital sex as they themselves become parents (Adelson; Bell).

TYPE E: Social change, but not by generations. There is great change evident in our society, but the change is not led primarily by generational conflict. All three generations are going through the social change, and to identify it with age group differences is to ignore the real ideological bases. Also, one must be aware of historical constancy in age group differences: there have always been certain differences, but today's are no greater and to call them a gap is a misnomer. The change is structurewide (Feuer, Adelson).

TYPE F: Solidarity will prevail over tangential differences. There are some apparent differences between children and their parents over largely peripheral issues that have to do with maturational factors. Despite such inevitable disagreements there is overwhelming solidarity between generations in most families; there is a basic, permanent, and constant solidarity between generations that will continue to develop (Campbell, Douvan and Adelson, Walsh).

THE POSING OF MORE REFINED RESEARCH QUESTIONS

As has been indicated, by now considerable work has been done in the study of generations; yet much of it is unsystematic and nonempirical. One can begin to build on what is accumulated and proceed to explore the uncharted areas. At the University of Southern California, a three-generational study is currently underway which will attempt to answer some of these questions.

It would seem that the first step toward collecting and ordering knowledge in this area would involve the systematic statement of important questions which remain to be answered. Perhaps the first question concerns the *nature and extent of differences between generational cohorts,* such investigations considered initially from outside the context of the family and its socialization implications. Despite imaginate cohort analyses using previously collected census and survey data (such as Cain, 1967, 1968; Cutler, 1968, 1969; Glenn, 1968; Zody, 1969) and despite the growing body of social-psychological studies of student activists, it is simply not known how much the variation *within* a cohort on a given set of behavioral attributes compares with the variation *between* cohorts. Nor is it known which kinds of attitudes, values, or norms exhibit greatest variation between age groups; or what part aging plays in the causation of differences that are apparently generational.

Second, and perhaps even more important, is the dearth of knowledge concerning the *within-family differences* between generations. Building on the pioneering work of Hill and Aldous (1969), one might ask: To what degree do parents and children share a similar perspective of intergenerational interaction; is the definition of situation shared across generational lines? What are perceived as major sources of disagreement and discussion; why is solidarity higher in some families than in others?

Third, the *antecedents or correlates* of high or low generational similarity and high or low cross-generational solidarity await more systematic investigation. What are the family structure patterns of parent–child dyads evidencing high similarity in attitudes, values, and norms? Can model socialization patterns be found that characterize conformity or rebellion? What is the effect of social mobility between generations on cross cohort differences? What is the influence of non-family socialization agencies, such as strong peer group membership, on intergenerational continuity? What is the effect of immigration, as in those families where socialization of the grandparental generation occurred in another society?

Finally, the *consequences* of high or low generational similarity or difference have only begun to be investigated (Aldous, 1965) either in terms of effects on individuals or in terms of the shape of broader social change. What does it mean to a parent, for example, to have a son who is extremely different from himself in opinions and basic life values? Is denial, or guilt, or a feeling of betrayal, or cheerful acceptance the more likely response? What does it mean to the son, who loses what Keniston and Erikson suggest may be of central importance to optimal personal development, a sense of continuity with the past? How do families cope with the inevitable instances of intergenerational conflict that occur within the family? Is it likely that continuity is deleterious in rapidly changing societies?

REFERENCES

ADELSON, J. 1970. "What generation gap?" *New York Times Magazine* (Jan. 18): 10 ff.

———— 1968. "The myth of adolescence: A polemic." Presented at the meeting of the Amer. Psychological Assn., San Francisco, September.

ALDOUS, J. 1965. "The consequences of intergenerational continuity." *J. of Marriage and the Family,* 26, 5:462–468.

———— AND R. HILL 1965. "Social cohesion, lineage type, and intergenerational transmission." *Social Forces, 43:* 471–482.

ANGEL, W. 1968. "Gaposis: The new social disease." *Vital Speeches* (August): 671–2.

BELL, R. R. 1966. *Premarital Sex in a Changing Society.* Englewood Cliffs: Prentice-Hall.

BENGTSON, V. L. 1969. "The 'generation gap': Differences by generation and by sex in the perception of parent–child relations." Presented at the annual meeting of the Pacific Sociological Assn., Seattle, April 24.

BERGER, B.   1960. "How long is a generation?" *British J. of Sociology 2:* 10–23.

BETTELHEIM, B.   1965. "The problem of generations," pp. 76–109 in E. Erikson (ed.) *The Challenge of Youth.* New York: Anchor.

BIRREN, J. E., AND BENGTSON, V. L.   1961. "The problem of generations: Emotions vs. reality." Presented at Senate Subcommittee on Aging, Santa Barbara, Calif. (Condensation in the *Center Magazine, 2*[2], 84–87).

BLOCK, J.   1970. "Rebellion re-examined: The role of identification and alienation." Unpublished, Institute of Human Development, Univ. of Calif.

BLOCK, J., HAAN, N., AND SMITH, M. B.   1970. "Socialization correlates of student activism." *J. of Social Issues, 26* (January): 25–38.

BUTLER, R. N.   1969. "Age-ism: Another form of bigotry." *Gerontologist 9*(4): 243–246.

CAIN, L. D.   1968. "Aging and the character of our times." *Gerontologist 8*(4): 250–258.

———   1967. "Age status and generational phenomena: The new old people in contemporary America." *Gerontologist 7* (2): 83–92.

CAMPBELL, E. Q.   1969. "Adolescent socialization," pp. 827–835 in D. A. Goslin (ed.) *Handbook of Socialization Theory and Research.* Chicago: Rand McNally.

CUTLER, N. E.   1969. "Generation, maturation, and party affiliation: A cohort analysis. *Public Opinion Q.*

———   1968. "The alternative effects of generations and aging upon political behavior: A cohort analysis of American attitudes toward foreign policy, 1946–1966." Oak Ridge, Tenn.: Oak Ridge National Laboratory.

DAVIS, K.   1940. "The sociology of parent–youth conflict." *American Sociological Review, 5*(4), 523–534.

DOUGHERTY, R.   1968. "Nixon unveils plan for youth service agency." *Los Angeles Times,* Part I (Oct. 17): 6.

DOUVAN, E., AND ADELSON, J.   1966. *The Adolescent Experience.* New York: John Wiley.

ERIKSON, E.   1968. *Identity: Youth and Crisis.* New York: W. W. Norton.

———   1965. "Youth: Fidelity and diversity," pp. 1–28 in E. Erikson (ed.) *The Challenge of Youth.* New York: Anchor.

———   1964. *Insight and Responsibility.* New York: W. W. Norton.

———   1959. "Identity and the life cycle." *Psychological Issues 1*(1).

———   1950. *Childhood and Society.* New York: W. W. Norton.

FEUER, L.   1969. *The Conflict of Generations: The Character and Significance of Student Movements.* New York: Basic Books.

FLACKS, R.   1967. "The liberated generation: An exploration of roots of student protest." *J. of Social Issues 23* (July): 52–72.

FRIEDENBERG, E.   1969a. "Current patterns of generational conflict." *Journal of Social Issues, 25*(2), 21–38.

———   1969b. "The generation gap." *Annals of the Amer. Academy of Political and Social Science, 382* (March): 32–42.

———   1965. *Coming of Age in America.* New York: Vintage.

———   1959. *The Vanishing Adolescent.* Boston: Beacon Press.

GAMSON, Z. F., GOODMAN, J., AND GURIN, G.   1967. "Radicals, moderates, and bystanders during a university protest." Presented at the meetings of the Amer. Sociological Assn., San Francisco, August.

GLENN, N., AND GRIMES, M.   1968. "Aging, voting, and political interest." *Amer. Soc. Rev. 33:* 563–575.

GOLDBERG, H.   1968. "Contemporary cultural innovations of youth: Popular music." Presented at the meeting of the Amer. Psychological Assn., San Francisco, August 31.

HAYAKAWA, S. I.   1968. "Mass media and family communications." Presented to the Seventy-Sixth Annual Convention of the Amer. Psychological Assn., San Francisco, September 2.

HEBERLE, R.   1951. *Social Movements.* New York: Appleton-Century-Crofts.

HILL, R., ALDOUS, J.   1969. "Socialization for marriage and parenthood," in D. Goslin (ed.) *Handbook of Socialization Theory and Research.* Chicago: Rand McNally.

KANDEL, D., AND LESSER, G.   1969. "Parental and peer influences on educational plans of adolescents." *Amer. Soc. Rev. 34* (April): 212–223.

KENISTON, K.   1968. *Young Radicals.* New York: Harcourt, Brace, & World.

———   1965. *The Uncommitted: Alienated Youth in American Society.* New York: Harcourt, Brace, & World.

KORNGOLD, B.   1968. "Contemporary culture innovations of youth: Needs or symptoms?" Presented at the meeting of the Amer. Psychological Assn., San Francisco, August 31.

LARSON, W. R.   1967. *Intrafamily Relationships and Adolescent School Adjustment.* A final report submitted to the U.S. Office of Education, on cooperative Research Project No. 1353 and S-044. Youth Studies Center, University of Southern Calif.

LARSON, W. R., AND MYERHOFF, B.   1965. "Primary and formal family organization and adolescent socialization." *Sociology and Social Research 50* (Oct.): 63–71.

Los Angeles Times   1969. "Reagan denounces Berkeley demands." (May 12).

LUBELL, S.   1968. "That 'generation gap'," pp. 58–66 in D. Bell and I. Krislol (eds.) *Confrontation.* New York: Basic Books.

MANNHEIM, K.   1952. *Essays on the Sociology of Knowledge.* London: Routledge & Kegan Paul.

MARIAS, J.   1968. "Generations: The concept." *International Encyclopedia of the Social Sciences 6:* 88–92. New York: Free Press.

MEAD, M.   1970. *Culture and Commitment: A Study of the Generation Gap.* New York: Basic Books.

MENTRE, F.   1920. *Les Generations Sociales.* Paris: Bossard.

MORIWAKI, S., AND BENGTSON, V. L.   1969. "Influence of sex lineage on intergenerational continuities." Presented at the Eighth International Congress of Gerontology, Washington, D.C.

MUSGROVE, F.   1965. *Youth and the Social Order.* Bloomington: Indiana Univ. Press.

MYERHOFF, B.   1969. "New styles of humanism: American youth." *Youth and Society, 1*(1), 151–177.

NEUGARTEN, B.   1970. "The old and the young in modern societies." *American Behavioral Scientist, 14*(1).

PINDER, A.   1926. *Das Problem der Generation in der Kunstgeschichte Europas.* Berlin.

REISS, I. R.   1968. "America's sex standards—how and why they're changing." *Trans-action 5*(4), 26–32.

RICHMAN, F.   1968. "The disenfranchised majority." *Greater Occasional Paper 1*(1): 4–14.

SEELEY, J.   1969. "Youth in revolt." *Britannica Book of the Year.* Chicago: Univ. of Chicago Press.

SIMMONS, J. L., AND WINOGRAD, B.   1966. *It's Happening.* Santa Barbara: Marc-Laird.

THOMAS, L. E., NEUGARTEN, B., AND KRAINES, R.   1970. Family correlates of student political activism. *Developmental Psychology,* Forthcoming.

TROLL, L.   1970. "The generation gap: Conceptual models." *Aging and Human Development, 1*(3).

TROLL, L. et al.   1969. "Similarities in values and other personality characteristics in college students and their parents." *Merrill-Palmer Q. 15*(4): 323–336.

Wall Street Journal   1968. "What troubles the older generation?" October 4.

WALSH, R.   1970. "Intergenerational transmission of sexual standards." Presented at the meetings of the Amer. Soc. Assn., Washington, D.C. September 2.

WESTBY, D., AND BRAUNGART, R.   1967. "Utopian mentality and conservatism: The case of the Young Americans for Freedom." Presented at the annual meeting of the Amer. Sociological Assn., San Francisco, August 30.

Some Socio-Cultural Factors in Adolescent–Parent Conflict: A Cross-Cultural Comparison of Selected Cultures

LAWRENCE SCHIAMBERG

The author reviews theories concerning parent-adolescent conflict in both technological and nontechnological societies and suggests educational implications for both generations.

Some level of adolescent–parent conflct has been virtually a constant factor in human societies. The problem of intergenerational relations has been so widespread as to have required some societal response, whether in the form of initiation rites and or rules governing intergenerational behavior.[1] It is generally during the period of adolescence that youth–parent conflicts are intensified because it is during this period that the youth must begin to make progress toward becoming an adult.

Several reasons have been suggested for the so-called "conflict of generations" in Western societies: (a) the different content of experience for youth of the present and for their parents when they were young; (b) the lack of clearly defined steps marking the recession of parental authority over children; and (c) the resulting differences between parents and youth on the psychological and sociological levels (youthful imagination versus adult experience, on the psychological level, and parental role as supervisor of child development versus child's need for independent experience on the sociological level.[2]

The brevity of these statements should not disguise the ultimate complexity of adolescent–parent conflict. For example, the idea of "different experiences" of youth and adults involves a large number of possible combinations, such as the particular style of family relationships, and lack of a sense of historical relatedness due to continual social change and particular traumatic events—to name two of the more general categories of experience. The main point of this paper is that adolescent–parent conflicts, or the so-called "conflict of generations" in the West, are not arbitrary and inscrutable but are directly related to the sociocultural background in which they

[1]S. N. Eisenstadt. *From Generation to Generation: Age Groups and Social Structure.* Glencoe, Illinois, Free Press, 1956.

[2]Kingsley Davis. "The Sociology of Parent–Youth Conflict." *American Sociological Review, 5,* August. 1940, pp. 523–535.

From L. Schiamberg, Some socio-cultural factors in adolescent–parent conflict: A cross-cultural comparison of selected cultures. Reprinted from *Adolescence,* 1969, 4(15), 333–360, by permission of the author and Libra Publications. Inc.

occur. This point will become somewhat clearer upon examination of several different cultures—their values, norms, and their handling of adolescent–parent conflicts.

However, before examining the "generation gap" in its cross-cultural perspective, an examination of the various explanations of the adolescent–parent conflict will serve to further clarify that point. Explanations of the conflict of adolescent and parent (father) have followed the pattern of initially treating the problem as an intrapsychic personality problem (Freud) and more recently emphasizing the equally important influence of the sociocultural milieu in helping to shape the personality.

Some Selected Theories

Perhaps the most famous explanation of the "conflict of generations" was Freud's notion of the "Oedipus Complex." Freud thought that the male youth's relationship with his father and, ultimately, with his culture, was determined by how well the son resolved the problem of identifying with his father versus his desire for sexual relations with his mother. The dilemma would hopefully be resolved when the adolescent son observed the father's dominance over the desired sexual object, the mother, and then would identify with the father as a source of power and control. These intrapsychic conflicts of the Oedipal period reappeared during the adolescent stage and then had to be permanently resolved.[3]

The weakness of the Oedipus complex theory is that it seems to underplay the fact that father–adolescent son relationships are conditioned largely by their social and cultural background. Freud's theory treats the problem of the "conflict of generations" from an intrapsychic point of view rather than as a problem of interpersonal relationships influenced by sociocultural norms and values. This is not to deny the existence of intrapsychic aspects of the problem but rather to suggest that Freud perhaps laid an undue amount of stress upon somewhat impressionistic and unverifiable constructs, such as the Oedipus complex.

Erik Erikson's notions of adolescent–parent conflict differ from Freud in that the latter places much more emphasis on the role of the Oedipus complex whereas Erikson emphasizes the social nature of the conflict.[4] Erikson's notion of adolescence involved the problem of establishing one's "ego identity." This concept primarily involved the individual's relationship to his parents and other individuals in his world, and the establishment of a general "stance" toward the world. Erikson was to some extent influenced by the work of cultural anthropology because he recognized that the method and content of adolescent ego identity would differ from culture to culture. Erikson did suggest that the achievement of adolescent ego identity had one element in common for all cultures: the adolescent must receive meaningful recognition of his achievements from his parents and from his society.[5]

Erikson recognized two major sources of conflict between adolescents and parents: (1) the failure of parents to accord recognition of adolescent achievement; and (2) adolescent revolt against the values and dominance of the parents. Erikson indicated that youths rarely identified with their parents during adolescence and often rebelled against their parents in their quest for ego identity. Ultimately, Erikson thought the adolescent must establish his ego identity by adopting and formulating a stance toward the world. Erikson seems to extend the Freudian concept of same-sex identification to include the social implications of a failure to achieve ego identity. Thus, in Erikson there is an emphasis upon the social nature of adolescent–parent conflicts, although he does not divorce himself from strict Freudian interpretation such as the Oedipus complex theory.

Perhaps the work of Kurt Lewin applies most specifically to the nature of adolescent–parent conflicts, since Lewin was concerned with both the stage of adolescence and the resolution of social conflicts. Lewin approached the problem of intergenerational conflicts from the point of view of his general theory of behavior which stated that behavior is a function of the person and the environment $[B=F(P.E.)]$. The sum of

[3]Sigmund Freud. *An Outline of Psychoanalysis.* New York: W. W. Norton & Co., 1940, pp. 25–33.

[4]Rolf E. Muuss. *Theories of Adolescence.* New York: Random House, 1962, pp. 34–39.
[5]Muuss, pp. 34–39.

all environmental and personal factors (motivation, needs, prception, etc.) in interactions is called the life space, and behavior is also a function of this construct [B=F(L.Sp.)].[6] Lewinian field theory recognizes that life spaces may differ between individuals and cultures. Field theory views adolescence as a transition from the life space of the child to the life space of the adult. Because of the rapid and somewhat abrupt shifts in the life space of the adolescent, he often becomes a "marginal man" with one foot in the world of childhood and the other in the world of the adult. The adolescent often experiences emotional tension due to the ambiguity of his social position. The resulting tension may affect adolescent–parent relationship and often produces conflicts over role expectations. Perhaps the most important contribution of Lewin to the study of intergenerational conflicts is his notion of the general cultural atmosphere or background for social situations: "In sociology, as in psychology, the state and event in any region depend upon the whole of the situation of which this region is a part.[7]

Some recent ideas on the relationship between personality and culture—and by implication the relationship between the generations—seem to have followed in the footsteps of Kurt Lewin. The background of parent–adolescent conflicts is seen to be interaction of the personality system and the sociocultural systems, which in turn are mediated by the family system.[8] The social system has certain functional prerequisites such as role differentiation, shared goals and values, and communication, while the personality system has certain requirements such as the satisfaction of needs and recognition of achievement. The family system mediates between the personality and social systems by ensuring the presence in individuals of societal goals and values and by providing an atmosphere in which the achievement of these goals is recognized. The socialization processes of the society—of which the family system is a prominent force—serve to create a con-gruence between the functional prerequisites of the society and the motivational patterns of the personality system.[9] Parent–adolescent crisis, if it does develop, occurs within this complex arrangement of personality, cultural, social, and familial variables. The problem of the conflict of the father with the male adolescent—the main concern of this paper—cannot then be divorced from this complex interrelationship of variables. Whether one approaches the problem from the viewpoint of a learning theory or a cognitive theory or any other point of view, the parent–adolescent relationship is ultimately limited by the nature of the particular sociocultural values in each particular culture.

The conflict of generations would seem to be best explained from a cultural anthropological view which recognizes that the parent–adolescent relationship is related not only to particular personalities and temperaments, and particular circumstances, but is also related to cultural and societal values and norms which influence the parent–adolescent relationship through the medium of the family. In light of this stance, it makes no sense to condemn industrialized Western societies for what appears to be a greater prevalence of such conflicts and rivalries, since many Western societies are so much more complex and more rapidly changing than some Eastern societies which apparently have less parent–adolescent conflict. Further, as Margaret Mead has indicated, the "Sturm und Drang" characteristic of American adolescence is perhaps the price we pay for our high level of technology and material welfare.[10]

In many of the cultures and societies to be discussed in this paper, Western technological innovations are beginning to reshape the society and, therefore, the parent–adolescent relationship. With increased industrialization in Eastern countries such as India and China, adolescent–parent problems begin to appear which bear a marked resemblance to those of the West. For example, in China, as more job opportunities have become available to adolescents, the traditional dependence of the young upon their elders has begun to

[6]Muuss, pp. 84–93.
[7]Kurt Lewin. *Resolving Social Conflicts.* New York: Harper & Row, 1948, p. 4.
[8]Aberle et. al. "The Functional Prerequisites of a Society" in Albert D. Vilman. *Sociocultural Foundations of Personality.* Boston: Houghton Mifflin Co., 1965, p. 396.

[9]Bert Kaplan (ed.). *Studying Personality Cross-Culturally.* Evanston: Row Peterson Co., 1961, p. 3.
[10]Margaret Mead. *Coming of Age in Samoa.* New York: William Morrow Co., 1928, p.

disappear and with it has gone the centuries-old tradition of unqualified respect for one's elders and ancestors.[11] A "generation gap" has begun to appear as the experiential worlds of Chinese youth have become different from the experiential world of their elders and ancestors. These experiential differences have formed a basis for more conflict between adolescents and their parents. When this situation in China (a situation which has not, as yet, permeated all of Chinese society) is compared with the United States—in which the so-called "computer revolution" is further extending the effects of industrialization—then perhaps it is not so surprising that differences of values and intergenerational conflicts are perhaps more prevalent in the West.

The question of adolescent–parent conflict has important ramifications for society at large and for the schools in particular. In Western societies, as is the case in many non-Western societies, the family is the primary influence on the developing child. However, in static (unchanging) societies parental influence is often continued into latter childhood and often into adolescence and adulthood, as children learn virtually all they need to know from their parents. However, in American society the schools have developed as a means of training youth for adult responsibilities (especially those skills necessary in a technological era). The schools (especially those devoted to higher education) in advanced technological societies serve to provide youth with the kind of information and skills which are not the specific function of the family or other societal institutions to transmit. If the schools serve only to transmit and teach technological and social skills without confronting the problem of adolescent–parent conflict and, more generally, the conflict of generations, then the problem can only become worse. The purpose of this paper is not to dispute whether the apparent "price" paid for social change is too high in terms of individual discontent, but rather to place the problem of adolescent–parent conflict in perspective: (1) by showing the intimate relationship between sociocultural values and methods of preventing adolescent–parent conflict in both non-

technological societies and in societies which are only beginning to be influenced by Western technology; and (2) to present some of the educational implications of adolescents and parents who are "out of step" with one another.

Some Selected Cultures

Indian society reflects certain characteristics of Eastern societies which have led to much lower levels of parent–adolescent differences and conflicts. Indian society has traditionally placed a great deal of emphasis on the quality of interpersonal relationships. Relatively little value is placed on the quality of material existence. Indian society has been relatively static for centuries, and as such the traditional values and norms of the society have remained unchanged and unchallenged. Generational gaps have not developed because life styles have remained constant for centuries.

A characteristic of Indian society which alleviates the strain of potential adolescent–parent conflicts and is consistent with the societal emphasis upon quality of interpersonal relationships is the Indian "extended family." This is the characteristic type of household in India.[12] The extended family allows for a number of interpersonal relationships whereas the nuclear family tends to produce more developed and intense relationships with fewer people. The extended family allows for more distribution of emotions and feelings over a greater number of family members, as compared with the nuclear family with fewer members, a potentially higher concentration of emotions per relationship, and therefore a higher likelihood of potentially explosive intergenerational relationships.[13]

In India the institution of "Asrama" insures the smooth transfer of authority from generation

[11]Marion J. Levy. *The Family Revolution in Modern China.* Cambridge: Harvard University Press, 1949, p. 155. (Human Relations Area Files: China, Source 8).

[12]The "extended" or joint family is to be distinguished from the "nuclear" family which is composed of a husband, a wife, and their children. An extended family is a group of nuclear families living together in the same household. The above definitions are taken from Stuart A. Queen, Robert W. Halsenstein, and John B. Adams. *The Family in Various Cultures.* Chicago: Lippincott Co., 1961, p. 12.

[13]Francis L. K. Hsu. *Americans and Chinese, Two Ways of Life.* New York: Henry Schuman, 1953, p. 28.

to generation. According to this tradition, sons owe complete obedience to their fathers, while the fathers are required to eventually relinquish their authority so as to avoid conflicts between adolescent males and their fathers. The Indian male is supposed to go through four Asramas, or "age grades" in Western terminology. As the age of eight the young enters the first Asrama or the celibate stage. During this period the child is guided by one or more instructors who teach him about the sacred, love, the arts, the use of weapons, and the profession which he will eventually take up.[14]

After his educatory period, the adolescent (age of twenty) is admitted into the next age grade—that of "householder." In this stage, he gets married, starts a home, and establishes himself in the profession for which he has been trained. This stage lasts until his own son reaches the "householder" stage or, if he has no children, until he is middle-aged (determined when his hair turns grey). At this point, he enters the third age grade, or "Vanaprasthasrama." During this stage the man is relieved of his household duties and is now free to devote his time to meditation or to worship. The man may live at home if he so desires, although an orthodox Hindu usually lives in a nearby house. The Vanaprasthasrama age grade ensures that by the time a man's son is able to enter the householder stage and accept the responsibilities of manhood, the man of the house is leaving the household, thus allowing a smooth transfer of authority. [15]

Underlying the social structure of the Asrama is the basic Hindu ideal of "dharma" (ideal duty) which consists of the right behavior appropriate to one's particular stage and station in life. According to the Hindu religion a man is born with three debts: (1) a debt to the gods; (2) a debt to the sages; and (3) a debt to his ancestors. The individual pays these debts by worship and ritual, learning and teaching, and by raising children.[16] These activities comprise the various age grades or asramas. Indian life is carefully organized so that each individual is constantly "paying" one of his three debts, while respecting his elders at all times.

Another underlying current in Indian life which reduces intergenerational tension is the emphasis on the ascetic life (as manifested in worship and meditation). Respect for the aged, retired Indian who devotes his last years to religious meditation is encouraged because of the widespread Hindu ideal of respect for the ascetic life. The Hindu belief that self-denial is superior to self-indulgence unites all Hindus in their respect for the aged and further contributes to the lessening of conflicts between adolescents and parents.[17] Respect for one's elders is an absolute requirement of behavior for adolescents in India.

The above description of the nature of the parent–adolescent conflict in the Indian family is perhaps most applicable to the more orthodox Hindus and higher caste families and somewhat less descriptive of lower caste families, Muslim communities in India, and families influenced by Western ideals of family relationships. Even for the orthodox Hindu families and the upper caste families, the pattern has been changing very slowly. With increasing trends toward urbanization and the greater availability of factory jobs, the adolescent has begun to liberate himself from complete dependence on the extended or joint family. For thousands of years the extended family has been the main economic force in Indian society. All members of the joint family operate as a single unit, contributing all their earnings to the entire extended family. One might expect greater resistance to this tradition, once individuals are able to establish themselves independently of the family. Although India is still far from being an industrialized nation, increasing industrialization and concomitant social change would appear to be factors in the breakdown of the traditional structure of adolescent–parent relationships.

Unlike the family structure of the United States or that of India, the traditional Chinese society (before the Communist takeover) placed great emphasis on differences of generation as the basis of role differentiation. In the traditional

[14]Irawati Karve. *Kinship Organization in India.* Deccan College Monograph Series: Poona, 1953, pp. 60–62.
[15]Karve, p. 62.
[16]Karve, p. 62.

[17]L. SS. O'Malley (ed.). *Modern India and the West.* London: Oxford University Press, 1941, p. 59. (Human Relations Area Files: India, Source 1).

Chinese society the father was respected not because he was older, or a "good father," but because he was of a different generation. The younger generation always had the burden of responsibility toward the older generation. Traditional Chinese society was a patriarchal society in which the men dominated the women and the older generation dominated the younger generation by control of the economic roles of the family. This control was often exercised by the older generation to restrain adolescents from leaving the household or otherwise causing problems, since these adolescents often had no alternative employment except that offered by their parents.[18] (This situation began to change in the twentieth century as Chinese cities became industrialized and more job opportunities were available to Chinese adolescents.) The fact that the traditional Chinese family was the primary economic unit in the society placed a great deal of power and authority in the hands of the older generation who controlled the extended family. Respect for one's elders by the Chinese adolescent was not only a traditional value of the society but was also a socioeconomic necessity.

Traditional Chinese society also had a hierarchical chain of power. Older brothers were more important than younger brothers and were responsible to their parents for insuring the proper behavior of their siblings. Through these chores and responsibilities, adolescents usually gained experience in controlling young children which would be of enormous assistance when raising their own children. In the determination of this power hierarchy, traditional Chinese society emphasized "particularistic" factors such as one's generation and the sequence of siblings. Certain Western societies (e.g., United States) place more emphasis on "universalistic" factors such as the ability to run a family.[19]

In comparison with the United States, the dominance of the older generation in the traditional Chinese society holds for both the early and later years of life. In American society the older generation dominates for the early years of growth and not necessarily for the later years.[20] This dominance of the Chinese youth and adolescents was the result of traditional Chinese inheritance customs. The land and property were not supposed to be divided among the children until the father died. No matter how ineffectively an old man carried out the household chores or the work in the fields, he was still recognized as the head of household with authority over all those of a younger age. This remained the case even though younger family members might, in fact, be doing more efficient work than the titular household head. The inheritance customs buttressed the tradition of ancestor worship and respect for one's elders. There was no problem dealing with the rate of recession of parental authority as in the United States, since parental authority was virtually a lifelong fact. Thus, three main factors established the locus of power in traditional Chinese society: (1) sex (males dominate); (2) generation; and (3) relative age (oldest siblings having preference).

From childhood on, the youth and adolescent was virtually immersed in a culture which stressed filial piety. There simply were no exceptions to the rule—that is, no successful exceptions. The child and the adolescent were confronted with examples of filial piety in their daily lives, in novels, textbooks, and in nursery schools. Veneration of the older generation and of one's ancestors was possible in traditional China because it was essentially a static culture in which the life experiences of one generation were almost identical with those of any other generation.[21] Perhaps the respect for age and experience rather than youth and imagination is best expressed by Confucius. When asked how to farm, Confucius replied: "I do not know as much as an old farmer."[22]

Respect for the aged was in part derived from the Confucian ideal that the good life consisted of the proper behavior between individuals. According to Confucius there were five types of interpersonal relationships: (1) the parent–child relationship; (2) the King–minister relationship; (3) the husband–wife relationship; (4) the older

---

[18]Marion J. Levy, p. 155.
[19]Marion J. Levy, p. 161.
[20]Marion J. Levy, p. 161.

[21]Ch'in-Kun Yang. *The Chinese Family in the Communist Revolution.* Cambridge, Massachusetts; Massachusetts Institute of Technology Center For International Studies, 1953, p. 150. (Human Relations Area Files: China, Source 70).
[22]Ch'in-Kun Yang, p. 150.

brother–younger brother relationship; and finally (5) the friend–friend relationship. Confucius felt that the highest form of respect that could be shown was between father and son. More specifically, that respect which the son showed for his father. Confucius felt that the father–son relationship was the archetypal pattern for the other four basic types of relationships. This Confucian ideal was in fact quite practical, in light of the traditional Chinese inheritance customs.[23]

The traditional precedence of the older generation has broken down in modern China. With the coming of industrialization and its emphasis on youth and adolescents as those best qualified to learn the new technological and factory jobs, the unqualified respect for the older generation began to deteriorate. The role of the traditional Chinese family as the educator of the young for occupational work is being usurped.

The gradual transition from an emphasis on age to an emphasis on youth was one of the primary trends which the Communist movement seized upon to gain support among Chinese youth. When the Communists finally gained control of China after World War II, they encouraged progressive young people to disregard existing kinship ties and to ignore the concept and practice of ancestor worship.[24] Soon progressive adolescents and young people became feared throughout China because any word from them to the Communist leadership of the practice of age prestige rituals could lead to stiff reprisals against the "guilty." Youth in "transitional" China have also rebelled against the traditional parental control of marriages and divorces. Marriage soon became focused upon the husband-wife relationship, the nuclear family (husband and wife rather than the clan), and on the free choice of one's mate. Thus, with the collapse of the family as the main economic unit in Chinese society and with the subsequent decline in age prestige, traditional adolescent respect for parents has begun to wane.

Indian and Chinese societies have traditionally had considerably less adolescent–parent conflicts primarily because the traditional concept of adulthood has been coherent and meaningful to the adolescents of these societies. There has been little difficulty in becoming an adult because the prerequisites for adult status were within the reach of virtually all adolescents. The only requirement was that adolescents become reasonably proficient in such tasks as working in the fields and caring for the young—tasks for which they had been trained all their lives. There were no frustrations involved in the choice of vocation, level of education, or style of life since there were virtually no alternatives to the existing social framework, nor any notion that society could be any different than it always had been. In short, where there were no choices and virtually everyone accepted the existing life styles, there were fewer individual frustrations—that is, fewer frustrations caused by having to choose between two or more alternative styles of life and accepting the consequences of that choice, but probably more frustrations in getting enough food—and fewer frustrations in interpersonal relationships and interpersonal role expectations.

The traditional simplicity and integrated social organization of China and India have permitted an emphasis on the quality of interpersonal relationships. In Erikson's terms, the attainment of "ego identity" has been so much easier in India and China that much smoother interpersonal relationships have been more likely to occur than in societies where ego identity is more difficult. Where there is greater agreement on the means and ends of life, and where adulthood is both possible and meaningful, adolescent–parent respect is greatly facilitated. Respect for one's elders and one's ancestors is more likely when one can be sure that Confucius' old farmer does, in fact, know more about farming than Confucius.

In some African societies the parent–adolescent relationship is linked primarily to an individual sense of reciprocity with the groups of which one is a member.[25] Principles of mutual rights and mutual duties—especially between the father and his adolescent son—run strongly through inter-

[23]Cornelius Osgood. *The Koreans and Their Culture*. New York: The Ronald Press Company, 1951, pp. 38–39. (Human Relations Area Files: Korea, Source 22).

[24]Ch'in-Kun Yang, p. 151. Also see the following for an analysis of the results of this policy: T.H. Chen, C. Wen-Hui, & Chen. "Changing Attitudes Towards Parents in Communist China," *Sociology and Social Research*, 43, pp. 175–182.

[25]Simon Ottenberg. *Cultures and Societies of Africa*. New York: Random House, 1960, p. 57.

personal relationships in many of the African societies such as the Tallensi.[26] Religious beliefs often further reinforce the influence of social groups ("spirits"— especially the spirits of the wrongdoer's ancestors—are frequently seen as forces of retribution.[27] Further, many African societies have clearly delineated systems of courts and methods of hearing disputes between the various clan members and between the various clans or joint families. Many African societies handle the problem of parent–adolescent conflict with clearly spelled out age grades or initiation ceremonies or some combination of the two (e.g., the pastoral Massai tribe). Other societies such as the Tallensi or the Mossi, lacking in highly specific age grades or initiation ceremonies, rely on other societal institutions or practices such as the principle of reciprocity (the societal norm of mutual duties and rights in interpersonal relationships, the practice of parent–adolescent avoidance, or refined methods of parent–adolescent dispute arbitration.[28]

In the social system of the pastoral Massai, the male sex is divided into boys, warriors, elders, and old men.[29] The first age grade ("boys") lasts until circumcision somewhere between the ages of thirteen and seventeen. Those who are circumcised automatically become members of a peer group of circumcised youth called by some distinctive name such as "white swords."[30] The newly circumcised youths do not become adults until they reach a senior age grade and then are allowed to marry. The newly circumcised live in a separate age-set village and are entirely under the authority of the elder age grades. Circumcision is thus only a first step to becoming an adult man. It might be thought of as the prerequisite for passage from childhood to adolescence, whereas marriage is the "rite de passage" from adolescence to adulthood.[31] Once the youth acquires a wife he becomes a "junior elder." Junior elders are mostly concerned

with family matters (their interests are mostly of a private nature) and they play a rather small role in tribal politics. Their major concern is to increase their status by having more wives and by having their own children circumcised and then initiated. Once junior elders have had one of their children initiated, they become "senior elders" with a full share in the tribal political life and assume the prime responsibility of initiating new members into Massai manhood.[32]

The major importance of the Massai system of age grades and initiation rites is that they regulate an individual's conduct in relation to those in similar or different age grades. The basic prerequisite for effective initiation ceremonies and age grades—the solidarity of the initiators in their concept of the role of an adult—is fulfilled in Massai society.[33] Unless this solidarity exists, initiation rites do not have a very powerful effect. Solidarity exists not only among the elders but also among the lower age grades, all of whom subscribe to the personality type preferred for each of the various age grades. These strong forces of cohesion among the various age grades direct attention away from inter–age grade struggles and channel it toward fulfillment of the specified goals of each age grade.

Not all societies require such rigid maintenance of age grades and "rites de passage" as do the pastoral Massai. For example, in the Tallensi society the transition from childhood to adulthood is a gradual process. The Tallensi do not have rigidly defined age grades but two rather loose criteria on which they determine the developmental level of an individual: the physiological criterion of pubescence and full physical maturity, and the economic criterion of development of skills requisite to doing a man's work in the fields. The attainment of adulthood in Tallensi society is based on a rather variable and somewhat flexible schedule. There is no social break to mark the transition from childhood to adulthood.[34]

For the Tallensi, the cornerstone of filial piety

[26]Meyer Fortes. *The Web of Kinship Among the Tallensi.* London: Oxford University Press, 1949, p. 209.
[27]Ottenberg, p. 58.
[28]Fortes, p. 209.
[29]A. C. Hollis. *The Massai: Their Language and Folklore.* Oxford: The Clarendon Press, 1905, p. 298. (Human Relations Area Files: Mossi, Source 1).
[30]Hollis, p. 298.
[31]Hollis, p. 298.

[32]B. Bernardi. *"The Age System of the Massai,"* *Annali Lateranensi,* 18. Citta de Vaticano: Pontificio Museo Missionanio Ethnologico, 1955, pp. 257–318. (H.R.A.F.: Massai).
[33]Frank W. Young. *Initiation Ceremonies—A Cross-Cultural Study of Status Dramatization.* Indianapolis: Bobbs-Merrill Co., 1965, p. 141.
[34]Fortes, p. 198.

is the basic notion that the bearing or begetting of a child is a difficult matter commensurate with a great deal of respect. Because childbearing is thought to be so difficult, children are taught to have respect for the fact that their parents brought them into the world, even though they may or may not have respect for their parents as persons. In this respect, the Tallensi believe that the bonds between the youth and the parents can never be obliterated or repudiated. The Tallensi concept of filial piety is a diffused norm rather than a specifically elaborated doctrine as in the case of the Chinese.[35]

The principle of reciprocity, or the mutual rights and duties of fathers and their adolescent sons, operates to prevent conflict between them.[36] In the parent–adolescent relationship, reciprocity operates in two notable instances to prevent conflict: (1) in the case of the use of the son's property by the father; and (2) in the arrangement of a marriage by the father. In the former case, if a man uses one of his son's cattle or goats he must eventually make an equivalent return. In the second instance, while the son is always under the authority of the father, it is the latter who arranges the son's marriage. Thus, the principle of reciprocity helps to reduce parent–adolescent conflicts by ensuring that, in the long run, mutual services and favors must balance.

Other means of reducing parent–adolescent conflict are held in common with the Mossi tribe of the Voltaic Republic just north of Ghana. The basic economic activities of the tribe include the production of livestock and cotton, and caravan trading. If a wife gives birth to a male child as her first born, the father sends the child away to live with the boy's maternal relatives until he reaches puberty. The father then has little contact or conflict with his future successor. This practice of initial removal of the newborn child is a rather drastic means of avoiding parent–adolescent conflict.

Since the Mossi firstborn males eventually inherit the wives of their fathers, it is often those wives who produce friction between fathers and their adolescent sons. In order to avoid conflict, Mossi firstborn sons are usually allowed to visit the family compound for important purposes only. It is an unfortunate circumstance when a father encounters his oldest adolescent son at the doorway of the household compound. In order to avoid this situation, the father or son usually shout something loud upon entering or leaving the household.[37]

Mossi fathers usually do not want to procure wives for their sons because the Mossi father sees the possession of a wife as representing the advantages of majority status. Since the son will gain this status only when the father dies, the antagonism between father and son is increased. It is not surprising that fathers often become extremely jealous of the development of their adolescent sons since this usually signals—at least in their minds—their eventual demise and decline in power. Mossi fathers are careful to avoid situations in which they are or could be directly compared with their adolescent sons. Often a Mossi father will not be seen walking with his eldest son in the village, lest someone accidentally fail to acknowledge their difference in age.[38]

Thus, in Mossi society the major indication of majority status and the major basis for adolescent–parent conflict is the possession of a wife by the adolescent. This state of affairs is further complicated by the fact that the eldest adolescent son usually inherits his father's wife upon the death of the father, and also because the adolescent youth remains completely dependent upon the father for obtaining a wife. (Adolescent sons do not possess the property to trade for a wife and must rely upon their fathers to get them one.) Interpersonal relationships between fathers and their adolescent sons are strained because of the social structure of Mossi society in which a confrontation between father and son is openly acknowledged, although adequate precautionary measures are taken. Perhaps the adherents of the Oedipal theory of generational conflict would point out that the very fact that the Mossi mothers are the subject of conflict between fathers and sons is evidence that the Oedipus complex produces adolescent–parent conflict. The problem

[35]Fortes, p. 171.
[36]Fortes, p. 207.

[37]Elliot P. Skinner. "Intergenerational Conflict Among the Mossi: Father and Son." *The Journal of Conflict Resolution, 5,* March, 1961, Ann Arbor, pp. 55–60.
[38]Skinner, pp. 55–60.

with such a position is that there is little or no objective evidence that what appears to be a manifestation of the Oedipus complex in Mossi society does in fact occur in other cultures with any kind of regularity.

Besides the Mossi practice of avoidance, their system of intergenerational conflict resolution helps to alleviate adolescent–parent conflicts. When a serious decision or problem arises between parents and their adolescent youth, the head of the extended family is consulted. No decision regarding such intergenerational problems is ever made without consulting the head of the extended family. This type of decision-making process helps to improve parent-adolescent relations by (1) insuring that adequate reflections and thought precede each decision, and (2) by preventing direct confrontations between parents and adolescents.[39]

Further supplementing the practices of avoidance and dispute arbitration in maintaining smooth relationships between parents and adolescents is the practice of shared adolescent discipline. Disciplining of Mossi adolescents is a shared responsibility between the father—the family head—and the head of the adolescent work group. After Mossi adolescents are circumcised at about the age of thirteen or fourteen, they join a "work group" composed of other youths recently circumcised. In the work group the youths perform work in the fields and are given their food and lodging for the seven-month period that they work there. During this work period the adolescents are responsible to the work group leader —usually an adult—for proper behavior and may be disciplined by the leader for improper actions. The division of disciplinary responsibility in this fashion reduces the possibility that conflict regarding disciplinary practices will develop between father and adolescent.[40]

Should the situation ever arise that the eldest adolescent has been given a wife, the son is required to leave the family household and build his own "soukala" or hut, even though he will eventually return to his father's house to inherit his property when the latter dies. The Mossi do this because of a strong belief that young married adolescents have a strong need for independence and that if the father were to keep his married son at his side, the latter might wish his father's death so that he could achieve independence.[41] (Mossi fathers maintain the right to control the lives of their children until the death of the children or the father. Mossi children rarely achieve independence until the death of the father, at which time the property is divided and the father's wives are inherited.)[42]

Thus, the problem of adolescent–parent relationships is kept within reasonable bounds by means of several rules of behavior which govern the relationship of the adolescent and the parent. Potential intergenerational rivalry is fostered primarily by the social custom of inheritance of wives. In order to prevent such conflict the following rules of behavior have been established: (1) the enforced removal of the eldest male child from the household; (2) the dispute arbitration process; (3) the divided disciplinary responsibility; and (4) the departure of the eldest married son from the household. The parent–adolescent conflict is rooted deeply in the structure and functions of the Mossi culture. The primary economic and social force in Mossi culture is the joint family. In order to maintain the solidarity of the family unit, the act of acquiring wives is reserved for the elders of the extended family— the father, and the clan chief or head. All marriages are arranged to enhance the extended family and to ensure that all new family members and new wives will remain loyal to the extended family. The inheritance of wives indicates not only the relatively low position of women in Mossi society but also serves to maintain the continuity and effective operation of the Mossi extended family by retaining effective women workers in the family unit. The code of behavior governing adolescent–parent relationships is the Mossi method of successfully integrating personal needs of both fathers and their adolescent sons with the functional prerequisites of a strong and efficient extended family.

---

[39]Skinner, pp. 55–60.

[40]Eugene Mongin. *Essay on the Manners and Customs of the Mossi People in the Western Sudan.* Paris: Augustin Challamel, 1921, p. 92. (Human Relations Area Files: Mossi, Source 2).

[41]Louis Tauxier. *The Black Population of the Sudan, Mossi and Gourounsi Country, Documents and Analyses.* Paris: Emile Larose, Librairie-Editeur, 1912, p. 49.

[42]Tauxier, p. 49.

In the Arab world the general guidelines for parent–adolescent relationships are laid down in the religious mores and teachings which pervade all aspects of Arab life. Muhammed is reported to have said: "Whoever has a son born to him, let him give him a good name, teach him good manners, and when he reaches puberty get him married. . . . if he reaches puberty and has not been married and falls into sin, it is the father who is responsible. . . ."[43] The Qur'an (holy book of the Muslim faith) advocates proper respect toward one's parents and states that filial piety is the highest form of good works. In practice these ideals are usually translated into a rather stern father who exercises his absolute authority over his children in arranging their marriages and ensuring that they do not "fall into sin," lest he be responsible. Adolescents are required to show absolute respect and obedience to their father.

Among Arab families there usually exists a close relationship between mother and youth and a rather loose one between father and adolescent boy. The Arab father has complete authority over both sons and daughters. Generally the father is the disciplinarian while the mother helps to keep the family together as an integrated unit and often acts as a buffer between the father and the adolescent. If the adolescent gets into any kind of trouble, help is usually sought from the mother rather than from the father. The parent–child relationship is usually a short one for girls, who generally marry at a rather early age and leave the household, whereas sons have an extended relationship with their parents. The son eventually marries and brings his wife with him to live with his family.[44]

The rights of Arab youth and adolescents are usually fixed by custom and/or law. The child has the right to food, care, and upbringing. The child has three types of guardianship: (1) guardianship of upbringing (tarbia) which is accomplished by the mother and usually ends when the child is seven or nine years old; (2) guardianship

of education (spiritual guardianship) which involves proper training in the values and rules of the society; and (3) guardianship of property which involves the maintenance of the adolescent's property until he reaches majority status.[45]

In the villages of Turkey, the male population is divided into four groups: (1) children; (2) unmarried youths (delikani); (3) young men (genc); (4) old people (ihtiyan). Marriage is the only necessary requirement to move from the delikani age grade to the genc stage. Passage from childhood to delikani is accomplished by growing a moustache, while passage from genc to ihtiyan is accomplished by growing a beard to accompany the moustache. Circumcision is a necessary requirement before one can marry.[46]

Villages in Turkey are made up of households containing extended families. Status in this society is designated by difference in age. Old people are held in greater esteem than the young. Respect for age difference is demonstrated dramatically at household dinners and community feasts. Old men and guests always sit in places of honor and are served first.[47] Adolescents must always address their elders with specific titles or kinship terms indicating their age grade, and are rarely permitted to address them with their actual names. Competition between adolescent and parent is further diminished by the social concept of status in Turkish life. One always outranks those in lower age grades. Status is determined by one's position in his age grade (a man is judged by his achievements in comparison with other individuals of his age).[48] In this manner, inter–age grade comparisons are usually avoided and are relatively insignificant if they occur at all. Such comparisons between adolescents and adults are relatively unimportant since both are virtually agreed on the basic goals of adolescence—to get the adolescent married and to prevent him from "falling

[43]Raphael Patai. "Relationship Patterns Among the Arabs," *Middle Eastern Affairs,* 5, New York: Council for Middle Eastern Affairs, Inc., 1951, pp. 180–85. (Human Relations Area Files: Middle East, Source 41)
[44]Patai, p. 184.

[45]Majid Khadduri and Herbert J Liebesny (eds.). *Law in the Middle East: Origin and Development of Islamic Law,* 1, Washington: The Middle East Institute, 1955, p. 155. (Human Relations Area Files: Middle East, Source 56.)
[46]Paul Stirling. *Turkish Village.* London: Weidenfeld and Nicholson, 1965, p. 223.
[47]Joe E. Pierce. *Life in a Turkish Village.* New York: Holt, Rinehart, and Winston, 1964, p. 83.
[48]Pierce, p. 84.

into sin." Thus, there is less intergenerational conflict than in the West because life experience in Turkey has been relatively static for hundreds of years. There is no conflict because there are no alternative styles of life.

Transmission of knowledge to the adolescent presents no real problem because this knowledge is virtually the same from generation to generation and specific social institutions have long satisfied this need. The most important semiformal situation for learning the values of the village culture and the role of man in village society are the evening meetings at the Muhtar's home (the Muhtar is the village head—usually an older experienced man).[49] The meetings are usually attended by all the males in the village although they are primarily directed at the adolescent males.

The relatively homogeneous values of the Turkish village, which promoted a smooth transition from adolescence to adulthood and which greatly lessened the incidence of parent–adolescent conflict, have nonetheless been threatened by social change. Problems have begun to arise due to the increasing number of youths going on to higher education after grade school and, therefore, not getting married at the customary age of about nineteen.[50] Most of the towns and villages now send their children to a "grade school" from which qualified graduates continue on to a junior high school and to a high school ("lise"). As of 1961, very few of the villagers had finished grade school.[51] However, with the increasing number of village children and adolescents who complete high school and continue on to some form of higher education, youths are delaying marriage. This failure to marry at the traditional age has perpetuated the status of Turkish adolescence such that, in the future, there may no longer be a clear and distinct difference between adolescents and adults. The implications of this social change for the adolescent–parent relationship are that experiential differences between adults and adolescents and the special opportunities afforded to the educated youth may, in fact, lead to a kind of "generation gap."

[49]Pierce, p. 91.
[50]Pierce, p. 91.
[51]Pierce, p. 91.

Summary, Conclusions and Observations

In conclusion, the behavior norms and role expectations provide the basis for the smooth adolescent–parent relationships surveyed in the several cultures presented in this paper. Nontechnological societies which have relatively clearcut and broadly accepted societal goals and values have less adolescent–parent conflict than societies in which individuals are confronted with the choice of many different occupations and life styles. This is not to suggest that the so-called generation gap has reached the critical stage in industrialized nations or that choice of life styles is a bad thing, but that where conditions exist which could create experiential gaps between parents and adolescents, the stage is set for more numerous intergenerational conflicts.

Surely, not all adolescent–parent conflicts are caused by social change or are avoided merely by the absence of social change. Personality variables undoubtedly play a role. Perhaps a solution of the generation gap lies in the development of certain cognitive styles which will promote understanding between the generations in the face of ever increasing social change. Perhaps a feasible method of partially alleviating the problem is for the school to assume some leadership responsibility in teaching individuals to accept change and to adapt to a world of ever increasing change and complexity in which the establishment of "ego identity" (a stance toward the world) in adolescence becomes ever more difficult. Perhaps what is needed—and is most difficult to develop in individuals—is a tolerance for uncertainty. As the rate of social change increases, the shape of the future becomes somewhat fuzzy and the schools become less certain of how to prepare people for that future. To the extent that this kind of situation exists, it would seem logical that the more successful individuals will be those who can tolerate and live with this uncertainty. David E. Hunt of the Ontario Institute of Educational Studies has developed a model of cognitive development which has its goal a conceptual style which permits numerous combinations of information processing, as opposed to monolithic or stereotyped categorization of information.[52] Higher conceptual levels are associated with more advanced information processing and with greater tolerance of frustration and uncertainty.

Perhaps also the school could exercise some leadership in reexamining some basic ideas of human development such as Maslow's notion of self-actualization. Maslow postulates two basic kinds of human needs: (1) deficit-needs, or those shared by all members of the human species (e.g., safety, love), and (2) idiosyncratic or self-actualization needs which are peculiar to each person.

Just as all trees need sun, water, and foods from the environment, so do all people need safety, love and status from their environment. However, in both cases this is just where real development of individuality can begin, for once satiated with these elementary, species-wide necessities, each tree and each person proceeds to develop in his own style, uniquely, using these necessities for his own private purposes. In a very meaningful sense, development then

becomes more determined from within rather than from without.[53]

As the distribution of wealth and the standard of living have increased, notions of self-actualization such as the acquisition of material goods have become somewhat less meaningful to a growing minority of so-called "alienated" youth. Although it may have been very meaningful for a man to work to provide food and shelter for his family during the depression of the 1930s, when food and jobs were hard to get, it is perhaps somewhat less meaningful to work to pay off a mortgage on a split-level suburban home. David Riesman has raised the poignant question: "Abundance, for what?"[54] Perhaps adolescent–parent conflict and the attendant generation gap might be eased if there were some reinterpretation of the notion of self-actualization to encompass the broad range of human possibilities.

[52]O.J. Harvey, David E. Hunt, and Harold M. Schroder. *Conceptual Systems and Personality Organization.* New York: Wiley, 1961.

[53]Abraham H. Maslow. *Toward A Psychology of Being.* New York: Van Nostrand Co., 1962, p. 31. Maslow presents a possible approach to the question of "self-actualization" by defining motivation in terms of two concepts: "self-actualizing" motivation and "deficiency" motivation.

[54]David Riesman. *Abundance, for What? And Other Essays.* Garden City: Doubleday, 1964.

Chapter 17: Suggested Additional Readings

BRITTAIN, C. V.   An exploration of the bases of peer compliance and parent–compliance in adolescence. *Adolescence,* 1967–68, *2*(8), 445–458. Brittain notes that adolescents are often involved in conflicting parent–peer expectations. He concludes, on the basis of his studies, that adolescents are influenced more strongly by parents in certain types of situations, and by peers in others. They rely on adults in more important, crucial decisions.

COUNT, J.   The conflict factor in adolescent growth. *Adolescence,* 1967, *2*(6), 167–180. The writer sees conflict as a built-in critical factor which may further, retard, or frustrate a youth's full personality development. Youth's elders are also in a state of conflict over their role as a receding generation. The writer suggests that a more intelligent management of adult–adolescent conflict would make for fewer cases of young adults who suffer from delayed adolescence.

DENISOFF, R. S., & LEVINE, M. H.   Generations and counterculture. *Youth and Society,* 1970, *2*(1), 33-58. Rock themes, past and present, are analyzed to determine evidence of generational conflict.

Dialogue between the generations.   *Harper's,* October 1967, *235*, 45–64. A group of college editors and writers look at the differences in the way the generations perceive each other and the major issues in American society today.

FEUER, L. S.   *The conflict of generations: the character and significance of student movements.* New York: Basic Books, 1969. The author, who writes from 40 years' experience with student movements, discusses basic causes of such movements, using illustrations from many countries.

FRIEDENBERG, E. Z.   Current patterns of generational conflict. *Journal of Social Issues,* 1969, *25*(2), 21–38. The generational conflict today is seen as different from that in the past. Youth have no desire to displace their elders; instead, they are fighting for their right to live outside the system.

HAAN, N.   Moral redefinition in families as a critical aspect of the generational gap. *Youth and Society,* 1971, *2*(3), 259–283. The author suggests that generational gap must be logically anticipated if humans are to improve upon, rather than merely reflect, their experience.

HERZOG, E., SUDIA, C. E., ROSENGARD, B., & HARWOOD, J.   *Teen agers discuss the generation gap.* U. S. Department of Health, Education and Welfare, Office of Child Development, Children's Bureau. Youth Reports #1, 1970. This article excellent insights into youth's reactions to the generation gap.

JENCKS, C., & RIESMAN, D.   The war between the generations. *Teachers College Record,* October 1967, *69*(1), 1–21. The writers trace the relationship between students and faculty down through the years and into the present. The problems of various types of youth are discussed, along with their implications for the colleges.

KLEIN, A. *(Ed.) Natural enemies: youth and the clash of generations.*   Philadelphia: Lippincott, 1969. This comprehensive book discusses why youth are rebelling and are seeking new values in love, politics and life styles. It brings together from both sides of the generation gap much provocative comment from 79 authors, including sociologists, psychologists, and anthropologists.

WEINER, I. D.   The generation gap–fact and fancy. *Adolescence.* 1971, 6(22), 155–166. The author reviews matters of "fact and fancy" relating to the generation gap. He concludes that the notion of such a gap has often been overgeneralized and that most young people, in fact, simply reflect the values of their families and communities.

18

Youth as Political Activists

Historically, student movements have been important political and social forces in many nations (Altbach, 1970). The European nationalist struggles of the nineteenth century had strong student support; and certain revolutionary movements—notably the German revolutions of 1848 and the various Russian upheavals—placed students in instrumental roles. In addition, students have played a significant, sometimes the most critical, political role in the developing areas of the world.

At least until the 1960s, the situation in the United States was quite different. True, in this nation we have pictured the adolescent as consciously planning for a better world—as dreaming dreams and sometimes acting upon those dreams; and this image has been accurate, except in the political sense. At least until the Vietnam situation and the civil rights movement became critical, politics was not a feature of the American teen culture. Even now, exchange students from other lands often comment on the relative political apathy of American youth.

What has accounted for the average American youth's apathetic, even negative, attitude toward politics? One factor has been the insulation of the teen culture from the strains of the larger culture that surrounds it. Another has been the relative stability of the American government. Still another is the example set by adults. Instead of arguing ideologies, say Stone and Church (1957), most American adults jostle each other in their anxiety to get into the political middle of the road. Consequently, youth have been deprived of things to rebel for, as well as against. Youth are even exposed to religions which are merely "well-adjusted working arrangements with reality [p. 318]."

Keniston (1962) describes youth's lack of concern for politics as the result of a retreat into the private sphere. He contrasts youth's general apathy toward political activity with the burgeoning of the arts on college campuses, and claims that this commitment to the aesthetic instead of the political follows from youth's feeling of helplessness in the face of powerful social and historical forces. Young people's vision and consciousness are split: one eye is on their own welfare, the other on some private utopia. They will be good organizational workers but lack the intensity of involvement which will upset "bureaucratic applecarts." The majority will be chiefly concerned with their own private sphere, which permits the greatest personal control. Their commitment and fidelity will be confined to the aesthetic, the sensual, and the experiential.

Youth's split consciousness, continues Keniston, bodes ill both for the individual and for society; few persons can maintain so ambiguous an outlook without psychological strain. Too, such privatism may provide greater short-run stability of society at the price of long-run stagnation. By exaggerating their own powerlessness, young people see "the system" as more unmalleable than it really is. Therefore, social changes will continue to occur haphazardly, rather than by conscious plan in accordance with the needs of society. We cannot afford such apathy, concludes Keniston; world problems are so acute that for the ablest college students to assume such an indifferent stance seems almost suicidal.

Brighter youth, writes Lifton (1962), are perhaps not so much apathetic as ambivalent in their attitude toward vanguard influences. They are attracted to liberating elements, yet are fearful of cultural confusion. Feeling hopelessly dislocated in the face of rapid and undigested historical change, they waver between near total commitment to causes and near total phobic avoidance of them. Such deliberate individuals do help put the brakes on more impulsive types who run about, seeking axes to grind. On the other hand, while such youths may never wreck society's ship, neither will they achieve miracles of reform or progress.

Parsons (1962) notes that American youths' susceptibility to political ideologies shifts with the prevailing winds. During the 1930s and 1940s, a limited number of youth were attracted to Communism. In the late 1960s, a similar resurgence of interest in politics took place, his time focused on specific issues—notably race relations, nuclear war, and the draft—rather than on broader ideologies. Intellectuals may deplore this indifference of youth to basic philosophies, but it simply reflects the apathy of the larger society. Intense political activity is most prominent in developing societies where intellectuals play a large role, or in those where major political transitions and reorganizations are in process; in these situations, youth more easily fuse a sense of personal destiny with social history.

However, Denney (1962) believes it is fortunate that most young people are not running pell-mell to redeem the social order. They seem aware of the tenor of their time and are neither frightened by dreadful freedoms nor oppressed by social tyrannies; and they have a talent for the "delayed reflex," which may prove an important resource in the politics of a nuclear age.

Halleck (1968) has identified various hypotheses which have been proposed to account for the political activism of the minority of students who do become involved. One hypothesis defines student activism as a function of some unfortunate characteristic of the protester himself, some consequence of his permissive upbringing, his family pathology, or the excessive affluence of the society in which he lives. Other hypotheses are sympathetic to the student, portraying him as a victim of, or as a crusader against, some external circumstances such as the war in Vietnam or civil rights discrimination. Still other theories propose such impersonal causes of student activism as the influence of the mass media and the stresses imposed by a technological society.

Rosenmayr (1968) points out that leaders of political movements have often catered especially to adolescents, because of their plasticity, and because convictions formed during the teen years tend to persist. Such leaders have recognized that the perpetuation of their movements depended upon bringing youth into their camp. After political goals were achieved, the movements have often evolved into instruments of social revolution. These traditions of activism, which originated during a nationalistic period, have proved hard to destroy. In many Asian countries, for example, these movements have their roots deep in society and student activism is considered quite legitimate. Meantime, the governments have come to use student groups as instruments of power and, in consequence, such groups have become a source of political power in society.

Bettelheim (1969) believes that adolescent revolt arises because society maintains young people too long in a status of dependency and too long deprives them of a feeling of mature responsibility. He also avers that much discontent stems from the failures of higher education, particularly from too large classes and the concomitant inferior instruction. As a result, students lose interest in furthering their education and seek group therapeutic experiences which will help them to find themselves. Other writers attempt to account, more specifically, for the student revolt of the 1960s. One of the prominent participants in the disturbances at the University of California at Berkeley portrayed such activities as personally exhilarating and satisfying. He described the days of revolt as distinguished throughout by "a fierce joy," "a sense of theatre," much "play acting," and "a sense of history, that one is himself participating in and helping to make history" (Rossman, 1968). Moreover, the activist feels that if society is significantly shaken up, its structure will somehow fall into place again with a more efficient network of interrelationships, like the aftereffect of massive electroshock therapy. The nature of this therapy derives from the heat of confrontation and the demonstration itself.

The Rowntrees (1968) attribute the political youth movement to young people's belief that they are being exploited both as soldiers and students. They feel themselves rejected by the dominant society and, in consequence, band together against adults. Nevertheless, the youth movement encounters certain difficulties because of the leaders' inexperience. Sometimes the youthful protesters look to older radicals for leadership, but these persons are often themselves bound by rigid ideas of class and organization. According to the Rowntrees, youth's present task "is to continue to unmask and confront the system that jeopardizes its own future" in order merely to preserve the status quo.

Using a somewhat different approach, Pitts (1971) seeks to account for student activism in terms of three social forces. The first, the civil rights movement, gave youths their initial experience with mass politics. The second force, the mass media—particularly the television networks and certain national news magazines (*Life, Time, Newsweek*)—dramatize political movements and portray sympathetically an ideology often shared by the students. The third force, the "hippyization" of antiwar students and the New Left (which led members of the political student movement to adopt the hippies' life style, dress and hair fashions, language, and sexual mores) gave these activist students a certain political identity. Uniting with these youth, many of the hippies thereupon renounced their own erstwhile nonviolence and political apathy; and the New Left also absorbed many of the drug and music cultists. When the mass media spoke of youth, then, they did not refer to the average clean-cut, all-American youth with his good parent relations, coolness toward drugs and promiscuous sex, and "a political outlook slightly to the left of Hubert Humphrey [Pitts, p. 224]," but to the youth who had adopted the hippie counter-culture. From this blending of youths interested in drugs, music, and politics emerged two further symbols of the counter-culture: the first, an assault on the puritan ethos; the other, a brand of political activism which subordinates effective action to personal exaltation of the participants.

Regardless of the cause of student activism, what is its residual worth? Are student activists really naughty big-little boys and girls who have discovered a game more exciting than cops-and-robbers? Many writers consider it desirable that youth concern themselves with politics. According to Riesman (1960), "far-reaching" changes" in "men's hopes and desires" are "necessary to create a better world [p. 225]." However, youth need a vision of a "viable and conceivable society," which should not become "fanaticism in pursuit of Utopian goals" nor "an Intellectual Swindle for True Believers." Keniston (1962) agrees with Riesman: "Society needs youthful activists. Each generation builds on relevant aspects of the past, yet creates new images of life which will provide points of constancy in a time of rapid change [p. 170]." In this way, the gap between generations is bridged. Moreover, asserts Parsons (1962), indictments of society by youth may be interpreted as a kind of campaign position which prepares them for their future role when they must take over the main responsibilities of society.

Stone and Church (1957) claim that youth cannot live comfortably with a set of ideas without first having tried out a variety of alternatives, no matter how irrational these alternatives may be. Dissatisfaction, unaccompanied by alternative ideas, may produce destruction. Youth who are merely against something are, to use Lindner's term, rebels without a cause. Rebellion is good when it is harnessed to idealistic goals, no matter how unworkable; but if blind and formless, it sours into cynicism or violence. Finally, Lifton (1962) notes that youth, with their fresher view of things, open up new possibilities in the universal task of "coming to grips with the ever accelerating, ever more threatening movement of history [p. 195]."

However, a few writers take a less favorable view of student activism, at least in its more violent forms. Indeed, notes Bettelheim (1969), there has been too little appraisal of the effect of student rebellion. Activists have often succeeded in paralyzing universities, while time and energy which should be devoted to more contructive matters are wasted in forestalling student–administration confrontations. Rubinstein (1969) finds certain paradoxes in student protest. For one thing, in their efforts to uphold individual freedom, student activists forcibly abridge the freedom of others. A second paradox is the activist's "intellectual anti-intellectualism" as opposed to his "dogmatic antidogmatism." While most student activists are above average in intelligence, they dogmatically refuse to compromise at any level. A third paradox exists in their rebellion against an authoritarian, politically-oriented society, while their own rebellious organization is shot through with all sorts of political tactics. Finally, even in climates of freedom and acceptance, the activists on seeking out issues to rebel against.

However, Rubinstein advises against extreme views of any sort about student activism. It is easy, he concludes, either to be too sympathetic toward the activists' somewhat romantic idealism on the one hand, or to be too condemnatory on the other.

Some authors call student activists "a prophetic minority"; others brand them "rebels without a program." Other opinions abound, and it is difficult to sift the wheat from the chaff in what one reads about student activism. Many expressed opinions have little or no nationwide data to support them (Abrahams et al., 1968). The truth is that we still lack adequate research about student activism, particularly concerning the social class and religious principles of students involved in it (Altbach, 1970). Pending such sober appraisals, activist events are apparently magnified and amplified by the network of almost instantaneous communication existing in modern Western society (Rubinstein, 1969). Meantime, student activists' activities are communicated to other student groups in "instant replay" or "instant regurgitation." Thus, each event tends to precipitate others in chain-reaction fashion, and everyone affected, whether student or member of the Establishment, sustains a certain psychic shock from the more violent activist episodes.

Whatever conclusions are reached about the current status of student protests must remain tentative because the whole situation is extremely fluid (Rubinstein, 1969). Even as these words are written youths' protests are waning, and younger youth are beginning to look on older youth—the standard-bearers of the activist movements—as having handled things pretty badly (U. S. News and World Report, 1971). Professor Michael Novak of the State University of New York observed: "Younger high-school students will seek some fresh, easy way to distinguish themselves from their older brothers and sisters. They will note that "consciousness expanding" drugs expanded few consciousnesses; that the politics of rage sated passions but improved the lot of few of the poor, and diminished the right wing and the police and the armies not at all; and that their older brothers and sisters, full of idealistic slogans, entered middle-age unprepared, embittered, isolated and by-passed (U. S. News and World Report, 1971, pp. 17–28).

From the vast number of selections dealing with youth's political activism, we have chosen for our first selection an article by Keniston, who reviews developmental studies of moral reasoning and relates them to the protest movement. Although most student activists are capable of high-level moral reasoning, there are exceptions. Moreover, concludes Keniston, a high level of moral reasoning does not guarantee moral behavior. In the second article, Flacks reviews the student movement in historical perspective and outlines the major themes of the present activists. He then discusses various hypotheses concerning the sociopsychological roots of student protests and cites research designed to test these hypotheses. Finally, he presents preliminary findings from his own research and suggests issues which have yet to be solved.

REFERENCES

ABRAHAMS, M. H. et al. Student protests: A phenomenon for behavioral sciences research. Science, 1968, 161(3836), 20–23.

ALTBACH. P. G. Student movements in historical perspective. Youth and Society, 1970, 1(3), 333–357.

BETTELHEIM. B.   The college student rebellion: Explanations and answers. *Phi Delta Kappan,* 1969, *50*(9), 511–514.

DENNEY, R.   American youth today: A bigger coast, a wider screen. *Daedalus,* 1962, *91,* 142–143.

HALLECK, S. L.   Hypotheses of student unrest. Address delivered to the American Association for Higher Education, Chicago, Illinois, March 4, 1968.

KENISTON, K.   Social change and youth in America. *Daedalus,* 1962, *91,* 167–170.

LIFTON, R. J.   Youth and history: Individual change in postwar Japan. *Daedalus,* 1962, *91,* 167–195.

LINDNER, R. M.   Rebel without a cause. New York: Grune & Stratton, 1944.

PARSONS, T.   Youth in the context of American society. *Daedalus,* 1962, *91,* 97–123.

PITTS, J.   The counter culture. *Dissent,* June 1971, 18, 216–229.

REISMAN, D.   The search for challenge. *Merrill-Palmer Quarterly,* July 1960, *6*(4), 218–234.

ROSENMAYR, L.   Towards an overview of youth's sociology. *International Social Science Journal,* 1968, *20*(2), 286–315.

ROSSMAN, M.   Breakthrough at Berkeley. *The Center Magazine,* 1968, *1*(4), 40–49.

ROWNTREE, J., & ROWNTREE, M.   The political economy of youth. *Our Generation,* 1968, *6*(1–2), 1–36.

RUBINSTEIN, E. A.   Paradoxes of student protests. *American Psychologist,* 1969, *24*(2), 133–141.

STONE, L. J., & CHURCH, J.   *Childhood and adolescence.* New York: Random House, 1957, 318–319.

US NEWS AND WORLD REPORT   End of the youth revolt. August 9, 1971, *71*(6), 26–31.

Student Activism, Moral Development, and Morality

KENNETH KENISTON

Keniston reviews recent research concerning moral development and, within this context, evaluates the moral level of student activists.

To discuss student activism today without immediately becoming involved in moral issues seems almost impossible. From the rhetoric of politicians to empirical research, judgments of moral praise or condemnation enter into (and frequently dominate) reactions to student protest. Political tracts, novels, research studies, biographies, and autobiographies that deal with student activism today generally emphasize the conflict between youth's personal morality (or immorality) and the immoral (or moral) practices of the surrounding world. Even the most thoughtful and scholarly analyses of contemporary student dissenters usually place them near one of two poles: "amoral-and-neurotic rebels" (2, 11, 42) or "fine-young-idealists-who-may-save-us-all." (36, 41) Whether we like it or not, the phenomenon of youthful protest seems to stimulate intense moral concerns in the beholder.

In the comments that follow, I will discuss data and interpretations concerning the moral development of politically active young men and women at a particular stage of life that coincides roughly with college and graduate school age. I will call this stage of life "youth." By speaking of "youth"

instead of late adolescence, I mean to suggest that the experience of those whom we awkwardly term "late-adolescents-and-young-adults" is in many respects different from the experience of younger adolescents but, at the same time, that it differs profoundly from that of adults. In other writings (19–22) I have argued that one of the characteristics of post-industrial societies is that they are beginning to sanction a previously unrecognized stage of development that intervenes between the end of adolescence proper and the beginning of adulthood. Not everyone passes through this stage: traditionally, most young men and women have had little real adolescence at all; and those few who have experienced adolescence as a developmental stage have usually entered adulthood immediately thereafter. But today, for a rapidly growing minority of young Americans—mostly college students, graduate students, members of the New Left, hippies, or in some cases military recruits—a previously unlabeled stage of development is opening up. This stage is defined sociologically by postadolescent disengagement from the adult society, developmentally by continuing opportunities for psychological growth,

K. Keniston, Student activism, moral development, and morality. Reprinted from *American Journal of Ortho-psychiatry,* July 1970, *40*(4), 577–592. Copyright ©, The American Orthopsychiatric Association, Inc. Reproduced by permission.

and psychologically by a concern with the relationship of self and society. It is this stage of life which I term the stage of youth.

In considering youthful activism and moral development, it is necessary to underline that moral development is not only an essential sector of development in its own right, but also a battleground upon which conflicts whose origins lie elsewhere are fought out. It is in fact arbitrary to isolate moral development from identity development, from ego development, from psychosexual development, from the development of intimacy, from new relationships with parents and peers, and from intellectual development. Nonetheless, moral development during youth has been more carefully studied than any other sector. In the work of Erikson (6–8), Lawrence Kohlberg (23–27), William Perry (37, 38), and Smith, Block, and Haan (3, 15, 17, 43, 44), we have accumulating evidence about the relationship between moral development and the often disruptive, idealistic, moralistic and anti-conventional behaviors of modern youth.

Moral Development and Socio-Political Activism

The early psychoanalytic account of superego development, though it still provides an essential underpinning for any study of the psychology of morality, clearly omits or neglects many of the dynamic and structural complexities of moral development in later life. In so far as the classical psychoanalytic account stresses only the formation of the superego through the introjection of the same-sex parent at the conclusion of the Oedipus complex (10, 13), it leaves out many subsequent changes in the superego and in morally determined behavior. Recently, psychoanalysts and others have shown greater interest in these changes. For example, it is now commonly recognized that during normal adolescence there can occur a "rebellion against the superego," by which the individual rejects not only his parents but that part of his own superego which is based upon unreflective internalization of their standards (4, 5). Other students of adolescence have emphasized the increasing integration of the superego and ego which can occur during this stage

and the greater elaboration of self-accepted moral principles, which form part of the ego ideal (4, 33).

Psychoanalysis has largely dealt with the genetic and dynamic aspects of superego development. Jean Piaget's account of moral development (39), in contrast, emphasizing changes in the logic or structure of moral reasoning throughout childhood. And more recently, Lawrence Kohlberg, in a series of brilliant studies, has modified and extended Piaget's work by developing a comprehensive account of developmental changes in the structure of moral reasoning (23, 27). Kohlberg finds that moral reasoning develops through three general stages. The earliest is the pre-conventional stage, which involves relatively egocentric concepts of right and wrong as that which one can do without getting caught, or that which leads to the greatest personal gratification. The preconventional stage is followed, usually during later childhood, by a stage of conventional morality, during which good and evil are first identified with the concept of a "good boy" or "good girl," and then with the standards of the community, i.e., with law and order. The individual in the conventional stage may not *act* according to his perceptions of what is right and wrong; but he does not question the fact that morality is objective, immutable, and derives from external agencies like parental edicts, community standards, or divine laws.

Kohlberg also identifies a third and final stage of moral development that is post-conventional—what Erikson has called the "ethical" stage (6, 18). This stage involves reasoning more abstract than that found in earlier stages, and it may lead the individual into conflict with conventional standards. The first of two subphases within the post-conventional stage basically involves the concept of right and wrong as resulting from a social contract—as the result of an agreement entered into by the members of the society for their common good—and therefore subject to emendation, alteration, or revocation. Conventional moral thinking views moral imperatives as absolute or given by the nature of the universe: social contract reasoning sees rules as "merely" convenient and therefore amendable.

Kohlberg identifies the highest post-conventional phase as that in which the individual becomes devoted to *personal principles* that may transcend not only conventional morality but even the social contract. In this stage, certain general principles are now seen as personally binding though not necessarily "objectively" true. Such principles are apt to be stated in a very high level of generality: e.g., the concept of justice, the Golden Rule, the sanctity of life, the categorical imperative, the promotion of human development. The individual at this stage may find himself in conflict with existing concepts of law and order, or even with the notion of an amendable social contract. He may, for example, consider even democratically-arrived-at laws unacceptable because they lead to consequences or enjoin behaviors that violate his own personal principles.

With the development of moral reasoning (as with all other sectors of development), precise ages cannot be attached to the attainment of specific stages. But Kohlberg's research indicates that those who attain post-conventional levels generally do so during later adolescence and in the years of youth. Figure 1 extrapolates from Kohlberg's research to give a rough indication of the timing of moral development, categorized according to his three general stages. The subjects on which this figure is based are middle-class American urban males: thus, at the age of 16 they are probably college-bound; at 20, they are likely to be in college; and at 24, many are in graduate schools. It is clear from Kohlberg's data that the highest (post-conventional) phases are *never reached* by most men and women in American society, who remain at the conventional stage. Even at age 24, only 10% of this middle-class urban male population have reached the personal principles phase, while another 26% are at the social contract phase.

Finally, Figure 1 indicates that between the ages of 16 and 20 the number of individuals in the pre-conventional stage increases. Kohlberg accounts for this increase by the phenomenon of "moral regression" as a routine developmental occurrence in many college students. Longitudinal studies conducted by Kramer (29) have documented the occurrence of such regression in a number of late adolescent and youthful subjects. In what Kohlberg has termed the "Raskolnikoff Syndrome," the individual moving toward post-conventional morality regresses to the earlier, pre-conventional (egocentric) stage in an apparent effort to free himself from irrational and ego-dystonic guilt. Interestingly, Kramer finds that such young Raskolnikoffs eventually return to the developmental track at approximately the point where they dropped off.

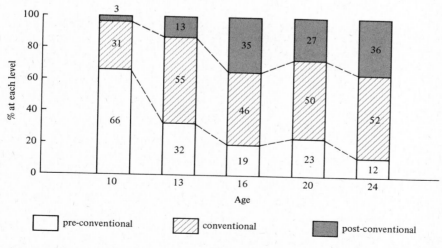

Figure 1. Level of Moral Reasoning and Age (Ss: middle class urban American males).
Percentages extrapolated from charts in Refs. 25 and 29. All percentages approximate; population sizes not stated in original.

The structure of moral reasoning is of course not all of moral development; conceivably an individual may reason one way, yet act in another. But several studies have demonstrated that the way a person reasons morally is closely related to his actual behavior under conditions of moral stress. Figure 2 presents some central findings about moral reasoning and behavior in situations of moral conflict. The Milgram experiment (34) is presented as an experiment in negative reinforcement. The subject is asked to administer high levels of electric shock to another experimental subject (actually a stooge). The stooge protests violently at the shock and eventually warns the subject that his heart condition makes the experiment dangerous. The great majority of college students and the noncollege population, when encouraged by the experimenter to continue to administer shock, do so despite the victim's protests. But Kohlberg (26) finds that 75% of the subjects at the stage of personal principles—the highest stage—refuse to continue shocking the victim, as compared to only 13% of subjects at all earlier stages. In another experiment, studying cheating behavior in sixth graders (30), only 25% of the conventional sixth graders did not cheat, while 80% of the post-conventionals did not cheat. In a study of college students (9), the corresponding figures were 58% and 89%. There is

strong evidence, then, that the level of moral reasoning is associated with the actual morality of behavior.

Figure 3 portrays the relationship between level of moral development and participation in student protest activities. This figure is based upon research done by Brewster Smith, Jeanne Block, and Norma Haan at the University of California at Berkeley (15–17, 43, 44). The subjects are male and female college students at Berkeley and at San Francisco State College. They are here divided into two groups: (1) the protesters, who have engaged in sit-ins, peace marches, picketing, and various forms of disruption or direct action over such issues as student freedom of speech, the war in Vietnam, or alleged racism in the university or in society: (2) all nonprotesting students, including political inactivists, apolitical fraternity and sorority members, and students who engage in social service activities but do not take part in protests.

The findings of the Berkeley research are complex, but as summarized in Figure 3, they indicate a marked difference in the level of moral development of protesters and nonprotesters in this college population. A clear majority (56%) of all protesters are at post-conventional levels of morality, whereas only 12% of nonprotesters have reached this level. The nonprotesters are

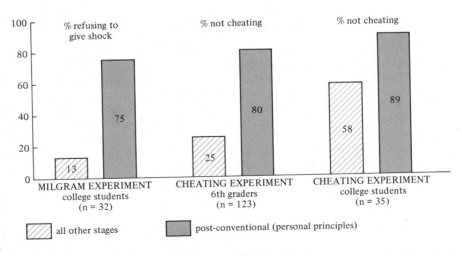

Figure 2. Level of Moral Reasoning and Behavior in Moral Stress Conditions. Data on Miligram experiment is from Ref. 26. Data on 6th grade cheating from Ref. 9. Data on college cheating from Ref. 30.

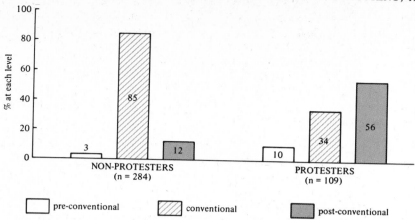

Figure 3. Level of Moral Reasoning and Socio-Political Protest (Ss: students at U.C. (Berkeley) and S.F. State).
Data is from Ref. 15.

overwhelmingly (85%) in the conventional stage —that is, they define morality as adherence to law and order, or as involving some concept of a "good boy" or "good girl." Only 36% of protesters are at the conventional stage. Interestingly, the proportion of protesters at the pre-conventional stage is also disproportionately large—10% of protesters as against 3% of nonprotesters. Kohlberg's writings suggest that such individuals may be in a state of moral regression (Raskolnikoffs), perhaps epitomized by certain variants of the hippie subculture.

The complexity of these data, however, are emphasized when we analyze them in a different way. Unlike Figure 3, Figure 4 distinguishes between the behavior of those at different levels of moral development, not between the moral development of those who behave in different ways. The behavior here studied was being arrested as a result of the Free Speech Movement sit-in in Sproul Hall at Berkeley in 1964. This analysis indicates that the proportion of pre-conventionals involved was about the same as the proportion of post-conventionals, although in absolute num-

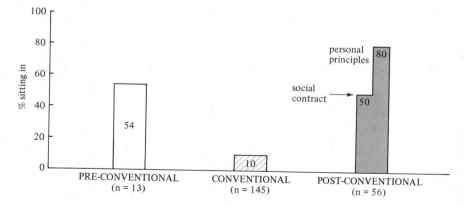

Figure 4. Level of Moral Reasoning and Participation in FSM Sit-In (Berkeley 1964).
Data is from Ref. 15. Not all Ss who sat in were studied. Therefore, extrapolations to all Ss sitting in should be made cautiously.

bers there were many fewer pre-conventionals in Sproul Hall. These findings make clear that level of moral development and socio-political activism are not correlated in a linear manner. They suggest that any protest will, depending on the issues involved, enlist supporters from several different levels of moral development.

This conclusion is supported by an unpublished study of Kohlberg's on the participants in the Harvard College sit-in in the spring of 1969 (28). Kohlberg predicted that at Harvard, unlike Berkeley, the students at the post-conventional level would *not* be overrepresented amongst those who sat in. He based this prediction on an analysis of the issues in the Harvard sit-in, which did not seem to him to involve a comparable appeal to abstract principles. His findings confirmed this prediction. These studies, then, do not indicate that high levels of moral development lead *automatically* to participation in all protests, sit-ins, confrontations, and disruptions. Rather they indicate that those who have reached higher levels of moral development are more likely to act in the service of their principles—protesting when their principles are at issue; refusing, also for reasons of principle, to take part in other protests and forms of activism.

Social Catalysts For Moral Development

I have so far presented research findings on the relationship between moral reasoning and socio-political activism. On the basis of such findings, we would predict that an increase in the proportion of the student population at post-conventional levels would also increase the likelihood of principled student socio-political activism. I will now argue, more speculatively, that modern social and historical conditions are providing new catalysts and facilitations for high levels of moral development, and that these new developmental attainments constitute *one* partial explanation of socio-political activism.

Kohlberg does not address himself specifically to the psychological or social catalysts of moral development. But his data makes clear that moral development is by no means guaranteed by aging, maturation, or socialization. Physical maturation

may make possible the development of post-conventional morality, but it obviously does not ensure it. And the pressures of socialization may in many instances militate *against* the development of a principled morality that can place the individual in conflict with his socializing environment—for example, with college administrators, with political parties, with the police, or with the present American Selective Service System. If neither maturation nor socialization guarantee moral development, how can we explain it?

Haan, Smith, and Block have provided us with a first account of some of the psychological antecedents of various levels of moral reasoning in late adolescence and youth (15–17). They report, for example, that students at the highest moral stage of personal principles "had a history of preparedness within politically liberal families who frankly experienced and examined conflict, and with parents who exercised their own rights as people, rather than the power and control that society automatically ascribes to them" (15). Their data—too complex to be summarized here—clearly indicate that family milieu during the preadolescent years plays an important role in facilitating or obstructing later moral development.

Here, however, I will not discuss the impact of these early experiences, but will consider the effects of more general social, historical, and political factors on adolescent and postadolescent changes in moral reasoning. That is, I will not consider why some individuals arrive in adolescence or youth already predisposed to develop to the post-conventional or "ethical" stages in moral development, but will discuss in a speculative way why post-conventional (ethical) moral reasoning may characterize a growing proportion of today's college generation in America and in the other advanced nations.

DISENGAGEMENT FROM ADULT SOCIETY. A prolonged period of disengagement from the institutions of adult society seems to facilitate moral development. Conversely, immediate entry into the labor force and early marriage with responsibilities for maintaining a family tend to constrain or obstruct moral development. Kohlberg's data, reported in Figure 5, showing higher modal levels of moral development in middle-class (college-bound or college) students than in lower-class

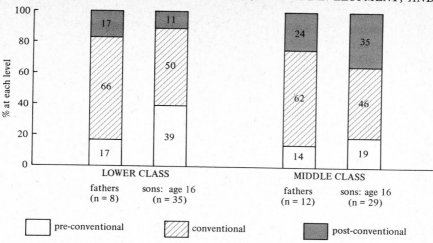

Figure 5. Level of Moral Reasoning and Social Class.
Data is extrapolated from charts in Ref. 26, derived from Ref. 29. All figures approximate. Percentages tabulated are of usage of moral reasoning at each level, averaged across Ss.

(noncollege) youth, are consistent with this hypothesis. For, in so far as an individual during or immediately after puberty or adolescence takes a job, marries, and has children, the opportunity for confronting and challenging conventional morality seems to lessen. The risks of unconventionality become greater; the price for departure from conventional morality, and especially for that moral regression which Kohlberg finds a frequent if usually temporary part of moral development, becomes too high for most individuals to pay.

CONFRONTATION WITH ALTERNATE MORAL VIEWPOINTS. William Perry, in his pioneering studies of ethical and intellectual development during the college years (37, 38), suggests that one prime catalyst for intellectual and moral development is confrontation with relativistic points of view in professors and fellow students. Such confrontations stimulate the student to abandon simple dualistic thinking about right and wrong, good and bad, truth and falsehood. He tends to move first toward a relativistic concept of morality and truth, and later, toward making personal commitments *within* a relativistic universe.

From a different perspective, Robert Redfield (40), in his discussion of the effects of the transi-

tion from peasant to urban societies, underlines the importance of culture contact in producing more high-level and synthetic ideologies (18, 35). The peasant, confronted in the city with others who hold conflicting moral viewpoints, may be compelled to reexamine his own, and to seek a post-conventional moral system that stands above and reconciles traditional moral pieties. Kohlberg's findings, reported in Figure 6, that post-conventional levels are almost never attained by age 16 in peasant societies, that they are more often attained by urban middle-class students in developing societies, and that they are most often attained in urban middle-class American society, support this line of reasoning. Put differently, an individual is more likely to move beyond a conventional moral system when he is personally confronted with alternative moral values, and especially when these are concretely epitomized in the people, the institutions, and the cultures among which he lives.

DISCOVERY OF CORRUPTION. A third catalyst for moral development, as for moral regression, is the discovery of corruption, hypocrisy, and duplicity in the world, especially in those from whom one originally learned the concepts of conventional morality. For example, disillusionment with

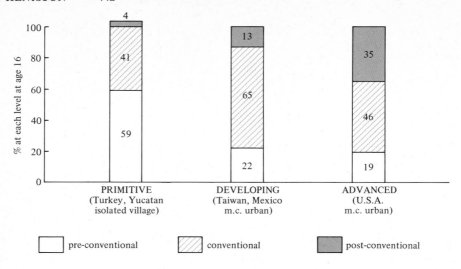

Figure 6.   Level of Moral Reasoning and Type of Society.
Figures are extrapolated from charts in Ref. 24. All percentages approximate; population sizes not stated.

parents—in particular the discovery of moral turpitude (or, in Erikson's [7] terms, lack of fidelity) in the parents' lives—may play a critical role in pushing the individual to reject the morality he learned from them. Obviously not all young men and women react identically to such discoveries. Some may accept them without regression: they will push the individual to higher stages of moral development. This advance seems especially likely if the discovery of corruption in the world is accompanied by growing awareness of one's own potential for corruption. Other youths, however, will react with at least a temporary regression to moral cynicism, in which they behaviorally flout and intellectually reject what they consider to be "hypocritical" conventional values.

Historical Pressures Towards Moral Development

Three social factors that may stimulate moral development in youth have been considered: continuing disengagement from adult institutions, confrontation with alternative moral viewpoints, and the discovery of corruption in the world. There is reason to believe that all three of these conditions obtain to an unusual degree today. In the extension of higher education, the cross-cultural implosion, and the pervasive reductionism of our age we have created important new catalysts, for better and for worse, for higher levels of ethicality, as for more marked moral regressions.

THE EXTENSION OF HIGHER EDUCATION. Our own era has witnessed an historically unprecedented influx of students to colleges and universities. To cite but one statistic, during the time of the Russian student movement in the middle of the nineteenth century, there were never more than 8,000 university students in all of Imperial Russia (12, 46). Today in America, there are 7,000,000 (almost 1000 times as many); while in Western Germany, France, and England there are by rough count 1,250,000. In most advanced nations of the world, the proportion of young people who attend colleges and universities is increasing logarithmetically; furthermore, this increase has largely occurred in the last two decades. The growing affluence of the highly industrialized nations permits them to keep millions of the young out of the labor force; the increasing need for high-level training in technological societies requires them to offer a university education to these millions.

Higher education does not, of course, inevitably entail moral growth. But one consequence of the prolongation and extension of higher education is that a massive group of young men and women have been disengaged for an increasingly protracted period from the institutions of the adult society, in particular from occupation and marriage. Freed of responsibilities of work, marriage, and parenthood, at least some find themselves in university atmospheres that deliberately challenge and undermine their pre-existing beliefs and conventional assumptions. Thus, the extension of youth via prolonged education on a mass scale probably tends to stimulate the development of post-conventional moral thinking.

CULTURE CONTACT AND THE CROSS-CULTURAL IMPLOSION. The individual who attends a liberal arts college or university is very likely to confront in his daily experience both peers and professors who preach and practice a different morality from the one he was brought up to take for granted. Many universities deliberately confront students with contrasting cultures that give allegiance to alien moral concepts, and deliberately provoke students to question the unexamined assumptions of their own childhood and adolescences. They thus push the individual away from what Perry calls "dualistic" thinking (37), away from an unthinking acceptance of conventional moral "truths'" and toward a more individuated moral position, at once more personal and more abstract.

But it should also be recalled that outside the university, as within it, we live in an age of extraordinary culture contact and conflict. The electronic revolution, coupled with the revolution in transportation, enables us to confront alien values within our living room or to immerse ourselves physically in alien cultures after a flight of a few hours. The days when one could live in parochial isolation, surrounded only by conventional morality, are fast disappearing. Conflicts of ideologies, of world views, of value systems, of philosophical beliefs, of esthetic orientations, and of political styles confront every thoughtful man and women, wherever he lives. If such confrontations stimulate moral development, then we live in an era in which technology and world history themselves provide new facilitation for moral growth. We are all today a little like Redfield's peasants who move to the city, living in a world where conflicting cultures and moral viewpoints rub against us at every turn. The urbanizing and homogenizing process has become worldwide: we live in an era of cross-cultural implosion. My argument here is that this cross-cultural implosion helps stimulate moral development.

CYNICISM AND REDUCTIONISM. Universities often undertake to expose the student to the gap between preaching and practice in society, in admired individuals, and even in the student himself. Whatever their many conformist pressures, universities in America and abroad also have another side: they have often been focal points of criticism of the surrounding society—institutional consciences that may collectively remind the surrounding society of its failure to live up to its ideals. To attend a university may systematically expose the student to the actual corruption that exists in the world, in representatives of the status quo, and even in himself.

But this exposure to corruption is today by no means confined to the university itself: ours is, in general, an age of skepticism with regard to traditional moral pieties and platitudes. Hypocrisy and corruption are constantly exposed at a cultural as well as an individual level. The debunking of traditional models and values is a favorite contemporary pastime; duplicity, dishonest, compromise, and deceit are widely reported. Many of our most powerful intellectual systems are highly developed in their capacity to debunk, reduce, and explain away the ideologies, values, and convictions of others. The sociology of knowledge, psychoanalysis, Marxism, philosophical analysis, cultural relativism, and a variety of other idea systems can all be readily used (or misused) for this purpose. Thus, even if the individual does not discover corruption in his own parents or immediate world, he is still hard put to avoid confrontation with the corruption that exists in the wider society. In an age of debunking, conventional morality tends to suffer: individuals are pushed to higher levels of moral development or to moral regression. The data suggest that student protesters are disproportionally drawn from just these two groups: primarily the morally advanced, but secondarily, the morally regressed.

Ethicality and Zealotry

My argument so far has been that new educational, technological, and historical factors today facilitate the development of post-conventional morality in larger and larger numbers of young men and women. Furthermore, post-conventional morality understandably characterizes many of those who are involved in principled protests against the conventional moral order and its institutions. We may therefore interpret worldwide student protest as *partly* a result of the fact that societies like our own are stimulating more individuals than ever before to higher levels of moral development. One aspect of the student movement must be seen as a result of a psychological advance, and not as a result of psychopathology or psychological retardation.

But how should we judge the development of a morality based on a commitment to ethical principles that are maintained even when they conflict with conventional moral wisdom? Is it really an advance? In evaluating the meaning of the highest levels of moral development, we are immediately confronted with a paradox. On the one hand, Kohlberg identifies such ethical reasoning with admirable men like Socrates, Gandhi, Lincoln, and Martin Luther King—men for whom devotion to the highest personal principles was paramount over all other considerations, and who as a result were moral leaders of their time. Yet on the other hand, especially during the past two cold war decades, we have been taught to view abstract personal principles with considerable mistrust—as a part of ideology not in the Eriksonian sense but in the highly pejorative sense (1). Such principles, it has been argued, are intimately—perhaps inevitably—related to the development of moral self-righteousness, zealotry, dogmatism, fanaticism, and insensitivity. In pursuit of his own personal principles, a man will ride rough-shod over others who do not share these principles, will disregard human feelings or even destroy human life. During the period when the "end of ideology" was being announced on all sides, when instrumental and consensus politics was being extolled, we learned to identify abstract personal principles with dogmatic and destructive moral zealotry. How are we to com-

bine these two perspectives? Do we see in Brewster Smith's findings confirmation of the view that student activists are dangerously moral zealots? Or do we adhere to Kohlberg's implication that such individuals are more likely moral heroes than despots?

The answer lies, I think, in recalling my earlier observation that the separation of the moral sector of human development from other sectors is analytic and arbitrary. Anna Freud (14) has taught us to think in terms of an ideal "balance" between what she terms "developmental lines" (sectors of development). Yet she has also shown that such balance is never found in practice, and that in any specific individual we always find retardations or accelerations of development within different sectors. Following Anna Freud's thinking suggests that whether the highest stages of moral reasoning lead to destructive zealotry or real ethicality depends upon the extent to which moral development is *matched by development in other sectors*. The critical related sectors of development, I submit, are those which involve compassion, love, or emphatic identification with others.

Most moral zealots, bigots, and dogmatists are probably best described, in Kohlberg's terms, as conventionalists, while others are perhaps permanent regressees to the Raskolnikoff Syndrome. But there are at least a few whom we know from personal experience or from history who seem truly post-conventional in moral reasoning but whose genuine adherence to the highest moral values is *not* matched by compassion, sympathy, capacity for love, and empathy (32). In such individuals, the danger of hurting men to advance Mankind, of injuring people in order to fulfill one's own moral principles, is all too real. We see this danger realized in the pre-Nazi German Youth Movement (31), where post-conventional morality often went hand in hand with virulent anti-semitism. Pascal put it well when he noted that "Evil is never done so thoroughly or so well as when it is done with a good conscience."

Thus, neatly to identify high levels of moral reasoning with any one kind of action, much less with human virtue, mental health, maturity, and so on is a serious mistake. What we might term "moral precocity" in youth—high moral development not attended by comparable development in other sectors of life—is often dangerous. The danger lies not in high levels of moral development in themselves, but in the retardation of other sectors of development. What is dangerous at *any* level of moral development, be it post-conventional, conventional, or pre-conventional, is the absence of a developed capacity for compassion, empathy, and love for one's fellow man.

No one phrase will adequately characterize the other developmental accomplishments that are essential to humanize the highest levels of moral reasoning. But the history of revolutions that have failed through the very ardor of their search for moral purity suggests that the combination of abstract personal principles with a humorless and *loveless asceticism* is especially likely to be dangerous. There are of course many kinds of asceticism, some of them mature, self-accepted, and benign. But there are other asceticisms that are based upon inhibition of the capacity to love, upon failure in the development of interpersonal mutuality, and upon absence of empathy. Often, these qualities are combined with ascetic self-denial based more upon unconscious fear and inhibition than upon self-accepted personal values.

Lewis Feuer's recent critique of student movements (11) identifies all student protesting activity (45) with the excesses of those student movements where high principles have been combined with asceticism, e.g., the prewar German Youth Movement. But if we examine the current American student movement, we find less ground for concern: however highly principled many of today's dissenting students may be, they are scarcely an ascetic lot.

In the end, then, we reach the paradoxical conclusion that morality is necessary but not sufficient; even the highest levels of moral reasoning do not alone guarantee truly virtuous behavior. Kohlberg's research, of course, shows that men who reason at an advanced level tend to act morally as well. And the Berkeley research suggests optimism about the high level of moral development of many or most student activists. Yet what is true for most is not true for all; and historically many crimes have been committed in the name of the highest principles, sincerely held. In the end, the findings of developmental psychology in the context of youthful political activism may merely return us to ancient truisms—mercy without justice is sentimental and effusive, while justice without mercy is cold and inhuman.

REFERENCES

1. BELL, D. 1959. *The End of Ideology.* Free Press, Glencoe, Ill.
2. BETTELHEIM, B. 1969. Obsolete youth. *Encounter, 23*(3): 29–42.
3. BLOCK, J., HAAN, N., AND SMITH, M. B. 1969. Activism and apathy in contemporary adolescence. *In Contributions to the Understanding of Adolescence,* J. F. Adams, ed. Allyn & Bacon, New York.
4. BLOSS, P. 1962. *On Adolescence,* Free Press, New York.
5. DOUVAN, E., AND ADELSON, J. 1966. *The Adolescent Experience.* John Wiley & Sons, New York.
6. ERIKSON, E. 1964. The Golden Rule in the light of new insight. *In Insight and Responsibility,* E. Erikson, ed. W. W. Norton, New York.
7. ERIKSON, E. 1965. Youth: Fidelity and diversity. *In The Challenge of Youth,* E. Erikson, ed. Anchor, New York.
8. ERIKSON, E. 1968. *Identity, Youth and Crisis.* Norton, New York.
9. FELDMAN, SCHWARTZ, BROWN, AND HEINGARTNER. Moral level and cheating in college students. Cited in Ref. 26.
10. FENICHEL, O. 1945. *The Psychoanalytic Theory of Neurosis.* Norton, New York.
11. FEUER, L. 1969. *The Conflict of Generations.* Basic Books, New York.
12. FOOTMAN, D. 1944. *Red Prelude: A Life of A. I. Zhelyabov.* Cresset Press, London.
13. FREUD, S. 1933. *New Introductory Lectures on Psychoanalysis.* Norton, New York.
15. HAAN, N., SMITH, M. B., AND BLOCK, J. 1968. Moral reasoning of young adults: Political–social behavior, family background, and personality correlates. *J. Pers. Soc. Psych. 10:* 183–201.
16. HAAN, N., AND BLOCK, J. 1969. *Further studies in*

the relationship between activism and morality. I. The protest of pure and mixed moral stages. Institute of Human Development, Berkeley, Calif.

17. HAAN, N., AND BLOCK, J. 1969. *Further studies in the relationship between activism and morality. II. Analysis of case deviant with respect to the morality–activism relationship.* Institute of Human Development, Berkeley, Calif.

18. KENISTON, K. 1965. Morals and ethics. *Amer. Schol. 34:* 625–632.

19. KENISTON, K. 1968. *Young Radicals: Notes on Committed Youth.* Harcourt, Brace, & World, New York.

20. KENISTON, K. 1969. Notes on young radicals. *Change,* Nov.–Dec.: 25–33.

21. KENISTON, K. 1969. You have to grow up in Scarsdale. . . . *New York Times Magazine,* April 27.

22. KENISTON, K. 1970. Youth as a stage of life. *In Psychopathology of Adolescence,* Zubin and Freeman, eds. Grune & Stratton, New York.

23. KOHLBERG, L. 1968. *Education for justice: A modern statement of the platonic view.* Burton Lecture on Moral Education, Harvard Univ., Cambridge, Mass.

24. KOHLBERG, L. 1968. The child as a moral philosopher. *Psychology Today,* Sept.: 25–30.

25. KOHLBERG, L. 1968. The concept of moral maturity. Paper presented at NICHD Conference on the Development of Values, Washington, May 15.

26. KOHLBERG, L. 1969. Continuities and discontinuities in child and adult moral development. Harvard Univ., Cambridge, Mass. Mimeo.

27. KOHLBERG, L. 1970. *Stages in the Development of Moral Thought and Action.* Holt, Rinehart & Winston, New York.

28. KOHLBERG, L. 1970. Personal communication.

29. KRAMER, R. 1968. Changes in moral judgment response pattern during late adolescence and young adulthood. Unpub. Ph.D. thesis, Univ. of Chicago.

30. KREBS, R. 1967. Some relations between moral judgment, attention and resistance to temptation. Unpub. Ph.D. thesis, Univ. of Chicago.

31. LACQUEUR, W. 1962. *Young Germany.* Basic Books, New York.

32. LAMPERT, E. 1965. *Sons Against Fathers: Studies in Russian Radicalism and Revolution.* Oxford Univ. Press, London.

33. LIDZ, T. 1968. *The Person.* Basic Books, New York.

34. MILGRAM, S. 1965. Some conditions of obedience and disobedience to authority. *Hum. Rel. 18:* 57–76.

35. MUMFORD, L. 1962. *The City in History,* Harcourt, Brace, & World, New York.

36. NEWFIELD, J. 1966. *A Prophetic Minority.* Signet Books, New York.

37. PERRY, W. 1968. Forms of intellectual and ethical development in the college years. Harvard Univ. Bureau of Study Counsel, Cambridge, Mass. Mimeo.

38. PERRY, W. 1968. Patterns of development in thought and values of students in a liberal arts college. Harvard Univ. Bureau of Study Counsel, Cambridge, Mass. Mimeo.

39. PIAGET, J. 1948. *The Moral Judgment of the Child.* Free Press, Glencoe, Ill.

40. REDFIELD, R. 1953. *The Primitive World and its Transformations.* Cornell Univ. Press, Ithaca, N. Y.

41. ROSZAK, T. 1969. *The Making of a Counter-Culture.* Doubleday, New York.

42. RUBENSTEIN, B., AND LEVITT, M. 1969. The student revolt: *Totem and Taboo* revisited. Paper delivered at Amer. Orthopsychiat. Assn. Meeting, New York, March 31.

43. SMITH, M. B. 1969. Morality and student protest. *In Social Psychology and Human Values.* Aldine, Chicago.

44. SMITH, M. B. 1969. The crisis on the campus. See ref. 43.

45. WALTER, R. 1968. *Student Politics in Argentina.* Basic Books, New York.

46. YARMOLINSKY, A. 1962. *Road to Revolution.* Collier, New York.

The Liberated Generation: An Exploration of the Roots of Student Protest

RICHARD FLACKS

Flacks reports data concerning the student movement and the activists involved in it. He considers the personality characteristics and value patterns of the activists and their antecedent experiences, and concludes by reviewing various questions relating to student protest which have yet to be resolved.

As all of us are by now aware, there has emerged, during the past five years, an increasingly self-conscious student movement in the United States. This movement began primarily as a response to the efforts by southern Negro students to break the barriers of legal segregation in public accommodations—scores of northern white students engaged in sympathy demonstrations and related activities as early as 1960. But as we all know, the scope of the student concern expanded rapidly

The research reported here stemmed from a coalescence of interest of the author and of Professor Bernice Neugarten of the Committee on Human Development of the University of Chicago. The author's interests were primarily in the student movement and the families and social backgrounds of student activists. Professor Neugarten's interests have been primarily in the relations between age-groups in American society. The plan to gather parallel data from students and their parents accordingly provided a welcome opportunity for collaboration. The research has been supported in part by grant #MH 08062, National Institute of Mental Health; in part by grants from the Carnegie Fund for the Advancement of Teaching and the Survey Research Center of The University of Michigan. I wish to thank Professor Neugarten, Charles Derber and Patricia Schedler for their help in preparing this manuscript; its flaws are entirely my own responsibility.

to include such issues as nuclear testing and the arms race, attacks on civil liberties, the problems of the poor in urban slum ghettoes, democracy and educational quality in universities, the war in Vietnam, conscription.

This movement represents a social phenomenon of considerable significance. In the first place, it is having an important direct and indirect impact on the larger society. But secondly it is significant because it is a phenomenon which was unexpected—unexpected, in particular, by those social scientists who are professionally responsible for locating and understanding such phenomena. Because it is an unanticipated event, the attempt to understand and explain the sources of the student movement may lead to fresh interpretations of some important trends in our society.

Radicalism and the Young Intelligentsia

In one sense, the existence of a radical student movement should not be unexpected. After all, the young intelligentsia seem almost always to be in

From R. Flacks, The liberated generation: An exploration of the roots of student protest. Reprinted from the *Journal of Social Issues*, Volume XXIII, No. 3, pp. 52–75, by permission of the author and publisher.

revolt. Yet if we examine the case a bit more closely I think we will find that movements of active disaffection among intellectuals and students tend to be concentrated at particular moments in history. Not every generation produces an organized oppositional movement.

In particular, students and young intellectuals seem to have become active agents of opposition and change under two sets of interrelated conditions:

When they have been marginal in the labor market because their numbers exceed the opportunities for employment commensurate with their abilities and training. This has most typically been the case in colonial or underdeveloped societies; it also seems to account, in part, for the radicalization of European Jewish intellectuals and American college-educated women at the turn of the century (Coser, 1965; Shils, 1960; Veblen, 1963).

When they found that the values with which they were closely connected by virtue of their upbringing no longer were appropriate to the developing social reality. This has been the case most typically at the point where traditional authority has broken down due to the impact of Westernization, industrialization, modernization. Under these conditions, the intellectuals, and particularly the youth, felt called upon to assert new values, new modes of legitimation, new styles of life. Although the case of breakdown of traditional authority is most typically the point at which youth movements have emerged, there seems, historically, to have been a second point in time—in Western Europe and the United States—when intellectuals were radicalized. This was, roughly, at the turn of the century, when values such as gentility, laissez faire, naive optimism, naive rationalism and naive nationalism seemed increasingly inappropriate due to the impact of large scale industrial organization, intensifying class conflict, economic crisis and the emergence of total war. Variants of radicalism waxed and waned in their influence among American intellectuals and students during the first four decades of the twentieth century. (Aaron, 1965; Eisenstadt, 1956; Lasch, 1965).

If these conditions have historically been those which produced revolts among the young intelligentsia, then I think it is easy to understand why a relatively superficial observer would find the new wave of radicalism on the campus fairly mysterious.

In the first place, the current student generation can look forward, not to occupational insecurity or marginality, but to an unexampled opening up of opportunity for occupational advance in situations in which their skills will be maximally demanded and the prestige of their roles unprecedentedly high.

In the second place, there is no evident erosion of the legitimacy of established authority; we do not seem, at least on the surface, to be in a period of rapid disintegration of traditional values—at least no more so than a decade ago when sociologists were observing the *exhaustion* of opportunity for radical social movements in America (Bell, 1962; Lipset, 1960).

In fact, during the Fifties sociologists and social psychologists emphasized the decline in political commitment, particularly among the young, and the rise of a bland, security-oriented conformism throughout the population, but most particularly among college students. The variety of studies conducted then reported students as overwhelmingly unconcerned with value questions, highly complacent, status-oriented, privatized, uncommitted (Jacob, 1957; Golden, et al, 1960). Most of us interpreted this situation as one to be expected given the opportunities newly opened to educated youth, and given the emergence of liberal pluralism and affluence as the characteristic features of postwar America. Several observers predicted an intensification of the pattern of middle class conformism, declining individualism, and growing "other-directedness" based on the changing styles of childrearing prevalent in the middle class. The democratic and "permissive" family would produce young men who knew how to cooperate in bureaucratic settings, but who lacked a strongly rooted ego-ideal and inner control (Miller and Swanson, 1958; Bronfenbrenner, 1961; Erikson, 1963). Although some observers reported that some students were searching for "meaning" and "selfexpression," and others reported the existence of "subcultures" of alienation and bohemianism on some campuses (Keniston, 1965a; Trow, 1962; Newcomb and Flacks, 1963), not a single observer of the campus scene as late as 1959 anticipated the emergence of the organized disaffection, protest and activism which was to take shape early in the Sixties.

In short, the very occurrence of a student movement in the present American context is surprising because it seems to contradict our prior understanding of the determinants of disaffection among the young intelligentsia.

A Revolt of the Advantaged

The student movement is, I think, surprising for another set of reasons. These have to do with its social composition and the kinds of ideological themes which characterize it.

The current group of student activists is predominantly upper middle class, and frequently these students are of elite origins. This fact is evident as soon as one begins to learn the personal histories of activist leaders. Consider the following scene at a convention of Students for a Democratic Society a few years ago. Toward the end of several days of deliberation, someone decided that a quick way of raising funds for the organization would be to appeal to the several hundred students assembled at the convention to dig down deep into their pockets on the spot. To this end, one of the leadership, skilled at mimicry, stood on a chair, and in the style of a Southern Baptist preacher, appealed to the students to come forward, confess their sins and be saved by contributing to SDS. The students did come forward, and in each case the sin confessed was the social class or occupation of their father. "My father is the editor of a Hearst newspaper, I give $25!" "My father is Assistant Director of the _____ Bureau, I give $40." "My father is dean of a law school, here's $50!"

These impressions of the social composition of the student movement are supported and refined by more systematic sources of data. For example, when a random sample of students who participated in the anti-Selective Service sit-in at the University of Chicago Administration Building was compared with a sample composed of non-protesters and students hostile to the protests, the protesters disproportionately reported their social class to be "upper middle," their family incomes to be disproportionately high, their parents' education to be disproportionately advanced. In addi-

tion, the protesters' fathers' occupations were primarily upper professional (doctors, college faculty, lawyers) rather than business, white collar, or working class. These findings parallel those of other investigators (Braungart, 1966). Thus, the student movement represents the disaffection not of an underprivileged stratum of the student population but of *the most advantaged* sector of the students.

One hypothesis to explain disaffection among socially advantaged youth would suggest that, although such students come from advantaged backgrounds, their academic performance leads them to anticipate downward mobility or failure. Stinchcombe, for example, found high rates of quasi-delinquent rebelliousness among middle class high school youth with poor academic records (Stinchcombe, 1964). This hypothesis is not tenable with respect to college student protest, however. Our own data with respect to the anti-draft protest at Chicago indicate that the grade point average of the protesters averaged around B-B+ (with 75% of them reporting a B− or better average). This was slightly higher than the grade point average of our sample of nonprotesters. Other data from our own research indicate that student activists tend to be at the top of their high school class; in general, data from our own and other studies support the view that many activists are academically superior, and that very few activists are recruited from among low academic achievers. Thus, in terms of *both* the status of their families of origins *and* their own scholastic performance, student protest movements are predominantly composed of students who have been born to high social advantage and who are in a position to experience the career and status opportunities of the society without significant limitations.

Themes of the Protest

The positive correlation between disaffection and status among college students suggested by these observations is, I think, made even more paradoxical when one examines closely the main value themes which characterize the student movement. I want to describe these in an impressionistic way here; a more systematic depiction awaits further analysis of our data.

ROMANTICISM. There is a strong stress among many Movement participants on a quest for self-expression, often articulated in terms of leading a "free" life—i.e., one not bound by conventional restraints on feeling, experience, communication, expression. This is often coupled with aesthetic interests and a strong rejection of scientific and other highly rational pursuits. Students often express the classic romantic aspiration of "knowing" or "experiencing" "everything."

ANTI-AUTHORITARIANISM. A strong antipathy toward arbitrary rule, centralized decision-making, "manipulation." The anti-authoritarian sentiment is fundamental to the widespread campus protests during the past few years; in most cases, the protests were precipitated by an administrative act which was interpreted as arbitrary, and received impetus when college administrators continued to act unilaterally, coercively, or secretively. Anti-authoritarianism is manifested further by the styles and internal processes within activist organizations; for example, both SDS and SNCC have attempted to decentralize their operations quite radically and members are strongly critical of leadership within the organization when it is too assertive.

EGALITARIANISM, POPULISM. A belief that all men are capable of political participation, that political power should be widely dispersed, that the locus of value in society lies with the people and not elites. This is a stress on something more than equality of opportunity or equal legal treatment; the students stress instead the notion of "participatory democracy"—direct participation in the making of decisions by those affected by them. Two common slogans—"One man, one vote"; "Let the people decide."

ANTI-DOGMATISM. A strong reaction against doctrinaire ideological interpretations of events. Many of the students are quite restless when presented with formulated models of the social order, and specific programs for social change. This underlies much of their antagonism to the varieties of "old left" politics, and is one meaning of the oft-quoted (if not seriously used) phrase: "You can't trust anyone over thirty."

MORAL PURITY. A strong antipathy to self-interested behavior, particularly when overlaid by claims of disinterestedness. A major criticism of the society is that it is "hypocritical." Another meaning of the criticism of the older generation has to do with the perception that (a) the older generation "sold out" the values it espouses; (b) to assume conventional adult roles usually leads to increasing self-interestedness, hence selling-out, or "phoniness." A particularly important criticism students make of the university is that it fails to live up to its professed ideals; there is an expectation that the institution ought to be *moral*—that is, not compromise its official values for the sake of institutional survival or aggrandizement.

COMMUNITY. A strong emphasis on a desire for "human" relationships, for a full expression of emotions, for the breaking down of interpersonal barriers and the refusal to accept conventional norms concerning interpersonal contact (e.g., norms respecting sex, status, race, age, etc.). A central positive theme in the campus revolts has been the expression of the desire for a campus "community," for the breaking down of aspects of impersonality on the campus, for more direct contact between students and faculty. There is a frequent counterposing of bureaucratic norms to communal norms; a testing of the former against the latter. Many of the students involved in slum projects have experimented with attempts to achieve a "kibbutz"-like community amongst themselves, entailing communal living and a strong stress on achieving intimacy and resolving tensions within the group.

ANTI-INSTITUTIONALISM. A strong distrust of involvement with conventional institutional roles. This is most importantly expressed in the almost universal desire among the highly involved to avoid institutionalized careers. Our data suggest that few student activists look toward careers in the professions, the sciences, industry or politics. Many of the most committed expect to continue to work full-time in the "movement" or, alternatively, to become free-lance writers, artists, intellectuals. A high proportion are oriented toward academic careers—at least so far the academic career seems still to have a reputation among many student activists for permitting "freedom."

Several of these themes, it should be noted, are not unique to student activists. In particular, the value we have described as "romanticism"—a quest for self-expression—has been found by ob-servers, for example Kenneth Keniston (1965b), to be a central feature of the ideology of "alienat-ed" or "bohemian" students (see also Keniston's article in this issue). Perhaps more important, the disaffection of student activists with conventional careers, their low valuation of careers as important in their personal aspirations, their quest for ca-reers outside the institutionalized sphere—these attitudes toward careers seem to be characteristic of other groups of students as well. It is certainly typical of youth involved in "bohemian" and aes-thetic subcultures; it also characterizes students who volunteer for participation in such programs as the Peace Corps, Vista and other full-time com-mitments oriented toward service. In fact, it is our view that the dissatisfaction of socially ad-vantaged youth with conventional career oppor-tunities is a significant social trend, the most important single indicator of restlessness among sectors of the youth population. One expression of this restlessness is the student movement, but it is not the only one. One reason why it seems important to investigate the student movement in detail, despite the fact that it represents a small minority of the student population, is that it is a symptom of social and psychological strains ex-perienced by a larger segment of the youth—strains not well understood or anticipated hereto-fore by social science.

If some of the themes listed above are not unique to student activists, several of them may characterize only a portion of the activist group itself. In particular, some of the more explicitly political values are likely to be articulated mainly by activists who are involved in radical organiza-tions, particularly Students for a Democratic So-ciety, and the Student Non-violent Coordinating Committee. This would be true particularly for such notions as "participatory democracy" and deep commitments to populist-like orientations. These orientations have been formulated within SDS and SNCC as these organizations have sought to develop a coherent strategy and a framework for establishing priorities. It is an empirical ques-tion whether students not directly involved in such organizations articulate similar attitudes. The im-pressions we have from a preliminary examination of our data suggest that they frequently do not. It is more likely that the student movement is very

heterogeneous politically at this point. Most par-ticipants share a set of broad orientations, but differ greatly in the degree to which they are ori-ented toward ideology in general or to particular political positions. The degree of politicization of student activists is probably very much a function of the kinds of peer group and organizational re-lationships they have had; the underlying disaf-fection and tendency toward activism, however, is perhaps best understood as being based on more enduring, pre-established values, attitudes and needs.

Social-Psychological Roots of Student Protest: Some Hypotheses

How, then, can we account for the emergence of an obviously dynamic and attractive radical movement among American students in this peri-od? Why should this movement be particularly appealing to youth from upper-status, highly edu-cated families? Why should such youth be par-ticularly concerned with problems of authority, of vocation, of equality, of moral consistency? Why should students in the most advantaged sec-tor of the youth population be disaffected with their own privilege?

It should be stressed that the privileged status of the student protesters and the themes they ex-press in their protest are not *in themselves* unique or surprising. Student movements in de-veloping nations—e.g., Russia, Japan and Latin America—typically recruit people of elite back-ground; moreover, many of the themes of the "new left" are reminiscent of similar expressions in other student movements (Lipset, 1966). What is unexpected is that these should emerge in the American context at this time.

Earlier theoretical formulations about the social and psychological sources of strain for youth, for example the work of Parsons (1965), Eisenstadt (1956), and Erikson (1959), are important for understanding the emergence of self-conscious op-positional youth cultures and movements. At first glance, these theorists, who tend to see American youth as relatively well-integrated into the larger society, would seem to be unhelpful in providing a framework for explaining the emergence of a radical student movement at the present moment.

Nevertheless, in developing our own hypotheses we have drawn freely on their work. What I want to do here is to sketch the notions which have guided our research; a more systematic and detailed exposition will be developed in future publications.

What we have done is to accept the main lines of the argument made by Parsons and Eisenstadt about the social functions of youth cultures and movements. The kernel of their argument is that self-conscious subcultures and movements among adolescents tend to develop when there is a sharp disjunction between the values and expectations embodied in the traditional families in a society and the values and expectations prevailing in the occupational sphere. The greater the disjunction, the more self-conscious and oppositional will be the youth culture (as for example in the situation of rapid transition from a traditional–ascriptive to a bureaucratic–achievement social system).

In modern industrial society, such a disjunction exists as a matter of course, since families are, by definition, particularistic, ascriptive, diffuse, and the occupational sphere is universalistic, impersonal achievement-oriented, functionally specific. But Parsons, and many others, have suggested that over time the American middle class family has developed a structure and style which tends to articulate with the occupational sphere; thus, whatever youth culture does emerge in American society is likely to be fairly well-integrated with conventional values, not particularly self-conscious, not rebellious (Parsons, 1965).

The emergence of the student movement, and other expressions of estrangement among youth, leads us to ask whether, in fact, there may be families in the middle class which embody values and expectations which do *not* articulate with those prevailing in the occupational sphere, to look for previously unremarked incompatibilities between trends in the larger social system and trends in family life and early socialization.

The argument we have developed may be sketched as follows:

First, on the macro-structural level we assume that two related trends are of importance: one, the increasing rationalization of student life in high schools and universities, symbolized by the "multiversity," which entails a high degree of impersonality, competitiveness and an increasingly explicit and direct relationship between the university and corporate and governmental bureaucracies; two, the increasing unavailability of coherent careers independent of bureaucratic organizations.

Second, these trends converge, in time, with a particular trend in the development of the family; namely, the emergence of a pattern of familial relations, located most typically in upper middle class, professional homes, having the following elements:

(a) a strong emphasis on democratic, egalitarian interpersonal relations;
(b) a high degree of permissiveness with respect to self-regulation;
(c) an emphasis on values *other than achievement;* in particular, a stress on the intrinsic worth of living up to intellectual, aesthetic, political, or religious ideals.

Third, young people raised in this kind of family setting, contrary to the expectations of some observers, find it difficult to accommodate to institutional expectations requiring submissiveness to adult authority, respect for established status distinctions, a high degree of competition, and firm regulation of sexual and expressive impulses. They are likely to be particularly sensitized to acts of arbitrary authority, to unexamined expressions of allegiance to conventional values, to instances of institutional practices which conflict with professed ideals. Further, the values embodied in their families are likely to be reinforced by other socializing experiences—for example, summer vacations at progressive children's camps, attendance at experimental private schools, growing up in a community with a high proportion of friends from similar backgrounds. Paralleling these experiences of positive reinforcement, there are likely to be experiences which reinforce a sense of estrangement from peers of conventional society. For instance, many of these young people experience a strong sense of being "different" or "isolated" in school; this sense of distance is often based on the relative uniqueness of their interests and values, their inability to accept conventional norms about appropriate sex-role behavior, and the like. An additional source of strain is generated when these young people perceive a fundamental discrepancy between the values espoused by their parents and the style of life actually practiced by them. This discrepancy is experienced as a feeling of "guilt" over "being middle class" and a perception of "hypocrisy" on the part of parents who express liberal or intellectual values while appearing to their children as acquisitive or self-interested.

Fourth, the incentives operative in the occupational sphere are of limited efficacy for these young people—achievement of status or material advantage is relatively ineffective for an individual who already has high status and affluence by virtue of his family origins. This means, on the one hand, that these students are less oriented toward occupational achievement; on the other hand, the operative sanctions within the school and the larger society are less effective in enforcing conformity.

It seems plausible that this is the first generation in which a substantial number of youth both have the impulse to free themselves from conventional status concerns *and can afford to do so.* In this sense they are a 'liberated" generation; affluence has freed them, at least for a period of time, from some of the anxieties and preoccupations which have been the defining features of American middle class social character.

Fifth, the emergence of the student movement is to be understood in large part as a consequence of opportunities for prolonged interaction available in the university environment. The kinds of personality structures produced by the socializing experiences outlined above need not necessarily have generated a collective response. In fact, Kenneth Keniston's recently published work on alienated students at Harvard suggests that students with similar characteristics to those described here were identifiable on college campuses in the Fifties. But Keniston makes clear that his highly alienated subjects were rarely involved in extensive peer-relationships, and that few opportunities for collective expressions of alienation were then available. The result was that each of his subjects attempted to work out a value-system and a mode of operation on his own (Keniston, 1965b).

What seems to have happened was that during the Fifties, there began to emerge an "alienated" student culture, as students with alienated predispositions became visible to each other and began to interact. There was some tendency for these students to identify with the "Beat" style and related forms of bohemianism. Since this involved a high degree of disaffiliation, "cool" non-commitment and social withdrawal, observers tended to interpret this subculture as but a variant of the prevailing privatism of the Fifties. However, a series of precipitating events, most particularly the southern student sit-ins, the revolutionary successes of students in Cuba, Korea and Turkey, and the suppression of student demonstrations against the House Un-American Activities Committee in San Francisco, suggested to groups of students that direct action was a plausible means of expressing their grievances. These first stirrings out of apathy were soon enmeshed in a variety of organizations and publicized in several student-organized underground journals—thus enabling the movement to grow and become increasingly institutionalized. The story of the emergence and growth of the movement cannot be developed here; my main point now is that many of its characteristics cannot be understood solely as consequences of the structural and personality variables outlined earlier—in addition, a full understanding of the dynamics of the movement requires a "collective behavior" perspective.

Sixth, organized expressions of youth disaffection are likely to be an increasingly visible and established feature of our society. In important ways, the "new radicalism" is *not* new, but rather a more widespread version of certain subcultural phenomena with a considerable history. During the late 19th and early 20th century a considerable number of young people began to move out of their provincial environments as a consequence of university education; many of these people gathered in such locales as Greenwich Village and created the first visible bohemian subculture in the United States. The Village bohemians and associated young intellectuals shared a common concern with radical politics and, influenced by Freud, Dewey, etc., with the reform of the process of socialization in America —i.e., a restructuring of family and educational institutions (Lasch, 1965; Coser, 1965). Although many of the reforms advocated by this group were only partially realized in a formal sense, it seems to be the case that the values and style of life which they advocated have become strongly rooted in American life. This has occurred in at least two ways: first, the subcultures created by the early intellectuals took root, have grown and been emulated in various parts of the country. Second, many of the *ideas* of the early twentieth century intellectuals, particularly their critique of the bourgeois family and Victorian sensibility, spread rapidly; it now seems that an important defining characteristic of the college-educated mother is her willingness to adopt child-centered techniques of rearing, and of the college educated couple that they create a family which is democratic and egalitarian in style. In this way, the values that an earlier generation espoused in an abstract way have become embodied as *personality traits* in the new generation. The rootedness of the bohemian and quasi-bohemian subcultures, and the spread of their ideas with the rapid increase in the number of college graduates, suggests that there will be a steadily increasing number of families raising their children with considerable ambivalence about dominant values, incentives and expectations in the society. In this sense, the students who engage in protest or who participate in "alienated" styles of life are often not "converts" to a "deviant" adaptation, but people who have been socialized into a developing cultural tradition. Rising levels of affluence and education are drying up the traditional sources of alienation and radical politics; what we are now becoming aware of, however, is that this same situation is creating new sources of alienation and idealism, and new constituencies for radicalism.

The Youth and Social Change Project

These hypotheses have been the basis for two studies we have undertaken. Study One, begun in the Summer of 1965, involved extensive interviews with samples of student activists and nonactivists and their parents. Study Two, conducted in the Spring of 1966, involved interviews with samples of participants, nonparticipants and opponents of the tumultuous "anti-ranking" sit-in at the University of Chicago.

STUDY ONE—THE SOCIALIZATION OF STUDENT ACTIVISTS

For Study One, fifty students were selected from mailing lists of various peace, civil rights, and student movement organizations in the Chicago area. An additional fifty students, matched for sex, neighborhood of parents' residence, and type of college attended, were drawn from student directories of Chicago-area colleges. In each case, an attempt was made to interview both parents of the student respondent, as well as the student himself. We were able to interview both parents of 82 of the students; there were two cases in which no parents were available for the interview; in the remaining 16 cases, one parent was interviewed. The interviews with both students and parents averaged about three hours in length, were closely parallel in content, and covered such matters as: political attitudes and participation; attitudes toward the student movement and "youth"; "values," broadly defined; family life, child-rearing, family conflict and other aspects of socialization. Rating scales and "projective" questions were used to assess family members' perceptions of parent–child relationships.

It was clear to us that our sampling procedures were prone to a certain degree of error in the classification of students as "activists" and "non-activists." Some students who appeared on the mailing lists of activist organizations had no substantial involvement in the student movement, while some of our "control" students had a considerable history of such involvement. Thus the data to be reported here are based on an index of Activism constructed from interview responses to questions about participation in seven kinds of activity: attendance at rallies, picketing, canvassing, working on a project to help the disadvantaged, being jailed for civil disobedience, working full-time for a social action organization, serving as an officer in such organizations.

STUDY TWO—THE "ANTI-RANKING" SIT-IN

In May, 1966, about five hundred students sat-in at the Administration Building on the campus of the University at Chicago, barring the building to official use for two and a half days. The focal issue of protest, emulated on a number of other campuses in the succeeding days, was the demand by the students that the University not cooperate with the Selective Service System in supplying class standings for the purpose of assigning student deferments. The students who sat-in formed an organization called "Students Against the Rank" (SAR). During the sit-in another group of students, calling themselves "Students for a Free Choice" (SFC) circulated a petition opposing the sit-in and supporting the University Administration's view that each student had a right to submit (or withhold) his class standings—the University could not withhold the "rank" of students who requested it. This petition was signed by several hundred students.

Beginning about 10 days after the end of the sit-in, we undertook to interview three samples of students; a random sample of 65 supporters of SAR (the protesters); a random sample of 35 signers of the SFC petition (the anti-protesters); approximately 60 students who constituted the total population of two randomly selected floors in the student dormitories. Of about 160 students thus selected, 117 were finally either interviewed or returned mailed questionnaires. The interview schedule was based largely on items used in the original study; it also included some additional items relevant to the sit-in and the "ranking" controversy.

SOME PRELIMINARY FINDINGS

At this writing, our data analysis is at an early stage. In general, however, it is clear that the framework of hypotheses with which we began is substantially supported, and in interesting ways, refined, by the data. Our principal findings thus far include the following:[1]

Activists tend to come from upper status families. As indicated earlier, our study of the Chicago sit-in suggests that such actions attract students predominantly from upper-status backgrounds. When compared with students who did not sit-in, and with students who signed the anti-sit-in petition, the sit-in participants reported higher family

incomes, higher levels of education for both fathers and mothers, and overwhelmingly perceived themselves to be "upper-middle class." One illustrative finding: in our dormitory sample, of 24 students reporting family incomes of above $15,000, half participated in the sit-in. Of 23 students reporting family incomes below $15,000, only two sat-in.

Certain kinds of occupations are particularly characteristic of the parents of sit-in participants. In particular, their fathers tend to be professionals (college faculty, lawyers, doctors) rather than businessmen, white collar employees or blue collar workers. Moreover, somewhat unexpectedly, activists' mothers are likely to be employed, and are more likely to have "career" types of employment, than are the mothers of non-activists.

Also of significance, although not particularly surprising, is the fact that activists are more likely to be Jewish than are nonactivists. (For example, 45% of our SAR sample reported that they were Jewish; only about one-fourth of the non-participants were Jewish). Furthermore, a very high proportion of both Jewish and non-Jewish activists reported no religious preference for themselves and their parents. Associated with the Jewish ethnicity of a large proportion of our activist samples is the fact the great majority of activists' grandparents were foreign born. Yet, despite this, data from Study One show that the grandparents of activists tended to be relatively highly educated as compared to the grandparents of non-activists. Most of the grandparents of non-activists had not completed high school; nearly half of the grandparents of activists had at least a high school education and fully one-fourth of their maternal grandmothers had attended college. These data suggest that relatively high status characterized the families of activists over several generations; this conclusion is supported by data showing that, unlike non-activist grandfathers, the grandfathers of activists tended to have white collar, professional and enterpreneurial occupations rather than blue collar jobs.

In sum, our data suggest that, at least at major Northern colleges, students involved in protest activity are characteristically from families which are urban, highly educated, Jewish or irreligious, professional and affluent. It is perhaps particularly interesting that many of their mothers are unique-

[1]A more detailed report of the procedures and findings of these studies is available in Flacks (1966).

ly well-educated and involved in careers, and that high status and education has characterized these families over at least two generations.

Activists are more "radical" than their parents; but activists' parents are decidedly more liberal than others of their status. The demographic data reported above suggests that activists come from high status families, but the occupational, religious and educational characteristics of these families are unique in several important ways. The distinctiveness of these families is especially clear when we examine data from Study One on the political attitudes of students and their parents. In this study, it should be remembered, activist and non-activist families were roughly equivalent in status, income and education because of our sampling procedures. Our data quite clearly demonstrate that the fathers of activists are disproportionately liberal. For example, whereas forty per cent of the nonactivists' fathers said that they were Republican, only thirteen per cent of the activists' fathers were Republicans. Only six per cent of non-activists' fathers were willing to describe themselves as "highly liberal" or "socialist," whereas sixty per cent of the activists' fathers accepted such designations. Forty per cent of the non-activists' fathers described themselves as conservative; none of the activists' fathers endorsed that position.[2]

In general, differences in the political preferences of the students paralleled these parental differences. The non-activist sample is only slightly less conservative and Republican than their fathers; all of the activist students with Republican fathers report their own party preferences as either Democrat or independent. Thirty-two per cent of the activists regard themselves as "socialist" as compared with sixteen per cent of their fathers. In general, both nonactivists and their fathers are typically "moderate" in their politics; activists and their fathers tend to be at least

[2]For the purposes of this report, "activists" are those students who were in the top third on our Activism index; "nonactivists" are those students who were in the bottom third—this latter group reported virtually no participation in any activity associated with the student movement. The "activists" on the other hand had taken part in at least one activity indicating high commitment to the movement (e.g. going to jail, working full-time, serving in a leadership capacity).

"liberal," but a substantial proportion of the activists prefer a more "radical" designation.

A somewhat more detailed picture of comparative political positions emerges when we examine responses of students and their fathers to a series of 6-point scales on which respondents rated their attitudes on such issues as: US bombing of North Vietnam, US troops in the Dominican Republic, student participation in protest demonstrations, civil rights protests involving civil disobedience, Lyndon Johnson, Barry Goldwater, congressional investigations of "un-American activities," full socialization of all industries, socialization of the medical profession.

Table 1 presents data on activists and nonactivists and their fathers with respect to these items. This table suggests, first, wide divergence between the two groups of fathers on most issues, with activist fathers typically critical of current policies. Although activists' fathers are overwhelmingly "liberal" in their responses, for the most part, activist students tend to endorse "left-wing" positions more strongly and consistently than do their fathers. The items showing strongest divergence between activists and their fathers are interesting. Whereas activists overwhelmingly endorse civil disobedience, nearly half of their fathers do not. Whereas fathers of both activists and non-activists tend to approve of Lyndon Johnson, activist students tend to disapprove of him. Whereas activists' fathers tend to disapprove of "full socialization of industry," this item is endorsed by the majority of activists (although fewer gave an extremely radical response on this item than any other); whereas the vast majority of activists approve of socialized medicine, the majority of their fathers do not. This table provides further support for the view that activists, though more "radical" than their fathers, come predominantly from very liberal homes. The attitudes of nonactivists and their fathers are conventional and supportive of current policies; there is a slight tendency on some items for nonactivist students to endorse more conservative positions than their fathers.

It seems fair to conclude, then, that most students who are involved in the movement (at least those one finds in a city like Chicago) are involved in neither "conversion" from nor "re-

Table 1. Students' and Fathers' Attitudes on Current Issues

Issue	Activists		Nonactivists	
	Students	Fathers	Students	Fathers
Per cent who approve:				
Bombing of North Vietnam	9	27	73	80
American troops in Dominican Republic	6	33	65	50
Student participation in protest demonstrations	100	80	61	37
Civil disobedience in civil rights protests	97	57	28	23
Congressional investigations of "un-American activities"	3	7	73	57
Lyndon Johnson	35	77	81	83
Barry Goldwater	0	7	35	20
Full socialization of industry	62	23	5	10
Socialization of the medical profession	94	43	30	27
(*N*)	(34)	(30)	(37)	(30)

bellion" against the political perspectives of their fathers. A more supportable view suggests that the great majority of these students are attempting to fulfill and renew the political traditions of their families. However, data from our research which have not yet been analyzed as of this writing will permit a more systematic analysis of the political orientations of the two generations.

Activism is related to a complex of values, not ostensibly political, shared by both the students and their parents. Data which we have just begun to analyze suggest that the political perspectives which differentiate the families of activists from other families at the same socioeconomic level are part of a more general clustering of values and orientations. Our findings and impressions on this point may be briefly summarized by saying that, whereas nonactivists and their parents tend to express conventional orientations toward achievement, material success, sexual morality and religion, the activists and their parents tend to place greater stress on involvement in intellectual and esthetic pursuits, humanitarian concerns, opportunity for self-expression, and tend to de-emphasize or positively disvalue personal achievement, conventional morality and conventional religiosity.

When asked to rank order a list of "areas of life," nonactivist students and their parents typically indicate that marriage, career and religion

are most important. Activists, on the other hand, typically rank these lower than the "world of ideas, art and music" and "work for national and international betterment"—and so, on the whole, do their parents (see also the relevant data presented by Trent and Craise in this issue).

When asked to indicate their vocational aspirations, nonactivist students are typically firmly decided on a career and typically mention orientations toward the professions, science and business. Activists, on the other hand, are very frequently undecided on a career; and most typically those who have decided mention college teaching, the arts or social work as aspirations.

These kinds of responses suggest, somewhat crudely, that student activists identify with life goals which are intellectual and "humanitarian" and that they reject conventional and "privatized" goals more frequently than do nonactivist students.

Four Value Patterns

More detailed analyses which we are just beginning to undertake support the view that the value-patterns expressed by activists are highly correlated with those of their parents. This analysis has involved the isolation of a number of value-patterns which emerged in the interview material, the development of systems of code categories related to each of these patterns, and the blind coding of all the interviews with respect to these categories. The kinds of data we are obtaining in this way may be illustrated by describing four of the value patterns we have observed:

ROMANTICISM: ESTHETIC AND EMOTIONAL SENSITIVITY

This variable is defined as: "sensitivity to beauty and art—appreciation of painting, literature and music, creativity in art forms—concern with esthetic experience and the development of capacities for esthetic expression—concern with emotions deriving from perception of beauty—attachment of great significance to esthetic experience. More broadly, it can be conceived of as involving explicit concern with experience as such, with feeling and passion, with immediate and inner experience; a concern for the realm of feeling rather than the rational, technological or instrumental side of life; preference for the realm of experience as against that of activity, doing or achieving." Thirteen items were coded in these terms: for each item a score of zero signified no mention of "romanticist" concerns,

Table 2. Scores on Selected Values by Activism (Percentages)

	Activists	Nonactivists
(a) *Romanticism*		
High	35	11
Medium	47	49
Low	18	40
(b) *Intellectualism*		
High	32	3
Medium	65	57
Low	3	40
(c) *Humanitarianism*		
High	35	0
Medium	47	22
Low	18	78
(d) *Moralism*		
High	6	54
Medium	53	35
Low	41	11
(N)	(34)	(37)

a score of one signified that such a concern appeared. Table 2 indicates the relationship between "romanticism" and Activism. Very few activists received scores on Romanticism which placed them as "low"; conversely, there were very few high "romantics" among the nonactivists.

INTELLECTUALISM

This variable is defined as: "Concern with ideas —desire to realize intellectual capacities—high valuation of intellectual creativities—appreciation of theory and knowledge—participation in intellectual activity (e.g., reading, studying, teaching, writing)—broad intellectual concerns." Ten items were scored for "intellectualism." Almost no activists are low on this variable; almost no nonactivists received a high score.

HUMANITARIANISM

This variable is defined as: "Concern with plight of others in society; desire to help others —value on compassion and sympathy—desire to alleviate suffering; value on egalitarianism in the sense of opposing privilege based on social and economic distinction; particular sensitivity to the deprived position of the disadvantaged." This variable was coded for ten items; an attempt was made to exclude from this index all items referring directly to participation in social action. As might be expected, "humanitarianism" is strongly related to activism, as evidenced in Table 2.

MORALISM AND SELF CONTROL

This variable is defined as: "Concern about the importance of strictly controlling personal impulses—opposition to impulsive or spontaneous behavior—value on keeping tight control over emotions—adherence to conventional authority; adherence to conventional morality—a high degree of moralism about sex, drugs, alcohol, etc.—reliance on a set of external and inflexible rules to govern moral behavior; emphasis on importance of hard work; concern with determination, 'stick-to-itiveness'; antagonism toward idleness—value on diligence, entrepreneurship, task orientation, ambition." Twelve items were scored for this

Table 3. Sons' and Daughters' Ratings of Parents by Activism (Percentages)

Trait of Parent	Males		Females	
	High Act.	Low Act.	High Act.	Low Act.
Mild–Stern				
Per cent rating mother "mild"	63	44	59	47
Per cent rating father "mild"	48	33	48	32
Soft–Hard				
Per cent rating mother "soft"	69	61	60	57
Per cent rating father "soft"	50	50	62	51
Lenient–Severe				
Per cent rating mother "lenient"	94	61	66	63
Per cent rating father "lenient"	60	44	47	42
Easy–Strict				
Per cent rating mother "easy"	75	50	77	52
Per cent rating father "easy"	69	44	47	37
(*N*)	(23)	(24)	(27)	(26)

variable. As Table 2 suggests, "moralism" is also strongly related to activism; very few activitists score high on this variable, while the majority of nonactivists are high scorers.

These values are strongly related to activism. They are also highly intercorrelated, and, most importantly, parent and student scores on these variables are strongly correlated.

These and other value patterns will be used as the basis for studying value transmission in families, generational similarities and differences and several other problems. Our data with respect to them provide further support for the view that the unconventionality of activists flows out of and is supported by their family traditions.

Activists' parents are more "permissive" than parents of nonactivists. We have just begun to get some findings bearing on our hypothesis that parents of activists will tend to have been more "permissive" in their child-rearing practices than parents of equivalent status whose children are not oriented toward activism.

One measure of parental permissiveness we have been using is a series of rating scales completed by each member of the family. A series of seven-point bipolar scales was presented in a format similar to that of the "Semantic Differential." Students were asked to indicate "how my mother (father) treated me as a child" on such scales as "warm–cold"; "stern–mild"; "hard–

soft"—10 scales in all. Each parent, using the same scales, rated "how my child thinks I treated him."

Table 3 presents data on how sons and daughters rated each of their parents on each of four scales: "mild–stern"; "soft–hard"; "lenient–severe"; and "easy–strict." In general, this table shows that activist sons and daughters tend to rate their parents as "milder," "more lenient," and "less severe" than do nonactivists. Similar data were obtained using the parents' ratings of themselves.

A different measure of permissiveness is based on the parents' response to a series of "hypothetical situations." Parents were asked, for example, what they would do if their son (daughter) "decided to drop out of school and doesn't know what he really wants to do." Responses to this open-ended question were coded as indicating "high intervention" or "low intervention." Data for fathers on this item are reported in Table 4.

Table 4. Father's Intervention—"If child dropped out of school" (Percentages)

Degree of Intervention	Activisim of Child	
	High	Low
Low	56	37
High	44	63
(*N*)	(30)	(30)

Another hypothetical situation presented to the parents was that their child was living with a member of the opposite sex. Responses to this item were coded as "strongly intervene, mildly intervene, not intervene." Data for this item for fathers appears in Table 5. Both tables show that fathers of activists report themselves to be much less interventionist than fathers of nonactivists. Similar results were obtained with mothers, and for other hypothetical situations.

Table 5. Father's Intervention—"If child were living with member of opposite sex" (Percentages)

| Degree of Intervention | Activism of Child | |
	High	Low
None	20	14
Mild	50	28
Strong	30	58
(N)	(30)	(30)

Clearly both types of measures just reported provide support for our hypothesis about the relationship between parental permissiveness and activism. We expect these relationships to be strengthened if "activism" is combined with certain of the value-patterns described earlier.

A Concluding Note

The data reported here constitute a small but representative sampling of the material we have collected in our studies of the student movement. In general, they provide support for the impressions and expectations we had when we undertook this work. Our view of the student movement as an expression of deep discontent felt by certain types of high status youth as they confront the incongruities between the values represented by the authority and occupational structure of the larger society and the values inculcated by their families and peer culture seems to fit well with the data we have obtained.

A variety of questions remain which, we hope, can be answered, at least in part, by further analyses of our data. Although it is clear that value differences between parents of activists and nonactivists are centrally relevant for understanding value, attitudinal and behavioral cleavages among types of students on the campus, it remains to be determined whether differences in family status, on the one hand, and childrearing practices, on the other, make an independent contribution to the variance. A second issue has to do with political ideology. First impressions of our data suggest that activists vary considerably with respect to their degree of politicization and their concern with ideological issues. The problem of isolating the key determinants of this variation is one we will be paying close attention to in further analysis of our interview material. Two factors are likely to be of importance here—first, the degree to which the student participates in radical student organizations; second, the political history of his parents.

At least two major issues are not confronted by the research we have been doing. First, we have not examined in detail the role of campus conditions as a determinant of student discontent (see the introduction by Sampson and the article by Brown for a further discussion of these institutional factors.) The research reported here emphasizes family socialization and other antecedent experiences as determinants of student protest, and leads to the prediction that students experiencing other patterns of early socialization will be unlikely to be in revolt. This view needs to be counterbalanced by recalling instances of active student unrest on campuses where very few students are likely to have the backgrounds suggested here as critical. Is it possible that there are two components to the student protest movement—one generated to a great extent by early socialization; and second by grievances indigenous to the campus? At any rate, the inter-relationships between personal dispositions and campus conditions need further detailed elucidation.

A second set of questions unanswerable by our research has to do with the future—what lies ahead for the movement as a whole and for the individual young people who participate in it? One direction for the student movement is toward institutionalization as an expression of youth discontent. This outcome, very typical of student movements in many countries, would represent a narrowing of the movement's political and social impact, a way of functionally integrating it into an otherwise stable society. Individual participants would be expected to pass through the movement on their way to eventual absorption, often at an elite level, into the established institutional order. An alternative direction would be toward the development of a full-fledged political "left," with the student movement serving, at least initially, as a nucleus. The potential for this latter development is apparent in recent events. It was the student movement which catalyzed professors and other adults into protest with respect to the Vietnam war. Students for a Democratic Society, the main organizational expression of the student movement, has had, for several years, a program for "community organizing," in which students and ex-students work full-time at the mobilization of constituencies for independent radical political and social action. This SDS program began in poverty areas; it is now beginning to spread to "middle class" communities. These efforts, and others like them from Berkeley to New Haven, became particularly visible during the 1966 congressional elections, as a wave of "new left" candidates emerged across the country, often supported by large and sophisticated political organizations. Moreover, in addition to attempts at political organizations, SDS, through its "Radical Education Project" has begun to seek the involvement of faculty members, professionals and other intellectuals for a program of research and education designed to lay the foundations for an intellectually substantial and ideologically developed "new left."

At its convention in September, 1966, SDS approched, but did not finally decide, the question of whether to continue to maintain its character as a campus-based, student organization or to transform itself into a "Movement for a Democratic Society." Characteristically, the young people there assembled amended the organization's constitution so that anyone regardless of status or age could join, while simultaneously they affirmed the student character of the group by projecting a more vigorous program to organize uncommitted students.

The historical significance of the student movement of the Sixties remains to be determined. Its impact on the campus and on the larger society has already been substantial. It is clearly a product of deep discontent in certain significant and rapidly growing segments of the youth population. Whether it becomes an expression of generational discontent, or the forerunner of major political realignments—or simply disintegrates—cannot really be predicted by detached social scientists. The ultimate personal and political meaning of the student movement remains a matter to be determined by those who are involved with it —as participants, as allies, as critics, as enemies.

REFERENCES

AARON, DANIEL *Writers on the left.* New York Avon, 1965.

BELL, DANIEL *The end of ideology.* New York: The Free Press, 1962.

BRAUNGART, R. G. Social stratification and political attitudes. Pennsylvania State University, 1966, (unpublished ms.).

BRONFENBRENNER, U. The changing American child: A speculative analysis. *Merrill-Palmer Quarterly,* 1961, *7,* 73–85.

COSER, LEWIS *Men of ideas.* New York: The Free Press, 1965.

EISENSTADT, SHMUEL N. *From generation to generation.* Glencoe: The Free Press, 1956.

ERIKSON, ERIK Identity and the life-cycle. *Psychological Issues.* 1959, *1,* 1–171.

ERIKSON, ERIK *Childhood and society.* New York: Norton, 1963, 306–325.

FLACKS, R. The liberated generation. University of Chicago, 1966. (mimeo)

GOLDSEN, ROSE; ROSENBERG, MORIS; WILLIAMS, ROBIN; AND SUCHMAN, EDWARD *What college students think,* Princeton: Van Nostrand, 1969.

JACOB, PHILIP *Changing values in college.* New York: Harper, 1957.

KENISTON, KENNETH *The uncommitted.* New York: Harcourt Brace, 1965a.

KENISTON, KENNETH Social change and youth in America. In E. Erikson (Ed.), *The challenge of youth.* Garden City: Doubleday Anchor, 1965b.

LASCH, CHRISTOPHER *The new radicalism in America.* New York: Knopf, 1965.

LIPSET, SEYMOUR   *Political man, the social bases of politics.* Garden City: Doubleday Anchor, 1960.

LIPSET, SEYMOUR   University students and politics in underdeveloped countries. *Comparative Education Review,* 1966, *10,* 320–349.

LIPSET, SEYMOUR, AND ALTBACH, P.   Student politics and higher education in the United States. *Comparative Education Review,* 1966, *10,* 320–349.

MILLER, DANIEL, AND SWANSON, G. E.   *The changing American parent.* New York: Wiley, 1958.

NEWCOMB, THEODORE, AND FLACKS, R.   *Deviant subcultures on a college campus.* US Office of Education, 1963.

PARSONS, TALCOTT   Youth in the context of American society. In E. Erikson (Ed.), *The challenge of youth.* Garden City: Doubleday Anchor, 1965.

SHILS, EDWARD   The intellectuals in the political development of new states. *World Politics,* 1969, *12,* 329–368.

STINCHCOMBE, ARTHUR   *Rebellion in a high school.* Chicago: Quadrangle, 1964.

TROW, MARTIN   Student cultures and administrative action. In Surtherland, R. *et al.* (Eds.), *Personality factors on the college campus.* Austin: Hogg Foundation for Mental Health, 1962.

VEBLEN, THORSTEIN   The intellectual pre-eminence of Jews in modern Europe. In B. Rosenberg (Ed.), *Thorstein Veblen.* New York: Crowell, 1963.

Chapter 18: Suggested Additional Readings

ALTBACH, P. G.   Student movements in historical perspective. *Youth and Society,* 1970, *1*(3), 333–357. The author relates changes in the character of student movements in Asia to corresponding changes in broad periods of history.

The art of rebellion.   *Teachers College Record,* 1967, *48*(6), 499–502. This article provides commentary about Albert Camus's, *The Rebel* (New York: Knopf, 1954), and gives the reviewer's reaction to methods of expressing rebellion. He suggests that perhaps the best sort of rebellion is a rational one with reasonable goals, not a demand for total change. Instead of suppressing dissent, the schools should encourage young people to raise questions and suggest answers, and to move, as Camus expresses it, "beyond nihilism" to moderation.

BETTELHEIM, B.   The college student rebellion: Explanations and answers. *Phi Delta Kappan,* 1969, *50*(9), 511–514. Bettelheim concludes that many students who may not be a serious danger to the country do constitute a menace to the universities. Moreover, the unfortunate behaviors of a few may lead to a fascist type of backlash.

BLOCK, J. H., & HANN, N.   Socialization correlates of student activism. *Journal of Social Issues,* 1969, *25*(4), 143. The authors report a study of the nature, scope, and patterns of political-social activity, moral orientation, and socialization antecedents, in samples of students recruited from the University of California at Berkeley and from San Francisco State College, and in representatives of several groups of Peace Corps trainees.

EISENSTADT, S. N.   Changing patterns of youth protest in different stages of development of modern societies. *Youth and Society,* 1969, *1*(2), 133–150. After outlining major characteristics of protest movements in earlier periods of modern societies, the writer considers new types of protest and their impact.

ERICKSON, E. H.   Reflections on the dissent of contemporary youth. *Daedalus,* 1970, *99*(1), 154–157, 172–175. The writer differentiates today's youthful dissent from protests of other times, and suggests methods of dealing with the protests of contemporary youth.

GREENE, M.   Moral education and dissenting youth. *The Record,* 1969, *71*(2), 227–229. The editor of *The Record* suggests that today's young rebels need help in learning what they want and how to secure what they want. Youth need to learn responsibility, to be liberated, to be moral, and to deal with current ambiguities.

GREENSTIEN, R. I., & TARROW, S.   Children and politics in Britain, France, and the United States. *Youth and Society,* 1970, *2*(1), 111–128. This account of children's reactions to certain hypothetical political situations points up the differences in value systems of children in widely different cultures.

HAAN, N.   Moral redefinition in families as the critical aspect of the generational gap. *Youth and Society,* 1971, *2*(3), 259–283. The adolescent's moral development is discussed in terms of family interaction, the generation gap, and contemporary society. A certain amount of disequilibrium in the individual is perceived as inevitable if he is to construct, rather than simply reflect, moral concepts. Somewhat different backgrounds are reported for three groups: the morally principled activists, the morally principled hippies, and the conventionally moral nonactivists.

HALL, M. H.   A conversation with Kenneth Keniston. *Psychology Today*, 1968, *2*(6), 16–23, 59. This interview with a scholar well known for his books about modern youth provides insight into the psychology of student activists today.

JENNINGS, M. K., & NIEMI, R. G.   Patterns of political learning. *Harvard Educational Review*, 1968, *39*(3), 443–467. Early socialization is portrayed as primarily concerned with inculcating appropriate cultural norms and motivations. Political values and commitments of early years are enduring, and the individual reaches a permanent plateau of political activity after early adolescence.

JOHNSTON, J. R.,   Student revolt and social revolution. *Educational Record*, 1970, *51*(1), 22–27. The student revolt is portrayed as the dominant instrument of social change, with a power base on campus and recruiting grounds among students and ghetto youth.

KERPELMAN, L. C.   Student political activism and ideology: comparative characteristics of activists and nonactivists. *Journal of Counseling Psychology*, 1969, *16*, 8–13. Activists and nonactivists are differentiated according to various personality traits.

ROSENBERG, R. R.   The apathetic majority. *Youth and Society*, 1970, *2*(2), 177–206. On the basis of a random sampling of 2500 students at a law college the author generalized the reasons for the political apathy of the vast majority of university students in Nationalist China. He considers the background of students, the nature of their school, and the individual differences among them.

ROWNTREE, J., & ROWNTREE, M.   The political economy of youth. *Our Generation*, 1968, *6*(1–2), 1–36. The Rowntrees describe the youth movement as an outgrowth of an imperialist system which exploits youth. Youth, in turn, band together and seek to confront and unmask the society that exploits them.

RUBINSTEIN, E. A.   Paradoxes of student protests. *American Psychologist*, 1969, *24*(2) 133–141. The author outlines some of the more recent interpretations of student unrest and raises additional questions about student protests.

SHAFER, S. M.   Political passions and rational actions. *Teachers College Record*, 1967, *48*(6), 471–479. After considering adult political behavior, the author describes contemporary concerns of young people, many of whom manifest more political commitment than any young generation in history. Through activating youth's awareness, enthusiasm, and social trust, and encouraging a feeling of high self-regard in individuals, he asserts, teachers can increase the number of youth who are capable of intelligent political activity.

SIGEL, R. S.   Essay Review: *Children and Politics. The School Review*, 1967, *75*(2), 228–236. This book systematically asks: What type of children know what about politics at what age, and what do they think of it? The study constitutes a pioneer work in the fast growing literature of political socialization.

SMITH, M. B., HAAN, & BLOCK, J.   Social-psychological aspects of student activism. *Youth and Society*, 1970, *1*(3), 261–288. This paper describes the results of a study designed to "shed light on the psychological basis of activism and alternative patterns of student orientation to the sociopolitical order."

TAYLOR, H.   The student revolution. *Phi Delta Kappan*, 1969, *51*(2), 62–67. The student movement in the United States is traced against the world background. It is necessary, says the author, for the universities to adjust to changing student needs.

THOMAS, L. E.   Family correlates of student political activism. *Developmental Psychology*, 1971, *4*(2), 206–214. Parents' political views, whether liberal or not, are related to their college-age children's political participation. A strong family influence on such activities was disclosed.

TRUMP, J. L. & HUNT, J.   The nature and extent of student activism. *Bulletin of the*

National Association of Secondary School Prinicpals, 1969, *53,* 150–158. In a national survey, three out of five secondary school principals reported a climate of student protest in their schools. Others anticipated such conditions in the future.

WARNECKE, S.   American student politics. *Yale Review,* 1971, *40*(2), 175–184. The author discusses the nature of student politics, its motives, and its values, and suggests how student political activism may be utilized to help universities function more effectively.

WRENN, R. I.   The authority controversy and today's student. *Personnel and Guidance Journal,* 1968, *46,* 949–953. Today's college campus is characterized by two extremes of expression: one, that of the hippie who withdraws into his inner world; the other, that of the activist who attacks existing problems.

ZOLBERG, A. R.   Youth as a political phenomenon in tropical Africa. *Youth and Society,* 1969, *1*(2), 199–218. The author develops a number of hypotheses concerning African youth as political activists, and suggests areas requiring further research.

part six

Cultural Variants in Adolescent Problems

19

Adolescents in American Subcultures

Each modern society has its own culture, comprising those customs, habits, attitudes, knowledges, and mores which distinguish it from other societies and which are shared by the individual members of the society. Within the larger society are subgroups, or subcultures, which possess not only all the distinguishing marks of the major culture but additional characteristic features of their own.

We have already commented on one such subculture, the American youth culture, formed by the age-grading of society. One variant of the youth subculture is the college student sub-culture, which may also have variants of its own. The college is viewed as a distinctive sociocultural system, with a value orientation that contains a variety of goals for the student (Gottlieb & Hodgkins, 1963).

Youth are also members of the subcultures of their own social classes. In recent years, one of the most widely studied variables in human development has been that of social class (Nagasawa, 1971). Apparently, modern American youth have high success goals regardless of their social class; nevertheless, cultural exposure to the middle class, as compared with cultural exposure to the lower class, more effectively prepares youth to function in societal systems where success-striving follows certain accepted rules.

In effect, for the lower-class youth, participation in the lower-class subculture substitutes for his lack of membership in the prevalent middle-class youth culture. To reduce the impact of their possible failure, youths in the lower-class subculture often revise their aspirations downward; perhaps they rationalize by establishing goals which involve less emphasis on success. Even youth in the upper-lower class, as contrasted with their middle-class counterparts, normally have a greater sense of powerlessness, a more fantastic attitude toward life, a lack of future orientation, and a greater impulse for "acting out." Most research studies show lower-class youth to be relatively nonverbal, antiintellectual, and poor in conceptual abilities (Pearl, 1965). What lower-class youth need, says Pearl, is "to be provided an opportunity to form groups which have a link with the future; which permit them to develop marketable competence; and in which they have the right to be wrong, the right to correct wrongs, and mostly, the right to belong [p. 108]."

The lower-class boy, especially, often lacks an adequate father model to help him prepare for his own adult role in the family. Lower-class children of both sexes often lack adequate contact with the male parent during their early years. In a study of parents' perceptions of children's televiewing habits (Martin and Benson, 1970), lower-class fathers demonstrated little involvement; by contrast, lower-class mothers attempted to control their children's use of television. Acceptance of the responsibility of fatherhood, the study disclosed, is more a function of education and social class than is acceptance of a mothering role, and an individual's success as a father tends to rise with his social class. On the other hand, the performance of the mother role is standard across social class and educational lines.

Traditionally, the lower-class youth has been spared some of the strains of adolescence—to put it another way, he has been spared the pains of membership in the youth culture. His parents have more willingly accepted him as an adult. He has felt free to leave school and seek a job. Consequently, he has had more spending money; and he has the opportunity to marry early and thus relieve his sexual tensions. While lower-class youth have envied upper-class youth in some respects, the reverse has also been true. Middle-class youth often adopt the clothes, verbal expressions, and music of the lower classes. Therefore, even as upper-class ways seep downward, so do lower-class ways filter upward (Stone & Church, 1957 p. 293).

Other American subcultures have developed according to race, or country of national origin. For example, until recently, Negro youth were almost wholly in the lower-class subculture; and like other members of their class, they had no youth culture. More recently, however, a Negro middle class has developed, whose children finish high school and often go on to college. Negroes have a growing interest in their origins in African areas, and black studies programs to explore the blacks' cultural heritage have been instituted in many colleges. However, perhaps now even more than before, the Negro teenager finds himself trapped between two cultures. When he had no hope of achieving the rewards of the larger, white-oriented culture, he often resigned himself to the way of life of his subculture. But now the black youth does have hope of achieving middle-class goals and more, and he resists being trapped in any stereotype mold. He wants the best of both worlds, his own Negro subculture and the broader white man's culture (Bernard, 1961).

Klinzing (1971) refers to the Negro as the invisible man in today's education, but the black individual is certainly more visible than before. Of course, many black youngsters still have problems of identity, of establishing a liking for self, of being comfortable with blackness, and of getting over a yearning to be white. As one writer stated, "to convince a black child that she is beautiful when every channel of value formation in this society is telling her the opposite is a heart-rending and well-nigh impossible task [Browne, 1968, p. 13]." According to Klinzing, the black youth must not try simply to become like the white man, because to do so might obliterate his own personality, debase his own experiences, and strengthen those forces that produce in him feelings of anonymity. Instead, black youths must seek collectively to establish a worthy identity for their race, and singly to define themselves as individuals. Of course, in these times, not only blacks but whites, too, have tended to become invisible. Thanks to the present-day passion for categorizing everybody, and to society's indifference to the uniqueness of the individual, youth of all races are in danger of becoming invisible.

Recently, the problems of minority groups, including Negroes, have been widely discussed and the conclusions reached have often been simplistic notions of what may be done to remedy the situation (Elder, 1970). However, the status of any minority group member hinges on unbelievably complex personal and social factors. For example, because of the frustrations Negro youth experience in the larger environment, they tend to retreat to the family; and this policy of withdrawal in turn strengthens the hand of those committed to policies of racial subordination.

Among the best descriptions of subcultural variants of adolescents in American society are those given by Hans Sebald in his excellent book, *Adolescence: A Sociological Analysis*. The excerpts given in our first selection briefly summarize separate chapters of Sebald's book relating to Negro, Jewish, Indian, and lower-class teenagers. The student who reads these four chapters in their entirety will find them both interesting and rewarding. Because of space considerations, only the summaries can be included here.

Regardless of race or social class, youth also dwell in the subculture of their particular locale, whether rural, small town, or urban. In certain respects, rural farm, rural non-farm, and urban youth are alike in experiencing parent–youth conflict; however, both rural youth and their parents are more traditional than their urban counterparts (Bealer & Willets, 1961). Farm youth are close to their parents, and the traditionally close-knit farm family persists. Particularly here, the characterization of adolescence as a period of rebellion against parental norms and rejection of traditional values is questionable; and the more remote the rural area, the less the youth rejects societal norms (Hathaway, Monachesi & Young, 1959). City-dwelling youth may be further subdivided into subcultures according to the section of the city in which they live, for various areas of the same city may be so different as almost to constitute different worlds. However, most city youth are alike in having access to certain cultural advantages, in living in an environment adapted largely to adults, and in experiencing, at close range, the tempo of change.

Cultural differences in a society vary not only by subgroups but also with the times. The America of the 1970s is certainly more different from the America of the 1900s than it is from the Japan of the 1970s. Changes that once would have taken a century now occur in less than a generation; what occurs in the present will soon be remote and outdated. While an individual moves through his personal life-stages, his social milieu is also changing; hence, in effect he experiences a succession of cultures. In a given country, these shifting cultures maintain certain core values for varying lengths of time; nevertheless, they also display distinctive differences. For example, in contemporary America the core values of economic achievement and generosity to less-favored nations have persisted, while respect for law and order, belief in the virtue of hard work, and sexual asceticism among females have declined. Moreover, since tomorrow has become totally unpredictable, sons can no longer depend, for their own future, on answers handed down by their fathers. Their education must be such that they will know how to devise new solutions for new-type problems.

Concerning the effect of various subcultures on adolescents in general, various issues suggest themselves. How fundamental are the variations in adolescents by subculture? How specifically may such variations be defined? There is much speculation and theorizing, but most of it lacks an empirical base. For instance, are the "disadvantaged" youth of the lower social classes as unfortunate as they seem from the perspective of middle-class observers? Perhaps they share advantages within their own milieu—for example, relative freedom from competitive pressure—of which the outsider is only dimly aware. Also, what sort of adaptations should the larger culture—and its agent, the school—make for teenagers of different subcultures? Should schools be racially integrated? Would it be better to accept the doctrine of pluralism, and to encourage youth of specific subcultures to maintain the values and ways of life characteristic of their families of origin; or should all young people be blended in the same sociocultural melting pot?

In the second reading selection presented here, Thornburg warns against overgeneralizing about youth, and describes three distinct peer categories: high school youth, college youth, and non-college youth. His article illustrates both basic respects in which youth tend to resemble each other and the broad range of ways in which they differ.

Finally, in the third selection, Gaier describes the present-day American adolescent as a new creation, or mutant, with his own concepts of alienation and life style. Gaier then differentiates the subcultural types of Negro-versus-white and rural-versus-urban; he concludes by discussing the American adolescent's special stresses and modes of coping with these stresses.

REFERENCES

BEALER, R. C., & WILLITS, F. K. Rural youth: A case study in the rebelliousness of adolescents in teen-age culture. In J. Bernard (Ed.) *Teen-Age Culture.* Philadelphia: The American Academy of Political and Social Science, November 1961, 338. pp. 63–69.

BERNARD, J. Teen-age culture: An overview. In J. Bernard (Ed.) *Teen-Age Culture.* Philadelphia: The American Academy of Political and Social Science, November 1961, 338, pp. 11–12.

BROWNE, R. The case for two Americas—one black, one white. *New York Times Magazine,* August 11, 1968, p. 13.

ELDER, G. H. Socialization and ascent in a racial minority. *Youth and Society,* 1970, 2(1), 74–110.

GOTTLIEB, D., & HODGKINS, B. College student subcultures: Their structure and characteristics in relation to student attitude change. *The School Review,* 1963, 71, 266–289.

HATHAWAY, S. R., MONACHESI, E. D., & YOUNG, L. A. Rural–urban adolescent personality. *Rural Sociology,* December 1959, 24, 331–346.

KLINZING, J. The invisible man and today's education. *Educational Forum,* 1971, 35(4), 431–438.

MARTIN, C. A., & BENSON, L.   Parental perceptions of the role of television in parent–child reaction. *Journal of Marriage and the Family*, 1970, *32*(3), 410–414.

NAGASAWA, R. H.   Social-class differentials in success-striving. *Pacific Sociological Review*, 1971, *14*(2), 215–223.

PEARL, A.   Youth in lower class settings. In M. Sherif and C. W. Sherif (Eds.) *Problems of Youth: Transition to Adulthood in a Changing World*. Chicago: Aldine Publishing Co., 1965, p. 89.

STONE, L. J., & CHURCH, J.   *Childhood and Adolescence*. New York: Random House, 1957.

Adolescence: A Sociological Analysis

HANS SEBALD

The brief summaries below taken from a longer article, provide thumbnail sketches of adolescents in four American subcultures—Negro, Jewish, Indian and lower class.

[The Negro Adolescent]

. . . These are . . . some of the major life conditions that influence the adolescent experience of the Negro in contemporary America.

(1) He carries with him the legacy of his slave forefathers, confronting numerous obstacles in his spasmodic progress to equality. His self-image is highly influenced by the awareness of his racial background and is beset with deprecatory connotations from which he finds it difficult to escape.

(2) The Negro population as a whole, and the Negro youth in specific, exhibit a singular lack of collective identity and solidarity. This collective passivity can usually be traced to the negative and self-debasing attitudes so often noticeable among Negroes. Such basic psychological preconditions may induce the Negro to project the rejection of himself to the rejection of the collectivity. In the case of most Negro teen-agers, especially lower class, this inability to form cohesive, stable, durable, and goal-oriented groups has frequently been observed. However, the Negro's traditional lack of collective cohesion is increasingly being modified by a sharpening of collective awareness and the growth of an assertive identity.

(3) Generalizations about the nature of one or a number of Negro youth subcultures are extremely difficult. Mid-20th-century America has seen a proliferation of Negro movements and orientations. Lower-class youth are characterized by personal, material, and frequently delinquent aggression. This behavior is a product of the unique combination of racial background, lower-class conditions, and ghetto living. A rising Negro middle class furnishes increasing numbers of youth who approach the issue of improving the Negro's lot by more rational and political means. Many educated young Negroes have joined protest movements to achieve integration and equality in peaceful ways. At the same time, such activities alleviate the problem of identity that is central to the modern Negro situation and is at the core of variegated expressions and ideological persuasions of Negro youth. Besides social activist subcultures, there are extremist Negro movements, the "black nationalists" and the "black internationalists," aiming at establishing black supremacy on a national or world basis, respectively.

(4) For most Negroes, family life is lower-class life and combines the insidious factors of lack of self- and other-respect, frequent family disruption, father-absence, illegitimacy, and ma-

From H. Sebald, *Adolescence: A sociological analysis.* New York: Appleton-Century-Crofts, 1968, 287–288, 303–304, 319, 346–347. Reprinted by permission of Meredith Corporation and the author.

tricentrism. In the process, masculinity is challenged and demeaned, burdening the young Negro male with extra problems of identity.

(5) The Negro adolescent is expected to make the transition from child to adult under additional conditions of conspicuous disadvantage and adversity. First, he is likely to be undereducated due to actual discrimination, segregated schooling that seldom equals the quality of white or integrated schooling, poor self-attitudes, defeatist perception of the educational institution resulting in the self-fulfilling prophecy, and finally, conditions of lower-class living in a ghetto where privacy, encouragement, and financial means for formal learning are limited. Second, his chances of finding a job are significantly reduced, and even if he finds employment, his wages are considerably below those of the white worker. However, the Negro female shows a trend of her own, more closely approximating and in some cases even exceeding the economic stature of her white counterpart. Third, parallel symptoms have been discovered in the realms of health, infant mortality, and life expectancy, showing evidence of the failure to bring mid-20th-century affluence and equal living standards to the American Negro.

[The Jewish Adolescent]

. . . Jewish youth contrasts sharply with the Negro youth. His ancestors came to the new continent not as slaves but as free men who participated widely in aspects of local and national life, some degree of anti-Semitism notwithstanding. The religiocultural heritage, though declining in salience, still helps to prevent Jewish youth from feeling the type of *anomie* and worthlessness that is common among the Negro population. The socioeconomic and educational standards of the Jewish people are ordinarily far above those of Negro families.

Generalization as to a uniform Jewish subculture is, however, difficult, since there are a number of distinct subgroups within. Discussion of the diversity as such is evaded, and focus delimitation reserves discussion to middle- and upper-middle-class Jewish youth, mostly of liberal religious orientation, who are characterized by many life conditions and behavior patterns that resemble those of their Gentile friends.

This assimilative process is helped along by a number of changing dimensions in the Jewish community. Over the past two to three decades, ecological shifts have resulted in de-ghettoization of Jewish living habits; religious convictions have partially faded into more secular and cultural values; declining anti-Semitism no longer challenges the Jewish subculture to bring forth united efforts to protect itself; Zionist zeal has changed into relatively dispassionate and usually merely verbal approval of the State of Israel; and endogamy, though still more consistently practiced than among most other religious groups, appears to be gradually losing its stringency.

However, these dynamic processes have still left enough ethnic uniqueness and, in fact, have added unique features through requiring the Jewish youth to adjust to them, so that some degree of generalization seems justified. Generalizability is particularly supported by an appreciable exhibition of familism among Jewish people and by continuing economic salience and cooperation within the Jewish community.

The conclusion that evolves from this discussion is that, in as far as adolescence refers to status discontinuity, the life conditions of the Jewish adolescent lessen, if anything, the difficulties of the transition to the adult status. The conclusion appears warranted in the light of the closer-knit family and kinship group that is able to provide a number of acceptable adult models; the security of a more stable family life that is not as frequently disrupted by separations, desertions, and divorces as in the Gentile population; some degree of economic "nepotism" and business "connections," which frequently facilitate finding jobs and entering professional careers for the Jewish youth; and a religiocultural tradition that is ever-present—though increasingly less frequently invoked—source for identity. The Jewish adolescent is thus in a better position than most of his Gentile friends to achieve personal identity and to overcome the intermittent social-structural discontinuity and unclarity of adolescence.

[The Indian Adolescent]

. . . It is . . . obvious that generalizations about Indian teen-agers *as a whole* are most difficult, if not unrealistic. Most contemporary Indian youth suffer psychological strain under the impact of cultural change. This is particularly true of Indian youth who fall into the category of marginal men. This type, unlike the others, especially the native, deviant, and acculturated types, is faced with a compound marginality that is ambiguous in respect to both ethnic identity and child–adult statuses. The polarity between the white and the Indian culture results in a suspension that is characterized by paradoxical pressures. It is this type of contrapuntal pressure that seems to immobilize the mid-20th-century teen-ager and impede his progress in either direction—the direction of the white as well as of the traditional Indian culture. In other words, the slow change of the psychological structure of the Indian teen-ager is usually due to the circumstance that neither sociocultural system—neither the white nor the Indian culture— is fully meaningful and acceptable to the contemporary Indian youth. As a result, the Indians as a distinct minority group are not, by any means, vanishing or being absorbed; unlike the Jews, for example, they are becoming an increasingly problematic minority group whose problems will continue to vex both the dominant white society and each new generation of Indians.

[The Lower-Class Adolescent]

. . . Life style and life chances of lower-class youth are significantly affected by a number of relatively unique economic, social, and cultural circumstances. One of the most influential conditions is the lower-class ethos, containing a number of *core concerns* that allow for value orientations and preoccupations that result in unique behavior patterns. Among the core concerns of the lower-class ethos are trouble, a preoccupation with the adversities and complications of life; toughness, a value encouraging fearless, defiant, and bravado acts that usually are meant to uphold an image of masculinity; smartness, the esteemed ability to outfox, "take," and "con" others; excitement, the search for variety of experience and expression to break the monotony of an otherwise deprived life style; fate, a belief in destiny reflecting the feeling of powerlessness; anti-intellectualism, a negative attitude toward abstractness and formal learning; and authoritarianism, the tendency to interpret social interaction in vertical dimensions.

Early acquisition of these core sentiments tends to prepare the youth to become a failure in situations requiring competition with middle-class peers or in general situations that confront him with middle-class demands. For example, the value of being tough and masculine frequently creates friction and disruptive conduct in the school setting. The belief in fate and the related feeling of being powerless in the face of middle-class demands make for poor motivation and defeatist attitudes in school. If the anti-intellectual propensity is added to this syndrome, it is easy to see why youth from the lower socioeconomic stratum are overrepresented among the truants, failures, and dropouts. Of particularly defeat-prone nature are the linguistic deficiencies of lower-class youth. His deficiencies in vocabulary, syntax, and idiom limit his perceptual capability and permit only gross intellectual distinctions and abstractions. This limited ability in abstract reasoning also shows in lower degrees of achievement motivation. While middle-class parents carry out early, regular, and insistent inculcation of the value of individual achievement, lower-class parents are irregular and indifferent in this respect. Although lack of achievement and success orientation is consistently correlated with lower socioeconomic background, researchers have discovered a number of intervening variables that—if operationally applied—are likely to produce a more sensitive and predictable correlation. Examples of such intervening variables include categorizing the pupil as either a college or a non-college prospect, the degree of parental domination, and the type of reference-group experience.

The educational establishment—middle-class in nature and outlook—is faced with the extremely difficult task of educating the lower-class youngster. A number of educators and behavioral scientists believe that this task can be successfully completed only when teachers become more sensitive toward the linguistic dilemma of the lower-class child, provide more realistic references that include the living conditions of the working man's family, appeal to the practical and motoristically-inclined learning preferences of the lower-class youth, involve the youth with deprived background in various role-playing techniques, and present themselves as identification-objects, implying that male teachers are needed to achieve a situation where the lower-class boy is less inclined to rebel and more able to identify.

Lower-class adolescence is distinguished from middle-class adolescence by more modest material implementation, more limited subcultural expanse and communication, less distinct fashions and fads, and an adolescent time span that usually is shortened by excluding prolonged educational and professional preparation. It appears that the close-knit gang, delinquent or nondelinquent, plays a prominent role in the life of the lower-class youth and functions as an effective bridge between child and adult status that, in a sense, tends to ease the adolescent transition.

Peers: Three Distinct Groups

HERSCHEL D. THORNBURG

In this article Thornburg describes, and attempts to account for differences in, the attitudes and value attitudes of three distinct peer groups: high school youth, non-college youth, and college youth.

Adolescents have vital concerns about the individuals and situations that affect their development. Of primary importance to each adolescent are (1) his society and his peers, (2) gaining self and social identity, and (3) social maturation. Most behavioral scientists agree that these factors are essential to the successful development of adolescents. They also recognize that these factors are worked out mostly within one's own world—among one's peers.

An article by Smith and Kleine (1966) reviews the literature about the adolescent and his world. The conflicting propositions are presented that (1) adolescents are an emphatically strong subculture and that (2) adolescent values do not differ significantly from their parents. In an extensive study of middle-class families, Elkin and Westley (1955) found very little difference between adult and adolescent values. Research among rural youth has reflected the same findings (Bealer, Willits, Maida, 1964). Yet, Coleman's studies (1961) show quite distinctly that there is an adolescent subculture which is the primary influence in adolescent social maturation. Research studies since Coleman support his findings (Strom, 1963; Cawelti, 1968; *Generations Apart,* 1969).

While controversy may surround the subcul-

ture vs. nonsubculture issue, most likely the proposition could be advanced that there is often too much emphasis being placed on the issue that might be no more than a natural rebellion of the adolescent and be less conflict- and anxiety-oriented if less were being said about it. Bandura (1964) expressed it in an article he wrote, "The story decade: Fact or fiction?"

Bandura's article focuses primarily on various sources of adolescent mythology. He attributes adolescent rebellion to superficial signs of nonconformity. He cogently parallels adolescent fad behavior with adult fad behaviors.

Mass media's ability to sensationalize adolescent behavior, especially deviant ones, is another perpetuation of the myth of significant adolescent–adult differences. Such a statement was attested to in the recent CBS report which asked college and non-college youth, "What scene stands out most vividly in your mind from the TV coverages you saw of the Vietnam war (*Generations Apart,* 1969, p. 34)?" Thirty-eight per cent of the college youth and 42 per cent of the non-college youth answered "killing and bodies."

Other statements and research evidence in Bandura's article make one aware that more could be done than is being done to minimize adoles-

From H. D. Thornburg, Peers: Three distinct groups. Reprinted from *Adolescence,* 1971, 6(21), 59–76, by permission of the author and Libra Publications, Inc.

cent conflict and accentuate more positive aspects of social development.

Some type of group behavior, i.e., cliques and crowds, is contributory in the pursuit of social maturation. The most recent investigation of adolescent social structure was done by Dunphy (1963) in which he found that nearly 80 per cent of our youth are involved is some form of group behavior. Figure 1 illustrates Dunphy's stages of group development in adolescence (1963, p. 236).

There are several reasons why group identification is so important to developing youth. One reason is to help youth in the process of emancipation. While Bandura (1964) suggests that most of youth's emancipation from parents has been more or less completed rather than initiated at adolescence, most writers believe that throughout adolescence there is a continuing emancipation process which is aided by peer association (Douvan and Adelson, 1966).

Group identification also spurs competition. Most adolescents spend much time in active competition. It serves an important developmental purpose when adolescents exercise their social maturation in spontaneous competition. Yet, not all adolescent competition is a result of growing up. Much of today's competition is affected by, sometimes even promoted by, the adult world since it is part of a society where so many attainments are necessary to success. However, the method of attainment can result in unhealthy competition. If adolescent competition is abused, it can produce lasting effects; it can become part of the individual's life style.

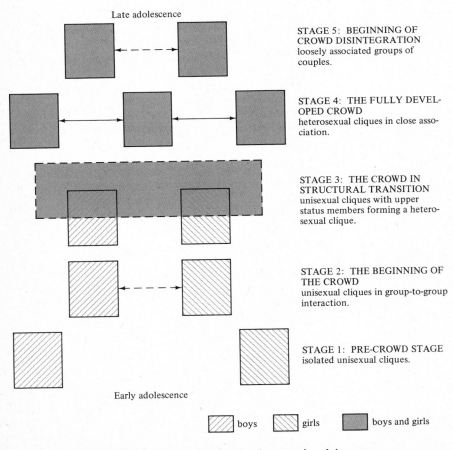

Late adolescence

STAGE 5: BEGINNING OF CROWD DISINTEGRATION loosely associated groups of couples.

STAGE 4: THE FULLY DEVELOPED CROWD heterosexual cliques in close association.

STAGE 3: THE CROWD IN STRUCTURAL TRANSITION unisexual cliques with upper status members forming a heterosexual clique.

STAGE 2: THE BEGINNING OF THE CROWD unisexual cliques in group-to-group interaction.

STAGE 1: PRE-CROWD STAGE isolated unisexual cliques.

Early adolescence

boys   girls   boys and girls

Figure 1. Stages of group development in adolescence.

A third aspect of group identification is conformity, about which psychologists are in considerable disagreement. Adolescent group identity may be linked to one's values; one's needs for acceptance or one's fear of rejection. Others identify because of a need to escape loneliness. Regardless of the reason, many adolescent groups do conform. Studies indicate that peer activity has the dominating effect on adolescent behaviors (Brittain, 1966; Cawelti, 1968; Coleman, 1961; Friesen, 1968; Musgrove, 1966). These studies do not preclude the fact that adults have significant effects on their youth (Meissner, 1965), but they do point out that peer influence is quite strong during adolescence.

Smith and Kleine (1966) observe that adolescents, just like adults, form smaller social units or reference groups, and these groups may vary in activities, sentiments, and behavioral norms. Such reference groups manifest their behavior through clique and gang-member activity. Youth does belong. Such is the process of social maturation.

Three Types of Peer Groups

There is increasing evidence that some distinct peer groups with varying attitudes and value references have emerged. The three groups are: (a) high school youth, (b) non-college youth, and (c) college youth. The differences are due to (1) distinctly different types of individual adolescent physical and intellectual functions, (2) the particular social and cultural milieu in which each adolescent develops, and (3) the attitudes and values of each adolescent peer affiliation.

HIGH SCHOOL YOUTH

Today, high school youth has basically the same type of peer relationships that earlier generation youth had. Most high school youth spend their time in breaking infantile ties, developing friendships, participating in high school activities and considering future plans. Parental, school and peer influences assist in this process. While there are many high school youth involved in student activism, drugs, and sex, they do it primarily as a means of identifying with some individual, clique, or gang. This results in some high school youth having stressful experiences. Yet, the primary focus is the continued resolution of developmental tasks (Garrison, 1966; Havighurst, 1952; Thornburg, 1970). Sherif and Sherif have stated, "Adolescents will find kicks in any activity—whether socially desirable or undesirable—that lets them act together on their own (1968, p. 6)." While this may very well apply to many high school youth, it is not the same type of motivation that triggers noncollege and college youth behavior.

NON-COLLEGE YOUTH

We have a majority of non-college youth. In fact, recent surveys place the proportion of non-college youth at around 80 per cent (Braham, 1963). Yet little is heard of this group and few studies have been done in which non-college youth were the primary focus. What are the values and attitudes of these youth? How do they differ from the high school youth? From college youth? From adults?

Non-college youth compared to college youth, in addition to the amount of education, are characterized by a stronger work orientation. They also tend to hold middle-class values, to be politically conservative, to be middle-income blue collar workers, to be religiously oriented (*Generations Apart,* 1969). Their life style is so much like their parents that one could strongly suggest that for this group, the generation gap is a myth. The impression is that today's problem may be a "fitting-into-society gap"—something that is far more difficult for college than non-college youth.

In April, 1969, CBS News undertook a study of the generation gap. It was conducted by the Daniel Yankelovich research firm. The survey, originally the subject of a series of television shows, has since been released as *Generations Apart* (1969). The sample consisted of 2,881 non-college youth and 723 college youth (17–23 years old); 310 non-college youth parents and 362 college youth parents. Parts of the youth profile will be reported here. The following summary statements will indicate differences existing between non-college and college youth and their parents.

(a) Question: Hard work will always pay off. (% that believe yes)

Answer: Non-college youth 79 College youth 56

NCY parents[1] 85 CY parents 76

(b) Question: Everyone should save as much as he can regularly and not have to lean on family and friends the minute he runs into financial problems. (% that believe yes)

Answer: Non-college youth 88 College youth 76

NCY parents 98 CY parents 90

(c) Question: Belonging to some organized religion is important in a person's life. (% that believe yes)

Answer: Non-college youth 82 College youth 42

NCY parents 91 CY parents 81

(d) Question: Competition encourages excellence. (% that believe yes)

Answer: Non-college youth 82 College youth 72

NCY parents 91 CY parents 84

[1]NCY stands for non-college youth.

Non-college and college youth were asked which of the following changes they *would welcome:*

Category	Non-College youth (%)	College youth (%)
(a) Less emphasis on money	54	72
(b) More emphasis on law and order	81	57
(c) More emphasis on self-expression	70	84
(d) More sexual freedom	22	43
(e) More vigorous protests by blacks and other minority groups	9	23
(f) More respect for authority	86	59

The statements and responses thus far have focused on traditional value statements. The survey indicates that non-college youth are more likely to agree with traditional value statements than college youth. Data also indicate that non-college youth values are more like parent values than are the college youth. If there is a significant difference between non-college youth and college youth values then it should reflect itself in areas in addition to traditional value statements. The following selected responses report the attitudes of non-college youth and college youth on society's institutions and restraints:

(a) Question: Having an abortion is morally wrong. (% agreeing)

Answer: Non-college youth 64 College youth 36

NCY parents 66 CY parents 50

(b) Question: Relations between consenting homosexuals are morally wrong. (% agreeing)

Answer: Non-college youth 72 College youth 42

NCY parents 79 CY parents 63

(c) Question: Pre-marital sexual relations are morally wrong. (% agreeing)

Answer: Non-college youth 57 College youth 34

NCY parents 88 CY parents 74

(d) Question: Extra-marital sexual relations are morally wrong. (% agreeing)

Answer: Non-college youth 77 College youth 77

NCY parents 92 CY parents 90

Additional questions were asked about restraints imposed by society which could or could not be accepted.

Category	Accept	Non-College youth	College youth
(a) Abiding by laws you don't agree with	easily	34	15
	reluctantly	55	74
	reject	11	14

Category	Accept	Non-College youth	College youth
(b) Conform-ing in matters of clothing and personal grooming	easily	54	33
	reluctantly	26	29
	reject	19	38
(c) Prohibition against marijuana	easily	72	48
	reluctantly	11	20
	reject	17	31
(d) Prohibition against LSD	easily	79	73
	reluctantly	7	11
	reject	13	13
(e) Power and authority of the police	easily	78	48
	reluctantly	27	42
	reject	4	10
(f) Being treated im-personally in a job	easily	21	9
	reluctantly	39	35
	reject	39	57

The statistics shown represent less than 10 per cent of the total questions asked by CBS News and do not include a political profile on youth presented in the report. But even in the questions not represented here, the non-college youth still indicate more significant differences in attitudes and values from the college youth. In summary, it could be said, as compared to college youth, that non-college youth are (1) more conservative, (2) more prone to traditional values, (3) more religious, (4) more respectful, (5) more work-oriented, (6) more money-oriented, (7) more patriotic, (8) more concerned about moral living, (9) more conforming, (10) more accepting of the draft and war, (11) less activism-oriented, (12) less sympathetic with activists, (13) less drug-prone, and (14) less sexually permissive (*Generations Apart,* 1969).

The behavior of non-college youth is not like that of high school youth. For the most part they are now involved in social integration more than social maturation. Their world is here. The responsibility they encounter to self and others makes them aware that it is here. It is not the idealism of high school youth or the world of the college youth. Many are married, most have jobs. The responsibility for maintaining a home and rearing a family is common. Life decisions are made on what they know and what they think is most appropriate at the time. Life is the ever-present daily experience of the non-college youth and his peers.

COLLEGE YOUTH

Perhaps the most unique and certainly the most controversial group of youth today are college students. These youths are characterized by their various institutional-challenging behaviors in which student activism, sexual freedom, and drug use are accentuated.

Most significant of their behaviors is the challenge they are presenting to the traditional conservative structure of life. As has been indicated by contrasting the non-college student with college youth, today's college student is less likely to adopt traditional standards and it is among this group that the generation gap, if any, most likely exists.

New ideas are emerging in college youth today. Some of these are ideas that focus on the educational institution. The challenges are based on the idea that college is not relevant to the needs of today's youth or society. R. W. Carry (1968) has suggested five emerging trends in attitude and thought about rules, education and youth. They are:

1. Trend one is away from the traditional view that it is the individual's responsibility to make the education offered him relevant. The emerging view is that it is the educational institution's responsibility to make its offerings relevant to the individual (Coleman, 1965).
2. Trend two is away from the traditional view that a rule is a rule, and right or wrong, it must be obeyed.
3. Trend three is away from the traditional view that rules were made for the purpose of insuring essential controls or for making a better educational environment. There is an emerging suspicion that many rules are made for the convenience of the educators (Goodman, 1968).
4. Trend four is away from the traditional view that modern youth "never had it so good" with so few demands and rules, to the emerg-

ing view that laws and processes purportedly protecting youth actually discriminate against them (Friedenberg, 1959).

5. Trend five is away from the view that we have adequate processes available to bring about changes in laws and rules in time to meet social pressures in a rapidly changing world. An emerging view is that riots or other less violent forms of confrontation are more effective in bringing about needed changes and that traditional methods are inadequate.

Perhaps it is the very college experience itself that these youth are having that has caused them to look for new definitions to replace old imperatives. Certainly, there is nothing wrong with youth expressing their concerns about contemporary issues and problems—and many things within our society *are* "bugging" our youth.

The focus of attention is on drugs, sex, the war, politics, hypocrisy, civil rights, police brutality, and the generation gap (Fort, 1968). Not much has been said about education, occupations, marriage, or other basic issues which endure far beyond a drug stage or a war stage.

Yet, in a recent survey, 94% of the college students said their college experience had the greatest effect on their life and values. Other events, i.e., the death of John F. Kennedy, Vietnam, and civil rights, have had significant effects, but not to the extent that college itself does (*Generations Apart,* 1969). [In] two research studies conducted by Thornburg (1969, 1971) in which youth were asked to express problems, issues, and concerns confronting them, education was the most frequently mentioned. The CBS Report found that college youth identified more with other students (88%) and other people of their own generation (83%) (*Generations Apart,* 1969). Therefore, it is hypothesized that (1) education is the most crucial factor in the college student's life and (2) the establishment of peer groups or subcultures at the college level is an essential part of college experience.

Gottlieb and Hodgkins (1963) have attempted to define the college student subculture by categorizing students into four areas: (1) the academic subgroup composed of students who want a good education and are willing to study in order to obtain it, (2) a vocational subgroup composed of those students pursuing primarily the same vocational choice, (3) a nonconformist subculture which concentrates on life and the issues of life, using the university setting as an avenue for their expression, and (4) the "collegiate," or the social group on campus, who are interested in social activities, athletic, sorority and fraternity functions, and the like.

A research article written by Lionel Lewis (1969) has looked at the value of college to these four different subcultures. Students falling within these subcultures were asked various questions about (1) intellectualism, (2) intellectual association, (3) autonomy, and (4) idealism. Students belonging to the academic subculture show strong interest in education, knowledge and understanding. Most of their leisure time was spent in intellectual or musical activities. In contrast, those belonging to the collegiate subculture spent most of their time in extracurricular and social activities. They also preferred courses where there was competition with other students for a final grade. Students in the vocational subculture were more practical-oriented. Their primary reason for being in college was to obtain a degree. Extracurricular and social activities meant very little to them. On idealism they had the lowest humanitarianism score of any of the four subcultures. (It may very well be that this particular subculture closely parallels the values of non-college youth.) Lewis found the non-conformist subculture to be interested in intellectual association and they also stated that an important reason for being in college was to develop the resources necessary to become an autonomous person.

Lewis has been able to advance the hypothesis proposed by Trow and Clark (1960) and Gottlieb and Hodgkins (1963) through analyzing basic values of various student groups. Within these subcultures there are a common set of ideals and behaviors. One group, the collegiates, primarily identify with their school. Characteristic of this group is a "social activities and minimal studying" philosophy. This group represents more accurately the social life and activity of the college campus. Within this group are strong peer attachments. Research by E. Jackson Baur focuses on such student peer groups and their academic development.

Baur's findings (1967) were categorized around (1) campus life, (2) relations with faculty, (3) studying, (4) the classroom, (5) student subcultures, and (6) honor students.

Baur found socialization to be the primary objective of both dormitory and Greek groups. Most activities were within their living groups, with Greeks emerging as the majority (87%) of campus-wide student leaders. While academic pursuits were not the main activity, interestingly, in most cases, in-group status was given to the persons with the highest grade-point average. Baur's analysis of social and academic life gives the reader a concise picture of campus life and its relation to peer affiliation and academic pursuits.

In conclusion, it must be remembered that while ideally, adolescence is the time in which the young make decisions about themselves, it is often difficult to do so in a changing society. Therefore, many of the attachments made are with other adolescents who also seek answers amidst change, violence and affluency. In the process of identity-searching some seek out adults; others seek only their own. Some adults will seek out youth; some will be rejected for doing so. But, whether it is high school youth, non-college youth, or college youth, each will seek out that which accommodates their need system. Some will conform; some will alienate themselves; some will find their place in society; and some will continue to allude to the generation gap.

REFERENCES

BANDURA, A. The Stormy Decade: Fact or Fiction? *Psychology in the Schools*, 1964, *1*, 224–231.

BAUR, E. J. Student Peer Groups and Academic Development. *College Student Survey*, 1967, *1*, 22–31.

BEALER, R. C., WILLITS, F. C., AND MAIDA, P. R. The Rebellious Youth Subculture—a Myth. *Children*, 1964, *11*, 43–48.

BRAHAM, M. Peer Group Deterrents to Intellectual Development During Adolescence. *Educational Theory*, 1963, *15*, 248–258.

BRITTAIN, C. V. Adolescent Choices and Parent–Peer Cross Pressures. *American Sociological Review*, 1963, *28*, 385–391.

CARRY, R. W. Youth Breaks the Rules. *Research Resumé No. 38.* Burlingame, Calif.: Proceedings of the 20th Annual State Conference on Educational Research, 1968, 124–125.

CAWELTI, G. Youth Assess the American High School. *PTA Magazine*, 1968, 62, 16–19.

COLEMAN, J. S. *Adolescents and the Schools.* New York: Basic Books, 1965.

COLEMAN, J. S. *The Adolescent Society.* New York: Free Press, 1961.

DOUVAN, ELIZABETH, AND ADELSON, J. *The Adolescent Experience.* New York: John Wiley, 1966.

DUNPHY, D. C. The Social Structure of Urban Adolescent Peer Groups. *Sociometry*, 1963, *26*, 230–246.

ELKIN, F., AND WESTLEY, W. A. The Myth of Adolescent Culture. *American Sociological Review*, 1955, *20*, 680–684.

FORT, J. Youth: How to Produce Drop-ins Rather Than Drop-outs. *Research Resumé No. 38.* Burlingame, Calif.: Proceedings of the 20th Annual State Conference on Education Research, 1968, 53–64.

FRIEDENBERG, E. Z. *The Vanishing Adolescent.* Boston: Beacon, 1959.

FRIESEN, D. Academic–Athletic–Popularity Syndrome in the Canadian High School Society. *Adolescence*, 1968, *3*(9), 39–52.

GARRISON, K. C. *Psychology of Adolescence.* New York: Prentice-Hall, 1966.

Generations Apart. New York: Columbia Broadcasting System, 1969.

GOODMAN, P. Freedom and Learning: The Need for Choice. *Saturday Review*, 1968, *51*(20), 73–75.

GOTTLIEB, D., AND HODGKINS, B. College Student Subcultures: Their Structures and Characteristics in Relation to Student Attitude Change. *School Review*, 1963, *71*, 289.

HAVIGHURST, R. L. *Developmental Tasks and Education.* New York: Longmans, Green and Company, 1952.

LEWIS, L. S. The Value of College to Different Subcultures. *School Review*, 1969, *77*, 32–40.

MEISSNER, W. W. Parental Interaction of the Adolescent Boy. *Journal of Genetic Psychology*, 1965, *107*, 225–233.

MUSGROVE, F. The Social Needs and Satisfactions of Some Young People: Part I—at Home, in Youth Clubs and at Work. *British Journal of Educational Psychology*, 1966 (Part I), *36*, 61–71.

SHERIF, CAROLYN, AND SHERIF, M. Seeking Thrills with the "In" Crowd. *PTA Magazine,* 1965, *60,* 5–6.

SMITH, L. M., AND KLEINE, P. F. The Adolescent and His Society. *Review of Educational Research,* 1966, *36,* 424–436.

STROM, R. D. Comparison of Adolescent and Adult Behavioral Norm Properties. *Journal of Educational Psychology,* 1963, *54,* 322–330.

THORNBURG, H. D. Environmental Concerns: An Assessment by Youth. In H. D. Thornburg (Ed.) *Contemporary Adolescence: Readings.* Belmont, Calif.: Brooks/Cole Publishing, 1971.

THORNBURG, H. D. Adolescence: A Reinterpretation. *Adolescence,* 1970, *5*(19).

THORNBURG, H. D. Student Assessment of Contemporary Issues. *College Student Survey,* 1969, *3*(1), 1–5, 22.

TROW, M., AND CLARK, B. R. Varieties and Determinants of Undergraduate Subcultures. Paper read at the annual meeting of the American Sociological Society, New York, 1960.

Adolescence: The Current Imbroglio

EUGENE L. GAIER

A readable and insightful article concerned with four topics: the adolescent as the new mutant; the Negro–white youth; the privileged youth; and the youth in the rural context.

Because the adolescent presently occupies a particularly intense place in American thought and feeling, he is projected as an individual who combines simultaneously the ambiguity of a charade with the unpredictability of the message in a Chinese fortune cookie. To the lay public, the adolescent is viewed as a Philistine living a life reminiscent of the luxury and smugness enjoyed by Marie Antoinette at Le Petit Trianon. He is undisciplined, given to childish outbursts, and an irresponsible person who has abandoned himself with complete license. He is the new leisure class; and he is the "beautiful people."

For his parents, the all-American normal adolescent of the '50s—what the magazine *Time* called the "Now" generation—can become whatever he wants to become. They reason, after all, that they have given him everything—many advantages—and surrounded him with the good life; should it be too much now to ask him to become the standard-bearer of his family? He need only gain admission to a prestigious university; that is all they ask. He is told not to be concerned with happiness; rather, they only want him to do well in school. Here, the parents reason again, "We are doing our best for him; we are sincere. Can't he just do well in school?" And as the parents repeat this leitmotif in loud tones, and increasing decibels, the adolescent believes he is even less understood.

In school, the middle class adolescent is viewed as a receptacle for enrichment; he is the repository for the latest educational techniques—proven or otherwise. He serves as a source of entertainment for the community; he is also expected to provide good copy for the sports pages of the local newspaper. If he does not meet these expectations, he may be sent to the school psychologist who is expected quickly to determine what is wrong. And the school is the place where these students spend three or four years on their way to the college of their choice. In fact, soon the conferring of the B.A. or perhaps even the Ph.D. may be constitutionally mandated and guaranteed in the Bill of Rights. And the lower class adolescent—too often viewed as the devil's own representative in the educational system and born of sin and evil—is perceived as being in school for the sole purpose of making the teachers' lives the living version of Dante's purgatory.

Through all this, the adolescent sees himself as unloved, rejected, and misunderstood—one

From E. L. Gaier, Adolescence: The current imbroglio. Reprinted from *Adolescence,* 1969, *4*(13), 89–110, by permission of the author and Libra Publications, Inc.

whose privacy is invaded at home, whose sense of dignity is violated at school, and whose behavior is assaulted by anyone over 25—at least if one can believe the writers of the academic Holy Trinity speaking for the American adolescent—Edgar Friedenberg, Paul Goodman, and David Riesman. The high school set feels exploited—especially where they may be made pawns in the solution of both political and social problems. The student feels compelled to exhaust himself in pursuit of status for his parents and his school. It he fails to engage in this type of activity, he may find himself in a setting that makes it untenable for him to remain in school. As a consequence, the *school dropout* becomes the *school pushout*.

In the following presentation, I would like to examine the process of the occupation of the adolescent as well as the preoccupation of both the youth subculture and the school. Specially, four topics will be discussed: a) the adolescent as the new mutant; b) the Negro–white youth; c) the privileged youth; and, d) the youth in the rural context.

A. Adolescents: The New Mutants

If one can look upon current literary output so heavily depicting the feelings and thoughts of the adolescent as some portent of the future, we might also employ these activities as the index for extrapolating the future. According to Fiedler (1967), the adolescent is the new mutant since he has become the nonparticipant of the past; he posits that they have become dropouts from history. The withdrawal from school, so typical of vast numbers of the adolescent generation and so puzzling to our own, is best understood as a symptom of their rejection of the notion of cultural continuity and progress, which the school system represents in institutional form. It is not simply a matter of the young rejecting what happened before them, as young people are often wont to do. What is relevant here is their attempt to disallow the very idea of the past, of their seeking to avoid recapitulating it step by step up to the point of graduation into the present. Fiedler points out that the new mutant—with a

logic of his own—denies all the apostles of reason, Freud as well as Socrates. He graphically states it this way:

Not only do they reject the Socratic adage that the unexamined life is not worth living, since for them precisely the unexamined life is the only one worth enduring at all. But they also adjure the Freudian one: "where id was, there shall ego be," since for them the true rallying cry is, "Let id prevail over ego, impulse over order," or in negative terms—"Freud is a fink!"

Perhaps an example cited by Fiedler may highlight one of the salient sources of friction between the adolescent and the adult. It is a platitude of the day that the generation gap is both source and reinforcer of this rankling situation. And it is also obvious that as long as parents continue to be older than their children, there will always be a generation gap. It also appears to be an arrangement that most parents and children find especially convenient—at least, of course, until the children take their place along the shelf of antique bodies.

Fiedler cites the incident of a community in southern California which was eager to close a particularly notorious cafe. When questioned by the town council about objections to the cafe's existence, one woman reported that each day as she walked past this eating house and looked in, she saw people she found particularly repellent "just standing there, looking nonchalant." And, in a way, her own improbable adjective describes a crime against much of the middle class world—the idea of "nonchaleur" or cool (as the futurists themselves would prefer to call it). In the vernacular of the '60s, the frequenters of this cafe were turning adults *on*, by turning them off! This is the essence of the life style of the adolescent as well as of the literary style to which the adolescent seems to respond. Or in Fiedler's words, this is "the offensive style of those who are not so much for anything in particular as 'with it' in general."

This is as far from the traditional concept of alienation, with its intense desire to end its connection, as it is from ordinary forms of allegiance. The new adolescent celebrates disconnection.

The beatnik was alienated from society and mad about it; the new youth—the mutant—is alienated and merely sad about it. Hence, one can take his choice of folk heroes. He accepts it as a necessary consequence of the industrial system which delivered him from work and duty, and of the welfare state which makes disengagement the last possible virtue. For the adolescent, there is also a more personal transformation: A radical metamorphosis of the western male—which was utterly unforseen in the decades before us, but is certainly now rampant.

In fact, whole school boards have disintegrated and collided with communities over the length of hair, tightness of trousers, shortness of skirts—as though adult groups have decided to focus on those things[1] on which they should disagree as perhaps an institutionalized way in which to preclude focus on things which are really of greater importance: relating to the students, helping them search for some kind of identification, preparing for some kind of adult-like behavior. All about, young males are beginning to retrieve for themselves the cavalier role once piously and class-consciously surrendered to women: *that of being beautiful and being loved.*

Whatever the mystique of the adolescent, adolescence is the period that Anna Freud (1936) labeled as the time when "a strong id confronts a relatively weak ego." Here, the adolescent must differentiate the self from the non-self, a first step in the process of identification—a stage through which the young person must pass to develop a sense of self-consciousness. And he does this through reality-testing his world, through his defensive behaviors, and through his search for a sense of identification. After all, the adolescent is early acquainted with the despair that comes from having to choose between the bad and the stupid, the detestable and the indifferent, and in his despair has nothing to say either to his parents or his teachers. That is, by so doing, the adolescent tends to avoid conflict. Conflict—where it is present—is largely unconscious conflict—undersurface resentments which do not necessarily

liberate or enlarge the personality, but which merely intensify docility towards the parents and school.

What is important here is this: even where the conflict has an "as-if" quality, it centers on trivia (or perhaps it seems that way only to the adult). They agree to disagree only on token issues—greatest of which are appearance, clothes—and in so doing are able to sidestep any genuine encounter of differences. And paradoxically, the adolescent through these as-if conflicts is not really deeply involved in ideological differences nor prepared to do much individual thinking involving issues of any generality. The beads-and-sandals syndrome may actually serve as a camouflage for involvement with genuine issues.

In a perceptive analysis of current youth cultures, the following view of this philosophy was presented (*The New York Times,* September 24, 1967):

> Having been children in an adult-centered world, they are now adults in a child-centered world. And how do they react to finding themselves in this historic riptide of values? By feeling guilty.
>
> How can parents live through the period when their hippie or demi-hippie is testing every parental value; when he is busily devaluing the sacrifices they have made; when, in an odd reverse of the historic wheel, his brooding presence is reminiscent of nothing so much as that of a Victorian chaperon as he counts each parental drink, each cigarette, each tranquilizer, each white lie, each hour "wasted" in front of television or in talks about non-ultimate matters, each mile above the speed limit. If the parents break the law by way of a car, the hippies argue they can break it by way of drugs.

The adolescent—despite his great potential—often ends up with less self-knowledge than his less hip contemporary or other parent. Trying directly to "find oneself" seems paradoxically less effective than first becoming the kind of person upon whom others can rely and then learning existentially from his revealing experience.

One clear difference between the current adolescent and his parents' youth (and they once were young!) is that the parents handled their

[1]Perhaps if school board members could grow long hair or buy tight pants in larger sizes, more empathy might be shown to the student body.

less colorful rebellion discreetly and in fear—if not of God, at least of their parents. The current adolescent—through his ambivalent behavior, pregnancies out of wedlock, drugs, etc.—or his unambivalent appearance—trumpets his rebellion and thus challenges his parents, if not God, to smite him down. In the words of one English wag, the only pre-marital experience current adolescents deny themselves is cooking.

B. Negro-White Contrasts

That the cultural and social determinants of the Negro adolescent in the social context differ widely has led a number of investigators to conclude that—at least until the recent riots provided contrary evidence—the Negro adolescent had acquired a compliant personality in his dealing with Whites, (Davis, 1941; Dollard, 1948; Davis, Gardner, and Gardner, 1941). In 1943, Powdermaker suggested that the special cultural conditions surrounding the Negro had forced him to channel his adaptive behavior in a fashion similar to that of a masochist, providing him with a way of appeasing his guilt feelings over his aggressive impulses, as well as a *modus vivendi* for adapting to the difficult cultural situation imposed on him.

Subsequently, the present author and his coworkers (Gaier and Wambach, 1960; Gaier and Littunen, 1961; and Gaier and White, 1965), employing a questionnaire patterned after Riesman (1950, 1952) initiated a series of investigations to assess the differences in modes of conformity of Southern White and Negro college students as reflected in their self-evaluation of personality assets and liabilities. At that time they were concerned with examining the behavioral and personality facets considered most positive and negative by two racially different groups of college students which might reflect social determinants of conformity. Assessment of the direction of differences in self-evaluation of personality assets and liabilities of Southern White and Southern Negro students with its accompanying conformity were made. On the basis of the data analysis the following conclusions were warranted: a) White males showed significantly fewer socially-oriented responses than White females and Negro males and females in the assets they believed they had; b) Socially-oriented responses were listed significantly more often than character- or achievement-oriented responses for all groups, though significantly less frequently for White college students; c) Southern Negro college students resembled their own female group more than White college men resembled their female group in terms of assets they believed they had; d) and Negro college men showed significantly fewer "achievement" responses than their White counterparts, with general profile similarity for both White and Negro women. More surprising in that sample of students was the failure to obtain significant sex role differences between the Negro and White groups as a whole. These differences undoubtedly exist, but the form of the questionnaire and/or similarity in educational background may have eclipsed or blurred any differentiation. Nevertheless, the findings were in line with Myrdal's (1944) observations that the

important thing is that the Negro Lower Class, especially in the South, has built up a type of family organization conducive to social health, even though these practices are outside the American tradition. *When these practices are brought into closer contact with White norms, as occurs when Negroes go to cities, they tend to break down partially and to cause the demoralization of some people.*

In her doctoral [dissertation] investigating selected psychocultural phenomena and vocational behavior of a defined subgroup of college students, Gilbert (1962) was concerned with the investigation of the significance of the sex of the parent having longer period of academic training on vocational behavior variables as evidenced by a selected group of Negro college students. The vocational behavior variables she studied were college persistence, college continuity, stated and inventoried vocational interest, grade-point average and final college graduation. Her study focused on the investigation of the dimension of the educational level attained by Negro mothers contrasted with the educational level of Negro fathers to ascertain which of these variables was more indicative of culturally-patterned preferences operating in the vocational socialization of Negro youth.

She posited that there would be significant differences in several aspects of vocational behavior evidenced by children from families where mothers had more or longer educational experiences than fathers; college persistence, college continuity, stated interests, inventoried interests, and academic potential and academic success. Her analysis revealed the following results:

1. Significant differences in college persistence were found between subjects in the MOTHER and FATHER groups as more of the matriculating students met the criterion for assignment to the MOTHER group.
2. MOTHER and FATHER subjects did not differ significantly in mean rates of college continuity.
3. Significant differences between academic potential were not evidenced for the two groups.
4. Contrary to expectation, there were differences in one of the indices of academic success, college graduation, which favored subjects in the FATHER rather than the MOTHER group. However, significant differences were not found for mean grade-point averages.

While definite conclusions might not be warranted, several tentative suggestions may be made in view of the observed data trends:

1. Vocational behaviors of subjects in the MOTHER and FATHER groups appear to reflect patterns central to (a) the psychocultural phenomenon, (b) sex role identification, and (c) parents' educational level.
2. A higher proportion of MOTHER group subjects made up more of the sample, stated commitments to a major field of study at time of entry to college, revealed less constriction in their patterns of major field preferences and evidenced a more homogeneous aptitude and achievement pattern on standardized tests.
3. Sex role identification seems to be reflected in assessment of academic potential and academic success where males in the FATHER group had higher mean achievement and aptitude scores. Similarly, aptitude and achievement performance was higher for females whose mothers had higher college status. College persistence was marked by more fe-

males in the MOTHER group but more males than females in the FATHER group.

The systematic limitation of opportunity has coerced talented Negroes to play angles and to search out devious ways to outwit this system which blocks their achievement. Exclusion from full participation has forced Negroes to distrust and to be distrusted, and to disregard some laws in order to survive.

Negro poverty is unique in every way. It grows out of a long American history, and it expresses itself in a subculture that it built upon an interlocking base of economic and racial injustice. It is a fact imposed from without, from white America (Harrington, 1962, p. 65).

Inferior education produces inferior educational development but the subsequent lack of performance on achievement tests does not necessarily indicate an inferior student or inferior ability as the defined expectation would have us believe. The inferior performance results from a constellation of forces.

The amorality of the larger society makes the amorality of the ghetto possible.

The ghetto is, in a manner, self-perpetuating, and while it encourages some for attempting to change, it rewards others for loyalty to things as they are. Inside the ghetto lie sources of energy that are ordinarily mobilized, overtly or covertly, to prevent change and to perpetuate and exploit the *status quo*. Outside the ghetto, too, are sources of energy that depend on the ghetto for their own security—all exploitation rests upon real or imagined advantages to exploiters. Therefore, any social action to transform the ghetto must expect to face apathy and hostility from both Negroes and Whites—for a ghetto can be a cocoon as well as a cage (Clark, 1965).

C. The Privileged Adolescent and/or The Privileged Class

Johnston and Rosenberg (1968) defined the privileged adolescent on the basis of parental education and status. As Keniston (1965) has remarked, the price of admission and permission to stay in the youth culture is readily rising academic performance. It not only requires individuals to be successful in the academic sphere, but also to be content with the status which denies them full economic and personal autonomy. Obviously, middle and upper class adolescents are at an advantage here—they do better in school and are more likely to have internalized values consistent with delayed childhood. It comes as no new insight that middle class parents place high premium on deferred gratification and generally agree that a principal cultural difference betwen social class is in regard to time orientation. The middle class parent continues to stress the postponement of gratification, the need to achieve high competence in academic skills, and produce high anxiety for status. These somehow point up the great concern for personal control as well as rational planning and the capacity to postpone short-run, small rewards for later, larger gains, all views that are highly congruent with the demands of extended adolescence and are nothing more than the contemporary behavioral manifestation of Freud's reality principle. Most relevant is that Johnston and Rosenberg point up that the theory that adolescents are widely rejecting the standards, guidance, and authority of their elders has yet to be supported for the middle class adolescents. After all, the privileged adolescent is still made up of a youth highly committed to traditional middle class definitions of success, one highly oriented to the rewards of the future, rather than to a cult of the present, and one which endorses rather than rejects the values of the parental generation. Johnston and Rosenberg (1968) thus conclude that middle class America is still "reporting itself very well."

D. The Adolescent: Rural-Urban Differences

In an attempt to examine the cultural determinants towards educational and occupational goals of two groups of adolescents—one in an urban setting and the other in a rural setting—graduating seniors in a large urban community and a small rural community were studied. In this study, Gaier and White (1965) were interested in testing the direction of the anomic–automatic axis that the senior high school students may move in. For example, does the person who has been strongly conformed by an inner-directed culture show a significant direction towards education? In examining the adolescent in the rural–urban axis, are there differences which transcend the cultural context, or does each cultural setting set up dimensions which will cast unique personality directions for the various members of the group?

The analysis of the data indicated that in line with Riesman's assessment of the orientation of subjects according to an inner-directed and other-directed personality hypothesis, the rural subjects appear to follow more frequently the old-fashioned virtues, principles, and philosophy of their parents. By contrast, urban youths apparently were more directed by group trends. This is not to suggest that rural youths were inner-directed isolates. While the individual may appear to be influenced by varying aspects of tradition, inner-directed and other-directed culture, Reisman's theory holds that one dominant socializing agent provides a given personality. Thus, while there is much overlapping among the categories, each individual lives in tune with the operative function of his culture. The rural sample emerged as more inner-directed, but the subsequent choosing of occupations and careers was in accord with the occupations and careers of their parents. In a sense, they rejected an interest in continuing formal education; in the same manner, their fathers and mothers have not fulfilled themselves in this way. Urban youth, on the contrary, perceived themselves as sensitive to group thinking and behavior. Since they were living in an environment in which their peers deemed continuing education as an important means of mobility, these youths were more concerned with college education. And it does seem apparent that those peer groups and parents influenced urban high school seniors to advance up the educational ladder as a basis for growth towards personal self-actualization as well as mobility.

Analysis of the personality assets obtained in studying these students were grouped into three major areas: Group Behavior, Character Traits, and Achievement. Rural boys, in comparison with urban boys, appeared to attach greater importance to character traits as assets of their fathers.

They indicated greater concern with attributes of their fathers. Both groups perceived equally the intellectual achievement of their fathers to the same small extent.

One of the most striking finds was rural girls placed absolutely no value on either their own intellectual assets or those of their fathers and mothers. Rural girls placed no onus on any intellectual inadequacy of their fathers and mothers and only a total value of 14 per cent in the fear of their own inadequacy. Since intelligence is received neither favorably nor unfavorably, one wonders if rural girls plan post–high school education for marriage reasons, for elevating social status, or merely for a means of avoiding the rural boys (only two per cent of the rural boys questioned noted any plans to attend college).

A much higher degree of identification existed between urban youths and their peer groups than for either of the groups in the rural population. This pattern is similarly extended to the perception of both their fathers and mothers. Thus, it would appear that greatest importance in the socialization process of the rural group is strongly reflected in the direction of Character Traits and Achievement. And the same percentages favor what this group of rural students liked best about their fathers and mothers.

Urban adolescents would be more sensitive to group control. They would more easily change their opinions and the opinions of their parents in order to be found more acceptable by the "significant others" in their peer groups and social cliques. The perception and success of future goals should reflect what the group considers important rather than a mere identification with the parental dictum. One of the most striking contrasts was in the high percentage of perceived value placed in physical achievement. Approval for the perception of parental physical assets was considerably higher for rural boys and girls. The rural sample appeared highly influenced by physical prowess and physical attractiveness to such a degree that the rural females were completely unconcerned with any kind of intellectual assets either for themselves or their mothers.

Of course, what the high influence of physical prowess and attractiveness may actually reflect is the great emphasis placed by adolescents in our culture on physical beauty. Perhaps the rural

sample studied placed greater emphasis on physical beauty than did urban females because the ideal of "the all American normal" in terms of beauty presented on the screen and TV advertisements is that beauty per se will insure both personal happiness and success in marriage. Little premium was placed on academic success, college degrees, or long-range career plans. This has been well-documented in studies spanning a generation of adolescent desires and aspirations. Although the urban seniors also listed physical attributes as worthwhile indicators of their own assets, they did indicate that their own assets were also distributed among factors of intelligence, self-confidence, and peer group acceptance.

When the liabilities of the students were broken down into three major groups, Group Behavior, Character Traits, and Personality, it was found that urban females attributed 80 per cent of their mothers' liabilities to character traits and only eight per cent to intellectual inadequacy. Were these urban girls expressing a behavioral identification in society but not an emotional identification because they did not wish to identify with the "bad character" of their mothers?

It is especially noteworthy that neither urban nor rural students perceived lack of specific abilities and fears of group behavior as meaningful liabilities within their social cultures, whereas group behavior characteristics were significant assets "belonging" to their respective adolescent societies. Among the personality liabilities "selfishness and conceit—arrogance" were of primary concern for the students in both schools, but to a marked degree for urban girls.

Rural boys were not as concerned about their own physical limitations and liabilities as were urban youth. But they were considerably more sensitive to physical defects of both parents than urban boys and girls. The highly prestigious value of physical assets, which rural youth demand for recognition in adolescent society, diminished within the scale of comparable liabilities. Even though the urban boys and girls appeared more concerned than rural youth about their own lack of achievement, nevertheless rural youth perceived a deficiency of personal achievement among their parents as more unfavorable than their urban counterparts.

Examination of the plans for adolescents in a

rural–urban society following the completion of high school is especially relevant here. When the plans of the seniors were compared, it was found not unexpectedly, of course, that urban adolescents are considerably more concerned about formal schooling than rural seniors. A greater percentage of rural girls desired business school courses than urban girls. Half of the rural sample of males would seek farming, military service, personal jobs, or unskilled employment; but only one-fifth of the urban sample stated these as work choices. The plans of the urban youth were more specific.

E. The Adolescent Imbroglio

Gertrude Stein, who many people have begun in a quiet way at least to believe is the mother of us all, somehow strikes the most telling blow for the adolescent conflict and paradoxes we have been discussing. In her recent play in New York, "In Circles," a girl says, "I have been deceived," upon which a brusque chorus replies: "No, you have been refused." Perhaps the refusal has come from the fact that the adolescent feels that the things that may be most important for him at a given time have somehow been pushed aside to give him more immediate things—or things that the parents feel he needs.

Pearson (1958) seems to imply that conflict is inevitable between adolescents and adults because of their psychic makeup. As he approaches puberty, the child again faces the Oedipal conflict with its frightening unconscious fantasies. This time, however, he cannot rely on repression and the abating of this instinctual drive to resolve the issue. Consequently, he may rebel, withdraw, or even consider his parents inferior. The adult also experiences psychic difficulties. The sight of his adolescent offspring may point out to him that physically and sexually he is past his peak, that many of life's goals are beyond his reach, and that in the near future, his child may be leaving home. Because his physique may not compare too favorably with his body ideal or the physiques of his peers, the adolescent may suffer a loss of self-esteem and self-love. This may also occur because of irregular growth which may cause the child to be awkward at times.

The problems created by the growth spurt are minor compared to those that arise because of the resurgence of the instinctual drives. According to Pearson, the ego and superego are unable to cope with the id at the onset of puberty; consequently, the human organism must take a few steps backward before it can stride forward. He attributes many of the adolescent's eccentricities—his preoccupation with food, his dieting, his love for horseplay—to regression to the oral and anal stages. This fits in nicely with Freudian theory.

Besides adapting to his growing body and the increase in his sexual drive, the adolescent must come to grips with the attitudes and mores of his culture. Pearson points out that society makes demands on the adolescent—he must be independent, responsible, chaste, etc.—and then turns around and passes laws and sets up customs that make these demands almost impossible to meet.

How does the ego strengthen itself to cope with the problems that arise in adolescence? Basically, the ego relies on the same methods it has used in the past—introjection and identification. Pearson is very persuasive when he tells how the ego strengthens itself by incorporating heroic ideals and group ideals.

In latency and in adolescence, the child eases many of his anxieties by having crushes on and identifying with adults. The child may incorporate the values and habits of a living, historical, or fictional person. Obviously, as Pearson points out, an identification can either help or hinder ego development. An identification with a person whose values no longer lead to success in our society—the traditional rugged individualist for example—can lead to disillusionment, cynicism, and maladjustment. Pearson seems to imply that live heroes are more likely to possess traits that will facilitate adjustment. He argues that the ego will unconsciously incorporate those characteristics that will aid in adjustment and reject those that are incompatible with the superego.

Group ideals are another important source of strength of the adolescent ego. The Oedipal conflict comes to the fore again just as the ego is having difficulty handling the rising instinctual drives. As a defense against the Oedipal conflict, the adolescent becomes more and more aloof from his parents; to strengthen his ego, he takes refuge in the group. Their values become his values. Because the group offers security and strength, teenagers tend to look alike, act alike and dress alike.

In the postpuberty stage, the teen-ager begins to seek his identity. Who am I? What are my interests, my capabilities, my limitations, and my needs? Identity, if it is ever attained, is found by the incorporation and the synthesizing of ego ideals.

If it is to reach maturity, the ego must strengthen itself by introjection and ego ideals, and must develop to the genital level of object relationships. Pearson traces this development from infancy to adulthood. The individual focuses on his mother in infancy; then on adults outside the family; on a best friend of the same sex in latency; and finally on members of the opposite sex. The teen-ager must give up his old cathexes and learn new ones. The development proceeds along these lines.

The defense mechanisms used by a teen-ager are an indication of his level of development. The best-friend stage is a defense against penis envy or castration fears. Negativism towards the parents, on the other hand, is a sign that the Oedipal conflict still has not been resolved satisfactorily. The defenses in the narcissistic stage center around the ego's attempts to maintain contact with reality. The keeping of a diary may be one way of doing this. Diaries, of course, also give a person an opportunity to indulge in role-playing. When the ego has left the narcissistic stage and is trying to protect itself against regression, it relies on fantasy and infatuation.

Many of the mechanisms used by American adolescents do reduce anxiety but do so at a high cost. Whereas European adolescents depend on asceticism or intellectualism, Americans seek relief in uniforms, i.e., the attitudes and the mores of the group determine how he will handle his instincts. The result is, according to Blos (1962), American youths rush into heterosexuality and pay for it by being emotionally shallow and by not learning their identity. Blos points out, however, that the youth who massively represses his instincts also pays a heavy price.

Though late adolescence is a period of relative calm, there are problems that have to be solved. The infantile conflicts and the sex drive are still around. Besides continuing to contend with these, he must now choose a vocation, and learn both social role and identity. The specific answers arrived at will be influenced by selected ego ideals and the culture.

After all, in childhood the body must be mastered; in latency, the environment; and in adolescence, the emotions. The developmental tasks of adolescence still include that resolving of bisexuality in early adolescence, the breaking away from early object ties during adolescence, and the finding of a life task, a social role, and an identity in late adolescence.

With her customary and expected insight, Marianne Moore may well offer the last word in dealing with any sub-culture—especially that of the young—as well as their tasks. In her poem, *To a Giraffe*, in which she spurs the reader to leave the periphery towards which we often stray because of our own tensions and hangups, she depicts the plight of the non-accepted world— and this is the world we have been discussing here —as follows:

When plagued by the psychological
a creature can be unbearable
that could have been irresistible;
or to be exact exceptional
since less conversational
than some emotionally-tied-in-knots animal.

After all
consolations of the metaphysical
can be profound. In Homer, existence
is flawed; transcendence, conditional;
the journey from sin to redemption, perpetual.

REFERENCES

BLOS, PETER   *On Adolescence*. Glencoe, Ill.: The Free Press, 1962.

CLARK, K. B.   *Dark Ghetto*. New York: Harper and Row, 1965.

DAVIS, ALLISON   American status systems and the socialization of the child. *American Soc. Rev.*, 1941, *6*, 345–54.

DAVIS, ALLISON, AND DOLLARD, JOHN   *Children of*

Bondage; The Personality Development of Negro Youth in the Urban South. Washington: American Council of Education, 1948.

DAVIS, ALLISON, GARDNER, B. B., AND GARDNER, M. R. *Deep South; A Social–Anthropological Study of Caste and Class.* Chicago: University of Chicago Press, 1941.

FIEDLER, L. The new mutants. *Partisan Review,* 1966.

GAIER, E. L., AND HELEN S. WAMBACH Self evaluation of personality assets and liabilities of Southern White and Negro students. *J. of Soc. Psychol.,* 1960, *51,* 135–143.

GAIER, E. L., AND LITTUNEN, Y. Modes of conformity in two subcultures: A Finnish-American comparison. *Acta Sociologica,* 1961, *5,* 65–75.

GAIER, E. L., AND WHITE, W. F. Modes of conformity and career selection of rural and urban high school seniors. *J. Soc. Psychol.,* 1965, *67,* 379–391.

GILBERT, JEAN *Psychocultural implications of vocational behavior of Negro college students.* Unpublished Ed.D. Dissertation, University of Buffalo, 1962.

HARRINGTON, MICHAEL *The Other America.* Baltimore, Maryland: Penguin Books, 1962.

JOHNSTON, J. W. C., AND ROSENBERG, L. In Adams, J. F. (Ed.) *Understanding Adolescence.* Boston: Allyn & Bacon, 1968, 318–336.

KENISTON, K. *The Uncommitted: Alienated Youth in American Society.* New York: Harcourt, Brace, 1965.

LITTUNEN, Y., AND GAIER, E. L. Occupational values and modes of conformity. Turku, Finland. *J. Soc. Psychol.,* 1960, *51,* 123–133.

MOORE, MARIANNE *The Complete Poems of Marianne Moore.* New York: Macmillan, 1967, 215.

MYRDAL, GUNNAR *An American Dilemma: The Negro Problem.* New York: Harper, 1944.

PEARSON, G. H. G. *Adolescence and the Conflict of Generations.* New York: Norton, 1958.

POWDERMAKER, HORTENSE The channeling of Negro aggression by the cultural process. *Amer. J. Soc.,* 1943, *48,* 750–58.

RIESMAN, DAVID *Faces in the Crowd.* New Haven: Yale Univ. Press, 1950.

RIESMAN, DAVID *The Lonely Crowd.* New Haven: Yale Univ. Press, 1952.

Chapter 19: Suggested Additional Readings

COLES, R.   Northern children under "desegregation." *Psychiatry,* February 1968, *31,* 1–15. The author, a research psychiatrist, studied Negro children living in the Boston area who were bussed to predominantly white schools. In general, they seemed to adjust very well, but in contrast with their counterparts in the South, evidenced more bitterness and anger toward white people. The white children displayed a wide range of emotions toward the Negroes, from scorn and rebuff to curiosity and friendliness.

DERBYSHIRE, R. L.   Adaptation of adolescent Mexican-Americans to United States society. *American Behavioral Scientists,* 1969, *13*(1), 88–103. Attitudes of Mexican-American adolescents are interpreted as reflecting their simultaneous membership in generally culturally-excluded minority worlds, especially within an urban setting.

EDINGTON, E. D.   Disadvantaged rural youth. *Review of Educational Research,* 1970, *40*(1), 69–85. This comprehensive survey of the research identifies the unique factors which cause rural youth to be disadvantaged.

ELDER, G. H.   Socialization and ascent in a racial minority. *Youth and Society,* 1970, *2*(1), 74–110. Elder discusses the black youth's problem of self-realization and socialization, including his individual aspirations, achievement training, parental attitudes, and family relationships. He also identifies and discusses the various sources of the youth's deprivation and frustration.

FRIEDENBURG, L. V.   Youth and politics in the Federal Republic of Germany. *Youth and Society,* 1969, *1*(1), 91–109. A review of the attitudes of West German youth toward politics suggests that attempts to establish a democratic society in that country are receiving increased encouragement from modern youth.

GURIN, P.   Motivation and aspirations of southern Negro college youth. *American Journal of Sociology,* 1970, *75*(4), 607–631. Findings among male students in ten predominantly black colleges indicated that these students' aspirations were positively related to achievement and failure-avoidance motives, but even more highly related to expectancies.

HOLZMAN, M., LURIA, Z., & SHERMAN, H.   Adolescent subculture: Endeavor, New England. *School Review,* 1968, *76*(2), 231–245. This study was designed to define the values and occupational goals of high school students in the Endeavor, New England, public schools, and to relate these values and goals to academic capabilities, performance, and home background.

KLINZING, J.   The invisible man and today's education. *Educational Forum,* 1971, *35*(4), 431–438. The author tells how society has frustrated the black man's realization of his potential and suggests what can be done to correct this situation.

MEREDITH, G. M.   Amae and acculturation among Japanese-American college students in Hawaii. *Journal of Social Psychology,* December 1966, *70,* 171–180. This study was designed to determine the differences between sansei (third-generation) Japanese-American college students and a comparable group of Caucasian-Americans on a set of basic personality dimensions.

NAGASAWA, R. H.   Social class differentials in success striving. *Pacific Sociological Review,* 1971, *14*(2), 215–223. The author reports the results of a study designed to determine differences, according to social classes, in youths' success as they moved through a simulated mobility system. He also considers the effect of cultural background on individuals' success striving and on final outcomes of their efforts.

SCHAB, F.   Adolescence in the South: A comparison of white and Negro attitudes about home, school, religion, and morality. *Adolescence,* 1968, *3*(9), 33–38. Responses from white and black high school students, almost all of whom attended racially segregated schools, were analyzed to determine similarities and differences in their attitudes about home, school, religion, and morality.

SOLLENBERGER, R. T.   Chinese-American child-rearing practices and juvenile delinquency. *The Journal of Social Psychology,* February 1968, *74*(Part I), 13–23. The investigator lived in New York's Chinatown for seven weeks and interviewed 69 Chinese mothers to determine those factors accounting for the low rate of delinquency among Chinese-American children. These appeared to include: abundant nurturance and protection in early childhood; a close-knit, mutually respecting family life; abundance of desirable adult models; and adult intolerance of child aggression.

20

Cross-Cultural Variants in Adolescents

The culture of a society—the combination of its habits, morals, customs, beliefs, and knowledge—leaves an indelible stamp upon those individuals who share it. Each culture is considered to have its distinguishing features, both for its society as a whole and for specific age groups within that society.

In all cultures, the way of life differs in varying degrees from one age-stage to another. Within a particular culture, the child, the adolescent, and the adult, in effect, live in different worlds, each with its separate identity. Persons at the same age-stage in different societies, however, may share many characteristics across cultural lines. Thus, teenagers living in the various cultures of the Western world resemble each other in many ways (Wylie, 1962). In general, they have more money and therefore greater independence from adults than do young people in the have-not countries. They have access to more material goods, not only necessities of life but luxuries such as cars or motor scooters, television, record players, and the like. Because their education is prolonged, school has a relatively large place in their lives.

However, youth in the Western cultures are also very different from each other in certain respects. For example, French children learn at an early age to respect the rules laid down by their society, while American youth are inclined to believe that they should test society's rules for themselves. Again, while in most Western societies youth have difficulty in achieving social and vocational maturity, in Australia, essentially a Western country, most youth have few problems in this area (Short, 1970). While a minority of Australian youth question all value systems, the majority simply accept their good fortune in being born into their particular society without entertaining grave doubts or questioning the society's goals. To date, however, there is insufficient research for us to assess what Australian society is doing for its youth or to form absolute judgments about their values and ideals.

Bernard (1962) has pointed out phenomena having special impact on adolescents in America. In general, he states, American adolescents are forced into a prolonged period of dependence upon adults—economically, socially, and intellectually. Education is prolonged; work opportunities are delayed; too early marriage is frowned upon. The rapid pace of societal change and technological advance has opened a wide gap between the generations, and communication between adults and youth grows more difficult. American adults, uncertain about their own morals and ethics, have communicated their confusion to youth; and adolescents are further confused by the conflict between ideals and reality which they perceive in the "real world." The adolescent male in America faces the uncertainty of obligatory military service: whether and when he will be called, and how long he must serve. In modern urbanized society, where the father may work at some distance from the home or may be absent entirely, many adolescents grow up largely under the control of women, deprived of adequate contact with adult male models. (However, a growing trend toward the employment of more male teachers in schools and the greater participation of fathers in family life, as their work week becomes shorter and their leisure time longer, may help to create a better balance of male and female authority figures for adolescents.)

Various writers suggest that American youth may actually benefit from the stresses placed upon them. In one study (Hsu, Watrous, & Lord, 1961), Chinese-American adolescents living in Hawaii were compared with Caucasian-American adolescents living in Chicago in terms of family culture patterns. The Chinese-American youth, reported this study, are inducted into the world of adults at an early age and simply conform to traditional institutions. By contrast, Caucasian-American youth are relatively insulated until adulthood and develop a more idealistic attitude toward life. When the Caucasian-American teenagers finally come face-to-face with an imperfect world, they experience a certain amount of trauma—which, by its very impact, stimulates them to try to improve matters.

The stresses which American culture places upon youth may have been overemphasized. While news media and researchers concentrate on adolescents with problems, creating the impression that well-adjusted teenagers are rare, in actual fact only about five percent of all adolescents act out their frustrations in a deviant manner.

When we look at affluent societies such as those of Australia and the United States, the question arises: Are our youth becoming too self-seeking and materialistic? Leichty (1963) reported that Vietnamese children feel a greater obligation to their families than do American children, and that the goals of American children are more selfish and materialistic than those of Vietnamese children. Perhaps as a consequence, American children's fears are more unrealistic than those of Vietnamese children. Walters and Stinnett (1971) raise the question whether in America we may have "stressed autonomy and independence in children as well as separatism from adults to the point that such emphasis has resulted in a tendency toward a self-centered orientation among children toward interpersonal relationships [p. 99]."

In contrast to America, certain other societies are dedicated to the social service ideal (Adler & Peres, 1970). For example, in a society such as Israel, whose very existence has been under constant threat throughout its brief history, it has been particularly important to instill in adolescents a sense of dedication to their society, especially in times of emergency. Such an orientation induces young people to come to the aid of their country and permits swift mobilization of the spiritual and mental resources of youth. Similarly, though for somewhat different reasons, the Soviets have organized young people for society's benefit and have demonstrated how the youth of a country may help to socialize the younger youth (Hahn, 1969). In Russia, the Komsomol, or Young Communists, help to organize the leisure time of younger people and to channel it toward social service, and away from possible antisocial behavior. The Russians are also attempting to solve the leisure time problem of youth by establishing cafés where young people may gather. These places become centers for political work as well as social areas where creative talents are encouraged.

In today's closely knit world, relationships between countries can be facilitated through an understanding of how young people become inducted into their various adult societies. Moreover, information about youth in the developing countries, though still sparse, helps us to appreciate the sort of world neighbors our own teenagers will have to deal with as adults. For example, youth in tropical African nations, like those in many other developing countries, tend to project conflicts of their own identity crisis onto the external world by way of ideological activities (Zolberg, 1969). Such youth tend to move to the extreme political left, though they vary among themselves in the position they assume. These youth movements have considerable autonomy in tropical Africa because the governments cannot afford the manpower (or police power) to keep them under control. As a result, the youth form a sort of political veto group, and sometimes are drawn into large-scale violence. However, only the better-educated youth, who constitute a minority, participate actively in these movements. About the political ideas of the less educated majority, we have little scientific information.

The question inevitably arises: What sort of culture is best for particular individuals, a highly advanced society or a more relaxed, primitive way of life? Civilization is often believed to place undue burdens on adolescents. By contrast, in primitive societies progress toward adult status is easy and uninterrupted; the child's life is patterned for him and troublesome choices need rarely be made. In Samoa, writes Margaret Mead (1935), growing up proceeds smoothly; the slow tempo of life, the close family ties, the single moral standard, and the relaxed attitude toward sexual expression, all constitute positive features in this primitive society. Since little privacy exists, facts of physical development are learned naturally. Life, including adolescence, says Mead, is easier in Samoa. However, primitive cultures do have their disadvantages. Civilization is static and individual potential remains unrealized. Besides, those features of primitive life which serve to reduce strain could hardly be superimposed onto advanced Western culture.

The first of the following reading selections, by S. N. Eisenstadt, defines youth as a universal phenomenon. The author identifies the basic elements of both primitive and traditional societies and finds they have much in common. In the last portion of his article, which is omitted here because of space considerations, Eisenstadt suggests that the framework of traditional societies is changing. For example, he perceives a "flattening of political–ideological motives and a growing apathy to them," and a growing meaninglessness of social relations, resulting from an age devoted to consumption and mass society.

The second selection, by Musgrove, relates youth as an age group to the larger English society. The author considers English youth from the historical perspective and compares them in certain respects to American and French youth.

REFERENCES

ADLER, C., & PERES, Y.   Youth movements and "salon societies." *Youth and Society,* 1970, *1*(3), 309–331.

BERNARD, H. W.   *Human development in Western culture.* Boston: Allyn and Bacon, 1962. Pp. 254–259.

HAHN, W.   The Komsomol Kollektiv as an agency of political socialization. *Youth and Society,* 1969, *1*(2), 219–239.

HSU, F. L. K., WATROUS, B. G., & LORD, E. M.   Culture pattern and adolescent behavior. *International Journal of Social Psychiatry,* 1961, *7,* 33–53.

LEICHTY, M. M.   Family attitudes and self concept in Vietnamese and US children. *American Journal of Orthopsychiatry,* 1963, *33,* 38–50.

MEAD, M.   *Sex and temperament in three primitive societies.* New York: Morrow, 1935.

SHORT, L. N.   Youth in Australia. *Youth and Society,* 1970, 1(3), 289–308.

WALTERS, J., & STINNETT, N.   Parent–child relationships: A decade review of research. *Journal of Marriage and the Family,* 1971, *33*(1), 70–111.

WYLIE, L.   Youth in France and the United States. *Daedalus,* 1962, *91,* 198–215.

ZOLBERG, A. R.   Youth as a political phenomenon in tropical Africa. *Youth and Society,* 1969, *1*(2), 199–218.

Archetypal Patterns of Youth

S. N. EISENSTADT

Eisenstadt considers youth as a universal phenomenon, with parallels between primitive and historical and modern societies. However, he also analyzes current social processes and indicates how they affect the basic archetypal elements of youth. A new configuration of youth is emerging with new possibilities and problems.

Youth constitutes a universal phenomenon. It is first of all a biological phenomenon, but one always defined in cultural terms. In this sense it constitutes a part of a wider cultural phenomenon, the varying definitions of age and of the differences between one and another.[1] Age and age differences are among the basic aspects of life and the determinants of human destiny. Every human being passes through various ages, and at each one he attains and uses different biological and intellectual capacities. At each stage he performs different tasks and roles in relation to the other members of his society: from a child, he becomes a father; from a pupil, a teacher; from a vigorous youth, a mature adult, and then an aging and "old" man.

This gradual unfolding of power and capacity is not merely a universal, biologically conditioned, and inescapable fact. Although the basic biological

processes of maturation (within the limits set by such factors as relative longevity) are probably more or less similar in all human societies, their cultural definition varies from society to society, at least in details. In all societies, age serves as a basis for defining the cultural and social characteristic of human beings, for the formation of some of their mutual relations and common activities, and for the differential allocation of social roles.

The cultural definitions of age and age differences contain several different yet complementary elements. First, these definitions often refer to the social division of labor in a society, to the criteria according to which people occupy various social positions and roles within any society. For instance, in many societies certain roles—especially those of married men, full citizens, independent earners—are barred to young people, while others—as certain military roles—are specifically allocated to them. Second, the cultural definition of age is one important constituent of a person's self-

[1] A general sociological analysis of the place of age in social structure has been attempted in S. N. Eisenstadt, *From Generation to Generation* (Chicago: The Free Press of Glencoe, Illinois, 1956).

Abridged from YOUTH: CHANGE AND CHALLENGE, edited by Erik H. Erikson, © 1961 by the American Academy of Arts and Sciences, © 1963 by Basic Books, Inc., Publishers, New York. Reprinted by permission.

identity, his self-perception in terms of his own psychological needs and aspirations, his place in society, and the ultimate meaning of his life.

Within any such definition, the qualities of each age are evaluated according to their relation to some basic, primordial qualities, such as vigor, physical and sexual prowess, the ability to cope with material, social, and supernatural environment, wisdom, experience, or divine inspiration. Different ages are seen in different societies as the embodiments of such qualities. These various qualities seem to unfold from one age to another, each age emphasizing some out of the whole panorama of such possible qualities. The cultural definition of an age span is always a broad definition of human potentialities, limitations, and obligations at a given stage of life. In terms of these definitions, people map out the broad contours of life, their own expectations and possibilities, and place themselves and their fellow men in social and cultural positions, ascribing to each a given place within these contours.

The various qualities attributed to different ages do not constitute an unconnected series. They are usually interconnected in many ways. The subtle dialectics between the unfolding of some qualities and the waning of others in a person is not a mere registration of his psychological or biological traits; rather, it constitutes the broad framework of his potentialities and their limits throughout his life span. The characteristics of any one "age," therefore, cannot be fully understood except in relation to those of other ages. Whether seen as a gradually unfolding continuum or as a series of sharp contrasts and opposed characteristics, they are fully explicable and understandable only in terms of one another. The boy bears within himself the seeds of the adult man; else, he must as an adult acquire new patterns of behavior, sharply and intentionally opposed to those of his boyhood. The adult either develops naturally into an old man—or decays into one. Only when taken together do these different "ages" constitute the entire map of human possibilities and limitations: and, as every individual usually must pass through them all, their complementariness and continuity (even if defined in discontinuous and contrasting terms) become strongly emphasized and articulated.

The same holds true for the age definitions of the two sexes, although perhaps with a somewhat different meaning. Each age span is defined differently for either sex, and these definitions are usually related and complementary, as the "sexual image" and identity always constitute basic elements of man's image in every society. This close connection between different ages necessarily stresses the problem of transition from one point in a person's life to another as a basic constituent of any cultural definition of an "age." Hence, each definition of age must necessarily cope with the perception of time, and changes in time, of one's own progress in time, one's transition from one period of life to another.

This personal transition, or temporal progress, or change, may become closely linked with what may be called cosmic and societal time.[2] The attempt to find some meaning in personal temporal transition may often lead to identification with the rhythms of nature or history, with the cycles of the seasons, with the unfolding of some cosmic plan (whether cyclical, seasonal, or apocalyptic), or with the destiny and development of society. The nature of this linkage often constitutes the focus round which an individual's personal identity becomes defined in cultural terms and through which personal experience, with its anguish, may be given some meaning in terms of cultural symbols and values.

The whole problem of age definition and the linkage of personal time and transition with cosmic time become especially accentuated in that age span usually designated as youth. However great the differences among various societies, there is one focal point within the life span of an individual which in most known societies is to some extent emphasized: the period of youth, of transition from childhood to full adult status, or full membership in the society. In this period the individual is no longer a child (especially from the

[2]The analysis of personal, cosmic, and societal time (or temporal progression) has constituted a fascinating but not easily dealt with focus of analysis. For some approaches to these problems, see *Man and Time* (papers from the Eranos Yearbooks, edited by Joseph Campbell; London: Routledge & Kegan Paul, 1958), especially the article by Gerardus van der Leeuw. See also Mircea Eliade, *The Myth of the Eternal Return.* Translated by W. R. Trask. New York: Pantheon Books, 1954 (Bollingen Series).

physical and sexual point of view) but is ready to undertake many attributes of an adult and to fulfill adult roles. But he is not yet fully acknowledged as an adult, a full member of the society. Rather, he is being "prepared," or is preparing himself for such adulthood.

This image of youth—the cultural definition of youth—contains all the crucial elements of any definition of age, usually in an especially articulated way. This is the stage at which the individual's personality acquires the basic psychological mechanism of self-regulation and self-control, when his self-identity becomes crystallized. It is also the stage at which the young are confronted with some models of the major roles they are supposed to emulate in adult life and with the major symbols and values of their culture and community. Moreover, in this phase the problem of the linkage of the personal temporal transition with cosmic or societal time becomes extremely acute. Any cultural definition of youth describes it as a transitory phase, couched in terms of transition toward something new, something basically different from the past. Hence the acuteness of the problem of linkage.

The very emphasis on the transitory nature of this stage and of its essentially preparatory character, however, may easily create a somewhat paradoxical situation. It may evolve an image of youth as the purest manifestation and repository of ultimate cultural and societal values. Such an image is rooted first in the fact that to some extent youth is always defined as a period of "role moratorium," that is, as a period in which one may play with various roles without definitely choosing any. It does not yet require the various compromises inherent in daily participation in adult life. At the same time, however, since it is also the period when the maximum identification with the values of society is stressed, under certain conditions it may be viewed as the repository of all the major human virtues and primordial qualities. It may then be regarded as the only age in which full identification with the ultimate values and symbols of the society is attained—facilitated by the flowering of physical vigor, a vigor which may easily become identified with a more general flowering of the cosmos or the society.

The fullest, the most articulate and definitive expression of these archetypal elements of youth

is best exemplified in the ritual dramatization of the transition from adolescence to adulthood, such as the various *rites de passage* and ceremonies of initiations in primitive tribes and in ancient civilizations.[3] In these rites the pre-adult youth are transformed into full members of the tribe. This transformation is effected through:

1. a series of rites in which the adolescents are symbolically divested of the characteristics of youth and invested with those of adulthood, from a sexual and social point of view; this investment, which has deep emotional significance, may have various concrete manifestations: bodily mutilation, circumcision, the taking on of a new name or symbolic rebirth;

2. the complete symbolic separation of the male adolescents from the world of their youth, especially from their close attachment to their mothers; in other words, their complete "male" independence and image are fully articulated (the opposite usually holds true of girls' initiations);

3. the dramatization of the encounter between the several generations, a dramatization that may take the form of a fight or a competition, in which the basic complementariness of various age grades —whether of a continuous or discontinuous type —is stressed; quite often the discontinuity between adolescence and adulthood is symbolically expressed, as in the symbolic death of the adolescents as children and their rebirth as adults.

4. the transmission of the tribal lore with its instructions about proper behavior, both through formalized teaching and through various ritual activities; this transmission is combined with:

5. a relaxation of the concrete control of the adults over the erstwhile adolescents and its substitution by self-control and adult responsibility.

Most of these dramatic elements can also be found, although in somewhat more diluted forms, in various traditional folk festivals in peasant communities, especially those such as rural carnivals in which youth and marriage are emphasized. In an even more diluted form, these elements may be found in various spontaneous initiation ceremonies of the fraternities and youth

---

[3]For a fuller exposition of the sociological significance of initiation rites, see Mircea Eliade, *Birth and Rebirth* (New York: Harper & Brothers, 1958) and *From Generation to Generation* (ref. 1).

groups in modern societies.[4] Here, however, the full dramatic articulation of these elements is lacking, and their configuration and organization assume different forms.

The transition from childhood and adolescence to adulthood, the development of personal identity, psychological autonomy and self-regulation, the attempt to link personal temporal transition to general cultural images and to cosmic rhythms, and to link psychological maturity to the emulation of definite role models—these constitute the basic elements of any archetypal image of youth. However, the ways in which these various elements become crystallized in concrete configurations differ greatly from society to society and within sectors of the same society. The full dramatic articulation of these elements in the *rites de passage* of primitive societies constitutes only one—perhaps the most extreme and articulate but certainly not the only—configuration of these archetypal elements of youth.

In order to understand other types of such configurations, it is necessary to analyze some conditions that influence their development. Perhaps the best starting point is the nature of the social organization of the period of adolescence: the process of transition from childhood to adulthood, the social context in which the process of growing up is shaped and structured. There are two major criteria that shape the social organization of the period of youth. One is the extent to which age in general and youth in particular form a criterion for the allocation of roles in a society, whether in politics, in economic or cultural activity—aside from the family, of course, in which they always serve as such a criterion. The second is the extent to which any society develops specific age groups, specific corporate organizations, composed of members of the same "age," such as youth movements or old men's clubs. If roles are allocated in a society according to age, this greatly influences the extent to which age constitutes a component of a person's identity. In such cases, youth becomes a definite and meaningful phase of transition in an individual's progress through life, and his budding self-identity acquires content and a relation to role models and cultural values. No

less important to the concrete development of identity is the extent to which it is influenced, either by the common participation of different generations in the same group as in the family, or conversely by the organization of members of the same age groups into specific, distinct groups.

The importance of age as a criterion for allocating roles in a society is closely related to several major aspects of social organization and cultural orientation. The first aspect is the relative complexity of the division of labor. In general, the simpler the organization of the society, the more influential age will be as a criterion for allocating roles. Therefore, in primitive or traditional societies (or in the more primitive and traditional sectors of developed societies) age and seniority constitute basic criteria for allocating social, economic, and political roles.

The second aspect consists of the major value orientations and symbols of a society, especially the extent to which they emphasize certain general orientations, qualities, or types of activity (such as physical vigor, the maintenance of cultural tradition, the achievement and maintenance of supernatural prowess) which can be defined in terms of broad human qualities and which become expressed and symbolized in specific ages.

The emphasis on any particular age as a criterion for the allocation of roles is largely related to the concrete application of the major value orientations in a society. For instance, we find that those primitive societies in which military values and orientations prevail emphasize young adulthood as the most important age, while those in which sedentary activities prevail emphasize older age. Similarly, within some traditional societies, a particular period such as old age may be emphasized if it is seen as the most appropriate one for expressing major cultural values and symbols—for instance, the upholding of a given cultural tradition.

The social and cultural conditions that determine the extent to which specific age groups and youth groups develop differ from the conditions that determine the extent to which age serves as a criterion for the allocation of roles. At the same time, the two kinds of conditions may be closely related, as we shall see. Age groups in general and youth groups in particular tend to arise in those

[4]See Bruno Bettelheim, *Symbolic Wounds, Puberty Rites and the Envious Circle* (Chicago: The Free Press of Glencoe, Illinois, 1954).

societies in which the family or kinship unit cannot ensure (it may even impede) the attainment of full social status on the part of its members. These conditions appear especially (although not uniquely[5]) in societies in which family or kinship groups do not constitute the basic unit of the social division of labor. Several features characterize such societies. First, the membership in the total society (citizenship) is not defined in terms of belonging to any such family, kinship group, or estate, nor is it mediated by such a group.

Second, in these societies the major political, economic, social, and religious functions are performed not by family or kinship units but rather by various specialized groups (political parties, occupational associations, etc.), which individuals may join irrespective of their family, kinship, or caste. In these societies, therefore, the major roles that adults are expected to perform in the wider society differ in orientation from those of the family or kinship group. The children's identification and close interaction with family members of other ages does not assure the attainment of full self-identity and social maturity on the part of the children. In these cases, there arises a tendency for peer groups to form, especially youth groups; these can serve as a transitory phase between the world of childhood and the adult world.

This type of the social division of labor is found in varying degrees in different societies, primitive, historical, or modern. In several primitive tribes such a division of labor has existed,[6] for example, in Africa, among the chiefless (segmentary) tribes of Nandi, Masai, or Kipigis, in the village communities of Yako and Ibo, or in more centralized kingdoms of the Zulu and Swazi, and among some of the Indian tribes of the Plains, as well as among some South American and Indian tribes.

Such a division of labor likewise existed to some extent in several historical societies (especially in city states such as Athens or Rome), although most great historical civilizations were characterized mainly by a more hierarchical and ascriptive

system of the division of labor, in which there were greater continuity and harmony between the family and kinship groups and the broader institutional contexts. The fullest development of this type of the social division of labor, however, is to be found in modern industrial societies. Their inclusive membership is usually based on the universal criterion of citizenship and is not conditioned by membership in any kinship group. In these societies the family does not constitute a basic unit of the division of labor, especially not in production and distribution, and even in the sphere of consumption its functions become more limited. Occupations are not transmitted through heredity. Similarly, the family or kinship group does not constitute a basic unit of political or ritual activities. Moreover, the general scope of the activities of the family has been continuously diminishing, while various specialized agencies tend to take over its functions in the fields of education and recreation.

To be sure, the extent to which the family is diminishing in modern societies is often exaggerated. In many social spheres (neighborhood, friendship, informal association, some class relations, community relations), family, kinship, and status are still very influential. But the scope of these relations is more limited in modern societies than in many others, even if the prevalent myth of the disappearance of the family has long since been exploded. The major social developments of the nineteenth century (the establishment of national states, the progress of the industrial revolution, the great waves of intercontinental migrations) have greatly contributed to this diminution of scope, and especially in the first phase of modernization there has been a growing discontinuity between the life of the children, whether in the family or the traditional school and in the social world with its new and enlarged perspectives.

Youth groups tend to develop in all societies in which such a division of labor exists. Youth's tendency to coalesce in such groups is rooted in the fact that participation in the family became insufficient for developing full identity or full social maturity, and that the roles learned in the family did not constitute an adequate basis for developing such identity and participation. In the youth groups the adolescent seeks some frame-

---

[5] A special type of age groups may also develop in familistic societies. See *From Generation to Generation* (ref. 1), ch. 5.

[6] For fuller details, see *From Generation to Generation,* especially chs. 3 and 4.

work for the development and crystallization of his identity, for the attainment of personal autonomy, and for his effective transition into the adult world.

Various types of youth organizations always tend to appear with the transition from traditional or feudal societies to modern societies, along with the intensified processes of change, especially in periods of rapid mobility, migration, urbanization, and industrialization. This is true of all European societies, and also of non-Western societies. The impact of Western civilization on primitive and historical–traditional peoples is usually connected with the disruption of family life, but beyond this it also involves a change in the mutual evaluation of the different generations. The younger generation usually begin to seek a new self-identification, and one phase or another of this search is expressed in ideological conflict with the older.

Most of the nationalistic movements in the Middle East, Asia, and Africa have consisted of young people, students, or officers who rebelled against their elders and the traditional familistic setting with its stress on the latter's authority. At the same time there usually has developed a specific youth consciousness and ideology that intensifies the nationalistic movement to "rejuvenate" the country.

The emergence of the peer group among immigrant children is a well-known phenomenon that usually appears in the second generation. It occurs mainly because of the relative breakdown of immigrant family life in the new country. The more highly industrialized and urbanized that country (or the sector absorbing the immigrants) is, the sharper the breakdown. Hence, the family of the immigrant or second-generation child has often been an inadequate guide to the new society. The immigrant child's attainment of full identity in the new land is usually related to how much he has been able to detach himself from his older, family setting. Some of these children, therefore, have developed a strong predisposition to join various peer groups. Such an affiliation has sometimes facilitated their transition to the absorbing society by stressing the values and patterns of behavior in that society—or, on the contrary, it may express their rebellion against this society, or against their older setting.

All these modern social developments and movements have given rise to a great variety of youth groups, peer groups, youth movements, and what has been called youth culture. The types and concrete forms of such groups vary widely: spontaneous youth groups, student movements, ideological and semipolitical movements, and youth rebellions connected with the Romantic movement in Europe, and, later, with the German youth movements. The various social and national trends of the nineteenth and twentieth centuries have also given impetus to such organizations. At the same time there have appeared many adult-sponsored youth organizations and other agencies springing out of the great extension of educational institutions. In addition to providing recreative facilities, these agencies have also aimed at character molding and the instilling of civic virtues, so as to deepen social consciousness and widen the social and cultural horizon. The chief examples are the YMCA, the Youth Brigades organized in England by William Smith, the Boy Scouts, the Jousters in France, and the many kinds of community organizations, hostels, summer camps, or vocational guidance centers.

Thus we see that there are many parallels between primitive and historical societies and modern societies with regard to the conditions under which the various constellations of youth groups, youth activities, and youth images have developed. But these parallels are only partial. Despite certain similarities, the specific configurations of the basic archetypal elements of the youth image in modern societies differ greatly from those of primitive and traditional societies. The most important differences are rooted in the fact that in the modern, the development of specific youth organizations is paradoxically connected with the weakening of the importance of age in general and youth in particular as definite criteria for the allocation of roles in society.

As we have already said, the extent to which major occupational, cultural, or political roles are allocated today according to the explicit criterion of age is very small. Most such roles are achieved according to wealth, acquired skills, specialization, and knowledge. Family background may be of great importance for the acquisition of these attributes, but very few positions are directly given people by virtue of their family standing. Yet this very weakening of the importance of age is always connected with intensive developments of youth groups and movements. This fact has several interesting repercussions on the organization and structure of such groups. In primitive and traditional societies, youth groups are usually part of a wider organization of age groups that covers a very long period of life, from childhood to late adulthood and even old age. To be sure, it is during youth that most of the dramatic elements of the transition from one age to another are manifest, but this stage constitutes only part of a longer series of continuous, well-defined stages.

From this point of view, primitive or traditional societies do not differ greatly from those in which the transition from youth to adulthood is not organized in specific age groups but is largely effected within the fold of the family and kinship groups. In both primitive and traditional societies we observe a close and comprehensive linkage between personal temporal transition and societal or cosmic time, a linkage most fully expressed in the *rites de passage*. Consequently, the transition from childhood to adulthood in all such societies is given full meaning in terms of ultimate cultural values and symbols borne or symbolized by various adult role models.

In modern societies the above picture greatly changes. The youth group, whatever its composition or organization, usually stands alone. It does not constitute a part of a fully institutionalized and organized series of age groups. It is true that in many of the more traditional sectors of modern societies the more primitive or traditional archetypes of youth still prevail. Moreover, in many modern societies elements of the primitive archetypes of youth still exist. But the full articulation of these elements is lacking, and the social organization and self-expression of youth are not given full legitimation or meaning in terms of cultural values and rituals.

The close linkage between the growth of personality, psychological maturation and definite role models derived from the adult world has become greatly weakened. Hence the very coalescence of youth into special groups only tends to emphasize their problematic, uncertain standing from the point of view of cultural values and symbols. This has created a new constellation of the basic archetypal elements of youth. This new constellation can most clearly be seen in what has been called the emergence of the problems and stresses of adolescence in modern societies. While some of these stresses are necessarily common to adolescence in all societies, they become especially acute in modern societies.

Among these stresses the most important are the following: first, the bodily development of the adolescent constitutes a constant problem to him (or her). Since social maturity usually lags behind biological maturity, the bodily changes of puberty are not usually given full cultural, normative meaning, and their evaluation is one of the adolescent's main concerns. The difficulty inherent in attaining legitimate sexual outlets and relations at this period of growth makes these problems even more acute. Second, the adolescent's orientation toward the main values of his society is also beset with difficulties. Owing to the long period of preparation and the relative segregation of the children's world from that of adults, the main values of the society are necessarily presented to the child and adolescent in a highly selective way, with a strong idealistic emphasis. The relative unreality of these values as presented to the children—which at the same time are not given full ritual and symbolic expression—creates among the adolescents a great potential uncertainty and ambivalence toward the adult world.

This ambivalence is manifest, on the one hand, in a striving to communicate with the adult world and receive its recognition; on the other hand, it appears in certain dispositions to accentuate the differences between them and the adults and to oppose the various roles allocated to them by the adults. While they orient themselves to full participation in the adult world and its values, they usually attempt also to communicate with this world in a distinct, special way.

Parallel developments are to be found in the ideologies of modern youth groups. Most of these tend to create an ideology that emphasizes the discontinuity between youth and adulthood and the uniqueness of the youth period as the purest embodiment of ultimate social and cultural values. Although the explicitness of this ideology varies in extent from one sector of modern society to another, its basic elements are prevalent in almost all modern youth groups. . . .

The Problems of Youth and the Structure of Society in England

FRANK MUSGROVE

The author discusses, in depth, the youth society in England, including historical backgrounds, popular theories, varieties of youth, and current social forces.

This paper is about power. The youth problem has usually been examined in terms of values. This obscures the real issues. Empirical research on the values of youth leads to the conclusion that the youth problem is a non-problem. Such a conclusion would astonish most young people in England today, their parents and teachers. They know they have a problem. My argument will be that it arises from the differential distribution of power among age groups. Its solution lies in the redistribution of power.

Investigations of the "youth culture" have become fashionable. They are misleading. They focus on the values and norms that operate among the young and emphasize the influence of the peer-group. In these inquiries the youth culture assumes many of the characteristics of a contra-culture, opposing and even inverting important values that are held in the adult world. The model of society that consciously or unconsciously lies behind these analyses is an integrative model: it assumes that every functioning social structure is based on a consensus of values among its members. The youth problem is explained as a failure of adjustment to the dominant values and symbols of a society; it is conceptualized in terms of value differences and its solution is seen as integration through more efficient socialization of the young. But in numerous investigations conducted in Britain, these alleged value differences have turned out to be largely illusory. The youth problem only begins to make sense when we employ a different model of society. The most serviceable model assumes that every society is based on the coercion of some of its members by others; and that conflict and change are universal features of social life (cf. Dahrendorf, 1959: 175–205).

The alleged divergence of values between the young and the mature is commonly ascribed to the extent and rate of social change. Social innovation, especially in the field of education, is stressed as a cause rather than a consequence of the tension between the young and their elders. It is true that the contrast between generational experiences is great in modernizing societies: the young have had more formal education; they have not so often endured great poverty; they have seen more television; and they have not so often been to war.

"The Problems of Youth and the Structure of Society in England" by Frank Musgrove is reprinted from *Youth and Society*, Volume 1, Number 1 (September 1969), pp. 38-58, by permission of the Publisher, Sage Publications, Inc., and the author.

And while many of an earlier generation spent their youth in man-sized communities, schools, and workshops, today the young experience associations which are quite different in scale: extensive suburbanization, the rapid growth in size and complexity of schools, universities, and industrial organizations have profoundly modified the texture of human relationships. Full-blooded love–hate relationships are ever less possible under the conditions of present-day organizational life; attenuated, calculative, and passionless relationships are needed in rational, finely co-ordinated large-scale associations.

It was Margaret Mead who gave us, more than twenty years ago, the classic analysis of the relationship between social change and divergent generational values. "Our system (of transmitting our culture through parents) might work smoothly in a culture which was changing very slowly," she said. "For an essential element in the system is that the child is expected to take the parent as a model for his own life style. In periods of rapid change . . . this requirement of the system is unattainable. The child will never be, as an adult, a member of the same culture of which the father stands as the representative during his early years." In consequence, "the socializing function of the age-group becomes very much intensified. . . . The surrogates who carry the cultural standards have changed. They are no longer the parents, omnipotent and belonging to another order of being, but one's everyday companions . . ." (Mead, 1948).

Identical, Not Conflicting Values

Actually, Margaret Mead was wrong. The inescapable conclusion of empirical research into values in England has been that this conflict in values is virtually non-existent. An English empirical study of the very "modelling" process to which Margaret Mead refers, shows clearly that average 15-year-old English boys and girls identify closely with their parents, rather than their peers. The study concludes that "the opinion sometimes expressed that adolescents are, in general, rejecting parental influence, receives no confirmation here" (Wright, 1962).

We have had other investigations recently in England which point to similar conclusions (Hancock and Wakeford, 1965). Those which have emphasized a distinctive youth culture have described divergent fashions in music and dress (on to which, in fact, adults themselves eventually converge); but they have detected little conflict in fundamental socio-moral values (Niles, 1968). Like Coleman's study in America (1961), they show a rejection of the values of teachers, "a thorough-going alienation from school" (Sugarman, 1967), but this is a different matter. (What needs explaining are not the deviations of adolescents, but the deviations of teachers, at least in their official attitudes and postures.) In rejecting teacher-values the young are commonly expressing agreement with the values of their parents (cf. Berger, 1963).

These English studies are broadly congruent with many which have been carried out in North America, for instance Riley and Moore's inquiry into teenage "other-directedness" (1961),[1] and Kahl's investigations of the attitudes and aspirations of "Common Man" boys (1953). Westley and Elkin's research (1957) in suburban Montreal led them to conclude that "adolescents, by the age of 14 or 15, have already internalized the ideals and values of the surrounding adult society . . . they do not reject adult values or participate in an anti-adult youth culture" (cf. Berge, 1964 and Vuchmich, 1964).

My own research in England points to a similar conclusion (Musgrove, 1963a). My most recent work in this area has been an investigation of the "reference groups" and "reference persons" of a population of English university students. Sixty-seven per cent of my sample mentioned members of their families—principally their parents—as the people most important in their lives. Only 19% referred to their friends. The people whose good opinion they valued, at least with regard to academic work, were parents: only 9% were bothered about the good opinion of their friends (and, indeed, only 12% about the good opinion of their teachers). And it was their parents above all whom they did not wish to disappoint by academic failure. In commenting on this work I felt constrained to point out, "This inquiry

---

[1]Compare with Webster et al. (1962) ". . . contrary to generally accepted theory, there was little evidence that adolescence had been a time of strife or rebelliousness for the majority of Vassar students."

raises doubts about the common assumption that late adolescence is a period in which parents rapidly decline in importance as 'reference persons' in their children's lives" (Musgrove, 1967).

Even the sexual revolution among the young turns out, in Schofield's survey, to be no revolution at all. Promiscuity occurs only in a small minority;[2] in fact the overwhelming majority of our teenagers appear not to have had sexual intercourse at all;[3] the young give massive support to the institution of marriage;[4] there is even widespread support for the double standard of sexual morality[5] to which most adults probably subscribe.

And yet in the past three or four years a significant and articulate proportion of the young have emerged from their private worlds to make a show of political activism without parallel since the thirties. In England the usual explanation has been in terms of the different value systems to which the young and the mature are supposed to subscribe. The idealism of the young has been contrasted with the gross materialism of their seniors. The Campaign for Nuclear Disarmament and the demonstrations by the young over Biafra and Vietnam have been "explained" in this sense. This explanation of the renewed political activism of the young proves on close scrutiny to be no explanation at all.

Recent studies of the politics of British youth have failed to reveal characteristically youthful political and social attitudes among young voters in general or young activists in particular. Analyses of surveys conducted by National Opinion Polls Limited in 1964 were expected to show "correlations of views with age—perhaps in the form of sharp discontinuities between the opin-

ions or behavior of the youngest age category (21–24) and the rest." No such correlations were established: the gross orientations of the several age groups were remarkably alike. "So far as voting intentions are concerned . . . the picture is clearly one in which the young are preponderantly following paths established by their elders" (Abrams and Little, 1965a).

A nation-wide study of young political activists suggests that activism itself, far from representing a rejection of parental socio-political values, is in fact an expression of solidarity with them.

> The further left a Young Socialist, the more likely he is to have actively radical if not revolutionary parents. . . . Indeed the principle of family succession is what emerges most clearly among the young activists of all parties. Four out of five young activists came from families with a record of political activity, 7 in every 10 support the same party as their most politically active parent.

The authors of this study conclude, "There is little reason to treat the young in Britain as a new political generation. The perceptions and orientations of the age-group as a whole are organized in an old frame of reference. . . . British youth has no collective political self-consciousness. There has been no breakthrough and there is little prospect of one" (Abrams and Little, 1965b).

There are indications that young political activists in America are more distant from their parents. But I have been struck by the studies of Berkeley students after the 1964 rebellion which indicate a situation not dissimilar to what we find in Britain. One study of a sample of Berkeley students showed that "those students who professed to be most in agreement with their parents on political issues and who discussed such issues most frequently, were most likely to approve of the Free Speech Movement" (Gales, 1966). Lipset has also assembled evidence which refutes the notion that student activists in America are expressing values counter to their parents'. "Studies of the background of activists," he writes, "indicate that the opposite, if anything, is true. They are much more often students who are acting out in practice the values which they have been taught by ideologically liberal parents . . ." (Lipset and Altbach, 1966). The conflict between the young

[2]". . . promiscuity, although it exists, is not a prominent feature of teenage sexual behavior" (Schofield, 1968: 231).

[3]"Our results have made it clear that premarital sexual relations are a long way from being universal among teenagers as over two-thirds of the boys and three-quarters of the girls in our sample have not engaged in sexual intercourse" (Schofield, 1968: 224).

[4]"Very few of our sample rejected the prospect of marriage; 6 per cent of the younger boys and 3 per cent of the older boys said at interview that they did not want to marry; hardly any of the girls (1 per cent in each age group) said they did not want to marry" (Schofield 1968: 102).

[5]Some 30% disagreed with the view that there is one standard of sexual conduct for men, another for women (Schofield, 1968: 108).

and the mature appears to be the product of consensus.

But we are using an irrelevant model of society for our analysis. The consensus model has led social analysts into an exploratory cul-de-sac. If the young and their elders do not differ substantially in values, they differ substantially in power.

It is my contention that the historical trend in England has been for the power of the young to decline. (By "the young" I mean people who are between 13 or 14 and their early 20's.) There are two major reasons for this: the first is the changing structure of the English population, the virtual disappearance of an "age pyramid"; the second is the changing structure of the economy, which has been ever less able to offer young people positions of significance.

These changing demographic and economic circumstances have profoundly altered the balance of power between the young and the mature. The young have been extruded from society; they scarcely belong to it; they are non-members. The contemporary problem of youth in England is essentially a boundary dispute. Outside the boundary of society the young are placed in a position of futility and irresponsibility, and are denounced for being futile and irresponsible. Theories of adolescence, of education and of work have been elaborated with great academic solemnity to explain and justify the extrusion of the young, which has occurred for quite other reasons. These theories have many of the characteristics of ideological tools which are used by the mature to maintain their power. They are effective instruments for boundary-maintenance.

Social Contract with an Adolescent Protectorate

I do not subscribe to a simple "zero-sum" notion of power (any more than I subscribe to the seventeenth-century mercantilist, or bullionist, theory of the balance of trade). Power does not necessarily serve only the sectional interests of those who wield it—though it may do so. The power of adults in general and of parents in particular was seen by John Locke in the late seventeenth century (in his *Second Treatise on Political Government*) as contractual. The young would submit to parental power only because they gained from it in welfare and protection.

Adolescence has been a "protectorate" administered by adults for the past two centuries. Our contemporary conflict has the character of a colonial revolt. The subordination of the adolescent —like the subordination of the African—was first justified by the claim to protect him. His subordinate status was a "protected status"—honourable and generally acceptable when protection was apparently needed. Adolescence was justified by society's corruption.

The ideas of adolescence and social corruption are closely linked in the writings of Rousseau: Emile must be withdrawn from the world. Shelley and Godwin wrote eloquently about the essential evil of society at that time. Late eighteenth-century anarchism and the concept of adolescence were both twins. Protective legislation in the nineteenth century—industrial, educational, and penal —dislodged the "young person" from the corrupting world of adults. Today, when society is reformed (and even our post-Mayo factories benign), adults have shifted their ground: the young need protection not from society, but from themselves. Psychological instead of social–moral theories now legitimize the dislodgement of the young. The legitimacy of the older social contract has been undermined by social amelioration. But the young are still denied power in two (related) senses; they are impeded in their access to positions in which they can require the compliance of others, regardless of age; and they are retained in positions in which their compliance can be expected by their elders. As the consensual basis of adult power is eroded, power is ever more likely to be based on force. It becomes apparent that the redefinition of society over the past two centuries has been less for the protection of adolescents than adults.

DEMOGRAPHY AND THE DISTRIBUTION OF POWER

The key to the distribution of power among age groups lies in demography. Attention has often been drawn to the narrowing base of the age pyramid: the young, it is argued, have acquired a scarcity-value and have consequently gained in importance (Bossard, 1954: 613; Ogburn and

Nimkoff, 1955: 337). It is true that in pre-industrial England, when only half the children born survived to puberty, children were not taken very seriously; a heavy investment in their training and education was a bad risk. But when they had proved their capacity to survive, by the age of 14, they were taken very seriously indeed: formal education and apprenticeship began at this time.

The middle and apex of the pyramid deserve at least as much attention as the base, for they regulate the flow of young people into the adult world: they are the key to the problem of succession. In seventeenth-, eighteenth-, and nineteenth-century England, children under ten constituted some 28% of the total population; in the mid-twentieth century, some 15%. But along with this narrowing of the base has gone a broadening of the apex: from the seventeenth to the nineteenth centuries, people over 50 years were some 15% of the population; today they are 30%.

But of still greater significance is the thickening in the middle—the bulge of men at the peak of their careers, in positions of power, in their 40's. People between 40 and 50 were probably some 7% of the population in the seventeenth century, 9% in the nineteenth century, but 14% today (Laslett, 1965: 103). As a proportion of the population, men of this age are twice as numerous today as they were in pre-industrial society. They block the access of the young to power. It is no longer an accurate metaphor to speak of an age pyramid at all: our population today resembles a column. The young are trapped at the bottom of a column of apparently indestructible and immortal middle-aged men.

In a typical village community of pre-industrial England, one-third of the children would be orphans in the sense that one or other parent had died. The expectation of life at birth in the seventeenth century was less than half of what it is today. The average age of the population was some 27 years. Life expectancies improved considerably at higher ages; but when a man married in his 20's he was unlikely to live to see even his eldest son reach fully adult years. He could expect perhaps 25 more years of life, compared with more than 45 today. Even among more affluent, titled people, mortality was high. The mean age at death of all the English aristocrats dying in the sixteenth and seventeenth centuries was in the early 30's.

To be orphaned at 15 or 16 may be a tragedy; it may also be an opportunity. Pre-industrial England was composed of a myriad of small-scale, family-based economic enterprises. England was, indeed, "a nation of shopkeepers"—in the sense of workshopkeepers. These family concerns faced a constant crisis of succession. If the children were young the widow might marry the apprentice (to be 18 and an apprentice was not entirely without its possibilities); or a son or a nephew in his teens might take over. Today a son of 17 or 18 would be unwise to live on his "expectations." Seventeenth- and eighteenth-century England abounded with young people who had quite realistic expectations of early succession to the headship of economic enterprises, small by modern standards, but the units or blocks of which society was composed. Allocation to social position was by death of the father or other kinsman: it was scarcely less certain and commonly much earlier than allocation by graduate school and Ph.D.

The population pyramid of an earlier age needed a broad base precisely because it was thin at the top. High mortality rates promoted large families, rather than vice versa (cf. Stevenson, 1920). Many were born when comparatively few survived: additional births were necessary to effect replacements. It is the rapid turnover of personnel that distinguishes pre-industrial from twentieth-century England. The exigencies of life were such that the very young were often called upon to carry heavy responsibilities and take their full place in society. The rates of mortality ensured a comparatively fluid boundary between the young and the mature.

EARLY INDUSTRIALIZATION AND OPPORTUNITY FOR YOUTH

Early industrialization in the first half of the nineteenth century brought the young even more extensively into society. The new industries had no superstructure of middle-aged and elderly managers; the mature were handicapped in this world of new techniques by irrelevant skills. While middle-aged handloomweavers starved, young men in their teens moved into senior positions in the new chemical, iron, and power-based textile industries. Robert Owen was an industrial manager in Lancashire at the age of 17. We can date a significant decline in the position of the young from the 1860s and 1870s. Technological change, and the growing tendency of middle-aged men to survive in the senior positions which they had entered young, displaced the young from an earlier role of central importance to the economy. The younger age groups were still expanding while mortality rates declined among adults (see Yule, 1906). Compulsory schooling came in the 1880s not because young people needed more formal education for important functions in a more complex economy, but because they no longer had any serious economic functions (see Musgrove, 1963b).

An explosive situation exists when we have a conjunction of high average life expectancies and a broad population base: when the age pyramid is thick in the middle, but still thicker—and thickening—at the bottom. And this is precisely the trend we have seen in the advanced industrial nations over the past 20 years. The notable exception is Japan, where the reverse tendency has been instituted by a deliberate and determined programme of birth-control (see Taeuber, 1964). The base of Japan's population pyramid is still much wider than that of American or Britain; and the conjunction of improved life expectancies and a continuing wide population base may have been a contributing factor in the considerable and continuing student turbulence throughout the past century of modernization (see Shimbori, 1968). The broad base of the pyramid persisted during the period of modernization and declining adult death rates. But this source of social tension is likely to disappear in the next 10 to 15 years as the base of the pyramid rapidly contracts. Japan may experience less unrest among the young—and perhaps less spectacular economic and social change—while Britain (and America) experience more.

England, like America, has had a different demographic history. The base of the population pyramid has contracted sharply since the late nineteenth century: in 1880 almost 37% of the English population was under the age of 15; today it is some 23%. But it is broadening again. In the 15 years after World War II, England had a depleted supply of young people in their teens, the product of a particularly low birth-rate in the thirties. Between 1945 and 1960 the young were remarkably quiescent. In the mid-thirties we had scarcely more than half a million births a year (599,000 in 1935); in 1947 there were some 800,000 births; in 1970 we shall probably reach this figure again; and in the 1980s we shall top a million births a year. This changing shape of the age pyramid is closely connected with the contemporary crisis of youth.

EXPANDING BASE AND CONTRACTING OPPORTUNITY

The Crowther Report of 1959, which recommended a later school leaving age, did so in large measure because of the probability of widespread unemployment among young people by the 1970s.[6] The Robbins Report on the universities produced no evidence that expansion was required by economic needs—indeed, it pointed out that some 20% of our science and technology graduates were misemployed (HMSO, 1963: 72). Subsequent official inquiries have pointed to the irrelevance to our economy of our output of scientists and technologists: 85% are specialists (as opposed to "generalists"); the economy requires only 40%.[7] And the university expansion has in fact seen a declining proportion of scientists and technologists, and a rising proportion of art students and social scientists[8]—for whom

[6]HMSO (1959) "After many years when juvenile labour has been relatively scarce, we are moving into a period when it will be relatively plentiful." ". . . the supply of young workers is going to rise relatively to the demand for them. . . . And whether or not the country as a whole continues to enjoy full employment, this is likely to mean that jobs for young people are going to be somewhat harder to find than they would otherwise have been." Disproportionate unemployment among adolescents has been a more marked feature of the American scene in the sixties. See Brill (1964).

[7]"Soon they [pure science graduates] will be coming out in a mighty wave looking for university jobs that don't exist. Now the expansion that provided their employment is over, new university jobs are only a fraction of those that were available three or four years ago. Many of them will head west [to America]. It is almost as if our educational system had built a conveyor belt to carry our most needed brains across the Atlantic" (HMSO, 1968a; compare with Rudd, 1967).

[8]Forty-six per cent of entering students in 1962 were in faculties of science and technology, 40% in 1966; 12% were in faculties of social science in 1962, but 22% in 1966. (HMSO, 1968b).

employment prospects are still less certain. Thus a greatly increased number of adolescents are in defined positions of subordination, in institutions which stand in loco parentis; and with ever less certainty of ordered advance to significant adult statuses. The overall balance of power has moved still further in favour of adults.

In the past decade—even in the past five years—we have seen a rapid increase in the number of older adolescents in full-time education. There is no single, simple reason for this. Some of the expansion is to be ascribed to greater national affluence: education is a consumer good which more people are pre-disposed to buy (or for which they are prepared to forego earnings). Some of the expansion, especially in scientific and technological education, is doubtless a response to a genuine demand by the economy for more highly trained manpower. But a substantial proportion of the expansion probably reflects the superfluity of the young in the contemporary economy—and to stay longer at school is one way of by-passing the more humiliating levels of rigidly age-graded occupational structures.

The statutory school leaving age is still 15 (it will be raised to 16 in 1973); but the number of young people remaining at school beyond this age has been rising rapidly. In 1870 only 1% of England's 17-year-olds were receiving full-time education, 2% in 1902, 4% in 1938, and 15% in 1962 (HMSO, 1963: 11). By 1980 it is expected to be more than 25% (Pearce, 1968); and some proposed reforms would raise it to 50% so that England would move into the position reached by America in 1940 (HMSO, 1959: para. 596). The universities themselves have expanded rapidly since the Robbins Report on Higher Education in 1963. The number of students has almost doubled in the seven years since 1960—from about 106,000 to some 200,000.

THE TEENAGE GHETTO AND SOCIAL CLUBS

The young are placed on the margins of society. They are inmates of a teenage ghetto (cf. Musgrove, 1968a). In England, youth clubs and junior departments of our political parties are important sectors of the ghetto. Since the publication of the Albermarle Report on the Youth Service in 1960

(HMSO, 1960)[9] a national network of clubs for young people between 14 and 20 has been extensively developed. They provide the young with a self-contained world; but it is no breakaway world—the English "Establishment" guides and directs it. The Church of England, "county" families, the Gentry, the Army and even Royalty are closely associated with the management of the Youth Service and invest it with the character-building ethos of a highly traditional upper-class morality.[10]

The junior departments of the political parties are at least related in a direct way to adult activities; but they can exist only if they disclaim any pretensions to actual power. The Young Conservatives are a social rather than a political association; the Young Socialists—as a recent study has shown—"are expected to be political but powerless; 'servants of the Party' who will carry the burden of constituency work without presuming to meddle with policy" (Abrams and Little, 1956). If they meddle—as the Streatham branch had the audacity to do in 1964—they are disaffiliated.

There are two important consequences of a major shift in the balance of power between age groups: one is diffuse disturbance, which arises from a diminution of "excitement control"; the other is more specific and focused disturbance, conducted with a programme of defined objectives, directed toward the seizure of power. The second is more likely to lead to purposive social change. We have seen in the past few years an increased turbulence on the frontier between the age groups of both the diffuse and the focused varieties.

The psychological and sociological apparatus for excitement control is extremely effective in advanced industrial societies—as we can see when we examine the lighter restraints in societies at an earlier stage of development. To show excitement in public (except in special enclaves like football fields) is shameful, unhealthy, immoral. The extreme differentiation of labour and interdependence of activities in our society demands and produces a heavy cover of restraints. The unremitting rationality required for the operation of our great bureaucracies leaves little scope for impassioned

---

[9]For the author's strictures on this report see Musgrove (1965: 154).

[10]For an investigation of the instrumental–moral aims of youth leaders see Musgrove (1966a: chap. 6).

and unpredictable behavior. Even the excitement of encounters between men and women has been brought under control, fitted into the orderliness of life. This excitement is limited to a single experience in the life of each person; it can be renewed only vicariously through an endless consumption of love stories and romantic movies.

But extreme excitement control is pre-eminently the product of egalitarian societies. When there exist great differences in status and power, excitement control is much more precarious. Excitement gets out of control in the gaps and openings, in the interstices of society. When there is a great difference in power between racial groups or between men and women, for example, the result is lynching and the Suffragettes. As women have acquired more equal power with men—chiefly by going out to work—the transactions between the sexes have become muted, unexciting, unimpassioned. A contrary trend is seen in the transactions between age groups: spontaneous, unreflected, and impassioned outbursts of behavior are more common. The breakdown of excitement control in the social vacuum between age groups means more drug-taking and experimental sex; music, dancing, and dress which lack form, structure, and line; excited gatherings in public places; and correspondingly unrestrained behaviour by policemen and other representatives of adult authority. These are counter-moves toward a relative loosening of restraint, which occur when specific changes take place in the structure of societies, especially in the distribution of power between age groups.

The position in early postwar Britain, when young people enjoyed a scarcity-value and fairly smooth and rapid access to adult statuses, was strikingly different. A survey of a representative sample of 18-year-old men showed excitement control operating with daunting efficiency. These young men were notable only for their "passive acceptance of the world around them" (Logan and Goldberg, 1953).[11] Their lives were charac-

terized by dull and stereotyped leisure routines, political and social apathy, a willingness to endure a boring present in return for secure jobs and adequate pensions in half a century's time.

Focused and programmed disturbance has developed principally among students in universities and colleges of art (but not among students in technical and teacher-training colleges). I think we must count as a "focused protest" the massive movement toward earlier marriage. (In 1921 some 5% of new husbands were under 21, 15% in 1965. For new wives the corresponding percentages are 15 and 41 [HMSO, 1967: 196–197].) This is the major adolescent rebellion of our time, the most significant invasion of the adult world, the most determined attempt to assume adult status. This in itself is a major social change, brought about principally by the unequal distribution of power between the age groups; and it typifies the conflict—a rebellion not to beat their seniors, but to join them.

But the assumption of this adult status has brought less power, not more. Adolescents are not in fact particularly well off, in spite of what has been written about their postwar affluence: they are 13% of the population over 14 years of age, but only 5% of consumer spending is in their hands (Abrams, 1961). Perhaps middle-class adolescents who marry are in especial difficulties in trying to maintain their customary style of life. They become heavily dependent on their parents as they establish a home and meet the expenses of their first babies. Married teenagers are often tied to their elders by a burden of indebtedness. In this sense the generation gap has narrowed (cf. Mead, 1962: 14–17; and Sussman, 1953: 18). The narrowing has placed married youngsters at the mercy of their parents.

Youth: An Interest Group and a Social Class

Clearly I have been considering youth in effect as a "social class," (and as a social class relatively independent of the social stratification system of adults). Especially in relation to the authority structure of their schools and colleges ("imperatively co-ordinated association" [see Dahrendorf,

[11]American university students at this time also appear to have been remarkably quiescent. See Jacob (1957: 1–2) "A dominant characteristic of students of the current generation is that they are gloriously contented both in regard to their present day-to-day activities and their outlook for the future. . . . The traditional moral virtues are valued by almost all students."

1959: 167 f.]), the young share latent and manifest interests and constitute a social class at least in the sense defined by Dahrendorf.[12] Youth constitute a quasi-group from which particular interest groups—the agents of conflict and change—are recruited. Our students are such an interest group, engaged in a "class" conflict. They say they are protesting about power. They are right. Of course they protest about other things, too: about university teaching and examining, capitalism, imperialism, technocratic values, bureaucracy, Biafra and Vietnam. But their central concern is power for themselves—both immediately, in their colleges and universities, and a few years hence, in the wider society. Their loudest cry is for "participation." Student rebellion has found its strongest support among those students who are unlikely to get very important or well-paid jobs.

Those students—of the arts, of the social sciences, and of art—may have personalities which predispose them to radicalism. But business courses and teacher-training also centre on the social sciences: students in these professional schools have been quiet. For the moment, at least, there are quite attractive jobs for them to go to.

POWERLESSNESS AND TENSION

The rebellious students in the Art Colleges at Guildford and Hornsey face an uncertain future (see Boston, 1968): they are not marching confidently into assured positions in adult society. Social science students at Essex, the London School of Economics, at Birmingham and elsewhere, are in a similar case. Their position is strikingly different from that of students even seven years ago, when our universities were truly elitist. In 1962, Zweig's investigations showed students as essentially "restrained": "They are not angry young men." Zweig reached the conclusion that: "University education is likely to strengthen the conservative forces in society . . ." (1963: 199).

[12] "By social class shall be understood such organized or unorganized collectives of individuals as share manifest or latent interests arising from and related to the authority structure of imperatively coordinated associations. It follows from the definitions of latent and manifest interest that social classes are also conflict groups" (Dahrendorf, 1959: 238; see also Winslow, 1968).

The faculty members had already moved to the Right (even at the London School of Economics [Lipset, 1963: 343]). In contrast with the thirties, they had been caught up in wartime and in postwar Britain in the nation's political power structure. Shils (1955) has examined the resurgence in postwar Britain of the aristocratic–gentry culture based on the London–Oxford–Cambridge axis. Our senior academics are not radical, embittered, alienated men: they are men of influence and power on Whitehall committees. A diminishing proportion of their more numerous students have any hope of similar positions.

French student rebels have explained their May Revolution of 1968 quite explicit in these terms. As one has said: "The unemployment among graduates of the faculties of letters and in scientific research proves that university reform is required and therefore also a reform of society in so far as the latter cannot itself ensure balanced development" (Bourges, 1968: 85). Among French university graduates, it is said, "there is an absolutely astonishing number of unemployed" (p. 45). "Our graduates find themselves in an impossible situation today, without outlets in society" (p. 88). But, if they succeed in gaining entrance into society, their radicalism deserts them: "Once students have left the university and become cadres [administrators]—those of them who can find employment—they are integrated into the social system to the point of no longer offering it any challenge" (p. 88).

French students have fought explicitly for "integration" with society. If they could not be "integrated," absorbed into its central concerns and pre-occupations, then they must change or overthrow it. But primarily they want a place within it—involvement in its ongoing business, social, political, and economic. Their aim has been to modify and even remove the boundary with the adult world. They aim to remove the distinction between student and worker. They would change the student role from a social transient to "a resident of society here and now" (Pinner, 1968). Disputes about social boundaries are inevitably disputes about social roles: contemporary disputes about the student role are essentially disputes about the boundaries of the adult world.

I have argued elsewhere, using historical and

comparative data, that the powerlessness of the young can be an important source of social tension and change (Musgrove, 1968b). Intergenerational conflict is a cause rather than a consequence of social change. When the young are integrated into the social structure and accorded high status, the tempo of social change is slow. In England today the powerlessness of the young is an obvious source of social innovation. Quicker routes into adult territory are attempted, particularly through early marriage. The heroes of youth are pop singers, song writers, and clothes designers who have achieved their positions young, without long years of adolescent servitude (see Sugarman, 1967).

Planned change is occurring because organized youth have put effective pressure on adult authorities. The Latey Report (HMSO, 1967) is the prelude to legislation which will lower the age of majority to 18. There will be no need for parental consent to marry at 18, and full contractual capacity will be attained at the same age. After a joint declaration by the Committee of University Vice-Chancellors and the National Union of Students (October 1967), the universities are bringing students into their highest councils.

And yet there is no radical change in the distribution of power positions. Only by completely re-phasing the life-cycle of man in modern societies could this be achieved. People would then move to and fro across the boundary of society throughout their lives: the longer expectation of life makes such an episodic life-style possible, the rapid obsolescence of knowledge makes it necessary. Men would have a number of quite different careers—and perhaps wives—in the course of their longer lives. Many would move into society much earlier than at present; and out again at intervals throughout life for refreshment, and re-styling as "re-treads," in educational institutions which would cater for people at all stages of life.

EDUCATION: A DEPOSITORY, NOT AN OPPORTUNITY

Such an interpenetration of the young and the mature might reduce the tension between the age groups and slow down tht tempo of change. But I do not think we need fear stagnation from these circumstances, because they will not come about.

Two developments are likely: the first is institutional, the second ideological. At the institutional level we shall probably devise educational agencies which are intended primarily to neutralize superfluous youth. The Crowther Report (HMSO 1959) recommended institutions for older adolescents which would not be vocational, nor preparatory for university education. They would be, in effect, depositories for the redundant young. The American junior college (as described by Clark, 1960) seems to be a similar institution for "cooling them out." Devices of this kind are still more urgent in developing Afro–Asian countries with their large populations of youth and ambitious educational programmes. Since they cannot be absorbed into the social order, a large proportion of educated Ghanaians, for example, are located on the margin of society in a Workers' Brigade (see McQueen, 1964; Hodge, 1964; Foster, 1965). Ceylon is inventing a similar mechanism (a National Youth Organization) for a similar purpose (see Passanake, 1969).

IDENTITY-PLAY AND ROLE DEPRIVATION

At the ideological level we shall further elaborate the theory of adolescence which has changed remarkably little since Stanley Hall. Hall knew that he was describing a non-existent creature: all his adolescents were "precocious"; and if all were, surely none could be (Hall, 1965).[13] We shall continue to justify an outside position for adolescents in terms of their alleged instability and lack of realism—although compelling English research in the past decade shows their stability of interests and strong sense of realism (cf. Liversidge, 1962; Veness, 1962; Katz, 1963). (One reason why we cannot easily manipulate them into studying science and technology is the persistence and stability of their values and attitudes [see Kelley, 1961]. Terman's retrospective study [1955] of gifted Californians indicates that adolescent stability may pose a similar problem in America). We shall place the young in socially marginal circumstances, without occupational roles, so that they can scarcely avoid a "crisis of

[13]For a discussion of the social function of theories of adolescence see Musgrove (1967).

identity"; and we shall advocate still longer exclusion from society as a cure—for identity-play and "experiences as-if."

We shall also justify their exclusion from employment because of the "culture-shock" which work allegedly gives (Dansereau, 1968). All the indications in English are that the shock is at school rather than work. Once again analysis in terms of values has diverted attention from the main issue: that the work role is a role in the adult world. A recent national survey of 15-year-old English boys and girls at school showed that 75% would rather be at work than at school; and among 16-year-olds at work, 90% preferred being at work to being at school (HMSO, 1968c; Musgrove, 1966b). This preference was based principally on the fact that at work they were treated as adults. My own research on 18-year-olds at the university and comparable 18-year-olds at work led me to the conclusion that the university was by far the more problematical (and perhaps damaging) social environment (Musgrove, 1968c). But a swollen population of university students, in positions of subordination and social irrelevance, may be the most effective device we have known for ensuring a sustained critique of society and a constant strain toward social innovation.

REFERENCES

ABRAMS, M. 1961. *Teenage Consumer Spending in 1959.* London: London Press Exchange.

ABRAMS, P., AND LITTLE, A. 1965a. "The young voter in British politics." *British J. of Sociology, 16.*

——— 1965b. "The young activist in British politics." *British J. of Sociology, 16.*

BERGE, A. 1964. "Young people in the Occident and Orient." *International J. of Adult and Youth Education, 16.*

BERGER, B. 1963. "Adolescence and beyond." *Social Problems, 10* (Spring).

BOSSARD, J. H. S. 1954. *The Sociology of Child Development.* New York: Harper & Row.

BOSTON, R. 1968. "Artburst." *New Society* (June 20).

BOURGES, H. 1968. *The Student Revolt: The Activists Speak.* London: Jonathan Cape.

BRILL, H. 1964. "Can we train away the unemployed?" *Labour Today, 3* (October–November).

CLARK, B. R. 1960. *The Open Door College.* New York: McGraw-Hill.

COLEMAN, J. S. 1961. *The Adolescent Society.* New York: Free Press.

DAHRENDORF, R. 1959. *Class and Class Conflict in Industrial Society.* London: Routledge & Kegan Paul.

DANSEREAU, H. K. 1968. "Work and the teen-ager." In A. E. Winder and D. L. Angus (eds.), *Adolescence: Contemporary Studies.* New York: American Book.

FOSTER, P. 1965. *Education and Social Change in Ghana.* London: Routledge & Kegan Paul.

GALES, K. E. 1966. "A campus revolution." *British J. of Sociology, 17.*

HANCOCK, A., AND WAKEFORD, J. 1965. "The young technicians." *New Society, 5* (January 14).

HALL, G. S. 1965. *Adolescence, 1.*

HMSO. 1968a. *The Flow into Employment of Scientists, Engineers and Technologists* (The Swann Report).

——— 1968b. *Enquiry into the Flow of Candidates in Science and Technology* (The Dainton Report).

——— 1968c. *Schools Council Enquiry 1: Young School Leavers.*

——— 1967. *Report of the Committee on the Age of Majority* (The Latey Report).

——— 1963. *Report: Higher Education.*

——— 1960. *Report of the Committee on Youth Services in England and Wales* (the Albermarle Report).

——— 1959. *Report of the Central Advisory Council for Education* (The Crowther Report).

HODGE, P. 1964. "The Ghana Worker's Brigade: A project for unemployed youth." *British J. of Sociology 15.*

JACOB, P. E. 1957. *Changing Values in College.* New York: Harper.

KAHL, J. A. 1953. "Educational and occupational aspirations of 'common man' boys." *Harvard Educational Rev. 23.*

KATZ, M. 1963. *Decisions and Values.* New York: College Entrance Examination Board.

KELLEY, P. J. 1961. "An investigation of the factors which influence grammar school pupils to prefer scientific subjects." *British J. of Educational Psychology.*

LASLETT, P. 1965. *The World We Have Lost.* London: Methuen.

LIPSET, S. M. 1963. *Political Man*. Mercury Books.

—— AND ALTBACH, P. 1966. "American student protest." *New Society* (September).

LIVERSIDGE, W. 1962. "Life chances." *Sociological Rev. 10*.

LOGAN, R. F. L., AND GOLDBERG, E. M. 1953. "Raising eighteen in a London suburb." *British J. of Sociology 4* (No. 4).

MC QUEEN, A. 1964. "Education, unemployment and African work." *Venture 16* (March).

MEAD, M. 1962. *Male and Female*. London: Penguin Books.

—— 1948. "Social change and cultural surrogates." In C. Kluckhohn and H. A. Murray (eds.). *Personality in Nature, Society and Culture*. New York: Alfred A. Knopf.

MUSGROVE, F. 1968a. "The adolescent ghetto." In *Youth, Work and Employment*. New York: T. Y. Crowell.

—— 1968b. "Youth and Social Change." In A. E. Winder and D. L. Angus (eds.). *Adolescence: Contemporary Studies*. New York: American Book.

—— 1968c. "Personal problems in learning environments." *Educational Research 10* (June).

—— 1967a. "University freshmen and their parents' attitudes." *Educational Research 10*.

—— 1967b. "Childhood and adolescence." In HMSO, *The Educational Implications of Social and Economic Change*. London: Schools Council Working Paper 12.

—— 1966a. *The Family, Education and Society*. London: Routledge & Kegan Paul.

—— 1966b. "The social needs and satisfactions of some young people." *British J. of Educational Psychology 36*.

—— 1965. *Youth and the Social Order*. Bloomington: Indiana Univ. Press.

—— 1963a. "Inter-generation attitudes." *British J. of Social and Clinical Psychology*.

—— 1963b. "Population changes and the status of the young since the eighteenth century." *Sociological Rev. 11*.

NILES, F. S. 1968. *The Influence of Parents and Peers on Adolescent Girls*. M.Ed. thesis, University of Manchester.

OGBURN, W. F., AND NIMKOFF, M. F. 1965. *Technology and the Changing Family*. Boston: Houghton-Mifflin.

PASSANAKE, D. M. P. B. 1969. "Deploying youth." *London Times* (January 8).

PEARCE, J. J. 1968 "The expansion of sixth forms." *Universities Q. 23* (Winter).

PINNER, F. 1968. "Tradition and transgression: Western European students in the Postwar world." *Daedalus 97* (Winter)

RILEY, N. W., AND MOORE, M. E. 1961. "Adolescent values and the Riesman Typology: An empirical analysis." In S. M. Lipsett and L. Lowenthal, *Culture and Social Character*. New York: Free Press.

RUDD, E. 1967. "Too many pure scientists." *New Society* (August 17).

SCHOFIELD, M. 1968. *The Sexual Behavior of Young People*. London: Penguin Books.

SHILS, E. 1955. "The intellectuals in Great Britain." *Encounter* (April).

SHIMBORI, M. 1968. "The sociology of a student movement: a Japanese case study." *Daedalus* (Winter).

STEVENSON, T. H. C. 1920. "The fertility of various social classes." *J. of the Royal Statistical Society*.

SUGARMAN, B. 1967. "Involvement in youth culture, academic achievement and conformity in school." *British J. of Sociology 18*.

SUSSMAN, M. B. 1953. "The help pattern in the middle class family." *American Soc. Rev. 18*.

TAEUBER, I. 1964 "Japan's population: Miracle or case study?" In S. Mudd (ed.). *The Population Crisis and the Use of World Resources*. Hague.

TERMAN, L. M. 1955. "Are scientists different?" *Scientific American 192* (January).

VENESS, T. 1962. *School Leavers*. London: Methuen.

VUCHMICH, M. N. 1964. "Values of Canadian young people." *International J. of Adult and Youth Education 16*.

WEBSTER, H. *et al*. 1962. "Personality changes in college students." New York: John Wiley.

WESTLEY, W. A., AND ELKIN, F. 1957. "The protective environment and adolescent socialization." *Social Forces 35*.

WINSLOW, R. W. 1968. "Status management in the adolescent social system." *British J. of Sociology 19* (No. 2).

WRIGHT, D. S. 1962 "A comparative study of the adolescent's concepts of his parents and teachers." *Educational Rev. 14*.

YULE, G. U. 1906. "On changes in the marriage and birth rates in England and Wales during the past half century." *J. of the Royal Statistical Society 69*.

ZWEIG, F. 1963. "The student in the age of anxiety." Heinemann.

Chapter 20: Suggested Additional Readings

BAHADOR, D., & ADDISON, W. S.   Youth at the crossroads: A comparison of American and Iranian adolescents. *Adolescence,* 1969, *4*(13), 1–18. This interesting comparison of adolescents in Iran and in the United States indicates the cultural bases of differences between them, and cites advantages and disadvantages of each nationality.

BEAUCHAMP, E. R.   Recent trends in the Japanese student movement. *Midwest Quarterly,* 1971, *12*(3), 257–267. The author discusses various Japanese student activists and defines differences in their goals, grievances, and modes of protest.

BETENSKY, M.   The role of the adolescent in Israeli collectives. *Adolescence,* 1967, *2*(7), 335–344. The author concludes that an individual does not achieve full identity at adolescence, but is given a defined status in the collective. By fulfilling the obligations accompanying this status, he prepares himself in the automatic junior community to advance to an adult level in the collective in the future.

CLARK, P. P., & CLARK, T. N.   Writers, literature, and student movements in France. *Sociology of Education,* 1969, *42*(4), 293–314. Changes in the student cultures of France are traced through this century. The man of letters has ceased to provide students with charismatic "Latin Quarter" leadership, while student leadership has gained.

HAHN, J. W.   The Komosomol Kollektiv as an agency of political socialization. *Youth and Society,* 1969, *1*(2), 219–239. The writer describes how the Komosol, or Young Communist League, whose members are between age 14 and 28, aids in the socialization of Soviet youth.

HICKROD, L. J. H., & HICKROD, G. A.   Communist Chinese and the American adolescent subcultures. In G. D. Winter & E. M. Nuss (Eds.), *Identity and Awareness.* Oakland, N. J.: Scott, Foresman, 1969. Pp. 280–288. Chinese and American adolescents are compared within the contexts of their separate cultures. This article offers a provocative, though somewhat disturbing, analysis of how societies mold their youth.

JOCANO, F. L.   Youth in a changing society. *Youth and Society,* 1969, *1*(1), 73–89. The author considers aspects of rapid change in the Philippines as they relate to youth. He also considers particular youth types including the street-corner groups, "liberated females," and university students.

KRAFT, I.   Child-rearing in the Soviet Union. *Children,* 1965, *12*(6), 235–238. Kraft says that little is known for certain about child-rearing in the Soviet Union, but he reviews what is known. He discusses family life, child-rearing patterns, and educational goals. In a number of cases, the points presented differ from general views Americans hold about life in Russia.

MCNASSOR, D.   Social structure for identity in adolescence: Western Europe and America. *Adolescence,* 1967, *11*(7), 311–344. McNassor draws a comparative picture of adolescent identity development in Europe and America. Although there are great differences among adolescents of European countries, the various nationalities have more in common than any one of them has with adolescents in America.

PETERSON, D. R. & MIGLIORINO, G.   Pancultural factors of parental behavior in Sicily and the United States. *Child Development,* 1967, *38*(4), 966–991. Child-rearing practices of American and Sicilian parents were studied by means of interviews. Few differences emerged in parental affection, but striking differences appeared in parental control, chiefly in the areas of sexual and aggressive behavior.

SHAW, M. E.   Attribution of responsibility by adolescents in two cultures. *Adolescence,* 1968, *3*(9), 33–38. Responses from white and black high school students, almost all of whom attended racially segregated schools, were analyzed to determine similarities and differences in their attitudes about home, school, religion, and morality.

SHORT, L. N.   Youth in Australia: a survey of background and problems. *Youth and Society,* 1970, *1*(3), 289–308. The author describes the thinking and activities of Australian youth, especially those in universities, and concludes that available research is insufficient to determine how well youth's problems are being solved.

STOODLEY, B. H.   Normative family orientations of Chinese-college students in Hong Kong. *Journal of Marriage and the Family,* 1967, *29*(4), 773–782. A random sampling of Chinese students was interviewed with reference to family norms. While adopting the Western norm of individual choice in marriage, these students only partially accepted Western norms of dating and romantic love. The students are in the mainstream of Western influence but observe certain proprieties of Confucian tradition.

TEFFT, S. K.   Anomy, values and culture change among teen-age Indians: an exploratory study. *Sociology of Education,* 1967, *40*(2), 145–157. A study of teenagers in several Indian tribes revealed that those in certain tribes had definite value systems. However, the Arapaho teenagers seemed unable to commit themselves to a set of values, a situation which might possibly be ascribed to anomy (a lack of norms) within their tribe.

Youth and Society.   See issues of this journal for frequent articles concerning youth in other lands.

21

The Youth and Society

A major issue relative to any discussion of youth in modern society concerns whether the teenager today is a victim of "the times." What specific price, if any, does youth pay for having been born on planet Earth in this particular era? What are the hazards facing youth in the contemporary world?

For one thing, writes Goffman (1959), the current mode of personality development requires the individual raised in an urban-industrial environment to play varied, often conflicting parts at different life stages, in the manner of varying personae appearing on an array of different stages in the theatre. As a result, serious questions arise concerning the individual's "real character" which may be concealed behind his "situational character." Present day urban-industrial adolescents experience a new style of socialization, one which is more impersonal, more abstract, and more complex than that encountered by any previous youth. It is hardly surprising, therefore, that many psychologists have identified as the number one psychiatric problem of our times the problem of identity (Sebald, 1968).

A second hazard of modern life is the modification of our traditional sense of time. Glasgow (1970), reporting a conversation with anthropologist Loren Eiseley, quotes Eiseley as declaring that there is no such thing as a total "now," in terms of "the time that exists in our heads (p. 90)." All those persons who presumably live in the here-and-now may actually be living in quite different time regions and areas philosophically. One person may live in the future, and another in the past, because of the different pace at which each lives. Some persons project more immediately into the present, while others linger in the past. Hence, one of an individual's problems is somehow to gear his own time clock to keep pace with those persons immediately around him without at the same time losing track of time elements in the world at large. Perhaps some individuals have more difficulty adjusting to other people because, as Eiseley states, "we really occupy quite different dimensions and some of us are walking like ghosts through the world of other people (Glasgow, 1970, p. 90)."

A third hazard derives from the population explosion, which may cause an individual to feel infinitely small in the total order of things and increase his subjection to group pressure. However, Milgram (1965) has pointed out that group pressures may have positive as well as negative effects, for example, by enhancing an individual's positive potential rather than the negative. Also, large-group living can result in more freedom for the individual by reducing his visibility, permitting him greater privacy, and offering him many alternative ways of life.

A fourth hazard for youth derives from today's apparently endless spasm of spectacular events, including space flights and walks on the moon. Loren Eiseley believes young people have come to think of science, and perhaps life, as a series of spectacular sporting events (Glasgow, 1970). Perhaps this generation is in danger of becoming jaded and bored and developing a "come entertain me" attitude toward life. An individual may lose his capacity for simple satisfactions when he constantly expects ever more remarkable scientific accomplishments. Caught up in a whirlwind of change, he becomes unable to stand still, even for a moment, to appreciate the quieter moods of life. This tendency may be especially marked among youth who, in almost any culture, normally like a change of pace and excitement.

However, other writers, among them Marshall McLuhan, have stressed the positive factors which accrue to life in our contemporary, automation-oriented society. According to McLuhan (1968), automation is "the invasion of the mechanical world by the instantaneous character of electricity (p. 301)." The mechanized technology of the industrial age has given way to a dramatically new electronic technology that is producing an electrically configured world, to which we must relate in completely new ways. The study of whole configurations of patterns—for example, those which make up a national economy, or a political system, or a culture—as contrasted with the mere collection of information which characterized the mechanistic period, will thus become man's responsibility for the new times.

This new age of automation and electricity—which McLuhan terms the electric age—has made obsolete a school curriculum of separate subjects because any subject treated in depth immediately relates to other subjects. If our school curricula persist in their present state of fragmentation, they will inevitably produce a citizenry unable to understand the automated world in which they live. In addition, "automation is information," and the future of work consists of "learning a living." McLuhan also notes that the erstwhile gap between work and leisure is closing; in the past, leisure meant the absence of work, or idleness, but during the present electric age we feel at leisure when we are most intensely involved, like the artists of past ages.

The electric age has covered the world with a global network of communication, and thanks to the mass communications media, we can react to the world as a whole. With magic gadgetry, events occurring vast distances away can be merged with the here and close-at-hand, and the future can be one with the present. In the same way, a great variety and expanse of operations within society can at once become a unified whole; that is, an individual does not have to experience such operations over a long period of time, in a fragmented manner, in order to comprehend them. Films and other visual aids not only speed up the learning process but provide more meaningful integration of knowledge both in space and in time. Indeed, the "entire world now reveals itself to us past and present, like a growing

REFERENCES

DUBOS, R. Stimulus response—we can't buy our way out. *Psychology Today,* 1970, *3*(1), 20–21, 86–87.

DUBOS, R. Man over-adapting. *Psychology Today,* 1971, *4*(9), 50–53.

GLASGOW, R. W. Ego and evolution—a conversation with Loren Eiseley. *Psychology Today,* 1970, *4*(5), 74–76, 90–96.

GOFFMAN, I. *The presentation of self in every day life.* Garden City, New York: Doubleday and Co., 1959.

KALVEN, H. The problems of privacy in the year 2000. *Daedalus,* 1967, *96*(3), 876–882.

MARIN, P. The open truth and fiery vehemence of youth: A sort of soliloquy. In H. Gadlin and B. E. Garskof (Eds.) *The uptight society: A book of readings.* Belmont, Calif.: Brooks-Cole, 1970. Pp. 352–365.

MC LUHAN, M. Automation: Learning a living. In A. E. Winder and D. L. Angus (Eds.) *Adolescents: Contemporary studies.* New York: American Book Co., 1968 pp. 229–308.

MILGRAM, S. Liberating effects of group pressure. *Journal of Personality and Social Psychology,* 1965, *1*(2), 127–134.

SEBALD, H. *Adolescence: A sociological analysis.* New York: Appleton-Century-Crofts, 1968.

WINDER, A. E., & ANGUS, D. L. *(eds.) Adolescents: Contemporary studies.* New York: American Book Co., 1968.

Hangloose Identity or Living Death: The Agonizing Choice of Growing Up Today

POVL W. TOUSSIENG

The author believes that many young people have been unable to find a workable ego-identity because they find no continuity between their life in the suburbs and the larger world. Youth are too honest and too stubborn to settle for a false compromise, and yet they cannot bridge the gap.

By combining insights from work in psychoanalysis and anthropology, Erik Erikson several decades ago formulated a theory of psychosocial development from birth into senescence which has had a monumental influence on all the behavioral sciences. The unique features of this theory are that psychic development is continuously viewed in interaction with the environment and the cultural setting, and that specific tasks are described for each developmental phase. The task of adolescence, crucial for reaching true adulthood, is the achievement of a firm ego identity.

Erikson (4) defines ego identity as follows: "Ego identity, in its subjective aspect, is the awareness of the fact that there is a selfsameness and continuity to the ego's synthesizing methods and that these methods are effective in safeguarding the sameness and continuity of one's meaning

for others." In other words, for a child to be able to develop a sense of having a stable meaning to others he must be able to count on a reasonable selfsameness and continuity in his environment, primarily in important adults around him and in his general culture. Youth growing up in today's atomic and electronic era, however, lives in a world that is changing so rapidly, so abruptly, and in such an unpredictable manner that the continuity and stability of the culture, as well as of the adults in that culture, have been severely affected if not practically destroyed.

Insecurity, bewilderment, and confusion are evident in many contemporary adults, although they desperately try to hide it. They vigorously deny that there is any need to make a change. They glorify the "good old days," and more and more savagely criticize and attack those adults and youngsters who struggle to find ways to help them adapt to the new, rapidly changing world, and to assimilate the many changes which already have occurred. A hundred million American adults regularly try to escape from all pain and all tension by resorting to alcohol or by taking

This paper is a condensed version of a presentation at the weekly Colloquium, Department of Psychiatry, Neurology and Behavioral Sciences, University of Oklahoma School of Medicine, Oklahoma City, Oklahoma, March 29, 1968.

From P. W. Toussieng, Hangloose identity, or living death: The agonizing choice of growing up today. *Adolescence*, 1968, *3*(2), 307–318.

tranquilizing drugs. These same adults are very upset about the two million or so youngsters who are experimenting with drugs and call them "escapists." Yet most, if not all, researchers agree that the true drug experimenters among the young are not trying to escape, but are actively seeking answers, particularly related to the question of how to learn to tolerate and integrate the intense and constant stimulation coming from a kaleidoscopic world. They want to learn to live with the pain rather than get away from it, as the adult majority is trying to do.

Unfortunately the escapist stance of most adults today leaves them caught in a vicious cycle of ever-increasing problems and fears. While denying their fear of change and difference, the adults also have to deny the need for change, and thus they become paralyzed and consequently cannot engage effectively in attempts to solve the crucial problems which face mankind today. As these problems are left unsolved, the emergency grows, causing more adult fears and further action paralysis.

The situation does not get any better when the panic erupts into frantic and desperate actions. These actions are becoming increasingly bizarre because they are dictated by the hope that the world can somehow be kept from changing or even that the calendar can somehow be turned back to the 19th Century. Examples of inappropriate reactions of adults to change can be seen in the intensity of emotion aroused by the U.S. Supreme Court decision regarding prayers in public schools, the exaggerated fear of even minor, but vocal, Civil Rights leaders and of the "hippies," and the increasing sadistic adult violence toward young people who openly express their wish to "change things."

Adult fearfulness and aversion to change keeps American Christian churches from making more than token gestures in moving from orthodoxy and towards the practice of Christian ethics, as demanded by many young people today. Even worse, adult control of the schools and of higher education is used to prevent any changes which might truly update the curriculum. As a result, it is becoming more and more difficult for students to find anything in their studies that is relevant to the world in which they live. Yet the world they are not supposed to know about is constantly kept before their eyes by the news media, particularly television, and by their own daily personal experiences.

In addition, an ever-increasing number of parents are quietly resigning from their parental duties. It is not because they do not care; they simply do not know how to respond to the present world, and feel unable to predict what the world will be like even ten years from now. Thus they do not know what to tell their children or how to prepare them for the future. Some parents hold on until their children have reached puberty, then turn them loose. Again, this does not reflect malice or lack of love on the part of the parents, but simply that they feel they have nothing more to offer. And so they turn their children over to other adults, who are considered "experts" or pose as such. These "experts" are primarily teachers and policemen, who, unfortunately, are as unable as the parents to guess what the future might hold for the children, and who are much more prejudiced and tied to the past than are most parents. The result is that many—if not most—contemporary children are left to find growth support from multiple, haphazard, and often totally inappropriate and irrelevant sources.

These developments are particularly unfortunate because, in recent decades, the onset of puberty is tending to occur earlier and earlier, and therefore hits many children at a psychosocially immature age. This would call for more, rather than for less, support during the years of puberty. The children who enter puberty early face a period of adolescence of up to 8–10 years, wherein they are too young to be adults and yet too old to be children. This long period is made even more difficult because of the intense adult pressure on most American children today to grow up in a hurry. Yet at the same time the adult world withholds all adult privileges from the youngsters until they have reached "legal age."

A further handicap to growing up today is that contemporary youngsters have an increasingly difficult time finding suitable adult models with whom they can identify. In addition, as pointed out by Friedenberg (5), schools place the adolescent under overwhelming pressure to accept and identify with patently outmoded values and techniques of living. If the adolescent is able to resist all these pressures, he has nowhere to turn for support and guidance but to other adolescents. In other words, the teenagers are left to raise themselves and each other—a task that would be difficult enough even if there weren't so much interference and sabotage. It is a tribute to our youth that they will manage to grow up under such circumstances.

Nowhere is the pressure on youth greater than in the middle-and upper classes of our society. Keniston's (6) penetrating study gives us a chilling picture of the psychological state of generally bright middle-class college students who have suffered no obvious psychological or social hardships while they were growing up but are unable to commit themselves to a career or to the society in which they have grown up. Keniston studied the influence on these students of their families and was less interested in the effect of society itself on his subjects. Nevertheless, many of his findings can be used to support the hypothesis that the struggle of bright and sensitive students in part, or maybe wholly, have resulted from their inability to usefully bridge the gap between the middle-class techniques of living (which they have been taught) and the techniques actually required in order to live successfully in what Daniel Bell (1) has called the "postindustrial society." The symptom picture which they present, especially their fears of caring for others and of making commitments to anything, corresponds closely to what Erikson (4) described as "identity diffusion," the antithesis of a firm ego identity. These students have not been able to find a workable ego identity; they cannot find any continuity between what they have been taught in their suburbs, and what the world in which they live is actually like and requires. They are too honest and too stubborn to settle for a false compromise, and yet they cannot bridge the gap.

Because these uncommitted students still are fighting valiantly they are less severe casualties of their unbringing than the very large group of middle-class youngsters who never have fought back. They have surrendered to adult pressure and allowed themselves to be fitted with a false identity, complete with well-worn but hopelessly outdated 19th Century values. In return for their surrender and submission, these youngsters are showered with praise, approval, and scholarships

by adults who in the existence of these "ideal kids," see hope that the future will bring no changes after all. The sad fact is, however, that these youngsters who go through all the "right" motions in their lives are totally out of touch with the real world. They hardly know that a real world exists. It is for this reason that I call them "the living dead."

Between the uncommitted and the living dead there is a large group of youngsters who engage in vigorously independent behavior. Many of these young people are considered delinquent by adult society because they are caught breaking some law. Although adults do not agree on the causes of delinquent behavior, most of them are convinced that delinquent youngsters have either moral or character defects, or are more or less emotionally disturbed. People who, like myself, have had considerable experience with delinquents do indeed find some of them disturbed or warped in their psychological growth. We also find that a large, ever-growing percentage of delinquents do not show sufficient evidence of disturbance to deserve a psychiatric label.

A closer look at these "bad" youngsters will reveal that their behavior represents a refusal to choose "living death." These youngsters are stubbornly, clumsily, dangerously, and often vainly searching, and what they seek is a workable ego identity that will lead to adult maturity in the style of the second half of the 20th Century.

Most of all, these young people—like a handful of honest contemporary adults—are searching for a new and reliable value system that can serve as a guide for and monitor of their behavior. They know their search behavior tends to get out of hand, and they desperately long for adult support and guidance in their search. Instead they receive punishment or "treatment" from adults who see their behavior as rebellious and destructive to the "established values of our society." This adult view is based on the delusion that there still is a sufficient number of people in modern society who try to live by the Judaeo-Christian values they insist they have. But the many adults who talk one way and act in another are all too apparent to today's youngsters. Because of this hypocrisy no honest teen-ager can possibly identify with these adults. It is even more preposterous to insist that adolescent delinquent behavior is "rebellion." How can anyone rebel against such nebulous figures?

There are other youngsters whose search is just as intense but does not express itself in antisocial behavior. Their behavior may even be quite constructive. In this category we have, for example, the youngsters who leave their parent's church in order to be able to practice, through unselfish service to others, what they consider to be the essence of the Judaeo-Christian ethics. These young people are invariably viewed as "rebels" and "revolutionaries" by their elders and are treated accordingly. These youngsters do not view themselves as rebels since they actually pursue their beliefs in a positive way. There is no hostility toward adults, and the adult institutions from which they have disassociated themselves, simply because the adolescents consider them irrelevant.

In discussing the topic of authority, a young college student, Karen Wullenweber (8) recently wrote:

> After all, we grew up on the heels of the Nuremberg Trials where men were condemned to death for following orders rather than their conscience . . . . We perceive in those issues in which we dissent some moral aspect which we insist must be taken into account and which isn't. . . . Why would any young person who is concerned about social justice, Civil Rights, the peace movement, and international relations want to commit himself to a Church which does not overtly prove that these are Her concerns too? . . . It is the authentic service which is in fact rendered that constitutes the actual source of authority. When this authentic service is neglected by the authority figure, the basis for obedience then drops out.

It is regrettable that so many adults view these developments with dismay and disgust or try to belittle the quest of the young people for a new identity and new values. In so doing, the adults force the youngsters to leave their homes, their churches and schools, and to expose themselves to many totally unnecessary and grave dangers. In the past few years, thousands of middle-class youngsters have felt compelled to run away from their suburban existence and eventually experi-

ment with potentially dangerous drugs in an attempt to find the answers in their lives.

There also are small groups of youngsters who seek and find their identity by rebelling against the older generation. These young people are found in the militant Civil Rights groups, in militant student groups, and in other groups sometimes referred to as the "New Left." John Dippel (3), recently retired editorial chairman of the *Daily Princetonian,* in discussing such "student power" groups states: "Spokesmen for student power have conveyed well an awareness of student identity, but have only slightly been able to mobilize this unity of identity into action." Thus the students do find an identity through their negative stance, but they cannot act because they are rebelling against dead issues. As useful as their identity is to them, it is a sham identity because it is based on rebellion without a cause—or even a target.

Nevertheless, even these young people are trying to fight rather than surrender to living death. Recent events at many major universities in the Western world demonstrate that rebellious students, because they will not surrender to the past, can come to represent as much of a threat to existing society as the youngsters who refuse to choose living death. This shows how little there is left of society's official structure.

Slowly and reluctantly, some adults are beginning to realize that police clubs and tear gas bombs cannot stop the calendar. Business firms are having difficulty recruiting promising college graduates because the graduates do not find that business is interested in society. However, business is quietly beginning to make changes in order to adapt to the wishes of these determined young adults. Large law firms have difficulty recruiting enough top students from the best law schools even though starting salaries have been raised substantially. Graduate schools have fewer applicants to choose from even though vastly greater numbers are graduated from college. College students are critical of professional people because they seem to be interested only in making money, or in immersing themselves in their special professional interests without regard for people or for society. Even universities, those magnificent museums of the past and of contempt for ethics and for humanity, are being forced by their students to face the issues of the day and to pay their respect to the dignity of human beings.

The young of today are not fooled when adults claim they are protecting them from dangers the adults fear. The world of many American adults caved in when the Russians launched their Sputnik long before an American satellite was sent into space. As a result, school curricula were made a lot tougher, and training for the eventual operation and invention of new hardware was stressed heavily in schools and colleges. Only the "living dead" youngsters and a handful of others are following the bugle call.

The cream of American youth is being sent to Viet Nam with the excuse that adults are trying to save them from having to live under communism. It is a magnificent tribute to the many American young men, who are not fooled by the adult flagwavers, that they remain undaunted and maintain a very high morale overseas. Adults are quick to say that this morale is due to superior indoctrination; but it is hard to detect any signs of brainwashing in communications received from the overwhelming majority of those young men who are or who have been in Viet Nam. A good example is the following poem, written by a young Marine, Stephen Brown (22) from Lindenhurst, Long Island, after he and his company had spent forty-five days at Con Thien under continuous shelling. The rest of the company agreed that this poem expressed their feelings better than anything else. (Incidentally, Con Thien means "Place of Angels.")

> Hill of the Angels
> —a fitting name;
> No bells can be heard,
> But they are there just the same.
> Lifeless and mud-clad,
> A body still warm.
> The Hill of the Angels
> Takes a mother's firstborn.
> Sky above is broken
> By shell red with heat
> And for what? Freedom?
> Our reason is gone,
> But for the hill of our angels
> Death goes on.

"Our reason is gone" reflects the skepticism of these young men; and yet they fight well, and do not become bitter and cynical. The explanation may lie in the fact that many of the young men going overseas see it as an opportunity to get to know themselves under the extreme circumstances of war. They hope to achieve a firm ego identity while learning to master the ever-changing, unpredictable, mortally dangerous and often totally overwhelming situations to which the war exposes them. It is striking how few Viet Nam veterans come back talking about the war; instead they talk about the way in which their experiences there have helped them grow up more than they could have managed in any other way. Thus the war, *because* of its risks and danger, is seen as an opportunity for growth.

Other young people seek that opportunity through LSD and other drugs which are known to involve grave risks, and still others take the big leap by enlisting in the Peace Corps and in Vista. These youngsters carry out what they feel they must do quietly, relentlessly, and without being impressed with the sacrifices they have to make. It is obvious that young men and women with that much strength cannot help but have a profound influence on what will happen in this country in the next ten to twenty years. They are likely to have the ability to build a bridge leading from the present to the future, and to formulate entirely new goals, values, and ways of life for all of us.

The older generation is keenly aware of this. It is obviously threatened by its lack of leverage to control the younger generation. The clear warning coming from the youngsters, that the present power structure in society will be put out of office *in toto* as sufficient numbers of youngsters reach voting age is an even greater threat to the older politicians. As a result, the older generation is increasingly mobilizing its police powers against the youth of today. The objective is not only to "stick" as many young people as possible with criminal records, but also to make it impossible for the more vocal and militant ones to finish their education. An ever-increasing number of young students are being mauled and mutilated by callous policemen who supposedly were trained to protect them. In the U.S., the right to bear arms via the draft is now being used as punishment—a death sentence without due process of law and allowing no defense. Thousands of American young men have been forced to go into permanent exile in foreign countries without even the prospect of a visit to the U.S. One may well ask how many young men, who are able and willing to think, a modern country can afford to lose just to keep the older generation in the saddle a few years longer.

It is inevitable, however, that youth must win out; and it is fitting that we listen to them as to what type of person they see as being able to live in the modern world. First of all, it is clear that youth believes that man must learn to struggle by himself against his fears and impulses before he can possibly bring out his potentials in a way which has real personal and objective meaning. Thus the growth process in children must allow opportunity for much more personal initiative while it still offers the children the necessary protection and support until they no longer need it.

In the years to come, discontinuity rather than continuity is likely to become the norm. In order to live in his environment, man will need an ego identity built on discontinuity rather than continuity; on change rather than on sameness. He must be able to tolerate his changing roles in and his changing meanings to his environment. A person's feeling of selfsameness and continuity will somehow have to include and base itself on all those changes and discontinuities. Thus ego identity will be built on the flexibility and adaptability of the ego as it changes roles in an ever-changing and flexible environment. Ethics, too, will need to be more flexible and adapted to changing situations. (Simmons and Winograd (7) have proposed the name "hangloose ethics.") The danger will still be identity diffusion, which would mean ego flexibility without adaption—an ego flexibility which is not meaningfully related to the environment most of the time.

Many young people today are trying to work out just such a new identity. They deserve, need, and want help from the older generation. Though most older people feel like the proverbial fish out of water in the new era they still have a wider perspective on many things. Young people are eager to listen to their elders, so long as they are not being given sermons or commercials. In order to remain human, mankind must achieve a meaningful identity as well as values and beliefs. The generation reaching adulthood now is deeply concerned about this very task, and is making major sacrifices to solve it. The future is thus in good hands, and there is hope for mankind.

REFERENCES

BELL, DANIEL. "The Postindustrial Society," In Ginzburg, Eli, Ed.: *Technology and Social Change.* New York: Columbia University Press, 1964.

BROWN, STEPHEN. *Daily Oklahoman,* Oklahoma City, Okla., October 9, 1967.

DIPPEL, JOHN. "Student Power." *Princeton Alumni Weekly,* 1968, *16,* pp. 10–15.

ERIKSON, ERIK H. "Ego Development and Historical Change," *Psychoanalytic Study of the Child.* New York: International Universities Press, 1946, *2,* pp. 359–396.

FRIEDENBERG, EDGAR Z. *The Vanishing Adolescent.* New York: Dell Publishing Co., 1959, pp. 223.

KENISTON, KENNETH. *The Uncommitted.* New York: Dell Publishing Co., 1965, pp. 500.

SIMMONS, J. L., AND WINOGRAD, BARRY. *It's Happening.* Santa Barbara: Marc-Laird Publications, 1966, pp. 174.

WULLENWEBER, KAREN. "Authority as Collegians See It." *St. Anthony Messenger,* 1968, 75:9, pp. 13–19.

Television and the Adolescent

MARC D. BARANOWSKI

Utilizing the currently available research, the author explores adolescents' tele-viewing habits and the various ways in which television influences teenage behavior.

Nationwide television programming first came to the United States in the late 1940's, and by the mid 1950's most American homes had at least one television set. Today's adolescents have grown up with television; it has always been available to them, and it is probable that most adolescents have never paused to consider what life might be like without the "tube." Indeed, such a consideration on the part of teenagers may be next to impossible, because the environment created by television has had such a total and all-encompassing effect on them that it is doubtful that they can really "escape" from it in order to study it. The parents of today's adolescents are in a much different position with regard to this particular medium. The over-thirty segment of the population, whether or not they know it and whether or not they like it, are aliens in television land. Television, like the moon rocket, is looked upon by most of these parents as one of the curious marvels of our technological age and is still regarded with some degree of amazement and wonder. They generally regard it not as a major influence in the creation of the environment, but rather as another of the many electronic gadgets to be reckoned with within that

environment. Television has thus had a much different and more influence on today's adolescents than on their parents, and this cannot be ignored in any analysis of present-day adolescent life. The purpose of this paper will therefore be to explore the ways in which adolescents use television and the ways in which it affects their attitudes and behavior.

Viewing Time

How much time do adolescents spend watching television? Young (28) surveyed junior high school students and found a range of 1½ to 5½ hours of television viewing daily. Witty and Kinsella (27), in their 1958 sample of Chicago-area high school students, found an average viewing time of 13 hours per week; interestingly enough, the parents of those adolescents averaged 19 hours of viewing time per week. Schneider (22) reported that some teenagers spend as much as 51 hours per week watching television. Schramm, Lyle, and Parker (23), in an extensive set of studies on the effects of television on children, found that in the sixth grade, when the child is entering the adolescent period, he averages between 2 and 2½ hours of viewing time per weekday and about 17

Grateful appreciation is expressed to William R. Looft for his valuable comments on an early draft of this paper.

Marc D. Baranowski, "Television and the Adolescent," *Adolescence*, Fall 1971, 6(23); 369–396.

to 18 hours per week. A peak of slightly over 3 hours per weekday is reached somewhere between the sixth and eighth grades. The amount of viewing time then decreases slowly and steadily and by the twelfth grade (about age 17), the adolescent is again watching an average of 2 to 2½ hours of television per weekday.

Why does the heaviest period of viewing occur between the sixth and eighth grades (age 11 to 13) and then drop off? Schramm and associates explain that the 11 to 13-year-old range, being the onset of adolescence brings with it new freedoms to stay up later in the evening, thus providing more viewing time. The gradual decrease in viewing time after this period is no doubt largely due to the social development of the adolescent. The television set is in the home, and home is not where most adolescents want to spend their time. Strivings for independence and increasing interest in the peer group, members of the opposite sex, and school activities generally mean less time for television. Radio listening also increases during this period and takes up some of the time previously set aside for television viewing. The Schramm *et al.* data suggest another reason for this decline. In the early school years, the more intelligent children tend to spend the greatest amount of time viewing television. But between the sixth and eighth grades the brighter children tend to drop from the ranks of the heavy viewers. In their sample of San Francisco adolescents, Schramm *et al.* found that the upper-third IQ children in eighth through twelfth grades spend over an hour per day less on television than the lower-third group. The researchers stated that their interviews with the more intelligent children indicated that by the time they are in high school, television has ceased being a challenge to them and they therefore appropriate less time to watching it.

Coleman (5) found that star athletes spend considerably less time attending to mass media (including television) than other students in those schools where athletics are highly rewarded; this trend was not evident in schools in which athletics are not highly rewarded. A similar pattern was found in relation to academic achievement: "scholars" spend less time viewing television than other students only if they attend schools at which scholastic achievement is highly rewarded. These data tend to support Coleman's "status frustra-

tion" hypothesis, which states that heavy mass media use occurs for an adolescent whose achievements are unrewarded. If the teenager's social system does not give him status or allow him positive self-evaluation, then he will turn to the mass media, where a negative self-evaluation is not so readily forthcoming. Coleman also found that television viewing is greater among adolescents from the lower social strata, and he felt that this may be due to the status frustration engendered by the low social position.

Schramm *et al.* (23) found a significantly greater percentage of working class tenth graders than middle class tenth graders in their "fantasy-oriented" group (high TV use, low print use excluding comic books and "pulp" magazines). These authors suggested that middle-class norms of self-betterment, activity, and future time orientation tend to push the middle class adolescent toward more "real-world" activities and leave him less time and less desire for television.

Even though the amount of television viewing decreases somewhat as adolescence progresses, teenagers do devote a considerable portion of their lives to the medium. A composite view of the data from the studies cited indicates that the "typical" high school student watches somewhere between 13 and 20 hours of television during any given week. Add to this the calculation by Hayakawa (10) which demonstrated that a child who has spent three to four hours per day in front of the set between the ages of three and 18 years will have accumulated over 22,000 hours of viewing time, and the data of Schramm *et al.* (23) indicating that from ages three to 16 the child spends more time in front of the television set than he spends in school. One must conclude that television is going to have some important effects.

Program Preferences

Perhaps a question more important than the one of *how much* television adolescents watch is the one of *what* they watch. Table 1 presents the favorite programs of adolescents as reported in the research of Atwood (1), Schramm *et al.* (23), and Witty and Kinsella (27). More recent data are not available.

Note that Table 1 lists program preferences. These are adolescents' favorite programs, but are

Table 1.   Favorite Programs of Adolescents, in Order of Preference

| 9th-12th Graders, 1958[a] | 12th Graders, 1958[b] | | High School Students 1963-1966[c] |
	Boys	Girls	
Maverick	Peter Gunn	77 Sunset Strip	I Spy
Gunsmoke	Maverick	Peter Gunn	Wild, Wild West
Steve Allen	77 Sunset Strip	Maverick	Dick Van Dyke
Shock Theatre	Rifleman	Playhouse 90	The Rogues
Father Knows Best	Science Fiction	Father Knows	The Fugitive
Playhouse 90	Theatre	Best	
Perry Como	Steve Allen	Loretta Young	Bonanza
American	Dick Clark	Dick Clark	Get Smart
Bandstand	Danny Thomas	Steve Allen	Shindig
Dick Clark	Gunsmoke	Ozzie & Harriet	Outer Limits
Meet McGraw		Bob Cummings	

[a]Witty and Kinsella (27), p. 520
[b]Schramm, Lyle, and Parker (23), p. 229.
[c]Atwood (1), p. 382.

these the programs that they regularly watch? There seems to be conflicting results on this point. Schramm *et al.* (23) found that diaries kept for them by their subjects indicated that teenagers' television viewing does tend to mirror program preferences. MacLean and Talbott (17) disagreed, for their data suggested that stated preferences are actually poor predictors of viewing behavior.

Program preferences can also be looked at in terms of types or categories of programs. In their 1958 San Francisco sample, Schramm *et al.* (23) found that for tenth grade boys the categories of favorite programs, in order of preference, were: Western, mystery, situation comedy, variety–comedy, adventure, and popular music; for girls the results were: popular music, situation comedy, mystery, Western, and variety–comedy. This list and Table 1 seem to indicate that adolescents go to television to be entertained; news programs, documentary series, and public affairs presentations are conspicuously absent from adolescents' lists of preferred programs and program types.

Schramm and associates reported other interesting findings regarding what adolescents watch. In one sample, they found that by the time children were in the sixth grade, 79 per cent of their viewing time was spent on programs which were best called "adult" in content. They also discovered that, in general, girls develop an interest in programs aimed at the adolescent and adult earlier

than do boys. Boys still tend to be watching cartoons and other juvenile programs when girls have already begun watching popular music shows and are swooning over television's latest detective or Western hero.

The study by Schramm *et al.* also indicated that parental influence on program preference is substantial during childhood but declines considerably during adolescence. The adolescent, in asserting his independence apparently tends to rebel against parents' advice on what programs to watch. At the same time he is being increasingly influenced by his peer group, and his viewing habits are likely to resemble those of his adolescent friends. Atwood (1) found that teenagers were somewhat better at predicting program preferences of their parents than were the parents at predicting preferences of their adolescent sons and daughters, although the accuracy of both groups was quite low.

Formulas and Stereotypes

At this point it is appropriate to look at the way in which television structures the content and information it presents. First of all, it appears that because of space and time limitations, television tends to simplify its material and therefore portrays life as considerably less complex than it really is. To facilitate this simplification, the medium works with formulas. O'Hara (21) described a formula as "the reduction of a basically complex situation to a few simplified elements, which appears to offer the receiver a ready solution to a problem" (p. 142). Formulas tend to give the viewer the impression that a successful philosophy of life can be reduced to a set of permanent rules such as "Work hard and you will succeed" and "Virtue is rewarded and evil punished." Television presents no insurmountable problems; to solve any problem one need only select the correct rule.

There is reason to believe that many viewers confuse reality with television fantasy. After a recent situation comedy "marriage," the actor and actress involved received several hundred wedding presents and cards from viewers wishing them a happy and successful married life. When the woman became "pregnant," the television couple received such advice as what hospital to go to and even how to avoid a miscarriage! While these sympathetic viewers may have been atypical, there is still the possibility that formula thinking interferes with a realistic and intelligent view of life. It can also lead to what O'Hara (21) called "bandwagon thinking"; that is, the person who has a problem does not seek a solution in terms of the problem itself, but he searches for an easy answer that has television-reinforced popular approval but is in actuality without depth or application to the problem.

An example of formula thinking can be found in television's treatment of good and evil. In television land, there are two types of actions: good and bad. Good actions are those which conform to the prevailing norms; bad actions are those which run counter to these norms. People can be classified according to their actions: Good acts are performed by good people and bad acts are performed by bad people. Violence and killing are justified when done by good people. Television, in fact, seems to condone violence carried out by "good" people as an efficient, practical, and natural way of settling problems. It is permissible for bad people to be killed because they deserve it, i.e., because they're bad. And, as O'Hara (21) pointed out, wrongdoers are rarely shown as motivated by anything besides selfishness; they are rarely depicted as being products of complicated situational and environmental forces.

Besides dealing in formulas, television, and especially television advertising, creates stereotypes and implies that the viewer should attempt to emulate them. Television advertising attempts to persuade the viewer to look upon himself primarily as a consumer of products. "Buy our brand and you will be like the glamorous, sexy female or popular he-man who uses the product in our ads," say the television product-pushers. But the stereotypes of the ideal as they are presented on television are without real substance and are also virtually unattainable for the majority of people who watch television. This can and no doubt does, lead to disappointment, insecurity and feelings of inferiority, especially for the adolescent, who is generally hypersensitive to the outward image he presents.

A related problem is that the scope of feelings and actions of the viewer may become limited to those which television deems appropriate. As O'Hara (21) observed.

> Stereotypes have the effect of conditioning reflexes in much the same way as Ivan Pavlov conditioned reflexes in dogs. When the bell rang, the dog salivated; when the situation occurs, the person accustomed to stereotyped reactions responds automatically. This, in turn, may lead to rigidity of mind as well as the automatic elimination of certain courses of action when the situation offers alternative responses (p. 201).

In addition to working with formulas and presenting stereotypes, television tends to distort through selective attention. This is especially true in its coverage of newsworthy events. Television tends to focus its cameras and microphones on extreme statements and actions; less inflamatory statements do not make the news. Abnormality in everyday life becomes the normal television news item. The cameras are trained on the protest marcher who throws a brick, not on the thousands who do not. Television can go even farther than this; it can "create" news. A striking example of this was reported by Skornia (26):

> The *New Republic* of October 14, 1957, reports (an) . . . event at Central High School in Little Rock. Quoting a *New York Times* story, the

item explained how, "egged on by one television crew," students were soon "hooting derisively in what quickly became a scene of violence, hate, and effigy-burning—one more of all too many examples where television causes or becomes part of news events instead of merely reporting them" (p. 33).

Thus it is clear that television news coverage does much more than just "report the facts."

The Effects of Television on Adolescent Development

This section will examine the range of possible effects of the medium, its content and its mode of presentation on specific problems of adolescent development. While not intending to diminish the importance of what has been presented so far, it would probably be appropriate at this point to present a comment by Maccoby (15):

The child is not a passive entity absorbing like a sponge whatever is offered to him. He is an active selector of what mass media materials he will expose himself to in the first place; and even during exposure . . . he deploys attention selectively, and what he remembers varies accordingly (p. 327).

The effects of the medium result from an interaction between the characteristics of television and the characteristics of those who watch it. Television, then, is not an all-powerful villainous force seeking to "put something over" on the unsuspecting adolescent, mesmerized by the movements on the screen. What the adolescent brings to television in the form of attitudes, values, and general outlook will to a great extent determine what he gets out of it.

SOCIAL INTERACTION

Adolescence is a period in which problems of interpersonal relationships and problems of relating self to societal patterns are becoming intensified. Peer group relations become very important because the teenager has greater independence and because he cannot always retreat to the security of

the family. This may also be related to the way in which the adolescent uses television and to the way it affects him. As previously noted, S. I. Hayakawa, famed semanticist, strike-breaker, and part-time college president, pointed out that an 18-year-old who has spent three to four hours per day in front of the television set since age three has lost approximately 22,000 hours of potential interaction with other people. As he stated,

For all the values television has, one thing you can't learn from it is interaction. Interaction . . . is an experience we all need. What happens to you if you've lost 22,000 hours of practice in interaction—interaction with your relatives, your grandma, your brothers and sisters, neighbors, and friends, and so on? . . . Perhaps you don't know how to interact. I get the feeling very, very often that some young people in their late teens today do not have an earlier generation's ability to relate to other people (10, p. 42).

This inability to relate to others may indeed be true, but it has not been conclusively demonstrated that television is the culprit. Research generally does reveal however, that television reduces the amount of social interaction in childhood and adolescence. When television was first introduced, it was often remarked that it had the effect of bringing the family together. But this may not really be "togetherness" for the adolescent. Demant (6) expressed this thought when he stated that group television watching "can no more be called a social activity than a number of monologues in the same room is a conversation" (p. 223).

A study by Himmelweit *et al.* (11) found that silent, personal viewing patterns were more characteristic of adolescents than any other age group. Blaine (3) felt that television not only inhibits family communication, but it can also physically separate the adolescent from his parents, especially if he has his own television set. Campbell (4), in his study of Australian adolescents, found that they spent smaller amounts of time entertaining, dancing, visiting, playing, and talking with friends three years after television was introduced into their homes as compared to before they had television. He suggested that this may have detrimental effects because of teenagers' need for the intimacy of family and peer-group relations. He also admitted, however, that his results may have been due to elements in the culture other than television.

Although the evidence seems to indicate that television tends to inhibit social interaction, the picture may not be as bleak as it seems. Various researchers, including Schramm *et al.* (23), have reported that adolescents indicated that one of the reasons they watch television is to learn appropriate ways to interact. Television, for instance, teaches them various ways of behaving, whether it be on a date, on the football field, or at home. Of course, it may be that television, with its preoccupation for violent and emotional content rather than thought-provoking analysis, teaches modes of interaction which are not entirely appropriate or beneficial for normal adolescent development.

PASSIVITY AND ESCAPISM

Much of the material on television depicts an unreal world, a fantasy world. Some condone this material because it provides opportunity for emotional release and relaxation. Others cry that it encourages passivity and escapist tendencies. Witty and Kinsella (27) quoted one parent as stating "TV is converting our children into a race of spectators" and another as saying "Life should be lived, not watched" (p. 575). Schramm *et al.* (23) and Hayakawa (10) compared viewing of television fantasy to drug use: Both are passive experiences which, while they may temporarily ease anxieties and frustrations, will hardly provide long-range solutions to human problems. Demant (6) suggested that the effect of getting the satisfaction of observation, news, and amusement without the effect of going out after them at some cost in money or energy may inhibit normal impulses to find significance and meaning in actual life experiences. Glynn (9) cited clinical evidence for the passivity effects of television:

The staff of a hospital for schizophrenic adolescent girls finds that these girls, insatiable in their demands, and yet themselves incapable of sustaining activity, want nothing so much as to be allowed endless hours of television. Without it they are soon noisy, unruly and frequently destructive. Significantly, the only other control of these girls is an adult who constantly directs them or organizes their entertainment for them (pp. 178–179).

Note, however, that these are the effects when dealing with schizophrenic adolescents who no doubt have abnormal tendencies to withdraw anyway. It is doubtful whether such evidence could be applied with much validity to normal adolescents.

Himmelweit *et al.* (11) found that television had little, if any effect on passivity of children of all ages. Viewers and those in a control group were rated equal by teachers in imagination and initiative. Studies by Schramm *et al.* (23) revealed that except for those rarer individuals who watched television five or more hours per day, there was no substantial change in adolescents' behavior in the direction of passivity. Therefore the most that can be said is that for those adolescents who have strong tendencies to withdraw or become passive, television provides an outlet for their behavior. The evidence, however, does not allow one to conclude that television *causes* passivity.

VIOLENCE AND AGGRESSION

Probably of more concern to parents than passivity is the possibility that television might cause adolescents to become aggressive and commit acts of violence. As previously noted, television does display generous portions of violence, and in many cases attempts to justify its use. Skornia (26) commented,

Television daily and nightly . . . shows people wiping out human life as if it were a great joke, as if human life were not sacred and as if this were having no effect on viewers, for whom it constitutes so large a part of the environment (p. 43).

To date, apparently no data are available concerning adolescents and television-mediated violence. Studies with children by Siegel (25), Lovaas (14), and Bandura, Ross, and Ross (2), suggested that viewing films depicting aggressive acts does not reduce subsequent aggressiveness in the children, but, in fact, often increases it. The general results of these and scores of studies similar to them conducted in other countries generally indicate that children who are exposed to media violence are more likely than those in control groups to act aggressively when given a chance to do so in a subsequent situation. Notice, however, that these are laboratory studies, not real-world situations, and involve young (and therefore probably not too well socialized in norms of nonviolence) children, not adolescents. Himmelweit *et al.* (11), engaged in research in England just after the introduction of television, found that viewers were no more aggressive or maladjusted than controls. They concluded that television is not likely to cause aggressive behavior, although "it could precipitate it in those few children who are emotionally disturbed" (p. 20).

It is important to recognize that one of the problems inherent in the study of media-induced violence concerns the behavioral variable to be measured. Certainly the aggressive acts observed by Bandura *et al.* (2) and Lovaas (14) have important social implications, but equally important are those reactions to televised violence which are not observable. An adolescent may be sitting quietly at his desk in the classroom, but concurrently he may be reveling in violent fantasies engendered by the late movie he viewed the previous evening. The inner world of the adolescent is likely to be markedly different from the behavioral world available to the measuring procedures of the experimenter.

In any case, it may be said with some certainty that television does not reduce aggressiveness in adolescents who watch it. But there is as yet no actual proof that television causes a person to be aggressive or violent. The danger exists, however, that television presents so much violence that viewers might come to regard it as normal and proper and therefore cease to condemn its use.

INTELLECTUAL STIMULATION

Is television intellectually stimulating for the adolescent? Does it help him to be more creative? Is television helping to rear a better informed generation? The answer to these questions seems to be "no," but with a few qualifications.

Television may be intellectually beneficial for many culturally deprived adolescents in our society. For them, the television screen is literally a window to the outside world. Whether or not the picture it presents is accurate, television does give these adolescents a view of life as it exists beyond the confines of the urban ghetto or depressed rural area.

But television certainly has delivered no new age of intellectual enlightenment. As Schramm *et al.* (23) pointed out, television is better at stimulating interest and contributing to existing interests than in stimulating intellectual activity or creation. Their research shows that television is helping to bring up a better informed generation, but only better informed about the fantasy-oriented content of television and not about such matters as public affairs and literature. Recall also their research which indicated that bright adolescents view less television than those of low intellectual ability.

Television tends to communicate life mainly in emotional rather than rational or intellectual terms. As O'Hara (21) observed,

Physical action takes precedence over thoughtful evaluation of the situation and is frequently used as a substitute for it. . . . The aim is to engage the emotions, not the mind—except in the superficial sense of requiring the passive attention of the receiver (p. 291).

One characteristic of an intellectual approach is depth analysis, and television rarely looks at anything in depth. For example, Skornia (26) stated that if one took every word spoken on all newscasts of any given television station in one day, eliminating duplication, this would add up to an average of only two newspaper columns; That can hardly be called penetrating intellectual analysis.

Demant (6) viewed television as potentially hampering creativity and intellectual growth. He felt that when people become habituated to looking at a medium which is as intellectually dead as television, they may develop a non-critical attitude and a disposition to "look without seeing."

Establishing an Identity

The adolescent faces the impending necessity of finding his place in the adult world. Stage five of Erik Erikson's eight critical stages of personality or character formation is called "identity versus identity diffusion." During this stage, which typically occurs during adolescence, the person is trying to form a picture of his environment, and at the same time he is attempting to separate himself from that environment in order to consolidate a unique identity as a human being. The adolescent must try to find out where he fits in society; he must somehow answer the question "Who am I?" In order to do this, the adolescent must learn something about the adult world and appropriate roles in that world. He often turns to television to help him do this; an adolescent may seek an identity by experimentally emulating television personalities.

What kind of adult models does television offer? It has already been mentioned that television contains an over-representation of violent, slick males and ostentatious females whose primary goals are to find husbands. The medium strongly implies that a woman cannot be considered happy or even normal unless she is married or has a strong desire to be married. In the world of television, whenever a woman faces a conflict between a career and marriage it is presupposed that she will choose married life and drop her vocational aspirations. And after she is married, the television wife–mother generally adheres to the saying "A woman's place is in the home" as if it were The Eleventh Commandment. The only time she is allowed out of the house without her husband is for motherly activities such as shopping trips, bridge parties, and hauling the children to school.

The typical TV husband fares no better. He is a rather bumbling, ineffectual, sincere, but not too intelligent creature of habit and routine. He is generally dominated (at least intellectually) by his wife, and as O'Hara (21) stated, "his position as head of the household is purely honorary or ceremonial, and he holds it solely on his wife's sufferance" (p. 264). Television parents are generally asexual. It is rarely even hinted that normal, happy marriage involves sexual intercourse; sexual passion and arousal are not depicted in TV marriages. And as media critic Gilbert Seldes once observed, on television "children are not born, they appear."

The television view of life also implies that men and women spend most of their day in leisure-time activities. People are not often shown working, except at exciting or glamorous jobs. The medium abounds in career information for the adolescent, but only if he wants to become a private detective, spy, defense lawyer, western sheriff, or thief. Routine tedious assembly-line jobs are never depicted, and worker–management friction is rarely seen.

The standard of living depicted on television is quite high. Advertisements reinforce this and ask the viewer to think of himself as a consumer of products. "You are what you own" say the ads; if you can't or don't buy their product, then you're somehow inferior because you have dandruff, bad breath, body odor, general lack of sex appeal, or countless other deficiencies.

Generally, then, television seems to present a distorted and erroneous view of adult life and adult roles. This unquestionably has implications for the adolescent seeking his identity. Patterning himself after television adults will not, in most cases, do much to aid him in successfully resolving his identity crisis. And advertising which begs him to answer the question "Who am I?" in terms of deodorants, mouthwashes, toothpastes, flashy clothes, and fast cars certainly will not help him to be a happy and psychologically healthy person. Fortunately, most adolescents have the ability to compare what they see on television to what exists in their actual environment, and in this way inaccurate views and beliefs can be dispelled. Nevertheless, it would seem that television has an obligation to present a more accurate and balanced picture of life, its roles, and its demands. Certainly a more honest and realistic view of marriage and careers with less reliance on typical male and female stereotypes would seem to be in order. It would also seem beneficial to de-emphasize the consumer-oriented definition of identity, but this may be very difficult to accomplish as long as large commercial enterprises sponsor programs. Furthermore, television has the responsibility to feature more minority group members, not in mock-white roles, but in their own environments with situations germane to their lives.

Activism and Social Change

Does television promote or inhibit social action and social change? Lazarsfeld and Merton (12) spoke of the "narcotizing dysfunction" of the mass media. They felt that through the fairly effortless reception of large amounts of mass communication, the viewer becomes informed about social problems but may mistake *knowing* about them for *doing* something about them. They suggested that "increasing dosages of mass communication may be inadvertently transforming the energies of man from active participation into passive knowledge" (p. 502). And they added that the media are financed by big business, which is fundamentally opposed to rapid social change, and the "he who pays the piper generally calls the tune" (p. 503). Schramm *et al.* (23) echoed this feeling and stated that the most likely social effect of television is no effect whatsoever.

On the other hand, Hayakawa (10) saw television as a strong force for social change. He proposed that television makes social events so vivid and immediate that it creates a sense of involvement not experienced with other media. Television can bring the war in Vietnam and racial injustice into the living room as no other medium can. It was his belief that television is primarily responsible for today's generation of youthful activists. Television, which has been with these people almost since birth, has made them more aware than previous generations of the problems and shortcomings of society. Hayakawa also claimed that television shows only the "show business" side of the democratic process and not its tedious, time-consuming inner workings; as a result today's adolescents, according to Haya-

kawa, become overly impatient with the democratic process when they do not get quick, dramatic, television-like solutions. Consequently, they turn to direct action. He added that television demonstrates to youth that acting directly is exciting and draws immediate public attention. This reinforces tendencies which adolescents already have.

Elkind (7) discussed a normal problem of development which he termed "adolescent egocentrism." This is the adolescent's "belief that others are preoccupied with his appearance and behavior" (p. 502). The adolescent is thus continually being an actor to his audience, whether that audience is real or imaginary. And television is an important audience; it demonstrates to the adolescent that the camera is indeed preoccupied with his appearance and behavior if they are suitably dramatic and out of the ordinary. Vice-president Spiro T. Agnew seems to agree; the *New York Times* (October 27, 1969) quoted him as saying:

> There is a direct relationship between the popularity of confrontation with young people and the fact that they were brought up on television, not books.
>
> They're conditioned to action and emotion, not words. This is a perfectly natural thing—every day they see action, violence, confrontation on television, and they are naturally more conditioned to action than logic.

Agnew's words appear to represent a political interpretation of the writings of media theorist Marshall McLuhan. McLuhan, who sees the media as being of the utmost importance in the shaping of our culture, observed that:

"The television environment is total and therefore invisible. Along with the computer, it has altered

TV "involves us in moving depth, but it does not excite, agitate or arouse. Presumably, this is a feature of all depth experience." (18, p. 337).

"The TV image requires each instant that we 'close' the spaces in the mesh by a convulsive sensuous participation that is profoundly kinetic and tactile, because tactility is the

"The TV image is of low intensity or definition, and

every
phase of
American
vision
and
identity"
(19, p. 134).

"The
student
of media
like the
psychiatrist,
gets more
data
from his
informants
than they
themselves
have
perceived.
Everybody
experiences
far more than
he understands. Yet it is experience, rather than
understanding, that influences behavior, especially in
collective matters of media and technology, where the
individual is almost inevitably unaware of their effect
upon him" (18, p. 318).

the conventionally
literate, that TV
presents an
experience for
passive viewers
is wide of the
mark. TV is above
all a medium that
demands a
creatively
participant
response"
(18 p. 336).

"The culturally disadvantaged child is
the TV child. For TV has provided a
new environment of low visual
orientation and high involvement that
makes accommodation to our older
educational establishment quite
difficult"
(18, ix).

interplay
of the
senses,
rather
than
the
isolated
contact
of skin
and
object"
(18, p. 314).

therefore
unlike
film,
it does
not
afford
detailed
information
about
objects"
(18, p. 317).
"For lack of
observing
so central an
aspect of the
TV image, the
critics of
program
'content'
have talked
nonsense
about
'TV violence.'
The
spokesmen of
censorious
views are
typically
semiliterate
book-oriented
individuals
who have no
competence in
the grammars
of newspaper,
or radio
or of film,
but who look
askew
and
askance
at all
non-book
media.
The simplest
question about
any psychic
aspect, even
of the book
medium, throws
these people
into panic
of uncertainty.
Vehemance
of projection

"TV
does
not
foster lineality
in
living"
(18, p. 321).
"The
children
in Watts (Calif.)
were quite right
in asking, 'Why

"Our children are striving to carry over to
the printed page the all-involving sensory
mandate of the TV image . . .
Pointlessly they strive to
read print in depth. They
bring to print all their
senses, and print rejects
them. Print asks for the
isolated and stripped-down
visual faculty not for the
unified sensorium" (p. 308).

should we go to school only to interrupt our education?"
Television is not a credit course in anything, but it
very definitely has the marks of a natural environment
in which
the child
forages
and finds
his way
as much
as any

Teenage clothing and styling "have
gone so tactile and sculptural that
they present a sort of exaggerated
evidence of the new qualities of
the
TV

Indian ever did in the out-of-doors" (19, p. 68).

mosaic" (18, p. 328).

"The young people who have experienced a decade of TV have naturally imbibed an urge toward involvement in depth that makes all the remote visualized goals of usual culture seem not only unreal but irrelevant, and not only irrelevant but anemic. It is the total involvement in all-inclusive *nowness* that occurs in young lives via TV's mosaid image. This change of attitude has nothing to do with programming in any way, and would be the same if the programs consisted entirely of the highest cultural content. The change in attitude by means of relating themselves to the mosaic TV image would occur in any event. It is, of course, our job not only to understand this change but to exploit it for its pedagogical richness. The TV child expects involvement and doesn't want a specialist *job* in the future. He does want a *role* and a deep commitment to society" (18, p. 335).

of a single isolated attitude they mistake for moral vigilance.

Once these censors became aware that in all cases 'the medium is the message' or the basic source of effects, they would turn to suppression of the media as such, instead of

seeking 'content' control. Their current assumption that content or programing is the factor that influences outlook and action is derived from the book medium, with its sharp cleavage between form and content" (18, p. 314).

. . . and the Generation Gap

The alleged "generation gap" is widely proclaimed today. It is rapidly becoming a favorite topic of women's magazines and PTA meetings. What role does television play in the generation gap? Erikson (8) identified television as "mediator between the generations" and claimed that it ". . . forces youth into being caricatures of the reflections of the images they had more or less experimentaly projected and drives the parents farther away from the eerie happenings" (p. 30).

It is Margaret Mead's (20) position that television, more than anything else, has brought about the confrontation between generations. She proposed that myths and half-truths which are firmly believed and taught by parents and teachers are destroyed by the actuality which television brings into the home. According to Mead, this basically unedited actuality gives youth a view of the world and an orientation very different from that

of their parents whose thinking is grounded in the edited views of writers and filmmakers.

And what about Marshall McLuhan? According to McLuhan's theorizing, it is inevitable that there exists a generation gap between television-raised and -oriented adolescents, seeking tactile depth experience and immediate involvement, and their "print-oriented" parents, with their linear surface approach and future time orientation. Is it completely true, as McLuhan proclaims, that "the medium is the message"? Some think not, at least not to the extent that McLuhan proposes. Macdonald's (16) view was that McLuhan has an ignorance of or lack of interest in cultural standards which are important in studying the media. He also submitted that McLuhan forces basically sound ideas to extremes of absurdity. Lieberman (13) commented on the "Cult of McLuhanacy" and charged that the defects in his theory include the total rejection of any role for media content and his lack of respect for the power of ideas, values, and emotions. But McLuhan's theory, perhaps the most comprehensive and intriguing theory on mass media in existence today, does provide some provocative and unique explanations for current adolescent behavior. At the very least, the ideas of McLuhan, as well as the others viewed in this paper, may help convince social scientists that an understanding of modern mass media is necessary for an understanding of today's adolescent.

REFERENCES

ATWOOD, L. E.   Perception of television program preferences among teenagers and their parents. *Journal of Broadcasting*, 1968, *12*, 377–388.

BANDURA, A., ROSS, D., & ROSS, S.   Transmission of aggression through imitation of aggressive models. *Journal of Abnormal and Social Psychology*, 1961, *63*, 575–582.

BLAINE, G. B.   *Youth and the Hazards of Affluence*. New York: Harper and Row, 1966.

CAMPBELL, W. J.   *Television and the Australian Adolescent*. Sydney: Angus & Robertson, 1962.

COLEMAN, J. S.   *The Adolescent Society*. Glencoe, Ill.: Free Press, 1961.

DEMANT, V. A.   The unintentional influences of television. *Cross Currents*, 1955, *5*, 220–225.

ELKIND, D.   Egocentrism in adolescence. *Child Development*, 1967, *38*, 1025–1034.

ERIKSON, E. H.   *Identity, Youth and Crisis*. New York: Norton, 1968.

GLYNN, E. D.   Television and the American character —a psychiatrist looks at television. In W. Y. Elliott (Ed.), *Television's Impact on American Culture*. East Lansing: Michigan State University Press, 1956.

HAYAKAWA, S. I.   Image and reality. *The Bulletin of the National Association of Secondary School Principals*, 1969, *53*, 35–48.

HIMMELWEIT, H. T., OPPENHEIM, A. N., & VINCE, P.   *Television and the Child*. London and New York: Oxford University Press, 1958.

LAZARSFELD, P. F., & MERTON, R. K.   Mass communication, popular taste and organized social action. In W. L. Schramm (Ed.), *Mass Communications*. (2nd ed.) Urbana: University of Illinois Press, 1960.

LIEBERMAN, B., & BEHAR, J.   In G. E. Stearn (Ed.), *McLuhan: Hot and Cool*. New York: Dial Press, 1967.

LOVAAS, O. I.   Effects of exposure to symbolic aggression on aggressive behavior. *Child Development*, 1961, *32*, 37–44.

MACCOBY, E. E.   Effects of the mass media. In M. L. Hoffman and L. W. Hoffman (Eds.), *Review of Child Development Research*. Vol. I. New York: Russell Sage Foundation, 1964.

MACDONALD, D.   In G. E. Stearn (Ed.), *McLuhan: Hot and Cool*. New York: Dial Press, 1967.

MAC LEAN, M., & TALBOTT, A.   Predictions of individual patterns of television viewing. Paper presented at the American Sociological Association, Los Angeles, August, 1963.

MC LUHAN, M.   *Understanding Media*. New York: McGraw-Hill, 1964.

MC LUHAN, M., & FIORE, Q.   *War and Peace in the Global Village*. New York: Bantam, 1968.

MEAD, M.   Our leaders do not understand television. *TV Guide*, Dec. 6, 1969, *17*, 10–15.

O'HARA, R. C.   *Media for the Millions*. New York: Random House, 1961.

SCHNEIDER, L.   Television in the lives of teenagers and their parents. Unpublished Ph.D. dissertation, University of Iowa, 1966. Reported in Atwood, L. E. Perception of television program preferences among teenagers and their parents. *Journal of Broadcasting*, 1968, *12*, 377–388.

SCHRAMM, W., LYLE, J., & PARKER, E. B.   *Television in the Lives of our Children*. Stanford: Stanford University Press, 1961.

SHAYON, R. L.   *Television and our Children*. New York: Longmans, Green, 1951.

SIEGEL, A. E.   Film-mediated fantasy aggression and strength of aggressive drive. *Child Development*, 1956, *27*, 365–378.

SKORNIA, H. J.   What TV is doing to America: Some unexpected consequences. *Journal of Aesthetic Education*, 1969, *3*, 29–45.

WITTY, P., & KINSELLA, P.   Children and TV—a ninth report. In J. M. Seidman (Ed.), *The Adolescent*. (Revised ed.). New York: Holt, Rinehart, & Winston, 1960.

YOUNG, G.   Operation video. *Clearing House*, 1950, *24*, 156–157.

Chapter 21: Suggested Additional Readings

BLAINE, G. B. JR.   *Youth and the hazards of affluence.* New York: Harper & Row, 1966. The author discusses the problems of high school and college youth, including such topics as drugs, family, sex and religion.

COLEMAN, J. S.   Social change: impact on the adolescent. *Bulletin of the National Association of Secondary-School Principals,* 1965, *49,* 11–14. Coleman indicates some of the structural changes occurring in our modern society and some of their consequences for adolescents.

KENISTON, K.   Youth, change and violence. *American Scholar,* Winter 1967, *37,* 227–245. This is an excerpt from the book *Youth Radicals: Notes on Committed Youth,* by a prominent writer about youth who teaches in the Department of Psychiatry of the Yale University School of Medicine. He gives his own interpretation of modern youth as related to forces of change and violence.

KOUPERNIK, C.   Refusal of an adolescent to accept the modern world. *Journal of Child Psychology and Psychiatry,* 1967, *8*(3/4), 233–240. The author reflects the case of a 16-year-old boy who refuses "frantically" all that is modern, including airplanes, missiles, nuclear bombs, liberal trends in the Catholic Church, pop singers, and everything exotic. Reference to these topics leads to anxiety, and the boy resorts to conjuratory rites to avoid contamination.

ROSZAK, T.   *The making of a counter culture: Reflections on the technocratic society and its youthful opposition.* Garden City, N. Y.: Doubleday, 1969. Roszak discusses why most youths act the way they do and portrays technology as the enemy. He also analyzes the essential ideas of many contemporary social critics.

SEBALD, H.   *Adolescence: a sociological analysis.* New York: Appleton-Century-Crofts, 1968. This systematic treatment of adolescence emphasizes the concept of role discontinuity and the existence of an adolescent sub-culture. Various adolescent sub-cultures are described in some detail.

WON, G., & YAMAMURA, D.   Expectations of youth in relating to the world of adults. *Family Coordinator,* 1970, *19*(3), 219–224, This paper reports a portion of a study intended to assess the orientation of youth to the adult world. The focus here is on how youth perceive and define their problems and how they desire to relate to the world of adults.

Glossary

acculturation: the process by which an individual learns the attitudes, modes of thinking, and behaviors characteristic of a larger social group or different culture

adolescence: the period of life from the beginning of puberty until maturity

affective: pertaining to feeling or emotion

age-stage theory: the concept that human development proceeds according to sequential and successively more mature stages, and that certain kinds of experience are needed for proper development at each of these stages

alienated youth: young people characterized by feelings of distinctiveness and isolation from the dominant social group

anaclitic: dependent on another for care and support

anal: pertaining to the anus or, in psychoanalytic terminology, to the infancy stage when toilet training is of major concern

analytic–descriptive style: the tendency to label items in terms of their objective attributes

androgen: a hormone secreted by glands in both sexes, but far more abundantly in males, which stimulates maleness of structure, function, and, to an unknown extent, behavior

anthropology: the comparative study of the chief characteristics of man, including somatic characteristics, social habits and customs, and language

asceticism: the self-denial of bodily satisfactions in the belief that concerns with them interferes with higher types of spiritual and intellectual achievement

automatizer: an individual who typically focuses on higher level conceptual behaviors while relegating routine perceptual–motor functions to the unconscious

autosexuality: narcissism, or sexual attraction toward oneself

beat: pertaining to a post–World War II expression of American Bohemianism, characterized by a loss of faith in western cultural traditions, and by nonconformist dress and behavior

beatnik: a member of the beat subculture; one who avoids conventional behavior and dress

bisexuality: having gonads of both sexes; having both active (male) and passive (female) sexual interests or characteristics

Bohemian: unconventional; arty

Bohemianism: a life-style characterized by unconventionality and interest in the arts

canalization: "setting the stage" to produce particular thoughts or behaviors

catalyst: a chemical which accelerates action without itself being consumed *celibate:* unmarried; abstaining from sexual intercourse

cervix: a neck-like part, as of the uterus

chromatin: granular protoplasmic substance found in the nucleus of plant and animal cells, which readily takes a deep stain

cognitive: pertaining to those processes by means of which an individual becomes aware of, and judges, objects and situations—for example, reasoning, learning, remembering, and problem solving

cognitive style: the characteristic way in which an individual organizes his approach to mental tasks, including specific ways of relating to the problem at hand

commune: a small community or administrative unit

concrete operations: the stage of cognitive or intellectual development at which the child is able to organize, classify, and otherwise reason logically about concrete, present objects and events but not yet about abstract concepts

congenital: present at or before birth, but not necessarily hereditary

contra-culture: a culture, or way of life, which develops within a larger culture and has no real substance of its own; its only function is to criticize the major culture, and its activities represent reactions to that culture

conventional stage: the second stage of moral development, usually beginning in later childhood, when good and evil are first identified with the concept of "good girl" and "good boy," and when the child identifies himself with the social standards, the law and order, of his social group

creativity: the ability to find new solutions, or novel syntheses of familiar ideas

critical period: a time during which particular experiences may have especially profound and enduring effects

cross-cultural research: studies which involve comparing the same variables as these are observed in more than one society or group

cryptorchid: an individual whose testes have not descended into the scrotum

cultural anthropology: the comparative study of man, especially his social habits and customs

cultural relativism: the theory that behaviors may best be understood through comparing them as they occur in different kinds of society

culture: the way of life—material and behavioral—of a society, including its customs, knowledge, beliefs, and morals

culture shock: trauma associated with having to adapt rapidly to radically changed social conditions

delinquency: a violation of legal or moral codes, especially by minors

demography: the study of human populations, including population trends, distribution, and differential birth rates in subcultural groupings

depolarized: reduced from a status of occupying exactly opposite positions in some continuum

developmental: pertaining to changes, both qualitative and quantitative, which occur during progress toward maturity

developmental task: a skill or problem, appropriate to a particular age-stage, whose mastery depends upon the groundwork laid during previous stages

developmental task theory: a conceptual approach based on the idea that an individual must master certain skills at each age-stage if he is to be ready for the next stage

dialectic: the art or practice of examining opinions or ideas logically, in order to determine their validity; logical argumentation

disadvantaged: persons who, because of some characteristic of the group to which they belong—for example, its social class, race, creed, or economic position—are denied the advantages normally enjoyed by members of the society

double standard: the existence or acceptance of distinctly different moral codes for the sexes

downward mobility: progression toward lower status in the social hierarchy

dual personality: a dissociative reaction characterized by the development of two relatively independent personality systems in the same individual

dyad: a pair, or twosome

ego: self, as distinguished from others; the aspect of the psyche which is conscious and most in touch with reality; in Freudian terms, the mediator between primitive impulses (id) and conscience (superego)

ego identity: a sense of uniqueness and significance as an individual

egocentrism: self-centeredness

ejaculation: the sudden ejection of a fluid, especially a seminal fluid, from the body

empirical: based on experience, careful experiment, and/or observation

epiphenomenon: a phenomenon occurring in conjunction with and dependent upon another

equivalence-range: the range of things which an individual treats in the same manner

erotic: relating to sexual feelings

ethic: moral code

etiology: the study of origins and causes

exhibitionism: the display of the body or its parts (particularly the genitals) for the purpose, conscious or unconscious, of arousing sexual interest

fetishism: a condition in which erotic feelings are excited by a nonsexual object such as a glove or handkerchief; the practice of regarding something with undue or disproportionate emotion

field-dependent: incapable of isolating an object from compelling background forces

field-independent: capable of isolating an object from compelling background forces

formal operations: the use of elements of mental construction such as relations among objects, which cannot be perceived because they are abstract, not concrete

genital: pertaining to the reproductive organs

genitalia: the reproductive organs

gerontocracy: government by the aged

gonads: the reproductive glands (ovaries and testes)

hallucinogenic: producing hallucinations or misinterpretations of stimuli in the environment

hard drugs: drugs usually associated with addiction, especially the opium derivatives and barbiturates

hermaphroditism: the condition of possessing both male and female sex organs (only one being functional in the human)

heterosexual: pertaining to cross-sex relationships

hippie: a member of a loose-knit nonconformist group which stresses universal love, is apt to make use of intoxicating or hallucinogenic drugs, and in general rejects both the goals and the outward mores (dress, living habits, etc.) of conventional society

hirsute: hairy; shaggy

homosexuality: sexual attraction toward members of the same sex *hoody:* (Schwartz and Merten): a category of youth in middle-class suburbia whose life-style is somewhat frivolous and irresponsible

humanism: a system of thought chiefly concerned with the interests and ideals of people

hyperadrenocotical: characterized by excessive secretion of anterior pituitary hormones

hypospadic: a male whose urethra opens into the underside of the penis or the perineum

hypothesis: an admittedly tentative explanation of a body of data made in order to draw out and test its logical consequences

id: in psychoanalytic terminology, the deepest, most primitive stratum of the mind; the fundamental, undifferentiated source of instinctual and motivational energy

identification: the process of merging one's goals with those of another, or modeling after another

identity: sense of uniqueness as a person and distinctiveness from others, equivalent to answering the question, "Who am I?"

ideological: concerned with ideology, or the doctrines and ways of thinking of a person or group

ideology: a system of values, ideas, and beliefs, characteristic of a particular group or culture

idiosyncratic: peculiar to the individual

incest: sexual intercourse between persons too closely related to marry legally

inguinal: of or near the groin

institutionalization: reduction to a system of established laws, customs, and practices

instrumental: directed toward the attainment of a goal

invert: one whose thoughts, feelings, interests, or behavior are typical of the opposite sex; frequently but not invariably a homosexual

laissez-faire ideology: a live-and-let-live philosophy

latency period: a stage in psychosexual development, between childhood and adolescence

leitmotif: originally, a brief musical phrase which recurs with a given situation, character, or emotion in Wagnerian opera; more generally, a dominant recurring theme

libido: in the psychoanalytic sense, the instinctive drives of the id; in a narrow sense the urge for sexual gratification; either constructive or destructive psychic energy

life style: the overall pattern of motives, coping techniques, and behaviors which generally characterizes an individual's behavior

longitudinal investigation: the study of the same individual or individuals over a considerable period of time

LSD (lysergic acid diethylamide): a powerful hallucinogen used on a limited basis in some types of psychotherapy, and also as a "consciousness-expanding" drug

marijuana: a substance derived from the plant *cannabis sativa* and smoked for its intoxicating effect

masochism: a tendency to find pleasure in being abused, or treated painfully, by another

masturbation: stimulation of the genitals by handling or other bodily contact, to obtain sexual satisfaction without intercourse

maturation: developmental changes due to heredity, in contrast to changes deriving from conditions of environment

menarche: the establishment or beginning of the menstrual function

mescaline: a poisonous alkaloid found in the "buttons" of the mescal cactus, which produces intoxication with delusions of color and music *modus vivendi:* manner of living; life style; often implies a compromise intended to by-pass some difficulty

monolithic: massively solid and uniform (derived from *monolith,* "one rock")

moral realist: one whose code of morals and ethics is based on practical, as opposed to abstract or idealistic considerations.

morals: standards of right and wrong as defined by society

multiple personality: the presence of two or more relatively distinct personality systems within one person

mutant: originally a new type, or sudden basic variation in genetic structure; more generally, such a new type or variation in character, life style, etc.

negative reinforcement: strengthening a particular response by punishing alternative responses

neurosis: a functional nervous disorder without demonstrable physical lesion

neurotic: having a tendency toward neurosis, or characterized by neurosis

nurturance: an attitude on the part of the parent, usually the mother, of warmth and assistance toward the child

Oedipus complex (Freud): the repressed desire of an individual for sex relations with the parent of the opposite sex. Specifically, the term relates to the boy's incestuous desire for his mother, but it often subsumes an analogous desire of the girl for her father (more properly called the Electra complex)

ontogenetic: relating to the origin and development of an individual organism

oral: pertaining to the mouth or to the infancy stage when the need for the satisfaction of hunger is of supreme importance

orgasm: the climax of sexual excitement, usually occurring, in conjunction with coitus

orgastic: pertaining to orgasm, or peak of excitement, in the genital zone

paraplegic: an individual with paralysis of the legs and lower part of the body, so that both motion and sensation are affected

pederasty: sexual intercourse between males via the anus

perceptual: pertaining to cognitive experience involving sensory stimulus

personal fable: an individual's complex of beliefs in his uniqueness and immortality, or the story he tells himself about himself

phallus: representation of the penis or testes, especially as a symbol in decoration or cult worship

phenomenologist: one who is primarily concerned with how others subjectively experience reality

phobia: an intense and persistent fear, usually out of proportion to the threat involved

positive reinforcement: strengthening, or stamping in, a particular response by rewarding it whenever it occurs

positivist: one whose system of philosophy in based on the positive data of sensory experience

postconventional stage: the third, or highest, stage of moral development, during which the individual adheres to personal principles, transcending not only conventional morality but even a social contract

preadolescent: one who is in the stage of development spanning approximately two years before puberty

preconventional stage: the first stage of moral development, which involves relatively egocen.ric or self-centered concepts of right and wrong: what one can do without getting caught, or what leads to greatest personal gratification

privatism: a tendency to focus attention on oneself and to disregard the welfare of others

product–moment correlation: the arithemetic mean of the sum of paired observations, measured from zero or from some other origin, which measures the degree of relationship between two or more series of observations

protestant ethic: a set of ideas about man's spiritual relationships supposedly characteristic of Protestant Christianity, which emphasizes hard work, personal stewardship, pleasurelessness, and individual enterprise

psyche: the human mind

psychedelic: pertaining to, or causing, hallucinations and perceptual distortions: e. g., psychedelic drugs, psychedelic music

psychoanalysis: a particular psychotherapeutic technique which involves in-depth penetration of the psyche

psychoanalytic stage theory: a system of beliefs based on the concept that psychosexual development procedes from infancy to adulthood according to certain rather well-defined stages

psychodynamics: the study of mental or emotional forces and processes, and their effect on behavior and mental states

psychosexual: pertaining to the mental aspects of sex

psychosis: fundamental lasting mental disorder

pubertal crisis: the emotional turmoil presumed to accompany the young adolescent's effort to adapt to a maturing body and feelings

puberty: the period during which the individual's reproductive organs approach readiness to function and secondary sex characteristics develop

pubescence: the time span of physiological development during which the reproductive system matures

Puritanistic ethic: (more commonly called Puritan ethic), a code of behavior characterized by stern, strict moral principles

random sample: a statistical population of subjects selected by methods which give each member of the population an equal chance to be drawn, and thus are presumed to provide an unbiased representation of the whole

rebus: a puzzle consisting of pictures of objects which, by the sound of their names, suggest words or phrases—thus, the picture of a chair followed by another of a man would represent the word "chairman"

reference group: those persons to whom an individual most intimately relates and from whom he derives his own status and standards

reinforcement: the process of motivating learning by rewarding the learner for producing the desired response

sadism: the practice of inflicting pain on others for the sake of personal satisfaction

self-actualization: the process of moving through advancing stages of motivation and organization to achievement of one's potential

sexual anomie: an attitude toward sexual behaviors characterized by impersonality and superficiality

siblings: offspring of the same parents

significant other: some person whose influence or operation is especially important to the individual concerned *sleeper effect:* the tendency of a trait, depressed for a time, to reappear

social identity: the pattern of characteristics distinguishing a particular individual in his interaction with others

socialization: the process by which an individual learns to behave like, and to get along with, others in his society and culture

social mobility: movement within a given society from one social class to another

social-sex role: the stereotyped composite portrait of male or female, defining the behavior patterns deemed proper for each sex

socie: (Schwartz and Merten), a member of relatively elite but conventional adolescent peer groups

sociocultural: pertaining both to society (the network of groups within which an individual lives) and to its culture (total way of life, including beliefs, knowledge, and material things)

sociology: the study of human society and its institutions and relationships

stage theory: see age-stage theory

stereotype: a preconceived, prejudiced picture of the members of some particular group

Sturm und Drang (German): Storm and Stress; a term often used to describe teen-age emotionality

subculture: a division of a cultural group consisting of individuals who share distinctive special cultural characteristics, while also sharing characteristics of the major culture

sublimation: the process of substituting for socially disapproved outlets, socially approved ones which satisfy the same need

superego: that part of the psyche which incorporates and reflects, largely unconsciously, the perceived ethical–moral standards of society; the conscience

syndrome: a group of symptoms characteristic of a particular disease or condition

tachistoscope: an apparatus designed for testing various mental functions, such as attention and memory, by brief exposure of visual stimuli

technology: the totality of the applied technical processes employed to provide the material goods, services, etc. of a society; especially, such processes in an advanced industrial society

transsexualism: a condition characterized by feeling like a member of the opposite sex

transvestism: practice of wearing, or desire to wear, clothing of the opposite sex

trauma: an experience which inflicts serious physical or psychological shock on the organism

value: in the ethical sense, the worth which an individual ascribes to a given object or activity

verbal protocols: records obtained by personal word-of-mouth interview

youth culture: all those attitudes, behaviors, and material objects which characterize, and set apart, persons in their teens and early twenties

youth: ordinarily an individual in his late teens, or perhaps early twenties, who has not yet assumed the responsibilities of adulthood

zooerasty: sexual intercourse with an animal